THE COLD WAR

THE
COLD WAR
A WORLD HISTORY

Odd Arne Westad

BASIC BOOKS

New York

Basic Books
Hachette Book Group
1290 Avenue of the Americas, New York, NY 10104
www.basicbooks.com

Printed in the United States of America
First Edition: September 2017
Published by Basic Books, an imprint of Perseus Books, LLC,
a subsidiary of Hachette Book Group, Inc.

The Hachette Speakers Bureau provides a wide range of authors for speaking events. To find out more, go to www.hachettespeakersbureau.com or call (866) 376-6591.

The publisher is not responsible for websites (or their content) that are not owned by the publisher.

Print book interior design by Cynthia Young.

Library of Congress Cataloging-in-Publication Data has been applied for.
Library of Congress Control Number: 2017939229
ISBN: 978-0-465-05493-0 (hardcover)
ISBN: 978-0-465-09313-7 (e-book)

LSC-C

10 9 8 7 6 5 4 3 2 1

In memory of
Oddbjørg Westad (1924–2013)
and
Arne Westad (1920–2015)

Contents

World Making

When I was a boy in Norway during the 1960s, the world I grew up in was delimited by the Cold War. It split families, towns, regions, and countries. It spread fear and not a little confusion: Could you be certain that the nuclear catastrophe would not happen tomorrow? What could set it off? The Communists—a tiny group in my hometown—suffered the suspicions of others for having different points of view, and perhaps—it was said often enough—different loyalties, not to our own country, but to the Soviet Union. In a place that had been occupied by Nazi Germany during World War II, the latter was a serious matter: It implied betrayal, in a region that was wary of treason. My country bordered the Soviet Union in the north and at the slightest increase in the temperature of international affairs, tension also mounted along the mostly frozen river where the frontier was set. Even in tranquil Norway the world was divided, and it is sometimes hard to remember how intense its conflicts were.

The Cold War was a confrontation between capitalism and socialism that peaked in the years between 1945 and 1989, although its origins go much further back in time and its consequences can still be felt today. In its prime the Cold War constituted an international system, in the sense that the world's leading powers all based their foreign policies on some relationship to it. The contending thoughts and ideas contained in it dominated most domestic discourses. Even at the height of confrontation, however, the Cold War—although predominant—was not the only game in town; the late twentieth century saw many important historical developments that were neither created by the Cold War nor determined by it. The Cold War did not decide everything, but it influenced most things, and often for the worse: The confrontation helped cement a world dominated by Superpowers, a world in which might and violence—or the threat of violence—were the yardsticks of international relations, and where beliefs tended toward the absolute: Only one's own system was good. The other system was inherently evil.

Much of the legacy of the Cold War centers on these kinds of absolutes. At their worst they can be seen in the American wars in Iraq and Afghanistan: the moral certainties, the eschewal of dialog, the faith in purely military solutions. But they can also be found in the doctrinaire belief in free market messages or the top-down approach to social ills or generational problems. Some regimes still claim authoritarian forms of legitimacy that go back to the Cold War: China is the biggest example, of course, and North Korea the most dreadful one, but dozens of countries, from Vietnam and Cuba to Morocco and Malaysia, have significant elements of the Cold War built into their systems of government. Many regions of the world still live with environmental threats, social divides, or ethnic conflicts stimulated by the last great international system. Some critics claim that the concept of never-ending economic growth, which may in the longer run threaten human welfare or even the survival of humanity, was—in its modern form—a creation of Cold War competitions.

To be fair to an international system (for once), there were also less injurious aspects of the Cold War, or at least of the way the conflict ended. Very few western Europeans or southeast Asians would have preferred to live in the type of Communist states that were created in eastern parts of their continental neighborhoods. And although the legacy of US interventions in Asia is usually roundly condemned, a majority of Europeans were and are convinced that the US military presence within their own borders helped keep the peace and develop democracies. The very fact that the Cold War confrontation between the Superpowers ended peacefully was of course of supreme importance: With enough nuclear weapons in existence to destroy the world several times over, we all depended on moderation and wisdom to avoid an atomic Armageddon. The Cold War may not have been the long peace that some historians have seen it as being.[1] But at the upper levels of the international system—between the United States and the Soviet Union—war was avoided long enough for change to take place. We all depended on that long postponement for survival.

How special, then, was the Cold War as an international system compared with other such systems in history? Although most world orders tend to be multipolar—having many different powers contending—there are some possible comparisons. European politics between the 1550s and the early seventeenth century were, for instance, deeply influenced by a bipolar rivalry between Spain and England, which shared some of the characteristics of the Cold War. Its origins were deeply ideological, with Spain's monarchs believing they represented Catholicism, and the English, Protestantism. Each formed alliances consisting of its ideological brethren, and wars took place far from the imperial centers. Diplomacy and negotiations were limited—each power regarded the other as its natural and given enemy. The elites in both countries believed fervently in their cause, and that the course of the centuries to come would depend on who won the contest. The discovery of America and the advance of science in the century of Kepler, Tycho Brahe, and Giordano Bruno made the stakes very high; whoever came out on top would not only dominate the future, it was believed, but would take possession of it for their purposes.

But apart from sixteenth-century Europe, eleventh-century China (the conflict between the Song and Liao states), and, of course, the much-explored rivalry between Athens and Sparta in Greek antiquity, examples of bipolar systems are quite rare. Over time, most regions have tended toward the multipolar or, though somewhat less commonly, the unipolar. In Europe, for instance, multipolarity reigned in most epochs after the collapse of the Carolingian empire in the late ninth century. In eastern Asia, the Chinese empire was predominant

3

from the Yuan dynasty in the thirteenth century to the Qing dynasty in the nineteenth. The relative lack of bipolar systems is probably not hard to explain. Requiring some form of balance, they were more difficult to maintain than either unipolar, empire-oriented systems or multipolar, broad-spectrum ones. Bipolar systems were also in most cases dependent on other states that were not immediately under the control of the Superpowers but still bought into the system in some form, usually through ideological identification. And in all cases except the Cold War, they ended in cataclysmic warfare: the Thirty Years War, the collapse of the Liao, the Peloponnesian War.

There is no doubt that the fervor of the confrontation of ideas contributed strongly to Cold War bipolarity. The predominant ideology in the United States, emphasizing markets, mobility, and mutability, was universalist and teleological, with the built-in belief that all societies of European extraction were necessarily moving in the same general direction as the United States. From the very beginning, Communism—the special form of socialism developed in the Soviet Union—was created as the antithesis of the capitalist ideology that the United States represented: an alternative future, so to say, that people everywhere could obtain for themselves. Like many Americans, the Soviet leaders believed that "old" societies, based on local identifications, social deference, and justification of the past, were dead. The competition was for the society of the future, and there were only two fully modern versions of it: the market, with all its imperfections and injustices, and the plan, which was rational and integrated. Soviet ideology made the state a machine acting for the betterment of mankind, while most Americans resented centralized state power and feared its consequences. The stage was set for an intense competition, in which the stakes were seen to be no less than the survival of the world.

THIS BOOK ATTEMPTS to place the Cold War as a global phenomenon within a hundred-year perspective. It begins in the 1890s, with the first global capitalist crisis, the radicalization of the European labor movement, and the expansion of the United States and Russia as transcontinental empires. It ends around 1990, with the fall of the

Berlin Wall, the collapse of the Soviet Union, and the United States finally emerging as a true global hegemon.

In taking a hundred-year perspective on the Cold War my purpose is not to subsume other seminal events—world wars, colonial collapse, economic and technological change, environmental degradation—into one neat framework. It is rather to understand how the conflict between socialism and capitalism influenced and were influenced by global developments on a grand scale. But it is also to make sense of why one set of conflicts was repeated over and over again throughout the century and why all other contestants for power—material or ideological—had to relate to it. The Cold War grew along the fault-lines of conflict, starting out in the late nineteenth century, just as European modernity seemed to be reaching its peak.

My argument, if there is *one* argument in such a lengthy book, is that the Cold War was born from the global transformations of the late nineteenth century and was buried as a result of tremendously rapid changes a hundred years later. Both as an ideological conflict and as an international system it can therefore only be grasped in terms of economic, social, and political change that is much broader and deeper than the events created by the Cold War itself. Its main significance may be understood in different ways. I have in an earlier book argued that profound and often violent change in postcolonial Asia, Africa, and Latin America was a main result of the Cold War.[2] But the conflict also had other meanings. It can be constituted as a stage in the advent of US global hegemony. It can be seen as the (slow) defeat of the socialist Left, especially in the form espoused by Lenin. And it can be portrayed as an acute and dangerous phase in international rivalries, which grew on the disasters of two world wars and then was overtaken by new global divides in the 1970s and '80s.

Whichever aspect of the Cold War one wants to emphasize, it is essential to recognize the intensity of the economic, social, and technological transformations within which the conflict took place. The hundred years from the 1890s to the 1990s saw global markets being created (and destroyed) at a dizzying pace. They witnessed the birth of technologies that previous generations could only dream about, some of which were used to increase mankind's capacity for the dominance and exploitation of others. And they experienced a singularly quick change in global patterns of living, with mobility and urbanization on the rise almost everywhere. All forms of political thinking, Left and Right, were influenced by the rapidity and voraciousness of these changes.

In addition to the importance of ideologies, technology was a main reason for the durability of the Cold War as an international system. The decades after 1945 saw the buildup of such large arsenals of nuclear weapons that—the irony is of course not lost on the reader—in order to secure the world's future, both Superpowers were preparing to destroy it. Nuclear arms were, as Soviet leader Joseph Stalin liked to put it, "weapons of a new type": not battlefield weapons, but weapons to obliterate whole cities, like the United States had done with the Japanese cities of Hiroshima and Nagasaki in 1945. But only the two Superpowers, the United States and the Soviet Union, possessed enough nuclear weapons to threaten the globe with total annihilation.

As always in history, the twentieth century saw a multitude of important stories developing more or less in parallel. The conflict between capitalism and socialism influenced almost all of these, including the two world wars and the Great Depression of the 1930s. Toward the end of the century, some of these developments contributed to making the Cold War obsolete both as an international system and as a predominant ideological conflict. It is therefore quite possible that the Cold War will be reduced in significance by future historians, who from their vantage point will attach more significance to the origins of Asian economic power, or the beginning of space exploration, or the eradication of smallpox. History is always an intricate web of meaning and significance, in which the perspective of the historian writing it is paramount. I am preoccupied with the part the Cold War played in creating the world we know today. But this is of course not the same as privileging the Cold War story over all other stories. It is simply to say that for a long period of time the conflict between socialism and capitalism profoundly influenced how people lived their lives and how they thought about politics, both at a local and a global scale.

Broadly speaking, the Cold War happened within the context of two processes of deep change in international politics. One was the emergence of new states, created more or less on the pattern of European states of the nineteenth century. In 1900 there were fewer than fifty independent states in the world, about half of them in Latin America. Now there are close to two hundred, which mostly share a remarkable degree of similarity in governance and administration. The other fundamental change was the emergence of the United States as the dominant global power. In 1900 the US defense budget stood, converted to 2010 US dollars, at around $10 billion, an extraordinary increase over previous years, thanks to the Spanish-American War and counterinsurgency operations in the Philippines and Cuba. Today that expenditure has expanded 100 times, to $1,000 billion. In 1870 US GDP was 9 percent of the world total; at the height of the Cold War, in 1955, it was around 28 percent. Even today, after years of reported US decline, it is around 22 percent. The Cold War was therefore shaped in an era of state proliferation and rising US power, both of which would help create the direction that the conflict took.

These international changes also ensured that the Cold War operated within a framework in which nationalism was an enduring force. Although believers in socialism or capitalism as social and economic systems always seemed to deplore it, appeals to some form of national identity could sometimes defeat the best-laid ideological plans for human progress. Time and again grand schemes for modernization, alliances, or transnational movements stumbled at the first hurdle laid by nationalism or other forms of identity politics. Though nationalism—by definition—also had its clear limitations as a global framework (witness the defeat of the hypernationalistic states of Germany, Italy, and Japan in World War II), it was always a challenge to those who thought the future belonged to universalist ideologies.

Even at the height of the Cold War, from 1945 to 1989, bipolarity therefore always had its limitations. In spite of their attractiveness on a global scale, neither the Soviet nor the US system was ever fully replicated elsewhere. Such cloning was probably not possible, even in the minds of the most fervent ideologues. What resulted in terms of societal development were either capitalist or socialist economies with strong local influences. In some cases these blends were much resented by political leaders, who wanted an unsullied form of their political ideals put in place. But—fortunately for most, it could be claimed—compromises had to be made. Countries like Poland or Vietnam both subscribed to a Soviet ideal for development, but remained in fact very different from the Soviet Union, just as Japan or West Germany—in spite of profound US influence—stayed different from the United States. A country like India, with its unique blend of parliamentary democracy and detailed economic planning, was even further from any kind of Cold War ideal type. In the eyes of their own leaders, and of their strongest supporters elsewhere, only the two Superpowers remained pure, as models to be emulated elsewhere.

In a way this is not surprising. Concepts of modernity in the United States and the Soviet Union had a common starting point in the late nineteenth century and retained much in common throughout the Cold War. Both originated in the expansion of Europe, and of European modes of thinking, on a global scale over the past three centuries. For the first time in human history, one center—Europe and its offshoots—had dominated the world. The Europeans had built empires that gradually took possession of most of the globe, and settled three continents with their own people. This was a unique development, which led some Europeans, and people with European ancestry, to believe that they could take control of the whole world's future through the ideas and technologies they had developed.

Even though this form of thinking had much deeper roots in history, its apogee was in the nineteenth century. Again, this should be no surprise: The nineteenth century was without doubt the era in which the Europeans' advantage over all others culminated in terms of technology, production, and military power. The confidence in and dedication to what some historians have called "Enlightenment values"—reason, science, progress, development, and civilization as a system—obviously sprang from the European preponderance of power, as did the colonization of Africa and of southeast Asia and the subjugation of China and most of the Arab world. By the late nineteenth century Europe and its offshoots, including Russia and the United States, ruled supreme, in spite of their internal divisions, and so did the ideas they projected.

Within the epoch of European predominance, its ideas gradually germinated elsewhere. Modernity took on different shapes in different parts of the world, but the hopes of local elites for the creation of industrial civilizations of their own extended from China and Japan to Iran and Brazil. Key to the modern transformation that they hoped to emulate were the primacy of human willpower over nature, the ability to mechanize production through new forms of energy, and the creation of a nation-state with mass public participation. Ironically, this spread of ideas that were European in origin signaled the beginning of the end of the epoch of European predominance; peoples elsewhere wanted modernity for themselves in order to better resist the empires that lorded over them.

Even within the heart of European modernity ideological contests were developing in the nineteenth century that, in the end, would blow the whole artificial concept of one modernity apart. As industrial society took hold, a number of critiques developed that questioned not so much modernity itself, but rather its endpoint. There had to be more, some claimed, to the remarkable transformation of production and society that was going on than making a few people rich and a few European empires expand in Africa and Asia. There had to be an aim that made up—at least in historical terms—for the human misery created by the processes of industrialization. Some of these critics linked up with others who claimed to deplore industrialization altogether and sometimes idealized pre-industrial societies. The dissenters demanded new political and economic systems, based on the support of ordinary men and women who were being thrown into capitalism's centrifuge.

The most fundamental of these critiques was socialism, a term that came into popular use in the 1830s but has roots back to the French Revolution. Its central ideas are public rather than private ownership of property and resources and the expansion of mass democracy. To begin with, quite a few socialists were looking back as much as forward. They celebrated the egalitarianism of peasant communities or, in some cases, the religious critique of capitalism, often connected with Christ's Sermon on the Mount: "Give to him that asketh thee, and from him that would borrow of thee turn not thou away."

But by the 1860s early socialist thought was coming under pressure from the thinking of Karl Marx and his followers. Marx, a German who wanted to organize socialist principles into a fundamental critique of capitalism, was more preoccupied with the future than the past. He postulated that socialism would grow naturally out of the chaos of economic and social change in the mid-nineteenth century. Neither the feudal order of old nor the capitalist order of the present could handle the challenges of modern society, Marx thought. They would have to be replaced by a socialist order based on scientific principles for running the economy. Such an order would come into being through a revolution by the proletariat, the industrial workers who had no property of their own. "The proletariat," Marx said in his *Communist Manifesto*, "will use its political supremacy to wrest, by degree, all capital from the bourgeoisie, to centralize all instruments of production in the hands of the state, i.e., of the proletariat organized as the ruling class; and to increase the total productive forces as rapidly as possible."[3]

Marx's adherents, who called themselves Communists after his *Manifesto*, in the nineteenth century never constituted more than small groups, but they had an influence far greater than their numbers. What characterized them were to a large extent the intensity of their beliefs and their fundamental internationalism. Where other working class movements sought out gradual progress and stressed the economic demands of the underprivileged they represented, Marx's followers stressed the need for relentless class-struggle and for conquering political power through revolution. They saw the workers as having no homeland and no king. They saw the struggle for a new world as having no borders, while most of their rivals were nationalist and, in some cases, imperialist.

Their internationalism and antidemocratic dogmatism were the main reasons why Marxists often lost out to other working class movements toward the end of the nineteenth century. In Marx's Germany, for instance, the setting up of a new strong unitary state under Bismarck in the 1870s was welcomed by many workers, who saw nation building as preferable to class-struggle. But Marx himself, interviewed from his comfortable exile in London's Haverstock Hill, condemned the new German state as "the establishment of military despotism and the ruthless oppression of the productive masses."[4] When the German Social Democrats in their 1891 program stressed the struggle for democracy as the main political aim, they were also roundly condemned by the Marxists. They had demanded "universal, equal, and direct suffrage with secret ballot in all elections, for all citizens."[5] Friedrich Engels, Marx's collaborator and successor, saw this as "removing the fig-leaf from absolutism and becoming oneself a screen for its nakedness." "This sacrifice of the future of the movement for its present may be 'honestly' meant," Engels said, "but it is and remains opportunism, and 'honest' opportunism is perhaps the most dangerous of all."[6]

By the 1890s Social Democratic parties had been established all over Europe and the Americas. Though sometimes inspired by Marxism in their critique of the capitalist system, most of them emphasized reform over revolution, and campaigned for the extension of democracy, workers' rights, and social services accessible to all. Quite a few had already developed into mass parties, linked to the trade union movements in their countries. In Germany, the Social Democratic Party received one and a half million votes in the 1890 elections, almost 20 percent of the total (though it got only a small number of parliamentary seats due to unfair election laws). In the Nordic countries the figures were similar. In France the Federation of Socialist Workers had already started gaining control of municipal governments in the 1880s. In spite of the critique by Engels and others, most Social Democratic parties were advancing democracy, while beginning to benefit from its fruits.

The global economic crisis of the 1890s changed all of that. Like the crisis of 2007–08, it started with the near insolvency in 1890 of a major bank, in this case the British Baring's, caused by excessive risk-taking in foreign markets. The City of London had known worse crises, but the difference this time was that the problem spread rapidly because of increased economic interdependence and came to infect economies throughout the world. The early 1890s therefore saw the first global economic crisis, with high unemployment (nearing 20 percent at one stage in the United States) and massive labor unrest. Many workers and even young professionals—who for the first time faced unemployment in high numbers—asked themselves whether capitalism was finished. Even many members of the establishment began asking the same question, as unrest spread. Parts of the extreme Left—anarchists mainly—began terrorist campaigns against the state. There were eleven large-scale bombings in France in 1892–94, including one in the National Assembly. Across Europe and the United States political leaders were assassinated: the president of France in 1894, the Spanish prime minister in 1897, the empress of Austria in 1898, and the Italian king in 1900. The following year US president William McKinley was assassinated at the Pan-American Exhibition in Buffalo, New York. Rulers the world over were outraged and fearful.

The unrest of the 1890s split the Social Democratic movements, just as they were facing unprecedented attacks from employers and governments. Strikes were crushed, often violently. Socialists and trade unionists were imprisoned. The fallout from the first global economic crisis set back the democratic developments of previous decades. It also produced a revitalized extreme Left among socialists, who saw democracy as nothing but window-dressing for the bourgeoisie. The young Vladimir Illich Ulianov, who came to call himself Lenin, had this background, as did many of the others who would drive the socialist and worker's movements in Europe to the Left in the first part of the twentieth century.

Different people within the workers' organizations drew different lessons from the crisis. Quite a few had expected capitalism itself to collapse as a result of the chaos created by the financial traumas of the early 1890s. When this did not happen, and—at least in some regions—the economy was again on the up in the latter part of the decade, mainstream Social Democrats were pushed further toward trade union organizing and processes of collective bargaining. They could draw on the lessons workers had learned from the crisis: that only an effective union could resist casual dismissals and worsening working conditions when an economic downturn struck. Union membership skyrocketed in Germany, France, Italy, and Britain. In Denmark the central board of trade unions in 1899 agreed to a system of annual negotiations over wages and working conditions with the employers' union. This long-term agreement, the first anywhere in the world, was the beginning of a model that would gradually spread elsewhere. It made Denmark one of the least polarized countries in the world during the Cold War.

The radical Left in Europe hated nothing more than the "class-treason" shown by the Danish Social Democrats in their September Agreement. Having been given a new lease on life by the crisis, the radicals were more convinced than ever that capitalism was coming to an end soon, as Marx had predicted. Some of them believed that the workers themselves, through their political organizations, could help nudge history toward its logical destination: Strikes, boycotts, and other forms of collective protest were not only means for improving the lot of the working class. They could help overthrow the bourgeois state. The 1890s therefore saw the final split between mainstream reformist Social Democrats and revolutionary socialists—soon again to call themselves Communists—which would last up to the end of the Cold War. The confrontation between the two would become an important part of the history of the twentieth century.

The emergence of politically organized workers' movements was a real shock to the established system of states in the late nineteenth century. There were, however, two other essential mobilizations brewing at the time that neither the political establishment nor their socialist opponents at first did much to engage. One was the women's campaigns for political and social justice, which grew in part as a reaction to early working class agitation for voting rights. Why, some were asking, should even educated bourgeois women be denied the right to vote, if illiterate male workers were enfranchised? Others saw some form of solidarity between women's demands—including for full economic rights or rights within the family—and the demands of the working class, but they were probably in the minority during the first wave of feminist agitation. The militancy of the movement, however, was striking, especially in Britain before World War I. Having been repeatedly denied their aim of full political emancipation, the suffragettes were beaten up by police and engaged in hunger strikes in prison. In a particularly shocking case a suffragette was killed by throwing herself under one of the king's horses at the races. They and their sisters ultimately won victories everywhere, but not as part of the socialist Left.

Growing at the same time as the women's movement were the anticolonial campaigns. By the 1890s the first shock of having been occupied and colonized was wearing off in parts of Africa and Asia. Armed with ideas and concepts adopted from the imperial metropole, but finessed for local use, the educated elites veered between benefitting from the colonial system and opposing it in the name of self-governance. Peasant movements also joined in opposing Western influence: the Tonghaks in Korea, the Boxers in China, or the jihadis in North Africa may have wanted a different world from their educated compatriots, but they, too, helped sow the seeds of anticolonial resistance. When the United States entered on its first Asian colonial adventure—in the Philippines in 1899—the local movement that opposed it consisted both of patricians and peasants. By the early twentieth century the first anticolonial organizations had already come into being: the Indian National Congress, the African National Congress in South Africa, and the precursors to the Indonesian National Party.

While the opponents of capitalism, colonialism, and patriarchy fought their battles against the establishment, global change was also taking place within the international system of states. In Europe and in East Asia, Germany and Japan strengthened their positions. But the most remarkable change was taking place around Europe's edges.

Europe—or, more precisely, parts of western Europe—had been militarily predominant on a world scale since the seventeenth century. Since the eighteenth century a few western European regions had also been economically paramount globally in terms of innovation, especially Britain, France, and the Low Countries. By the late nineteenth century, however, the huge continental states on the fringes of Europe—empires of a special kind—were catching up with and in some areas overtaking the key European countries. Russia and the United States were very different in terms of politics and economic organization. But both had expanded over vast distances to conquer enormous amounts of territory from the peoples on their borders. The United States had grown ten times from its original size in the 1780s, from 375,000 square miles to 3.8 million. Russia had also grown fast since the beginning of the Romanov dynasty in 1613, and on an even grander scale: From roughly 2 million square miles to 8.6 million. Britain and France of course had huge colonial possessions, too. But these were noncontiguous, and mostly settled by indigenous people—they were much harder to benefit from economically and to keep under control in the longer run.

As we shall see later in this book, ideas and a sense of destiny played essential roles in Russian and American expansion. Elites in both countries believed that their states were expanding for a reason, that the qualities they possessed as peoples earmarked them for predominance within their regions and—eventually—on a global scale. In reaching for predominance, both elites felt that they were fulfilling a European mission. Having come from European ancestry, they were in a sense engaged in projects to globalize Europe, to bring it all the way to the Pacific. Some of their intellectual leaders also believed that in the process they were making their own people more European, more centered on European values and more willing to bear the burden of empire in an imperial age. But at the same time there were those, in both countries, who saw their expansion as fundamentally different from that of the European empires. While the British and French were searching for resources and commercial advantage, the

Russians and Americans had higher motives for their expansion: to spread ideas of enterprise and social organization, and to save souls, in politics as well as in religion.

The role of religion is important both on the American and Russian side.[7] While the position of organized faith was already in decline in Europe (and in many other places, too) by the end of the nineteenth century, Russians and Americans still saw religion as has having a central place in their lives. In a certain sense, there were similarities between American Evangelical Protestantism and Russian Orthodoxy. Both emphasized teleology and certainty of faith above what was common in other Christian groups. Being unconcerned with concepts of original sin, both believed in the perfectibility of society. Most importantly, both Evangelicals and Orthodox believed that their religion inspired their politics in a direct sense. They alone were set to fulfill God's plan for and with man.

In different ways both the American and the Russian entries into global affairs were colored by the contest each of them had with the dominant world power of the late nineteenth century, Great Britain. Americans resented Britain's trade privileges abroad and found its proclaimed principles of free trade and freedom of investment to be sanctimonious and self-serving. In spite of the admiration that many elite Americans had for British ways, by the 1890s the two countries were increasingly rivals for influence, not least in South America, the continent that first witnessed the rise in US global power. In Russia, too, the British world system was seen as the main obstacle to its rise. Since the Crimean War of the 1850s, when a British-led coalition checked Russian control of the Black Sea region, many Russians viewed Britain as an anti-Russian hegemon, intent on foiling their country's ascendance. British and Russian interests clashed in Central Asia and in the Balkans, and in 1905 British support was seen as instrumental in Japan winning its war against Russia. Unlike the United States, Russia did not see the economic development that could launch it as a potential successor state to Britain as a global capitalist hegemon. But in the combination of territorial expansion and economic backwardness lay the germs of Russia's rise—in its Soviet Marxist form—as a global antisystemic power.

EVEN THOUGH THE Cold War represented the international emergence of the United States as the successor to Great Britain, it would be entirely wrong to see this succession as peaceful or smooth. For most of the twentieth century, the United States was a revolutionary influence on world politics and on societies abroad. This is as true for its impact on Europe (including Britain) as for Latin America, Asia, or Africa. Henry James was not far off the mark when in the 1870s he saw his American hero as "the great Western Barbarian, stepping forth in his innocence and might, gazing a while at this poor effete Old World and then swooping down on it."[8] The United States was an international troublemaker, who at first refused to play by the rules British hegemony had established in the nineteenth century. Its ideas were revolutionary, its mores were upsetting, and its doctrinarism dangerous. Only as the Cold War was coming to a close did US hegemony begin to sit comfortably on a global scale.

The Cold War was therefore about the rise and the solidification of US power. But it was also about more than that. It was about the defeat of Soviet-style Communism and the victory, in Europe, of a form of democratic consensus that had become institutionalized through the European Union. In China it meant a political and social revolution carried out by the Chinese Communist Party. In Latin America it meant the increasing polarization of societies along Cold War ideological lines of division. This book attempts to show the significance of the Cold War between capitalism and socialism on a world scale, in all its varieties and its sometimes confusing inconsistencies. As a one-volume history it can do little but scratch the surface of complicated developments. But it will have served its purpose if it invites the reader to explore further the ways in which the Cold War made the world what it is today.

1

Starting Points

The Cold War originated in two processes that took place around the turn of the twentieth century. One was the transformation of the United States and Russia into two supercharged empires with a growing sense of international mission. The other was the sharpening of the ideological divide between capitalism and its critics. These came together with the American entry into World War I and with the Russian Revolution of 1917, and the creation of a Soviet state as an alternative vision to capitalism. As a result of world war and depression, the Soviet alternative attracted much support around the world, but it also became a focus point for its enemies and rivals. By 1941, when both the USSR and the United States entered World War II, the Soviet Union was internally more powerful than ever, but also more isolated internationally. The wartime interaction between the Soviets, the United States, and the greatest of the nineteenth-century powers, Great Britain, would determine the future framework for international relations.

While the Soviet Union opposed world capitalism, the United States became its leader, though under circumstances that no European would have dreamed about a generation earlier. The history of the world in the late nineteenth and early twentieth centuries is first and foremost a history of the growth of American power, economically, technologically, and militarily. In the fifty years between the American Civil War and World War I, the US gross domestic product

(GDP) multiplied more than seven times. Its steel production, which in 1870 had been at only 5 percent of British levels, by 1913 was four times that of Britain. By that year, the United States had the most industrial patents of any country in the world. The combination of technological change and abundant natural resources created a juggernaut of capitalist development that, within a generation, would put all competitors to shame.

Part of the US success was how its massive economic power intersected with the daily lives of American citizens. Other rising powers in history had seen their rise mainly benefit their elites, while ordinary people had to be satisfied with the scraps left at the table of empire. The United States changed all that. Its economic rise created a domestic consumer society that everyone could aspire to take part in, including recent immigrants and African-Americans, who were otherwise discriminated against and had little political influence. New products offered status and convenience, and the experience of modernity through goods produced by new technology defined what it meant to be American: it was about transformation, a new beginning in a country where resources and ideas fertilized each other through their abundance.

In the late nineteenth century, concepts of uniqueness, mission, and abundance came together to create a US foreign policy ideology of great force and coherence. In its own mind, the United States was different from other places: more modern, more developed, and more rational. Americans also felt an obligation toward the rest of the European-dominated world to help re-create it in the US image. But while few Americans doubted that the United States was a more advanced form of European civilization, they were divided about what kind of power this advantage entitled them to. Some still believed in the framework established by the American Revolution: that it was the example set by US republicanism, thrift, and enterprise that would affect the rest of the world and make peoples elsewhere want to restart the European experience, the way Americans themselves had done. Others believed that in a world of expanding empires the United States had to lead from the front. Instead of only acting as an example it had to intervene to set the world right; the world needed not only American ideas but American power.

Ideas and power came together at the turn of the century with the US victory in the Spanish-American War. Though the war lasted less than four months, the United States got a colonial empire that included the former Spanish possessions of the Philippines, Guam, Puerto Rico, and Cuba. The first US governor of the Philippines, William Howard Taft, made the islands an experiment in what he saw as an American type of development: capitalism, education, modernity, and orderliness. When elected US president in 1908, Taft stressed the beneficial role US capital could play abroad, in the Caribbean, Central America, or Pacific Asia. But he also underlined the plentiful opportunities for US companies to earn money abroad and the government's duty to protect them. Taft's "dollar diplomacy" was a sign of his country's global ascendance.

BY 1914 THE United States was a world power. But its leaders were still uncertain about their country's role on the world stage. Should the American purpose be effective intervention or effective insulation? Was the main aim of American power to protect its own people or save the world? These debates came together in President Woodrow Wilson's decision to join World War I in 1917. Wilson believed that part of the US mission was to help set the world right. His policy toward Mexico, where he intervened twice, was based on the principle that it was in the interest of the United States to push its southern neighbor toward constitutionalism and an American form of democracy. Wilson's sympathies were entirely with the Allied Powers, headed by the British, French, and Russians, fighting against the Central Powers led by Germany and Austria-Hungary. What pushed him to intervene was German submarine warfare against international shipping between the United States and the Allied countries. In his declaration of war, Wilson promised to "vindicate the principles of peace and justice in the life of the world as against selfish and autocratic power" and make the world "safe for democracy."[1] His rhetoric during America's short war in Europe focused on the need to battle against chaos and unrest, and to preserve freedom, for men, for commerce, and for trade.

Wilson was the first southerner elected president since before the Civil War, and his views on race and the US mission reflected those held by white men of his time. To the president, part of America's global task was to gradually improve the ability of others to practice democracy and capitalism. For this mission, Wilson thought in terms of a clear racial hierarchy. White Americans and western Europeans were already well suited for the task. Central, eastern, and southern Europeans had to be prepared for it. Latin Americans, Asians, and Africans had to be enlightened and educated through guidance or trusteeships until they could really start to take responsibility for their own affairs. To Wilson, who was essentially a liberal internationalist, the capacities to make rational political decisions and to make economic decisions went together. Only those who had mastered the latter would master the former. The American role was to prepare the world for a time when such decisions would universally be made, and when a peaceful equilibrium would be promoted through trade and free economic interaction.

While the United States, at least in the eyes of most of its citizens, came to fulfill the promise of capitalism and the market, Russia in the late nineteenth century was for many about the negation of these values. Though business and industrial production expanded under Tsar Nicholas II's reign (1894–1917), both the government and much of the opposition attempted to find alternatives that would not take Russia through the furnace of a market transformation. Throughout the nineteenth century, the Russian Empire relentlessly expanded from eastern Europe to central Asia to Manchuria and Korea. Just as many Americans believed in a continental definition of their country, well before any such possibility existed, many Russians felt their destiny was to forge a dominion from sea to sea, from the Baltic and the Black Sea to the Caspian and the Pacific. Empires such as Britain and France might have expanded through sea power, but Russia aimed at creating a contiguous land empire, settled by its own people, in a territory almost twice the size of the continental United States.

Inside this new Russia, old and new ideas wrestled for primacy. Sometimes they came together in surprising combinations. The tsar's advisers often denigrated the market as a pollution of the values that upheld Russian-ness and empire: hierarchy, authenticity, empathy, and religion, as well as learning and culture, were being lost in a frenzied search for material advantage. Even those who did not support the tsar felt that natural, direct, genuine forms of personal interaction were being lost, and might be replaced by inauthentic and foreign ways of living. All of this fueled anticapitalist resistance in Russia both on the Right and the Left in the years before World War I. The few who believed in the ideas of liberal capitalism were often lost in the melee.

In this anticapitalist chorus in Russia, the Social Democratic Party stood out as one of the movements that linked the empire to broader trends in Europe. Founded in 1898, the party's background was in Marxist thinking, which of course connected it to significant parts of the labor movement in Germany, France, and Italy. Already before its Second Congress, in 1903, the tsar's police had driven most of the Social Democratic leaders into exile abroad. And so the Second Congress convened in London, where the party split into two factions, the "majority" (Bolsheviks in Russian) and "minority" (Mensheviks). The split was as much personal as political. Many party members resented the personal control that Lenin, now the head of the Bolsheviks, was trying to install over the party organization. The split contributed to chaos among the tsar's opponents. Lenin was not a man of easy compromise.

Since well before the London Congress, Lenin had sustained his followers on dreams of a Russian revolution and the conquest of state power. He was born Vladimir Illich Ulianov in 1870, into a liberal bourgeois family in a town five hundred miles east of Moscow. The key moment in his young life came in 1887. His older brother, Aleksandr, a member of a Left-wing terrorist group that planned to assassinate the tsar, was arrested and executed. Vladimir soon joined a radical student association and read voraciously not just in Russian but in German, French, and English. In 1897 he was arrested and banished to Siberia, where he took his nom de guerre, Lenin, from the river Lena. Living in a peasant's hut under police surveillance for three years, he read, wrote, and organized. In his first major published work, *What Is to Be Done?*, from 1902, he quotes an 1852 letter from the German socialist Ferdinand Lassalle to Marx: "Party struggles lend a party strength and vitality; the greatest proof of a party's weakness is its diffuseness and the blurring of clear demarcations; a party becomes stronger by purging itself."[2] Released from exile, Lenin was ready for battle.

THE FIRST OPENING for the Russian revolutionaries came very unexpectedly. In 1905, the Russian empire lost its war against Japan, and the shock of defeat set off massive antigovernment demonstrations in Moscow and St. Petersburg. In the capital the socialist Lev Bronshtein, who called himself Trotsky, led an autonomous workers' council (a soviet), which opposed the authorities. All the Russian opposition demanded free elections and the introduction of some form of parliamentary democracy. The tsar gave in to a few of the demands, but he and his advisers tried to control the government and steer it away from a dependence on the new elected parliament, the Duma. The Bolsheviks participated in the 1905 events, but Lenin did not believe in elections as the road to socialism. Combined, the Bolsheviks and Mensheviks never gained more than 5 percent of elected representatives.

The wider world around the turn of the century was in a state of increasing social and political tension. New conflicts were gradually gnawing away at the optimistic European vision of a future imbued by scientific rationalism, gradual progress, and new opportunities. The economic crisis of 1893 had hit particularly hard in the United States, with increases in unemployment and decreases in working-class income that were to last for several years. While more territory in Africa and Asia was being colonized in a relentless hunt for resources, markets, and prestige, the first organized anticolonial movements appeared in India, South Africa, southeast Asia, and the Middle East. But in spite of this dissonance, which led to increased class conflict and armed resistance, the concept of a better tomorrow held fast in Europe and in the European offshoots elsewhere. There had been no all-European war for close to a hundred years, and most people assumed that rational thinking, commitment to people's welfare, and economic interdependence would prevent one in the future. The new century would surely get a few hiccups, but the overall path to progress was linear and permanent.

1914 changed all of that. As they marched their young men off to war, European elites began a form of collective suicide that would kill off many of them and deprive those still left of much of their wealth and their position in the world. World War I was the beginning of a thirty-year European civil war that would give rise to revolutions, new states, economic dislocation, and destruction on a scale that nobody at the start of 1914 would have thought possible. More than fifteen million died in World War I, most of them European men in their prime. More than twenty-one million were wounded. In France, GDP declined by 40 percent, in Germany by more than twice that. The Austro-Hungarian and Ottoman empires vanished. Britain introduced the rationing of food for the first time in its history.

But worse than the physical effects of total war were its psychological consequences. A whole generation of Europeans learned that killing, destroying, and hating your neighbors were regular, normal aspects of life, and that the moral certainties of the nineteenth century were mainly empty phrases. They learned to distrust the existing order, which had led them into a war that had no victors and no noble purpose. After the battle of the Somme in 1916, one young Welshman wrote in his diary: "It was life rather than death that faded into the distance, as I grew into a state of not-thinking, not-feeling, not-seeing. . . . Men passed me by, carrying other men, some crying, some cursing, some silent. They were all shadows, and I was no greater than they. Living or dead, all were unreal. . . . Past and future were equidistant and unattainable, throwing no bridge of desire across the gap that separated me from my remembered self and from all that I hoped to grasp."[3]

It was the World War I generation who went on to shape the Cold War. All the elements of the Great War were in it: fear, uncertainty, the need for something to believe in, and the demand to create a better world. The desperation created by total war in Europe and the fear that it would spread to much of the rest of the globe was in the minds of all those who experienced it, regardless of where they experienced it. Major Clement Attlee, later British prime minister, fought in Turkey and Iraq. Captain Harry Truman fought in the important Meuse-Argonne offensive. Second Lieutenant Dwight D. Eisenhower trained soldiers for the front. Konrad Adenauer, later West German chancellor, was mayor of war-stricken Cologne, Germany's fourth-largest city. Joseph Stalin, who created the Soviet Union, castigated the war from his revolutionary exile in Siberia. Ho Chi Minh, the Vietnamese Cold War revolutionary, saw France reduced and formed his country's first independence movement. They all grew out of the disasters of World War I.

The Communist challenge to the capitalist world system also started with the Great War. The war split Social Democratic parties everywhere into prowar and antiwar camps. Some Social Democrats supported the war efforts out of a sense of obligation to the nation. But in Germany, France, Italy, and Russia, minority socialists, including the Russian Bolsheviks, condemned the fighting as a conflict between different groups of capitalists. Karl Liebknecht, the only socialist who voted against the war in the German parliament, bravely argued that "this war, which none of the peoples involved desired, was not started for the benefit of the German or of any other people. It is an imperialist war, a war for capitalist domination of world markets and for the political domination of important colonies in the interest of industrial and financial capital."[4]

Revolutionaries such as Liebknecht and Lenin contended that soldiers, workers, and peasants had more in common with their brothers on the other side than with their superior officers and the capitalists behind the lines. The war was between robbers and thieves, for which ordinary people had to suffer. Capitalism itself produced war and would produce more wars if it was not abolished. The answer, the ultra-Left proclaimed, was a transnational form of revolution, in which soldiers turned their weapons on their own officers and embraced their comrades across the trenches.

The Great War jump-started the destinies of the two future Cold War Superpowers. It made the United States the global embodiment of capitalism and it made Russia a Soviet Union, a permanent challenge to the capitalist world. The outcome of the conflict therefore prefigured the Cold War as an international system, even though much was to happen before the full bipolarity of the late twentieth century came into being. The radical Communists emerging from World War I were not the only challengers to capitalism, however. The Italian Fascists (Partito Nazionale Fascista) and the German Nazis (Nationalsozialistische Deutsche Arbeiterpartei) came out of the same Great War cauldron. But it was the birth of Communist power in the world's biggest empire that set the course for the longest conflict of the twentieth century, through the state it created and through the impact it had elsewhere.

The Bolshevik takeover in Russia came because the empire, a wartime ally of France and Britain, was weakened by the war. As 1917 began, the situation at the front was dismal, with no victory in sight. The liberal opposition was tarnished among the population because of its support of the war. When the Russian monarchy was overthrown in a revolution in March 1917, the influence of the Bolsheviks was limited. But the liberal-socialist coalition that came to power after the revolution could not end the war or deal with its catastrophic economic effects. Lenin's slogan "Land, Bread, Peace," as well as his popularity among other socialists because of his opposition to the war, increased his political sway. In November 1917, with the provisional government further weakened through infighting, the Bolsheviks pulled off a coup d'état and took power in Petrograd (St. Petersburg) and Moscow.

The October Revolution, which, following the old Russian calendar, was the Bolshevik term for their November coup, began a profound transformation of Russia. In 1918 the Bolsheviks chased out the elected constitutional assembly and established the Russian Socialist Federative Soviet Republic. The civil war that followed, between the

Bolsheviks' Red Army and a multifaceted anti-Bolshevik White Army, killed two million people. The Bolsheviks gradually, and very surprisingly, even to themselves, were able to turn the military tide to their advantage. In 1922 the Russian Soviet republic became the centerpiece of the Union of Soviet Socialist Republics (USSR), a federation of sixteen republics carved out from the former empire, all ruled by the Bolsheviks. Lenin's followers, who now called themselves Communists, won the war because they had genuine support in the population, most of whom did not want to go back to the discredited old imperial state. Liberals and socialists, who had provided many of the leaders in the struggle against Lenin's coup, had to depend on tsarist officers for military support, and that cost them much esteem in the eyes of the population.

The Bolsheviks' coming to power horrified elites in the countries that had been Russia's allies in World War I. To them, the Bolsheviks were a nightmare within a bad dream: not only did Lenin end Russia's war against Germany, he proclaimed that the supreme aim of his state was revolution in *all* European countries, preferably by violence, as had happened in Petrograd. The allies intervened in the Russian civil war at first to help those non-Bolsheviks who wanted to continue to fight against Germany and Austria-Hungary. But the intervention soon became directed against the Bolshevik regime itself. The foreign forces remained in place after the European war ended in 1918. Their Russian protégés were militarily unreliable and politically weak, and the interventions ultimately had little effect. But they did convince new recruits to the Bolshevik cause that the capitalist world would not hesitate to use arms against them if given a chance. Lenin's regime could now rightly call itself the defender of Russia against foreigners.

THE END OF the war saw the United States as the main economic and political power in the world. It alone held a surplus of credit and industrial supplies. The war also ended with the United States as the world's foremost moral authority in politics. In his Fourteen Points, describing American war aims and peace terms, President Wilson had proclaimed that the United States fought for a just world, not simply for national advantage. As a state built on ideas and principles, it stood above mere nation-states. It believed that all competent nations had the right to self-government and to participation in a new world organization, the League of Nations. When the United States intervened against the Bolsheviks in Russia in 1918, it claimed to do so because it would "render such aid as may be acceptable to the Russians in the organization of their own self-defense."[5] In reality, US elites were as horror-struck by Lenin's rule as were the Europeans. It was rare to see, either in the press or in Congress, a reference to the Communists that did not include terms such as "murderers" or "savages." Wilson, himself more cool-headed, saw the Soviet project as a competing form of internationalism to his own variant.

Just as the USSR in the 1920s would give up on immediate revolution in Europe, the United States soon gave up on Wilson's dream of rearranging Europe through the League of Nations. But the isolationism that America is often blamed for in the 1920s and '30s was never a reality. More Americans than ever before went abroad to Europe and elsewhere. The cultural exchange, and the exchange in goods and services, between America and the rest of the world increased sharply. In Europe, Asia, and Latin America, US consumer products were all the rage: cars, washing machines, vacuum cleaners, radios, and films did more to transform families and societies than did most political projects. Even in an era dominated by high tariffs and import restrictions, US foreign trade and investment increased sharply. From the 1920s on, the financial center of the world moved from Great Britain to the United States, from London to Wall Street.

Nowhere was this increased US influence more striking than in Europe. For centuries European elites had been the arbiters of global taste and purpose. In Russia, in America, and in the colonized world, the ideal of the English gentleman or the learned French *philosophe* ruled. But in the interwar years, America brought change to Europe in ways nobody could have foreseen before World War I. US ways of conducting business replaced old European traditions: on crucial matters such as management styles and accounting methods, and also—though more gradually—principles of investment. In factories the assembly line, pioneered by Henry Ford in Detroit, objectified output and linked man and machine. Fordism, meaning synchronization, precision, and specialization in production, also spread to other spheres of life, and the technological approach to organization was taken up not just by western European liberals, but by Fascists, Nazis, and Soviet Communists.[6] But the Americanization of Europe went further than the assembly line in advanced production. Attitudes and ideals were also gradually changing. The concept of holding a job with regular hours and regular pay was foreign to most Europeans at the turn of the century. Even for those who worked in industry, older, more paternalistic mores applied, as did rules set by guilds or home-town associations. Aristocrats never held a job, of course, but neither did the peasants and laborers over whom they lorded. Europe had been changing in this sense for a very long time. But the Americanization of the post-1918 era capped the turn toward a market economy with distinctive US characteristics.

The rapid change created by war and its effects gave rise to an extraordinary climate of fear among many people in Europe and elsewhere. The most destructive of these fears centered on individual or national humiliation and destitution. It was claimed that radicals, Jews, capitalists, Communists, or neighboring states were out to exploit those who had already suffered and sacrificed in the Great War and its aftermath. In Europe the fear gave rise to nationalist authoritarian movements such as Fascism and Nazism. But it also created new forms of antirevolutionary thinking that focused on the threat that Communism and the Russian revolution posed to religion, individual liberty, and social advancement through self-improvement. In the United States, the Red Scare of 1919–20 led to arrests and deportations of suspected radicals, restrictions on the freedom of speech, and federal assistance for employers to break strikes and workers' protests. In 1920, Seattle's mayor, Ole Hanson, embodied the Scare:

> With syndicalism—and its youngest child, bolshevism—thrive murder, rape, pillage, arson, free love, poverty, want, starvation, filth, slavery, autocracy, suppression, sorrow and Hell on earth. It is a class

government of the unable, the unfit, the untrained; of the scum, of the dregs, of the cruel, and of the failures. Freedom disappears, liberty emigrates, universal suffrage is abolished, progress ceases, manhood and womanhood are destroyed, decency and fair dealing are forgotten, and a militant minority, great only in their self-conceit, reincarnate under the Dictatorship of the Proletariat a greater tyranny than ever existed under czar, emperor, or potentate.[7]

In the United States and Britain, liberalism split under the pressure of war and radical challenges. In ways similar to what would happen after World War II, many liberals joined with conservatives in a wave of antirevolutionary activism. Winston Churchill, in 1920 still a Liberal member of Parliament, said, "In every city there are small bands of eager men and women, watching with hungry eyes any chance to make a general overturn in the hopes of profiting themselves in the confusion, and these miscreants are fed by Bolshevist money. . . . They are ceaselessly endeavoring by propagating the doctrines of communism, by preaching violent revolution, by inflaming discontent, to infect us with their disease."[8] Only a few liberal skeptics remained. While criticizing the methods the Bolsheviks used, the philosopher Bertrand Russell believed that "the heroism of Russia has fired men's hopes."[9] For Russell, in the early years of the Russian Revolution, the possibility for a better world explained its attractiveness.

In the interwar years, many people felt a great betrayal. Instead of the good life, their countries' elites had given them war. Instead of increased opportunity, they got unemployment and more exploitation. In the colonies, many local leaders concluded that the war and the subsequent economic crises proved that the Europeans only cared about themselves, not about progress for those they ruled overseas. Soviet Communism seemed a viable alternative to war, destitution, and oppression. The new Communist International organization (the Third International, or the Comintern), set up by Lenin in 1919, included brand-new Communist parties in many countries, constructed after the Bolshevik model. It defined national Communist parties simply as branches of the Comintern, under a strong, centralized, Soviet leadership. Ho Chi Minh, the Vietnamese anticolonial activist who would eventually lead North Vietnam, wrote, "At first, patriotism, not yet Communism, led me to have confidence in Lenin, in the Third International. Step by step, along the struggle, by studying Marxism-Leninism parallel with participation in practical activities, I gradually came upon the fact that only Socialism and Communism can liberate the oppressed nations and the working people throughout the world from slavery."[10] The voice of Communist revolution, wrote the Norwegian poet Rudolf Nilsen, called out to "burning hearts" everywhere:

Yes, give me the best from amongst you, and I shall give you all.
No one can know till victory is mine how much to us shall fall.
Maybe it means we shall save our earth.
To the best goes out my call.[11]

The call of the Comintern was heard throughout a world that was tired of war and colonial oppression. Most Communist parties began small and formed alliances with other, larger movements. For example, the Chinese Communist Party (CCP), founded in 1921, worked with the Guomindang, the National People's Party, a much bigger nationalist group founded in 1919 by the physician and revolutionary Sun Yat-sen. In Iran, where an ill-fated Soviet republic had been set up in the north in 1920, the Communist Party was forced underground, where its members concentrated on setting up trade unions and urban organizations. In South Africa, its Communist Party, also founded in 1921, appealed "to all South African workers, organized and unorganized, white and black, to join in promoting the overthrow of the capitalist system and outlawry of the capitalist class, and the establishment of a Commonwealth of Workers throughout the World."[12] It later worked within the African National Congress (ANC) and provided many of the leaders in the struggle against apartheid. The Comintern linked all of these parties together and, gradually, helped turn them into instruments of Soviet foreign policy. But the Communist International had an influence that went beyond just the Communist parties themselves. The first global anti-imperial movement, the League Against Imperialism, set up in Brussels in 1927, was, for instance, funded and mostly organized by the Comintern.

While dreamers dreamed of a Communist revolution that would save the world, Lenin and his successors began constructing socialism in their new state. But the plans went awry almost immediately. Not only did the economy collapse, as wealthy and educated people fled the Communist regime and untrained political devotees replaced them; but the civil war, the war against foreign intervention, and the bloody invasions of Soviet power into former parts of the Russian Empire that had declared themselves independent all cost the regime dearly. By 1920 it was reduced to confiscating food from peasants to transport to workers in the cities. Lenin's decision the following year to test out market incentives in order to get the economy going again, the so-called New Economic Policy (NEP), was never more than a tactical ploy and was abolished as soon as it had brought immediate results. The low point for the Communists was a costly and badly fought war against Poland, in which the USSR lost much territory that used to be part of the Russian Empire to the new Polish state. The Polish victory forestalled Soviet attacks on the Baltic republics of Lithuania, Latvia, and Estonia, which now solidified their independence.

But for the Soviet leaders the failure of revolution elsewhere in Europe was even worse than the loss of territory for the Soviet state. A core idea behind Lenin's seizure of power in 1917 had been that his revolution would soon be followed by others in more socially and technologically advanced parts of Europe. Together they would form a continent-wide Soviet Union fueled toward a higher stage of modernity by European know-how and Russian resources, including its revolutionary discipline. But there were to be no successful revolutions elsewhere. In Berlin, an uprising of Left-wing socialists was crushed in January 1919, and its leaders—Karl Liebknecht among them—were murdered. The Bavarian Soviet Republic lasted a mere twenty-seven days before it was defeated in May 1919 by remnants from the German Army in the streets of Munich. In Hungary, the center of the eastern part of the former Austro-Hungarian Empire, the Communists held out the longest. But in August 1919 the

Hungarian Soviet Republic went down in flames in the face of invading Romanian troops supported by France and Britain. Preoccupied with its own civil war, the USSR could do nothing to help. By the early 1920s it was clear that no other Communist revolutions would follow that in Russia, at least not anytime soon. But the deep enmity of the victorious powers against the Soviet Union would remain. The outlook seemed bleak for Moscow's new rulers.

Even so, the Communists gradually managed to stabilize the Soviet government, albeit in a different form from what they had first thought. After Lenin's death in 1924, the party organization was led by Iosif Dzhugashvili, a Georgian Communist who called himself Stalin, the "man of steel." Born in 1878 in a small town in rural Georgia, Stalin had very little formal education. From the age of twenty-one, he worked for Lenin and his party, specializing in the most dangerous jobs such as bank robberies and occasional assassinations. By 1922, Stalin had become general secretary of the Communist Party, meaning head of the central party administration. Six years later he had defeated all his political rivals to become uncontested master of the party and the Soviet state. While doing so, Stalin and his followers had probably saved the government they represented. How did they do this? They could rely on the abundant natural and human resources of the former empire. They had the organizational ability of the Communist Party to use those resources. They employed centralized power and economic and social planning for greater efficiency. Finally, they used terror against enemies, real and imagined. Stalin's aim was a totalitarian society, in which everyone followed one will and one set of aims in pursuit of socialist construction. And although he never entirely managed to build such a society, the state that had Stalin as its leader seemed an impressive machine to friends and foes alike.

The human cost of Stalin's state-building was immense. Lenin had set a bloody pattern by executing at least one hundred thousand people without any form of judicial process.[13] Most were killed simply because they were "class enemies" or had worked for the old regime. Lenin had also instituted the one-party dictatorship and intolerance toward any opposition. But Stalin, the man his closest associates called *vozhd*, the Boss, took these murderous and anti-democratic principles to genocidal lengths. The campaigns against Trotsky and those who had supported him in the inner-party struggle after Lenin's death set the pattern in the late 1920s. Then came the terrible campaign against kulaks, rich peasants, to "exterminate them as a class" and thereby ease the transfer of all land into public hands. In the 1930s millions of innocent Soviet citizens were arrested, imprisoned, deported, or shot. The total figures are hard to estimate. At least ten million Soviet people were killed by Stalin's regime from the late 1920s up to his death in 1953. Twenty-three million were imprisoned or deported. In addition, at least three million died in the Ukrainian famine, which the regime did much to provoke and nothing to prevent. Massacres and executions of Poles, Karelians, Baltic peoples, or peoples of the Caucasus are impossible to estimate in numbers, but are rightly characterized as genocide. The Soviet regime under Stalin was savage to its own people and to other peoples alike, in ways that did nothing to contribute to the economic growth it recorded.

How could the Soviet system, based on terror and subjugation, appeal to so many people around the world? The Great Depression provided the opportunity. If it had not been for capitalism doing so very badly, Communism would not have won the affection of large numbers of dedicated and intelligent people everywhere. In the eyes of many, capitalism had already produced war and colonial enslavement. After the stock market crash in 1929, it produced poverty, too, even in the most advanced industrial economies. The Soviets did not do so well, at least not after the mid-1920s, although the regime managed to survive. But world capitalism was seemingly intent on self-destruction in the 1930s. In the first three years after the crash, world GDP fell by about 15 percent, and it stagnated after that. Overall capitalism had a very bad run in the first half of the twentieth century. It was easy to inflame world opinion against it and in favor of ideals of social justice and defense of local communities, even when such values were presented by thugs and murderers.

The Soviet Union was not the only collectivist challenger to liberal capitalism in the interwar years. In Italy, the Fascists, headed by Benito Mussolini, claimed that their combination of nationalism and socialism was the way forward. In Munich in 1923, just four years after the defeat of the Bavarian Soviet Republic, a young German extremist, Adolf Hitler, tried to grab power on behalf of his Nazi Party. Hitler failed at first, but his party built on its extreme nationalism, anticapitalism, and anti-Semitism to present an alternative both to the liberal Weimar Republic and its Communist challengers. In the 1928 elections the Nazis still got less than 3 percent of the vote. After the worldwide economic crisis hit Germany, with 40 percent unemployment and inflation spiraling out of control, in 1930 the Nazis got 18 percent and two years later 37 percent, making them by far the biggest party in the country. Hitler took over the German government in 1933 and made the country a one-party state, like the Soviet Union and Italy. A number of eastern European, Asian, and Latin American countries also moved toward one-party dictatorships. By the mid-1930s, it seemed that not only capitalism but also political pluralism were dead or dying everywhere except in Britain and its dominions, and in the United States.

The new one-party states formed a collectivist challenge to capitalist ideals. Though they shared a disdain for individual freedom and democratic practices, for the bourgeoisie, and for Social Democratic mass parties, they saw each other as worst enemies because each aspired to exterminate any rival ideology on its territory and because, for most of them, their nationalisms were constructed in opposition to the nationalisms of their neighbors. The exception to the latter was the Soviet Union, which under Stalin constructed a very peculiar form of national identity, idealizing the Soviet state as the natural "homeland" of workers everywhere while also drawing on symbols of the Russian past to gain support at home. Communism was fundamentally different from Fascist and Nazi ideologies in this sense: in spite of Stalin's visibly prioritizing the Soviet state, Communist ideology was internationalist, not nationalist. It was authoritarian and ruthless, while at the same time appealing to global solidarity and social justice. Communists in Europe and elsewhere were often among the bravest and most unselfish opponents of Fascist dictatorships in their own countries, while refusing to speak out against oppression in Stalin's USSR.

As Nazism and Fascism grew stronger, Stalin's Communists prevented working-class organizations from joining together to resist them. Between 1928 and 1935, the Comintern defined Socialists and Social Democrats as "Social Fascists," telling workers everywhere that there was really no difference between Adolf Hitler and German democrats such as the liberal Gustav Stresemann or the Social Democrat Hermann Müller. However unreasonable this view was, most Communists were willing to follow it. Young German Social Democrats, such as Herbert Frahm (who during the Cold War became chancellor of West Germany under the name Willy Brandt), condemned Communist attacks on the other parties of the Left and blamed them for indirectly assisting Hitler's rise. The German Communist Party, which by 1932 had three hundred thousand members and one hundred representatives in the Reichstag, stuck with Stalin's views, summarized by the Comintern: "Fascism is a militant organization of the bourgeoisie resting on the active support of Social Democracy. Social Democracy is objectively the moderate wing of Fascism."[14]

As international tensions rose in the mid-1930s, Stalin consolidated his hold on the Communist Party and the Soviet state. He was already firmly in charge, but in his suspicious mind he convinced himself and others that there were large-scale plots afoot to undermine Communist power from within the USSR. Stalin turned on all who could seem a threat to him. Arresting, deporting, or executing perceived class enemies was of course nothing new in the Soviet Union. But the late 1930s Great Purge, as it became known, was also directed against Communist Party members. By 1937 nobody was safe. Close to a million people were executed for crimes that were largely invented by the regime. Many times that number died during the decade from deliberate starvation, overwork in labor camps, or from neglect and ill-treatment during large-scale deportations. Among those arrested were almost all of the original leaders of the

Bolshevik party. It was as if Stalin's rule could not be safe unless all those who had been witness to his rise were eliminated. Nikolai Bukharin, who had been Lenin's favorite colleague, was arrested and executed in 1938. After having been tortured and, presumably, out of a perverted loyalty to the party he had helped found, Bukharin agreed to sign a confession written in part by Stalin himself: "I am guilty of treason to the socialist fatherland, the most heinous of possible crimes, of the organization of kulak uprisings, of preparations for terrorist acts and of belonging to an underground, anti-Soviet organization. . . . The extreme gravity of the crime is obvious, the political responsibility immense, the legal responsibility such that it will justify the severest sentence. The severest sentence would be justified, because a man deserves to be shot ten times over for such crimes."[15]

The Moscow trials did little to dampen the faith of Communists elsewhere. Most of them believed in Stalin's claims: that he had saved the USSR from attacks by its enemies. In the Spanish Civil War, Communists from all over the world met up to help fight the forces of General Francisco Franco. With the help of Hitler and Mussolini, Franco was trying to unseat the constitutional government in Spain and set up a Fascist dictatorship. It was not only Communists who offered their help to the Spanish government; anarchists, trade unionists, and Social Democrats joined, too. But the democratic powers refused to get involved, and soon Franco's forces were on the march toward Madrid. In the spring of 1939, the final resistance was crushed. But before that happened the Communists had had a complete falling-out with the other internationalists in Spain. Following Stalin's instructions, the Soviet advisers spent as much time organizing Communists to fight against Social Democrats, anarchists, and (suspected) Trotskyists in Spain as they spent on fighting Franco. The experience of the lost war against Franco taught Communists and Social Democrats much about what divided them. But it also taught both that Britain, France, and the United States were unlikely to stand up to Hitler except in the most extreme circumstances.

The latter half of the 1930s is rightly called the age of appeasement. Britain had lost its leading role, and its elite was not inclined to confront the buildup of Hitler's power. France was militarily weak and politically divided. The United States had no appetite for getting involved in another war in Europe. Hitler swallowed first Austria (in 1938) and then the western part of Czechoslovakia (in early 1939). The British, French, and Americans did nothing to stop him. Leaders in those countries hoped that Hitler's territorial demands were satisfied, and some of them expected a German-Soviet war to follow. Many British Conservatives were not unhappy with the prospect of the two dictatorships tearing each other to pieces. Very few listened to the likes of Winston Churchill, who, in spite of his visceral anti-Communism, had realized that only cooperation between France, Britain, and the Soviet Union could stop Hitler's expansion. Stalin's desperate attempts at negotiating a collective security arrangement with the western powers came to nothing.

In Britain, France, and the United States, more attention was paid to welfare than warfare in the 1930s. Leaders in all three countries realized that if the disastrous social effects of the Great Depression were not ameliorated, their political systems would be threatened from within, from the same kind of forces that had taken power in Russia, Germany, Italy, and Spain. In Britain the government introduced unemployment benefits, commenced a program of public works, and doubled overall welfare spending. France went even further, with obligatory insurance arrangements and regulated working hours set by the state. The new administration of Franklin Delano Roosevelt in the United States broke with the policies of its predecessors and launched what it called a New Deal. The president termed it "a tremendous adjustment of our national life." It meant using unprecedented methods of planning and government regulation to provide relief and stabilize the economy. In his methods, FDR drew on great American campaigns from the past: the progressive welfare movement at the turn of the century and the mobilization of all of US society to fight World War I. The New Deal was a campaign of great political intensity, intended to jump-start the economy by getting people back to work. Roosevelt's intention was not to abolish capitalism, but to use the state to strengthen it so that its critics both on the Right and the Left could be outplayed and outnumbered.

Roosevelt's policies divided America. Most supported him, and he won four presidential elections in a row. But a vocal minority detested his policies and saw them as socialist and authoritarian. His foreign policy was equally contentious. Right after becoming president in 1933, FDR had established diplomatic relations with the Soviet Union. Much was made of this at the time (and later) by both the president's enemies and friends, but in fact Roosevelt did little beyond what Britain, France, and even Germany and Italy had done a long time before: recognize the Soviet regime as a reality that would not soon go away. By the late 1930s, FDR understood that Nazi Germany was the greatest threat to international peace, but he had to work hard to get US public opinion to accept that German aggression might also be a threat to the United States. A massive majority of Americans, 95 percent in 1936, thought that the United States should stay out of any war in Europe.[16] The memory of US intervention in World War I, which most people regarded as a failed crusade, hung heavy over FDR's foreign policy.

Knowing that at least some western leaders would gladly sacrifice the USSR to German aggression, Stalin made the move that would unleash World War II. In August 1939 he signed a treaty of nonaggression with the enemy he feared most, Adolf Hitler. The pact was not just about not attacking each other. It was also about dividing parts of eastern Europe between the two dictators: western Poland went to Hitler, while the pact allowed Stalin to invade eastern Poland, Finland, the Baltic states, and Romania. Even if the details of the unlikely compact were not fully known at the time, the deal between the two archenemies led to incredulous and furious reactions all over the world. "Whatever the agreement means," editorialized the *New York Times*, "it is not peace; it serves only to aggravate the crisis."[17] Hitler attacked Poland on 1 September. Two days later, because of their defense agreement with the Poles, Britain and France declared war on Germany. On 17 September, the Soviets moved into Poland from the east.

At first, the new European war seemed so slow-moving that it got called the Phony War. Both sides were wary of the enormous sacrifices the World War I offensives had demanded. Stalin stubbornly planned to cash in on his pact with Hitler, even though there were plenty of warnings that the Nazis were preparing an attack on the Soviet Union. The new war, the vozhd told his followers, was "between two groups of capitalist countries—(poor and rich as regards colonies, raw materials, and so forth)—for the re-division of the world. . . . We see nothing wrong in their having a good, hard fight and weakening each other. . . . Next time, we'll urge on the other side."[18] In the spring of 1940, eight months after it broke out, the Phony War ended and the real one began as German forces occupied the Netherlands and Belgium, broke through the French lines, and attacked Denmark and Norway. France capitulated on 18 June. For an agonizing year, Britain would be left alone to face a Nazi Germany that dominated the continent. For the British, as for most people in German-occupied Europe, the Soviets seemed to be on the German side.

For Communists everywhere the pact between Moscow and Berlin was the first serious test of their faith. Most stuck with the Soviet version: that World War II, like World War I, was a war between capitalist robbers and thieves, in which Communists had no part. The pioneering folk singer Woody Guthrie, then a Communist sympathizer working in California, was fired from his first radio job for refusing to condemn Stalin.[19] But for French, Dutch, Czech, or Norwegian Communists, who saw their societies take the full brunt of the Nazi occupation, the fiction was hard to keep up. On the coast of Norway, some Communists joined with other Leftists to fight the German presence. "Our country must again become free," they declared in July 1940. "Fight against the forces of darkness, which want to destroy our national independence, to tie our people down as slaves, and to abolish the rights we have gained through hard struggle."[20] But the Communist Party leaderships did not accept such behavior. The Bulgarian Communist Georgi Dimitrov, the head of the Comintern, instructed the French Communist Party that "this is not a war of democracy against fascism; this is an imperialist, reactionary war on the part of both France and Germany.

In this war a position of national defense is not a correct one for the French Communists."[21] Stalin even sent German Communists, who had fled Hitler's oppression, back to prison in Germany, because he wanted to show his good faith to Hitler.[22]

Hitler, however, had never wavered in his long-term plan to attack and destroy the Soviet Union. But he needed to find the right time for violating his treaty with Moscow. In the summer of 1941, with most of Europe occupied, Britain isolated, and no signs of a direct American involvement in the war, Hitler deemed that the moment had come. On 22 June 1941, 117 German divisions crossed into Soviet territory, and the Nazi air force devastated Soviet airfields. Stalin was so shocked that for hours he refused to believe he was facing an all-out German offensive.[23] On 29 June, he growled to his closest comrades, "Lenin founded a great state, and we fucked it up."[24] The German attack continued. By November 1941 Hitler's troops conquered Belorussia, the Baltic states, and western Ukraine. They laid siege to Leningrad (formerly St. Petersburg, or Petrograd) and stood less than six miles from Moscow.

The years since 1914 had turned many things upside down. World War I had devastated Europe and opened up a set of challenges from radical anticapitalist movements that wanted to transform the world in a collectivist direction. In the colonial countries, resistance was brewing. The United States had become the world's most powerful country, but, except in an economic sense, it was uncertain of its global role. The ideological Cold War, Communism versus capitalism, had intensified, but it had not yet created a bipolar international system of opposing states. By 1941 it was Nazi Germany, driven by an aggressive nationalist ideology, that seemed to benefit most from this state of affairs. But while the Germans had reached most of their European objectives, they had not managed to knock Britain and the USSR out of the war. The two holdouts, diametrically opposed as they were in ideological orientation, would now make an alliance of convenience that would defeat their wartime enemies and redraw the map of the world.

2

Tests of War

World War II, which lasted six years, set the framework for half a century of Cold War. For much of the war, the Soviets, the British, and the Americans were allies. But the defeat of their common enemies—Germany, Italy, and Japan—meant that the conflict between Communism, led by the Soviet Union, and its opponents, led by the United States, became the new central focus of world politics. The dramatic loss in status and influence of the two main European colonial empires, first the French and then the British, led to the United States becoming by far the world's most powerful country. The outcome of World War II assured American global hegemony, with the Soviet Union and the Communist parties it had inspired as the only major challenge remaining.

While it is important to understand the role of World War II in creating the Cold War international system, it is equally important not to reduce that great war only to a prelude for what was to come. From a US perspective, World War II was predominantly about defeating German and Japanese expansionism in Europe and Asia. But even so, the question often asked—why was there later a Cold War when the United States and the USSR could be allies in World War II?—is the wrong question. The two were accidental allies in a global war brought on by their mutual enemies. In June 1941 Germany had attacked the USSR, and that December Japan attacked the United States. The Grand Alliance between the USSR, the United States, and Great

Britain did not consist of a long period of working together for common aims, as most successful alliances do. It was a set of shotgun marriages brought on by real need, at a time when each of them had to find help to defeat immediate threats.

Winston Churchill, British prime minister since 1940, gave voice to this dilemma when he addressed the nation via radio after the Nazi attack on the Soviet Union, Operation Barbarossa, on 22 June 1941. Never even mentioning the Soviets or Stalin by name, Churchill still declared a de facto alliance with Moscow:

> The Nazi regime is indistinguishable from the worst features of Communism . . . [and] no-one has been a more consistent opponent of Communism than I have for the last twenty-five years. I will unsay no words that I've spoken about it. But all this fades away before the spectacle which is now unfolding. The past, with its crimes, its follies and its tragedies, flashes away. I see the Russian soldiers standing on the threshold of their native land. . . . It follows, therefore, that we shall give whatever help we can to Russia and to the Russian people. . . . [Hitler's] invasion of Russia is no more than a prelude to an attempted invasion of the British Isles.[1]

Stalin knew that his regime was very lucky to receive foreign aid. Just as he had expected uprisings against his dictatorship across the Soviet Union after the German surprise attack, he had expected Britain and the United States to concentrate on their own defense and leave Russia to its fate. Stalin's views were not surprising. Not only had his pact with Hitler helped unleash World War II, but— shielded by the pact—his forces had invaded eastern Poland, occupied the Baltic states, and attacked Finland. European memories of the peak of Soviet terror in the 1930s were still fresh, as was intelligence information about Soviet supplies of fuel and oil to the Germans in 1939 and 1940. In 1941 there was ample reason not only for conservatives, but for liberals and Social Democrats as well, to see Hitler and Stalin as two thieves in the same market, two dictators leading cruel regimes, which were the deadly enemies not only of free market capitalism but of independent workers' organizations and of representative democracy.

But foreign leaders realized that the only chance for Britain to survive the war, barring a US entry, was for the Soviets to resist the German forces as long as possible. And for that to happen, the USSR had to receive British and American support and aid. As Churchill quipped to his private secretary on the day of the invasion, "If Hitler invaded Hell I would make at least a favorable reference to the Devil in the House of Commons."[2] As it turned out, Churchill (and Roosevelt) would say much more positive things about Stalin and the Soviet regime later in the war than anyone could have expected in the summer of 1941. But in that crucial year all that mattered was the ability of the Red Army to continue to fight. British military leaders, however, had little belief in Soviet military capabilities. The chief of the Imperial General Staff told the prime minister that "I suppose they will be rounded up in hordes."[3] And to begin with they were. By the winter of 1941–42 the unified armed forces of Nazi Germany, the Wehrmacht, had taken 3.5 million Soviet prisoners. Behind German lines many civilians collaborated freely, especially in the Baltic states and in Ukraine, where significant portions of the population saw the German occupation as a liberation from Soviet rule. Atrocities against Jews were common. Hitler equated Bolshevism with Jewish rule and called his war against Stalin a "crusade to save Europe" from a Judeo-Bolshevik threat. Romanian, Hungarian, Croatian, Slovak, Finnish, and Spanish forces joined the Germans in the first months of the offensive.

The German attack on the Soviet Union also brought Britain and the United States closer together. Roosevelt regarded (rightly, based on past performance) his new British colleague as a jingoist and buffoon, who would not be an easy partner for any foreign nation. But FDR also realized, very quickly, that Churchill would fight to the bitter end against Nazi Germany. There would be no surrender. Meanwhile, FDR himself, increasingly concerned with attacks on his anti-Nazi policies within the United States, which he interpreted in a deeply partisan way as a continuation of his political opponents' battles against the New Deal, was willing to nail his colors to the mast of the British ship. By dedicating his Administration's foreign policy to the survival of Britain by any means other than direct US military intervention, Roosevelt could get back at his domestic political enemies for being unpatriotic or worse. The Lend-Lease agreements with London, signed into law on 11 March 1941, put the almost limitless US industrial production capacity at the disposal of the UK war effort. It was war by any other means than the use of US soldiers in Europe. From 1941 to 1945, the United States delivered $31 billion (close to half a trillion in 2016 dollars) worth of equipment to the United Kingdom: ships, aircraft, oil, and food. After Germany attacked the Soviet Union, FDR extended Lend-Lease there. "We are at the moment," Churchill and Roosevelt told Stalin in a joint telegram, "cooperating to provide you with the very maximum of supplies that you most urgently need. Already many shiploads have left our shores and more will leave in the immediate future."[4]

In September 1941, after three months of war on the Eastern Front, most observers still expected the Soviet Union to collapse, either through a military breakdown or through internal uprisings, just like in 1917. A couple of months later they were no longer so sure. The defense of Moscow and Leningrad, organized by Stalin and his generals, was tenacious. The German supply lines were overextended and their losses increased. German racial policies made it difficult to recruit from among the local populations. Hitler's murderous obsession with exterminating Jews and Communists in the vast occupied areas deflected from the German military advance. And winter was setting in, with temperatures down to forty degrees below. The German soldiers had not prepared to fight under such conditions. Hitler had told them that the offensive would be over quickly, as had happened against France.

When the Germans failed to defeat the Soviets in the fall of 1941, the international situation changed fundamentally. A sudden invasion of Britain became much less likely. In occupied Europe, people began to hope that Germany could after all be defeated. Germany's allies and friends in Europe—Italy, Hungary, Romania, and Spain—were discouraged, and some of their leaders began to wonder about how to settle with the British or with the Soviets.

But the biggest impact of the stalemate on the Eastern Front was on Japan. No longer believing that the Soviet Union would collapse or even be an easy target for their forces, Tokyo reoriented its aggressive strategy southward and eastward. Its own war with China had been dragging on for four years. Japanese leaders now decided to land a devastating blow to European interests in Asia and secure access for itself to crucial southeast Asian raw materials.

In December 1941, the Japanese attack on the main US naval base in Hawaii, Pearl Harbor, and on European colonies in Asia meant that American forces joined in the fighting in the east and soon also in Europe. Even though the US Navy's top strategists had been deeply concerned with the Japanese naval buildup in the Pacific, nobody had expected an all-out attack on US facilities. What followed was even more shocking. Within six months, Japan had taken control of all of southeast Asia and stood at the gates of British India. In the wake of the victories of its Japanese allies, Germany rashly declared war on the United States. The Axis Powers, as Germany and its partners were called, now controlled most of Europe and much of Asia. But through their reckless pursuit of power, they had also brought together against them the most powerful coalition of forces the world had ever seen.

The US stock-taking of its new Soviet allies was important for what was to follow. Britain was a known quantity in the United States. Although many Americans disliked the British for their class system, their colonialism, and their snobbish way of looking down their noses at "upstart" former colonials in North America, a common language and common cultural and political traditions linked them. The Soviet Union was very different. Having entered the war, many Americans hoped that the common cause would help make the Soviets more "democratic" and the Soviet Union more like the United States. US government propaganda presented an image of heroic Russians fighting a devilish enemy. For some Left-wingers, in the United States as elsewhere, the Soviet and then the American entry into the war, involuntary as they may both have been, was an enormous relief, and held out hopes for a future in which the two countries could work together both to defeat Hitler and to build a better world. Woody Guthrie, who had lost his first radio job for refusing to condemn Stalin over the German-Soviet Nonaggression Pact, now could sing about taking his union gun into battle and ending a world of slavery: "You're bound to lose / You Fascists bound to lose!"[5]

The Fascists may have been bound to lose. But the three newfound allies approached each other warily. In Stalin's mind, there was no fundamental difference between Britain and the United States, on the one hand, and Hitler and the Japanese on the other. Any alliance with ideological enemies would be temporary and brittle, Stalin thought, and would only survive as long as the others needed the Soviet Union for their own purposes. Even with the United States in the war, Stalin expected his capitalist allies at some point to seek a separate peace with Nazi Germany, leaving his Communist country in the lurch.[6] As Stalin's Red Army slowly began to push back the German divisions, at tremendous cost in lives and materiel, the Soviet leader constantly demanded that his allies set up a second front against Germany in northwest Europe. The fact that he did not get it until June 1944, after nine million Soviet soldiers had been killed, was to Stalin proof of British and American perfidy and hostility.

But if Stalin distrusted and disparaged his allies, the Soviet Union was increasingly dependent on their support for its survival. In all, goods and weapons worth $11.3 billion ($180 billion in 2016 dollars) reached the USSR between June 1941 and September 1945. Five thousand sailors died in shipping the aid to Soviet harbors. Some of this materiel was crucial to the Soviet war effort. Locomotives and railcars helped transport troops. Dodge trucks became the mainstay of Soviet logistics in their great tank battles both against Germany and later against Japan. Canned rations produced in Ohio and Nebraska kept millions of Soviets from starvation. Stalin thought, not unreasonably, that the Soviets paid for these supplies in blood on the battlefield. But he also knew that the American supplies were of such great importance to the Red Army's fighting capabilities that he could not under any circumstance endanger their continued provision. Stalin therefore had a very concrete motive for continuing to cooperate with his allies as long as the war lasted and, if possible, for the long period of time it would take to rebuild the Soviet Union after the war ended.

The main political negotiations among the allies during the war took place at a number of summit meetings. At Tehran in November 1943, Yalta in February 1945, and Potsdam in July 1945, the leaders of the three major Allied powers participated. But in addition there were a number of bilateral meetings: Churchill traveled to meet Roosevelt three times before the prime minister's first visit to Moscow in August 1942. Churchill's visit with Stalin was essential. If the head of world Communism and the dyed-in-the-wool anti-Communist could reach practical agreements, then the alliance between the three incongruous partners would probably hold, at least for the duration of the war against Germany. The positive outcome of the first meeting in Moscow showed the degree to which Britain and the USSR, both struck by German power, depended on some form of cooperation for survival. But during their conversations, Stalin passed up few opportunities to chide his ally for British (and US) lack of a land offensive against Germany. According to British minutes of an August 1942 meeting at the Kremlin, "Stalin suggested that higher sacrifices were called for. Ten thousand men a day were being sacrificed on the Russian front. . . . The Russians did not complain of the sacrifices they were making, but the extent of them should be recognised."[7]

At the Tehran summit in November 1943, a pattern was set that would last until the war was over. The Soviet role had changed from supplicant to demander. In January 1943 the Red Army had broken the German offensive at Stalingrad. From the summer of 1943, Soviet forces were on the attack along several broad fronts toward eastern Europe. The often-promised second front in France had not happened, even though Allied forces had landed in Italy in September. On the Asian side, Japan was still on the offensive in China, while US forces were slowly pushing Japan's Imperial Army back across the Pacific. Most importantly, by the end of 1943 the United States had mobilized fully for war both in Asia and in Europe. In the year to come, the United States would produce 300,000 military planes and 529 large warships. Germany's production was 133,000 and 20; Japan's, 70,000 and 90. In the first three months of 1943 the United States produced as much overall shipping tonnage as Japan did in total during seven years of war. The Soviet Union was on the offensive in Europe, but the country itself was devastated. The United States was untouched, and its GDP had almost doubled since 1939.

In their discussions at Tehran, Stalin attempted to set the agenda because he knew that the Americans now wanted something from him. A Soviet attack on Japan could save hundreds of thousands of American soldiers' lives in the Pacific, not to mention in the battles that would follow an invasion of the Japanese home islands. Roosevelt also had his mind set on a postwar world organization—what became the United Nations—in which he wanted Soviet participation. Given the increasing weakness of the British economic and political position, many of the key points of the conference were settled by Stalin and Roosevelt without Churchill's direct participation. On the afternoon of 1 December 1943 Stalin came to see Roosevelt in the US president's quarters in the Soviet embassy in Tehran, into which FDR had moved for security reasons. In their conversation, the US president agreed to move Poland's borders two hundred miles west, at the expense of Germany, and keep the eastern borders for Poland that Stalin and Hitler had agreed to in 1939. FDR also agreed to the incorporation of the Baltic states into the Soviet Union. He only asked Stalin to keep the deal secret, so that it would not adversely affect his chances for reelection in 1944. FDR believed that little could be done for these countries anyway; at the end of the war the Red Army would be in control of their territories unless Britain and the United States were willing to fight the Soviets over them (which they were not).[8] Roosevelt got Stalin's agreement to enter the war against Japan after the defeat of Germany.[9]

When the Yalta summit was held in February 1945, the military situation had changed even more in the Soviets' favor. Budapest fell to the Red Army during the conference. Soviet advance forces ended up standing less than seventy miles from Berlin as the conference was still going on. Even so, Yalta was not an all-out victory for Soviet interests. Roosevelt, physically weakened by illness, got Stalin to repeat his firm commitment to enter the war in east Asia no later than three months after the defeat of Germany. He also got Soviet membership in the new world organization he had proposed, the United Nations. Churchill, on his side, got the creation of a French occupation zone in postwar Germany, although the Soviets and the Americans had opposed it before the conference. The British wanted it because they sought to restore France's position as a Great Power, in order to fortify against postwar Soviet control in Europe after a US withdrawal. Stalin got little that he had not achieved by military force already. The Allies agreed to build on a Communist-based Polish government, already in place in Warsaw after the Red Army occupation, not on the Polish government-in-exile based in London. The Soviets would be compensated for their efforts in Asia by getting some of their prerevolutionary rights in northeastern China (Manchuria) returned to them. The Chinese had not been asked their opinion in the matter.

A major Soviet concession, at least in the eyes of Roosevelt and Churchill, was agreeing to a joint Declaration on Liberated Europe. But the declaration was long on principle and short on detail. It promised the peoples of Europe the right to "create democratic institutions of their own choice" and "to choose the form of government under which they will live," including "the earliest possible establishment through free elections of Governments responsive to the will of the people." It also talked about "the restoration of sovereign rights and self-government to those peoples who have been forcibly deprived of them."[10] The American and British leaders expected the Soviets to at least go through the motions of "democracy" and "elections" in the parts of Europe occupied by the Red Army. It was more than a fig leaf. Leaders in London and Washington needed these concessions both for their own public opinion and as a sign of trust among allies. But they did not think they could alter the facts on the ground in eastern Europe. "It is the best I can do for Poland at this time," FDR told his advisers at Yalta.[11] Churchill went further. As he told his Cabinet after returning from the Crimea, "Stalin I'm sure means well to the world and Poland" and would deliver the "Polish people [a] free and more broadly-based gov[ernmen]t to bring about [an] election."[12]

Even battle-hardened politicians can give in to wishful thinking as a long war is coming to an end. Roosevelt and Churchill wanted peace after the war, and they hoped Stalin would help them deliver that peace. But their oversell of the Yalta agreements in their own countries increased the risk of conflict rather than reduced it. Stalin had no intention of allowing Western-style elections in Poland. After occupying the eastern part of the country in 1940, his secret police had executed twenty-two thousand Polish officers, policemen, officials, landowners, factory owners, lawyers, and priests and buried them in mass graves, such as at Katyn. The Soviets knew that any elections in Poland would produce an overwhelming majority against them and the government they had created. But the problem was not only the Soviet relationship with Poland. The Stalin who signed the declaration on democracy and national rights in Europe was the same man who had launched a new democratic constitution for the USSR in 1936, the year in which his regime executed at least three hundred thousand of its own citizens. He was the same man who was purported to have written a theoretical book on Marxism and the "national question," full of nice-sounding phrases, while sending whole nations to exile or death. The point was not so much that Stalin could not be trusted. The point was that the Soviet regime could not have introduced democratic elections in eastern Europe even if it had wanted to. It was not of that kind.

Stalin learned quickly how to conduct war on a grand scale, even if he left most of the concrete planning to his generals. Because of the ferocity of the German attack, the Soviet leader believed (for the first and only time) that Russian officers were (by necessity) loyal to him and the Communist regime, and he started a massive campaign of Russian nationalist propaganda in order to keep things that way, at least for the duration of the war. The word "revolution" was replaced by "nation" in Communist self-promotion; it is not for nothing that Russians still know World War II as the Great Patriotic War. It is hard to know whether Stalin's own views changed much. His megalomania certainly grew. More than ever before, the Soviet Union became an instrument of his personal power. It is also clear that Stalin relished the personal recognition that his alliance brought him. To be dealt with on equal terms by a British aristocrat and the president of the most powerful country on earth was pleasing to a former bank robber from small-town Georgia. But Stalin's wartime interaction with his allies did not change his outlook on the world, which remained crudely Marxist. Those who benefitted from capitalism, he thought, would always oppose the Soviet experiment and try to extinguish it. Therefore there would be conflict, including wars, between the Soviets and their opponents in the future. For now, however, all that mattered was the survival of Soviet power in the USSR and, if militarily possible, its extension into central Europe. Communist revolutions in Europe could wait, Stalin thought, until the European peoples were ready for them. The view in Moscow in 1945 was that the Red Army could further such revolutions, but it could not guarantee them.

Stalin hoped that his alliance with the United States and Britain would last for several years after the war ended. His country was a disaster in 1945. The physical destruction was immense, as were the human losses. Stalin knew that the Soviet Union needed peace if it was to recover. He feared the consequences for his own party if people were forced to live in misery even after the war was over. But Stalin was never quite sure what peace really meant, or whether his and Communism's international opponents were willing to let him rest. There was no opposition to his dictatorship in the Soviet Union, and Stalin had a hard time imagining any opposition coming out of the new regions his Red Army had conquered. These countries might not be ripe for Communism yet, he thought, but they could be guided toward it by his authority and the example of the Soviet state. The British and Americans would extend their form of capitalism into the heart of Europe. Stalin would, at least over time, attempt to do the same with his system. It was both an ideological and strategic imperative. "This war," Stalin told his Yugoslav Communist admirers in April 1945, "is not as in the past; whoever occupies a territory also imposes on it his own social system. Everyone imposes his own system as far as his army can reach. It cannot be otherwise."[13]

For ordinary Russians, the Great Patriotic War meant that Stalin and the Communist Party became symbols for the defense of the country. In the 1930s Stalin may have symbolized modernization, social justice, and the welding together of the Soviet Union into a new kind of state, but he and his henchmen were still outsiders. One, whom I later spoke to, told me about their sense of having stolen a country and got away with it. In a 1933 poem, Osip Mandelstam had described the *vozhd* as "the Kremlin's mountain yokel." Perhaps it was the line "the huge laughing cockroaches on his top lip" that cost the poet his life. But many shared his sense of insult at a "foreign" regime led by a Georgian imposing its authority on Russians.[14] The ferocity of the German attack, Hitler's policy of extermination in the occupied areas, and, maybe most importantly, the ability of the Soviet regime to fight foreign invaders, had changed much of that. In 1945 Stalin's dictatorship could be seen as representing the Russian nation simply through having fought, and in the end defeated, the German invasion. Even the Russian Orthodox Church—an institution for which the original Bolshevik approach in 1917 had been to burn its churches, if possible with worshippers inside—blessed the Soviet regime in 1945. "The Russian people accepted this war as a holy war," said one of the church leaders, "a war for their faith and for their country. . . . Patriotism and Orthodoxy are one."[15]

The pride of the Russians in the victory over Nazi Germany was also reflected in how others viewed the Soviets. In many parts of Europe the Red Army was seen as the real liberator of the continent from Nazi rule. In northern Norway, where Soviet troops entered in 1945, fishermen and their families emerged from hiding with banners praising Stalin and the Red Army. In Czechoslovakia, which had suffered six long years of German occupation, people embraced the Soviet soldiers as they marched through. In eastern Europe, many saw the Red Army as a Slav army liberating them from German racial oppression. But even outside their zones of occupation, Stalin and the Soviets were hailed as the liberators of the continent.

In France, quite a few who had condemned Communism in the 1930s now saw it in a more positive light because of the amount of Soviet sacrifice in the war against Hitler. Support for Communist parties in western Europe had never been greater. Most of the new Communists were young people who had come of age during the war. In their eyes Communism and the Soviet example were first and foremost about much-needed reform in their home countries. They wanted full employment and social services. Women who had joined the workforce during the war did not want to be forced back into patriarchal domesticity. Communists were genuinely admired by many for their role in the resistance to German occupation, including by people who regretted their own failure at taking up weapons. Now Nazism and Fascism were dead, and Europe could renew itself. In spite of the Soviets' bloody past, Communism had a model ready for Europe's transformation.

The sense of the need for change was also very visible outside of Europe as World War II was coming to an end. If the First World War had sounded the death knell for Europe's world domination, the Second World War made its abolition a necessity, not least for Europeans themselves. Young people in Europe who had survived the war were far more preoccupied with welfare in their own countries than in what happened to their colonies. Crucially, large numbers of them no longer believed that their own income and status were dependent on the maintenance of colonial control overseas. At the same time anticolonial resistance was on the increase, especially in Asia. Reeling from the war against Germany and Japanese attacks in the east, in 1942 Britain had offered India self-government as soon as the war was over. But independence leader Mohandas Gandhi, known as the Mahatma, or "Great Soul," refused to budge on his demand for immediate independence. In 1942 he launched the Quit India Movement, which aimed at making use of British wartime weakness to drive them out of the subcontinent. Gandhi wanted no compromise. Churchill's offers "have shown up British imperialism in its nakedness as never before," Gandhi wrote. The British "desire our help only as slaves . . . it is harmful to India's interests, and dangerous to the cause of India's freedom, to introduce foreign soldiers in India," even to fight Hitler and the Japanese.[16]

Further east, colonialism also seemed in free fall. In Indonesia—a new territorial concept coined by nationalists for all the southern islands of southeast Asia, as well as Malay-speaking regions of the mainland—the anticolonial leader Sukarno worked with the Japanese occupiers to secure independence from the Netherlands. In Vietnam, also a new term for all Viet-speaking regions that had been colonized by France, the Communist Ho Chi Minh established an independent state, with himself as president. The US government had promised the Philippines its independence before the war and used the promise to mobilize against the Japanese occupation of the islands. In Iran and Egypt nationalists protested against imposed British control. For many people in these countries, Nazism and Japan were not the main problems. The problem was European colonialism in all its forms. Working with Berlin and Tokyo could even help hasten the day of independence and national self-determination. The Atlantic Charter, issued by Roosevelt and Churchill in August 1941, seemed to some non-European nationalists too reminiscent of Woodrow Wilson's World War I idealism, even if it inspired others. In the charter, the two countries pledged to "respect the right of all peoples to choose the form of government under which they will live; and they wish to see sovereign rights and self government restored to those who have been forcibly deprived of them."[17] This, Indian, Indonesian, and Algerian nationalists claimed, must be as true for their countries as it would be for such white European countries as Czechoslovakia, Poland, Denmark, and France.

For most Americans, the Atlantic Charter summed up the principles for which they fought. The United States had been attacked by Japan and Germany, they thought, because these countries' leaders hated the principles to which America had dedicated itself. World War II, in the American view, was a battle for individual liberty, constitutional order, and the American way of life. As in World War I, it was the enemies of these principles who had unleashed global war, and the United States had yet again to sacrifice the lives of its young men to attempt to set the rest of the world right. Toward the end of World War II, there was in America, across the political spectrum, a deeply felt sense that the country had earned the right to lead by example and that the world needed to be reformed along US lines if yet another war was to be avoided.

The growing US impatience with being challenged on any major issue even by its allies was in part a reflection of American power as the war was ending. The United States had outproduced and outfought its enemies. By mid-1945 the US Navy was bigger than all the world's other navies combined, and US bombers had devastated Berlin, Dresden, Tokyo, and Yokohama. As the war ended, more than 60 percent of all the world's heavy aircraft were American. No enemy bombers ever hit the US mainland. Both because of its productive power and because it was untouched by warfare, the US economy in 1945 reigned supreme. It now accounted for more than half of the world's manufacturing capacity. It held two-thirds of the total financial reserves available, providing it with the world's only stable currency and therefore the one in which all global trade was denominated.

President Franklin Roosevelt had no grand plan for what the world ought to look like after the war had ended. When he died, suddenly, on 12 April 1945, his focus was still squarely on fighting the war. The conflict in Europe had not yet ended, although German military power was fading fast. Japan showed no sign of surrendering. Roosevelt still wanted a Soviet entry into the war against Japan in order to spare American lives if an invasion of the Japanese home islands should be necessary. Supremely self-confident to the last, FDR had no doubts that he would be able to manage his relations with his allies as the war came to an end, and after that, too. In spite of rising tension with the Soviets, especially over the future of Poland, Roosevelt was convinced that the wartime alliance would muddle through, not least because of his own charisma, political suaveness, and ability to avoid overall confrontation (sometimes through being economical with the truth, both to his allies and his own people). Political defeat at home, not to mention death, simply did not figure in his calculations.

Because FDR had managed to transmit this confidence in his own durability, if not immortality, to his Administration, Vice President Harry S. Truman had the worst day of his life as he was sworn in as president upon Roosevelt's sudden demise. The new US president had been abroad only once, seeing combat as a captain in France during World War I, and FDR had never drawn him into any foreign policy decision-making. Now Truman suddenly had to take charge of the most powerful country on earth just as the war was ending. Like his predecessor, the new president believed that the Grand Alliance would remain in place after the defeat of Germany, but he lacked the tools FDR had counted on to make it happen: personal charm, strategic (and moral) flexibility, and knowledge of world affairs. Down-to-earth, middle-class Truman was, in other words, closer both to the behavior and the outlook of most of his countrymen than his patrician predecessor had been. He was also more convinced that the United States had the power to set things right, and with that conviction came an impatience when being challenged. Both FDR and Truman disliked Communism, but from the very beginning of his presidency, the new president saw Communism as a challenge to the United States, as an undesired alternative to a US-led world order. Truman wanted to strike deals with Stalin, but only if the latter behaved according to a US view of how the world was supposed to operate.

Hitler committed suicide on 30 April and Germany capitulated unconditionally on 7 May 1945. With the Führer dead and the country in ruins, Hitler's generals had nothing left to fight for. The endgame had come quickly, with Soviet forces rushing in from the east and US and British forces from the west and south. While all sides attempted to end up in control of as much land as possible, as long as the war lasted military considerations generally overrode the competition for territory. US and Soviet soldiers hugged and drank together, teaching each other songs from home, when they first met up by the River Elbe north of Leipzig. It would take more than forty years for Americans and Soviets to be able to mingle so effortlessly again.

The heads of the three main victorious states met outside Berlin, the capital of defeated Germany, from 17 July to 2 August 1945. At the small town of Potsdam, where the Prussian kings had their summer palaces, Stalin yet again played the host, as he had at Yalta and Tehran. But even if it was Soviet forces who had taken the German capital, Stalin wanted to avoid a clash with his allies over the occupation regime in Germany. At Potsdam the Soviet leader mainly wanted US and British acceptance of his country's predominant position in eastern Europe. Both Roosevelt and Churchill had given him reason to believe that would be the case. But at Potsdam, Stalin was the only constant of the three leaders. When the meeting convened, FDR was dead, and Truman took his place. During the conference, the Conservatives lost the British general elections to the Labour Party, so on July 26 Prime Minister Clement Attlee replaced Churchill in Potsdam. Stalin distrusted Truman and Attlee from the beginning—Truman because Soviet intelligence reports stressed his anti-Communism and Attlee because he represented the Right wing of the British Labour movement, the old enemies of Communists everywhere. The Soviet leader knew, however, that he held two trump cards. His troops occupied half of Europe. And the war in east Asia was still not over. The new US president, like the old one, needed Soviet assistance to defeat Japan.

The Potsdam Conference is testimony to how fast global events can move, especially when a great war is coming to an end. The participants were not much preoccupied with Germany. Hitler was dead and his country defeated. The agreement on temporary zones of occupation, demilitarization and denazification, reversal of all German annexations, and moving Polish borders west at Germany's expense (so that Stalin could keep his conquests of 1939) were easily arrived at. Tehran and Yalta had set the pattern on these matters, and Stalin was secretly relieved to find that those agreements still stood. The attention of all three main participants had moved to war in east Asia and to the political settlements in liberated Europe. Stalin knew that Truman's eagerness to get the USSR into the war against Japan would help with other matters, maybe also in Europe. The US development of nuclear weapons, which Truman alluded to during their conversations, came as no surprise to Stalin; his spies had been following the

US development of the atomic bomb since 1942. There is no evidence that the Soviet leader felt threatened by the US atomic monopoly in 1945, even though it made him speed up his own nuclear program. The Red Army had ten million soldiers in Europe, though Stalin, prior to Potsdam, had started transferring troops to east Asia in preparation for an attack on Japan. Stalin had just survived the biggest war in human history and emerged as its victor. He may have had forebodings about the future (he always did), but at Potsdam he was brimming with self-confidence and gusto. Truman believed he could take the measure of the man, and that negotiations with the Soviets were possible. "I can deal with Stalin," the new president confided to his diary. "He is honest—but smart as hell."[18]

The Potsdam Conference spent a great deal of time avoiding making decisions for the future. It was a waiting game: the war in Asia was still on, Truman and Attlee were new in power, and Stalin wanted to solidify the gains he had already made on the battlefield in Europe and, as a consequence thereof, at Tehran and Yalta. The British and Americans expected elections in Soviet-occupied eastern Europe and at least a pro forma adhesion to principles of democracy there. But at the moment the material challenges of the peace were enormous. All across the continent, great masses of people who had fled from the war were trying to get back home. Big cities were in ruins. Millions had no food or fuel. It is not surprising that there was a general feeling that political resolutions could wait. But while leaders hesitated on the big issues, decisions were being made on the ground, in part as a result of conflicting visions of how societies should be reorganized after the war had ended.

THESE CONTESTS HAPPENED throughout Europe, but it could still be argued that the Cold War began in Poland. There, Stalin's policy of imposing strict Soviet control clashed with the wishes of his allies and those of the great majority of Poles. Britain had gone to war with Germany over the fate of Poland in 1939, and it would be hard for any British government to accept Soviet occupation and dictatorship in that country. Churchill was led by the exigencies of war and a great deal of wishful thinking about Stalin's intentions to accept the Soviet plan for a reorganization of the Polish government over the heads of the Poles themselves. But this was only a first step in the Soviet campaign to bring Poland to heel. When the Poles had rebelled against the Germans in Warsaw in the summer of 1944, the Red Army deliberately stopped its offensive outside the Polish capital, allowing the Nazis to destroy the Polish Home Army. Stalin reckoned that the fewer Polish officers alive, the better for Soviet control of the country. When the Red Army was finally ordered to take Warsaw, a quarter of a million Poles had already been killed by the Wehrmacht and the SS and most of the city had been razed to the ground. Even so, after entering the Polish capital, Stalin's secret police kidnapped many of the surviving leaders of the resistance and shipped them off to Moscow for a typical Stalinist show trial. Stalin had instructed the Soviet judges to give them "light" sentences, as a favor to his great power allies. All but a few were to die in captivity anyway.

As all of this went on in Warsaw, US views of Soviet behavior started to change. Roosevelt had become increasingly concerned with the Polish issue; his main concern had been the disdain for foreign opinion with which the Soviets handled matters in Warsaw. His successor saw matters in more concrete terms. Harry Truman believed that the Yalta agreements on Poland ensured democratic freedom and an inclusive transition government that would prepare free elections. The Soviets were not living up to their commitments, Truman thought. As a result, the new president's first meeting with Soviet foreign minister Viacheslav Molotov, twelve days after FDR's death and three months before Potsdam, had been quite frosty. "The President said that he desired the friendship of the Soviet Government," reads the official US record, "but that he felt it could only be on the basis of mutual observation of agreements and not on the basis of a one way street."[19] "I gave it to him straight," Truman told a friend afterward. "I let him have it. It was the straight one-two to the jaw."[20]

Poland seemed a dividing line to Allied leaders. Churchill, who had less at stake in the final stages of the war in Asia, moved effortlessly back to some of his earlier views of the Soviets. On 12 May

Churchill sent Truman a personal message, in which for the first time a western leader used a term that would define the Cold War, "Iron Curtain":

> An iron curtain is drawn down upon [the Soviet] front. We do not know what is going on behind. There seems little doubt that the whole of the regions east of the line Lubeck–Trieste–Corfu will soon be completely in their hands . . . as this enormous Muscovite advance into the centre of Europe takes place. . . . It would be open to the Russians in a very short time to advance if they chose to the waters of the North Sea and the Atlantic. . . . Surely it is vital now to come to an understanding with Russia, or see where we are with her, before we weaken our armies mortally or retire to the zones of occupation.[21]

Increasingly concerned about Soviet behavior in the east, Churchill wanted US and British troops to remain in the positions they had had when the war ended. Truman turned him down, ordering a withdrawal to conform with the lines of responsibility previously agreed with the Soviets. As a result, hundreds of thousands of Germans fled west to avoid the Soviet zone of occupation. But Truman was concerned enough to send Harry Hopkins, FDR's trusted adviser and a champion of cooperation with the Soviets, to Moscow to try to convince Stalin of the error of his ways. Hopkins was already dying of cancer, and the grueling trip to Russia took the best out of him. He still tried his hand with the Soviet dictator, though. "I told Stalin," Hopkins reported to Truman, "that I personally felt that our relations were threatened and that I frankly had many misgivings about it and with my intimate knowledge of the situation I was, frankly, bewildered with some of the things that were going on."[22] Stalin would not budge. He accused the British of muddying the waters in US-Soviet relations. Even though mainly conceived as part of US postwar cost-cutting, Truman's abrupt termination of the Lend-Lease arrangements with the Soviet Union right after victory in Europe in May 1945 had also helped convince Stalin that he was facing a new attitude in

Washington. He did not know whether it was the end of the war in Europe or the coming of a new president that had caused it. Stalin had been on his best behavior at Potsdam. But his suspicions were up. "Poland! What a big deal!" Soviet foreign minister Molotov noted in February 1945. "We are unaware," Molotov continued, "of how the governments in Belgium, France, Germany, etc. are organized. No one consulted us, although we don't say we like one or another of these governments. We didn't interfere because this is the zone of operations of British and American troops!"[23]

In the rest of eastern Europe, which lay within the Soviet lines of occupation, Stalin's irritation with his Great Power partners showed more clearly. In Bulgaria he accepted a more radical line from the local Communists in early 1945; hundreds of key opponents of the Communist-led Fatherland Front, which ruled the country after the Red Army invaded, were executed and more than ten thousand sentenced to prison terms. Most of these had served in Bulgaria's wartime government, which had been an ally of Hitler's Germany. Neither the Allies nor most of the Bulgarian public therefore protested much. But these were not trials of collaborators as seen in western Europe. In Bulgaria, the Soviets and local Communists established a pattern in which all opposition to Communist control of the government was by its very nature defined as Fascist and therefore subject to imprisonment or worse. Inside the Soviet Union, more than a million Balts and Caucasians, including the whole Chechen population, were deported to Siberia and to the Russian Far East as the war came to an end. The Soviet regime did not want to take any chances with unreliable population groups in its border areas.

Stalin did not have a master plan for what to do in eastern Europe when the war was over. But the Communists there were loyal only to him and provided the ultimate guarantee for Soviet control if relations with the United States and Britain were to break down. And in the spring of 1945 Stalin increasingly fell back on what his Marxism told him about his erstwhile allies. Already in January he had warned against believing in any continuing community of interest between Moscow and the west. "The crisis of capitalism has manifested itself in the division of the capitalists into two factions—one fascist, the other democratic," he told a group of visiting Yugoslavs and Bulgarians. "The alliance between ourselves and the democratic faction of capitalists came about because the latter had a stake in preventing Hitler's domination, for that brutal state would have driven the working class to extremes and to the overthrow of capitalism itself. We are currently allied with the one faction against the other, but in the future we will be against the first faction of capitalists, too."[24]

One of the biggest surprises the Soviets got in 1945 was the Labour Party victory in the British general election. Stalin may have distrusted Winston Churchill and seen in him the embodiment of British upper-class rule, but Winston was the devil he knew, just as he knew, through his spies, that the old Conservative had formed a bit of a sentimental relationship with Stalin as a fellow survivor and victor in World War II. Besides, there was already bad blood between British Labour and Soviet Bolshevism. The leaders of the Labour Party—Clement Attlee, who now became prime minister, and Ernest Bevin, who became foreign secretary—detested the Communists within their own trade union movement; Moscow's supporters were responsible, both thought, for splitting the movement in the 1920s and 1930s. Bevin, an unskilled worker who had come to prominence as the head of the biggest of the British trade unions, the Transport and General Workers' Union, had fought Communist influence there and elsewhere relentlessly. In his postwar dealings with Stalin and Molotov, Bevin saw many of these battles repeated on an international scale. Molotov, said Bevin later, was like a Communist in a local Labour Party branch: if you treated him badly, he made the most of the grievance, and if you treated him well, he put up the price next day and abused you. A cabinet colleague viewed Bevin as "full of bright ideas, as well as earthy sense, but dangerously obsessed with Communists."[25]

The Soviets hated British Labour back with equal fervor. In the Soviet documents of the era, there is nearly no sense of opportunity in the news that a Left-wing party, some of whose key union leaders and intellectuals had long-established contacts with Moscow, had won the

British elections. Stalin and his lieutenants sensed that Labour's dedication to building a Social Democratic welfare state could be the worst challenge to Communist aspirations not only in Britain—none of them were so deluded as to expect a Communist revolution in London anytime soon—but also in the rest of western Europe. Soviet foreign affairs experts presumed that the capitalist countries would be hit by an economic crisis after the war ended and that competition among them therefore would increase, as had happened after the First World War. European Communist parties could benefit from the ensuing impoverishment of the workers, since it would prove that no capitalist system could deliver what the working class wanted. The efforts of Social Democrats to reform capitalism was therefore, in the Soviet view, at best irrelevant and at worst counterproductive. Only countries that consciously patterned themselves on the Soviet experience, which had shown that it could deliver full employment and economic growth, would gain in economic terms from the war's end.

The US perspective on conditions in Europe after the war ended was almost the diametric opposite of that of the Soviets. Americans feared the effects of an economic collapse and lasting poverty in Europe, one that could perhaps spread worldwide. While the Soviets expected revolution after the war, because the end of World War I had created the Russian Revolution, most Americans feared such revolutionary prospects. In their minds, World War I and the Great Depression had created Communism and Fascism, the enemies of America. Polls taken in the autumn of 1945 showed that the majority of Americans wanted their country to act to relieve the despair and poverty that had produced ideologies abhorrent to the American mind.

But American opinion polls also showed a contrary trend to this engagement with the world. Throughout the first postwar years, the vast majority of Americans felt their country had sacrificed enough in terms of blood and direct effort to stem the rot in Europe and Asia. Like Europeans and Asians, postwar Americans wanted their government to concentrate on improving living conditions at home. Essentially they wanted to get their boys in uniform back as quickly as possible. Fearful of the isolationist thinking that had emerged after

World War I and mindful of the fact that the United States had not entered World War II until it was attacked by Japan, the Truman Administration wanted to balance the obvious need for the United States to engage internationally after the war was over with the need to placate its voters back home. It could do so, the president himself believed, by using its enormous economic resources to alleviate want elsewhere and get foreign economies going again.

World War II had led to a wholesale transformation of the global economy. As we have seen, the rise of the United States as the center of world economic affairs had been ongoing since the early twentieth century, and had sped up during the interwar years. But it was World War II that made long-term change into a rapid transformation. The American economy had almost doubled in size during the war. In contrast, almost everywhere else lay devastated. In Japan, across the country a quarter of all buildings were destroyed—in Tokyo more than half. Its industrial output was below one-third of prewar figures. In China industrial production was down by more than 60 percent compared to 1937. In the Philippines, the Asian country most devastated by World War II, total economic output was just above 20 percent of what it had been in 1941.

During the war the Roosevelt Administration had realized that it needed to make use of its unique position to create a postwar world that would work better for the United States. FDR's key idea was to perpetuate the wartime alliances against Germany and Japan, while also creating a world organization to which all countries could belong. The United Nations, a term that Roosevelt used interchangeably for the Allied Powers and for the wider group of nations he wanted to put together, was founded as an organization in 1945, with its headquarters first in London and then in New York. In form, the UN was a compromise between two strands in the late president's own thinking. One was idealist: to create a truly global forum, which could assist progressive reform everywhere while keeping the peace. The other was realist: to create a forum through which the allied Great Powers could cooperate and, if necessary, force others to do their bidding. The first aim was realized through the UN General Assembly, which at the beginning had fifty-one members, among them twenty Latin American republics. The second was constructed through the UN Security Council, which had just five members—the United States, Britain, the USSR, France, and China—and in which each had a veto against any proposal made. Only the Security Council could issue resolutions binding for all UN member states, including for sanctions or military action. Neither Stalin nor the British had much faith in the new organization, but each went along to please their mighty American partner. In 1945, nobody could foresee the global role that the UN was to play as the Cold War took hold.

One of the new world organization's main duties was to deal with global economic issues. As the most powerful economy, the United States wanted free trade and access to markets abroad. But it also wanted increased stability in the world economic system. At Bretton Woods in New Hampshire in July 1944, the main allied industrial countries had signed a set of agreements that led to the establishment of an International Monetary Fund (IMF), to provide loans that could bridge a country's imbalance in payments, and an International Bank for Reconstruction and Development, which later became part of the World Bank. But the most basic element of the Bretton Woods system, as it came to be called, was tying all other major exchange currencies to the US dollar at fixed parities. The Bretton Woods agreements gave the United States a massive opportunity for international trade and for influencing the economies of other countries. But it should not be forgotten that, just like the political division lines in Europe and Asia, the agreements were the outcome of what the war had already created. In the longer run, the United States got neither the opportunity nor the stability that it wanted from Bretton Woods. But the agreements did provide a system, of sorts, to legitimize the advent of the United States as the world's economic behemoth.

Given its unique position, could the United States have done more to avoid international conflict in the wake of World War II? A lot of different countries resented the consequences of America's rise but learned to live with it because they had to, for both political and economic reasons. Lines from a ditty much circulated in the British Foreign Office in 1945 went something like this:

> *In Washington Lord Halifax*
> *Once whispered to Lord Keynes,*
> *"It's true they have all the money-bags*
> *But we have all the brains."*[26]

But by 1945 London had to accept that Washington had eclipsed it, by a wide margin, as the center of global power. Britain needed US financial assistance and, if it could get it, US protection against what it saw as the rise of Soviet power in Europe and Asia. Already in 1945, the Truman Administration—as its own relations with Moscow soured—did not need to impose its view in the matter on western European and British leaders. They were as concerned by Stalin's policy as were any group in Washington. British foreign secretary Bevin in 1945 told everyone who wanted to listen, including Soviet foreign minister Molotov, that "it was the Soviet government which was making things difficult."[27]

Although the United States and the Soviet Union were wartime allies, some form of postwar conflict was next to inevitable. Leaders of the two countries had seen each other as adversaries ever since the Russian Revolution of 1917, and in some cases even before that. Stalin's policy of prioritizing control of eastern Europe over good relations with his allies contributed significantly to the weakening of the Grand Alliance as the war was coming to an end, as did his wartime atrocities, for instance in Poland, and his megalomania. Soviet ideology stood in the way, too, since it considered a future conflict with the capitalist world as unavoidable and predicted that intense revolutionary upheavals would occur in the postwar era. On the US side, there was little patience with the Soviet Union not recognizing the preponderance of the United States in international affairs. President Truman did not have the political agility and personal charm of President Roosevelt, and his key advisers, who long had been advocating a tougher line on the Soviets, led him to make decisions that pointed toward the containment rather than the integration of the Soviet Union. As we shall see, it was containment that made postwar conflict into a Cold War. Truman did not understand FDR's policy of attempting to tie Moscow to international arrangements and treaties. As the strongest power, the United States should have done more to keep open channels of communication, of trade, and of cultural and scientific exchange. Stalin would probably have chosen isolation anyway. But the intensity of the conflict, including the paranoia that it later produced on both sides, might have been significantly reduced if more attempts had been made by the stronger power to entice Moscow toward forms of cooperation.

It has to be realized, though, that such judgments can only be made with hindsight. It is not surprising that in spite of the absolute predominance of the United States, many people feared Soviet power, especially in Europe. The Red Army had vast forces on that continent in 1945. In terms of numbers and proven capability they outgunned everyone else. Soviet behavior in eastern Europe spread foreboding. Some say that Stalin was indeed terrible to his own people, but rather limited and traditional in his foreign policy aims. That may be so, at least on some issues. But by 1945 Stalin had taken his behavior into the heart of Europe and into China and Iran, too. Soviet actions in these parts precipitated changes in US policies, and they frightened others who glimpsed them from afar. By themselves, these actions may not have precipitated a Cold War. But they certainly made postwar containment against the Soviet Union much more likely.

3

Europe's Asymmetries

For anyone who had known Europe in 1914, or even in 1939, the devastation wrought by five years of total war would have been overwhelming. Hitler's vainglorious attempt at conquering the continent had wrought destruction on a scale unprecedented in Europe's long history of war and peace. From the Greek islands to the high north of Scandinavia, cities had been firebombed, fields and orchards burned, and people killed and buried in mass graves. Forty million had died. At least as many were refugees or emerging from German concentration camps. The Nazi genocide of six million Jews was the single greatest crime of the war, in a horrible category all its own. The Holocaust also led to widespread dislocation and chaos in regions where significant Jewish populations had been removed. Starvation was widespread: in the Soviet Union, Hungary, Poland, and parts of Germany, more than half the population were slowly dying from hunger as the war ended.

Even if most of Europe was hungry, tired, and terrorized in 1945, the situation was worst in the east. Along an enormous belt of land between the Norwegian Arctic and the southern Balkans, the war between Germany and the Soviet Union had left cities completely devastated and people dead or dying. More than 1,700 towns were almost totally destroyed in the USSR. Cities like Budapest, Minsk, or Kiev were more than 80 percent uninhabitable. In his letters home, a young American relief worker tried to give words to the destruction he witnessed in Warsaw: "Wherever you walk here it is hunks of buildings standing up without roofs or much sides, and people living in them. Except the Ghetto, where it is just a great plain of bricks, with twisted beds and bath tubs and sofas, pictures in frames, trunks, millions of things sticking out among the bricks. I can't understand how it could have been done. . . . It's something that's so vicious I can't believe it."[1] The world most Europeans had lived in prior to 1914 had ceased to exist. In its place had come death and destruction, and a lack of faith in old ideas.

The Cold War between capitalism and Communism, and between the United States and the Soviet Union, fit the European disaster to a T. Not only had the military outcome of the war left the Americans and the Soviets in command of the continent, but Europeans, hungry for a miracle, or just plain hungry, looked to Washington or Moscow for answers. For now, in a moment unique in Europe's modern history, most of the continent was reduced to a supine waiting on events outside its control. Europeans wanted a lasting peace. They wanted rapid reconstruction. They wanted a future that was fair, efficient, and economically successful. In other words, they wanted to get as far away from the disasters of the 1930s and '40s as possible, and Communism or American capitalism were each offering a way out.

And a way out was needed immediately. Europe in 1945 had come to a standstill. Although the physical infrastructure could be rebuilt, there was a deeply felt sense that things were not moving forward, that the situation after the war ended was going from bad to worse. The continent was facing a humanitarian crisis on a scale that Europe had not seen since the seventeenth century. Within the prewar German borders alone there were around seventeen million displaced people: concentration camp survivors, slave laborers, German refugees from the east, or people who had fled because their homes had been destroyed. They were all hungry and all trying to get to somewhere they could not go. All forms of order had broken down, and it was every man, woman, and child for themselves. A Polish girl trying to get home was struck by the scale of it: "Germany in 1945 was one huge ants' nest. Everyone was moving. This was how the eastern territories of Germany looked like. There were Germans escaping from the Russians. There were all these prisoners of war. There were some of us [Poles]—not that many, but still. . . . It was really incredible, teeming with people and movement."[2]

Even in rich countries that had not experienced hunger for at least three centuries the situation seemed hopeless. In the Netherlands the population in the main cities got fewer than eight hundred calories of food per person per day; the prewar average had been close to three thousand. The Dutch hunger winter of 1944–45 killed at least twenty-two thousand people and its effects were felt long afterward.[3] Getting starving people to contribute to production was next to impossible, and relief—in the Netherlands as elsewhere—could only come from the outside. But in spite of massive attempts by the new UN Relief and Recovery Administration (UNRRA), large parts of Europe still did not have enough to eat by 1947.

The disasters that had befallen Europe put the prestige of the new masters of the continent—the Americans and the Soviets, or the Superpowers as Europeans had started calling them—into sharp relief. Their military power was unquestioned, but unlike Britain—which also had considerable military power in Europe in 1945, but seemed old and exhausted—they could also provide new models of development for the future. Much of the hope for change rode on such inspiration from the outside. Even though the Americans could contribute much more in terms of material supplies, Soviet prestige and Stalin's personal standing were built on the Red Army's central role in defeating Nazi Germany. Whoever could beat the German war machine and conquer Berlin must be a very advanced country, many Europeans believed.

World War II brought total collapse to National Socialism and Fascism. Right-wing Fascist-style authoritarian governments in the Spain of Generalissimo Francisco Franco and the Portugal of António de Oliveira Salazar survived only because they had been neutral during the war. For collectivism and anticapitalism, Communism was the only game in town. Not only had the Soviets played a key role in defeating Germany, but Communist parties elsewhere had often been at the forefront of the resistance against occupation and Nazi rule. In war, four years is a very long time. Many people had forgiven or forgotten Stalin's pact with Hitler, and the erstwhile Communist slogans against "the imperialist robber war" had been drowned out by the post-1941 heroism of the Red Army and local Communist partisans.

In western Europe it was the hope for change that fueled allegiance to the Communist cause. Almost no European wanted to go back to systems that had created two world wars and a profound economic crisis. The hope was for better, and the Communists—with their blend of anti-Fascism, social justice, and reflected glory from the Soviet war effort—carried high the banners of hope. They were by far the biggest party organization in France (with 900,000 members) and in Italy (1.8 million). In the first postwar western European elections, the Communists made inroads everywhere. In Norway they got 12 percent of the vote, in Belgium 13 percent, in Italy 19 percent, in Finland 23.5 percent, and in France almost 29 percent. Their leaders insisted on representation in government, which they got in most of the national-unity cabinets formed after the war was over. They wanted to have a decisive influence on politics in the future, paving the way for a social revolution coming out of the demands of the working class. But the Communist leaders did not believe in immediate revolutionary upheavals in postwar western Europe. Reflecting the advice they were getting from Moscow, they did not want to mount an outright challenge to the existing governments when US and British troops were still in control and could crush such rebellion out of hand.

But even the most powerful Communist leaders in western Europe—Maurice Thorez in France, Palmiro Togliatti in Italy—could not hold back waves of social upheaval that deprivation and degradation spread across the continent. In Italy, workers took control of factories and peasants occupied land. Both there and in France there was political violence against established elites, against people who had collaborated with the Nazis or the Fascists and against those who had not, but happened to own a factory or had a noble title. Some were dragged out of their houses and beaten to death. The elites were seen as responsible for everything that had gone wrong in their countries.

Communist government ministers had their hands full campaigning for social stability and a return to work. France's revival, Thorez said in a speech in October 1945, "depends on our own efforts, the union of all republicans strengthened by the union of the working class."[4] Rebuilding came first, the Communist leader argued, and through rebuilding would come political hegemony for the Left. But some local Communists saw things differently. The government "and the rest, to hell with them. I only have one boss, and that's Stalin," yelled a Communist partisan in southern France as he and his men arrested and beat up local noblemen.[5]

But Stalin, as well as Thorez and Togliatti, at first believed that revolutionary action in western Europe could destroy the Communist parties as well as sound the death knell for the faltering Soviet alliance with the United States and Britain. Stalin expected conflict with the capitalist states and, eventually, Communist revolutions in Europe. But after the end of the war the Soviet Union itself was in ruins. Stalin could not risk a confrontation with his allies while the Soviet Union was weak. Better then, Stalin thought, to express hope of future cooperation while the American and British imperialists fought over the spoils of war on their side. The biggest threat to the Soviet Union, Stalin felt, was if the imperialist countries made a common front against it. The initial postwar Soviet policy on western Europe was designed to avoid such a coming together of its enemies.

In Greece, an ongoing civil war served as a warning to the Soviets and European Communists of what could happen if they acted too soon. When the Axis Powers occupied Greece in 1941, the country's Left formed a National Liberation Front. The front gradually came under the control of the Greek Communist Party, and its armed wing, the Greek People's Liberation Army (ELAS), fought both the Germans and other Greek parties. As the Germans withdrew in late 1944, the British arranged for a coalition government and gradual integration of ELAS into the Greek army. But when the Communist units refused to fully disband, the coalition broke down. After the police opened fire on a Left-wing rally in Athens in December 1944, killing twenty-eight civilians, ELAS fought back. The British responded by aerial bombardments of Communist strongholds in Athens. Out-gunned in the capital and advised by the Soviets to seek a compromise, the Greek Communist leaders agreed to dissolve ELAS in the spring of 1945. Fighting continued in some areas, mostly provoked by Right-wing attempts at driving peasants off the land they had occupied during the war or punishing ELAS soldiers who had fought against them. Six thousand Greek National Liberation Front activists fled across the northern border to Communist-held Yugoslavia.

The Greek disaster led Stalin to demand that other Communists, from China to Italy, not act prematurely. While the Soviets believed that World War II would create revolutions, just as Lenin had taught about the first world war, they expected them mainly in those parts of Europe where the Red Army could help protect them, meaning in the east. Stalin's view was that other Communist parties had neither the experience nor the theoretical understanding to take and keep power on their own. Only when they were guided by the Soviet Union and protected by the Red Army would they stand a chance of permanently defeating their enemies. The Soviet leader remembered well the "Soviet republics" that had sprung up all over Europe, from Finland to Hungary and Bavaria, after 1918. They had, the Soviet leader was fond of explaining, quickly been snuffed out by a better-armed and better-organized Right-wing, supported by the imperialist countries. What made the 1940s different, Stalin believed, was the existence of the Soviet Union as a political and military great power.

The Soviet strategic position in Europe in 1945 was truly remarkable, if one compares it with Russia in 1918 or at any point since the end of the Napoleonic wars. In little more than a year, since the spring of 1944, the Red Army had broken all resistance on the way from deep inside the Russian plains to a line that ran roughly from Lübeck and the Danish island of Bornholm through the middle of Germany and Austria to the Adriatic. The Soviet Union was now in central Europe. The breakdown of Hitler's Third Reich had happened so suddenly that there was little resistance to Soviet control in areas behind Red Army lines. In some countries, such as Bulgaria, Yugoslavia, and Czechoslovakia, the Soviets were generally welcomed as liberators. In others, including Hungary, Poland, and the Baltic states, they were seen as conquerors. It all depended on the locals' historic experience with Russia and the Soviet Union. It also, of course, depended on the degree to which local authorities and populations had collaborated with the Germans. But with Hitler's Reich gone, the Soviets had total military preponderance in eastern Europe. Even those who had reason to hate and distrust them thought twice about challenging them in 1945.

Stalin had yet to make up his mind, though, about what to do with the vast regions of Europe now under his control. Although his political judgment told him that none of the countries were ripe for revolution in the Soviet sense, he hoped that the presence of the Red Army and Soviet civilian advisers would strengthen the Left and enable the Communists to gain significant influence. The Soviet example might steer these countries toward socialism, the Kremlin leaders thought. But in the meantime eastern Europe was important as a buffer zone against any possible American and British imperialist attack on the USSR. Stalin was convinced that Soviet influence had to remain there, although he wanted to keep it in place in ways that did not cause a break with the Americans and the British. The Soviet Union had to rebuild. And until that rebuilding was in place, Stalin hoped to avoid aggression from his World War II allies.

Soviet planning for postwar eastern Europe left much to be desired. The Kremlin had been so preoccupied with fighting the war that there was little time for thinking through postwar scenarios. Much like the United States and Britain—but not nearly at the same level of detail—the Soviets had produced some contingency plans for how to avoid mass starvation and mass flight in eastern Europe as their forces advanced. But even more so than in the west, the course of war defeated the best laid plans. By mid-1945 the Red Army was in control of far more territory in Europe than almost anyone in Moscow had expected. Red Army commanders sought out local authorities who could establish a modicum of order and help with the supply situation, including for their own troops. In some regions, where warfare had been less intense or where the local population welcomed the Soviets as Slavic liberators from German tyranny, these tactics worked reasonably well. But the Red Army's atrocities in war zones, or in non-Slavic countries that had opposed the USSR (Hungary, Romania, and of course Germany) made it difficult even for those who wanted to collaborate with the new masters to work with them there.

The killings, rapes, and robberies that soldiers in the Red Army carried out against the civilian population did much to impede Soviet ability to govern in eastern Europe. In Germany, Soviet soldiers raped hundreds of thousands of women, possibly as many as two million in total. These horrendous experiences were compounded by destruction, theft, and wanton killings of unarmed civilians. By mid-1945 there were very few families in the Soviet occupation zone of Germany who had not experienced Red Army brutality, as had many people in most zones that the Soviets moved into. A young German girl from East Prussia was among a group of refugees who were attacked:

> Terrible hours followed, particularly for the women. From time to time, soldiers came in, also officers, and fetched girls and young women. No shrieking, no begging, nothing helped. With revolvers in their hands, they gripped the women round their wrists and dragged them away. A father who wanted to protect his daughter was brought into the yard and shot. The girl was all the more the prey of these wild creatures. Towards morning, she came back, terror in her child-like eyes. She had become years older during the night.[6]

Soviet leaders tried to excuse their soldiers' behavior by pointing to the systematic cruelty of the Germans and their allies inside the USSR during the war. Some Soviet propagandists and officers egged the soldiers on in their savagery. For them it was a question of revenge. But even for Stalin, who easily turned against his subordinates when they engaged in behavior he considered counterproductive to his aims, Soviet war crimes were a nonissue. He told a group of Yugoslav Communists who complained about Red Army conduct, "One has to understand the soul of the soldier who traveled three thousand kilometers of battle from Stalingrad to Budapest. The soldier thinks that he is a hero, everything is permitted, he is allowed to do anything, he is alive today and might be killed tomorrow, [and] he will be forgiven. The soldiers are tired, they are worn out in the prolonged and difficult war. It is wrong to take the point of view of a 'decent intellectual.'"[7] The Americans, British, and French also committed war crimes at the end of the war in Europe. But they paled in comparison with Soviet actions, which affected millions of families and left a legacy of hatred for future generations.

Eastern European Communists therefore started their postwar agitation under difficult circumstances. Communism had never been strong in the region, except perhaps in Czechoslovakia, where the prewar party had gathered some 10 percent of the votes in free elections.[8] Elsewhere the support for the Communist parties had been minuscule, and the dictatorships in eastern Europe had been Right-wing, nationalist, anti-Communist, and authoritarian. Even though they discounted the effects of their own army's behavior, Soviet leaders saw the weakness of eastern European Communism rather clearly. They believed that the social and economic conditions for advanced socialism were not in place, at least not yet. In some countries it would be hard to achieve even with Soviet support and guidance. The first Soviet reports to come back from eastern Europe in 1945 reported quite negatively on local political conditions, especially—as could be expected—in Poland and Hungary. Stalin himself dismissed the potential for home-grown revolution with a down-home metaphor: "Communism would fit Poland as a saddle on a cow," he told Harry Hopkins, Roosevelt's envoy, in 1944.[9]

What, then, was the form of government in eastern Europe that the Soviets were looking for? Having no experience with pluralism at home and regarding "bourgeois democracy" as a sham, they naturally sought authoritarian regimes that excluded the Soviets' wartime and prewar enemies, that obeyed Stalin's instructions, and included the local Communist parties. Given that there had been little love for Stalin in the region in the past and that the Communists were weak, this meant a very narrow base to rule from. Already by the fall of 1945 the Soviets found that they did not have the instruments in place to secure future influence in eastern Europe after the withdrawal of the Red Army.

Bulgaria is an example of what this meant in practice. After the collapse of the old pro-German regime, the hastily assembled Fatherland Front coalition government increasingly came under the control of the Bulgarian Communists. Though few in numbers, they used their special relations with the Red Army to take command of the ministry of the interior and the police. Thousands of the Communists' Right-wing political opponents were tried by People's Courts set up by the new government or organized by Communist activists locally. Many were sent to prison camps or executed. But though the Communist Party grew in influence and in support, most Bulgarians still favored the Peasants' Party, a Left-wing agrarian reform group that had joined in the Fatherland Front. In a country where more than 80 percent of the population were peasants it could hardly have been otherwise.

The Bulgarian Communists therefore faced a dilemma. The Soviets told them that the right form of government for Bulgaria, at its stage of development, was a "democratic" coalition government, meaning a government of the Left that could rule efficiently and was beholden to Moscow. Georgi Dimitrov, former head of the Comintern who had moved home to take control of the Bulgarian Communist Party, was told that it was fine for the Communists to expand their influence but not to break away from "unity" with the Peasants' Party and other "progressive" forces. But at the same time peasant leaders were becoming increasingly critical of the Communists and their plans, which included the rapid industrialization of Bulgaria. In May 1945, the Communists engineered a split within the Peasants' Party, with a small pro-Communist faction breaking away. The majority, headed by the formidable Nikola Petkov, resigned from the government and ran on a separate ticket in the October 1945 elections. After much voter intimidation and outright fraud, the Communist-dominated Fatherland Front won. From then on

Dimitrov was in charge. He made the country a People's Republic, meaning a republic under Communist control; forced the Social Democrats to merge with the Communists; and detained the main leaders of the non-Communist opposition. Meanwhile, Petkov was arrested, sentenced to death, and hanged in 1947.

The concept "People's Republic" was a Soviet invention from 1924, created for use in Outer Mongolia, a territory in eastern Asia under Red Army control that Moscow could not integrate as a full Soviet republic without serious problems with the Chinese who had ruled there for centuries. But the People's Republic concept fit the situation in eastern Europe, too. Stalin did not want to integrate the eastern European countries into the Soviet Union; doing so would be an unnecessary provocation for the Americans and western Europeans. It would also mean large numbers of sullen, resistant peoples inside Soviet territory. People's Republics became halfway houses: they could become fully Communist, but not entirely Soviet. Even by the beginning of 1947 Stalin had not made up his mind about a model for the composition of future eastern European governments. He preferred coalition governments, headed by powerful Communist parties. Marxist-Leninist political theory told him that the "revolutions" in eastern Europe were "national-democratic" revolutions, not socialist ones. Full Communist rule would happen when circumstances permitted, that is, when the Communist parties had won full hegemony over the working class.

Romania posed a particular challenge for Soviet policies. It, too, had been a German ally, imitating the Nazis by murdering hundreds of thousands of Jews and Roma. It switched sides only in August 1944, when the war was going very badly for Hitler. The Communist Party there was weak and faction-ridden and did not have a key leader such as Dimitrov in Bulgaria. Worse, in Stalin's view the Romanian party was dominated by "non-Romanians"—basically, Jews and Hungarians—who would not be recognized as "national" leaders. By the end of the war the Red Army had full military control, with a million Soviet soldiers stationed in Romania. But where to turn for effective local leadership? The Soviets decided to install a coalition government, as in Bulgaria, with the Communist Party in control of the ministry of justice and therefore the police. The young Romanian king, Michael, protested. Michael was regarded as a national hero after dismissing the pro-German leadership, but the Soviet emissary Andrei Vyshinskii gave him no choice. "You have two hours and five minutes to make it known to the public that [the government] has been dismissed," the Soviet deputy foreign minister barked at the king. "By eight o'clock you must inform the public of [the] successor."[10] In November 1945 the Communist-led coalition won an election through widespread intimidation and fraud. Two years later it forced the king to abdicate. The government announced that a new People's Republic of Romania was up and running.

Bulgaria and Romania may have been tricky for the Soviets to control, but they paled in comparison with the real test, which was Poland. The Soviets were generally hated in this largest of the European countries that had now come under their military control. Imperial Russia had lorded it over parts of Polish territory since the eighteenth century. The Soviet Communists had fought and lost a war against Poland in the early 1920s. Stalin and Hitler had invaded the country and divided it between them in 1939. Then, after having congratulated the Germans on their conquest of Warsaw, Foreign Minister Molotov explained to his partners that the USSR "intended to take the occasion of the further advance of German troops to declare that Poland was falling apart and that it was necessary for the Soviet Union, in consequence, to come to the aid of the Ukrainians and the White Russians."[11] In the course of this "aid," the Soviets had introduced a reign of terror in the part of Poland they had occupied up to 1941, when their German partners betrayed them. Then, in 1944, the Red Army had stood silently by as the Germans slaughtered the desperate Polish resistance in Warsaw. Quite a record on which to create a friendly neighborhood ally.

And still Stalin believed his regime could build a new Poland, with the Polish Communist Party (PPR), however weak, playing a significant role. One element involved a curious mixed army. After Hitler invaded the Soviet Union, the Red Army began recruiting Polish soldiers to fight the Nazis. Most of these men came straight from Soviet prison camps, where they had been since 1939. Not surprisingly, Stalin soon realized that keeping such an army on Soviet soil was a bad idea. He quietly let the British send most of these Poles to fight in the Mediterranean under command of the Polish government-in-exile. But some remained, forming the Polish Army in the USSR, fighting under Red Army command. They were a combination of Communists, Leftists, eastern Poles, and those who simply wanted to fight the Germans closer to home than on faraway battlegrounds in North Africa or Italy.

In January 1945, before the Yalta Conference, the Soviets had established a provisional government of the Republic of Poland, ignoring the government-in-exile, with which it (understandably) had bad relations. At Yalta, the powers had agreed to a merger of the two governments and free elections in Poland as soon as possible. It was an attempt at a compromise that made nobody happy, but it was based on military facts on the ground: the Red Army was in full control of Poland. President Roosevelt's chief of staff, William Leahy, pointed out to the president privately that Stalin's promise was "so elastic that the Russians can stretch it all the way from Yalta to Washington without ever technically breaking it."[12] The new "coalition" government in Warsaw was a marvel of Communist dissimulation: technically it had a non-Communist majority, including some ministers who had returned from London, but in reality it was controlled by Polish Communists under Soviet tutelage.

The big question for the Polish Communists after the war was how to increase their public appeal. History counted against them. The brutal behavior of Red Army soldiers did not help. Even the man the Soviets handpicked as the head of the Polish Communist Party, Władysław Gomułka, noted that "the mistakes that the Soviet organs have committed with regard to the Poles (deportations) have influenced the public opinion . . . ; given these attitudes, there is a danger that we might be accused of being Soviet agents and subjected to isolation."[13] But the Communists also had clear advantages. They had the Red Army and the Polish Army in the USSR to support them in case of trouble. They had international recognition for their government. Their own party may have been in bad shape, but so were all other political parties. They had the advantage that the main treaty with the Soviet Union was signed before the coalition government came into office, and before the crucial decision to incorporate former German territory into Poland and cede Polish lands in the east to the Soviets had been made by the Great Powers at Yalta. The Polish Communists and their allies could therefore claim that they were making the best of a difficult situation: they claimed to stand not just for a rapid modern transformation of a war-torn country, but also for stability and independence.

The Polish Communists had some takers for their message, improbable as it may sound. As everywhere else in eastern Europe, people were tired of fighting and starving. They might not like the new government, but it represented authority and stability. At the end of 1945, Stalin told the Polish Communists they were not taking enough credit for their achievements. "It is ridiculous that you are afraid of accusations that you are against independence. . . . You are the ones who built independence. If there were no PPR, there would be no independence. You created the army, built the state structures, the financial system, the economy, the state. . . . Instead of telling them all that, you are saying only that you support independence. The PPR turned the USSR into an ally of Poland. The arguments are right there at your feet and you don't know how to make use of them."[14] But not only Stalin thought that the Polish Communists were in a much improved situation. Many Poles who disliked the Soviets and the local Communists accommodated themselves to the regime. The Polish-Lithuanian writer Czesław Miłosz, then thirty-five, who later wrote one of the most scathing—and accurate—analyses of the accommodation of intellectuals in eastern Europe—agreed to serve in the new government's foreign ministry. "I was delighted," Miłosz wrote, "to see the semi-feudal structure of Poland finally smashed, the universities opened to young workers and peasants, agrarian reform undertaken and the country finally set on the road to industrialization."[15]

Meanwhile the Communists' attempts at securing their control of the Polish state and Polish society continued. In mid-1946 they managed, by hook and by crook, to get a majority in a referendum supporting land reform and nationalization of basic industries. During that year the Communists gradually, with Soviet assistance, outmaneuvered their Left-wing coalition partners and marginalized them. A few brave politicians—such as Stanisław Mikołajczyk, the leader of the centrist Polish People's Party—attempted to hold them back, and the Polish Catholic Church complained about the country being ruled by atheistic Communists. But no one in Poland had a strategy to prevent Communist domination. Neither did Britain nor the United States. Both the new British foreign secretary Ernest Bevin and US secretary of state James F. Byrnes kept reminding the Soviets of their obligations to arrange free elections in Poland. But neither man believed that Stalin would have known how to organize a free election even if he had wanted to. And Stalin did not want the Poles to vote freely because he knew that in spite of the Communist advances there was no chance they and their allies could win. When Stalin finally agreed to elections in January 1947—ironically first and foremost in a belated attempt at placating the other Great Powers—the Soviets and the Polish Communists made sure that not a vote was counted that should not be. With deception and coercion and the exclusion of opposition candidates on trumped-up charges, the Communist-led Democratic Bloc claimed to have won more than 80 percent of the vote. Opposition leaders ended up in prison or in exile. But the Soviets were still not secure. One of their officials in Poland, in charge of culture, reported to Moscow that he was continuously working to "suggest to the Poles the thought that only in friendship with the USSR will they achieve peace and economic prosperity, that any other path spells trouble for them; . . . to promote the economic and military power of the USSR; [and] to dispel slanderous statements about the backwardness of Soviet culture and technology." But he could report little progress.[16]

Czechoslovakia and Hungary were the most developed of the countries the Red Army occupied after 1944. Before 1918, Hungary had been a key part of the Austro-Hungarian Empire, which dominated central Europe. During World War II, its authoritarian Right-wing government had allied itself with Nazi Germany, with disastrous consequences as the war ended. The Soviets shot their way through eastern Hungary to the capital, Budapest, which was then subjected to a devastating siege. When the Hungarian government tried to arrange a cease-fire, local Fascists rebelled and fought on alongside the Germans until the German surrender in May 1945. Even more than its neighbors, the Hungarians had got the short end of the stick: not only had the country been devastated by war, but its elites had not managed to change sides in time. As a result, Hungary was occupied not only by the Red Army, but by the Romanians, with whom the country had a number of overlapping territorial claims.

Stalin's view of Hungary was colored by the sad fate of the short-lived Hungarian Soviet Republic in 1919 and by what he saw as the strength of the political Right. He instructed the Hungarian Communist leaders who returned from Moscow in order to reestablish their party in Budapest to be careful. Do "not be sparing with words, [but] do not scare anyone," the Boss admonished. "Once you gain strength you may move on."[17] The land reform policies of the coalition government that took over running the country after the German capitulation did prove popular, and the Communists thought they could take much of the credit. They bragged about their influence to Stalin. The Soviet leader, however distrustful he was of the Hungarian party's predominantly Jewish leadership, allowed elections to go ahead in Hungary in the fall of 1945, on the assumption that the Communists would do well. It is also likely that Stalin intended his generosity toward the Hungarians to reduce tension with his allies while he made up his mind about the country's future.

The Hungarian election of 1945 became a disaster for the Communists. By all ordinary measurements they did well by getting 16 percent of the vote in a country where they had not existed a few months previously. But with the Soviets expecting them to do much better and—worst of all—the Right-wing Smallholders' Party getting more than 50 percent, Stalin feared he might lose control of a country that was on the edge of his new sphere of influence. He instructed his old comrade Marshal Kliment Voroshilov, the Soviet representative in Hungary, to insist that "the Communists receive the Interior Ministry; recommend that two posts of deputy prime minister be created additionally and that these be awarded to the Communists and the Social Democrats; pay attention mainly to ensuring that those entering the new Hungarian government from the Smallholders' Party and the Social Democrats should be people also acceptable personally to the Soviet government."[18]

By issuing this ultimatum, the Soviets secured considerable Communist influence in the new government. In spite of its majority of votes, the Smallholders' Party was still hostage to Communist policies because of Soviet manipulation and because they believed that confronting the Communists would risk Moscow's goodwill concerning Hungary's territorial aspirations. Hungary's economic situation was precarious, and with Moscow blocking Budapest from applying for American loans, outside assistance could only come from the USSR. By mid-1947 Hungary's Communists, led by the inveterate Stalinist Mátyás Rákosi, felt that they had decimated their coalition partners enough through arrests, deportations, and intimidation for another election to take place. In August 1947 the Communist Party and its Left-wing allies won 60 percent of the vote after much rigging. With increased confrontation with his former allies looming, Stalin gave his blessing to the new regime, even though he remained unsure of whether the Hungarian Communists could manage the situation.

Between 1944 and 1947 Soviet policies in eastern Europe gave rise to much conflict with the United States and Britain. But American and British policies—in part in response to Moscow's behavior in the east—also helped convince Stalin that only through Communist regimes could Soviet control of eastern Europe be made secure. With Soviet military control already in place, it is likely that a Sovietization of eastern Europe would have happened at some point whatever the policies of others had been. There were a number of very weak states along the Soviet European borders, mostly remnants of the Austro-Hungarian Empire that had collapsed back in 1918. After the German breakdown in 1945, Soviet control seemed probable. But there is no doubt that the advent of a Cold War between the Soviets and the United States made complete Communist takeovers everywhere in eastern Europe more critical and urgent for Moscow. By 1947, Stalin may still have believed that his neighbors were not ready for socialism. But he had concluded that only Communist rule could deliver the kind of security the Soviet Union wanted.

After the Potsdam Conference, Britain and the United States repeatedly protested the Soviets' behavior in the countries they occupied at the end of the war. The regular meetings of the allied foreign ministers became increasingly confrontational, even though the Truman administration realized that it did not have the power to change Soviet policies in areas that the Red Army controlled. The president wanted postwar demobilization to go ahead, bringing US troops back from Europe. But the United States and Britain, working increasingly closely with each other, clashed verbally with the Soviets over reparations from Germany and Italy, over the content of the peace agreements with Romania, Bulgaria, and Hungary, and over the question of the Italian city of Trieste, which had been occupied by the Yugoslav Communists at the end of the war. The short-tempered British foreign secretary, Ernest Bevin, was furious with his Soviet colleague, Molotov, at a Paris meeting in the summer of 1946. It appeared to him, Bevin said, that "the procedure of this conference was not to decide anything." The Russian coolly retorted that "Bevin should not underestimate his services in helping to produce that result."[19] In Washington, President Truman wrote that he was "tired of babying the Soviets."[20]

By the spring of 1947 many Europeans and most US policy-makers had become fixated on a seemingly relentless pattern of Soviet expansionism in eastern Europe. Never mind that this was not how matters may have seemed from Moscow or from within the eastern European countries themselves. In all of these places developments seemed more contingent, more diverse, and generally more chaotic. Still, in the west, many who had lived through the 1930s noted similarities with Nazi expansionism. And there was the scale of it: Soviet control seemed to be imposing itself over half of Europe. In spite of Stalin only acting in countries that had come under Red Army control, there was no clear limit to "eastern Europe" in the minds of many Europeans or Americans. Were Finland and Norway fundamentally different from Czechoslovakia? Were Greece and Turkey different from Bulgaria and Yugoslavia? From the far vantage point of today it may indeed seem so, and Soviet aims therefore seem more limited. But such demarcation lines were hard to see for those who had grown up with a more diverse Europe, where division lines between east and west did not readily exist.

From the start of his tenure, President Truman believed that the Soviets were expansionist in nature, but also that they would not take the risk of a complete break with the United States and Britain. But over the next two years, Truman started to doubt his original judgment. He was furious over Soviet behavior in eastern Europe, where he felt that Stalin had reneged on promises given to FDR about establishing democracies there. He also believed the Soviets were increasingly engaging in confrontational conduct not only in Europe but in Asia, too. Many leaders whom Truman respected were fueling his suspicions. In a March 1946 speech at Westminster College in Fulton, Missouri, where he was introduced by Truman himself, former British prime minister Winston Churchill spoke again about immediate danger. Its motifs, especially the idea of an "iron curtain descending across the continent," he had rehearsed in his letter to Truman a year before. But this was public. The old lion roared:

> From Stettin in the Baltic to Trieste in the Adriatic, an iron curtain has descended across the Continent. Behind that line lie all the capitals of the ancient states of Central and Eastern Europe. Warsaw, Berlin, Prague, Vienna, Budapest, Belgrade, Bucharest and Sofia, all these famous cities and the populations around them lie in what I must call the Soviet sphere, and all are subject in one form or another, not only to Soviet influence but to a very high and, in many cases, increasing measure of control from Moscow. . . . In front of the iron curtain which lies across Europe are other causes for anxiety. . . .

The future of Italy hangs in the balance. . . . In a great number of countries, far from the Russian frontiers and throughout the world, Communist fifth columns are established and work in complete unity and absolute obedience to the directions they receive from the Communist centre. Last time I saw it all coming and cried aloud to my own fellow-countrymen and to the world, but no one paid any attention. . . . We surely must not let that happen again.[21]

Churchill's warning was echoed by a young and talented US diplomat, George F. Kennan, who had served in Moscow during the war. Kennan's Long Telegram, as it became known, sent from Moscow on 22 February 1946 to the State Department, became an influential, widely distributed document in the Administration. In it Kennan described Moscow's policy as inherently aggressive and expansionist because of its Marxist-Leninist ideology. While the Russian people preferred peace, they were held hostage by a party that exploited traditional Russian insecurities against the more advanced parts of Europe. The past had told Russians that only through destroying an enemy could security be achieved. And the current Soviet aim was to weaken foreign powers, through splits and subversion, until Moscow's predominance was complete:

We have here a political force committed fanatically to the belief that with the US there can be no permanent modus vivendi, that it is desirable and necessary that the internal harmony of our society be disrupted, our traditional way of life be destroyed, the international authority of our state be broken, if Soviet power is to be secure. This political force has complete power of disposition over energies of one of world's greatest peoples and resources of world's richest national territory, and is borne along by deep and powerful currents of Russian nationalism. In addition, it has an elaborate and far flung apparatus for exertion of its influence in other countries, an apparatus of amazing flexibility and versatility, managed by people whose experience and skill in underground methods are presumably without parallel in history.[22]

But Kennan, as did his superiors in Washington, believed that war could be avoided. Stalin was not taking unnecessary risks. And the USSR was still much weaker than the United States and had significant internal problems. Containing the Soviet threat, however, meant that the Truman Administration had to become more forward in its foreign policy:

> We must formulate and put forward for other nations a much more positive and constructive picture of the sort of world we would like to see than we have put forward in the past. It is not enough to urge people to develop political processes similar to our own. Many foreign peoples, in Europe at least, are tired and frightened by experiences of the past, and are less interested in abstract freedom than in security. They are seeking guidance rather than responsibilities. We should be better able than Russians to give them this. And unless we do, Russians certainly will.[23]

George Kennan's message was more a summing up of where many US policy-makers were already heading than an innovative policy prescription. It was also in parts contradictory: the Soviets were inherently aggressive but also able to compromise. But for officials hungry for ways of explaining an increasingly complicated world, it resonated. In spite of some compromises being reached at the Paris foreign ministers' meeting, other worries, such as a new flare-up of the Greek civil war and new Soviet demands on Turkey, darkened the picture in late 1946. Truman was increasingly concerned that the Soviets were planning to take control of the Black Sea Straits and help the Communists win in Greece. Such a breakthrough would put the Soviet Union in control of the eastern Mediterranean. It would also be a serious blow to Britain, the traditionally predominant power there, at a time when the British domestic economic situation seemed to be going from bad to worse. In a calculated attempt at getting the United States to back up London's interests in deeds as well as words, the British Labour government formally appealed to Truman for assistance.

The US president now faced some tough choices. Though the economy had avoided the postwar slump that many had predicted, Truman's Democrats had fared badly in the November 1946 midterm elections, with the Republicans taking control of both Houses of Congress for the first time since 1932. In the campaign, his opponents had castigated Truman for being too preoccupied with helping foreign countries and for being too soft on Stalin and the Communists. With public opinion moving in different directions at the same time, Truman felt that the situation called for bold leadership. Although the president knew little about foreign affairs and understood even less, his temperament as well as his political instincts provided a way forward. Truman had been looking for means by which to confront the Soviets. In Greece and Turkey he found one. In March 1947 he addressed a joint session of Congress, in which he asked for up to $400 million ($4.3 billion today) in immediate US economic and military assistance to the two countries. "The very existence of the Greek state is today threatened by the terrorist activities of several thousand armed men, led by Communists, who defy the government's authority," Truman said.

> We shall not realize our objectives . . . unless we are willing to help free peoples to maintain their free institutions and their national integrity against aggressive movements that seek to impose upon them totalitarian regimes. This is no more than a frank recognition that totalitarian regimes imposed upon free peoples, by direct or indirect aggression, undermine the foundations of international peace and hence the security of the United States. . . . I believe that it must be the policy of the United States to support free peoples who are resisting attempted subjugation by armed minorities or by outside pressures.[24]

Truman's new secretary of state, General George C. Marshall, whom the president called the most admired man in America, put the situation even more starkly in a closed meeting with Congressional leaders. "We have arrived at a situation which has not been paralleled since ancient history," Marshall and his deputy, the suave, self-confident Dean Acheson, told them, according to a summary of the meeting. "A situation in which the world is dominated by two great powers. Not since Athens and Sparta, not since Rome and Carthage have we had such polarization of power. It is thus not a question of pulling British chestnuts out of the fire. It is a question of the security of the United States. It is a question of whether two-thirds of the area of the world . . . is to be controlled by Communists."[25] The Administration was following the Republican internationalist senator Arthur Vandenberg's advice to Truman: it was only through "scaring the hell out of the American people" that the White House could get what it wanted. And Truman's address—known later as the Truman Doctrine—frightened Congress enough to grant the president's wishes.

While the Soviets were busy subduing eastern Europe and the Americans debated their future role abroad, western Europe's economic situation continued to deteriorate. Very different from expectations in Washington or London, the supply situation in most of France and the Low Countries, not to mention in Germany and Italy, had not improved as the military and political situation stabilized. Instead, the winter of 1946–47 was among the worst Europeans had ever experienced, with dwindling food stocks, unstable currencies, and diminishing industrial outputs. In a note to his boss Secretary Marshall, the undersecretary of state for economic affairs, William Clayton, laid out the stark realities in May 1947:

> It is now obvious that we grossly underestimated the destruction to the European economy by the war. We understood the physical destruction, but we failed to take fully into account the effects of economic dislocation on production . . . Europe is steadily deteriorating. . . . Millions of people in the cities are slowly starving. . . . Without further prompt and substantial aid from the United States, economic, social and political disintegration will overwhelm Europe. Aside from the awful implications which this would have for the future peace and security of the world, the immediate effects on our domestic economy would be disastrous:

markets for our surplus production gone, unemployment, depression.[26]

To remedy the situation, and to rescue both the western European and the US economies, Truman decided on a gamble. He would ask Congress for an unprecedented grant for European reconstruction. Presented in June 1947 by Secretary of State George Marshall, and henceforth known as the Marshall Plan, the scheme would provide over $12 billion ($132 billion in 2016 dollars) over four years to European countries that signed up to receive it. The conditions seemed unrestrictive: the recipient countries would need to cooperate with each other, open up their economies for outside reporting, and accept American envoys who would help decide where the aid should be allocated. Washington knew that American control (and benefit) would mostly be secured through the Europeans buying US goods for what they received. The main western European countries jumped at the opportunity. The same month France and Britain invited other countries to assemble in Paris to discuss a European response to the American offer. The USSR and the eastern European countries were invited, too. Given the tense situation that existed, Truman expected the Soviets to turn the offer down. But he was willing to take the risk, since not to do so would have made the Marshall Plan a too obvious instrument for waging a Cold War against Moscow.

Stalin hesitated. On the one hand the Soviets and east Europeans needed funds for reconstruction, even more than what the west Europeans did. On the other hand he sensed a trap. Stalin first sent Foreign Minister Molotov to Paris with a large delegation, only to order them to walk out after a few days. Accepting the plan, Molotov declared in Paris, would lead to American hegemony in Europe and a divided continent. When the Czechoslovaks still seemed eager to explore the US offer, Stalin lambasted their pro-Soviet prime minister Klement Gottwald, leaving him shaking: "He reproached me bitterly for having accepted the invitation to participate in the Paris Conference. He does not understand how we could have done it. He says we acted as if we were ready to turn our back on the Soviet Union."[27]

Moscow made its views clear to all eastern European governments: American assistance would be regarded as an anti-Soviet act.

One of Stalin's main anxieties around the Marshall Plan was the future of Germany. After the war ended, the country and its capital, Berlin, had been divided into four zones of occupation, with the Soviets taking control of the eastern part. Stalin believed that a neutral, or in the best case, socialist, Germany was the key to Soviet influence in Europe. In spite of what he often told his foreign interlocutors, he was not primarily concerned with German revanchism; he knew that Germany was removed as a serious military force in Europe for a long time to come. But he was concerned that the western powers—above all the United States—might turn the German territory they controlled into an arsenal for a future confrontation with the Soviet Union. The others ruled the richer part of Germany. And if they integrated it into the Marshall Plan, they would control it permanently. Stalin wanted to avoid such an eventuality, even if it meant depriving his own people and all those of eastern Europe of much-needed aid.

The controversy over the Marshall Plan reminded Stalin about the need to bring Czechoslovakia fully to heel. Even if he had not done so, the Czechoslovak Communists would have been there to remind him. By far the most powerful Communist party in east-central Europe, it had received 38 percent of the vote in a free election in 1946, making it the biggest party in the Czech lands, including in the capital, Prague. Much of the extraordinary support for Communism in Czechoslovakia was an effect of the failure of Britain and France to support the country against the German occupation of 1938–45. The feeling, which went much beyond the Communists, was that the western powers could not be trusted and that the Soviet Union was a necessary and often admired partner. Ever since 1945, the party leaders had pushed for a Czechoslovak revolution—the seizing of total power by the party and its affiliates—but until the autumn of 1947 Stalin refused to give his go-ahead, preferring a coalition government. With a more hard-line policy coming from the Soviets, the Czechoslovak Communists concluded that they had the all clear, and in February 1948 they struck, using the threat of civil war and Soviet intervention to force the aging president, Edvard Beneš, to appoint a government fully controlled by the Communist Party. The police and security services, already in Communist hands, began rounding up "enemies of the people."

The Czechoslovak coup was a shock to many in western Europe, far beyond the anti-Communist Right. Czechoslovakia's inclusion in a Soviet sphere had in no way been seen as a given by other Europeans. There was also—especially in Britain and France—a sense of the need to stand up for the Czechoslovak people, who had been so appallingly betrayed in 1938. Most important was the feeling within the non-Communist western European Left—socialists and social-democrats—that Soviet expansionism and Communist militancy now were a direct threat to them and not only to the old elites. In Norway, for instance, where the ruling Labor Party was traditionally one of the most Left-leaning Social Democratic parties in Europe, Prime Minister Einar Gerhardsen spoke out against the Soviets and the local Communists: "The events in Czechoslovakia have not only aroused sorrow and anger among most Norwegians, but also fear and alarm. Norway's problem is, as far as I can see, primarily a domestic problem. What could threaten the freedom and democracy of the Norwegian people is the danger that the Norwegian Communist Party represents at any given time. The most important task in the struggle for Norway's independence, for democracy and the rule of law, is to reduce the influence of the Communist Party and the Communists as much as possible."[28]

The Norwegian Communists, few in number and already politically isolated, had no chance to counter the might of a well-organized and unsparing Social Democratic movement. It was a pattern that repeated itself all over Scandinavia, in the Low Countries, and in Austria after the Czechoslovak coup.

Part of the weakness of many western European Communist parties stemmed from new instructions from Stalin. It had become clear to him that the main postwar conflict would not be between the remaining capitalist powers, but between the capitalist world, headed by the United States, and the Soviet Union. Now, in this new state of things, an old weapon would be retooled. In September 1947, the Communist International, the Comintern, which had been dissolved during the war as a gesture of goodwill—with the war on, it did not make much sense to seek to foment revolution among your allies—was resurrected as the Cominform (Communist Information Bureau). At its inaugural meeting at Szklarska Poręba on the Polish-Czechoslovak border, Stalin's deputy for issues of ideology, Andrei Zhdanov, made clear the Boss's current thinking with a decisive clarity:

> The crusade against Communism proclaimed by America's ruling circle with the backing of the capitalist monopolies, leads as a logical consequence to the attacks on the fundamental rights and interests of the American working people . . . to adventures abroad in poisoning the minds of the politically backward and unenlightened American masses with a virus of chauvinism and militarism, and in stultifying the average American with the help of all the diverse means of anti-Soviet and anti-Communist propaganda—the cinema, the radio, the church and the press. . . . The strategic plans of the United States envisage the creation in peacetime of numerous bases and vantage grounds situated at great distances from the American continent against the USSR and the countries of the new democracy. America has built, or is building, air and naval bases in Alaska, Japan, Italy, South Korea, China, Egypt, Iran, Turkey, Greece, Austria and Western Germany. . . . Economic expansion is an important supplement to the realization of America's strategical plan. American imperialism is endeavoring . . . to take advantage of the post-war difficulties of the European countries, in particular the shortage of raw materials, fuel and food in the Allied countries that suffered most from the war, to dictate to them extortionate terms for any assistance rendered.[29]

Stalin suspected that the western European Communist parties were being seduced by the Americans and the local elites. The leaders of the French Communist Party "have fallen prey to the fear that France would collapse without American credits," he told his inner circle at a drunken party at his dacha in August 1947. At the Szklarska Poręba meetings the next month, the verbal attacks continued. The Soviets entrusted the Yugoslavs with launching a stinging attack on their comrades in western Europe: "After the war, certain communists thought that a peaceful, parliamentary period of appeasement of the class struggle was ahead—there was a deviation towards opportunism and parliamentarism, in the French party, the Italian party, as in other parties."[30]

By the beginning of 1948 a Cold War system of states was being established in Europe. A lot was still unclear, but the main characteristics were known. Communist parties would be in political control of the countries occupied by the Soviet Union at the end of World War II. The United States would remain involved in European affairs. Britain's role was permanently reduced. Most of the western European Left would side with their governments against the Communists and the Soviets. Although neither the Soviets nor the Americans wanted war in Europe, military tension was likely to grow. The American government was increasingly thinking of European and world politics in terms of containment of the Soviet Union and Communism. Soviet leaders—essentially Stalin himself—were choosing security and ideological rectitude over any potential for limited cooperation with the United States and Britain. And while Europe was changing politically in dramatic ways, the reconstruction of its economies and social structure was taking longer than anyone had expected.

4

Reconstructions

During the 1940s and early 1950s, Europe and the rest of the world were being reconstructed in ways that would have been hard to recognize from the early part of the century. Some of this reconstruction was physical, made necessary by the ravages of war. But there was also a political and intellectual reconstruction going on, which put the Cold War between Communism and capitalism, and between the Soviet Union and the United States, at the center of world affairs. For people in most parts of the world it was increasingly as if the great power conflict had something to do with them, often at the personal level. Over and over again, events that were in origin local and specific metamorphosed into manifestations of a global struggle. The main reason for this was that both the Soviets and the Americans—as Kennan had pointed out in his Long Telegram—stood for models of human endeavor that had universalist pretensions. The Nazis had tried to rule through extermination. The colonial empires had ruled through exploitation and racial oppression. But the undoubted cruelty that both emerging Superpowers were capable of—nuclear extermination of cities or millions sent to labor camps—was offset in people's minds by the promise each held of a better life, especially for those in the many parts of the world who had gone through hell in the first decades of the twentieth century. The reconstruction that took place in the first years after the war ended was psychological as well as physical, and it privileged a Cold War competition for people's minds.

At first, agendas changed rather subtly, and then—as wartime attempts at cooperation faded from memory—the changes happened more and more quickly. One good example is the United Nations, the brainchild of President Roosevelt, the world organization through which he wanted to make up for the US failure to help build peace and prosperity after World War I. To begin with, the UN concentrated on rescue and relief operations in Europe and Asia; through the UN Relief and Recovery Administration much was achieved, mainly with US funding. The UN agencies dealing with food and health, the Food and Agriculture Organization and the World Health Organization, began work to study and ameliorate famine and epidemics with support by both Superpowers, and without much overt Cold War interference. Even the new world economic institutions, the International Monetary Fund and the World Bank, launched relatively smoothly, although the United States—as the biggest provider of funds—kept control of who could receive funding. Stalin at first regarded the UN simply as a concession to his wartime American partners and took little interest in its proceedings, except through the UN Security Council, where the Soviet Union used its veto to block resolutions it did not like.

It was the Americans who first discovered how the UN could serve their Cold War purposes. The text of the UN's Universal Declaration of Human Rights was passed in 1948 by a coalition of American New Dealers, western European liberals, and postcolonial elites, with the Soviets unable to block it. They in the end abstained from the vote, along with seven other states. Forty-eight voted in favor. The Chilean representative summed up the conflict in distinct terms: "The views expressed by the Polish representative and shared by the USSR delegation resulted from a different conception of life and man. The draft declaration rested on the assumption that the interests of the individual came before those of the State and that the State should not be allowed to deprive the individual of his dignity and his basic rights. The opposing conception was that the rights of the individual must give precedence to the interests of society."[1] The declaration may not have had much practical significance in the first decades of the Cold War, but its adaptation was a victory for the United States over Soviet concepts of rights.

While words could be made into weapons at the UN, science could be made into weapons at the world's top universities and laboratories. In 1945, some observers thought that the invention of nuclear weapons would prevent armed conflict in the future. The consequences of war would simply be too great. But the Truman Administration did not heed calls for shared control of the frightful new weapons through the UN. Instead, the US military gradually began integral planning for the use of atomic bombs in warfare. "Plan Broiler" from November 1947—one of the first complete war plans against the Soviet Union drawn up by the US Joint Chiefs of Staff—envisaged thirty-four atomic bombs dropped on twenty-four Soviet cities. The White House and top military commanders were aware of the terrifying gulf that separated nuclear weapons from conventional weapons, in spite of calls from some officers and members of Congress to make atomic bombs more readily available at the potential frontlines of a war with the Soviets. Truman had read the medical reports coming in from tests made on survivors of Hiroshima and Nagasaki. The atomic bomb was not just another weapon, and the Administration was uncertain both about production and control. Still, having a nuclear monopoly gave the Americans confidence, and boosted their willingness to develop a global strategy. By the end of 1949 more than two hundred bombs had been produced, and twenty B-29 bombers had been modified to carry them.

For the Soviet Union the US nuclear monopoly was an immediate threat, even though neither Stalin nor his American counterparts believed that atomic weapons by themselves would win a war. Outwardly the Soviets used the US refusal to share nuclear technology as part of its "peace campaign," portraying the Truman Administration as warmongers, hell-bent on nuclear destruction. Internally, Stalin had started a crash program to develop a Soviet nuke. Using a combination of Soviet physics' prowess and intelligence gathered from spies within the US program, the plans made rapid progress. The first test in August 1949 was an example of what Soviet science could achieve.

Even though the Soviets were only able to develop five or six atomic bombs over the first couple of years, it started an arms race in which Moscow seemed to be catching up with Washington. In November 1952 the Americans tested the first thermonuclear weapon, the so-called hydrogen or H-bomb, a nuclear weapon 450 times more powerful than the bomb that had destroyed Hiroshima in 1945. The Soviets tested a similar weapon only nine months later.

The US invention of nuclear weapons made most Americans feel that their country had unique power and responsibility in the world. After the Soviets got their nukes, it also created a sense of American vulnerability. The change from isolationist American attitudes in the 1920s and '30s was palpable. Government propaganda explains just a part of this change. The experience of having been attacked at Pearl Harbor, of having fought in Europe and the Pacific during World War II, as well as the legacies of an activist state at home during the New Deal, contributed to making Americans more interventionist in their approach. Even though those in charge in the White House were Democratic liberals, they were joined in their Cold War policies by many Republicans. The Marshall Plan, a massive US investment in the future of Europe, passed a Republican-controlled House with only 74 members voting against. The assistance to Greece and Turkey was opposed by 107 congressmen. Even Republicans like Robert Taft, who had been a standard-bearer for noninterventionism in the 1930s (and who later was to oppose both NATO and the Korean War) voted for Truman's economic and military aid plans. From a US perspective, the Cold War was a bipartisan initiative.

Instead, the main challenge to Truman's decision to confront the Soviet Union came from the Left. And it was not much of a challenge. Roosevelt's former secretary of agriculture, Henry Wallace—a Democratic Party grandee who regarded himself as a leader of the Left—decided to form a separate party for the presidential elections in 1948. "The bigger the peace vote in 1948," Wallace said in declaring his candidacy, "the more definitely the world will know that the United States is not behind the bi-partisan reactionary war policy which is dividing the world into two armed camps and making inevitable the day when

American soldiers will be lying in their Arctic suits in the Russian snow."[2] Even though it was supported by some Democrats who felt that Truman was moving away from the legacies of the New Deal by breaking the wartime alliance with the USSR, Wallace's campaign was undermined by his own haplessness as a candidate and the rather shrill US Communist Party support for his cause. To everyone's surprise, Truman narrowly won the election against the Republican Thomas Dewey. Wallace's Progressives scored 2.5 percent of the vote, less than Strom Thurmond's Southern segregationists ticket.

Truman's second-term foreign policy was marked by increasing tension with the Soviets, the collapse of a US-supported government in China, and the outbreak of the Korean War. This was the time when the Cold War was militarized, both from a Soviet and American perspective. Truman's administration struggled to put together a comprehensive and global strategy for fighting what everyone hoped would remain a shadow war with the Soviets. There was never much doubt in the president's mind that the struggle was *both* against the Soviet Union and Communism globally. And he had little time for those among his own advisers—such as George Kennan—who warned against a global militarization of the conflict. Kennan was replaced as director of the State Department's Policy Planning Staff in 1949, and his successor, the more hawkish Paul Nitze, put together a document that attempted to set out a US Cold War strategy.[3] Later known as NSC-68, the paper was radical in its recommendations and would probably not have come to reflect the Administration's policies if it had not been for the outbreak of the Korean War three months after it was first presented.

The direction of NSC-68 focused on the need for dramatic increases in US defense spending and on American willingness to intervene globally. It encouraged economic and psychological warfare as well as covert operations to target the Soviet enemy and its allies. It wanted a dramatic increase in US intelligence-gathering capabilities and in money spent on internal security and civil defense. It was even foolhardy enough to suggest that tax increases and cuts in domestic programs would be necessary to pay for these expenses. The purpose was to put the United States on war footing in a conflict that could last for a very long time.

Still, the most striking aspect of NSC-68 was not its practical suggestions but the view of the enemy that it represented. "The defeat of Germany and Japan and the decline of the British and French Empires have interacted with the development of the United States and the Soviet Union in such a way that power increasingly gravitated to these two centers," Nitze and his colleagues explained.

> The Soviet Union, unlike previous aspirants to hegemony, is animated by a new fanatic faith, anti-thetical to our own, and seeks to impose its absolute authority over the rest of the world. Conflict has, therefore, become endemic and is waged, on the part of the Soviet Union, by violent or non-violent methods in accordance with the dictates of expediency. . . . The [Soviet] design . . . calls for the complete subversion or forcible destruction of the machinery of government and structure of society in the countries of the non-Soviet world and their replacement by an apparatus and structure subservient to and controlled from the Kremlin. To that end Soviet efforts are now directed toward the domination of the Eurasian land mass. The United States, as the principal center of power in the non-Soviet world and the bulwark of opposition to Soviet expansion, is the principal enemy whose integrity and vitality must be subverted or destroyed by one means or another if the Kremlin is to achieve its fundamental design. . . . Our free society finds itself mortally challenged by the Soviet system. No other value system is so wholly irreconcilable with ours, so implacable in its purpose to destroy ours, so capable of turning to its own uses the most dangerous and divisive trends in our own society, no other so skillfully and powerfully evokes the elements of irrationality in human nature everywhere, and no other has the support of a great and growing center of military power.[4]

The long-term US aim, NSC-68 maintained, is to create "a fundamental change in the nature of the Soviet system, a change toward which the frustration of the design is the first and perhaps the most important step. Clearly it will not only be less costly but more effective if this change occurs to a maximum extent as a result of internal forces in Soviet society." But to begin with the United States should concentrate on internal and external defense:

> It is quite clear from Soviet theory and practice that the Kremlin seeks to bring the free world under its dominion by the methods of the cold war. The preferred technique is to subvert by infiltration and intimidation. Every institution of our society is an instrument which it is sought to stultify and turn against our purposes. Those that touch most closely our material and moral strength are obviously the prime targets, labor unions, civic enterprises, schools, churches, and all media for influencing opinion. The effort is not so much to make them serve obvious Soviet ends as to prevent them from serving our ends, and thus to make them sources of confusion in our economy, our culture, and our body politic.[5]

As a document, NSC-68 was itself a product of a new US foreign policy coordination process centered on the White House. The National Security Council (NSC) was set up by President Truman in 1947 in order to link the various foreign policy, military, and intelligence bodies within the executive branch. At first the NSC was intended primarily as a step toward providing better and more consistent advice to the president. But, bowing to bureaucratic necessities, it increasingly took on key functions of consultation, deliberation, and—at least to some extent—policy-making. As the Cold War intensified, the NSC became the main coordinating body for how to conduct it within the US government. On intelligence, likewise, Truman aimed for centralization and effectivization. The Central Intelligence Agency (CIA), established by the same act that set up the NSC, aimed at bringing together the various intelligence-gathering bureaus and agencies that existed within the US government. In this it failed, since different branches of military intelligence as well as the signals intelligence bureau (later renamed the National Security Agency, or

NSA) remained outside CIA purview. But the new agency still became a key instrument of US Cold War capabilities, both through spying and through covert operations.

As US capacity increased and expanded, so Britain's decreased and contracted. The agenda for the British government in the late 1940s and early 1950s was much narrower than its victory in World War II should have allowed for. Britain was still a great power with global interests. But it did not have the economic capacity to sustain its status for much longer. As the war ended, Britain was broke. It had lost one quarter of its national wealth, meaning that its expenditure for World War II was roughly twice that of World War I. When Churchill had spoken of all-out mobilization against the Nazis, his government had really meant it: Britain had borrowed (from the Americans), sold off foreign assets, and sacrificed civilian production at home to keep the war going. It had won, but at a cost that was too great to bear for Britain's prewar position. In order to pay back its debts and rebuild at home—not to mention prepare for the welfare state that the Labour government had promised—the UK had to introduce rationing for most goods and cut back dramatically on its overseas military engagements. Still, it was not enough. People had to line up for hours in order to get basic supplies. Bombed-out Londoners had to wait on average seven years to get a new home.[6]

Politically, Clement Attlee's government was caught in a quandary. For a while it kept on pretending that Britain could be the balancing force on the European continent, helping to contain Communism, while gradually allowing for more freedoms in the Empire and building a welfare state at home. In reality it had to choose, and—understandably enough—opted for the latter. By 1950 the British withdrawal from east of Suez was in full swing; India and Pakistan had become independent in 1947, southeast Asia was soon to follow, and Britain's position in the Middle East and the Mediterranean was much reduced. One should be careful, though, with making Britain's international weakness in the 1950s total: it still had one of the largest armies and navies in the world, it had the prestige of having stood up to

Hitler when nobody else would or could, and it had—successfully it seemed—hitched its wagon to that of the world's main power, the United States. The British may have felt that they were treated dismally by their big ally and resented the slide in their country's international prestige. But, whether they voted Labour or Conservative, they were also aware that they were getting something back: free medical care for all, universal pensions, and family allowances mattered in what was still one of the most class-ridden societies on earth.

If life in Britain was topsy-turvy after the war, its former enemy had had its existence almost obliterated. Germany was a wreck in 1945, and it took a long time for its people to begin moving out of the physical and psychological ruins Hitler had left behind. Even though German industrial production in 1945 was less than 20 percent of what it had been before the war, the psychological scars were worse than the material destruction. The Germans had, in 1933, joined up with a disastrous political project. Right to the end of the war they had embraced the lie, and the Nazi breakdown was therefore utterly demoralizing. What was the purpose of work, if death and devastation were its wages? Getting any form of economic activity going again in post-war Germany was difficult, and in the first years Germans were dependent on handouts from the victorious powers. The only way of obtaining goods beyond the bare necessities was through the black market.

The allies had a hard time deciding what to do with Germany. The French and some Americans suggested its total dismemberment as a state; one American plan proposed the abolition of its industrial potential and its reinvention as an agricultural economy. Agreeing to zones of occupation was the easy part at first. The Soviets got 40 percent in the east (reduced to 28 percent when Stalin transferred German territory to Poland). The remainder was shared between Britain (in the northwest), the United States (in the south), and a smaller zone in the southwest for France. Very soon the discussion about Germany's long-term future was overwhelmed by its immediate needs. None of the occupying powers wanted to contribute more to the German economy than what they were getting out of it—"paying reparations to the Germans," as the cash-strapped British put it. To make things worse for the western Allies, the Potsdam agreements allowed the Soviets to receive some of their reparations from the western zones. So while the Americans in reality were paying for the upkeep of the former enemy, the Soviets—who contributed much less in their zone—were busy dismantling surviving German industries in the Ruhr and shipping them east.

In May 1946 the US military governor, General Lucius D. Clay, unilaterally suspended reparation deliveries from the American zone. The British did the same three months later. The Soviets were furious, but could do little about it. Neither could they hinder the Americans and the British from joining their two zones, for economic purposes, at the end of 1946. The so-called Bizonia was supposed to be a temporary measure. But in reality it laid the foundation for a separate West German state. At the Moscow foreign ministers' meeting in March 1947, it became clear that both the two main western allies were edging closer to Kennan's view from 1945, when he had argued that "we have no choice but to lead our section of Germany . . . to a form of independence so prosperous, so secure, so superior, that the East cannot threaten it."[7] By mid-1947, after the authorities in Bizonia had in effect given up on the de-Nazification of German industry, some economic activity had restarted in western Germany, but it did still not show any signs of an economic recovery.

As on so many other matters, Stalin found it difficult to decide what Soviet postwar policy toward Germany should be. He had learned from his mentor Lenin that Germany was the big prize for socialism in Europe; only with a Communist Germany, Lenin had believed, could the Soviet Union continue to exist in the long run. But instead of going socialist, Germany had been taken over by the Nazis in the 1930s and, after Stalin's attempts at accommodation had failed, had started a war in which the USSR itself almost succumbed. Even in defeat, Germany was therefore a big opportunity as well as a big danger. If a neutral Germany could gradually be linked to the Soviet Union, then the Cold War in Europe would be won. But if the Americans succeeded in turning the part of Germany it occupied—the richest and best developed part—into an arsenal for a US-led attack on the USSR, then Communism would be stamped out. Stalin therefore had to be cautious not to misstep, again, on Germany.

As so often happens, indecision led to passivity. For a crucial year Stalin let events in Germany float. He allowed his soldiers to introduce a regime of terror in the east, not exactly conducive to the future establishment of socialism. He seemed more preoccupied with looting what could be of use to the Soviets than with establishing order in his occupation zone. If the Soviet zone, after the initial chaos, for a while seemed to work better than the west, this was due not so much to Stalin as to Red Army administrators and the German Communists who had come back with them. They were more than ready to take over the centralized planning systems that had existed in Nazi Germany and to rely on them in order to get basic infrastructure and production going wherever possible. After a while former Nazi officials at the lower levels—those the Soviets decided not to put on trial—also found it remarkably easy to collaborate; the Communist ideas of planning were not, after all, that different from those of their former masters.

Publicly, however, the new east German authorities held high the banner of anti-Fascism. They were the "good Germans"; the bad Germans, plenty of them, were all collaborating in the western occupation zones, or so German Communist propaganda claimed. Many Left-wing Germans fell for the disinformation, especially intellectuals and artists, some of whom moved east, including top names in German literature like Stefan Heym and Bertolt Brecht, who both moved there from wartime exile in the United States. In the spring of 1946 the Soviets and the German Communists forced the Social Democrats in the east into a Socialist Unity Party (SED), in which the Communists under Wilhelm Pieck and Walter Ulbricht had full control. Again, some non-Communist Left-wingers joined enthusiastically, believing that they thereby made up for the failure of the German Left to cooperate against Hitler in the 1930s. Most Social Democrats were made of sterner stuff, however, and fought to keep their party separate, even if it meant relocating to the western occupation zones. Still, the SED scored enough successes for Stalin to be convinced that there would be a future for Soviet political influence in a united Germany.

The reasons why Stalin wanted a united Germany were exactly the same reasons why the United States, by 1947, did not. A functional German state would have to be integrated with western Europe in order to succeed, Washington found. And that could not be achieved if Soviet influence grew throughout the country. This was not only a point about security. It was also about economic progress. The Marshall Plan was intended to stimulate western European growth through market integration, and the western occupation zones in Germany were crucial for this project to succeed. Better, then, to keep the eastern zone (and thereby Soviet pressure) out of the equation. After two meetings of the allied foreign ministers in 1947 had failed to agree on the principles for a peace treaty with Germany (and thereby German reunification), the Americans called a conference in London in February 1948 to which the Soviets were not invited. Before the meeting started, it was clear that the Americans and British had agreed between themselves on German currency reform and on elections in Bizonia. The French reluctantly joined in the plans. As Bevin explained to Parliament,

> Germany cannot be allowed to remain a slum in the centre of Europe. On the contrary, our policy is that she must contribute to her own recovery and keep herself, and give her share to European recovery. That is the best way to get Germany to make reparations for the devastation that she caused in the war. In accordance, therefore, with the London recommendations, Germany has been incorporated into the European Recovery Programme [the Marshall Plan]. . . . She will receive her share of aid under this programme, but in turn she must produce and be enabled to pay her share into the common pool. She cannot do it unless we proceed apace with economic rehabilitation. We must give her the tools to work with if she is to make a contribution.[8]

The division of Germany was therefore in some respects a result of the Marshall Plan. The United States regarded it as crucial to its own security to get the European economies going again. The Soviet Union and the Communist governments had, understandably, no wish to join in European recovery plans headed by the United States and implemented by US officials. The necessity of including the western part of Germany, under control of the western Allies, into the Marshall Plan therefore meant its separation from the east. The new deutschmark was a symbol of this division, and it was a dramatic step. First the western Allies agreed on a new German central bank. Then, in June 1948, they wiped out public and private debt by setting ceilings on how much old currency could be fully converted into Deutschmark. And then they pegged the new currency to the US dollar at a low exchange rate, while abolishing price controls in the western zones. The effects were spectacular. Overnight the black market virtually disappeared. Goods reappeared in the shops and production began to increase. Workers were unhappy because their wages did not increase. And savers were furious because—for the second time in the lifetimes of some—their savings were decimated. Angriest of all were the Soviets, who were now forced to introduce a separate currency in the east in order to prevent their zone being flooded with the former currency, now worthless in the west.

West German currency reform was an integral part of the Marshall Plan, which in itself was a part of the integration of western Europe into a US-led capitalist economy. It was the completion of a process that had begun in the early part of the twentieth century, with the gradual transfer of technology, production, and management methods, and instruments for trade and investment. But it was also a response to the crisis that had been created by depression and world war. Like the New Deal in the United States, the Marshall Plan was an attempt at getting production going again, using whatever instruments were available. US advisers, many of whom were old New Dealers themselves, were willing to accept European government controls, planning, and even nationalizations if it helped put people back to work and bring goods to market. At the core of the project, though, was the realization that the capitalist market had not existed in Europe during the war and had mostly been a disaster before it. If markets, banking, and belief in private property were to be resurrected, the United States had to offer economic assistance to Europe.

It is hard to say exactly how much Marshall Plan aid assisted with European postwar recovery, in spite of its $12 billion size (roughly $150 billion in today's money)—about 1.5 percent of the US GDP per year. It is likely that some growth would have begun anyway, though more in some countries and regions than others. But its psychological effect was massive everywhere. Western Europeans started believing in public and private institutions again, making spending possible and increasing employment and productivity. In economic terms, it made up for the trade deficits with the United States, which otherwise would have had a debilitating effect on European economies. It made claims for reparations from Germany less important. And it abated balance of payment difficulties between European countries, helping to get inter-European trade going again. Between 1947 and 1951 production grew on average 55 percent in Marshall Plan countries.[9]

The recipients at first approached US offers of aid gingerly. Some did not like the inclusion of Germany. Others believed that it amounted to a wholesale US takeover of the European economies. Resistance was found mostly at the far side of the Right and the Left. The Communists protested—violently, in some cases, as when dockworkers in Marseilles and Naples prevented the off-loading of American ships. "The European worker listens listlessly while we tell him we are saving Europe, unconvinced that it is his Europe we are saving," according to one US Marshall Plan official.[10] But traditional European elites were not too happy, either. They felt that the Americans were out to upset established social order and wipe out their positions within their own societies. They saw American table manners, raunchy music, and black soldiers as a threat to their European culture.

The meeting of minds was most often between American officials and the emerging European Christian Democrat or Social Democrat leaders. The Americans insisted that the Europeans themselves should decide on the details of how Marshall Plan funds should be spent, within the frameworks established by Washington. In Britain, some of the funds were used for food imports, alleviating the shortages created by the war. In Germany and France much money was spent on the import of heavy machinery to restart industries. Everywhere governments used the new funds available for reconstructing what the war had destroyed; photos of smiling families in front of their new apartment block rising from the rubble were much used to counter Communist slogans that the Marshall Plan was simply preparation for a new war. The budget guarantees US aid offered enabled western European governments to begin constructing their modern welfare states; without it, there certainly would not have been the surpluses necessary for new social expenditure or, for that matter, for government investments in infrastructure, which helped tie the western part of the continent together.

For Americans and western European governments alike, a major part of the Marshall Plan was combatting local Communist parties. Some of it was done directly, through propaganda. Other effects on the political balance were secondary or even coincidental. A main reason why Soviet-style Communism lost out in France or Italy was simply that their working classes began to have a better life, at first more through government social schemes than through salary increases. The political miscalculations of the Communist parties and the pressure they were under from Moscow to disregard the local political situation in order to support the Soviet Union also contributed. When even the self-inflicted damage was not enough, such as in Italy, the United States experimented with covert operations to break Communist influence. The Italian election in April 1948 pitted a US-funded Christian Democracy, heavily supported by the Catholic Church and the Vatican, against a Soviet-funded and Communist-led Popular Democratic Front. Both camps were led by Italians from outside Italy: the Christian Democrat leader Alcide De Gasperi, born in Austria and not an Italian citizen until he was almost forty, against Palmiro Togliatti, the Communist leader who had spent almost twenty years in exile in the USSR. The CIA got

Italian-Americans to write letters to their relatives at home, agitating against the Communist threat, while engaging in dirty tricks' campaigns against Communist candidates. In the end the Christian Democrats won almost 50 percent of the vote. They would probably have won anyway, since the Communist coup in Czechoslovakia two months before drove a lot of voters away from the Left. But the 1948 elections symbolized the first occasion when the CIA had engaged in a big covert operation against its enemies, and the Agency was very pleased with the result.

In France the Communist Party had been thrown out of government in May 1947 after they refused to support the French reconquest of its Indochinese colonies. The French Communists, led by Maurice Thorez, had long been caught between being a responsible party leading the country and getting a more radical course of change. Their position in France was very strong; the sense that the old elites had failed during the war drove young people to the Communist party. Its support among intellectuals and students was particularly powerful, but it also had a solid working class base in the trade unions. In addition, it was helped by the positive image of the Soviet Union held by many French people—the Soviets had, after all, defeated Nazi Germany (which France itself had spectacularly failed to do). Even anti-Communist intellectuals such as Raymond Aron admitted that "every action, in the middle of the twentieth century, presupposes and involves the adoption of an attitude with regard to the Soviet enterprise."[11] But the French Communists went so far in supporting the Soviet Union's ever-changing policies that they isolated themselves, in spite of being the biggest political party and the only one with mass popular support. They got no succor from Stalin. The Boss "considers the policy of the Fr[ench] party entirely wrong," the former Comintern chief Georgi Dimitrov wrote in his diary after another evening of drinking at Stalin's dacha. "Its leaders have fallen prey to the fear that France would collapse without American credits. The Communists should have left the government with the explanation that they are against the betrayal of France's independence, instead of waiting to be thrown out."[12]

Stalin's advice to the French showed him at his most disingenuous. In 1945 he had advised the French Communist Party (PCF) to work within a parliamentary system. With Great Power relations in tatters, he now turned on them because they had followed Soviet instructions. But he was right about the rest of French politics (except the Communists, who remained his most loyal followers whatever opprobrium he threw at their party). The new French leaders—General Charles de Gaulle, who had resigned in a huff in 1946, and those of the Fourth Republic who followed him—were entirely dependent on US aid. Since almost all Frenchmen still believed that their country was a Great Power, this was a difficult position to be in. Germany had humiliated France in 1940. The United States was, in the eyes of many Frenchmen, humiliating France now simply by being in a so much more powerful position than France itself was. "The United States . . . is infatuated with its own weight," wrote the philosopher Jean-Paul Sartre. "The richer it is, the heavier it is. Weighed down with fat and pride, it lets itself be rolled towards war with its eyes closed."[13]

But while French anti-Americanism was shared by many Frenchmen outside of the Communist Party, its government became increasingly closely linked with the United States. Marshall Plan aid was crucial for France, which mostly spent it making long overdue investments in French industry, thereby laying the groundwork for an industrial revival in the 1950s. But the links with Washington were also essential in security terms. The leaders of the Fourth Republic knew that in case of war the Red Army would be heading straight for Paris. American influence may be a danger to France's soul, but Soviet power was a danger to its heart. And France needed assistance against what its leaders saw as a distinct security threat. In March 1948 its government signed the Brussels Pact with Britain, the Netherlands, Belgium, and Luxembourg, providing for mutual assistance in case of an attack by others. But it was clear to many non-Communist French leaders—with Soviet forces standing only one hundred miles from the Rhine—that this was not enough. After the Czechoslovak coup and the crises over Germany, French leaders who at first had wanted to work with the Communists—such as the wartime head of the French

resistance, Georges Bidault, who had insisted on Communist participation in his postwar government—sought a US commitment to
French security. Bidault became a key figure among European Christian Democrats in the discussion about a western European defense
treaty with the United States.

The Soviet reaction to western economic policies in Germany
helped convince French leaders that the Soviets and not the Germans
would be the biggest threat to their country's security in the future.
Stalin was furious about the introduction of the deutschmark and
what he saw as US attempts at keeping Germany divided for its own
purposes. He wanted to strike back, but in a manner that did not risk
outright war with the western countries. The German strategy arrived
at in Moscow in 1948 was split into many different parts. Stalin wanted
to solidify his grip on the east by taking full control of Berlin. He also
began reaching out to "real Germans," as he put it, those who had followed Hitler and the NSDAP, through Soviet-sanctioned nationalist
propaganda in Germany against the United States. If German nationalism could prevent US control of western Germany, then it would
objectively serve Soviet interests. The National Democratic Party of
Germany, set up under Communist control in the east in order to at-
tract former Nazis to the Soviet cause, declared in its program: "America violated the Treaty of Potsdam and plunged us Germans . . . in the
biggest national distress of our history. . . . But the American war may
and shall not take place! Germany must live! That's why we National
Democrats demand: the Americans to America. Germany for the
Germans. . . . Peace, independence and prosperity for our entire German fatherland."[14]

Alongside their propaganda for a plebiscite on the unification and
neutrality of Germany, Soviet and German Communists developed a
somewhat rudimentary plan for forcing the western powers out of
Berlin. Stalin had stressed the centrality of Communist control of
Berlin in order to show the Germans that unification could only happen under the auspices of the Soviet Union. In the spring of 1948 Red
Army commanders had started harassing western Allied transports
heading in and out of the German capital. In June, after the

introduction of the new currency, the Soviets prohibited its use in Berlin and threatened sanctions against the western zones. With Berlin as an island within Soviet-held territory, such threats held some credibility. When the deutschmark started appearing in Berlin, the Soviets cut off all surface traffic between western Germany and the capital. In the days that followed they also terminated all deliveries of food or electricity to western Berlin. Stalin had decided on the first real showdown of the Cold War.

The Berlin blockade, which lasted for almost a year, was a Soviet political failure from start to finish. It failed to make west Berlin destitute; a US and British air-bridge provided enough supplies to keep the western sectors going. On some days aircraft landed at Tempelhof Airport at three minute intervals. Moscow did not take the risk of ordering them to be shot down. But worse for Stalin: the long-drawn-out standoff confirmed even to those Germans who had previously been in doubt that the Soviet Union could not be a vehicle for their betterment. The perception was that Stalin was trying to starve the Berliners, while the Americans were trying to save them. On the streets of Berlin more than half a million protested Soviet policies. When the SED chased councilors from other parties out of City Hall, located in east Berlin, they reconvened in the west and elected a Social Democrat mayor, the formidable trade unionist Ernst Reuter. Communist and Social Democrat workers fought each other in the streets, with the latter giving as good as they got. The young Willy Brandt, a German Social Democrat who had taken up arms against Hitler's regime and who returned to Berlin in 1946 as a Norwegian officer, helped organize the resistance. But even he was in doubt about the final outcome: "Would the western democracies risk a world war in the interest of a few million Berliners?" Brandt wrote.[15]

The need to reassure not just Berliners but other Europeans about US staying power was a key reason why the Truman Administration in the fall of 1948 began discussing a formal alliance treaty with the countries in western Europe. The President was fully aware of how difficult such a process would be. Americans were not naturally given to forming foreign alliances in peacetime—its founding fathers had warned against any "entangling alliances," especially with European powers. Many voters were resentful of the United States taking on Europe's problems and paying for them through their tax bill. And a majority of Americans were still against any permanent foreign stationing of US troops. Opinion in western Europe was also divided. Some believed that their countries should try to act as a bridge between Soviets and Americans, and not join one side against the other. For people on the Left, especially, it was tough to consider joining the United States—a country they saw as the home of freewheeling capitalism—in an alliance against eastern Europeans who themselves professed to be socialists.

But by 1949 fear seemed to rule out all other considerations. Truman managed to get a coalition together in Congress for a North Atlantic Treaty Organization (NATO), an integrated alliance that included a mutual defense obligation. Though much time was spent in Washington on discussing who in Europe could join, what was most remarkable was how European governments lined up to get inside quick. In Italy and France, their Christian Democrat and liberal governments delivered their countries for NATO. In Britain and the Low Countries both labor parties and conservatives were in favor. Even in Scandinavia, with its long tradition of neutrality, Danish and Norwegian Social Democrats steamrolled applications for membership through their parliaments. The Norwegian ambassador to the United States explained that "Norway learned her lesson in 1940. . . . Today [it] does not believe that neutrality has any relation to the facts of life."[16] The most curious addition was Portugal, which was neither a democracy nor a World War II ally. But both Britain and the United States viewed the Portuguese Atlantic islands as essential bases in case of a war against the Soviets. In April 1949 the treaty was signed in Washington.

The initial effects of NATO in Europe were neither military nor political. They were substantially psychological. Non-Communist western Europeans started to believe that the United States would not withdraw from the continent anytime soon. This meant that Europe would remain divided. But it also meant security against a Soviet

attack. The setting up of NATO was not about a civilizational definition of a European core ("from Plato to NATO," as some put it—even
though Greece would not join until 1952). It was about stability on a
continent that had been going through hell for more than a generation. If the purpose of NATO—as its first general secretary, Lord Is-
may, is said to have quipped—was to "keep the Americans in, the
Soviets out, and the Germans down," then this was a purpose with
which the majority of western Europeans agreed around 1950. The
exception, of course, were the Communists, who protested everywhere. Togliatti condemned his government in the Italian parliament:
"We say 'no' to the Atlantic Pact, 'no' because it is a pact of preparation for war. We say 'no' to your policy, a policy of hostility and aggression against the Soviet Union. We say 'no' to the imperialist
intrigues which you are plotting to the harm of the Italian people,
their independence and their liberty, and we shall do everything in
our power to unmask this policy of yours and make it a failure."[17]

The speed with which NATO was brought about was in part a reflection of the military weakness of the United States and its new allies on the ground in Europe. The advice President Truman had got
from the Joint Chiefs of Staff was clear: US troops could not defend
continental western Europe against the Red Army, even if the atomic
bomb were to be used. At best, the Americans would be able to hold
on to bridgeheads in Italy and the French west coast, and help protect
Britain as an air base for bombing raids against the Soviets, while
waiting for reinforcements to arrive from North America. The Soviets
were in a position to establish full control of all of Europe within less
than two months, the Joint Chiefs reported. The Berlin Blockade had
changed the perspectives of the US military dramatically. General
Clay, for instance, told his superiors in Washington of his feeling that
war "may come with dramatic suddenness."[18] Although historians
have found no evidence of Soviet planning for an offensive war until
the 1950s, and though the alarmism expressed by some US generals,
Clay included, was also fed by their wish for Congress to approve
higher levels of military spending, there is no doubt that there was a
real fear of war among US military planners from mid-1948 on. They

assumed it would be a global war, with Soviet offensives not just in Europe, but in the Middle East and east Asia, too. US war planning was itself increasingly global, implying an almost universal perception of threat as well as an expansion of US capabilities, especially in terms of aerial warfare. But underlying it all was also a rising assumption of US global interest, in which events in Europe and North America were linked to those in other parts of the world in a systemic sense.

With preparations for war came fears of domestic subversion. The link had been made many times before in US history: the Red Scare after World War I or the internment of Japanese-Americans during World War II were just recent examples. The public witch hunt against Communists and other Left-wingers in the 1940s and 1950s had equally damaging effects. Charges of disloyalty, most of which were entirely unfounded, drove many knowledgeable and gifted experts away from government service. Joseph McCarthy, the demagogic and hyperbolic Wisconsin senator who through his speeches on the Senate floor came to symbolize anti-Communist paranoia, did more damage to US interests than any of Stalin's covert operations. In February 1950 McCarthy claimed that he had evidence of 205—later corrected to 57—Communists working in the State Department, and denounced the president as a traitor who "sold out the Christian world to the atheistic world."[19] The series of hearings and investigations, which accusations such as McCarthy's gave rise to, destroyed people's lives and careers. Even for those who were cleared, such as the famous central Asia scholar Owen Lattimore, some of the accusations stuck and made it difficult to find employment. It was, as Lattimore said in his book title from 1950, *Ordeal by Slander*. For many of the lesser known who were targeted—workers, actors, teachers, lawyers—it was a Kafkaesque world, where their words were twisted and used against them during public hearings by people who had no knowledge of the victims or their activities. Behind all of it was the political purpose of harming the Administration, though even some Democrats were caught up in the frenzy and the president himself straddled the issue instead of publicly confronting McCarthy.

McCarthyism, as it was soon called, reduced the US standing in the world and greatly helped Soviet propaganda, especially in western Europe.

One effect of McCarthyism was that public hysteria made investigations into genuine spy networks more difficult. Since the 1930s there had been a substantial Soviet intelligence presence in the United States, just as in the main European countries. These agents—some ideological, some blackmailed or bribed—had provided important information to Moscow during World War II, and their activities were stepped up as the Cold War took hold. Stalin demanded that the Soviet intelligence services—known for most of the Cold War as the Committee for State Security (KGB) and its military counterpart, the Main Intelligence Directorate of the Red Army (GRU)—deliver information about US war plans against the USSR. Because of the rising frenzy in the United States, Communists or ex-Communists were easy targets to recruit. A British spy of German origin, the physicist Klaus Fuchs, provided intelligence on the US nuclear project on which he worked. Fuchs continued to spy after returning to Britain in 1946 until he was arrested in 1950. There were several hundred such spies in the United States, though few as important as Fuchs. As US counterintelligence in the late 1940s gradually cracked Soviet codes—a top-secret enterprise known as Operation Venona—many of these spies were arrested. But since Venona was to be kept secret (even, it turned out, from President Truman), its results did little to allay public fears of Communist subversion.

The alarm that the Cold War created in the United States paled in comparison to the spasms that the Soviet Union and eastern Europe went through. Up to Stalin's death in 1953, denunciations, purges, and show trials were the order of the day. This was of course nothing new in Soviet history; in many ways it was a repeat of what had happened on several occasions since the Bolshevik revolution and that had peaked in Stalin's great terror of the 1930s. World War II had intensified Stalin's suspicions and the Cold War brought them to another peak. The first problem was the hundreds of thousands of soldiers who returned from German prison camps; could they be trusted?

More than a third of them were marched straight from German to Soviet prison camps. Then there were those who had lived under German occupation; most were investigated and many, including all Communist officials there, were sent to the camps. Even victorious Red Army soldiers returning from the battlefront were seen as suspect. They may have glimpsed ways of life abroad that were inconsistent with Soviet visions of the future. One careless statement about German living standards or Czech culture could be enough to land them in prison upon their return.[20]

The worst crime of the Soviet 1940s was the mass deportations of whole peoples or population groups from the western USSR to the east. During the war more than a million Soviet Germans were deported to the east, plus another million Muslims from the Caucasus and the Crimea (Chechens, Ingush, Kalmyks, Tatars, Turks, and others). They were regarded as security threats. One-fifth of them died in the first three years after deportation. Then, as the Red Army advanced westward in 1944, mass deportations from the Baltic states, Ukraine, and Belorussia began. In eastern Poland, now incorporated into the Soviet Union, the Communists completed the Soviet deportations of the old elite that Hitler had interrupted in 1941. In the early 1950s the Soviet population controlled by the Chief Directorate of Camps (GULag) reached its peak of over two and a half million prisoners.

Some groups continued to resist, especially in Ukraine and the Baltic states. Ukraine, which had been part of the Russian Empire and was taken over by Communist forces after the 1917 revolution, had come under German control in 1941, and Ukrainian nationalists used the opportunity to declare independence from the Soviet Union. While Ukrainian autonomy remained a sham under German occupation, many Ukrainian nationalists continued to fight against the Red Army after the Nazi withdrawal. The Organization of Ukrainian Nationalists (OUN) existed in the Soviet Union until 1950, when its leader, Roman Shukhevych, was killed. While the OUN was feared for its collaboration with the Nazis and its atrocities against Poles and Jews, some Ukrainians still regarded it as the champion of independence and sovereignty. Soviet countermeasures were brutal. Between 1944 and 1952 as many as six hundred thousand people were arrested in western Ukraine; about a third of these were executed and the rest imprisoned or exiled. The fierce Soviet response probably did as much to keep resistance alive as the waning military power of the OUN.

In the Baltic states—Estonia, Latvia, and Lithuania—the return of the Red Army also provoked lasting resistance. Having become independent from Russia in 1918, the three countries were occupied by the Soviets in 1940, after Stalin's pact with Hitler. The occupation was vicious, and the German invasion in 1941 had been greeted with relief by many Balts, who now turned their wrath on Russians and other local minorities, including Jews. The German defeat meant the return of the Red Army and the start of another round of bloodletting. In all three Baltic countries resistance coalesced around former officers, most of whom had collaborated with the Nazis; they were known collectively as the "Forest Brothers." The fighting lasted for almost a decade and cost up to fifty thousand lives, mostly in Lithuania. Around 10 percent of the entire adult population of Balts was deported or sent to Soviet labor camps between 1940 and 1953.

As had been the case in the 1930s, external pressures led Communism to turn in on itself in the late 1940s. These inner purges started with the conflict with Yugoslavia, a completely unnecessary clash that was created by Stalin's indecision and paranoia. The Yugoslav Communists were the only eastern European party that had taken power by its own devices after World War II. Not only had the party's partisans held their own against the Germans, they had also defeated the Croatian militias and, after the war ended, the Chetniks under Draža Mihailović, a conservative, royalist movement mostly of Serbian extraction. The Yugoslav Communists were led by the flamboyant and energetic Josip Broz, who called himself Tito, a veteran organizer of mixed Croatian and Slovene parentage who had spent several years in the Soviet Union. In 1946 Tito had declared a socialist Federal Republic of Yugoslavia ideologically aligned with the Soviet Union.

Tito was profuse in his praise of Stalin and wanted to be known as the keenest and most powerful disciple the *vozhd* had in eastern Europe. In the postwar years the Yugoslav Communists were always the first to criticize what Stalin thought ought to be criticized, whether it was US policies in Europe or the foibles of western Communist parties. But Tito's approach awakened Stalin's suspicions, as did the very fact that the Yugoslav Communists were not dependent on the Soviets for their power at home. In 1945 Stalin criticized Tito for his occupation of the Trieste region, which had created a crisis with the British and the Americans. He also felt that the Yugoslavs were too radical in supporting the Communist rebellion in Greece. Most fundamentally, perhaps, the flamboyant, intense personality of Tito himself irritated Stalin, as did the fierce loyalty the Yugoslav leader had among his followers. Communism could only have one head, Stalin thought, and set out to put Tito in his place.

The ostensible cause for the chastising was a plan for a Balkan federation. Such plans had existed for a very long time, but the fact that so many countries in the region had turned Communist after 1945 breathed new life into the idea. Both Tito and the Bulgarian Communist leader Dimitrov had discussed these plans with the Soviets. In September 1946 Stalin had told Dimitrov "that Bulgaria and Yugoslavia will unite in a common state and play a unified role in the Balkans."[21] As the plans matured, the Yugoslavs and the Bulgarians kept the Soviets informed and sought their advice. Then, out of the blue, Stalin turned on them. At a hastily convened meeting in Moscow in February 1948, the Soviet leader accused them of systematic errors and "leftist infatuations," having taken an "improper and intolerable course" in planning their union.[22] The Bulgarians immediately fell to foot. The Yugoslavs hesitated. Before they could respond formally, the Soviets unilaterally withdrew all their advisers from Yugoslavia. A week later Stalin and Molotov sent a letter in which they claimed that Tito had turned anti-Marxist, that he was ignoring the class-struggle, and that he was slandering the Soviet Union. The Balkan federation plans were now used to prove that Tito had planned to take over neighboring countries. Tito fought back. Having lived in Moscow during Stalin's purges in the 1930s, he believed that if he did not, then not just his political career but his life would be forfeited. In June 1948 the Cominform expelled the Yugoslavs, accusing them of revisionism and of having instigated a terrorist regime. They had, the resolution stated, been "betraying the cause of international solidarity of the working people." It called for "healthy elements" inside the Yugoslav Communist party to overthrow Tito. The first break among Communist parties was out in the open.

Stalin had expected Tito's regime to fall at his command, if not immediately, then during the first few months after his break with the Yugoslavs. When this did not happen, the Soviets started a set of purges among Communists elsewhere in eastern Europe who could be suspected of disobedience, now or in the future. The victims were chosen more or less randomly, but always among Communists who had shown initiative of their own and who were popular within their own parties. Sometimes they were picked because they were easier to portray as outsiders: Jews, national minorities, or people who had spent time abroad. In Hungary László Rajk, a Jewish Communist who had fought in Spain, fitted the pattern perfectly. Rajk, who himself as minister of the interior had been responsible for sending thousands to their deaths, was accused of being a Titoist spy and an agent of imperialism. He was shot in October 1949. In Bulgaria Dimitrov's second in command, Traicho Kostov, was executed two months later. The two main intended victims in Poland and Romania, Gomułka and Ana Pauker, survived because it took time to collect "evidence" against them and Stalin died before their show trials could begin. Rudolf Slansky, the general secretary of the Czechoslovak Communist Party, was not so lucky. In his confession, well rehearsed before the trial, a harrowed Slansky agreed with everything the prosecution claimed: "As the enemy of the Communist Party and the people's democratic regime, I formed the Anti-State Conspiratorial Center at the head of which I stood for several years. In this center of ours I concentrated a number of various capitalist and bourgeois-nationalist elements. My collaborators became agents of imperialist espionage services, that is of the French, English, and particularly of the American services . . .

aimed at liquidating people's democratic order [and] restoring capitalism." Slansky was executed in December 1952.

Utterly unbelievable and therefore ridiculous, these confessions contributed to the loss of faith in Communism in western Europe. But in eastern Europe, and in the Soviet Union itself, it is difficult to say if they made a difference. Unless one's family or friends were directly hurt by the purges and show trials, most people chose to concentrate on the reconstruction of their country, which might give a better life for their children and grandchildren, if not for themselves. The Communist order seemed there to stay, and in spite of small signs of everyday resistance to the dictatorships, conformity ruled. One reason for people's acquiescence was that the Communist authorities were able to deliver on some of their social and economic promises, especially during the era of reconstruction. The Communists were good at coordinating resources because they had no market or civil society to interfere with their dispositions. Housing, for instance, was rebuilt more easily in eastern Europe, even though much of the building was of poor quality. Social services, such as health care and care for the aged, were developed more quickly. Overall, the economies of eastern Europe grew more rapidly than those in the west during the first postwar years. But they started from a much lower position, and growth was greatest in the least developed economies (such as Bulgaria) and lowest in the more developed (such as Czechoslovakia). The fact that the economies grew at all is as much a testimony to the willingness of ordinary people to work as to Communist abilities to organize, especially given Soviet looting and the loss of western markets and technology imports.

In the Soviet Union itself it took a long time to improve people's livelihoods. No other country had suffered the wartime loss of so much of its productive capacity as the USSR. The first postwar years were dire; in 1946 there was a famine in parts of the country (unreported, of course, in Soviet media). Even though the Soviet authorities did not expect a new war, at least not soon, they liked the wartime command systems for the economy and kept them in place. The result was an economic system even more regimented than in the 1930s, with production quotas set out in miniscule detail. The priority was heavy industry; steel plants and machinery production were always top of the list. Still, on its own terms, Soviet output returned to its pre-war capacity remarkably quickly. A significant reason for this was simply peace: in one way or another Russia had been at war, internally or externally, through wars, civil war, collectivization, or purges ever since 1914. Even though Stalin had in no way given up on political campaigns, he understood that another round of this right after World War II would have been too much to dish out. With at least the semblance of peace, Soviet production was able to catch up on the backlog of unrealized potential and seemingly make great strides from the late 1940s on.[23]

FOR MANY PEOPLE, reconstruction after World War II also meant getting used to a new way of seeing the world. The Cold War had its roots, of course, in the early parts of the twentieth century, and as an ideological divide, its shadow had long fallen on much of European and global history. But it was in the intense first years after the war that the conflict between Communism and capitalism was imposed almost everywhere as the predominant worldwide clash. As people were busy rebuilding their lives—getting a roof over their heads, feeding their children, finding work—they found that they were increasingly doing so within a framework defined by the Cold War. They may not have felt that they were part of the conflict, but they could not avoid being touched by it. It created strictures and opportunities they had not seen before, whether in war or in peace. And gradually, the Cold War connected different parts of the world in ways and purposes that had not been obvious in the past.

5

New Asia

When World War II ended in Asia, Japan lay with its back broken, and most of the continent faced profound revolutions. In China, Korea, and Vietnam, the Communist parties had improved their positions immensely during the war, and were ready to contest for power. In Indonesia and India, radical nationalist groups were pushing for full independence from their Dutch and British colonial masters. The continent was hit by a perfect storm: not only was Japan gone as an expansionist great power, but the European empires were breaking down fast as well. For the first time in at least a hundred years Asians would be able to determine their own fate, this time under the banners of nationalism and democracy—concepts first imported from Europe, but given distinct local twists. The new Asian revolutions did not so much look back as forward, toward full autonomy, modernization, and state-building.

The revolutionary storm that hit Asia in the wake of the war had three main currents. The colonial powers and their local allies fought on to keep their positions, or at least keep some of their economic gain, by handing over power to elites with whom they could negotiate. But their front lines were broken; in China all foreign privileges had already been handed back during the war (except in Hong Kong and Macao), and in India the British—as a measure of desperation at a time when Japan was set to invade from the east—had promised autonomy to the country after the war was over. The two new

Superpowers, the United States and the Soviet Union, both opposed colonialism (at least as long as it was not their own) and pushed for rapid and full European withdrawals. Most important of all, no European country could any longer afford to keep its colonial system in place; their populations wanted reconstruction at home, not further expenditure on what seemed futile and morally indefensible positions abroad. Within a decade, colonialism had gone from being the pride of most Europeans to one of their many problems.

Across Asia, nationalist movements were positioning themselves to take power. Most of their leaders combined ideas of a nation, often represented by its past glory, with concepts of modernization and state planning. Many had some form of socialist orientation, though their contacts with the Soviet Union had been limited. In the two biggest countries, China and India, the main nationalist groups (the Chinese National People's Party, or Guomindang, and the Indian National Congress) were large organizations with many factions, both headed by charismatic leaders. Their political orientations were based on state-centered systems of planning under a strong executive, but both confronted the Communist parties within their own borders. In Indonesia—an archipelago of seventeen thousand islands with diverse cultures and histories—the imagined new state was based on an entirely new concept of nation, a national homeland for all indigenous people, with its core in the colony the Dutch had put together in the nineteenth century. The creators of the Indonesian idea were fueled by the notion that in southeast Asia the concepts of being indigenous and being Muslim were identical, and that all southeast Asian Muslims belonged in one united, centralized state. Just at the time when the Cold War came to dominate international affairs, Asian nationalists saw their new nations breaking through.

In all key Asian countries from Japan to Iran, Communist parties emerged from World War II as the main alternative to the nationalist movements. Ordered by the Comintern to oppose the Japanese in the east, most Communists there had been able to gain patriotic credentials of their own during World War II. But, even so, they were not able to cooperate easily with the more nativist nationalist leaders, in part—ironically—because some nationalists believed the Communists' war efforts had been dictated by Soviet and not national aims. In some places, where the Japanese had been seen as harbingers of an anti-European revolt, the Communists were seen as untrustworthy allies of Asian nationalism. Even so, the Communist parties had expanded everywhere. In China the party claimed to have a million members and a large army under its command. In Indonesia the party was the largest political organization in the country (in spite of its leaders' political incompetence). In India the party dominated the trade unions and had significant influence in the most populous region, Bengal. Even in Japan the party polled more than 10 percent support in the first election after the new constitution. While still minorities, the Communists had reason to believe that they would play a major role in guiding the future destinies of their countries.

The strategic situation in Asia in 1945 is easy to sum up. In the east, US forces had occupied Japan, landed fifty thousand troops in China, and taken control of Korea south of the thirty-eighth parallel. As part of the war, the United States had also landed soldiers on islands in the larger region, from Okinawa to Borneo, and across the Pacific. Britain, with Australian help, had taken over the main cities in southeast Asia from the Japanese. After they finally entered the war against Japan on 9 August 1945, the Soviets had conducted a three-week blitzkrieg, ending up in possession of all of the Chinese northeast (Manchuria), the islands north of Japan, and the northern half of Korea. In the west, Britain and the Soviets had already invaded and occupied Iran in mid-1941, with the Soviets holding the areas north of Tehran. The British were in charge of the rest of the Middle East. It was the imperialist powers that had benefitted the most from the collapse of Japan and Germany, but it was also clear that the British were grossly overextended in 1945. They could not even take effective control of their own former Asian colonies, not to mention independent Asian states or those colonies that had belonged to others. Just like in Europe, Britain needed the cooperation of other powers—predominantly, the United States—to pursue its interests in Asia.

Immediately after 1945, US policy-makers were as preoccupied with parts of Asia as they were with Europe. The United States had, after all, fought World War II because it was attacked by an Asian power. The Americans had had 350,000 casualties in all in the Pacific war, and the sacrifice was not easily forgotten. Twenty thousand of the deaths occurred in the battle for one southern Japanese island, Okinawa, in mid-1945. The future of Japan after capitulation was understandably seen as crucial for the United States, but so was the future of China, whose cause many Americans had felt intimately connected to as an ally during the war. On the western side of the continent, the United States saw Iran as a key state for the years to come; the country had a long border with the Soviet Union and was the most powerful in the oil-rich Persian Gulf region. American leaders believed they could help rescue the Iranians from the clutches of foreign imperialism, British or Soviet, and secure stable oil supplies for its European allies in the process. In addition to historical and strategic reasons for US involvement, US leaders often believed that they could contribute to the political and economic modernization of Asia after the war in ways no European power could or would. If Asia was ripe for revolution, Washington wanted to be at the forefront of it, helping to lead the world's most populous continent in the direction of independence, wealth, and modernity.

The United States was the main ally of the western European countries in the Cold War, and especially of Britain and France, the two powers that had the largest colonial empires. But colonialism as a principle was not popular in the United States in 1945, since most people saw it as conflicting with the principles of democratic government and with the cause of freedom, in which name the war had been fought. Like its predecessor, the Truman Administration at the end of the Pacific War wanted to see a speedy transfer of power to local elites in Asia, and it was willing to challenge its European allies to reach that aim. But it was not only high principle that led US policy. The Americans also wanted access to market opportunities that colonial preferences had barred them from during the interwar years. And they were fretful about the opportunities that could be given to radicals and Communists if independence for the colonies were too long postponed; the self-centered Europeans, the State Department often argued, could not see the larger Cold War implications of their actions. The universalist heart of the Cold War drove Americans to have strong views on countries and territories that had, only a few years earlier, meant little to Washington.

For the Soviet Union, revolution in Asia meant both opportunities and risks. Lenin had taught that although Marx had been right in putting European revolutions at the center of the overthrow of capitalism, supporting national movements in Asia was a way of putting pressure on the whole imperialist system. Such assistance could thereby hasten the revolutions in Europe that were key both to Soviet security and to the future of humankind. Stalin had taken over this perspective, but with an emphasis on Soviet security. After the lack of international revolutionary success in the interwar years and the searing experience of World War II, Stalin did not want to risk unnecessary confrontations with the United States and Britain over peripheral areas. In 1945, the Soviet leader still hoped that the Soviet Union could reach what he saw as its limited aims in Europe without such conflict. If so, there was no reason to exacerbate tension with his allies over issues that were less important to Soviet foreign policy overall.

But the postwar Soviet leadership also understood that the revolutionary potential in Asia that had been kindled by Japan's collapse could not be overlooked as an element in Soviet foreign affairs. Moscow's role, most of them thought, was to channel this potential in the direction of coalition governments that were anti-Japanese and—at the very least—neutral in the worldwide, long-term conflict between capitalism and socialism. The nascent Communist movements in Asia needed time to build proper organizations, educate cadres, and learn from the USSR. Moscow needed to set aside part of its own meager resources to assist with these processes, many leading Communists argued. But it also needed to spend more time studying the class composition and ideologies of the nationalist and Left-wing parties in Asia in order to avoid making mistakes. With his usual skepticism, Stalin was often on the side of those who argued that the Soviets had to be careful with spending money and materiel on untrust-worthy groups and uncertain political prospects in Asia, when so much else was at stake. Based on his reading of Soviet (and Russian) history, the *vozhd*'s view was that there was only one Asian country that really mattered to Moscow in the short run. That country was Japan. And it was there, ironically, that the Soviets seemed to have the least prospect for direct influence when the war ended.

IN AUGUST 1945 Japan was a country in ruins. Its wooden cities had been burned to cinders by American firebombs. In Tokyo less than one-third of the city remained standing, and even that was badly damaged by bombs. Just one B-29 raid, in the night of 9 March 1945, set off a firestorm that killed at least one hundred thousand people, overwhelmingly civilians. The cities in the south, Hiroshima and Nagasaki, had been attacked with nuclear weapons. One hundred twenty thousand were killed instantly, and more died slow and agonizing deaths from radiation. Everywhere infrastructure was in chaos, millions were homeless or living as internal refugees. Then, as the empire collapsed, almost three million Japanese refugees from abroad came to a home country many of them had never seen and where there was little welcome for them. If there was one thing Japan did not need in 1945 it was more hungry mouths to feed. Food rations were already well below starvation point, lower even than the terrible diet the Japanese had been offered by their own government prior to the collapse.

The Japanese, understandably, blamed their own leaders as much as the foreigners for the disasters that had befallen them. The common people had been promised prosperity, land, and glory; what they got was death and misery. The Japanese people had shown discipline, cohesion, and an immense willingness to sacrifice for what they had been told was the common good during the war. Now, in the fall of 1945, the wages for the loyalty they had shown became clear. A country that had not seen a major war for three hundred years lay devastated. No wonder there were huge demonstrations outside the imperial palace in central Tokyo, with people calling out to the emperor: "What will you have for dinner?" In May 1946 the so-called

"Give Us Rice" mass meetings, organized by the leaders of the Japanese Left—most of whom had just emerged from the previous regime's prison camps—demanded "revolutionary changes" and "a democratic government."[1]

The Truman Administration was clear from the outset that it did not want to share postwar control of Japan with any other allied nation. The United States, the president believed, had borne the brunt of the war against Japan and was the only country capable of reforming it (the Chinese would be loath to agree). True, a commission was set up, with pro forma participation by other allies, including Australians and New Zealanders. But power was solely in the hands of the Americans. General Douglas MacArthur, the old soldier who had fought his way back into Asia at the end of the war—against both the Japanese and the staff of the US Department of the Army—had been named Supreme Commander of the Allied Powers, and all authority in the occupied country emanated from his office. MacArthur wanted to see Japan transformed; he believed the country's wartime aggression stemmed from a deep cultural propensity for violence, authoritarianism, and, as he often put it, "ant-like behavior" that separated Japanese from Americans (and from anyone else, for that matter). Japan's polity and economy had to be completely rebuilt, so that barriers could be created for the forms of behavior to which the Japanese were prone, and so that they could be made into reliable allies of the United States in the global conflict with Communism that the general was sure would come.

The radicalism of the reforms that the United States imposed on Japan is often not understood today. The initial postsurrender directive issued by President Truman in August 1945 called for the country to be completely demilitarized, its territory limited to the home islands, and its new constitution written by the occupiers. This constitution would include "the freedoms of religion, assembly, speech, and the press. . . . The existing economic basis of Japanese military strength must be destroyed. . . . [The United States would] favor a program for the dissolution of the large industrial and banking combinations . . . [and encourage] the development of organizations in labor, industry, and agriculture, organized on a democratic basis."[2] MacArthur may have been a very conservative US general, but his orders were to carry out a revolution in Japan, with elements that smacked distinctively of the New Deal policies of the FDR generation.

To the surprise of most Americans, the new freedoms proposed for the Japanese were eagerly seized by the Japanese themselves. As soon as they were allowed to do so, Japanese men and women set up trade unions, self-help organizations, and political groups. Schools and universities began to teach curriculums that emphasized democracy and public participation, very different from the wartime staple of nationalism and emperor-worship. Many saw Japan's old elites as delegitimized by the support they had given to a disastrous policy of expansion. They called themselves nationalists, but had destroyed the nation, many believed. When Truman's advisers on Japan insisted on keeping Emperor Hirohito in place, in spite of his obvious responsibility for waging aggressive war, they claimed that removing him would make the country ungovernable. But that view was more based on an orientalist sense of Japanese devotion to absolute authority— reinforced, of course, by the experience of fighting the war—than on the rapid changes taking place in postwar Japanese society.

By 1947, the impact of the Cold War had begun to change minds in Washington about the best approach to Japan. The political Left in Japan increased its support from 22 to more than 30 percent of the vote in the April 1947 elections, and although less than 4 percent was for the Communist Party, there was no doubt that political radicalism was increasingly in vogue. Most Japanese believed that the main victors in the war, the Americans and the Soviets, jointly stood for democracy; why else, some Tokyo journalists noted, should the Americans introduce reforms that opened opportunities for the Left? But General MacArthur had already in 1946 issued a stern warning to the increasingly vocal socialists: "If minor elements of Japanese society are unable to exercise such restraint and self-respect as the situation and conditions require, I shall be forced to take the necessary steps to control and remedy such a deplorable situation."[3] George Kennan, visiting in 1948, was struck by how the lack of political stability and economic development in Japan served as a drag on US global policies. He called for a swift end to further reform and a "relaxation" in the purge of wartime perpetrators. He also called for a "limited re-militarization of Japan" if the Soviets were not "extensively weakened and sobered" or "Japanese society still seems excessively vulnerable in the political sense" by the time of a peace treaty.[4]

The so-called "reverse course" by the Americans gave Japanese conservatives back some of their self-confidence. They could build on a Japanese society in which the majority was becoming increasingly preoccupied with stemming economic decline. The leaders of the Right seemed to have the better skills to get factories going again, and to organize supplies of rice to the cities. Those few on the Right who had fallen out with the wartime militarists proved especially popular. Yoshida Shigeru, a former diplomat who had been arrested for trying to force an early Japanese surrender, became prime minister in 1946 and stayed on for most of the time until 1954, though strongly challenged by the Left. From late 1948 thousands of Left-wing teachers, civil servants, and trade unionists were thrown out of work in a reverse "Red purge." That their own people were blacklisted when those who had been charged with war crimes now walked free: this infuriated and radicalized the Japanese Left. In the 1949 elections the Communists got more than 10 percent of the vote.

The occupation of Japan gave the United States a unique opportunity to shape a former enemy into a long-term auxiliary. Both the period of reform and the antiradical policies that followed were aimed at the same purpose: to refashion Japan in the American image. It was, of course, the US military victory in the Pacific War that made this possible. But it was also dependent on shutting out the other victorious powers—and chiefly the Soviet Union—from any real role in the occupation that followed. Stalin was angry at the brazen exclusion of his country from the occupation force, but he was not surprised. It was, after all, the kind of behavior he himself had shown in eastern Europe. And he did not expect Truman to do him any favors. Stalin's policy was to instruct the Japanese Communist party to oppose the US occupation and to argue that only a Japanese socialist revolution and an alliance with the Soviet Union could resurrect Japanese independence. But he also held out a hand to Japanese conservatives: if they wanted back the northern Kuril Islands, which the USSR had occupied at the end of the war, and if they wanted to trade with Communist China, then the road to such settlements went through Moscow.

The Communist victory in China and the outbreak of the Korean War in the summer of 1950 changed the strategic situation in eastern Asia. Before, Japan had been an asset to the United States primarily because of its long-term economic (and possibly military) potential. After the North Korean attack, especially, Japan was all the United States had in the region, and the country played a key role in staging and supplying the US Army's counteroffensive in Korea. The war made Washington decide to enter into a peace treaty with Japan as soon as possible, so that the US got a permanent foothold in Japan, and Japan assumed some of the responsibility for its own defense. Truman insisted that the Japanese government first agree to a bilateral security treaty with the United States, which committed Tokyo to have the Americans as their only ally and gave Washington the right to bases in Japan entirely outside the local government's purview. US forces, said the treaty, would contribute to "the security of Japan against armed attack from without, including assistance given at the express request of the Japanese government to put down large-scale internal riots and disturbances in Japan."[5] Yoshida also had to declare that Japan would not enter into any agreements with the Chinese Communist government. Only then could the peace treaty be signed. The Soviets, predictably, refused to sign it, and China was not even invited to the meeting.

Over time, Japan would develop into the most important US ally for fighting the Cold War. Not only did it serve as an unsinkable aircraft carrier off the coast of mainland Asia, but it was also in the late 1940s already central to US military planning, which assumed an offshore strategy for US military predominance in the region. Later, the most important part of the US-Japanese alliance was to become the economic interaction and support Tokyo provided for US Cold War strategies. But in the first years of the alliance, this was still in the future. As Asia became an evermore important part of US foreign policy, the main American concerns remained over the stability of the Japanese political system and Tokyo's willingness to defend itself against Communism, foreign or domestic.

FOR MOST CHINESE the twentieth century had been a topsy-turvy experience. Their country had gone from being an empire in the early century to becoming a republic, to becoming an anarchic collection of competing regimes, to becoming a republic again. The latest incarnation of the Chinese state, from the 1930s on, was a modernizing dictatorship led by Chiang Kai-shek and his National People's Party, the Guomindang. But the Japanese attack in 1937 had challenged Chiang's hold on power, and allowed his domestic competitors to re-emerge. While the Guomindang was fighting for its life (and China's) against the Japanese onslaught, these competitors had been gaining ground. First among them was the Chinese Communist Party (CCP), which Chiang had been able to drive almost out of existence by the mid-1930s. Without much direct contact with Moscow, the CCP had been able to transform itself during the war into a significant national party. Fighting the Japanese when it had to and the Guomindang when an opportunity arose, the CCP in 1945 stood ready to wrestle with Chiang's Nationalists for the leadership of China.

The war against Japan had offered the Chinese Communists their opportunity to flourish. But it was their leader, Mao Zedong, who made sure that they gripped that opportunity to gain power. Mao was a brilliant, swashbuckling commander with a strong commitment to social justice and a deep hatred for "old China" as he saw it—backwardness, superstition, and patriarchy. He wanted to create a "new China," which was modern and socially just at the same time. His main ideal was Stalin's Soviet Union, a country he had never visited but which he idolized as anti-imperialist, revolutionary, and progressive. By early 1945, Mao's forces were ready to link up with the Red Army in north China, as part of a Soviet intervention that they expected to come soon, and thereafter to challenge Chiang Kai-shek for supremacy.

But the end of the war in China came in ways neither Mao nor his opponents had expected. Stalin hesitated in attacking Japan for so long that Mao was close to despair. The CCP was forced to begin contemplating a postwar China in which the United States was the predominant foreign power, a scenario most definitely not to its liking. Then, in August 1945, everything happened at once. Atomic bombs fell on Japanese cities. The Soviet Union finally attacked Japan and occupied northeast China, also known as Manchuria, and the northern part of Korea. Japan capitulated. All of a sudden the power that had driven China to the edge of extinction was no more. Mao ordered Chinese Communist forces into Manchuria to grab as much territory from the humbled Japanese as they could. His party seemed poised for major successes.

Then everything went wrong for the Chinese Communists. The Americans ordered the Japanese, who still held vast areas of China, to surrender *only* to Chiang's forces. Using his status as the head of China's internationally recognized government, Chiang negotiated a deal with Stalin, in which the Guomindang was given control of Manchuria in return for concessions to the Soviets for future economic and military activities there. Even worse, the Chinese living along the eastern seaboard—the most populous regions of the country, which had been occupied by Japan during the war—welcomed Chiang's forces back as liberating heroes when they arrived aboard American transport planes. Mao seemed set to lose on most counts.

The Chinese Communists obviously would not take this lying down. Ignoring Soviet orders, Communist soldiers made their way into Manchuria anyway. As tension mounted in the fall of 1945, President Truman sent America's number one wartime hero, General George C. Marshall, to mediate in China. Stalin at first asked the CCP to cooperate with the mediation, for two main reasons: the Soviet leader saw no chance for a successful Communist revolution in China, and he needed Chiang's continued cooperation in order to make use of the concessions he had wrestled from China earlier in the year. Stalin's thinking was not so much about sacrificing revolution in China for Soviet gain as it was about getting some advantages for the Soviet Union (and therefore for Communism) instead of getting no advantages. But the CCP would not cooperate. As the party refused to give way to Chiang, military clashes intensified. The Americans increasingly threw their weight behind the Chinese president, who—emboldened—dragged his feet on implementing China's agreement with the Soviets. With American pressure mounting, and Cold War tensions erupting elsewhere, Stalin abruptly decided to withdraw his forces from Manchuria in March 1946, probably knowing that by doing so he threw the military advantage in the region to the Chinese Communists. He may have thought that this would force Chiang back to the negotiating table. Instead it set off a civil war that engulfed all of China for the next four years.

Chiang Kai-shek was hell-bent on dislocating the CCP from Manchuria. His mission was to unite the country under his leadership, and to resurrect it as a political and military great power. In order to do so, he thought, the CCP had to be crushed. His all-out US-assisted offensive against the Communists in late 1946 and 1947 came close to succeeding. But then he and his party overreached. With increasing Soviet support, the Communist troops—now reconstituted as the People's Liberation Army (PLA)—began attacking Nationalist supply lines in Manchuria. While Chiang continued to pour his best, US-equipped troops into the region, the military equation there slowly changed. By late 1947 PLA marshal Lin Biao's troops began an overall offensive. In early 1948 the Guomindang's main forces were trapped in the northeast, to be picked off one by one by the PLA. The war started to go badly for Chiang Kai-shek.

While Chiang got into trouble on the battlefield, he also began weakening his own position in the cities and in other areas controlled by his government. Chiang was a man in a hurry. He wanted too much too fast. First and foremost he wanted to build a strong central government, which could guide and fund an economic and social revival for China. Instead, his precipitous actions hurried the downfall of his regime. By mid-1948 the peasantry deserted him because they resented seeing their sons press-ganged into the army for a cause that seemed increasingly hopeless. The landowners gave up on the Guomindang because Chiang seemed intent on bringing his own men into their provinces to rule them. The bourgeoisie turned against the government because it drove them into penury through inflation and corruption. The working class in the cities—among whom the Guomindang had some support and the CCP none—was the last group to run away from the regime, but in 1949, when the CCP armies overran all of China, few workers came forward to die for the Nationalists.

The Truman Administration—never keen on Chiang's government to begin with, but much preferring it over the Communists—also abandoned its wartime ally. Already in 1948 the president's advisers made it clear that there was no way in which the Nationalists could win, except through a direct US military intervention. And under pressure elsewhere, especially in Europe, there was no way the US president would sanction a landing of US troops to fight in a civil war in mainland Asia, even if he believed such a war to be winnable. George Marshall, now back in Washington as secretary of state, had warned both Chinese and Americans that simply resupplying Chiang's armies would not do the job. Chiang is faced "with a unique problem of logistics," Marshall coldly told the Chinese ambassador Wellington Koo. "He is losing about 40 percent of his supplies to the enemy. If the percentage should reach 50, he will have to decide whether it is wise to supply his own troops."[6]

While the Americans distanced themselves from Chiang, though never cutting him off fully, the Soviets drew closer to the CCP. By early 1948 Soviet military aid was coming into Manchuria, and Red Army instructors trained PLA officers both there and in the Soviet Union. It is likely that the PLA would have won the civil war even without Red Army assistance. But Soviet aid was politically important to the CCP. It proved that the "great master" of Communism in Moscow, Joseph Stalin himself, now accepted the party's policies, and that he would help a new Chinese Communist state come into existence.

While Chiang Kai-shek fled to Taiwan, the island off China's coast that had been under Japanese direct rule since the late nineteenth century, Mao in October 1949 set up a new government in Beijing. In spite of Soviet appeals for caution, Mao declared it a People's Republic, like the Soviet satellite states in eastern Europe. He also insisted on setting out on a pilgrimage to Moscow right after the new People's Republic of China (PRC) was declared, ostensibly to help celebrate Stalin's seventieth birthday. In reality, what Mao wanted was an alliance with the USSR against US attempts at undermining his revolution. The great master grudgingly permitted it. Stalin did not trust the "class-basis" of the Chinese Communists. They were peasants, he concluded, rather than workers. Theirs was a "national" rather than a socialist revolution, and they should govern in alliance with the national bourgeoisie, at least to begin with. Deeper down Stalin distrusted the CCP for coming to power on its own rather than being dependent on the Soviet Red Army. As he grew older, he increasingly suspected anything and anyone he could not directly control. Mao got his alliance but was not happy about being treated as a curiosity rather than as the great master's foremost disciple, which he so much wanted to be.

The new state the CCP set out to build was formed in the Soviet image. The party pretended that their government was a coalition, mainly to please Stalin and the Soviet advisers. But its new constitution highlighted the leading role of the CCP and lauded the "indestructible friendship with the great Union of Soviet Socialist Republics." In reality there was no doubt: the CCP ruled China, and it set out to purge those who might disagree with its way forward. "We stand for the dictatorship of the proletariat and peasantry under the leadership of the Communist Party, for a people's dictatorship, because workers and peasants make up 90% of China's population," Mao told the Soviets. "Such a regime will provide democracy for the people and dictatorship for the landlords, bureaucratic capital, and imperialists. We call our regime a new democracy, based on the union of workers and peasants under the leadership of the proletariat, represented by its vanguard, the Communist Party."[7]

The revolutionary violence that the new regime unleashed on China had three main purposes. Mao wanted to break the power of the traditional elite in the countryside and the bourgeoisie in the cities. He wanted to insulate China from non-Communist foreign influence by driving out foreigners and banning their newspapers, books, and films. And he wanted to mobilize China's youth, through mass campaigns, to build a new socialist republic patterned on the Soviet Union. The outbreak of the Korean War in the summer of 1950 may have made these purges bloodier than they otherwise might have become. But all the key elements were there from the beginning, borrowed straight from Stalin's campaigns of the 1930s in the Soviet Union, not least the province-wide quotas of how many counterrevolutionaries had to be found and eliminated. Almost two million people were killed in the first two years of CCP rule, even as the Soviet advisers warned against rashness.[8]

In spite of the brutal and often meaningless crimes of the new regime, Chinese did flock to its banner in large numbers. Many believed Mao's version, that after hundred years of weakness, the Chinese people had finally stood up. Nationalism was the order of the day, and so many Chinese desperately wanted a country they could be proud of. If Communism was the wave of the future, then China would have to accept it, or even be at the forefront of it, they thought. Fighting the war in Korea against the United States helped fuel Chinese nationalism. But Mao's project, and the stories he told about how all of China's past pointed toward this moment of Communist victory, also had a more profound appeal. It fitted with the image of collective action and collective justice that leaders had been fond of promulgating for much of Chinese history. To some, who felt that they had let their country down through wars and confrontations in the first half of the twentieth century, the Communist revolution was a kind of cleansing: it might have used methods that were incomprehensible or even inhuman, but the revolution gave them the opportunity to immerse themselves in something bigger than the individual, something meaningful, something that would, eventually, set China right.

The power of the Chinese revolution was felt far outside the borders of China itself. In southeast Asia, anticolonial revolutionary parties were encouraged and emboldened. In Korea, Kim Il-sung's Communists felt that they, too, could now reunify their country by force. Even in Japan, where elites had regarded Chinese Communism as a deadly threat, nationalists secretly rejoiced at seeing Asians taking power by themselves, in spite of US opposition. Among Chinese diasporas, many who had had little affinity with Communism celebrated the advent of a strong government in China.[9] In India and in Europe, the Chinese revolution was seen as a major shift in world politics. The nationalist prime minister of newly independent India, Jawaharlal Nehru, told his parliament that "it was a basic revolution involving millions and millions of human beings . . . , [which] produced a perfectly stable government, strongly entrenched and popular."[10] French newspaper editorials—across the political spectrum—commented on the swiftness of the transition and how it strengthened Communism as an ideology everywhere. In Le Figaro, the French anti-Communist intellectual Raymond Aron observed, with much portent, that "the conquest of the former Chinese Empire by a revolutionary party professing an ideology of Western origin, which has now become the official religion of a Eurasian empire, constitutes a historic event, paradoxical at first sight and still unpredictable in its consequences. . . . The example of China, after that of Russia, shows that Marxism, created by Marx for post-capitalist societies, has a better chance of success in pre-capitalist societies."[11]

In the United States the overall reaction was more one of profound shock. Since the early part of the twentieth century, the few Americans who were preoccupied with such matters had seen their country as a benevolent guide for China, helping and assisting the country as it entered the world stage. This view had reached its zenith during World War II when the United States and China had been allies, fighting the Japanese together, in order—interested Americans thought— to free China and enable it to join the United States as a obliging world power. Franklin Roosevelt had often spoken of China as one of the future "world policemen," around which the United Nations system should be based. Now US dreams and investments seemed to be in tatters. But instead of blaming their own foreign policy, many US officials found that the Chinese were to blame. They were seen as ungrateful and devious, spurning generations of US assistance for them.

The Cold War implications of the Communist takeover in China were immediately visible to the Truman Administration. China had joined the Soviet Union in an alliance directed against the United States. While there were some who believed nationalist pressures eventually would drive the alliance apart, the majority view was one of alarm, dismay, and betrayal. The Korean War of course intensified the loathing of the Chinese Communists; Truman noted in 1951 that "as long as I am president, if I can prevent it, that cut-throat organization will never be recognized by us as the government of China."[12] But even before the outbreak of war in Korea, NSC-68 had warned that "the Communist success in China, taken with the politico-economic situation in the rest of South and South-East Asia, provides a springboard for a further incursion in this troubled area."[13]

The alarmism of the Truman Administration was not enough for the president's critics. By the late 1940s, most Republicans had shed their isolationist image and become ardent Cold Warriors, accusing Truman of being soft on Communism abroad and at home. The US "loss of China" provided them with ammunition. As Truman sought Congressional funding for his Cold War doctrine in Europe, first-term Republican congressman Richard Nixon made the case for a global Communist threat, which he believed the Democratic Administration had ignored: "What is the difference between the spread of Communism in China and Red influences in the eastern Mediterranean? . . . [Are we] going to make the same mistake as we did in China by sending pinks and fellow-travellers to fight Communism and sabotage our announced program? And, if we are going to combat Communism in Greece and Turkey, should we not also clean house here at home and remove Communists and fellow-travellers from positions of power in our governmental departments and labor unions?"[14] Linking up with Joe McCarthy, whom he joined in the US Senate in

1950, Nixon charged the Democrats with the United States losing China to the Communists.[15]

AS NORTHEAST ASIA was being transformed through war, occupation, and revolution, southeast Asia was going through its own transfiguration. Unlike the region to its north, almost all of southeast Asia had been colonized by outside powers during the nineteenth and twentieth centuries. Indochina had come under French control, while most of the southern archipelago had been taken over by the Dutch. The British ruled Malaya and Burma. The Americans—latecomer imperialists—had taken possession of the Philippines. Only Thailand remained precariously independent. But in the first few years after 1945 this established order was turned upside down. The veteran Communist Ho Chi Minh declared Vietnam's independence in August 1945. The same month, the radical nationalist Sukarno proclaimed the new sovereign state of Indonesia, covering all the territory the Dutch had colonized. In Burma, Aung San negotiated a British withdrawal in January 1947. Both Sukarno and Aung San had collaborated with the Japanese. Aung San, a former Communist and leader of an intensely nationalist group, had set up the Burma National Army in Japan, and only switched sides in March 1945, when he constructed the abundantly named Anti-Fascist People's Freedom League, together with the Burmese Communist Party. Sukarno had launched his five principles for the new Indonesian state—nationhood, internationalism, democracy, socialism, and faith—in Japanese-occupied Jakarta, and worked with the Japanese until they capitulated. He then set about constructing a new country, irrespective of Dutch designs on returning to their colony after the collapse of Japan.

But there was to be no easy way to independence and nationhood, as the Indonesian example shows. After the Japanese surrender, British forces occupied the main Indonesian cities. London decided to let the Dutch take back their former colony. Indonesian resistance grew, culminating in the battle of Surabaya in November 1945. Six hundred British soldiers, including their commander, Brigadier Aubertin

Mallaby, died for the Dutch right to return. More than nine thousand Indonesians were killed. Surabaya was a reminder both to the British and the Americans of the strength of southeast Asian nationalism, and they urged the Netherlands to settle for a loose affiliation with Indonesia. When the Dutch in 1947 attempted to overthrow the young republic by force, the British refused to support them, and the Americans were caught in a quandary. They were afraid that forcing a Dutch withdrawal from southeast Asia would weaken the government in the Netherlands itself and provoke social and economic instability there. But they were even more worried that the longer the Dutch "police operation" in its former colony went on, the more would nationalists such as Sukarno have to give way to the policies of the powerful Indonesian Communist Party. In the end, the Indonesian Communists solved the US policy dilemma by launching an ill-fated armed uprising against the leaders of the Indonesian republic. When the Dutch tried to make use of the chaos on the Indonesian side to reinforce its intervention and arrest some of the Indonesian leaders, the Truman Administration put its foot down. While threatening to cut off economic aid to the Netherlands, Washington supported a UN Security Council resolution demanding that the Indonesian republic's leadership be reinstated. The Dutch agreed to give Indonesia independence by the end of the year.

The saga of Indonesian sovereignty shows two important links from the Cold War to a rapidly decolonizing world. The first is that in most places outside of China and its immediate neighbors, Communist parties were no match for more popular and better-organized nationalists. And China itself may have been an exception simply because the Japanese had already done so much damage to the Communists' enemies, the Guomindang under Chiang Kai-shek. The second is that the United States, generally, was more preoccupied with preventing Communist gains than with supporting its western European allies in retaking their former colonies. When a US Administration became convinced that the latter stood in the way of the former, it would act even against its own allies. The problem, as the Cold War progressed, was that in ideological terms it became harder and harder for US political leaders to distinguish between radical nationalism and Communism. Both were seen as anti-American, and the policies of radical nationalists were believed to pave the way for the Communists (in spite of much evidence to the contrary).

Vietnam was, with the possible exception of Korea, the only former Asian colony where Communism was the choice of the predominant pro-independence leaders. One reason, ironically, was the integration of Vietnamese elites into French culture and education, from whence the post-1914 generation took over the radicalization that was prevalent among French youth, too. The internationalism of Soviet Communism appealed to many in the Vietnamese independence movement. It gave them a chance to show why and how their struggle for self-rule was of global importance, on par with what was happening in France itself. Ho Chi Minh, the key leader connecting Vietnam to the Cold War, also symbolized this link between Vietnamese nationalism and Communist internationalism. Ho was born in 1890 and attended a French lycée in Hue. Fascinated by the world outside of Vietnam, Ho traveled to France, Britain, and the United States, where he worked in menial jobs—among them as a waiter at the Carlton Hotel in London—and studied in his free time. Having campaigned unsuccessfully for Vietnam's independence at the Versailles conferences after World War I, he became a founding member of the French Communist Party and went on to work for the Communist International, the Comintern, in Moscow and then in China and southeast Asia from 1923 to 1941. Only then did he return to Vietnam, where he sensed that France's defeat in World War II provided an opportunity to break his country free from colonial rule. Ho and the organization he headed, the Viet Minh, short for the League for the Independence of Vietnam, fought the Vichy French and the Japanese, never trusting Tokyo's promises of postwar independence for Vietnam and following instructions from Moscow to put pressure on the Japanese Imperial Army.

When the Japanese suddenly capitulated in August 1945, Ho, like Sukarno, immediately struck for Vietnamese independence. In an attempt to build on wartime Great Power cooperation and avoid US support for his enemies, Ho put his declaration into an international perspective: "'All men are created equal. They are endowed by their Creator with certain inalienable rights; among these are Life, Liberty, and the pursuit of Happiness.' This immortal statement was made in the Declaration of Independence of the United States of America in 1776. In a broader sense, this means: All the peoples on the earth are equal from birth, all the peoples have a right to live, to be happy and free." Like Mao in China, Ho believed that the Communist revolution in Vietnam, which would follow the Viet Minh's taking of power under Communist leadership, could only be prevented by US intervention against them. Ho may have thought about parallels from the French history he had studied. If Paris was well worth a mass for the Protestant king Henry IV, then the Vietnamese revolution could well be worth a quotation from the Declaration of Independence by the Communist Ho Chi Minh.

If it had not been for the French determination to return to Vietnam after the war, Ho may well have been right. One key reason why the United States did get involved in matters in Vietnam (and the rest of Indochina) was that the French forces continued to fight Ho's Viet Minh until the Korean War broke out. At first, Washington took a dim view of the French recolonization of Indochina, even though successive French governments were hard at work trying to convince Truman that the fighting there was a conflict between Communism and "the Free World." But with the war in Korea raging, and with Chinese Communist support for the Viet Minh becoming increasingly evident, neither Truman nor Eisenhower who succeeded him felt that handing Vietnam over to Ho Chi Minh was a defensible proposition. The problem was that the battles in the north of Vietnam were increasingly going against the French, and in May 1954 they suffered a massive defeat at Dien Bien Phu, attacked jointly by Viet Minh fighters and Chinese heavy artillery.[16]

For the new Eisenhower Administration, Dien Bien Phu was a massive problem in Cold War terms. The United States had supported France both directly and indirectly during the outdrawn battle. It had supplied weapons and aircraft to the French, and toward the end, two

US Air Force squadrons of B-26 bombers had attacked Vietnamese targets around the battle area. Still, the French had lost, the government in Paris had collapsed as a result, and Pierre Mendès-France, the new Left-leaning French premier, wanted to withdraw from Indochina as soon as possible. Eisenhower refused to put US soldiers on the ground. "Any nation that intervenes in a civil war can scarcely expect to win unless the side in whose favor it intervenes possesses a high morale based upon a war purpose or cause in which it believes," the president said. In private, he criticized the French, accusing them of having used "weasel words in promising independence and through this one reason as much as anything else, have suffered reverses that have been really inexcusable."[17] But he also warned against letting the Communists come to power in Vietnam. "You have the specific value of a locality in its production of materials that the world needs," Eisenhower told reporters as the 1954 international conference on Indochina was gathering. "Then you have the possibility that many human beings pass under a dictatorship that is inimical to the free world. Finally, you have broader considerations that might follow what you would call the 'falling domino' principle. You have a row of dominoes set up, you knock over the first one, and what will happen to the last one is the certainty that it will go over very quickly. So you could have a beginning of a disintegration that would have the most profound influences."[18]

Another possible domino that both Truman and Eisenhower worried about was India. Washington had generally applauded British prime minister Attlee's decision—imposed on him by a deteriorating economy at home and expanding protests against British rule—to grant India early independence after World War II. Far better, Truman thought, to hand over to Indian nationalists than wait for conditions favoring the Communists to grow. But the Americans were also, from the beginning of independence in 1947, skeptical of the political orientation of some of India's leaders, and especially of the predominant party, the Indian National Congress. "He just doesn't like white men," Truman complained after having met Nehru the first time.[19]

For Nehru, his US problem was far bigger than the Americans' India problem. The Indian National Congress, which he represented, was an anticolonial movement, founded in 1885, which aimed at Indian independence, anti-imperialism, and Asian solidarity. Its thinking about social and economic development was distinctly socialist; Congress believed in centralized planning and a state-led economy, and its main political aim was to abolish India's terrifying rural poverty. Nehru himself combined the feeling of superiority a Cambridge education had left in him with a deep sense of social justice and national purpose. He also believed firmly that Asian leaders had to stand together to abolish colonialism and take responsibility for global affairs. Although never attracted by Communism as an ideology, Nehru and many of his colleagues had a long-standing fascination with Soviet development models, which they regarded as more appropriate for India than any form of capitalism. From the very beginning of his tenure as prime minister, Nehru viewed the United States as an impatient and immature Superpower with a missionary zeal, and as a potential troublemaker for postcolonial Asia.

Nehru's view of a benign India ready to take its position on the world stage had been severely dented by the violence surrounding his country's independence from Britain. As it became clear that parts of India's Muslim minority would break away and form their own state, Pakistan, on the country's western and eastern borders, masses of refugees started to move in either direction. Seventeen million were displaced and at least half a million died as a result of interethnic violence. In Punjab, especially, defenseless refugees—Hindus, Muslims, and Sikhs—were attacked by mobs from outside their own religious communities. Rape was common. The relationship between India and Pakistan was poisoned as a result, and the other countries that came out of British decolonization in south Asia—Burma, Nepal, Bhutan, and Ceylon (now Sri Lanka)—all looked with suspicion at the behavior of their big neighbor India. Nehru's Congress government was born into a difficult foreign policy region.

Eisenhower worried about India's allegiance in Cold War terms, though he was wary of spending too much on foreign aid to that country. The State Department appealed for increased funding for India. "There is no time to lose," said the department's Office of South Asian Affairs in 1952. "Communist gains in the recent elections in India show clearly that the conditions our program is designed to combat are being successfully exploited by Communist agents. . . . [i]f South Asia is subverted it will be only a matter of time before all of the Asian land-mass and over a billion people will be under Communist domination, and our national security will face an unprecedented threat."[20] US aid to India (and to its neighbors) did gradually increase. But the political relationship between the two giant countries—both democratic heirs to a British political culture—showed few signs of improving.

Further west in Asia, matters were threatening to develop in an even more negative direction for the United States. Since World War II Washington had been preoccupied with securing oil supplies from the Middle East to its allies in Europe and east Asia. French and British decolonization in the region threatened to create the kind of political instability that could upset such supplies, which the Cold War had made even more significant. Still, the Truman Administration was hopeful that power could be handed over to moderate nationalists, mostly from the local royal families, who could be depended upon to fight Communism and continue to work with foreign oil companies to deliver oil. Saudi Arabia promised such cooperation, as did Iraq, both led by conservative monarchs. But although both Syria and Egypt seemed to be moving in a pro-western direction, the conflict in Palestine threatened to undo US aims in the Middle East. Like Muslims in Pakistan had done the year before, Jews in Palestine in 1948 declared their own state, after a vote in the UN General Assembly recommended the partition of the territory, which both the United States and the USSR had voted in favor of. Truman argued, against most of his foreign policy advisers, that early recognition of Israel was necessary both for Cold War and domestic political reasons. The president's preference had been for a federated or binational Palestine. In a diatribe in his personal diary, he wrote, "The Jews, I find are very, very selfish. They care not how many . . . get murdered or mistreated, as long as the Jews get special treatment. Yet when they have power, physical, financial or political neither Hitler nor Stalin has anything on them for cruelty or mistreatment to the underdog."[21] But in spite of his anti-Semitic attitudes, he worried that not recognizing Israel would open it up for Soviet influence and cost him votes in the presidential election in the fall.

As soon as Israel was declared in May 1948 the country was attacked by armies from the Arab states. The civil war in Palestine became an international war, which Israel won. It took control of much of the territory that according to the partition plan should have gone to Palestinian Arabs, while Jordan and Egypt took over the Palestinian West Bank and the Gaza Strip. The Palestinian civil war thereby became a permanent affliction in international affairs, which would have a major influence on the Cold War. It also soon brought the Cold War directly into the Middle East, as both Israelis and Arabs were looking for allies in their conflict with each other. Of course, the Cold War in the Middle East was about more than the Palestinian issue. But the permanence of that conflict did make it an unavoidable aspect of all foreign involvement in the region.

In 1945, though, the biggest concern in the Muslim world for both Superpowers was Iran. After the German attack on the Soviet Union in 1941, the Soviets and the British had occupied Iran in order to prevent any possible cooperation between Germany and Iranian nationalists. A major aim was to keep control of the Iranian oil production, through the monopoly of the Anglo-Iranian Oil Company (AIOC; later British Petroleum, or BP). The occupation further alienated the majority of Iranians, and gave the Soviets the opportunity to support Azeri and Kurdish separatist movements in their northern occupation zone against the central government in Tehran. Having secured agreement for the continuation of the AIOC monopoly, the British withdrew their forces by early spring 1946. But, much like he did in China, Stalin decided to hold out for a better deal with the Iranians. Meanwhile, Azeris and Kurds declared their own autonomous republics in northern Iran, with Soviet support.

US and British attempts at forcing the USSR to withdraw from Iran in the spring of 1946 constituted one of the first Cold War crises. "Tell Stalin that I had always held him to be a man to keep his word. Troops in Iran after Mar[ch] 2 upset that theory," Truman instructed his Soviet ambassador when the Red Army had not withdrawn by the UN deadline. The ambassador delivered the warning, adding that "it would be misinterpreting the character of the United States to assume that because we are basically peaceful and deeply interested in world security, we are either divided, weak or unwilling to face our responsibilities. If the people of the United States were ever to become convinced that we are faced with a wave of progressive aggression on the part of any powerful nation or group of nations, we would react exactly as we have in the past."[22] Stalin was furious. When the Iranian prime minister, the nationalist Ahmad Qavam, held out against Soviet demands for economic agreements, the Soviet leader ordered his diplomats "to wrench concessions from Qavam, to give him support, to isolate the Anglophiles, thus, and to create some basis for the further democratization of Iran."[23] Stalin's contradictory orders did little good for Soviet diplomacy. When the Red Army did withdraw, under US pressure, in May 1946, Qavam lost no time in breaking every promise he had given to the Soviets. In December 1946 Iranian troops took control of the north, and the Azeri and Kurdish leaders who did not escape to the Soviet Union were publicly executed. The Iranian Communist Party, the Tudeh—the biggest Communist group in the Middle East—suffered a setback from which it was hard to recover.

IN IRAN, AS elsewhere in Asia, Soviet policy was riddled with contradictions. Stalin wanted to support the Communist parties, but did not in a single case believe that they were ready to carry out revolutions on their own. When he was proven wrong, as in China, he spent more time worrying about the "real"—meaning potentially discordant—content of these massive political transformations than designing plans for their further development. But he also wanted to exploit Soviet power to get material advantages from Asian states. In part because he suspected their revolutions were bourgeois nationalist, rather than socialist, he pushed so hard for such concessions that he put the local Communists on the defensive. It was not easy to explain to the population in Iran that the Communists were against all foreign oil concessions, except the Soviet ones. Or for Mao Zedong to explain to the Chinese that the Soviet comrades wanted to keep special privileges for themselves in China's northern provinces.

In some cases the Soviet Union seemed more preoccupied with acting as a spoiler to US or British interests than developing a long-term policy of its own. The recognition of Israel is a case in point. In spite of his own deep-seated and escalating anti-Semitism, Stalin believed that it was more important to create difficulties for Britain's position in the Middle East than to stick with the earlier Soviet policy of creating a secular unified state in Palestine. In his instructions, the Soviet UN ambassador Andrei Vyshinskii—who may have wondered what was going on in Moscow—was told not to be "alarmed by a large minority of Arabs in the Jewish state, provided that it is less than 50 percent. This situation will not threaten the existence of an independent Jewish state, since the Jewish element in the state will inevitably increase."[24] Stalin's views on the Cold War played a key role in the creation of the state of Israel, in ways that the Soviets would soon regret.

Still, what mattered more in Asia was the Soviet model for development, rather than Stalin's foreign policy initiatives. From China to Israel, ruling parties were influenced by what they saw as Soviet achievements with regard to economic and social progress. State planning, national industries, and collective agriculture played a key role in government programs all over Asia. As we have seen, such policies were not foreign to western European governments either, at least not during the initial phase of postwar reconstruction. But in the new, postcolonial Asia the inspiration was more often taken directly from the Soviet experience. While deploring its lack of freedom, Nehru praised the Soviet Union for having "advanced human society by a great leap," citing its achievements "in education and culture and medical care and physical fitness and in the solution of the problem of nationalities—by the amazing and prodigious effort to create a new world out of the dregs of the old."[25] Nehru quoted the Indian poet and Nobel Prize winner Rabindranath Tagore, who in his deathbed message lauded "the unsparing energy with which Russia has tried to fight disease and illiteracy, and has succeeded in steadily liquidating ignorance and poverty, wiping off the humiliation from the face of a vast continent. Her civilization is free from all invidious distinction between one class and another, between one sect and another. The rapid and astounding progress achieved by her made me happy and jealous at the same time."[26]

THE UNITED STATES was as hesitant as the Soviet Union when approaching the new Asia, but even more bound by links to the European colonial past. Ironically, for a country that often highlighted its own anticolonial heritage, postwar US Administrations mostly failed to prioritize anticolonialism over Cold War concerns. And even when it did push European powers toward decolonization, as with the Netherlands in the case of Indonesia, it was mainly because the assumed Cold War consequences of not doing so were greater than their opposite. This failure of imagination had many reasons. The sense of a racial hierarchy, in which Europeans were at the top, influenced US policy-making. Concepts of religion likewise: those who believed in Christianity, both in Europe as well as Asian converts, ought to be defended against those who did not. And economic interest played a role, though increasingly as a systemic concern. Washington wanted to promote access to raw materials and future markets for the United States and its allies. In Asia as in Europe, US policy in the early Cold War was more oriented toward the expansion of capitalism as such than toward a unique preservation of US national economic advantage or the interests of specific US companies.

By the end of the Chinese civil war, if not before, both the US government and its critics at home subsumed all other concerns in Asia to the exigencies of the Cold War. The future in Asia did not look bright to most American leaders. Before the Korean War and well before his campaign for the presidency, General Eisenhower had noted to himself that "Asia is lost with Japan, P[hilippine]

I[slands], N[etherlands] E[ast] I[ndies] and even Australia under threat. India itself is not safe!"[27] The fear of the consequences of a Viet Minh victory in Vietnam came out of such apocalyptic Cold War concerns. So did the decision to intervene in Korea, though Korea also gave the Americans a chance to strike back against what they saw as a pattern of Soviet aggression everywhere. The Korean War combined Superpower confrontation with Asian nationalism. It was an Asian civil war, but also the biggest campaign of the Cold War.

6

Korean Tragedy

The war in Korea and its effects were perhaps the biggest calamities of the Cold War. They devastated a country and enchained a people. Their direct consequences are with us today and will last long into the future. And, worst of all, this was an entirely avoidable war, created by the intensity of ideological conflict among Koreans and a Cold War framework that enabled Superpower interventions. The Korean War symbolized the Cold War conflict at its most frightening. Extreme, barbaric, and seemingly inexhaustible, it reduced Korea to a wasteland and made people all over the world wonder if their country might be next for such a disaster. It therefore intensified and militarized the Cold War on a global scale.

The origins of the Korean War linked the late nineteenth century collapse of Chinese power in east Asia with the rise of Cold War ideological conflict. The fall of the Qing Empire, with which Korea had long been associated, opened the way for Japanese imperialist expansion across the region. The first country to be taken over was Korea, after China lost the 1894–95 war against Japan. By 1910 Korea was fully annexed to Japan, as an integral part of its empire. The Japanese administration did its best to stamp out Korean identity. The royal palace in Seoul was demolished and Japanese became the medium of instruction for all higher education. Tokyo even tried to force Koreans to wear Japanese dress and assimilate in social codes and family life. But at the same time, just like in the European empires that the

Japanese admired and feared in equal amounts, there was widespread segregation of colonizers and colonized. Most Koreans understood that they could never become full members of the Japanese Empire, even if they had wanted to.

From the beginning, the occupation of Korea gave rise to nationalist resistance. For many young Koreans, the real insult of the Japanese takeover was that it came just as they were formulating their own views of their country's future. Some of them went into exile, and the nationalisms they conceived there were intense and uncompromising, as ideal views of one's own country formed abroad often are. Korean nationalists wedded themselves not only to defeating Japan and liberating their country but also to building a future, unified Korea that was modern, centralized, powerful, and virtuous. Korea, they believed, could not only produce its own liberation but would stand as an example for other downtrodden peoples.

Throughout World War I and its aftermath, Korean nationalists argued that the principles of national self-determination should also extend to Asians. But with Japan being on the winning side in the war, their calls stood little chance of being accepted. The exiled Korean nationalists who traveled to Paris for the 1919 Peace Conference were bitterly disappointed. Not only did they fail to get foreign recognition, but Japan seemed to have the support of the United States and Britain for its Korean policies. With Japan joining in the attempts at isolating the new Soviet state, neither Washington nor London wanted to risk a falling-out with Tokyo over Korea. In Korea the disappointment led to rebellion, which was put down by the Japanese with great loss of Korean life.

One of the Korean nationalists who was shattered by the failed campaign for Korean nationhood in Paris was Syngman Rhee. Born in 1875, Rhee had spent six years in prison for nationalist activities. He then moved to the United States, where he was the first Korean to get a US PhD (from Princeton in 1910). Rhee was a tireless editor and publisher of nationalist texts during his long exile in the United States. At the core of all of them was the need to get US support for the just Korean cause. Appealing to Woodrow Wilson in 1919, Rhee had called out: "You have already championed the cause of the oppressed and held out your helping hand to the weak of the earth's races. Your nation is the Hope of Mankind, so we come to you."[1] Twenty years later Rhee had still not given up hope of US support. Right before Pearl Harbor he published a book predicting that Japan would attack the United States and that the best hope for a US victory would be an alliance with nationalists on the Asian mainland, including (prominently) in Korea.

Rhee envisioned Korea as a modern country that embraced its Confucian past. The president of the Republic of Korea in exile, as he now styled himself, wanted a Korea invigorated by US technology and management methods, but within the constraints of traditional virtues. As much as he hated the Japanese, he despised Korean radicals who wanted a socialist country after liberation. They were nothing but stooges of the Russians, Rhee thought. Just like some Koreans had joined up with the Japanese, others had ended up in bed with the Soviets. To Rhee they were defectors who had to return to true Korean nationalism, which—with US assistance—would build a new nation under his leadership.

To Rhee's increasing desperation, his campaigns in the United States during World War II did not make much more progress than those during the war twenty years before. The Americans concentrated on the war effort and on the alliance with China, with little time for Rhee and his associates, who did not seem able to deliver anything of vital interest for winning the war. The State Department considered Rhee a nuisance. But he kept in touch with US intelligence, which believed that Rhee's anti-Communism might make him useful as soon as the war was over. By 1945, Rhee's attention had already shifted from the Japanese to the Soviets. "The only possibility," he told his US friends, "of avoiding the ultimate conflict between the United States and the Soviet Republics is to build up all the democratic, not communistic, elements wherever possible now."[2]

Syngman Rhee was right about who his competitors for allegiance in postwar Korea would be. Ever since 1919, Korean Communism had developed, against the odds, as the alternative to the

Korean nationalism that Rhee represented. Like elsewhere in Asia, the Russian Revolution had been an inspiration for many Koreans, with its promise of modernity, equality, and respect for national rights. The first Communist groups were set up among Koreans in Siberia in 1918, and by the early 1920s the movement had spread to Korea itself as part of the underground resistance. A Korean Communist Party was organized in Seoul in 1925 but quickly became a focus-point for the Japanese police, and hundreds of party activists were arrested. The repression led to increased factional infighting, which, in the late 1920s and '30s, got entangled in Stalin's murderous purges in the Soviet Union. Korean Communism was to have no easy future.

A Korean Comintern agent, sent clandestinely to Korea to report on the situation there in the late 1920s, found large numbers of youth ready to join the Communists. "They regard the USSR and Comintern as their saviors from Japanese imperialism," he reported. Unfortunately they had "only superficial familiarity with Marxism," being mainly "former students and intellectuals who came from the ranks of the bourgeois independence movement." Their activities suffered from "theoretical chaos and long term mostly unprincipled factional strife."[3] In 1928 the Comintern closed down the Korean Communist Party, believing it was better to educate Korean cadres in Moscow and send them back later to set up a proper Communist movement. But during the purges of the late 1930s all top Korean Communists in Moscow were arrested and shot, accused of being Japanese spies. In 1937 almost two hundred thousand Soviet Koreans living in the USSR's Pacific regions were forcibly deported to central Asia. Stalin's fear of a fifth column in Soviet Asia was more important than his dedication to revolution in Korea.

Among the Korean Communists who survived the double whammy of Japanese and Stalinist oppression was a small number that had joined the Chinese Communist underground in neighboring Manchuria. One of them was Kim Il-sung, a young Korean from a Presbyterian family who had settled in Manchuria in 1920, when Kim was eight years old. Kim joined his first Marxist group at seventeen, and was jailed several times for his activities. At nineteen, he became a member of the Chinese Communist Party (CCP) and soon after was fighting against the Japanese with a small band of guerillas. Five years later he was already a bit of a mythical hero among Koreans in China, largely because the guerrilla group he now commanded had been able to survive Japanese operations against it. But slowly the Japanese were catching up, and in 1940 Kim and his surviving comrades slipped across the border to the Soviet Union. When Germany attacked there the following year, Kim volunteered for the Red Army. He returned to Korea in 1945 as a Soviet officer, proudly displaying the Order of the Red Banner, usually given for extraordinary heroism in combat.

The Korea to which Kim returned was a country in flux. At the Cairo Conference two years earlier the Allied powers had jointly agreed to restore Korean independence after the war was over. When the USSR attacked Japan, at the last minute, Washington and Moscow had agreed to zones of occupation on the peninsula, divided by the thirty-eighth parallel: the Soviets to the north and the Americans to the south. The dividing line was simply supposed to be a wartime arrangement to facilitate the Japanese capitulation. Nobody in 1945 believed that the division would be permanent, least of all the Koreans themselves.

In both zones the liberators turned to people known to them to help organize administration and supplies. Even though the Americans often found him unreliable and irksome, Syngman Rhee was a choice that was hard to avoid in the US zone. He had plenty of nationalist legitimacy and an organization that could operate on the ground. Rhee did become the central political figure in the south with US aid, but even so, political clashes with his American sponsors intensified. Rhee wanted international recognition for his government, based on a movement he called the National Society for the Rapid Realization of Korean Independence. Washington was still hoping, at least up to mid-1947, that an agreement with Moscow would pave the way for reunification and national elections.

In the Soviet zone there was nobody with Rhee's Korean or international stature. Instead, the Soviets turned to the thirty-three-year-old

Kim Il-sung, primarily because they believed that he would be fully subservient to Soviet interests. But they also chose him because of his proven leadership skills and because he had none of the political drawbacks of the more established Korean Communists, who had either been part of 1920s factionalism or joined in the 1930s Soviet purges. Kim showed both his loyalty and his acumen during his first few months in power—though he also made it clear that he and his Communist colleagues aspired to the leadership of all of Korea, not just a part.

Up to the end of 1947 Soviets and Americans both continued toying with proposals for Korean self-governance under an international trusteeship as a way to avoid a conflict between the two powers over control of the peninsula. It is likely that Stalin did not fully give up on such an approach until the end of 1948. What cemented the division of Korea was the stubborn unwillingness of Rhee and Kim to agree to any plan that did not help reunify Korea under their own rule, along with the intensification of the Cold War elsewhere in the late 1940s. When the United States gave in to pressure from Rhee and other anti-Communists to allow separate elections in the south in May 1948, the die was cast. Rhee had already started persecuting Communists, trade unionists, and other Leftists. His victory in the elections was almost a foregone conclusion.

The change in US thinking about Korea was not just a passive reflection of the global Cold War. It was influenced by strategic concerns about the position of the Korean peninsula with regard to both China and Japan. In China the tide of the civil war was turning against the American ally Chiang Kai-shek, and the CCP began aiming for national power through conquest. In Japan the United States needed to create a regime capable of defeating the domestic Left and form a lasting alliance with Washington. In both cases Korea was crucial. A presence there would preserve a US foothold on the mainland in case China fell to the Communists, and help the United States defend Japan. It would also, over time, make the Japanese government more self-confident by securing its strategic position. Having a leadership in southern Korea linked to the United States therefore became more and more significant for both US military and civilian planners in the late 1940s.

Stalin was less focused on Korea up to 1949, mainly because he struggled to reconceptualize the Soviet role in China as the CCP, to his great surprise, turned the civil war to its advantage. Potentially having China within the Communist camp was a prospect it took some time getting used to, for the Soviet *vozhd* as for everyone else. Stalin distrusted the Chinese Communist leaders in spite of their open devotion to him and to the USSR. But he was of course alert to the enormous strategic opportunities a Communist regime in China would offer. His policy of providing assistance to the CCP in the final stage of its takeover also incorporated Korea. Having Soviet-controlled northern Korea as a rear base area for CCP forces fighting in Manchuria was of crucial importance to Communist success there. The Soviets also helped organize Korean volunteers to fight for the CCP.

Syngman Rhee declared the Republic of Korea (ROK) in Seoul after the May 1948 elections. Kim Il-sung followed up by declaring a new state from his northern capital Pyongyang in September. Making it a "People's Republic" was not enough for Kim; he named it the Democratic People's Republic of Korea (DPRK), in line with the slogans used at the time. The new governments got the blessing of their respective Superpower sponsors. Ironically, Stalin and Truman seem at the time to have believed that the creation of separate states made war less likely. In any case, both Soviet and US troops were withdrawn from the Korean peninsula soon after the new regimes were set up.

As they solidified their governments, the Korean regimes made preparations for confronting each other. In the north, the Communists under Soviet guidance restored much of the industrial capacity that the Japanese has concentrated there. They also carried out a land reform plan that took land away from landlords, most of whom had worked closely with the Japanese, and put it in the hands of those who farmed it. The land reform secured support for the regime among peasants, and improved food supplies across North Korea. But it also contributed, with other Communist political campaigns, to hundreds of thousands of refugees fleeing to the south.

In South Korea, Rhee continued the crackdown on his enemies, who now extended to many liberal political leaders who had no sympathy with Communism. He crushed a Communist-led rebellion in the southern Jeju Island with great loss of life. ROK troops executed not just suspected guerrillas but their families and in some cases whole villages. The guerrillas, mostly locals who could draw on a sense of separate identity on the island, fought on for more than a year before the rebellion was over. Elsewhere in South Korea strikes were broken up and independent organizations outlawed under the National Traitor Act.

Beginning in late 1948 tension increased along the thirty-eighth parallel. Both sides had plans for attacking across the dividing line, and almost constant skirmishes contributed to a state of alarm in Seoul and Pyongyang. What held Rhee and Kim back was that their Superpower patrons would not support their plans for reunifying the country by force. The Americans saw themselves well served by the status quo. The Soviets focused on China. Kim Il-sung made at least two, possibly three, concrete proposals to Stalin for an attack on South Korea before June 1950. In turning down one of them, in September 1949, the Moscow great master told Kim that "it is impossible to acknowledge that a military attack on the south is now completely prepared for and therefore from the military point of view it is not allowed":

> We, of course, agree with you that the people are waiting for the unification of the country. . . . However, until now very little has been done to raise the broad masses of South Korea to an active struggle, to develop the partisan movement in all of South Korea, to create there liberated regions and to organize forces for a general uprising. . . . Moreover, it is necessary to consider that if military actions begin at the initiative of the North and acquire a prolonged character, then this can give to the Americans cause for every kind of interference in Korean affairs.[4]

Kim was of course unhappy, but could not act without the Soviets. Then, after the CCP victory in China, Stalin slowly began to change his mind. According to Soviet documents, there were at least five reasons why this happened. The success of the Chinese Communists altered the strategic picture. It also showed that the Americans were reluctant to intervene on the Asian mainland. In addition, Stalin was increasingly annoyed by the lack of success he had against the United States in Europe; the Berlin Blockade fiasco showed that in full. Based on reports he had been receiving from his main representative in Pyongyang, Terentii Shtykov, who had headed the Soviet occupation of Korea and became the first ambassador to the DPRK, the balance of forces between north and south was now in favor of the Communists. And according to Stalin's experience with US patterns of action in Europe, this would not always be the case. Finally, Korea was a perfect test case for the "internationalism" of the new CCP regime in China. If they went along with a green light to Kim Il-sung for an attack, then they would have proven themselves revolutionaries in practice, not just in theory.

Stalin's eagerness to let the Chinese prove their mettle was stimulated by his knowledge that Mao was not keen on a war in Korea. The Chinese leader had told the Soviets so several times. If Mao had a foreign priority in Asia, it was to help the Viet Minh win decisive victories over the French in Indochina. Korea, in Mao's mind, could wait. The Chinese needed time to rebuild their own country and their own forces, and Korea was too close for comfort to the richest areas of Manchuria and, for that matter, to the Chinese capital, Beijing. So when Stalin accepted the need for urgent reunification of Korea by force, during Kim Il-sung's visit to Moscow in April 1950, the Boss also instructed Kim to travel immediately to Beijing to get Mao's blessing for the undertaking. It was a typical Stalin kind of test, reminiscent of the impossible choice he had given Tito in Yugoslavia two years earlier: If Mao said yes, he would sign on to an offensive on his own borders over which he had little say. And if he said no, he would have proven himself to be less of an international revolutionary leader than Chinese propaganda indicated.

But Mao could not say no. He was a Communist internationalist who believed that it was the CCP's duty to help revolutionaries elsewhere. He also viewed Stalin as the undisputed head of the international Communist movement and could not countenance an open challenge to the vozhd's authority. Most important of all, the Chinese had just reunified their own country by force. How could he refuse the Korean Communist younger brothers the right to do the same?[5] When Kim Il-sung arrived in Beijing in May 1950, Mao still double-checked with Moscow first to ensure that Stalin had indeed given his express go-ahead. Moscow confirmed. "In a conversation with the Korean comrades, Filippov [one of Stalin's code names] and his friends expressed the opinion that, in light of the changed international situation, they agreed with the proposal of the Koreans to move towards reunification."[6] Mao told Kim that the Koreans had China's support, too. But he warned his guest that foreign imperialist intervention might make his task more difficult than Kim Il-sung assumed.

The preparations for an attack on the south began as soon as Stalin had given his go-ahead. There were still hundreds of Red Army military advisers in Korea, and more arrived in May and June. It was mainly the Soviets who drew up the plans for the offensive, and they based it on their highly mobile campaigns against Germany and Japan at the end of World War II. Large amounts of mobile artillery and tanks were sent from the USSR, with technical staff to prepare and maintain the weapons. Stalin had made it clear to the Koreans that this would be their war, but that the Soviet Union would assist as best it could. Kim assured him that victory would be won within weeks, since hundreds of thousands of Koreans in the south would rise up against the regime there as the northern army crossed the thirty-eighth parallel. The time for the attack was set for late June.

How could the normally cautious and realistic Stalin have sanctioned an attack on an area that he knew Washington regarded as being within its sphere? The main reason was that the aging Soviet leader was increasingly getting caught in his own delusions. The late-1940s' purges of Communists in eastern Europe, the many "plots" discovered against Stalin in the USSR, and the treatment of the Yugo-slavs and Chinese all point in the same direction. Though the vozhd may have been somewhat deranged all along—and his constant scheming against his associates and complete disregard for human life certainly indicate that—before, at least, there had been some method to the madness. Stalin's ability to work exceptionally hard, obtain the necessary information, and understand how other people thought had, at least in part, compensated for the intricacies of his mind. But by the late 1940s he had started taking leave of the flawed but careful reasoning that lay behind his earlier decisions. Increasingly he acted on his own whims and regarded himself as being omniscient, at least as far as strategy went. Other reasons, such as mixed signals in Washington about US plans to defend South Korea, the first Soviet nuclear test, and Soviet anger over being stymied in Berlin, probably played a role in the decision. But the Korean War came from Stalin's change of mind. If he had not given the go-ahead to Kim, there would have been no war.

At dawn on 25 June, the North Koreans attacked on a broad front across the thirty-eighth parallel. The plan was to capture Seoul and then to encircle the South Korean army in the central part of the country. Over the first week chaos and confusion reigned on the South Korean side. Seoul fell on the third day of the offensive, and Rhee fled toward the south. The South Koreans lost three-quarters of their fighting troops, mostly through defections. The encirclement plan proved unnecessary because resistance was so light, although about twenty thousand of Rhee's soldiers did manage to flee to the southeastern coast. Both sides committed atrocities as the fighting developed. Rhee's regime massacred Leftists held in their prisons. The North Koreans executed ROK officials as they advanced. US military advisers fought on the side of the South Koreans from the very beginning, and small US reinforcements arrived from Japan during the second week of the war. Still, in late July Kim Il-sung reported to Moscow that he expected the war to last less than a month.

Although the North Koreans held the upper hand militarily, the international reaction to the war already made Kim's prediction unlikely. Across the world the attack was seen as an element in the Cold War and not simply a domestic Korean affair. Given the degree to which the Cold War had become the organizing element in world affairs, such a reaction was not surprising. In Washington, President Truman immediately decided that the war was a case of outright Communist aggression, carried out to further reduce US influence in Asia and to test the will of the United States and its allies on a global scale. He ordered US forces to resist. The president also introduced a resolution at the UN Security Council that condemned the North Korean attack, determined that it was "a breach of the peace," and ordered an immediate withdrawal. The resolution passed unopposed because the Soviets were boycotting the council on account of the US refusal to seat the People's Republic of China (PRC) there. The following week the Security Council passed a follow-up resolution, which called for all UN members to "furnish such assistance to the Republic of Korea as may be necessary to repel the armed attack." It established a unified UN military command in Korea, to be led by the United States. The UN resolutions were gigantic victories for the Truman Administration. Not only did they give legitimacy to a US offensive in Korea, but they also required other countries to assist in the operation.

In the meantime the Soviets were standing on the sidelines. They claimed that the North Korean "counter-attack" was a response to a US/South Korean plan to invade the north. Even though his diplomats asked him to do so, Stalin refused to send his UN ambassador back to the Security Council to block the second resolution, which the USSR could easily have vetoed. Stalin sent instructions to keep a low profile diplomatically, while waiting for the war to conclude militarily. Even so, it is clear that the Soviet leader was rattled by the swift reaction from Washington. The Soviets kept hoping that the offensive would be over before the Americans would be able to intervene in force. But they, and the Chinese, began to understand that such an outcome was unlikely.

Because in spite of their rout of the South Korean army, the North Koreans did not quite succeed in finishing them off. As the remnants arrived in the southeast, they were joined by ever more powerful US forces from Japan. Together they were able to establish a perimeter around the city of Busan and hold it against the northern offensive. The failure to take Busan made alarm bells go off in Beijing. Mao now expected some kind of US counterattack. The Soviets remained more optimistic. As late as mid-August the Red Army general staff reported to Stalin that they expected the war to be over soon. They were wrong. By early September the US and South Korean forces were beginning to break out of the perimeter moving north.

Then, in a daring move that in one stroke undid the North Korean gains, US-led forces carried out a successful amphibious landing at Inchon, close to Seoul, on 15 September. US general Douglas Mac-Arthur, the head of the occupation forces in Japan whom Truman had put in charge of the offensive in Korea, insisted on landing that far north both for political and strategic reasons. He wanted to liberate Seoul, but also to threaten to cut off North Korean troops in the south of the peninsula. MacArthur succeeded more than even he could have imagined. The Inchon landings took Kim Il-sung's forces by surprise. They then prioritized the defense of Seoul over protecting the strategic corridors farther south. Seoul fell after a week's hard fighting. By then Kim's forces in the south were all but detached from their supply lines northward. Under pressure both from the west and the south, and as well as from intensifying US air strikes, Communist troops in South Korea started to buckle. By 1 October they fled for the thirty-eighth parallel, with only a few units able to conduct an orderly retreat. Close to one hundred thousand surrendered.

MacArthur, who had been given extensive control over how to fight the war, now called for a full and unconditional North Korean capitulation. With authorization from Washington, US and allied forces crossed into North Korea on 7 October. In Moscow, Stalin was furious and accused the North Koreans of incompetence and his own military advisers of criminal negligence. But he was still not willing to intervene to help Kim. Instead he sent a message to Mao on 1 October where Stalin, as often on receiving bad news, claimed to be on vacation and not fully au courant with events. But he had learned that "the situation of our Korean friends is getting desperate." "I think that if in the current situation you consider it possible to send troops to assist the Koreans, then you should move at least five-six divisions toward the 38th parallel at once," the Boss opined.[7]

Mao knew, of course, that Kim was in bad straits. He also knew that his countrymen were tired of war and that an intervention in Korea against US forces would be a risky undertaking, putting it mildly. Still, the Chinese leader was in an ebullient mood. He had just won a great civil war and, although he had to fight for it, he had got the recognition from the Moscow master that he craved. Crucially, he also believed that revolutionary China would most likely have to fight a war against the United States at some point anyway. The imperialists hated and feared the Chinese revolution, Mao thought. He just could not believe that the United States, as the head of the imperialist camp, would let a country as important as China leave their zone without a fight.

The Chinese leadership had been preparing for a possible intervention in Korea since well before the North Korean attack happened. As soon as he knew there would be war, Mao had moved forces from the south up to Manchuria, and he had placed some of his best commanders there. Still, there were many other military priorities for the new state. The war in Korea had made some of them more difficult, such as the immediate takeover of Taiwan, where Chiang Kai-shek's rump government had taken refuge. Mao was not surprised when he learned that the United States had moved naval vessels into the Taiwan Straits to protect Chiang shortly after the outbreak of the war in Korea. After all, Mao regarded the war as part of a global confrontation between Communism and its opponents, just as Truman did. But he was concerned that China would have to prioritize its commitments and aid Kim ahead of other tasks closer to his heart: taking over Taiwan, aiding the Communists in Vietnam, or more fully integrating Tibet or Xinjiang into the PRC.

The CCP leadership met in emergency sessions from 2 to 5 October 1950 to decide on the Chinese intervention. Mao was clear from the very beginning that he wanted Chinese forces to move into

North Korea. Stalin had requested it. The Chinese Communists owed the Koreans a debt of gratitude from the civil war. Mao himself had promised Kim assistance if needed. And, in general, Mao believed China should not be afraid of war. It was better to fight now than to wait until the Americans were at China's borders. Mao's whole life had been about war. The chances of him waiting this one out were very low.

But as North Korean resistance broke against the US counterattack, others in the CCP Politburo had second thoughts. At the first meeting on 2 October there was considerable reluctance at Mao sending the telegram he had prepared welcoming Stalin's request. After further discussion, Mao had to change course, informing the Moscow boss that "we now consider that such actions may entail extremely serious consequences," and therefore declined the request for an immediate intervention.[8] Mao Zedong may have been the leader of the Chinese revolution, but in the Politburo, he was still only the first among equals. This would change soon. Evidence suggests that Mao already the next morning regretted having given in to the Politburo majority, and convened an extended meeting of Central Committee members to discuss further. He also brought in Marshal Peng Dehuai, whom he had already chosen to head the Chinese expeditionary force, to argue in favor of intervention. Armed with yet another and more urgent request from Stalin to intervene, on 5 October Mao was able to get the Politburo to overturn its previous decision and agree to send up to nine divisions to fight in Korea.

Stalin was well informed about the decision-making process in Beijing. In his message to Mao of 5 October, he had echoed Mao's own attitude, saying that "if war cannot be avoided, then let it come now, not several years hence when Japanese militarism will have recovered and become an ally of the United States."[9] Stalin also promised full Soviet support for a Chinese intervention. Having made Soviet aid part of his argument to his colleagues, Mao sent Premier Zhou Enlai to Stalin's dacha on the Black Sea to negotiate the details directly with the Boss. Stalin was still concerned that too visible a Soviet participation would draw the USSR directly into the war. In spite of his earlier promises to Mao, he would not commit much air support until well after the Chinese intervention had taken place. The Chinese hesitated. Stalin told Kim on 12 October that since the Chinese would not send troops, the DPRK leaders and their remaining forces should evacuate Korea and retreat northward. The following day Mao, again overruling his Politburo colleagues, made the final decision to intervene.

While Stalin and Mao prevaricated, the UN military advance continued. South Korean forces had entered the north on 1 October, and US troops followed them on 9 October. Pyongyang fell to the UN on 19 October. The Chinese had signaled to the United States on 3 October that they would intervene if American troops crossed into North Korea, but Washington paid no heed. Truman's and MacArthur's aim was to force the North Koreans to surrender. The PRC forces, constituted as the People's Volunteer Army, entered Korea the same day as the North Korean capital fell, with about two hundred thousand men. US intelligence knew they were there, but had no idea about their numbers. The Chinese first turned on the South Korean forces along the border and destroyed them. Then, on 1 November, they attacked the US First Cavalry Division near Unsan. The Americans seem to have been wholly unprepared. More than one thousand US soldiers were killed. Mao was surprised about the outcome, and ordered the Chinese troops to wait for reinforcements before proceeding. This led General MacArthur to his biggest miscalculation of the war, ordering an offensive against the Chinese troops whom he still believed were few in number.

The result was a complete disaster for the UN forces. The Chinese counterattack not only destroyed the offensive, with heavy losses on both sides, but it also gradually forced a UN retreat. In December the UN was entirely pushed out of North Korea. On 4 January 1951 Seoul fell to the Communist forces for a second time. General MacArthur argued, increasingly publicly, that the United States had to take the war to China. In Washington, the Joint Chiefs of Staff began discussing using nuclear weapons to end the war. Truman hesitated. He worried about the Korean War drawing crucial

US military resources from Europe, which in the president's mind was far more important for the Cold War. He also worried about MacArthur challenging his authority as commander in chief. When a letter from MacArthur to the Republican leader in the House of Representatives criticizing the Administration was read out on the House floor, Truman had had enough. On 11 April he fired the garrulous general. Truman, in usual style, explained later that "I fired him because he wouldn't respect the authority of the President. I didn't fire him because he was a dumb son of a bitch, although he was, but that's not against the law for generals. If it was, half to three-quarters of them would be in jail."[10]

In mid-March, UN forces retook Seoul for the second time, and their forces were able to establish and hold a fragile front line very close to the thirty-eighth parallel. The Chinese tried to dislodge them in April but failed, mainly due to US air superiority. Losses on the Chinese side kept rising. In the spring offensives of 1951 their casualties were sometimes ten times those of the UN forces. Just in two weeks in May/June the Chinese army lost forty-five thousand to sixty thousand men. Chinese units also started to run out of supplies. By June Mao was ready for a cease-fire based on the status quo. But Stalin demurred. "A drawn out war," the Soviet leader argued unscrupulously, "gives the possibility to the Chinese troops to study contemporary warfare on the field of battle and . . . shakes up the Truman regime in America and harms the military prestige of the Anglo-American troops."[11] Mao did not want to seem more eager for compromise than the Boss. Syngman Rhee, now again operating out of the ruins of his capital, enjoined the UN not to settle before his people were fully liberated. There was to be no easy peace in Korea.

When the Chinese attacked US troops in the fall of 1950 people everywhere thought that they were heading fast toward World War III. A fifteen-year-old in Connecticut wrote to President Truman at the outbreak of the war to tell him how she could not sleep when she heard planes passing overhead, "afraid any minute we all would be killed."[12] Countless others, in North America, Europe, and Asia, must have felt the same way. The US Administration hoped they could keep the war contained. Truman realized that he had to strike a balance between using Korea to get public support in the United States for a global containment policy and increased military expenditure, while avoiding a full-fledged war scare. Always given to hyperbole, Truman at first struck that balance badly. In an address to the American people in December, the president claimed that "our homes, our Nation, all the things we believe in, are in great danger": "This danger has been created by the rulers of the Soviet Union. . . . In June, the forces of communist imperialism broke out into open warfare in Korea. . . . Then, in November, the communists threw their Chinese armies into the battle against the free nation. By this act, they have shown that they are now willing to push the world to the brink of a general war to get what they want. This is the real meaning of the events that have been taking place in Korea. This is why we are in such grave danger."[13]

With an ever-larger number of Americans believing that global war might break out very soon, the anti-Communist excesses that had started in the 1940s went into overdrive at home. Senator McCarthy and his supporters, such as the freshman senator from California, Richard Nixon, attacked the Administration for being soft on Communism within the United States. The government responded by having loyalty boards investigate millions of employees. They were asked what civic groups they belonged to, what reading habits they had, and whether they knew any Communists. Thousands of journalists, artists, and ordinary workers were blacklisted and prevented from getting jobs because they refused to join in the frenzy. Teachers and other public employees—in one state even postal workers and grave diggers—were required to swear oaths of loyalty to the Constitution.

In Europe, too, the Korean War intensified the Cold War. Western European leaders worried that Korea was just a Soviet test case. France's Charles de Gaulle wondered whether "these local actions were tests . . . to prepare for the 'great shock' of a final push through Europe. Of course, Europe is the central, pivotal region to complete the unification of the Eurasian sphere under Soviet domination, with the loss of freedom as a consequence."[14] The French Communists, for their part, followed the Soviet line: "Clear Provocation of War from the Puppets of Washington in Korea," screamed the headline of their newspaper *L'Humanité* the day after the North Korean attack. "The People's Army strikes back victoriously against the aggression of South Korean troops!"

But the conflict had other effects as well. Fears of nuclear warfare spread. In some western European countries radicals were blacklisted from work just like in the United States, although levels of persecution in western Europe never got close to what Communist regimes had imposed in the east. The South Korean cause itself never had much resonance in western Europe, and Soviet and Communist propaganda, saying that the war was a US attack on an innocent people, did have some effect. Most people simply wanted the conflict to end before it spread to their part of the world.

In Japan, close to Korea and with its history of colonialism there, the reaction to the war was one of both fear and opportunity. Most Japanese were afraid that the war would spread to their islands, through a Soviet nuclear attack or a Chinese invasion. There were significant antiwar protests. Japan, after all, was the only country in the world that had already suffered a nuclear attack. But among political leaders and businessmen there was also a sense of opportunity. They knew that the war would make the United States more dependent on Japanese support, and that Japanese industry was in a better position than anyone else to supply the US armies in Korea. Japan did experience a significant economic upturn during the war. Even more importantly, the war ended the US occupation and made Japan a valued ally of the United States. Syngman Rhee and other South Korean leaders hated the thought, but the fact was that their regime could not have been rescued without Japanese assistance.

In the Third World no country or movement did much to support the US cause. India insisted, from the very beginning, on an end to the war and a withdrawal to the thirty-eighth parallel. Others were even more critical. Comments and editorials in the Middle East and statements by African liberation movements asked not unreasonable questions about US policy. Why had the United States intervened immediately against North Korea, when it did little to throw France out of Algeria or end apartheid in South Africa? The first major apartheid law, the Population Registration Act, was signed the same week as the Korean War broke out. And yet South African forces participated on the UN side in Korea. Though it was not known at the time, it was aircraft from the South African fighter squadron that killed Mao Zedong's son Mao Anying, who served as an officer in Korea, in November 1950.

For the Truman Administration it mattered more that it had succeeded in putting together an international coalition than who served in it. Because of the unprecedented UN mandate, sixteen countries sent troops to Korea. The biggest contingents came from Britain, Turkey, the Philippines, and Thailand. France, Greece, and the Low Countries also sent troops, as did some countries of the British Commonwealth (Canada, Australia, and New Zealand). Still, almost 90 percent of the UN troops in Korea were American. Even more importantly, all UN troops fought under US command.

But while the war in Korea may have helped America's international alliances, it probably did even more to facilitate Sino-Soviet cooperation. After the Chinese intervention took place, the Soviets stepped up their assistance, supplying much of the materiel the Chinese and North Korean forces needed. The Soviets also sent more military advisers and, crucially, more airplanes and anti-aircraft artillery. From April 1951 Stalin allowed Soviet pilots to fly combat missions, as long as they stayed within North Korean airspace. Around eight hundred Soviet pilots flew in Korea, mostly in MiG-15 fighter jets, which were the most advanced Soviet aircraft available. During the war both the level of cooperation and the mutual confidence of the Chinese and the Soviet side increased substantially, in spite of occasional disagreements over tactics among the three allies.

The Korean War also had a profound influence on China domestically. In 1950, the Chinese had longed for peace after almost twenty years of war. There was substantial dissatisfaction with having to send young men to war again, this time abroad. Even some soldiers de-murred. They asked themselves why they had to be marched from southern China all the way up to Korea to fight in a foreign war, just after victory had been achieved at home. As casualties rose, some even harder questions were asked. A Chinese captain at the battle of Chosin Reservoir remembered "when we moved up the hill just twelve days ago . . . two hundred young men were running and jump-ing, full of energy and heroic dreams."

> Tonight there were only six of them. Tired and wounded, they moved slowly down the hill. Covered by dust and blood, their faces and arms were black like charcoals. Their uniforms were ragged, shabby, and torn at the elbows. They looked like ghosts walking in the dark. . . . My lieutenants, sergeants, and privates had followed me from China all the way to Korea. [Most] could never go back to their homes and see their families. They were only nineteen or twenty years old, and dropped their last blood on this foreign land.[15]

In Korea the destruction was immense. Most parts of the country had been consumed by war at least twice during the campaigns. All the cities were in ruins. About half the population were refugees. Most production had been destroyed and there was widespread hunger throughout the war. Those who tried to hang on in the cities faced a grim fate when war rolled back in. In the second battle for Seoul, "the artillery duels were taking a terrific toll of Korean civilians," according to news reports. "All day and all night women, little children and old men were being brought by pushcart, oxen or litter into the regimen-tal command post in the pathetic hope that the frantically busy doc-tors could pause long enough to tend to them."[16]

Even though armistice talks started in the summer of 1951, the war itself rolled on for two more dreadful years, without any meaningful military gains being made by either side. Neither the UN forces nor the Chinese and North Korean commanders were willing to gamble on a large-scale offensive that might yield little or nothing at all. But the armistice talks were also going nowhere. One sticking point was how to handle the prisoner of war issue. The Chinese and North Koreans insisted on repatriation of all prisoners, even those who did not want to return. The Americans maintained that they would repatriate only those who wanted to go back. Meanwhile, the prisoner of war camps in the south developed into veritable battlegrounds of their own, where Communist groups fought anti-Communist wardens put in place by the Americans and the South Koreans. In one of them,

> In early 1952, the brigade leader, Li Da'an, wanted to tattoo every prisoner in Compound 72 with an anti-Communist slogan. . . . He ordered the prisoner guards to beat those who refused the tattoo. . . . One prisoner, however, Lin Xuepu, continued to refuse. . . . Li Da'an finally dragged Lin up to the stage. . . . "Do you want it or not?" Bleeding and barely able to stand up, Lin, a nineteen year old college freshman, replied with a loud "No!" Li Da'an responded by cutting off one of Lin's arms with his big dagger. Lin screamed but still shook his head when Li repeated the question. Humiliated and angry, Li followed by stabbing Lin with his dagger. After Lin finally collapsed, Li opened Lin's chest and pulled out his heart. Holding the bleeding but still beating heart, Li yelled to all the prisoners in the field: "Whoever dares to refuse the tattoo will be like him!"[17]

Neither Rhee nor Kim wanted an armistice. They still insisted that all of the country had to be "liberated." And, crucially, Stalin had no interest in letting the war end. The more the Americans were bogged down in Asia, the better it was for his positions in Europe.

Already by early 1951 the war was getting increasingly unpopular in the United States, with two-thirds of Americans believing that the United States should pull out of Korea altogether.[18] The news media increasingly asked hard questions about the purpose of the war. Calling Korea "a miserable country to die in," in January 1953 one reporter let his readers know that where he was, "three of our men got it last night." One of them had "graduated from a small southwestern college last August. Korea in October. Dead in January. . . . They were killed near a bend in the Imjin River between two hills we've named Chink Baldie and Pork Chop."[19] In less than four days in mid-February 1951, the United States had more than 1,300 battle casualties.

The state of the war contributed to Harry Truman's decision not to run again for president in 1952. General Dwight Eisenhower, who ran on the Republican ticket, promised an early end to the war, through tough measures if necessary. But he had no recipe for how to do so. When he won the election, Eisenhower mixed threats (including about considering the use of nuclear weapons) with blandishments (putting pressure on the South Koreans to accept a cease-fire). Right after his inauguration, Eisenhower agreed to an exchange of wounded prisoners without any preconditions. He also signaled an interest in comprehensive Indian proposals for a cease-fire.

Then, on 5 March, the news came that changed everything. Stalin had died. On 1 March the dictator had, as often before, had a late meal with cronies at one of his dachas outside of Moscow. The next day there was no sound from his apartment. Under strict orders never to enter uninvited, the guards did not dare open the door until about 10:00 p.m. They found Stalin laying on the floor. He had had a massive stroke, which immediately incapacitated him. As his successors tried to pull things together, while warily keeping an eye on each other, the one matter on which they did agree was to end the Korean War. They regarded its continuation as dangerous and unnecessary, and hoped its end would signal to the United States an intent to lessen tensions.

The Communist leaders who inherited Stalin's Soviet Union were right that the Korean War had grown increasingly dangerous, even after the front lines stopped shifting. One of the most significant effects the war had on the Cold War was to militarize the conflict on a global scale. The US defense budget more than doubled, with only part of that increase going to fight the war in Korea. NATO, which up to the summer of 1950 had been mainly a political organization, now started becoming an integrated military force. US military assistance to Britain and France intensified, as did US determination to re-arm West Germany. Nuclear weapons programs were put into high gear.

Perhaps most important was the perception, promoted by the Eisenhower Administration, that US commitment to protect associates abroad had to be total. The Cold War was a zero-sum game. Any further reasoning invited enemy attack.

The Korean armistice was signed almost exactly three years after the war broke out. The Communist powers accepted most of the proposals that had been holding up negotiations before. It had been a useless and terrible war for everyone involved. Worse, though, were the consequences for Korea itself. The country was devastated. Three and a half million Koreans had died or been wounded in the war. Ten million were dependent on food aid. Just in the south, there were at least one hundred thousand orphans without any known living relatives.[20] Those Koreans who could return to their towns and villages saw death and despair everywhere. Their foreign allies attempted to ameliorate the situation, in return for integrating "their" Korea into their respective alliance systems. But for the Koreans themselves the war was a national catastrophe, leaving scars that have not yet healed and miseries that have not yet gone away.

7

Eastern Spheres

From the 1940s to the 1960s one alternative world covered the globe from the Arctic through the center of Europe to the Adriatic, and from there through the Caucasus and central Asia to Korea and the city of Vladivostok on the Pacific Ocean. That city's name, meaning "the conqueror of the east," now symbolized Communist victory in a very large part of Eurasia. But the Communist world did not stop there. From Vladivostok it moved south, through China, the most populous country on earth, to end off the shores of Vietnam, in the South China Sea. What is remarkable about this world is how it was connected. It was not just a security alliance, such as NATO was for the north Atlantic states. It was an integrationist political and economic project, built on a common understanding of how the world worked and how it ought to be changed. It based itself on the teachings of Marx and Lenin, and on the practices that had developed in the Soviet Union under Stalin. It was fiercely protective of its unity and committed to supporting the Soviet Union in the Cold War. It was, or so it seemed, a full-fledged alternative to capitalism and a rebuke to those who believed the United States was the great victor of the Second World War.

Everywhere, the imposition of Communist rule was based on military power. In eastern Europe and North Korea the Soviet Red Army helped put Communist regimes in place. In China, Yugoslavia, and Albania, local Communist armies took power on their own.[1] But in all cases their leaders identified the Communist military takeover with a socialist revolution. They left behind Marx's concepts of capitalism under bourgeois rule gradually developing the foundations of socialism. Like Stalin, they believed that Communist regimes could create socialism in their own countries, especially since the Soviet Union had blazed a path for such development. But the realization of socialism under Communist rule would have to happen in stages, so as to conform to the Marxist elements of Stalinism. The regimes were therefore forced to claim that they at first represented a "national" revolution, which would then later go on to develop socialism, because that was the best for the nation. With a dishonesty remarkably similar to private companies claiming that they are acting for the public good, Communists claimed to be acting for all the nation, even though their programs were blatantly intent on empowering some social classes and marginalizing others.

Among the biggest difficulties for Communists in power everywhere was their claim to stand for the international. The future, they said, belonged to the proletarians and the peasants—to classes, not to nation-states. The problem was that for many ordinary people in the 1940s and '50s, a strong nation-state was what they wished for most. The war had shown what would happen to those groups who did not have the protection of their own state. The massive bloodletting in eastern Europe, the mass murders of Jews and Roma, and the moving of borders had made it possible for Poles, Hungarians, or Romanians to claim their countries to be nation-states. The Communists, even when professing to carry out a "national" revolution, also had to stand for internationalism, especially since Moscow made that the test case for the loyalty of each Communist regime. From the very beginning, therefore, the Communists had a troubled relationship with concepts of nation and nationhood, or even state independence.

The Communist parties were minorities everywhere. The Hungarian Communist party, for instance, had only around three thousand members when the war ended.[2] They therefore had to depend on surveillance and the use of force to stay in power. The techniques they used were copied from those developed by the Bolsheviks after the

Russian Revolution or, in some cases, from the Nazis or the authoritarian regimes of the interwar years. Although workplace dismissals, expropriations, secret arrests, labor camps, and terror against real or imagined opponents were used everywhere, there were big differences in the number of people who died. In China, as we have seen, more than two million were killed in the first two years of Communist rule. In Hungary the number was about five hundred, and in Czechoslovakia less than two hundred. The difference is probably explained both by the character of the regime and by the situation the leaders were in. In China there had been a long civil war, turning into an international war in Korea, while in Czechoslovakia violence in the taking of power had been relatively slight. But the Chinese Communists also believed in a swift transformation of their country, and liked to use the phrase that one cannot make an omelet without breaking eggs.[3] As seen from Prague, the realization of Communism was a slower concoction.

In all of the Communist states, there was of course much change over time. Even though the Communist parties were in power, they still had to build a state and get some form of cooperation from the population. While Stalin was alive, it was hard to get on with these essential tasks, because the aging dictator took them through a series of increasingly capricious campaigns, purges, and changes in policy. After Stalin's death in 1953, the eastern European regimes turned toward stability and economic growth. This deliberate lessening of tension by the Communists made protest more possible, as in East Germany in 1953 or Poland and Hungary in 1956. But it also made it easier for the population to collaborate with the regimes. For most people, after all, the Communist regimes were simply the new authorities, and socialism increasingly the new normality. Over time a degree of mutuality between rulers and ruled developed. Those in power at the lower levels could fashion official policy to suit them. Workers used solidarity with their workmates to carve out space free from direct Communist interference. But more and more people also participated in the regime's organizations, events, or festivals. By the early 1960s some form of uneasy truce had arrived between rulers and ruled, in the Soviet Union itself as well as in eastern Europe (but not in China, where Stalinist-style campaigns were intensified rather than abated).

IN SPITE OF all the geographical and economic differences among new Communist states, the Communists set off in similar directions everywhere. At the beginning there was much that could be based on common models, often lifted directly from Soviet practices. Most of the Communist countries were heavily agricultural, so their leaders wanted to maximize state income from the land. They therefore decreed collectivization so the state could keep the profit from agricultural production and control the farmers politically. They also believed that the Soviet model had shown collective farming to be more effective, more industrial, and therefore more modern than individual farms. But collectivization was often resented by farmers, who believed they would do better in working their own land themselves. Much as in their relationship with the nation, the Communists were caught in a developmental quandary with regard to agriculture. They argued that collective farming was the future, just at the very moment when many farmers, from eastern Europe to China, had begun to sell their produce for cash, and therefore saw opportunities in linking up to the capitalist market.

The methods by which Stalin and his henchmen had pushed through Soviet collectivization in the 1930s had been one of the worst crimes of his regime. No other Communist state acted with the same degree of ruthlessness, possibly because even the Soviets had become alert to the costs. All over eastern Europe collectivization progressed slowly, and in Poland the process was a complete failure; the Communist government there simply gave up on account of massive resistance by farmers—Polish collective farms never covered more than 10 percent of the country's arable land. Elsewhere collectivization continued apace, with a mix of incentives and pressure. For some farmers, especially in the less developed countries, incentives such as access to technology were important. The new policies also appealed to some of the collective values of rural society. But nowhere did farmers give up their right to own their own land without some form of resistance. Even in China, where the main phase of collectivization was completed in record time in 1955 and where it had been preceded by massive terror against the bigger landowners, many peasants did demur. Given a choice, they would have preferred to own the land they cultivated.

The central tenet of Communist economic change was industrialization. The pattern again was taken from the Soviet Union. Only by industrializing fast could a country become socialist and modern. The policy had an obvious appeal: in countries on the European periphery, where there was a profound sense of having fallen behind, and in countries outside of Europe, such as China, Korea, and Vietnam, rapid industrialization seemed indeed to be the way forward. Everyone was bewitched by the extraordinary role of Soviet industrial production in destroying Nazi Germany. The emphasis was always on heavy industry: steel, machinery, shipyards, and on the mining and drilling that served such industries. Big enterprises had the priority, and almost all investment went to capital projects. Consumer goods were lacking, and for those that were available, shortages and queuing were the rules from the very beginning of Communist governments.

The ideal was that all economic activity should be run by the state, and that the measure of the economy was production volume, not competition or exchange. Planning and centralization therefore played a big part in all Communist economies. As we have seen, elements of planning were not uncommon for the postwar era even among non-Communists. But the difference was the totality of the plan: in the Communist world it covered everything, from household consumption to steel production. By the early 1960s, 100 percent of the national income in the USSR and Bulgaria was produced by state and collective enterprises, and most other Communist countries had similar figures.[4] Private ownership was abolished through expropriations.

A fully planned economy was based on the government deciding the priorities for production. Government ministries then issued production quotas, which factories strove to fulfill. The allocation of raw materials, energy, and workers was decided centrally, based on calculations of how much was needed to achieve the quotas on time. Transport, repairs, or new machinery were requested by the individual factory and decided on, according to political priority, by state institutions allocated such tasks. Investment and output were imagined to be in perfect balance, and resources therefore utilized to the utmost. Distribution replaced the market as a mechanism of dividing the output. No factories ever closed, and no workers were laid off. There was therefore full employment at all times. The country was a socialist economic machine, the purpose of which was to maximize production.

Reality, of course, diverged rather substantially from this economic ideal, as did capitalist practices from free market thinking in nonsocialist countries. Although much was achieved in terms of increasing production during the first decades of full economic planning, mainly in industry (socialist agriculture always lagged behind), growth slowed later. Some of this is undoubtedly explained by the first phase of growth being pushed forward simply by unrealized potential from earlier decades. The resource advantages of centralization in an underdeveloped economy played a part in initial successes, as did the enthusiasm of workers to rebuild and see their factories and countries succeed. But there were also inefficiencies built into the planned economy, which became more glaring as economies matured. There was a lack of efficient allocation, innovation, and product differentiation. There was also a lack of incentives for workers, and a lack of economizing or preservation of resources, natural or industrial.

With industrialization came urbanization, and the transformation of peasants into workers on an unprecedented scale. Bulgaria, for example, was predominantly rural in 1945. Less than a quarter of the population lived in cities. By 1965 that figure was doubled, and more than half the population worked in industry. This process was replicated—although usually at a slower rate—all over the Communist states. As all processes of rapid social change, it had its push and pull factors. For many, the opportunity to live in a city and to learn new skills was attractive. But some were driven out of their villages by the effects of collectivization or by Communist party pressure to join the ranks of industrial workers. Aspiring to be a worker was a badge of honor in all Communist-ruled states.

The Communist regimes constructed new centers of production, which were supposed to be ideal sites for factories and for workers. In these new towns—Nowa Huta in Poland, Dimitrovgrad in Bulgaria, or Sztálinváros (Stalin City) in Hungary—socialist planning efforts were taken to the extreme. Big plants were built in the cities, with modern apartments for workers in high-rise buildings close by. Schools and kindergartens were run in cooperation between city authorities and the factories where people worked, as were clinics, sports grounds, and concert halls; evening classes were offered for workers who wanted to further their education. All was free of charge or available for a nominal fee. No wonder people such as Mateusz Birkut, the impoverished hero of Polish director Andrzej Wajda's magnificent film *Man of Marble*, flocked to the new socialist towns in great numbers. Though many of their hopes were to be dashed, for the emergent working class in eastern Europe or in China, such initiatives symbolized a future that they found attractive.

For most workers the transition to socialism held out considerably fewer rewards. Though everyone appreciated job security and a steady income—especially those who had experienced the 1930s—living conditions were still poor and the shortages of consumer goods and sometimes even food clashed with socialist ideals of plenty. Even worse was the lack of working-class autonomy. All over eastern Europe workers had tasted influence and power of their own in the immediate postwar years. In some areas factory councils had taken over the running of plants or negotiated deals with the owners. By the late 1940s Communist trade unions came in and took over workers' organizations, and officials appointed by the authorities were the new bosses. They set production quotas after instructions from above, and workers had little influence on their daily existence. Workers protested everywhere, with some condemning the Communists as Nazis in disguise. Gradually, in the post-Stalin era the authorities tried to buy off workers' protests through accepting lower levels of productivity and increasing subsidies on food and rent.

One of the biggest changes throughout the Communist world was in the position of women. All over eastern Europe and eastern Asia the position of women had been governed by patriarchal traditions that gave them little say over resources, work, or family affairs. In areas that had had a taste of capitalism, new opportunities for women were mixed with increased social and economic exploitation. The Communist parties set out to change this sorry state of affairs, and at first many women were able to benefit from the new policies. Access to education, work, and child care improved dramatically in many places. So did women's control of their own lives. The right to divorce and availability of birth control made for big changes in gender relations. But women were still kept out of political leadership positions, and as the regimes wanted to increase their populations, many women found themselves increasingly caught between work and duties to their families. The dual burden on women turned out to be as troublesome in societies that called themselves socialist as they were in the capitalist countries, and the on-going conflict between progressive ideas and traditional norms at least as intense.

Part of the reason why Communist regimes cherished women's return to the domestic sphere after first having enabled them to make other choices was the gradual militarization of society. The Cold War played a significant role in this. As was the case in the capitalist countries, the Communists needed new soldiers for their armies, and falling birth rates did not serve that purpose. But the Communists' fondness for the military was not only connected to defense. Many Communists admired military organization as a supreme form of modernity. For them, or at least for those who had never served in the military themselves, military organization equaled efficiency and the maximum use of resources. It was the principles of the assembly line and of planning put into practice on a grand scale. Enormous new military parade grounds came to define Communist states. To many Communists, in Stalin's Russia and Mao's China especially, society ought to be organized as a machine that worked in a military manner, with commands being executed, positions conquered, and enemies destroyed. Such societies had no use for those with their own agendas or for doubters or dissenters.

The idea about the tight organization of society and the state often led to the idolization of the supreme leader, the symbol of the collective efforts. Such adoration was hard-wired into the Communist system, although it took different forms under different circumstances. In the worst cases leaders used it to establish a personal dictatorship, as in the cases of Stalin or Mao Zedong, or the "little Stalins" who emerged all over eastern Europe during the *vozhd*'s rule. North Korea under Kim Il-sung was another crude example. The Soviet national anthem claimed, "We were raised by Stalin to be true to the people, To labor and heroic deeds he inspired us!" But even when the cult of the leader was less intense, the hierarchical and authoritarian remained. Rituals and festivals, and even shrines, were set up to honor the leader. Though atheist in principle, it is hard not to suspect a certain craving for the sacred in Communist attachment to their high priests and the political theory they represented.

For those who could not believe, or were excluded from the fold, Communism was grim and repressive. Surveillance was the order of the day. The regimes had spies who helped them control the population. To begin with, at least, a wrong word could get you into big trouble. As often happens, for instance in the United States during the McCarthy era, some people made use of reporting on others to settle private scores. But the Communist parties went further than sheer control. Whole social or ethnic groups were suspected of enemy activity and excluded from society. Class enemies, of course, included the former aristocracy or those who owned property, shops, or factories, but also teachers, writers, or people with foreign or minority background. In Stalin's last years, Jews were singled out for persecution. The point was to force everyone to conform to Communist ideals, though as time went by, a mere passive conformity gradually became enough. In the Soviet Union, campaigns against enemies peaked as the Cold War hardened in the late 1940s, even if mass executions ended. The population in forced labor camps, under the GULag system, reached its highest number, about two and a half million people, in the early 1950s.

Even though resistance was hard, people obviously did resist. Under the rule of the great dictators Stalin or Mao, or even Kim Il-sung, in most people's minds conformism won over resistance time and again because the price paid for opposition was so great. But after Stalin's death in 1953, people began to oppose the authorities in greater numbers, especially in the Soviets' newly won empire in eastern Europe. Most of this was everyday workers' resistance: shirking work, pilfering from the factory, boycotting Communist marches or festivals, reading forbidden literature, or cursing the government when sitting around the kitchen table at home. Some went further, organizing underground meetings or distributing leaflets. Troubling for the authorities, most often it was not the hated bourgeoisie that committed such infractions. It was the sons and daughters of the working class, the very group the Communists pretended to represent. Sometimes the government cracked down, and the perpetrators of such small liberties ended up in prison or labor camps. Overall, however, the governments in eastern Europe managed to hold the fort through warning people off, or by playing up fears of Soviet intervention or German revanchism.

But in East Germany in 1953 resistance boiled over into open rebellion. It began in June when workers in Berlin demanded better working conditions and better pay. When the Communist government prevaricated, forty thousand protesters assembled in East Berlin and marched on the party headquarters. A general strike was proclaimed. On 17 June the Communists panicked and called in armed police, supported by Soviet troops. At least one hundred people died in the fighting, and several thousand were arrested. The number of skilled workers departing for West Berlin, already high, increased sharply. In Moscow, the new post-Stalin leaders understood that their German problem had not gone away.

Behind the workers' protest in East Germany lay years of dissatisfaction with Communist rule. First, there was the Red Army terror in 1945–46, and the removal of industrial machinery as reparations to the Soviet Union. Then, the 1948 Berlin Blockade increased the sense of isolation in the Soviet occupation zone. When the Soviets and the German Communists agreed to set up a new German state within the Red Army zone of occupation in October 1949, they did so based on the de facto division of the country that the currency reforms had created. Although most Germans in the east longed for a united Germany free of foreign occupation, the disasters they had been through also made them realists. They wanted to make the most of the situation in the new Communist German Democratic Republic, which was supposed to be a socialist workers' state. Among some workers there were hopes for increased autonomy and better livelihood. Famous German writers such as Bertolt Brecht and Stefan Heym returned to settle in East Germany. Heym, who had fought in the US Army during the war, wrote a letter to President Eisenhower, in which he renounced his US citizenship, condemned the war in Korea, and returned the Bronze Star he had been awarded for bravery. For Brecht and Heym, the German Democratic Republic was the good Germany.

But the German Communists, as Communists in governments elsewhere, wanted to accentuate production over workers' participation. They were not keen on the involvement of intellectuals, except as mouthpieces for the regime. The East German leader Otto Grotewohl, in his speech at the founding of the GDR, told his audience that reconstruction was the main business of the new regime: "The German cities, towns and villages which have been destroyed, the ruined houses and factories will not rise up again if the German people simply twiddle their thumbs. All true Germans must therefore work together to overcome the consequences of the war as quickly as possible, and to reconstruct a free, democratic and peace-loving Germany."[5]

The unrest in Berlin and other East German cities in 1953 came as a result of the regime's impatience. By again increasing the output quotas for industry, the Communists reminded the workers that the party would construct socialism through their hard work. During the first part of the demonstrations, the workers' demands were therefore mainly economic: "Away with inflated norms!" "Increase wages now!"

"Reduce food prices!" But soon the slogans changed to the political: "For free elections!" "Release all political prisoners!" "Freedom of speech!" After the rebellion had been crushed, the East German Communists blamed foreign agitators for the unrest, claiming that the rebellion had been a "fascist coup attempt": "Through their agents and other people bought by them . . . , the aggressive forces of German and American monopoly capital succeeded in influencing parts of the population in the capital Berlin and some other places in the Republic to strike and demonstrate," said the Communist Central Committee.[6] They wanted the population to rededicate itself to hard work. Bertolt Brecht wrote scathingly, in a poem he did not dare publish at the time, about how the Communist leaders claimed that the people had failed the government and had to work hard to regain its trust. Would it not then be simpler, the old satirist wrote of his own regime, if "the government dissolved the people / and chose another?"[7]

The dilemma between satisfying workers' pent up demands and defending the socialist state was precisely the challenge of the new Soviet leadership after Stalin. The group that had come to power— Georgii Malenkov as premier, Lavrentii Beriia as head of the secret police, Nikita Khrushchev as party first secretary, Viacheslav Molotov as foreign minister, Nikolai Bulganin as defense minister—feared the collapse of Communist rule as much as they feared and distrusted each other. Through his brutality and the respect he commanded, Stalin had been the guarantor of Communist rule and the final adjudicator of all things political. With him gone, his Kremlin successors all agreed that tension had to be reduced and compromises found if the Soviet state and its alliances were not to be seriously threatened. The first signal of new policies was the sudden release of the Jewish doctors arrested by Stalin, who were accused of trying to murder him and other Soviet leaders. Beriia, as the former head of the secret police, may have tried to cover his own tracks by announcing that this and other cases were violations of "socialist legality." Unnerved by Beriia's vigorous involvement in policy-making, the other leaders conspired against him, and he was arrested in July 1953 and executed by the end of the year. According to several witnesses, General Pavel Batitskii, the commander of the Moscow Air Defense Region, shot the most feared man in Russia through the head at close range when he would not willingly walk to the execution ground.[8]

The killing of Beriia, who had been the symbol of Stalinist repression, did little to enable the surviving leaders to find new policies. Even the freeing of some of Stalin's prisoners was controversial. Hearing of the doctors' release, a female railway worker wrote a complaint, oozing anti-Semitism and allegiance to the great leader: "We lost our great friend and father, our beloved Iosif Vissarionovich [Stalin], and the tears on our face will still not dry, the trepidation in people's hearts over our future had not calmed, when the stunning news spread, and the terrible thought pierced people's brains—enemies of the people are free. They once more have the right to commit their dark acts, to wreck mankind's peaceful work, and to receive praise and rewards from their American-English bosses."[9]

Even so, the new leadership, among whom Nikita Khrushchev slowly emerged as the head, went ahead with gradually setting free many of those imprisoned in the GULag. While labor camps would continue to exist right up to the end of the Soviet Union, Khrushchev removed them as a key part of the country's economy, which under Stalin had been completely dependent on prison labor. Hundreds of thousands of prisoners—political protesters, petty thieves, foreign soldiers, those who belonged to the "wrong" nationality, and those many who had no idea why they had been arrested—started to emerge from the camps, and struggled to get home or find a new place in society. These are the people the Russian Nobel laureate Aleksandr Solzhenitsyn immortalized in *One Day in the Life of Ivan Denisovich* and the process Ilya Ehrenburg called "The Thaw." But Khrushchev himself later admitted that the new leaders "were scared—really scared. We were afraid that the thaw might unleash a flood, which we wouldn't be able to control and which would drown us."[10]

Nikita Khrushchev was born close to the Russian-Ukraine border in 1894, and moved from his village to the industrial city of Donetsk when he was fourteen. With less than four years of formal schooling, he was lucky to get a job as a metal fitter's apprentice. He joined the local Soviet when it was set up in 1917, and fought with the Red Army in the civil war, in which his first wife died. After the civil war he combined political posts in the Ukraine with evening studies of technical subjects. He was an active participant in carrying out Stalin's purges in the 1930s and during World War II served in political roles on the front against Germany, ending as party leader and premier of Ukraine. Here he carried out the Communist revenge against those who had worked with the Germans or sought independence. In Stalin's final years he was the party boss of Moscow and ever closer to the dictator himself. Underestimated and sometimes mocked by his rivals for power because of his lack of schooling and his boorish manners, Khrushchev outmaneuvered them all and became the top leader—now called First Secretary—of the Communist Party in 1953 and head of the government five years later.

In his first years in power Khrushchev had to work closely with his colleagues to formulate policy. Among their biggest challenges were eastern Europe and China. Khrushchev was intent on strengthening the alliance with the Chinese. To his advisers he often commented that Stalin had been crazy not to immediately embrace the Chinese revolution. "We will live like brothers with the Chinese," he was fond of saying, and his first major foreign trip was to Beijing, where he massively increased Soviet economic support for China.[11] Eastern Europe seemed more difficult. The new Soviet leaders understood that some of Stalin's policies had created the resistance that had boiled to the surface after his death, not just in East Germany but elsewhere as well. But they were also afraid that the East German rebellion could be repeated elsewhere if they were not careful. By late 1953 they had therefore developed what they called a "new course," which was intent on reform without weakening the Communists' monopoly on power.

The main parts of the reform program were reducing the number of people who were arrested or otherwise excluded from society, amnesty for most political prisoners, cuts in heavy industry and defense industry output, and improvements in the production of food and consumer products. Not all of these measures were welcomed by the eastern European party leaders, whom Khrushchev often ridiculed as "little Stalins." Only one of them the Soviets managed to curtail straight away: the old Stalinist Mátyás Rákosi in Hungary. He was already during the Beriia interregnum forced to share power with Imre Nagy, who had previously been criticized as a "nationalist deviationist." And even in Hungary the changes were temporary. By 1955 Rákosi had maneuvered himself back into power.[12] But Khrushchev still pushed hard for political changes. He met with the eastern European leaders and warned them that they faced a catastrophe if they did not reform. But most eastern European Communists resisted, concerned that reform would be interpreted by their populations merely as weakness. They often and correctly explained to a furious Khrushchev that they had simply implemented orders coming from Moscow before.

In spite of the lack of wholehearted support for his new course from the eastern European leaders, or perhaps because of it, Khrushchev and the other Soviet leaders decided to expand the integration processes in the eastern bloc. The new bosses in the Kremlin had been watching the rise of western European and NATO integration closely, and they wanted the same advantages for their alliances. The result was the setting up of the Warsaw Pact in 1955 as a countercheck to NATO, and a stepping up of economic coordination through the Council for Mutual Economic Assistance. Many eastern European leaders initially thought these were just new ways of dictating and controlling them by Moscow. But they soon realized that Khrushchev had more of a genuine mutual integration in mind. Although he insisted on the paramountcy of the Soviet Union as the oldest and biggest Communist state, the new Soviet leader understood that effective military and economic cooperation would have to involve a bit of give and take.[13] By the late 1950s eastern bloc summit meetings no longer just involved the others being ordered around by the Soviets. Real discussions started to appear, with a sense of common purpose as well as disagreements.[14]

The biggest surprise of Khrushchev's early years in power was his 1954 decision to normalize relations with Yugoslavia. Stalin's pet object of hatred in his final years was the Yugoslav leader Tito, whom

Soviet propaganda referred to as "the stinking head of a fascist clique" and "a prostitute for Anglo-American imperialism."[15] All eastern European leaders whom Stalin had purged were routinely called Titoists, in addition to other epithets. At least twice the Boss had seriously considered invading Yugoslavia. But other priorities had intervened, and Tito had, reluctantly and in desperation, sought support from the United States and western Europe, which had kept his regime afloat. The Yugoslav leader therefore hesitated to respond to Moscow's overtures, until Khrushchev himself showed up in Belgrade in May 1955 to apologize in person for Soviet actions. "We studied assiduously the materials on which had been based the serious accusations and offenses directed at that time against the leaders of Yugoslavia," he told Tito. "The facts show that these materials were fabricated by the enemies of the people[;] detestable agents of imperialism who by deceptive methods pushed their way into the ranks of our party."[16] Khrushchev blamed Beriia. Tito welcomed the visit, but would have none of it. Stalin himself was to blame, he said.[17]

Khrushchev was slowly coming around to the same position himself, and not only with regard to Yugoslavia. In February 1955 he had Malenkov, his nearest rival for party power, demoted from the premiership. In July, after returning from Belgrade, he attacked Molotov for adhering too closely to Stalin's line. "I will frankly say," Khrushchev told the Central Committee, "that I believed Molotov's word on everything, [and] like many of us, thought that he was a great and experienced diplomat. Sometimes you'd look and then reason and think: Damn it, maybe I am missing something!"[18] Molotov was replaced as foreign minister the following year. But in spite of all this infighting, none of the defeated leaders were executed, arrested, or even thrown out of the central committee. Khrushchev had something bigger in sight: a break with the Stalinist past and a reinvigoration of Lenin's party, thereby shortening the road to Communism.

His opportunity came at the Communist Party's Twentieth Congress in February 1956. It was the first such Congress since Stalin's death, and Stalin had never bothered much with them—there had been no Congress between 1939 and 1952. Khrushchev had prepared a speech that would stun the Soviet and foreign Communists assembled there. The speech was held at the end of the Congress, to a closed session of delegates and high-ranking party members who had been released from Stalin's prisons. It was therefore dubbed "the secret speech," but there was little doubt that Khrushchev expected it to eventually be made public. He got up to speak just after midnight. "Quite a lot has been said about the cult of the individual and about its harmful consequences," he began. "The negative characteristics of Stalin . . . transformed themselves during the last years into a grave abuse of power . . . which caused untold harm to our party. . . . Stalin acted not through persuasion, explanation, and patient cooperation with people, but by imposing his concepts and demanding absolute submission to his opinion. Whoever opposed this . . . was doomed to removal from the leading collective and to subsequent moral and physical annihilation."

While the audience gasped in astonishment and trepidation, Khrushchev continued his indictment. While Stalin had begun as a servant of the party, he had become a despot, the first secretary said, who engaged in "the most cruel repression, violating all norms of revolutionary legality." He spoke of Stalin's intolerance, his brutality, and his coldheartedness, and pointed out that the majority of all delegates at the Seventeenth Communist Party Congress, in 1934, had later been arrested as counterrevolutionaries. Khrushchev listed some of those who had been unjustly arrested or executed by name. And it had all been for nothing, Khrushchev argued. Stalin had left the country woefully unprepared for World War II. The victory in 1945 had been the people's, the party's, and the Red Army's, not Stalin's.

But Khrushchev's worst indictment was reserved for Stalin's postwar behavior. Then, the new leader said, "Stalin became even more capricious, irritable, and brutal; in particular his suspicion grew. His persecution mania reached unbelievable dimensions. Many workers were becoming enemies before his very eyes. . . . Everything was decided by him alone without any consideration for anyone or anything." The break with Yugoslavia was Stalin's fault, as were the postwar purges. "You see to what Stalin's mania for greatness led. He had completely lost consciousness of reality; he demonstrated his suspicion and haughtiness not only in relation to individuals in the USSR, but in relation to whole parties and nations."[19]

In the audience, some fainted, though the majority cheered wildly. The Polish party leader Bolesław Bierut had a heart attack and died when he read the text. Communists everywhere were profoundly shocked when they heard about the speech. Their whole lives they had been defending Stalin and the USSR against what they considered slander. Now their key leader told them, and the whole world, that Stalin's accusers had been right. Some, in western Europe where they had the freedom to do so, left the Communist parties. Others rejoiced in the supposed return to Leninism. Mao Zedong told the Soviet ambassador that Stalin had always approached the Chinese with "distrust and suspicion." Stalin had "continued to believe more in the power of the Guomindang than of the Communist Party," said Mao, adding that he himself had been treated like a "Chinese Tito."[20] For Mao, as for other Communists, some hard questions had to be asked, however, even if they initially felt relieved by the criticism of Stalin. Where had the other Soviet leaders, including Khrushchev himself, been while Stalin had "violated all norms"? And could not the criticism of Stalin be carried too far, so that the principles of Communist rule—not to mention their own positions—could be undermined?

In the summer of 1956 the worst fears of the Communist leaders were confirmed. As so often, it began in Poland. On 28 June around one hundred thousand workers gathered in the city center of Poznan to demand lower work quotas, lower food prices, and the freedom to organize independently of the Communist Party. They were met with brute force by the Polish army, commanded by the defense minister, Konstantin Rokossovsky, who up to 1949 had been a general in the Soviet Red Army. Up to one hundred striking workers were killed, and nearly one thousand arrested. But the crackdown did little to stem unrest elsewhere in the country. Most worrying from Moscow's perspective, a number of Polish Communists joined in the calls for reform and to replace the party's leadership. Matters came to a head at an 8 October Central Committee meeting, at which the Communist reformer Władysław Gomułka, recently released from prison, was elected the head of the Polish Communist Party. Faced with incidents all over the country in which ordinary people demanded free elections, religious freedom, and the withdrawal of Soviet troops, Gomułka promised an end to repression and a more open society, including talks with the church. He also wanted to remove Soviet advisers from Poland and increase food subsidies for workers.

Khrushchev was alarmed. On 19 October he led a top-level delegation from the Soviet party leadership to Warsaw to discuss matters face to face with Gomułka and the new Polish leadership. The Soviets attacked the Poles for allowing news stories critical of the Soviet Union to be published. Gomullka retorted that the same was happening in the Soviet Union itself after the Twentieth Congress. "What frightens them?" Gomułka wrote in his own abbreviated summary of Khrushchev's reply. "It's not [about] insults, as much as the threat of us [Polish Communists] losing power. The slogan of the youth: away with Rakossovsky [sic], is a blow against the army. How are we [the Soviets] to reconcile [Soviet-Polish] friendship with the demand to recall officers, Soviet officers. They can't be thrown out all of the sudden. Do Soviet officers imperil [Polish] sovereignty? If you [the Poles] consider the Warsaw Pact unnecessary—tell us. Anti-Soviet propaganda does not meet any resistance."[21] But Gomułka would not give in, and both sides realized that an open break would imperil the position of both. With the situation tense, and with Polish youth chanting anti-Soviet slogans in the streets, cheering Gomułka on, the Red Army units in Poland were put on full combat readiness.

By late October 1956, though, the Soviet leaders found that events in Poland were much overshadowed by graver circumstances in Hungary. There, the Stalinist leader Mátyás Rákosi, who had seen his power circumscribed on Beriia's orders in 1953, had defeated the reformists and regained his former authority. After Khrushchev's February speech, the majority in the Communist Party, supported by Moscow, toppled Rákosi and replaced him with Ernő Gerő, a party leader no less Stalinist but more to the Soviets' liking. Independent student clubs had sprung up all over the country to discuss Hungary's future. But little had happened on the streets until news came through from Poland that Khrushchev had agreed to a compromise with Gomułka, in which Soviet advisers would be removed and more open debate allowed. On 23 October the Hungarian Writers' Union, joined by some of the student clubs, placed flowers on the monument to a Polish-Hungarian revolutionary hero from 1848. They recited a patriotic poem:

> On your feet, Magyar, the homeland calls!
> The time is here, now or never!
> Shall we be slaves or free?
> This is the question, choose your answer!-
> By the God of the Hungarians
> We vow,
> We vow, that we will be slaves
> No longer![22]

As the crowd grew, someone cut the Communist symbols from a Hungarian flag, and a throng of about twenty thousand people marched behind the new banner toward the parliament building. By nightfall they were ten times as many, chanting slogans against Soviet occupation and for political freedom. When Gerő took to the radio to condemn the rally, the demonstrators responded by toppling a large statue of Stalin in downtown Budapest. Another group of protesters attacked the radio headquarters. State security officers opened fire on the crowds. The Hungarian revolution had begun.

With the situation out of control in Budapest and many other Hungarian cities, the Soviet leadership met with eastern European Communist leaders in the Kremlin. After Gerő had appealed for Red Army intervention, Soviet troops had already begun to cross the border in the early morning of 24 October. In Moscow the leaders discussed the situation, trying to find ways of avoiding an armed conflict. "In the case of Poland," Khrushchev said, "it is necessary to avoid nervousness and haste. It is necessary to help the Polish comrades straighten out the party line and do everything to reinforce the union among Poland, the USSR, and the other people's democracies." But in the Hungarian case the situation was extremely serious. Khrushchev still expected that it could be contained without bloodshed. He said that Communists everywhere needed to "think about the problems in greater depth. We must realize that we are not living as we were during the [Comintern], when only one party was in power. If we wanted to operate by command today, we would inevitably create chaos. . . . Ideological work itself will be of no avail if we do not ensure that living standards rise. . . . In our country they also listen to the BBC and Radio Free Europe. But when they have full stomachs, the listening is not so bad."[23]

With Soviet support, the Hungarian Communist Party made Imre Nagy the new prime minister. He was an unconventional but effective Communist leader who had been purged by the party several times in the past. But the situation in Budapest and elsewhere only worsened. A general strike had been declared. Workers' councils and revolutionary committees took power from local authorities and took over arms depots and police stations. With orders only to protect major public institutions, the Red Army was mostly bystanders. Nagy believed that compromises needed to be made with the protesters, hoping that they would join with him in seeking peaceful reform. With this in mind, he extracted several concessions from the Soviets: Red Army troops would be withdrawn, there would be an amnesty for all revolutionaries and a legalization of their organizations, and the hated state security bureau would be dissolved.

But the concessions came too late. The people in Budapest and other cities had begun to organize their own authorities and armed groups. The youth, especially, were celebrating their newfound freedom. Some Hungarian army units began to cross over to the rebel side. After Soviet troops opened fire on protesters in front of the parliament building, killing at least one hundred, the mood turned increasingly ugly. There were pitched battles between Red Army soldiers and Hungarian rebels all over Budapest, and the civilians fighting to protect their barricades refused to give in. Nagy was playing for time.

He begged the Soviets to withdraw their troops immediately, saying that he and the Hungarian Communists would be able to restore order on their own. Khrushchev wanted to reduce the violence and avoid a full-scale invasion. On 30 October the new Soviet foreign minister, Dmitri Shepilov, who had replaced the dogmatic Molotov in the summer of 1956, declared that "with the agreement of the government of Hungary, we are ready to withdraw troops. We will have to keep up struggle with national-Communism for a long time."[24]

While the Hungarian and Soviet governments were negotiating, people were taking power into their own hands all over Hungary. Revolutionary committees began to administer basic services, and organized the fighting. The old political parties were reestablished. Some Communist party headquarters were attacked and set on fire, and the remaining offices of the security services were raided. A number of security officers were executed on the spot. Around the headquarters of the security service in Budapest the fighting was particularly fierce. When Red Cross personnel tried to evacuate the wounded, they, too, came under fire from inside the building. Then, a reporter wrote, the "youngsters took over": "They were magnificent; fifteen, sixteen, seventeen year old kids. They ran in there with no protection at all. A kid ran in, half bent over. He put a man on his back and dragged him to shelter. Now, many were at it. Young boys in twos, flat on the ground, some pulling stretchers, getting to the wounded and dragging them back. Nothing could stop them."[25]

When the main building of the hated security services was finally occupied, the revolutionaries showed no mercy: "Six young officers came out, one very good-looking. Their shoulder boards were torn off. They wore no hats. They had a quick argument. 'We're not so bad as you think we are. Give us a chance,' they were saying. . . . Suddenly one began to fold[;] they were going down the way you'd cut corn. Very gracefully. They folded up smoothly, in slow motion. And when they were on the ground the rebels were still loading lead into them."[26]

Reports of the attacks on Communists made the Soviet leaders change their mind. It became clear to them that Nagy would not be able to stabilize the situation, and that both the Communist regime in

Hungary and the integrity of the Soviet bloc were waning quickly. The day after they had decided to withdraw their troops, the Soviets turned around and ordered a massive military intervention to crush the rebellion. Khrushchev's rethinking was also fueled by the advice of other eastern European Communists and the Chinese in favor of an invasion, and by the NATO powers being distracted by the Suez Crisis, which was unfolding at the same time. Overall the concrete response of the Americans and the western Europeans had been limited. For Eisenhower the prospect of intervening in the Soviet bloc was a nonstarter, even though some foreign radio stations, such as Radio Free Europe, were encouraging the Hungarian revolutionaries.

The Soviet invasion forced Nagy to make the toughest decision of his life. In the end, and in spite of a checkered career that included a time as a Soviet secret police informer, he sided with the revolutionaries. His government unilaterally withdrew Hungary from the Warsaw Pact and declared the country's neutrality.[27] Nagy also appealed for UN intervention. It was, of course, to no avail. Nagy's last broadcast was in the early morning of 4 November: "Today at daybreak Soviet forces attacked our capital with the obvious intention of overthrowing the lawful democratic Hungarian government. Our troops are in combat. The government is at its post. I notify the people of our country and the entire world of this fact."[28] Soon afterward the radio station issued its final appeals for help. Then it went off air. When it reappeared in the evening it was in the hands of a new Hungarian government, led by János Kádár, installed by the Soviets.

The aftermath of the crushing of the Hungarian revolution was deeply depressing for Europeans. It showed that the division of the continent into power blocs was there to stay. The United States and its allies had no plans for "liberating" the eastern Europeans, in spite of occasional rhetoric about the "roll-back of Communism." And Khrushchev's attempts at liberalization inside and outside the Soviet Union were landed a heavy blow by his own hands. Two hundred thousand Hungarians fled west, twenty thousand were arrested, and 230 executed, including Prime Minister Nagy and several of his close associates. In western Europe, as a direct result of Hungary, the

Communist parties lost strength, some of them irrevocably. And in the east most opponents of the regimes concluded that they could not win through open rebellions against Moscow. Unless international circumstances changed, the road to reform would have to be gradual.

But the eastern European Communist regimes also drew lessons from Hungary. Repression would have to be balanced against real improvements in people's living conditions. Subsidies for food, housing, and health care had to be stepped up. Any increase in work quotas had to be avoided, even if it meant borrowing money abroad to offset low productivity. In Poland Gomułka engaged in much nationalist rhetoric against a German revanchist threat—centering, of course, on West Germany and not on the "friendly" East Germany next door. But he also opened up Polish society so that most people felt freer than before. In Hungary the new leader, Kádár, initially reviled as a quisling by most Hungarians, with Soviet consent moved away from the Stalinist terror of the past. Kádár gradually made his country the most "liberal" eastern European state, with larger plots of private land, less state interference, and freer travel than anywhere else. But neither Gomułka nor Kádár wanted to remove the Communist dictatorship or the close alliance with the Soviet Union. They may have been cabbage or goulash Communists, as they were often derided to be. But they remained Communists all the same.

Nikita Khrushchev survived the Polish and Hungarian events politically, although by a hairsbreadth. In 1957 he stared down a coup attempt in the Central Committee, in which most of the old Stalin coterie conspired against him. It became their, not his, political end. Molotov was packed off as ambassador to Mongolia. Malenkov and Stalin's old-time associate Lazar Kaganovich were made factory directors in Kazakhstan and in the Urals, respectively. In 1961 they were all expelled from the Communist Party. Khrushchev, in the most symbolic act of his career, had Stalin's body removed from the mausoleum on Red Square, where it had been laying next to Lenin, and hastily reburied along the Kremlin wall. The Soviet leader continued to believe that he could create a new and reformed Communism, harking back to the Leninist ideals of the past. But Poland and Hungary had told him that it would have to be without political reforms that could endanger the whole Communist edifice.

Instead Khrushchev turned to the expansion of Soviet plans for agriculture, science, and technology. In spite of its gigantic size, the Soviet Union had always had problems with its food supply, mainly because its collective farms lacked productivity. It was also held back by its biologists, who, mainly for ideological reasons, clung to the teachings of Trofim Lysenko, a Soviet geneticist who believed in the inheritance of acquired characteristics. Khrushchev was convinced that bigger and better collective farms would solve the problem. He proposed to develop "virgin lands" in northern Kazakhstan and western Siberia to produce more wheat. Beginning in 1954, almost two million people from the western Soviet Union migrated to the new giant farms in the east. Some were sent there by the government. Others were attracted by promises of better wages and living conditions. Yet others were caught up in the ideological fervor of developing new lands for Communism and for their country. The tasks they faced were overwhelming. Within a territory half again as large as California or Sweden, they had to build successful farms from scratch. Leonid Brezhnev, a young Communist technocrat from the Ukraine who later became general secretary of the Soviet Communist Party, described the challenges he and others faced: "Selection of sites for the centers of the new state farms; the reception and accommodation of hundreds of thousands of volunteers in country that was still totally unprepared for human habitation; the urgent building of tens and later hundreds of state farm settlements; the selection of many thousands of specialists; the building of close-knit, harmonious collectives out of a heterogeneous mass of people; and the actual plowing of the virgin soil and the first spring sowing. And this had to be done not gradually but all at once, simultaneously."[29]

The virgin lands campaigns delivered good results at first, but ultimately failed. The kinds of wheat selected were not suited for the arid and cold conditions in the new regions. Irrigation plants did not deliver enough water and infrastructure was slow to develop. Nutrient depletion withered away the soil. Some areas saw wind erosion create massive dust bowls. The environmental outcome was grim, with lakes drained, soil eroded, and mono-cropping inviting weed and pest infestations. By the 1970s some of the new collective farms looked like ghost towns, and breadlines returned to the Soviet cities. What remained of the virgin lands campaign and similar Soviet campaigns in central Asia, Siberia, the Caucasus, and in Soviet eastern Europe was a mixture of peoples and cultures, which added to the deportations Stalin had carried out in creating truly multicultural sites throughout the Soviet Union. In Kazakhstan there were more Russians than Kazakhs in 1970; in Turkmenia and in Estonia, only about two-thirds of the population were Turkmen or Estonians. The rest came from population groups all over the Soviet Union, though the main part of the migrants tended to be Russian.

But it was not only agriculture that was supposed to benefit from virgin lands. One of Khrushchev's grander schemes was the building of a new city for science and technology in Siberia, Akademgorodok. "We hoped very much that by coming to virgin lands we could start everything from scratch, according to international scientific standards, instead of waiting for God-only-knows how long in Moscow's old established institutions," said a young physicist who arrived in Akademgorodok in 1961. "We wanted to catch up with the West."[30] And catch up they did, at least in some fields, as Soviet nuclear science had already demonstrated. By the late 1950s Soviet electromagnetics, hydrodynamics, and quantum electronics were as developed as in any other country, and in some fields, such as space exploration, the Soviets were pushing ahead. In 1957 they launched the first satellite, Sputnik, which orbited the earth in 96 minutes, doing 1,500 orbits in all. The feat elated Soviet leaders and frightened Americans and western Europeans, who believed that the Communists could weaponize their satellites and thereby win the Cold War. They tended to forget that a large portion of the Soviet population could only watch the satellite streaking through the sky from their place in the breadline or from their derelict collective farms.

8

The Making of the West

Eastern Europe was remade by Communism, western Europe was remade by capitalism. In the 1950s and '60s western European countries were transformed almost beyond recognition by widespread social and economic change. The pace of the change was dizzying for many. European writers and novelists, an Albert Camus in France or a Heinrich Böll in Germany, describe how quickly former lives were left behind. A Norwegian poet saw a great river that uproots everything and forces it all downstream, into a wider world. For many western Europeans, that river was the entrance to a better life: richer and healthier, with better jobs, education, and social welfare than before. Even those who deplored the loss of the old were often seen luxuriating in the new: striking French dockworkers drinking Coca-Cola, British aristocrats enjoying American-style central heating. The close encounter between the United States and western Europe set off changes, some of which seemed superficial but which would nonetheless alter the European continent forever.

Part of the reason for the success of the new were the disasters of the old. After Europe's calamitous half century, *any* stability would do, even one that was imposed by outside powers through the Cold War. Although few Europeans admitted any responsibility for what had gone wrong, most still realized that continuing the way they had done before was impossible. While almost everyone wished for a welfare state in which governments influenced the commanding heights of the economy, most also believed that private enterprise should play a role in the economy of the future. Even the Left was divided on that question. The Communists, of course, wanted a transition to full government ownership of the means of production, but Socialists, Social-Democrats, and Labourites may have wanted, at times, to nationalize key services and industries, but rarely wanted the state to take over the corner store. All western European countries set out a role for the market in their economies. But they wanted capitalist *successes* to help the overall economy, not failures like in the 1920s and '30s.

The rescue of capitalism in western Europe, and its expansion as integrated markets, was therefore dependent on a great deal of hybridity. Even more so than in the United States during Roosevelt's New Deal, European governments wanted market expansion within clear rules and regulations set by the governments themselves. And while the New Deal was always presented as an emergency measure, state-controlled capitalism in Europe was supposed to be a lasting compromise between state, capital, and labor. Indeed, some of its power came from that sense of compromise, which was a faculty that had been lacking in Europe during the past two generations. Both Christian Democratic and Social Democratic politics had an appeal to national cooperation and cohesiveness as a core part of their strength.

The role of the United States in all of this was of course central, though not at all times in ways that its critics or closest supporters imagined. As we have seen, significant changes had been underway in Europe itself since the early part of the century, in social mores, products, and consumption. They had been held back by the unprecedented misfortunes of 1914 to 1953, from Sarajevo to Seoul, when disasters always seemed to be right around the corner (and often were). Compared to the Soviet role in eastern Europe, in western Europe it is much more difficult to disentangle what was US influence and what would have happened anyway. Apart from the crucial US role in helping European elites back on their feet through the Marshall Plan and defending them from what they and the Americans saw as a clear and distinct Soviet threat, it is hard to tell what came from within and what came from without.

The point about the postwar Americanization of western Europe is therefore less about its comprehensiveness than its relative suddenness. Processes of integrating US and European economies had been underway during the interwar period. But the challenges of the 1930s had held them back. US private investment in Europe was very limited (and would remain so up to the 1960s). Even though US business methods and products had proliferated in interwar Europe, knowledge about each other was strikingly deficient, especially on the European side, where US history or politics were barely understood. This was especially true in the main European countries: France, Germany, and Britain. Scandinavians, Greeks, and Italians, who were more likely to have relatives in the United States, knew more about the country. Overall it was an important relationship, but not a close one.

The concept of "The West" was therefore meaningless before the 1950s. There were plenty of public references to a common heritage: Greece, Rome, Christianity, and badly disguised remarks about race. But there were no instruments of cohesion before military, economic, political, and cultural interaction sped up in the postwar era. These placed the United States at the center of western Europe's consumer revolution, through its music, movies, and fashion as much as through its political ideals. An imagined America made it possible for many western Europeans to escape from restrictions of class, gender, or religion. The United States was therefore part of a European revolution that was in many ways as deep, and more lasting, than the Soviet impact in the eastern half of the continent.

THERE WERE THREE main reasons why the western European economic transformation sped up in the 1950s. One was simply a catch-up created by nondevelopment in the past. Europe in 1914 had been the center of the world economy. Europeans had the desire and most of the knowledge needed to get back in the economic and technological forefront. What had held them back was bad politics, which led to catastrophes on a scale the continent had not known since the seventeenth century. There was therefore plenty of pent-up demand for housing, goods, services, and high-quality and stable food supplies. Production would get going as soon as there were credit and functional currencies. And the US presence secured both of these preconditions, fast, through the Marshall Plan, the international financial institutions, and bilateral agreements.

The United States was also integral to providing the security needed for the economic transformation to take place. Although this need was more psychological than real—the USSR was not planning to attack western Europe—its satisfaction was still necessary in order to move forward. Too often in the past people had been told to build things up, only to see them torn down again. What Europeans needed was confidence in the future, and the US security presence supplied that, at least for the critical period when the foundations for European development had to be laid.

Finally, there was the ability to cooperate across lines that had so often divided Europeans in the past. Some of this came out of sheer need. With people on the verge of starvation, it was a lot harder to appeal for strikes and lockouts, especially when governments worked hard to integrate labor and capital through forms of social compromise. This was especially true since there was very little leadership for the substantial minority of western Europeans who distrusted capitalism altogether. Even the Communist parties had appealed for their supporters to participate in national reconstruction, and the only way they could do so was through the political and economic system devised by their governments. Gradually, the idea and practice of transnational European integration also began to take hold, providing the critical element that took western Europe from reconstruction to reemergence.

Not all of it was a success story, of course, even though in light of the experience of Europe's previous generation it is easy to present it as such. Cold War conformity meant that dissent was sometimes suppressed. The past was often swept under the carpet, not only in Germany and Italy, but also in France, where the crimes of the Vichy government were overlaid with unifying narratives of heroic resistance. In Spain and Portugal, which were still under fascist governments, the past was not even past. There, as elsewhere in western Europe, minorities faced a harsh assimilation policy, sometimes carried out in the name of national security. Many women and young people felt that the demands of reconstruction and economic growth made it even less likely for them to have a public voice than had even been the case during wars and depression. And, most important of all, the transformation was happening only in one half of the continent, which may have made it simpler to achieve, but also created questions about its overall long-term significance.

Cold War western Europe was built on two international pillars. One was military cooperation with the United States through NATO. The other was economic and political integration through agreements among western European countries. To some extent Atlantic and European links went hand in hand. The United States had been militarily predominant in western Europe since 1944, and as NATO became more of an integrated military alliance because of the Korean War, US predominance became institutionalized. Both Americans and Europeans were careful, however, to set up deliberative bodies that conveyed the impression of a democratic alliance, in which all members had an equal say. But, besides security delivered by US military prowess, the most important European aspects of NATO were the access that member states had to buy weapons (most often through US credits) and train their own forces internationally. NATO became a school through which western European countries gradually, but increasingly, obtained the sense of a common purpose.

Not all of the military cooperation was plain sailing. One big question was what to do with West Germany. After the Korean War broke out, the Americans became increasingly insistent that they wanted West Germany to re-arm as part of the Western alliance. The Europeans, understandably, demurred. The plan they devised in 1950 to overcome the problem, the European Defense Community, which would have integrated German forces under a common European command, was far too complex to work in practice. It collapsed in 1954, when the French, whose government had originally proposed the plan, refused to ratify it. The following year West Germany joined NATO as a full member.

The other big issue was to how to handle the command of nuclear weapons in western Europe. By the late 1950s the Europeans wanted more of a say within NATO over military strategy, and especially over planning for nuclear warfare. Since 1954, based on the experience in Korea, NATO decided as part of its doctrine that it could respond even to a non-nuclear Soviet attack on western Europe by using nuclear weapons. This was in part general deterrence and in part recognition of Soviet superiority in conventional forces. Britain had become a nuclear power in 1952 and France tested its first nuclear weapon in 1960. Some political leaders, both in western Europe and the United States, wanted more nuclear cooperation in Europe, in part because they feared West Germany might also be tempted to develop its own weapons. Still, a US proposal for a sea-based nuclear Multi-Lateral Force (MLF), operated and commanded jointly by the United States and western Europeans, collapsed in 1964. The British and, especially, the French wanted to keep their nuclear autonomy. Some feared *any* German involvement in nuclear matters. As the US singer-comedian Tom Lehrer put it in his "MLF Lullaby":

> Once all the Germans were warlike and mean,
> But that couldn't happen again.
> We taught them a lesson in nineteen eighteen,
> And they've hardly bothered us since then.[1]

How to deal with Germany was also at the center of plans for Europe's economic recovery. By 1950, much helped by the Marshall Plan, the western European economies seemed to have stabilized, but all of them were still far from the goal of significant and stable growth. Some European and American leaders believed that the only way such growth could be created was by closer European economic integration. One of the effects of long years of wars and depression was to have broken up the transnational markets that had helped make Europe rich in the first place. But given the status of the national economies in western Europe in the late 1940s, it was unlikely that such markets would reconstitute themselves, at least anytime soon. So, as with the national economies, governments set out to organize frameworks within which international economic cooperation (and competition) could thrive.

The road toward European economic integration was formed by the coming together of many different paths. One starting point was the institutions of the Marshall Plan itself, and especially the Organization for European Economic Cooperation. Set up in 1948 to help administer US assistance across borders, the OEEC also helped remove quotas on private trade and make currencies convertible. It also assisted in reducing tariffs and floated the idea of a customs union, which could lead to a European, or possibly Atlantic, free trade area. The latter was a step much too far for most western European politicians in the early 1950s, concerned as they were with balances of trade and currency restrictions. But combined with the security emergency of the Korean War and the growth of NATO, which from 1952 also included Greece and Turkey as members, the OEEC was a starting point for European integration on a grander scale.

Even more important was the European Coal and Steel Community (ECSC), which was formed by France, West Germany, Italy, and the Low Countries in 1951. The plan was the brainchild of the former French prime minister Robert Schuman, who also served as foreign minister from 1948–53. He and his collaborators designed a supranational authority with control of a common market in mining and steel production in all the member countries, which meant mainly in France and Germany. The ECSC was intended as an alternative to a long-term French occupation of parts of Germany to harness its industrial potential. Instead, Schuman believed, all of western Europe could benefit from cooperation between France and Germany, both in Cold War terms, by increasing and regulating strategic production, and in terms of economic development. Jean Monnet, the Frenchman who was the first head of ECSC, also made sure that it had a social purpose, through subsidies for miners and workers, and that its institutions pointed toward wider European integration in other fields as well.

The beginning processes of western European integration were created by one-third idealism and two-thirds practical necessity. It was a Cold War project from the very beginning, seeking to improve western European strategic production and cohesion while faced with the threat from the east. It also took many of its models of integration from the United States, where Monnet had spent several years. At its core it was about Europe's economic recovery, which its founding fathers believed would be impossible without a high degree of integration. But it was also an idealistic project, created to move away from the French-German antagonism that had dominated European politics at least since 1870. Cold War pressures concentrated the minds of European policy-makers and made cooperation necessary. The form that cooperation took, for Schuman, who himself hailed from the Franco-German border areas, or Monnet, a European federalist since the 1920s, was determined by their pan-European outlooks. "World peace cannot be safeguarded without the making of creative efforts proportionate to the dangers which threaten it," began Schuman's declaration of 1950: "The pooling of coal and steel production should immediately provide for the setting up of common foundations for economic development. . . . The solidarity in production thus established will make it plain that any war between France and Germany becomes not merely unthinkable, but materially impossible. . . . This proposal will lead to the realization of the first concrete foundation of a European federation indispensable to the preservation of peace."[2]

Although most western European leaders had reservations about the concept of a full European federation, a majority of them, especially among Christian Democrats, agreed that the ECSC created a foundation to build on. Even Winston Churchill, back as British prime minister after the 1950 elections, had called for a "United States of Europe," though he had doubted that the British Commonwealth would be part of it. In 1956 a committee under Belgian foreign minister Paul-Henri Spaak set out proposals for what a year later became the Treaty of Rome, creating the European Economic Community

(EEC). The EEC built directly on the ECSC. It had the same member states and the same supranational approach to economic integration. But it had a much wider remit, and would, over the generation that followed, remake western Europe as a unifying economic zone.

The biggest Cold War problem inside western Europe was how to handle the German question. From the setting up of the Federal Republic of Germany in 1949, there had always been a suspicion that West German leaders would give up on Western cohesion in order to strike a deal with the USSR on reunification. The idea was not far-fetched. Mistrust of Germans, any Germans, went together with the knowledge that under Cold War conditions such a deal was the only means through which the Germans could achieve what other Europeans assumed were their most cherished aims. But the assumption of German pliability toward the Soviets foundered on the thinking of the West German *Bundeskanzler* (premier) Konrad Adenauer. A conservative Christian Democrat from Rhineland in the west of the country, Adenauer wanted reunification, but he wanted his Germany's integration with the Western powers even more. Adenauer was keenly aware of how enticing the siren song of reunification, even under Communist conditions, could be to some of his countrymen. He therefore at all times prioritized cooperation with the French and with the Americans. "For us, there is no doubt that we belong to the western European world through heritage and temperament," he had said already in his first declaration as German premier.[3] And Adenauer became a constant in West German politics, remaining chancellor until 1963, when he was eighty-seven years old.

But what really gave credence, to Germans and other Europeans alike, to Adenauer's *Westbindung* (attachment to the West), was the extraordinary recovery of the West German economy that started around 1950. The *Wirtschaftswunder*, the German economic miracle, had many causes. Marshall Plan assistance and the linking of the deutschmark to the US dollar was one. The gradual integration of the West German economy into a western European framework was another. Perhaps most important was the US decision to shield the Federal Republic of Germany from the full effect of wartime debt and postwar reparations. The FRG had to pay some reparations, and the dismantling of some German industries and compensatory takeover of patents and technology continued until the early 1950s. But the cumulative burden of excessive debt never came into play. As a result, West Germany was even freer than some of its new Western partners to plan for further expansion as its economy began to grow.

The social transformation the Wirtschaftswunder created was one of the biggest stories of postwar Europe. In 1945 all of Germany was a bombed-out disaster zone. Ten years later most people had jobs that paid well enough for their families both to consume and to save. Industries and infrastructure were approaching prewar levels. Housing was being rebuilt at astonishing rates. West German banks had credit available and the country's currency and interest rates were stable. The West German economy grew by more than 5 percent year on year during the 1950s and '60s. It was the highest growth rate of any major European economy, more than twice that of Britain, for instance.

While structural causes explain the fundamentals of West Germany's Cold War economic expansion, it was the psychological effects of the Wirtschaftswunder that ensured its amplification and perpetuation. It was more than a generation since Germans had last been able to believe that their own work was translatable into wealth, happiness, and stability for their families. In the 1950s, as they sensed this was at last becoming possible, they threw themselves into production with a vengeance. West Germans worked longer hours than most Europeans, and productivity expanded rapidly. As a result, their purchasing power almost doubled from 1950 to 1960, and the rapid expansion continued into the 1960s.

But Germany was not the only western European country that saw high growth rates in the 1950s and '60s. France, in spite of the political instability of the Fourth Republic, had substantial growth, as did the Benelux countries and Scandinavia. The economic expansion in Italy was very strong, though unevenly spread in terms of rewards, both geographically and socially. Overall the effect of the economic transformation of western Europe was not just to rescue capitalism, which had seemed to be the issue in the 1940s, but to dramatically expand it as part of people's lives. As industrialization and urbanization continued, more people were drawn into economic exchanges as workers and consumers. In 1950, a third of all Frenchmen worked the land. Twenty years later it was less than 10 percent. But, different from the late nineteenth-century wave of industrialization, there was little political radicalization. The French Communist Party lost a third of its voters during the two first postwar decades.

There were several reasons why Communism lost out as a political alternative in western Europe. Members of the Communist parties were persecuted both at work and in society as the Cold War intensified. When the crimes of Stalin and his cohort became universally known, and especially after the 1956 uprising in Hungary, the parties started to lose members. Except in Italy, where domestic inequity made up for foreign tumults, Communism was not such an attractive alternative anymore in democratic states. But the main reason for the crisis in European Communism was not so much political as social. As many western European countries began dramatically expanding social welfare for their citizens, the need for revolution seemed ever less obvious to most of the working class.

As we have seen, the origins of the European welfare state goes back to the ideological conflicts of the late nineteenth and early twentieth century. But its main expansion was in the 1950s and '60s. For some, including European and Soviet Communists, this was a surprising development, given the US predominance in western Europe. They had interpreted the Marshall Plan as an attempt at Americanizing the European economies, both for the benefit of US business interests and in order to push free market solutions. Instead, what western Europe got, mostly with US blessing, was state-centered solutions, in which government regulations determined the shape of the national economies. Western Europe's postwar decades of rapid economic growth were created in an environment of state control.

The main reasons this was possible were the Cold War emergency and the lessons of the immediate past. The Cold War, both domestically in western Europe and between East and West, mandated centralized states in which quick decisions could be made for the defense of the established political order. But it also demanded that the powerful western European working classes could be bought off from industrial unrest and independent political activism through guarantees for social progress. Christian Democrats and Social Democrats agreed that part of the reason for the continent's hitherto unhappy century was the past inability to integrate the working class into the body politic. Now firmly in power, they believed that the only way this deficiency could be remedied was through social programs that gave workers a stake in the nation. While Christian Democratic parties were closer to the national elites than Social Democrats were, at least to begin with, they both ended up putting in place large-scale social security programs, as well as government-mandated, branch-wise bargaining over wages and working conditions in industry. Limitations to the workweek, paid vacations, and regularized pensions all came out of state-imposed initiatives, as did, somewhat later, comprehensive medical and disability insurance.

US support for such government-centered development plans can also be explained by the Truman Administration's realization of just how bad the situation had been all over Europe in the 1940s. If the choice was between chaos, opening up for Soviet subversion, and government-imposed order, it was not difficult to make, for Truman in Europe or for later US administrations elsewhere in the world, in spite of American ideological predilections. Many US representatives in postwar Europe (as well as in postwar Japan) had backgrounds in the United States' own experiments with state-led initiatives during the New Deal. Granted, western European initiatives went much further toward state planning than anything implemented long-term in the United States. But, even so, Americans were not wholly unused to measures through which the state regulated economic activity. And in western Europe, for the time being, these controls made sense: limiting private profit helped secure necessary reinvestment. Providing welfare prevented political radicalization. And economic pluralism within the NATO alliance meant that US predominance became less visible, and therefore probably more effective.

US predominance was visible, and increasingly so, within the consumer revolution that accompanied western European economic growth. It was not so much that the products Europeans desired were always made in the United States. They were often produced at home or, increasingly, in Japan. But the goods and the marketing that sold them were often American in origin. For many Europeans, the United States appeared to be a highly desirable society, affluent and abundant, and always one step ahead of old-fashioned and restrictive Europe. This positive view of America seemed to increase the more Europeans got to know about the country. The expansion of transatlantic travel was important in that regard, as were plentiful US information agencies and scholarships.

Even more important was American influence in Europe through its music, movies, and fashion. Unlike the Soviet efforts at gaining a cultural influence, there was little that was centrally planned about this. The State Department and the CIA tried to make sure that "healthy" American films and literature were spread abroad, but their successes were limited. Instead, company marketing and consumer responses ruled the roost. The ability of US film studios and record producers to make their output inexpensive and plentiful, while Europe suffered all kinds of shortages, also gave imports an advantage. In 1947, for instance, only forty French films were made, while 340 were imported from the United States. Though the music of Elvis Presley or the movies of Marlon Brando or James Dean were not set up to be propaganda for the American way of life, young Europeans liked them, in part because of their rebelliousness. Wearing T-shirts and blue jeans merged a form of protest against convention with identifying with US movies. In the mid-1950s, American and European teenagers were more united by Brando than by NATO.

Where US officialdom had more of an influence was in terms of support for European organizations and institutions. Encouraged by the government, American philanthropy, such as the Ford or Rockefeller foundations, gave grants that remade many western European universities and research centers. The CIA provided funding for organizations such as the Congress for Cultural Freedom, which was set up to combat Communist influence among writers and artists. And government-backed links with American labor unions, to the greatest extent the AFL/CIO, helped convince some European Social Democrats that US society was less Right-wing and antilabor than what they had imagined. Even so, unofficial cultural links were more important than anything governments did to further US soft power in western Europe during the Cold War.

Changes for the European world seemed to come from all sides during the postwar era. Besides the ideological division of the continent and the increase in US influence, the gradual loss of its overseas colonies transformed western Europe. In 1945 Britain, France, Portugal, Spain, Belgium, and the Netherlands all claimed substantial overseas possessions. Around three times as many people lived in the European colonies as lived in western Europe itself. By 1965, except for those of Portugal, there were very few colonies left. The readjustment needed to facilitate this transition inside Europe—economically and perceptually—was considerable. One issue was to accommodate Europeans who returned from former colonies, or populations from the colonies who chose to remain in the metropole. Another was getting used to the much reduced global status of their own countries. For Britain and for France, especially, this was a tough transition. But keeping up the pretensions of being Great Powers demanded more than these countries could afford. "There is no way that we will take the path of least resistance and allow France to fade away," General de Gaulle told his countrymen in 1963.[4] In terms of world power, however, fading away is a pretty accurate description of the role of the former empires during the Cold War.

Besides the situation within the continent itself, the changes in the global economy in the mid-twentieth century also assigned Europe to a secondary role. In 1950 the United States was the hegemon of world capitalism. It produced around a third of the combined global economic output. The US dollar was the only currency used for large international transactions. The capital that went into international banks was mainly from the United States. US industries were substantially more technologically advanced and productive than those in

Europe. And Americans, on average, lived longer and better lives than Europeans, in spite of the postwar western European recovery.

This unique position of the United States came about in a world that was primarily based on managed trade and investment. Governments set quotas and tariffs, regulated capital flows and currency levels, and decided how national incomes were to be spent. Successive US administrations pushed for trade and investment liberalization, but were careful with pushing too hard for fear that such US pressure could complicate Washington's building of Cold War alliances with other capitalist countries. The United States therefore was at the center of a global capitalist economy that had to be managed for Cold War purposes. The reconstruction of this economic system was in the US interest, even if that meant putting aside a few of the most immediate opportunities that existed for Americans making profits overseas. The hegemonic moment for the United States was circumscribed by Cold War contingencies that spread all over the world, among which links with western Europe were central but not always decisive.

Successive US administrations believed that western European integration was in the American interest. They assisted in the recovery of the economy and strengthened the European commitment to other multilateral institutions, first and foremost NATO. The Americans were never overly concerned that a more united Europe would become a competitor to the United States. In the 1950s that did not seem likely to happen anytime soon. And the improvement in common security that came with European economic growth was more important anyway than narrow US self-interest, at least in the short run. If western Europe got richer by building large and integrated markets after American models, that was a good thing for everyone concerned. As John Foster Dulles, soon to become US secretary of state, had declared in 1948, "a healthy Europe" could not be "divided into small compartments." It had to be organized into a market "big enough to justify modern methods of cheap production for mass consumption."[5]

If Europeans hungered for recovery, Americans longed for stability. For more than twenty years, US voters had faced one emergency after another: the Great Depression, the New Deal, wars in Europe and Asia, and the Cold War. In 1952 they voted for stability and normality under General Dwight D. Eisenhower, the first professional military man to head the US government since Ulysses S. Grant in the 1870s and the first Republican president since the onset of the national crises. Eisenhower was an internationalist and a Cold Warrior who believed that the United States needed to confront the USSR and Communism worldwide. In his campaign, he had argued for the need to win in Korea and for "rolling back" Communism in Europe and Asia. But his main rhetoric was intended to assure Americans that they were safe under his leadership, and that the United States would defeat its enemies if it put its own house in order through national unity, fiscal discipline, a strong defense, and clear international priorities.

Intent to move away from the Cold War as a national emergency, Eisenhower ended up institutionalizing it as policy and doctrine. On the Korean War, the new president simply got lucky. Stalin's death removed the last hindrance for a negotiated armistice. But Eisenhower believed that projections of US strength would prevent what he saw as Soviet adventurism in the future. Confirming Truman's overall containment strategy, Eisenhower wanted to reinforce it by increasing US nuclear capacity and readiness. He also upgraded the CIA's covert operations and used them to overthrow governments the president saw as inimical to US Cold War interests, such as in Iran in 1953 and in Guatemala the following year. Eisenhower saw the Cold War as a total contest that would last for a long time, and in which US purpose and readiness would remain the critical element.

But the new president also believed, firmly, that the United States could fight the Cold War without making too many compromises with regard to its domestic affairs. A fiscal conservative, Eisenhower preferred developing nuclear deterrents as a less expensive alternative to large standing armies and massive amounts of conventional weapons. As Dulles explained in January 1954, "We want for ourselves and for others a maximum deterrent at a bearable cost": "Local defense will always be important. But there is no local defense which alone will contain the mighty land power of the Communist world. Local defenses must be reinforced by the further deterrent of massive retaliatory power. . . . The way to deter aggression is for the free community to be willing and able to respond vigorously at places and with means of its own choosing."[6]

The turn toward a policy of massive nuclear retaliation meant preparing for strategic warfare on a scale that so far had seemed unimaginable. Eisenhower set in motion a dramatic buildup of US atomic capabilities, in what he called his New Look policy. On his watch, the United States developed intercontinental ballistic missiles (ICBMs) and submarine-launched ballistic missiles (SLBMs). The Pentagon also initiated large-scale intelligence-gathering programs, including secret overflights of Soviet territory, to gather information on targeting and enemy capabilities. In addition, the administration stepped up the deployment of tactical and medium-range nuclear missiles to US bases in Europe and Asia. When criticized for the inflexibility of the US strategic stance, the president responded that the United States had effectively deterred any Soviet attack on itself or its allies. Eisenhower had no doubt that the US capacity to wage nuclear warfare against the Soviets vastly outmeasured anything they could do against the United States. His New Look policy enabled him to get deterrence on the cheap and without, the president hoped, too much of a militarization of US society.

Throughout his presidency, Eisenhower feared the political consequences of making his country into a garrison state, with its budgets geared toward military procurement and its politics dominated by foreign threats. After having been supported by Senator McCarthy in the election campaign, Eisenhower turned on him when the senator in 1954 expanded his attacks on subservience to Communism in the US Army. The president was "very mad and getting fed up—it is his Army and he doesn't like McCarthy's tactics at all."[7] By the end of the year McCarthy had been censured by the Senate and removed as a force in US politics.

The censure of McCarthy removed the foremost symbol of the hysterical style of Cold War politics in the United States, though it did little to damage the anti-Communist cause. McCarthy had already become an embarrassment across the spectrum of American politics. What remained after him was still a sense of mission on a global scale, on behalf of democracy, religion, and free markets. Confronting Communism was for most Americans in the 1950s part of their country's fundamental quality, and a campaign that had to be won at home and abroad. A very wide consensus, comprising people who would call themselves either liberals or conservatives (a distinct minority), was in favor of fighting the Cold War as part of an American undertaking to improve global affairs. The Communists, so the thinking went, were trying to take over a world that by natural direction and God-given foresight was the Americans' to modernize and make better. The Cold War was therefore an unprecedented struggle for the soul of mankind.

For many Americans, the need to fight the Cold War abroad was allied with a sense of achievement at home. Economic conditions were improving, as were salaries, housing, and access to consumer goods. The middle class expanded rapidly, and more and more people moved out of the cities to new houses in the suburbs. Political leaders from both parties portrayed the fight against Communism as the defense of all that Americans had achieved materially, socially, and politically. Religion played an important role in Cold War rhetoric. Communism was portrayed as God-less radicalism, and clergy and religious activists who had been persecuted in eastern Europe were often brought over to the United States to bear witness to what was going on behind the Iron Curtain. A large majority of Americans believed that their families and their communities were under direct threat from Communist subversion in the United States, although not many of them could think of specific instances when such things had actually happened. Given that the Communist Party of the United States by the mid-1950s was reduced to only around five thousand active members, the chances of ever meeting one of them was indeed limited.

The stability, predictability, and caution that characterized Eisenhower's America did not suit all Americans. Some felt, rightly, that they were excluded both from economic and social progress. African-Americans had been discriminated against ever since slavery was abolished, and neither the New Deal nor the prosperity of the 1950s did much to improve their lot. As the civil rights movement expanded, more and more people drew unfavorable comparisons between American campaigns for freedom worldwide and the obvious oppression of African-Americans and other people of color at home. Roy Wilkins, the director of the main civil rights organization, the NAACP, put it charitably, but well, when he characterized the president as "a fine general and a good, decent man, but if he had fought World War II the way he fought for civil rights, we would all be speaking German today."[8] Diplomats from the new African states, who were subject to racial harassment and segregation in Washington and across the country, were less charitable in their reports back home.

Another group that benefitted little from Eisenhower's Cold War America were women who wanted to construct their own lives outside the confines of family and housework. During the war many women had found rewarding jobs in industry and services. But the emphasis on family values and child-rearing during the Cold War had forced a large number out of the workplace and back to primary roles as wives and mothers. Some women found the conformity of American society during the 1950s stifling. Toward the end of the decade both female employment rates and women's participation in organizations and in politics had begun to increase. But the biggest breakthrough came in 1960, when the contraceptive pill became widely available. Access to effective birth control, decided on by women themselves, transformed family life in Cold War America, and would gradually open up for a much more active participation in society. But social conservatives condemned the effects the pill had on population numbers and on young people's sexual behavior. Christian preachers, both Catholics and Evangelicals, claimed that birth control was the work of the Devil, alongside Communism, "free love," and homosexuality.

The 1950s emphasis on material well-being and social conformity led to a fair amount of restlessness, not just among disadvantaged groups. Many young people were wondering if they could do more and experience more than what was visible on the path that their parent's generation had laid out for them. The unease was both political and cultural. Tastes in music, movies, literature, and fashion became more daring as the decade wore on. Some people wondered if they could do more for their country, including help fight the Cold War more effectively. Many liberals feared that the United States was falling behind the Soviet Union in the international competition for hearts and minds. The Cold War had after all been as much, if not more, of a liberal political project than a conservative one. A young Democratic senator from Massachusetts, John F. Kennedy, in 1958 claimed that President Eisenhower was more preoccupied with balancing the budget than defeating the USSR. As a result, Soviet military strength was overtaking that of the United States, creating "a peril more deadly than any wartime danger we have ever known."[9] The president dismissed Senator Kennedy as an inexperienced political opportunist.

Eisenhower has rightly been praised for moving the United States away from the political hysteria of the early Cold War. But if the president was not a Cold War hysteric, neither was he someone who could conceive of a world without the confrontation with the Soviet Union. Eisenhower lacked the imagination and the political will to think about ending the Cold War after Stalin's death. When the new Soviet leaders attempted to normalize their relations with the West, through ending the Korean War, reducing their troop levels in Europe, and talking about peaceful coexistence, the US president hesitated. John Foster Dulles and his brother, the CIA director Allen Dulles, believed that Khrushchev's charm offensive was just that: an attempt at getting the West to lower its guard while the Soviets increased subversion worldwide. Given the strength of anti-Communism at home, not least in his own party, Eisenhower did not want to risk useless meetings with the Soviets. Even the old Cold Warrior Winston Churchill encouraged the president to extend a hand to the Soviets. "Would it not be well," he asked Eisenhower in April 1953, "to combine the re-assertions of your and our inflexible resolves with some balancing expression of hope that we have entered upon a new era. A new hope has I feel been created in the unhappy bewildered world. It ought to be possible to proclaim our unflinching determination to resist communist tyranny and aggression and at the same time though separately to declare how glad we should be if we found there was a real change of heart and not let it be said that we had closed the door upon it."[10] But Eisenhower did not believe the motives of the Soviet leaders had changed much, and resisted any pressure for a summit meeting until mid-1955.

The 1955 Geneva discussion among the leaders of the wartime alliance was the first such meeting since 1945. Eisenhower had agreed to the summit because of Soviet willingness to support both a settlement in Indochina and the reunification of Austria, which had been divided into occupation zones since World War II. Though the conversations were civil, no major breakthroughs were had. The Americans concluded, somewhat correctly, that the power struggle among Soviet leaders after Stalin was still ongoing. When meeting with the Soviet premier, Nikolai Bulganin, President Eisenhower "raised the question of the satellite [states]": "He explained that there were literally millions of Americans who had their roots and origins in Central Europe. The status of the satellites was a matter of very genuine concern to him. This was not a question on which we could be silent. Bulganin indicated that it was a subject which it would do no good to pursue at this conference: it would require time and an improvement in the atmosphere."[11]

The Hungarian revolution at the start of Eisenhower's second term led to a severe setback in East/West relations. It was not until the end of his presidency that Eisenhower began thinking about possible changes in his Soviet policy. In his 1959 State of the Union address he spoke at length about strengthening the institutions of peace, and the following year, his last as president, Eisenhower agreed to a summit meeting with Khrushchev in Paris in May. The purpose of the conference was to discuss a reduction of tension in Europe, and predominantly the German issue. Eisenhower also hoped that by setting the summit in Paris, he could help bring the mercurial de Gaulle, now

back as president of France, into a united NATO approach to the Soviets on European security problems. With some of his closest advisers, Eisenhower had begun to prepare a more positive response to
Soviet proposals of a ban on testing new types of nuclear weapons.
The president may have hoped for a breakthrough in these negotiations in Paris.

If so, Eisenhower never got the chance to test Soviet intentions.
On 1 May 1960, the Soviet air force shot down an American U-2 spy
plane, which had been traversing the USSR on its way from Peshawar
in Pakistan to Bodø in Norway. Khrushchev was furious. But the Soviet leader also knew how to play to the gallery. While the Americans,
awkwardly, were trying to lie about it being a meteorological mission
gone wrong, the Soviets put the pilot, who had been rescued, on show
in Moscow. Gary Powers admitted he had been on an espionage flight
for the CIA. Khrushchev relished the propaganda bonanza. But he
could not make up his mind about cancelling the Paris summit, which
began two weeks later. In the end Khrushchev flew to Paris, but under
pressure from party hardliners, he at the last minute refused to meet
Eisenhower. Already under fire from the Chinese for being weak on
imperialism, the Soviet leader could not risk having a summit meeting under these circumstances.

China and Asia were very much on the minds of leaders both in
the USSR and the United States as Eisenhower's presidency drew to
a close. The US president felt that he had solidified the West and
given it a common purpose on which to confront the Soviet Union
and its allies. But he was much less certain about US positions in
Asia. The president feared the expanding power of China, and believed Beijing would attempt to spread Communism to Southeast
Asia. "If the Communists establish a strong position in Laos, the
West is finished in the whole southeast Asian area," Eisenhower told
his chief advisers just before stepping down.[12] He gave little credence
to reports of a fundamental and lasting Sino-Soviet split. The Cold
War in Asia "is like playing poker with tough stakes and . . . there is
no easy solution," the president told his successor, John F. Kennedy,
when he met him at the White House in January 1961.[13] Eisenhower

lamented "the Communist influence on Chinese troops, pointing out their ability to get much higher morale among the under-developed peoples than seemed to be the case of the Western Allies."[14] Having secured the West, the United States seemed about to open a new chapter in the Cold War.

9

China's Scourge

There is a strange symmetry to China's twentieth century, and much of it is linked to the ideological Cold War. At the beginning of the century, China's republican revolution was overtaken by Communism and conflict. And at the end of the century, Communism was overtaken by money and markets. In between lay a terrible time of destruction and reconstruction, of enthusiasm and cynicism, and of almost never-ending rivers of blood. What marks these Chinese revolutions most of all is their bloodthirst: according to a recent estimate, seventy-seven million Chinese died unnatural deaths as a result of warfare or political mass-murder between the 1920s and the 1980s, and the vast majority of them were killed by other Chinese.[1]

The People's Republic of China (PRC), the Communist state that Mao Zedong and his party set up in 1949, had promised peace and development as its main aims. Instead they took their countrymen almost immediately into a new war in Korea, in which it suffered at least eight hundred thousand casualties. By the summer of 1953, when the Korean war ended, China was an exhausted country, which had to face up to a massive task of reconstruction after almost twenty years of continuous warfare. The Chinese leadership had decided that the Soviet Union was to be its model. It was firmly convinced that the future on a global scale belonged to socialism, and that China's close alliance with the Soviets would help put their country at the forefront of world progress. Mao and his comrades were of course also convinced that Moscow's military assistance helped them protect their revolution against rapacious US imperialists. The Korean War had proven that to them, even though they had not always been satisfied with the level of Soviet support during the fighting. After all, Mao pointed out, the Chinese were doing the fighting and dying on behalf of the socialist bloc, including the North Koreans and the Soviets themselves.

Communism was to be China's weapon for modernization, according to the party's propaganda. It would make the country rich and strong. But Mao's agenda went further than the creation of a modern, wealthy country. He wanted to transform Chinese society and people's ways of thinking. It was "old China" that was to blame for the country's weakness, Mao thought, more than even British, Japanese, or American imperialists. He liked to compare traditional, Confucian forms of thinking to women with bound feet, hobbling along while being disdained by others. His "new China," on the other hand, should be youthful, progressive, and militant. Those who stood in the way were "pests" to be exterminated; landlords, priests, and capitalists were holding China back on purpose, in order to serve their own interests. They had to go, as did all those forces that blocked the new society the Communists would create. For Mao this was a millennial struggle. It was China's last chance to redeem itself and retake its rightful position in the world.

At first, in the 1950s, Chairman Mao and his leadership group believed that China's progress could only come within the Soviet-led community of Communist states. But by the latter part of the decade, doubts had set in. Soviet-style development seemed all too slow for Mao. He wanted to see China excel in his own lifetime. After 1956, the Chairman believed for a while that Khrushchev's attempts at reforming the Soviet bloc and making it more equal and diverse could satisfy China's needs. But Soviet criticism of China's fast-forward development plans disabused him of such notions. Amid conflicts over domestic development as well as international affairs, the Sino-Soviet alliance floundered. By the early 1960s the concept of "brother states" was gone, to be replaced with an enmity so deep that it almost led to war at the end of the decade.

Most of the 1960s saw China alone, internationally isolated and descending into ever deeper political campaigns to satisfy Mao's thirst for societal transformation. Economic progress suffered. The Great Proletarian Cultural Revolution, proclaimed by Mao in 1966, made politics the judge of all things. "It is better to be Red than to be an expert," was one of its slogans. The result was a chaotic society, in which violence and dislocation were rife. By the end of their second decade in power, the Chinese Communists presided over a country that appeared on the verge of civil war. China's entry into the Cold War seemed to deliver the opposite of what most Chinese had expected.

THE CHINESE COMMUNIST Party (CCP) had been a war-fighting organization for most of its life span. Although it had begun to get some experience in civilian administration as it took over territory during the 1946–50 civil war, it was very unprepared to preside over a complex society with more than six hundred million inhabitants, at least sixty ethnic groups, and a geography that spanned from a dry and cold north to a subtropical south. The Communists had not administered a city until they took Harbin, up by the Soviet border, in 1946, and they were deeply distrustful of places like Shanghai, Wuhan, or Guangzhou—cosmopolitan cities where the Communists, who had been based in the countryside for a generation, had little influence. Some CCP members were so disgusted with the filth—physical and moral—they found in Shanghai when they conquered the city in 1949 that they wanted to abolish it and herd the population into the countryside where they could reform through hard menial labor. Mao in the end decided against such excesses; he wanted to use the cities as showcases for the transformational power of Chinese Communism.

Mao Zedong was sixty years old when the Korean War ended. He reckoned that he had ten more years to influence China, and he wanted progress fast. By 1953 Mao had fully embraced the principles of centralized and structured planning, Soviet-style, that his main colleagues Liu Shaoqi and Zhou Enlai stood for, and was happy to let younger, Soviet-educated experts run the day-to-day aspects of the economy. Though a perfectionist in military campaigning, in peacetime, Mao was never much of a details man. But he did want to impress on younger comrades his concerns about time running out. China needed to catch up with the West, and thereby become a more useful partner of the other Communist countries. Although he mostly refrained from saying it aloud, Mao felt that China should become a leader among Communist parties and countries, and be the closest partner of the Soviet Union itself. After Stalin's death, he was the most senior Communist leader around. But China, and he himself, had to earn such a position, Mao thought. A rapid socialist transformation would be the best proof of China's dedication to the cause.

The Chinese Communists would have to begin in the cities. Although in charge of a peasant-based army, Mao had never doubted that his party would become a proletarian one as the Chinese working class matured. Now, all of a sudden, the Communists found themselves in charge of cities in which they had very little organization among workers. Like in eastern Europe, some of these workers had taken power for themselves in their factories as war and civil war came to a close. The Communists faced the double task of restoring industrial production and organizing workers in Communist-led trade unions. The strategy they chose, much influenced by their Soviet advisers, was one that combined cajoling and pressure with promises of material rewards for workers as soon as industrial production got going again. All industry had to adhere to the national plan, and the party appointed managers and directors. In cases where the owners had fled or were suspected of having been in league with Japan or Chiang Kai-shek, plants were confiscated by the state. But planning was more important than ownership in the early People's Republic. It took up to the late 1950s before all industry was nationalized.

In their campaigns in the cities, the CCP was much helped by the enthusiasm of many young, urban, middle-class Chinese. Though some of them had joined the party already during the civil war, most had not, and were now eager to make up for that by showing their patriotism and dedication to the Communist cause. They were at the forefront of campaigns dealing with public health, sanitation, or education, or in the party's crusades against social vice such as prostitution, drug use, or gambling. Together with those who had been trained in the party's base areas during the war, these young educated Chinese staffed the PRC government departments and institutions. While more senior cadres stood for purges, arrests, or executions, the young adherents showed off the romantic side of Communism, with their nationalist-infused enthusiasm for reform and reconstruction.

The rapid transformation of China in the 1950s would not have been possible without Soviet aid. The Soviet assistance program for China was not only the biggest Moscow ever undertook outside its own borders. It was also, in relative terms, the biggest such program undertaken by any country anywhere, including the US Marshall Plan for Europe. The total from 1946 to 1960 amounted to around $25 billion in today's prices, a little bit less than 1 percent of the Soviet GDP yearly. But in reality the costs were much higher than this. The sum does not include technology transfers, salaries for Soviet experts in China, or stipends for Chinese students in the USSR. Even if we subtract the roughly 18 percent that came from Soviet allies and around 15 percent that the Chinese eventually paid back, we are still dealing with a program so vast in scope that it had a major impact on both countries.

Even though the first agreements for Soviet aid to the CCP were formed during the Chinese civil war, it was Nikita Khrushchev who really cranked the program up to its unprecedented size. To Khrushchev, Stalin's unwillingness to form a closer relationship with the Chinese was a sign of the old boss's increasing madness. Khrushchev himself saw unlimited opportunity. The alliance of the world's biggest country with the most populous one would propel Communism to global victory, he thought. The potential for cooperation in terms of resources and human talent was boundless. And China could be transformed in the Communist, meaning the Soviet, image, by the free will of its own leaders and its own people. It was an occasion far too good to pass up for Khrushchev.

It was not surprising, then, that the new Soviet leader's first foreign visit in 1954 was to Beijing. The Chinese capital, into which the famously rustic Mao had reluctantly moved after the Communist victory, was made to look its best in preparation for its prominent guest. To Mao, it was important that Khrushchev had chosen China as his first destination. It was also important that the Soviet leader came to see him, rather than the other way around, as had been the case four years earlier under Stalin's rule. But even more significant were the gifts Khrushchev had chosen to bring along. He promised a steep increase in Soviet aid to China, both civilian and military. One-third of all projects under the first Chinese Five Year Plan were to be built and paid for by Soviet or eastern European assistance. But Khrushchev also accepted a more equal relationship between the two countries: Soviet privileges in Chinese border areas would be abolished, and "joint companies," set up at Stalin's insistence, would be transferred to Chinese ownership. He even promised to share Soviet nuclear technology with the Chinese.

Khrushchev also agreed to send more Soviet advisers to China. Throughout the 1950s these advisers played a key role all over the Chinese central administration, regional and provincial governments, and major industrial enterprises. For young Soviet experts it became popular to go to China. They had good conditions there. But they also filled a real need on the Chinese side to replace the losses from war or exile. Soviet experts advised on every aspect of life in new China— from working with youth and women, national minorities, or law and imprisonment, to education, technology, and military training. Overall the cooperation worked out well. The Chinese looked at the Soviets as models for what they wanted to become: educated, dedicated, and efficient. Of course there were cultural clashes, and sometimes the Chinese resented what they saw as Soviet attempts at lording it over them. But on the whole the Sino-Soviet alliance was a formidable Cold War challenge to the predominance of the West.[2]

One key influence that the Soviets had was in military affairs. More than ten thousand officers in the People's Liberation Army (PLA) were trained in the Soviet Union, and countless more were trained by Red Army instructors in China. The result was a modern Chinese army that looked increasingly like the Red Army, that served the same purposes internally, and fought wars more or less in the same way. This new PLA served three major purposes. First, it was intended to be an effective fighting force, trained in the latest Soviet military doctrines and equipped with the best weapons the Soviets and eastern Europeans were willing to offer. Second, it was to be a laboratory for educating young Chinese men to serve in a new world of socialism. And third, the army was intended to help build China's civilian development projects, just like the Red Army had in the Soviet Union in the past.

Educational reform was another main Soviet influence. The Chinese wanted to emulate education as it had developed in the Soviet Union, with an emphasis on science and technology, but also with broad grassroots programs for literacy, numeracy, and politics. A main point was to get education to fit in with the Five Year Plan. The government set the aims of how many engineers, chemists, and other specialized groups were needed every year. The candidates for entry were selected according to political, class, and achievement criteria; they had to be both bright and Red. The Education Ministry underlined the need to be able to predict the numbers of people who would be available to send to work in plants and mines every year—just as in the Soviet Union in the 1930s, students were often given a specific future work assignment as early as their second year in college (even though the authorities rarely found it necessary to inform the students themselves of what lay in store).

The Soviets were aware of the problems the CCP had with governing the cities. They contributed their advice on urban planning. The socialist city had to be modern, planned, productive, and secure for the Communist elite. Broad avenues and big urban squares facilitated the mobility of workers from home to the factory and back, but they also could come in handy in case the PLA needed to enter a city center to crush a counterrevolutionary rebellion. For Beijing—the new national capital and therefore the showcase for Communist planning—the 1935 General Plan for the Reconstruction of Moscow served as a concrete model. On one occasion, somewhat to the horror of Soviet advisers, the Chinese planners simply superimposed a transparency of the Moscow plan on a map of old Beijing. The Ming Dynasty city had to give way to socialist high modernism. The center itself would be rebuilt, with the massively enlarged central plaza at its heart (now known as Tian'anmen Square). A new avenue for military parades—called, with some irony, the Avenue of Eternal Peace— would bisect the old city. In Beijing as a whole, one million old houses should be destroyed each year, and two million new ones built. The city should aim for the same population density as Moscow, with the majority of its inhabitants being industrial workers (a group that had been only 4 percent of the workforce in 1949).

Not only the national center, but also the peripheries would be re- constructed according to Soviet advice. Policy toward minorities or "nationalities" was an area of particular importance to the Chinese Communists. They wanted them counted, categorized, and, first and foremost, controlled. An issue of particular concern was that more than half of these groups lived in more than one country. The poten- tial for subversion of Chinese interests seemed legion, especially since the CCP's relationship with Tibetans, Mongols, Uighurs, Kazakhs, and others had not always been easy in the past. They wanted to use the experience of the Soviets in handling minority issues to their own advantage. The issue had to be dealt with carefully, though, by both sides, since some of these minorities lived in the borderlands between China and the Soviet Union itself.

The CCP's insistence on "recataloging" its inventory of ethnic groups, combined with the unprecedented period of regional and local autonomy created by the wars of the early twentieth century, made for unexpected results in the 1950s. In the great counting of peoples, local agency sometimes combined with the intricacies of Marxist-Leninist theory to give new opportunities to marginal groups. The breakdown into fifty-six nationalities in China was hap- hazard and often a product of decisions made across a table in Bei- jing. But it still meant that some groups who had never had their own institutions suddenly found themselves to be one of China's peoples, with representation all the way up to the National People's Congress (China's parliament). Though Communist political repression could hit anyone within China's borders, recognition as a separate nationality gave some degree of protection from the most vicious aspects of PRC political campaigns, at least until the Cultural Revolution began in 1966.

In spite of having come to power at the head of a peasant army, the CCP took its time in dealing with rural issues. It waited six years, for instance, before taking the leap into the full collectivization of agriculture. There were several reasons for this measured approach. Soviet advice had been to go slow, and not repeat some of the errors of collectivization in USSR and in eastern Europe. Many Chinese peasant leaders were skeptics. They knew full well how peasants had joined the revolution in order to get their own land. Taking it away from them could be politically dangerous. But Mao's impatience, supported by younger CCP members who regarded collectivization as de rigueur for a Communist state, in the end won the day. By 1956 most land in the central areas was collectivized, growing to almost 90 percent of all Chinese agricultural produce. By all indications collectivization in China had been a major success both politically and economically.

Mao Zedong pondered the apparent successes of collectivization, and then drew the wrong lessons from them. He started to believe that the CCP had been too hesitant in carrying out major economic reforms tout court. Maybe, the Chairman thought, China was holding back too much, paying too much heed to the advice of planners and Soviet-trained economists. Perhaps he needed to be bolder, to move more quickly, as the CCP and its army had done in war?[3] For now he held his tongue, at least in public. But after Khrushchev's speech at the Soviet Twentieth Congress in 1956, which criticized the dogmatism of the Soviet past and stressed that all Communist countries had to find their own way to socialism, the Chairman became more and more outspoken in stressing China's unique position and its need to speed up its social and economic transformation.

What jolted Mao into action were the crises in Poland and Hungary in the autumn of 1956. He and many of his advisers thought that the reason workers in eastern Europe had rebelled was that the Communist parties there had not paid attention to local conditions. They had also been too slow and reluctant in offering the forms of advanced socialism that would have won the workers' support. The answer to Hungary was, in other words, not less socialism, but more socialism, especially since the CCP leadership feared that China itself could be vulnerable to the kinds of unrest that had happened in eastern Europe. Workers, especially, were not happy with their lot in China, and reports of strikes came in daily in the aftermath of the Hungarian revolution. Among such demonstrations, the party center noted, "some were led by party members and youth league members; chairmen of . . . unions participated in some; some were . . . stirred up by antirevolutionaries. In many cases, the masses' blood was up, with even some administrative leaders yelling '[we] have to fight till the end.'"[4]

Mao's response was first to open up for criticism of party practices, to "let hundred flowers bloom," as he put it. For a few heady weeks in the spring of 1957, Chinese in all walks of life were allowed—and in some cases encouraged—to give voice to their own opinions. Then, fearful of the barrage of criticism that hit them, the party leaders backtracked and launched an "anti-Rightist" campaign to punish those who had dared to come forward. The "hundred flowers" criticisms had been of three major kinds. Some felt that the party was too bureaucratic and dogmatic. Others attacked the lack of basic political freedoms in China. And the third group claimed that the party was not nationalist enough; the CCP, they said, put Soviet interests over those of China. With the venturesome critics now on their way to labor camps or worse, Chairman Mao began preparing a push for advanced socialism, which he hoped would let the Communists regain the popular enthusiasm of the wartime era.

The Great Leap Forward, as he called it, was to become the most lethal Communist campaign of all time, though it started as shock therapy to increase industrial production. Mao's concern was that China was not catching up with advanced countries fast enough. The steady progress of the first Five Year Plan was good, but it was not sufficient, Mao thought. China could do better if it relied on its own strength and initiative. Other Communist leaders, who ought to have known better—such as President Liu Shaoqi, Premier Zhou Enlai, and the head of the party apparatus, Deng Xiaoping—got caught up in increasingly harebrained development plans that would, the Chairman promised, catapult China into Communism.

The Great Leap was based on Mao's preoccupation with the power of the human will. Never properly materialist in a Marxist sense, Mao always believed that all progress depended on the willingness and ability of people to carry out socialist transformation. If such plans were not successful enough, it was because the full human potential had not yet been mobilized. China could combine a rapid development in agriculture with massively increased industrial output through the use of manpower, Mao decreed. It should "be possible for China to catch up with advanced capitalist countries in industrial and agricultural production in a period shorter than what had previously been predicted," he explained in the spring of 1958. "China could catch up with Britain in ten years, and with the United States in another ten years."[5]

The core units of the Great Leap were the People's Communes, set up all over China in the summer of 1958. The planning methods of previous years were thrown overboard, and the new Communes were given entirely unrealistic production targets. The country's steel production was set to double in a year, and rural Communes had to contribute to the steel targets. Sometimes, out of desperation, they did so simply by melting down their agricultural tools. Millions of peasants were taken away from their fields during the time of sowing and reaping to work on poorly planned building or irrigation projects. Inspired by the Soviet virgin lands campaign, the CCP sometimes forced peasants to leave their own fields and move to new areas where they had no means of survival. Inside the Communes discipline and collectivism were taken to the extreme. Children were housed in separate dormitories so their parents could dedicate themselves entirely to production.

In the winter of 1958 many people went hungry as they slaved away at Mao's new schemes. In the spring of 1959 they started dying of starvation. By the time the nightmare eased, in 1961, at least forty million had died, most of them from a combination of overwork and lack of food. Eyewitnesses described it all. In Xinyang, a formerly rich city in Henan Province, frozen corpses lay in the roads and in the fields. Some of them were mutilated. Surviving locals blamed wild dogs. But the dogs and all other animals had already been eaten. Instead, humans had turned to eating the flesh of their own kind to survive.[6]

Mao refused to back down. When honest party members reported on the disaster, he had them purged. One was the Korean War hero and marshal Peng Dehuai, who spoke up in the summer of 1959. The Soviet advisers, some of whom had at first believed that the Chinese might succeed in their Great Leap, very soon quietly started to warn about the consequences. Mao brushed them off. "The Soviet Union has been building socialism for 41 years, and it couldn't make a transition to socialism in 12 years. They are now behind us and already in panic," the Chairman said.[7] At the Communist Party of the Soviet Union's Twenty-first Congress in 1959 Khrushchev warned, "Society cannot jump from capitalism to Communism without experiencing socialist development. . . . Egalitarianism does not mean transition to Communism. Rather it only damages the reputation of Communism."[8]

As Mao's China moved to the Left in search of rapid development and political rectitude, foreign policy issues also started damaging the Sino-Soviet relationship. During the height of the alliance, the Soviets and the Chinese had worked closely together in the international arena. In 1954 they had forced the Vietnamese Communists to accept a settlement at the Geneva Conference. In 1955, China had been the spokesman for the Communist camp at the Afro-Asian Bandung Conference. In 1956 they had not only agreed on the invasion of Hungary but also jointly disciplined North Korea's Kim Il-sung for his inner-party purges. But Mao's increasing anti-American rhetoric and his insistence on the inevitability of war had begun to rile the Soviets. They worried that China was out of tune with their own charm-offensive vis-à-vis the West.

One key reason for Moscow's worry was the Chinese refusal to further integrate into the Soviet bloc, militarily and economically. Up to 1958 it was China that had pressed for such integration, with the

Soviets holding back, in part because they feared that China's enormous population would prove a strain on the Soviet and eastern European economies. But when the Soviet Ministry of Defense in the summer of 1958 had proposed a few relatively routine steps of military coordination, such as Soviet-operated early-warning systems and naval communication transmitters in China, Mao had reacted furiously. "I could not sleep, nor did I have dinner," he told the surprised Soviet ambassador Pavel Iudin.

> You never trust the Chinese! You only trust the Russians! [To you] the Russians are first-class [people] whereas the Chinese are among the inferior who are dumb and careless. . . . Well, if you want joint ownership and operation, how about having them all—let us turn into joint ownership and operation our army, navy, air force, industry, agriculture, culture, education. Can we do this? Or [you] may have all of China's more than ten thousand kilometers of coastline and let us only maintain a guerilla force. With a few atomic bombs, you think you are in a position to control us.[9]

The Soviets were understandably horrified at Mao's rant. Against the advice of his colleagues, Khrushchev rushed to Beijing to soothe his irate revolutionary colleague. Mao subjected the Soviet leader to lectures on the impotence of US imperialism, but was unwilling to enter into much concrete discussion. Khrushchev returned to Moscow convinced that he had contained the crisis, only to find that the PRC started to shell Guomindang-held offshore islands just two weeks after he left Beijing, deliberately provoking a crisis with the Americans. Even though Mao had alluded to his desire to "liberate" Taiwan, the Chinese military action had not been discussed during the visit. The purpose seems to have been to warn both the Soviets and the Americans that China was capable of independent action. Khrushchev again stood up for the Chinese in public, but inwardly he was furious. Mao called an abrupt end to the confrontation over the islands a couple of months later. He lackadaisically declared that the PRC in the future would shell Guomindang-held territory only every second day, so Chiang Kai-shek's soldiers could venture outside occasionally for some sun and fresh air. In Moscow, some Soviets started questioning the Chairman's mental stability.

Other crises followed, even though the alliance still seemed in workable shape, at least from the outside. In China, Mao Zedong had to deal with the fallout from the Great Leap and had less time for foreign affairs. From the summer of 1959 on, however, it seems as if the Chairman in his own mind began to connect his domestic troubles with his Soviet problem. Those Chinese who were challenging his Great Leap policies, he thought, did so because they were too wedded to the Soviet path of development. If they succeeded in going back to Soviet ways, they could destroy his revolution. Mao therefore began sending his closest associates notes that criticized the Soviets but also took aim at those who doubted the Great Leap. "At the beginning of the construction of the Soviet Union, the speed of industrial development was very high. Later, . . . [it] has decreased. Soviet planners constantly lowered the speed of development. [This shows] their right-deviationist thinking."[10]

If the Soviets were "Right-deviationists," then the alliance was obviously in some form of trouble. It was one of the most serious charges one could make against a fellow Marxist. Mao followed up with further accusations of the same sort. When Khrushchev, after much preparation, went on the first ever visit of a Soviet leader to the United States in 1959, Chinese media more or less ignored it, while stepping up their anti-American propaganda. Worse, Beijing got itself embroiled in a series of border incidents with India around the same time, giving much ammunition to anti-Communists both in Asia and in Washington. Although Delhi was probably about as much to blame for these clashes as Beijing, Khrushchev was incandescent, both about the timing and about the target. The Soviets had spent much time and many rubles buttering up Nehru and the nonaligned Indians. Now Moscow's Chinese allies seemed intent on throwing it all away.

Very unwisely, Khrushchev again insisted that he himself go to Beijing and set things right. This October 1959 visit backfired badly. Last time he had visited, Mao had tried to humiliate Khrushchev.

Among other carefully selected indignities, the Chairman had enticed him into a swimming pool, well aware that the Soviet leader could not swim. This time the humiliation was verbal. Meeting with the whole Chinese top leadership, everyone of them (except Mao himself, of course) took turns at insulting Khrushchev. Foreign Minister Chen Yi called him a term-serving opportunist, someone who supported India and therefore also the bourgeoisie. Khrushchev gave as good as he got. "You should not spit on me from the height of your Marshal title," he fumed at Chen Yi, one of the ten marshals of China's civil war. "You do not have enough spit! We cannot be intimidated! What a pretty situation we have: On one side, you [still] use the formula [the Communist camp] headed by the Soviet Union. On the other you do not let me say a word!"[11] The meetings ended in acrimony.

By late 1959 Mao had concluded that the Sino-Soviet alliance had to go. He noted to himself that Soviet "revisionism" could "last for a very long time (over ten years, for example). . . . We resisted the fallacies of our friends [the Soviets] . . . , [but now] our friends together with the imperialists, the counter-revolutionaries, and the Tito revisionists organize an anti-China chorus." But even in isolation, "in eight years China will have finished the initial constriction of [its] industrial system. . . . The Chinese flag is bright red."[12] At international Communist meetings in the spring of 1960 the Chinese attacked the Soviets openly. That summer, Khrushchev's patience snapped. He abruptly withdrew most Soviet advisers from China. Mao complained publicly, but in private he welcomed his counterpart's rash action. It would remove Soviet influence in China, and enable him to explain to his people why Sino-Soviet cooperation—the principle on which his Communist party had been founded—had broken down.

In the early 1960s it was not easy for the Soviets, the Chinese, or anyone else to see how completely the Sino-Soviet alliance was coming to an end. Most people—except Mao himself and some of his younger followers—expected this to be a temporary quarrel. Both sides were fundamentally Marxist, and would therefore join together again, it was thought. Some cooperation continued for a while. The Soviets offered food assistance when the full extent of the Great Leap disaster was becoming clear in 1961. Military and intelligence cooperation lasted at least until 1963. But Khrushchev was sulking and found it hard to reach out to the Chinese. Mao, on his side, reveled in China's new isolation. After some hesitation in the wake of the Great Leap, he now declared his own return to setting the party's ideological agenda and moving it further to the Left. As so often before, Mao's poetry indicated where he wanted to go:

> Only heroes can quell tigers and leopards
> And wild bears never daunt the brave.
> Plum blossoms welcome the whirling snow;
> Small wonder flies freeze and perish.[13]

Nationalism helped in Mao's plans. His version was that where all other countries had failed, China would succeed. This is what most Chinese liked to hear. Even those who had worked with Mao for almost a generation did not understand that the break with the Soviets would take China in a disastrous direction. Even less did they see that it sealed their own fate. The public hero-worship of the Chairman was intense. Mao was clever enough to push the leaders whom he suspected of wanting a return to the safety of 1950s-style economic planning, like Liu Shaoqi or Deng Xiaoping, to the fore in criticizing the Soviets. By publicly attacking moderation, gradualism, and traditional Marxist economics, these leaders helped dig their own graves, in a few cases quite literally, as China descended into another round of internecine bloodletting in the 1960s.

In the meantime China's foreign policy floundered. Mao spoke about his country leading the Third World, but the real Third World treated China with increasing mistrust, not least because of its constant attempts to teach others how to behave. Beijing's support for minority Communist parties, often in violent conflict with both the "official" Soviet-backed Communists and nationalist regimes, did not help either. Even so, China's Third World strategy initially did pay a few dividends. The Communist regimes in Vietnam and North Korea, and in Cuba, felt that China's emphasis on sovereignty and national development suited them better than the lectures they received from Moscow, and therefore for some time were closer to Beijing's points of view. The suave premier Zhou Enlai visited Africa, handing out aid that post-Leap China could hardly afford, but which Mao insisted had to be given to compete with the Soviets. But by 1965 almost all of China's Third World links had soured. Mao's insistence that cooperating with China meant breaking fully with the Soviets was unacceptable to other leaders. And whoever did not adopt China's views were immediately characterized by Beijing as "very arrogant and conceited," as in the case of Algeria's radical leader Ben Bella in 1965.[14]

But the real disaster for China's Third World relationships was the 1962 border war with India. This was a conflict that had been a long time coming. Although China and India had cooperated for a while after their states were reconstituted in the late 1940s, a decade later they were locked in enmity. The causes were many. China suspected, with some justification, Nehru's government to be sympathetic to Tibetan nationalists. India feared that Chinese control of the Himalayas would put New Delhi at a dangerous strategic disadvantage. But the most basic problem was that the Chinese Communists always viewed Nehru's Indian state simply as a colonial construct, something less than a real country. Nehru, on his side, saw Chinese-style revolution as a threat not just to his wishes for India's development, but to the security of all of Asia. "The Indians," Zhou Enlai had told Khrushchev in 1959, "[have] conducted large-scale anti-Chinese propaganda for forty years."[15]

The war broke out when Indian military mountain patrols moved into disputed areas of the Himalayas in October 1962. Chinese soldiers tried to force them out, and both sides started shooting. The Indians were on the offensive first, but the PLA managed to get large reinforcements in, which pushed the Indian army back. When the fighting ended the Indians had been thoroughly routed, and the Chinese took control of the disputed region. The war was a shock to all of Asia, and not least to the members of the recently formed Non-Aligned Movement, which had India as one of its principal members.

But the main effect was to further isolate China, who, largely because of its bellicose language, was seen as the aggressive party.

Increasingly cut off and exposed to one man's whims, China began its long descent into the Cultural Revolution. First Mao turned on those who had tried to stabilize the situation after the Great Leap and who had not understood the need for a full break with the Soviets. "There was a connection between revisionism at home and abroad," Mao said.[16] In 1962 he lambasted China's president Liu Shaoqi for having started down the revisionist road. Wang Jiaxiang, the veteran diplomat who had dared suggest that China ought not to have too many enemies at the same time, was called "a deviant Rightist."[17] But Mao himself did not know how to reawaken the revolutionary spirit that he now felt to be absent. In 1963 and 1964 the Chairman bided his time. He concentrated on strengthening his personal dictatorship, while reaping the rewards of China's progress in science and technology, most of which had come about as a result of Soviet aid. A major breakthrough was China's first nuclear test in 1964. The man who had derided nuclear weapons as "paper tigers" when China did not itself possess them, now admitted to his colleagues that he felt much safer when others feared China more.

In 1965 Mao first turned to settling old scores. A historian and playwright had written a historical play back in 1959 indicating through allegory that during the Great Leap righteous officials had been persecuted while sycophants had been promoted—a pretty accurate description of reality. Six years later Mao wanted him punished, along with his boss Peng Zhen, the dour mayor of Beijing. Peng, an old revolutionary hard-liner, resisted. A furious Mao decided to "rectify" China's intellectual life and crack down on "deviationists" in the capital. In November 1965 he left Beijing and began traveling around the country, never staying long in one place. He was not to return for nine months. While in Hangzhou, one of his main residences, he lectured people there: "You should gradually get into contact with reality, live for a while in the countryside, learn a bit. . . . There's no need to read big tomes. It's sufficient to read little books and get a bit of general knowledge."[18]

With Mao out of Beijing, his underlings did their best to guess what his plans were. Peng Zhen was dismissed, as were the heads of the CCP party apparatus and of the PLA's general staff. Mao's wife, Jiang Qing, and a number of younger associates of Mao got more and more influence over policy-making. Lin Biao, a brilliant but mentally unstable strategist from the civil war, had been made defense minister during the Great Leap. In 1966 he was also made Mao's second in command. Together the new leadership group launched an attack on the old party institutions: "Those representatives of the bourgeoisie who have sneaked into the Party, the government, the army, and various spheres of culture are a bunch of counter-revolutionary revisionists. Once conditions are ripe, they will seize political power and turn the dictatorship of the proletariat into a dictatorship of the bourgeoisie. Some of them we have already seen through; others we have not. Some are still trusted by us and are being trained as our successors, persons like Khrushchev for example, who are still nestling beside us."[19]

It sounded similar to Stalin's postwar purges. But Mao wanted to go further. In July 1966 he was filmed swimming the Yangzi River, probably to show that at the age of seventy-two he was still fit and healthy. Then he returned to Beijing. Schools had been suspended so that students could read the new directives and attack the teachers they suspected of being counterrevolutionaries. Mao's return was triumphant.

Meeting with the students, Mao instructed them to "bombard the headquarters" and form Red Guards to defend the revolution. Those following the capitalist road were planning to take power, he said. But the most striking instruction from the Chairman was about where these enemies were to be found. They were inside the party, Mao claimed. By the autumn of 1966 senior party leaders, pinpointed by Mao, were attacked in their homes by Red Guard youth. President Liu Shaoqi was dragged through the streets and publicly humiliated. Deng Xiaoping was luckier. He was kept in solitary confinement, and then sent to the south to work as a manual laborer in a tractor factory. Through all of this, the police and the army stood aside, and chaos reigned on the streets.

President Liu Shaoqi's wife, Wang Guangmei, was kidnapped by Red Guards at the height of the chaos and tortured. "We want you to put on the dress that you wore in Indonesia," they shouted at her.

Wang: That was summer. . . . Interrogator: Rubbish! We know nothing about such bourgeois stuff as what is good for summer, winter, or spring. . . . We'll give you ten minutes. . . . What's your opinion of Liu Shaoqi's fall from grace? Wang: It is an excellent thing. In this way, China will be prevented from going revisionist. . . . Wait a moment. . . . (She is pulled to her feet and the dress is slipped on her.) [Red Guards] Reading in unison [from Mao]: "A revolution is not a dinner party, or writing in an essay, or painting a picture, or doing embroidery. . . . " Wang: You violate Chairman Mao's instructions by saying . . . (Wang Guangmei is interrupted and forced to wear silk stockings and high heeled shoes and a specially made necklace. She is photographed. . . .) Interrogator: By wearing that dress to flirt with Sukarno in Indonesia, you have put the Chinese people to shame. . . . Coercion is called for when dealing with such a reactionary bourgeois element as you. . . . [Red Guards] reading in unison [from Mao]: "Everything reactionary is the same: if you don't hit it, it won't fall.")[20]

Mao's plan for the Great Proletarian Cultural Revolution, as he called his new purge, was to deepen the processes of change through removing the old party leadership and appealing directly to the country's youth to make revolution. He wanted to fundamentally remake China and remake the Chinese. His ideal was a new type of man and woman, free from family, religion, and old culture. Only such a person, Mao claimed, would be strong enough to complete the transformation of China. He raged against the party he had led for thirty years. It had held him and the country back. Now time was running out. Mao felt a need to complete the work he had begun as a young man.

The Cultural Revolution looked different seen from the top and the bottom of Chinese society. Seen from above it was a purge like those in eastern Europe or the Soviet Union. Leaders were removed from power, ritually humiliated, and killed or sent away. But seen from below it became a carnival of released tension, in which personal grudges and aspirations could be played out after decades of intense change. Some rebelled against authority and authoritarianism, mostly oblivious to the fact that they did so through supporting Mao's rule, the most absolute authority of all. Others could simply show and act upon their dislike for their neighbors, fellow students, or workmates. Factions and factionalism abounded. In Wuhan, in the summer of 1967, for instance, two Red Guard groups fought each other for power, first with slogans, then with fists and knives, and finally with machine guns and 122 mm howitzers looted from army barracks and depots.

One of Mao's intentions in the Cultural Revolution was to set the young against the old. In a country where tradition venerated the elderly, their hold on society needed to be broken for Mao's vision of "new China" to be complete. Red Guards, sometimes as young as twelve or thirteen, were encouraged to report on their parents or grandparents. At times older members of the family were captured as a result of such denunciation, beaten, or sent away to labor camps. One family in Beijing, who I know, saw both the father and the grandfather taken by Red Guards after they had been reported on by the youngest son. The boy, fourteen at the time, participated in their public humiliation and torture. The grandfather died as a result. The pattern was repeated a million times over across China. Though most of those who were "struggled against" survived, normal family life understandably did not.

Minorities were among the worst hit groups in the Cultural Revolution. In Chinese-ruled Inner Mongolia, at least twenty thousand people were killed as Chinese Red Guards hunted members of the "Inner Mongolian People's Party." This phantom party, which probably never existed at all, was claimed to be a counterrevolutionary, separatist organization, specializing in assassinating Red Guard leaders. In Tibet, Communist atrocities went even further. Monks were beaten or killed. Age-old artwork was thrown on the fire. Red Guards, flown in by helicopter, dynamited or fired missiles against temples and monasteries. Parts of the country were in a state of civil war for years, as Tibetan groups counterattacked. In Guangxi, in the south, Zhuang people (and some Chinese, too) ate their enemies, deemed counterrevolutionaries, in staged cannibalistic events.[21]

As can be imagined, China's descent into chaos during the cultural revolution also led to chaos in foreign policy. Mao believed that diplomats and foreign affairs experts were among the worst sinners in betraying his revolution. All ambassadors were recalled to Beijing for political reeducation, and most of them never returned to their stations. Instead the Foreign Ministry was taken over by younger diplomats and other employees, including a former janitor who had set up a Red Guard unit, who spent their time conducting political study sessions and engaging in "struggle" against senior leaders. China's foreign minister, Chen Yi, was denounced in front of large crowds. The British embassy in Beijing was attacked and set on fire, while the Soviet and eastern European embassies were besieged by thousands of Red Guards, who shouted antirevisionist slogans through loudspeakers night and day. Even China's closest allies, North Vietnam and North Korea, had had enough of the chaos. They summarily arrested Chinese advisers who organized pro–Cultural Revolution marches in their countries and shipped them back to China. After one especially egregious incident in Pyongyang, in which Chinese students had criticized Kim Il-sung for not studying Mao's works well enough, the North Koreans exploded. "Our people are indignant at the arrogant behavior of the Chinese. The Chinese . . . are behaving like hysterical people . . . they are not able to avoid responsibility for the criminal actions damaging the interests of the DPRK."[22]

As political relations between China and the Soviet Union deteriorated, tension at their long border increased. Already in 1962 there had been clashes between border guards as Chinese Kazakhs attempted to flee across to Soviet Kazakhstan to avoid the effects of the Great Leap Forward. Two years later, Mao laid into the Soviets over the border issue. "More than one hundred years ago," he told visiting Japanese Communists, "[the Russians] occupied the entire area east of Lake Baikal, including Khabarovsk, Vladivostok, and the Kamchatka Peninsula. That account is difficult to square. We have yet to settle that account."[23] Mao used the conflict with the Soviets to ratchet up support for his domestic positions, even though he did not foresee war with the Soviet Union.

When the Cultural Revolution started, Chinese Red Guards began setting up loudspeakers in the border zones, where they berated the Soviets for following their "revisionist" leaders. But in 1969 these tensions suddenly took a turn for the worse. After Chinese and Soviet soldiers had clashed repeatedly over an island in the middle of the Ussuri River, which both sides claimed, the Chinese ambushed a Soviet border patrol and killed around sixty troops on 2 March. On Moscow's orders, the Red Army counterattacked two weeks later, but were unable to dislodge the Chinese from the still-frozen river region. Large-scale artillery shelling from both sides ensued. In Moscow, there was a real fear of war. Some Soviet military experts recommended taking out the Chinese nuclear installations as a precaution, but the Politburo held back. The Soviet premier tried to call the Chinese leaders, but the young Chinese operator refused to connect him with either Zhou or Mao. The operators were told to shout antirevisionist slogans down the line whenever the Soviets tried to call.

But Mao's bluster concealed a fear much worse than the one felt in Moscow. The Chinese leader ordered his side to hold fire. But he also worried that the Soviets would launch a full-scale nuclear attack on China. It was one thing to provoke the Red Army at the border in order to show at home how the Cultural Revolution had made the country more powerful. It was something very different to risk the survival of China. As the Soviets sent reinforcements to the border and warned that Moscow would retaliate against further provocations, including with the use of nuclear weapons, a full-scale war scare broke out in Beijing in the fall of 1969. Even though Zhou Enlai and the Soviet premier held talks to moderate the tension, in early October Mao ordered all party, government, and military leaders to leave Beijing. All over China, Communist cadres left the cities to go to the countryside and prepare for war. Lin Biao, in an even more disordered mood than usual, suddenly ordered China's military to move to the highest alert. The crisis passed. But it did remind Mao, forcefully, of how unprepared China was for a real war and how erratic his new leadership group was.

The Chairman had already begun reining in some of the worst Cultural Revolution extremists. The army was sent in to restore order in the cities and on university campuses, and some of the most vocal Red Guards were sent to prison camps or to do manual labor, following the many they themselves had mistreated over the previous three years. The Soviet war scare pushed Mao further in the direction of reducing tension in China. But the Chairman was also fearful of any policy that would "reverse the verdict," as he himself put it, on the Great Leap and the Cultural Revolution. Both were still good, Mao insisted. He came to depend on advisers who were a mix of Cultural Revolution leaders, such as his own wife, Jiang Qing, or the Shanghai Leftists Zhang Chunqiao and Yao Wenyuan, as well as more traditional CCP figures who paid lip-service to Mao through the disasters of the 1960s, such as the premier, Zhou Enlai. The leaders who had been purged were ordered to stay out of view, while Mao—bizarrely—sometimes would call on them privately for advice in their provincial hideaways.

With China poor and isolated, and with the Cold War having caught up with Mao through the Soviet war scare, the Chinese leader temporarily reduced his revolutionary zeal and agreed that more emphasis had to be put on production and overall economic development. In the early 1970s, as the international climate changed considerably, Chinese managers and officials tried to put things back together again after Mao's campaigns. But the country still drifted from crisis to crisis. The worst was in September 1971, when Vice-Chairman and Defense Minister Lin Biao, Mao's chosen successor, panicked and attempted to flee to the Soviet Union. Convinced that Mao was out to get him, the increasingly deluded "closest comrade-in-arms" of the Chairman boarded a military plane with his wife and son, ordering it to fly toward the border. When asked by Premier Zhou whether the plane should be shot down, Mao shrugged: "Rain has to fall, girls have to marry, these things are immutable; let them go."[24] Lin's plane crashed in Outer Mongolia, killing all onboard.

Lin's betrayal buried any hopes in the population at large that the Cultural Revolution could be turned to any positive effect. What followed was profound cynicism, especially among younger people. Through their whole lives they had joined in Mao's campaigns, one more intense and life-changing than the other. They had learned to revere the Chairman as a god. Their role was to help him create a new and better China. Now all seemed in ruins. Even though few were prepared to rebel, people certainly reverted to old standards where they could. Corruption and nepotism increased considerably. Although orders to intensify the revolution kept coming from Beijing, not many were eager to listen anymore. Mao's vision of a Herculean new Chinese man had turned out to be a monster.

THE COMMUNIST REVOLUTION and the Cold War had transformed China, though not always in the directions its leaders or its people had expected. The most important change was the death of "old China," a patriarchal community of farmers, merchants, and officials that had been in decline since the nineteenth century and was finally killed off by the Communists. Instead had come a hybrid society, with some Chinese and some foreign elements. Marxism, the rulers' political theory, was of course a foreign import, as was the Communist Party. New thinking about family, education, technology, and science came from abroad. What was most distinctly Chinese about the Chinese revolution was its preoccupation with human transformation, willpower, and the need to find "correct" ideas and solutions to society's ills. In ways that were increasingly visible to many Chinese in the 1970s, it was Mao's preoccupation with ethos over practical gain that had led the revolution astray. China's lack of resistance to other forms of foreign influence toward the end of the Cold War was directly linked to this self-inflicted wound.

Seen from above, Mao's campaigns had all the hallmarks of Stalinist purges, similar to what had gone on in the Soviet Union and eastern Europe. Leaders of the Communist party were singled out for criticism, publicly humiliated, and executed or exiled through some quasi-legal process. The charges were entirely trumped up and the procedures were aimed at centralizing power. The president of the country, Liu Shaoqi—as loyal a party member as could ever be imagined—was beaten and tortured in public before being sent to Kaifeng during the 1969 war scare. There he died from mistreatment. Mao wanted to be fully in command on his own.

But there was also another side to the Cultural Revolution. As chaos increased on the streets, the authorities started losing control. Mao was of course in favor of Red Guards attacking those he wanted to purge. But by 1966 millions of young people had started traveling the country in the revolutionary cause. Although much of their days were spent chanting moronic slogans or otherwise inconveniencing the peasants, their travels did allow them get a sense of the state of the country. For most, and especially for young women, this was their first time outside of paternal control. Some of them made use of it to begin thinking for themselves, even about taboo topics that could not be raised in public, on issues from sex and gender roles to economics and politics. A part of China's post–Cold War transformation came out of this Red Guard generation and its experiences.

Outside of China, Mao's Cultural Revolution madness was picked up by rebellious students and others who believed it could be used to challenge authority in their countries. China's Stalinist purges are therefore sometimes, without reason, conflated with 1960s youthful rebellions elsewhere. One of the more bizarre twists was in western Europe, where a few intellectuals formed Maoist groups. They believed one could worship Chairman Mao and be antiauthoritarian at the same time. In wealthy Norway, for instance, students formed a group that called itself the Workers' Communist Party (Marxist-Leninist). They believed that "the Chinese Communist Party and People's China, both domestically and internationally, are stronger than ever before. . . . Never has interest in China and friendship with China been so extensive [in Norway]."[25] But even if some intellectuals celebrated China's tragedy, most Europeans could not have cared less. No Maoist party ever got more than 1 percent of the popular vote in elections.

The most important international effect of China's Maoist era was to kill off forever the idea that Communism was monolithic. This had of course already become clear to most when Stalin threw the Yugoslavs out of the eastern bloc in 1948. But China was, quite literally, on a different scale. The enmity between the Chinese Communists and the Soviets had the potential to transform international politics and break Cold War dualism. This could not happen as long as China seemed mainly preoccupied with tearing itself apart in a Cultural Revolution. But as soon as the country started to emerge from that morass, the potential for new global constellations also began to become visible.

10

Breaking Empires

The Cold War was born as an ideological contest in Europe and the European offshoots, Russia and the United States. In the second half of the twentieth century that contest came to interact with the processes surrounding the collapse of the European overseas empires. Europe had been predominant in international affairs for at least two centuries. But as the post–World War II re-creation of Asia had shown, this position of primacy could no longer be taken for granted. And in the 1950s and '60s decolonization sped up, so that by 1970 the number of independent states had increased almost four times since 1945. They all wanted to have their say in how the world was run. And they were not willing to conform to the bipolar Cold War system without a struggle for their own interests.

Out of this encounter between Cold War and decolonization came the Third World movement. It was so named by its protagonists in homage to the Third Estate, the rebellious underdog majority of the French Revolution of 1789. But its aims were very contemporary. Leaders of newly independent states, such as Indonesia's Sukarno or India's Nehru, believed that the time had come for their countries to take center stage in international affairs. Europeans, a small minority in the world, had dominated for far too long, and had not done a good job of it. Not only had they produced colonialism and two world wars, but within colonialism they had created a political and economic system that only served the interests of Europeans. The talents, opinions, cultures, and religions of the vast majority of the world's people had been neglected. Now the time had come for the disenfranchised to take responsibility not just for their own liberated countries, but for the world as a whole.

To Third World leaders the Cold War was an outgrowth of the colonial system. It was an attempt by Europeans to regulate and dominate the affairs of others, to tell them how to behave and what to do. Even though many in the newly independent states distrusted capitalism because it was the system their colonial masters had tried to impose on them, in most cases they were not ready to embrace Soviet-style Communism as an alternative. It seemed far too regimented, too absolutist, or simply too European for postcolonial states. Even when attempting to learn from the Soviet experience, as many did, for instance in India or Indonesia, the Third World agenda implied independence from the power blocs. As developed at the 1955 Afro-Asian Bandung Conference, this agenda stressed full economic and political sovereignty, solidarity among former colonial countries and liberation movements, and peaceful resolution of conflict, followed by nuclear disarmament.

For the Superpowers this was a perturbing spectacle. The United States increasingly put its own national experience at the core of its perception of global development. As the Cold War hardened, countries that did not conform to US visions of liberty and economic growth were believed to be sliding toward a Soviet orientation. The Soviet Union, on its side, believed that any "third" position was simply a stage on the way to socialism and eventually the Soviet form of Communism. No wonder non-Europeans saw significant similarities between the two Superpowers, in spite of their ideological rivalry. Indeed, leaders such as Ahmed Ben Bella in Algeria or Kwame Nkrumah in Ghana compared the demands the Superpowers made on them to colonialism in its latter phase. The Americans and the Soviets wanted political and diplomatic control, but also sought development within the framework that the Superpowers could offer. They were thieves on the same market, even though the US bid for control was much more powerful, and therefore more pervasive, than anything the Soviets could muster.

THERE WERE TWO main reasons why decolonization happened on such a wide scale in the 1950s and '60s. The first was the social and economic exhaustion of the colonizing powers. In 1910 a European man, especially if he was French or British, could still safely assume that he was on top of the global pile. He may have been poor in his own country, or felt threatened by suffragettes or revolutionaries. But it was his country that had set the global agendas for as long as he could remember. The world economic system was created to make him produce and consume. His culture and his religion were assumed to be the envy of the world. And others, who were not Christian Europeans, who did not possess the Europeans' science or technology, or military skills, or well-honed and ruthless administrations, were seen as distinctly inferior.

Compare this with a generation later, in 1945. The European countries were exhausted by warfare and their inhabitants had themselves begun to doubt their centrality in the world. With what right did they rule others, when they could not avoid repeatedly tearing their own continent to pieces? Principles of racial superiority—at least those openly stated—now had a bad name. Hitler had seen to that. And was not the primary duty of a young Englishman or Frenchman to his own battered country, rather than to faraway places? Resources were scarce, and almost all Europeans wanted them spent at home.

The second reason for decolonization was the rebellion against foreign rule in the colonies. Although it is unlikely that any anticolonial movement would have been able to throw the Europeans out by force alone, these movements increased the cost of colonialism and made the enterprise less popular at home. Organizations such as the Indian National Congress or the South African National Congress aimed for national independence and a basic restructuring of the economy to serve the native inhabitants of their countries. They wanted their peoples to be recognized as a new driving force in world history, not as second-class citizens in their own countries.

The disasters of the two world wars and the global depression focused these movements politically and magnified their support. Until the 1920s almost all of them were minority phenomena, with leaders who had a hard time convincing their countrymen to take the risk of challenging colonial rule. But thereafter they increased in size and significance, not least because the colonial powers tried to stamp them out by force. India's Jawaharlal Nehru had been imprisoned by the British, as had Gandhi, his political mentor. Sukarno, Ho Chi Minh, and Ben Bella all spent time in prison and exile. They became heroes to their peoples, and their anticolonial rhetoric began to be picked up by many young men and women, often from prominent families, often trained at the best European or American colleges.

These processes of retrenchment and resistance had been underway since the start of the century, although they came to the fore after 1945. The Cold War influenced both, though it did not determine them. The global economic restructuring, which gradually privileged the United States, was an important factor in the collapse of formal empires. So was the Soviet support for liberation movements and the radicalization of some of them due to the Soviet example. But most important was the Cold War at home in Europe, the need for Britain and France to strengthen their own defense, to align with the United States, and the fear, especially in France, that long-term disorder in the colonies would contribute to radicalization at home. By the early 1960s, when the focus for the Cold War was shifting to the Third World, the conflict had already for a long time played itself out both among colonizers and colonized.

The history of how the Cold War influenced decolonization in economic terms is strange and somewhat incongruous. British and French high imperialist ideology of the late nineteenth and early twentieth century had been built on the prospect of improvement for all inhabitants of their empires, and implied a move away from the naked exploitation of earlier years. But wars and depression had made the metropoles more dependent on their colonies in economic terms, not less. They therefore attempted to reconstitute some of the mechanisms that would favor the Europeans, but found it difficult to do.

Imperial preference systems counted not only as key examples of what the Americans thought was wrong with colonialism—restrictions against free trade and US access to foreign markets—but they also alienated indigenous elites who had taken the imperial reformers at their word. But on the whole these measures did not correspond to changing global realities. The United States and other countries, rather than Britain and France, were gradually becoming more important for economic development in the colonies. Meanwhile, economic cooperation and trade in western Europe was becoming more important for the British and French. It was a discordance that could not last.

The role of the United States was crucial in the process of decolonization during the Cold War. Most Americans believed that colonialism was a bad thing. The country had won its own independence in a rebellion against Britain. Colonial control meant less freedom and free trade, both concepts that Americans cherished. But most white Americans also suspected that nonwhites were not capable of governing themselves unless assisted by people of European origin. This fear increased during the first phase of the Cold War. With another Superpower vying for their attention, Washington was terrified that postcolonial leaders, easily tempted, would fall into the Soviet bloc. Anticolonial instincts would therefore have to be tempered by Cold War concerns in US foreign policy.

US support was the main reason why the European colonial empires did not all collapse in the 1940s, but went on for another two (or, in the Portuguese case, three) decades. After 1945, no European country was financially capable of keeping its colonial possessions given the poor state of their own economies and their defense needs in Europe. The chimera of colonialism could only be continued as long as the United States was willing to underwrite these countries' other expenses at home. All of the colonial countries were of course aware of this, and did their best to present their reluctance to decolonize as part of a common struggle against Communism. US policy-makers, getting used to working with their western European allies in NATO committees and other international organizations, far too rarely questioned the motives of their partners. Washington's own anti-Communist focus mostly overrode its anticolonialism, except in cases where it was blatantly obvious that failing to decolonize would stimulate Communist groups, such as in Indonesia and India. When the British falsely claimed that the Kenyan nationalist Jomo Kenyatta was controlled by Communists, or when the French claimed the same for Guinean leader Sékou Touré, the Americans did not protest, even though their own intelligence agencies told them that it was untrue.

Both during the Truman and the Eisenhower Administrations, the Americans were also wary of contributing to the loss of prestige that letting go of their colonies would lead to for the European powers. Such a development could threaten stability in Europe and make the western Europeans less effective in helping to fight Communism both on their own continent and on a global scale. The fact that these governments were completely dependent on US loans did not make things better. It rather made them worse. The British and French resented the supplication and subservience to the United States that their economic weakness had led to, and suspected the Americans of having their own designs on their overseas territories. Impoverished at home, empire still made them great powers. Britain without empire was only "a sort of poor man's Sweden," as one British colonial administrator put it.[1]

Still, the writing was on the wall for the European empires after 1945. Even with significant US support, the combination of economic weakness at home and rising resistance in the colonies determined the outcome. The governments in Britain and France that completed decolonization were not of the socialist Left. They were the British Conservatives, led by Winston Churchill, Anthony Eden, and Harold Macmillan, and the French nationalist Right-wing government of Charles de Gaulle. They regretted the loss of the colonies but realized they had no choice. As the last British governor-general of Nigeria, Sir James Robertson, viewed it in 1959: "The trouble is that we have not been allowed enough time; partly this is because we are not strong enough now as a result of two world wars to insist on having longer to build up democratic forms of government, partly because of

American opposition to our idea of colonialism by the gradual training of people in the course of generations to run their own show: partly because of dangers from our enemies, the Communists, we have had to move faster than we should have wished."[2]

On the US side, an increasingly global military strategy and the need to facilitate access to key resources and raw materials were big concerns in the decolonization process. US leaders increasingly saw their country as engaged in a worldwide campaign against Communism and responsible for building global capitalist structures that worked well. A US network of military bases was necessary in this struggle, as was securing the availability of resources for the economic rebuilding of western Europe and Japan. By 1960, the United States had global access to bases that furthered its military superiority, and many of these came courtesy of the colonial powers. In addition to the British and French stations around the world that the United States could use in case of war, it leased its own bases in colonial territories from Ascension Island to the Azores and Bermuda. French-controlled Morocco had a US base. And Diego Garcia, a British-held island in the Indian Ocean, remained British after decolonization, mainly so that a massive US military base could be constructed. The 1,200 people who already lived on Diego Garcia were evicted.

Throughout the Cold War US leaders were concerned that the Soviets would be able to control, directly or indirectly, the raw materials on which America's allies depended for their economic well-being. Such fears were a main reason why radical Third World nationalism, which included proposals for economic nationalization, production planning, and export restrictions, was conflated with Communism or Soviet influence. The Cold War in resource terms was about absolute control. Anything that assisted the enemy in getting an influence over vital resources in strategic or economic terms was a challenge to the United States. This was of course particularly true for access to metals vital for the military industry. In the 1940s the most significant of these was uranium, used to produce nuclear weapons. The United States tried to get exclusive access to uranium ore from Belgian-ruled Congo and from South Africa, although it soon became clear that the metal was so scattered in occurrence that monopolizing access was very hard.

The most important strategic resource during the Cold War was oil. The first half of the twentieth century had seen its rise from a minor source of energy to becoming the substance that made modern states work. Armies depended on it for transport, and civilian economies depended on it for production. The Soviet Union became self-sufficient in 1954, so it was not competing with the West for access to foreign oil for its own sake. But the post-Stalin Moscow leaders knew how dependent US allies were on oil imports for their economic development. In western Europe dependence on oil for energy consumption increased from less than 10 percent in 1945 to over a third in 1960. In Japan the figures were even more striking: from 6 percent to 40. Eight-five percent of western Europe's imports came from the Middle East already by 1950. For the United States, which up to 1970 relied primarily on its own production for domestic use, controlling access to Middle Eastern oil was therefore still of major strategic importance.

The main oil producers in the Middle East were Iran, Iraq, Saudi Arabia, and the Gulf states. These were all countries in which Britain had been the predominant foreign power in the first part of the twentieth century. With British power waning, British-led oil companies were struggling to hold on to their positions. In Iran, for example, nationalists were pushing for more of an Iranian stake in the Anglo-Iranian Oil Company (AIOC), the biggest producer in the country, which operated the world's largest oil refinery at Abadan. Even though both profit-sharing arrangements and working conditions for Iranians were blatantly unfair, AIOC and the British government refused to change them. The result was the election of a nationalist government in Iran, led by Mohammed Mossadegh, committed to the nationalization of the oil industry.

At first, US advice to the British was to compromise. In Saudi Arabia, where the Arabian-American Oil Company (ARAMCO) was the main producer, the US government had successfully pushed for a 50/50 percent sharing of profits between the Saudi monarchy and the

American owners. But neither the Iranians nor the British accepted the US proposals. Instead, the conflict intensified. On 1 May 1951 the Iranian Majlis, the national assembly, voted to nationalize the oil industry, with compensation for current owners. The British initiated an embargo on Iranian oil and appealed to the United States for support. London argued that nationalization of Iranian oil entailed a strategic danger to the West. In the wings of Tehran politics, they claimed, waited the powerful Iranian Communist party, the Tudeh, which would benefit politically from the nationalization campaign.

The Truman Administration hesitated, though it was increasingly won over by some of the British arguments. Even so, Iranian prime minister Mossadegh was no Communist. He had been a staunch critic of the Soviet occupation of northern Iran, and attacked the Tudeh on that issue in 1944, saying that "if you claim to be Socialist, then why are you ready to sacrifice the interest of your own country for the sake of Soviet Russia?"[3] But Washington worried about long-term effects and about instability in the region. As the embargo started having severe economic effects inside Iran, opposition to Mossadegh grew. His response was to suspend the Majlis, and to rely increasingly on the Iranian Left, including the Tudeh, for the support of his policies.

The Eisenhower Administration decided to join with Britain in a covert operation to remove Mossadegh's government. Using contacts in Iran as well as paid agents, the CIA organized a stream of misinformation and staged rallies. In some cases the CIA paid Iranians to pose as Tudeh members attacking Islamic preachers or the advisers of the monarch, the Shah. The purpose was both to create unrest on the streets and to unify the conservative opposition against Mossadegh: the Shah, the Islamic clergy, and the military. The stage-managed coup, which came in August 1953, almost failed when the young Shah, Reza Pahlavi, lost his nerve and fled the country. But the military stepped in, arrested Mossadegh, and crushed the Tudeh party. Pahlavi flew back to Tehran accompanied by the US director of central intelligence, Allen Dulles. For the next twenty-six years the Shah ruled Iran as an autocrat, closely allied with the United States.

In spite of US skepticism about British motives, the Iran coup had seen the two countries closely aligned. They had also been working together over the British-declared "emergency" in Malaya, where British forces from the late 1940s battled and defeated a Communist-led workers' rebellion. While the United States supported Britain's warfare in Malaya, Washington stepped up its own campaign against a Left-wing rebellion in the Philippines. In spite of US protestations against colonialism, the Philippines had in reality been held as a colony by the United States since 1898. During the Japanese occupation, the Philippine Left had carried out the bulk of the resistance struggle and, when the war was over, campaigned for a fairer deal for peasants and workers. Granted their independence from the United States in 1946, Philippine leaders refused the Left's demands. Later US forces and the Philippine army fought a rebellion by the People's Liberation Army, the Huks. But by 1954 both the Malayan National Liberation Army and the Huks had been defeated.

It was Western intervention in the processes of setting up new independent states that gave rise to the Third World movement. Anticolonial activists only gradually began using the term, until the Martinican activist Franz Fanon popularized it in his book *The Wretched of the Earth* in 1961. But its contents were visible much before: the belief that non-Europeans now had the primary responsibility not just for their own countries, but for the future of the world. The idea that solidarity among newly decolonized states would create a power bloc out of the world's majority peoples. And the concept that the Cold War showed how arrogant, irresponsible, and out-of-touch with global developments the United States and its European allies were. The Soviet bloc came in for criticism as well. But it was the Eisenhower Administration that bore the brunt of Third World ire.

The Afro-Asian conference in Bandung, Indonesia, in 1955 became a focus point for Third World ideas. The Bandung Conference had a long pedigree. Since the early twentieth century anticolonial activists had been gathering across borders to create transnational networks of resistance. By the 1950s a number of key leaders had a transnational background: the Martinican Fanon fought French colonialism in Algeria, and the Trinidadian George Padmore played an important role in the creation of Ghana as an independent country. But at Bandung the new states were in focus. In his opening speech, Sukarno stressed the responsibilities the postcolonial states had to work together, defeat colonialism, and prevent nuclear war. "We are often told 'Colonialism is dead,'" the Indonesian president told his audience from twenty-nine different countries and even more nationalist parties and liberation movements.

> Let us not be deceived or even soothed by that. I say to you, colonialism is not yet dead. How can we say it is dead, so long as vast areas of Asia and Africa are unfree. . . . Colonialism has also its modern dress, in the form of economic control, [and] intellectual control. . . . War would not only mean a threat to our independence, it may mean the end of civilization and even of human life. There is a force loose in the world whose potentiality for evil no man truly knows. . . . No task is more urgent than that of preserving peace. Without peace our independence means little. The rehabilitation and upbuilding of our countries will have little meaning. Our revolutions will not be allowed to run their course.[4]

Those who met at Bandung came from very different backgrounds. China was represented by the smooth premier Zhou Enlai, though others kept the Chinese at arms' length because of their close alliance with the Soviets. Iran, Iraq, Turkey, and Japan attacked what they saw as anti-American views at the conference. But the main countries in terms of the dynamism of their leaders and their role within their regions were Indonesia, India, and Egypt. Their views had a decisive impact on the final communiqué, which stressed human rights, sovereignty, nonintervention, and resistance against Great Power domination. And their leaders—Sukarno, Nehru, Nasser—hoped that Bandung was just the first step in setting up cooperation among postcolonial states as an alternative to the Cold War.

The spirit of Bandung got its first test in the Middle East in the summer of 1956. At the head of a new radical military government,

Egyptian leader Gamal Abdel Nasser was frustrated by fruitless nego-tiations with the Americans over loans. He resented that Egypt, long under British domination, still was forced to accept substantial for-eign influence. Nasser wanted the Suez Canal, bisecting his country, to revert from British and French to Egyptian control, not least so that Egypt could benefit more from the substantial income from the canal. The United States urged negotiations. When London and Paris both declined, Nasser seized control of the canal zone in a sudden military operation on 26 July 1956. The Egyptian code word for the immediate start of the operation, cleverly woven into a lengthy Nasser speech in Alexandria, was *Lesseps*—the name of the French engineer who had designed the canal in the 1860s.

In his Suez speech, Nasser summed up the injustices imperialism had committed not only against Egypt, but against all Arabs. Arabs had been second-class citizens in their own countries; they had been divided, or evicted, like the Palestinians. But no longer. In a speech laden with references to Bandung and anticolonial solidarity, Nasser declared a new Arab unity, of which Egypt and Syria would form the initial parts, but which all Arab states could join. "Since Egypt has declared its free and independent policy, the entire world has its eyes fixed on Egypt," Nasser said. "Everyone takes account of Egypt and the Arabs. In the past we were wasting our time in the offices of [for-eign] ambassadors . . . , but today, after we are united to form a single national front against imperialism and foreign intervention, those who disdained us began to fear us."[5]

The British and the French reacted with fury. To British prime minister Anthony Eden, Nasser was another Hitler, or at least a Mus-solini. Together with the Israelis, London and Paris came up with a harebrained conspiracy, by which Israel would first invade Egypt. Then the British and French would intervene, claiming to separate the warring sides. Finally, as a simple addition, they would retake the Suez Canal. The Israelis went into action 29 October 1956, just as—in another theater—the Hungarian crisis reached its peak. French and British forces invaded Egypt on 5 November. With fighting in the ca-nal zone, the crisis escalated. President Eisenhower was enraged. He had been kept completely in the dark about the plans of his allies, and now felt that he had "just never seen great powers make such a complete mess and botch of things."[6] Particularly after the removal of Mossadegh, Washington was eager to avoid being seen as an opponent of nationalism in the region. This was especially true for the Arab countries, where the CIA feared that any display of British and French colonialism would give the local Communists a leg up against more "healthy" nationalist forces.[7]

The United States demanded an immediate cease-fire and the withdrawal of all foreign troops. The president let the British know that if they did not comply, the Americans would refuse to sell or transport oil to them, much more important now that the Suez Canal was closed, and cancel further loans to prop up the flagging British economy. When Eden hesitated, the US Treasury hinted that they might start selling British pounds, thereby further weakening a currency already in near free fall. Eden and his French colleague Guy Mollet, threatened by similar measures, capitulated and withdrew. The Israelis, chastised by the US president in ways that shocked Prime Minister David Ben-Gurion, followed a few months later. They only complied after Eisenhower had gone public with his complaint. In a television address to the American people, the president asked whether "a nation which attacks and occupies foreign territory in the face of United Nations disapproval [should] be allowed to impose conditions on its own withdrawal? If we agree that armed attack can properly achieve the purposes of the assailant, then I fear we will have turned back the clock of international order."[8]

There were many reasons for Eisenhower's fury. His sense of betrayal after not having been informed by his allies was strong. The United States, after all, saw itself as the leader of the "free world." Eisenhower suspected that the invaders had timed their operation to coincide with the US presidential vote, in which he was seeking reelection, thereby hoping for a weaker US response. The co-incidence with the Soviet invasion of Hungary also jarred, since it invited people across the world to compare the two actions. Eisenhower's assistants feared that the attack on Egypt would make it easier in the future for the Soviets to gain a foothold in the Middle East. But the most important concern was the European powers' willingness to sacrifice larger Cold War interests to achieve short-term, narrow, national gain. For Eisenhower this was a deadly sin, since it, in his mind, deflected from the purpose for which the United States was fighting the Cold War.

The outcome of the Suez crisis was also manifold. It made it abundantly clear, if further confirmation was needed, that Britain and France could no longer take independent action in foreign affairs against the will of the United States. For both countries this was a visible setback for national prestige, even though the realities of the matter had been clear for more than a decade. But Suez also showed that public opinion in the postcolonial world counted, and, as with Hungary, there was a price to pay for displaying naked power too openly. Speaking to the Indian parliament, Nehru summed it up: "The use of armed forces by the big countries, while apparently [achieving] something, it has really showed its inability to deal with the situation. It is the weakness which has come out."[9] With characteristic panache, Nehru told them, "The greatest danger which the world is suffering from is this Cold War business. It is because the Cold War creates a bigger mental barrier than the Iron Curtain or brick wall or any prison. It creates barriers of the mind which refuses to understand the other person's position, which divides the world into devils and angels."[10]

After Suez, decolonization sped up, both because of further British and French weakness and because it had become increasingly clear that the future for the two countries lay in Europe and in the transatlantic alliance, not in Africa or Asia. France had been forced out of Indochina in 1954 and was fighting a colonial war in Algeria that was going badly and attracted unwelcome American criticism. Elsewhere the French withdrew reluctantly. The governments of the Fourth Republic were caught among competing priorities: Being anti-Communist (while also wanting to appear radical); resenting US domination (while also fearing US abandonment); and embracing European integration (while also fearing a drop in French independent power and prestige). The French governments wanted US support, and therefore reported on the threat of Communism in independence movements from Senegal to Madagascar to Tahiti. But they also feared that the United States was out to replace France in its former colonies. French intellectuals denounced US imperialism, while some of them found it hard to abandon France's own colonialism, which—by strange twists of terminology—was supposed to be more moral, involved, committed, and "authentic" than any other. France knew Africa; the Americans did not, was an often underlined perception in French newspapers. But the subtext—that "knowledge" entitled continued exploitation—was as little said out loud in Paris as in London.

Some Frenchmen and other Europeans, and a smaller number of Africans, believed that the colonial empires could still somehow be transformed from within. They believed in an integrationist form of a British Commonwealth or *Union française*, where democratic values and the culture of the metropolitan state could be embraced by the former colonials, creating what some Parisian intellectuals called *Eurafrique*. Everyone, regardless of race, would be a citizen with equal rights, the argument went. The closeness of the colonizers and the colonized was substantially greater than among different countries in Europe. Why should progressives support European integration, while encouraging disintegration overseas? Not understanding that it was much too late for such an argument, the French Communists, for instance, went through considerable political contortions on the issue. The French Communist Party (PCF) wanted to see the "liberation" of the colonies, but not their separation from France. "The right to divorce is not followed by the obligation to divorce," declared PCF leader Maurice Thorez.[11]

For the main leaders in the colonized world in the 1950s and '60s, the issue was not promises of future integration but decolonization and anticolonial solidarity. The issue of race was essential. Colonialism was in its essence a racist project, and the lack of US support for full decolonization reminded many Third World leaders of racial oppression against African-Americans in the United States. But the

European Left was also to blame. In his 1956 resignation from the PCF, whom he had been elected to represent in the National Assembly ten years earlier, the black Martinican writer Aimé Césaire castigated the Eurafrique idea: "Look at the great breath of unity passing over all the black countries! Look how, here and there, the torn fabric is being re-stitched! Experience, harshly acquired experience, has taught us that we have at our disposal but one weapon, one sole efficient and undamaged weapon: the weapon of unity, the weapon of the anticolonial rallying of all who are willing, and the time during which we are dispersed according to the fissures of the metropolitan parties is also the time of our weakness and defeat."[12]

Nowhere was the weapon of unity more tested than in the Algerian struggle for liberation. Different from the British case, where all colonies (except, some people would say, Ireland, Scotland, and Wales) were far away overseas, Algeria was linked with France by the Mediterranean. The country had been invaded by the French in the 1830s, and by the late 1950s had around 1.2 million European settlers in a total population of eight million. Anticolonial rebellions had been frequent, and the National Liberation Front (FLN) began a campaign of armed struggle against the French in 1954. The French government responded with a massive anti-guerrilla operation, during which atrocities were committed on both sides. At its peak, France kept half a million soldiers in Algeria, most of whom could be paid only because of US support for the government in Paris. Even so, the operation did not succeed in rooting out the FLN, which by 1957 controlled significant parts of the country.

In May 1958 a military coup by French officers in Algiers threatened to split not just Algeria, but France as well. The officers, and the settlers who supported them, insisted that there could be no negotiations with the FLN. They demanded that General Charles de Gaulle, unconstitutionally, return as French president. To underline their military power, the rebels took control of Corsica and threatened to march on Paris. De Gaulle, who had been out of power since 1946, returned as the savior of the (French) nation, declaring his anti-Communism and his commitment to keeping Algeria a part of

France. But even if given near dictatorial powers, he could do little to change the tide of the Algerian war.

De Gaulle spent four years trying to keep Algeria French. In the end he failed because the Cold War priorities of the United States had little time for France's last colonial war. On the contrary, the Americans found de Gaulle difficult and suspected his war to be lost already. The FLN conducted very skillful diplomatic offensives, in which they challenged the anticolonial credentials of the United States. Why would a nation itself born in a struggle against empire not condemn the French occupation of Algeria? De Gaulle struck back at Washington's hesitation, declaring that France would have to acquire its own nuclear weapons, since the United States and the Soviet Union were obviously out to divide the world between them, and diminish France. The Eisenhower Administration did not think de Gaulle could afford to break with the West, but worried about the impact its alliance with France had elsewhere. "As long as the Algerian conflict continues," a National Security Council study concluded in 1959, "France will be a liability in U.S. relations with the Afro-Asian bloc, as well as in the Middle East."[13]

The British Conservative government, which had sworn never to abandon the British Empire, ended up giving eight countries independence between 1958 and 1962. In most cases the process was peaceful, even though the new postcolonial governments often found it difficult to sustain their authority. Ghana had been the first African colony to gain independence, in 1957. There, the charismatic nationalist leader Kwame Nkrumah became the first prime minister, though Nkrumah was keen on getting a more prominent place in the liberation of Africa than just being the head of one small country. In spite of his declared commitments, de Gaulle played the same role for the French colonies as the Conservatives had done on the British side. In French West Africa, Guinea became independent in 1958 and declined all association with the former metropole. Fourteen more French territories became independent between 1958 and 1962. In Algeria, de Gaulle also capitulated in the end. Unable to win the war, and under strong international pressure, Paris agreed to withdraw its forces and grant independence to its former colony. The FLN took power in Algiers in the summer of 1962, a radical anticolonialist government that was intent on symbolizing the power of the Third World.

For the Soviet Union, the view of the world also started to change in the late 1950s. The Soviet state was founded on the principle of world revolution and the overthrow of imperialism and other forms of feudal and capitalist oppression. In the first decades of Soviet rule, the prospect of "revolution in the east" had taken on an increasing significance, especially since "revolution in the west" failed to materialize. The Comintern set up schools and training institutes in the USSR for Communists from outside of Europe, and they helped organize parties and Communist groups in Asia, Africa, and Latin America. The Communist University of the Toilers of the East, a sort of finishing school for Asian revolutionaries, had been set up in Moscow in 1921, with branch campuses in Baku, Irkutsk, and Tashkent. It trained an astonishing array of leaders, including the head of the Indonesian Communist Party, Tan Malaka; China's Deng Xiaoping; and Vietnam's Ho Chi Minh (who would later serve as a Comintern agent all over southeast Asia and southern China). During the interwar period, Soviet universities attracted anti-imperialist students from most Asian and some African countries, with especially large groups from China, Vietnam, India, the Middle East, and Turkey. Not all of these were Communists, but all of them were attracted to the Soviet Union because of its proclaimed opposition to colonialism and European domination.

Lenin's stated policy of creating "united fronts" with non-Communist Left-wingers and anti-imperialists, especially in the colonized world, paid great dividends for Soviet foreign policy and for the radicalization of the anticolonial movement. Even the turns and twists of the Comintern in the late 1920s, as Stalin secured his hold on the Soviet Communist Party, did little lasting damage to the attraction of working with the Soviets for a common cause. For anticolonialists, the Soviet Union was both an inspiration as a social and economic model, and a source of practical support. For many Soviets, especially of the younger generation, helping the anti-imperialist struggle added luster to lives that were becoming harder at home. And for the Communist leadership, supporting anticolonial revolution made strategic sense, even if it was not led by their ideological brethren. It was a way of hitting the imperial centers in Europe—London, Paris, Brussels—which could not be achieved through a weak Communist movement in Europe.

The perceived closeness of the Communist cause and the anti-imperial one was witnessed at a number of conferences from the 1920s to the 1940s. One starting point was the first International Congress against Imperialism and Colonialism held in Brussels in 1927. The conference had been planned by German Comintern agents, primarily the colorful Willi Münzenberg, a master of setting up united-front organizations. Münzenberg used the anti-imperialist campaigns in China, led by the Guomindang, as the summons to the meeting. The conference had attracted international participants ranging from anti-imperialist Europeans, such as Albert Einstein and Henri Barbusse, to Jawaharlal Nehru; Song Qingling, the widow of the first Chinese president, Sun Yat-sen; and other Asian, African, and Caribbean activists. A number of US civil rights organizations were represented, including African-American and Puerto Rican groups. Very soon the Comintern handlers lost control of the proceedings, which turned into a denunciation of European control rather than the celebration of the links between anticolonialism and socialism that they had hoped for. The Senegalese Communist Lamine Senghor stressed that his primary commitment was to the replacement of empires by democracies that embraced racial equality: "Slavery is not abolished. On the contrary it has been modernized. . . . We know and ascertain that we are French when they need us to let us be killed or make us labor. But when it comes to giving us rights we are no longer Frenchmen but Negroes."[14]

The difficulties the Soviets had with controlling global anti-imperialism was also seen in their problems with handling the multinational empire they had inherited from the tsars. At first, the Communists encouraged the non-Russians (and especially the non-Europeans) to take up leading positions in their own areas, which were made into Soviet republics or autonomous regions. Groups such as the Tajiks or the Uzbeks, who had been conquered by the Russian empire in the nineteenth century, were now told that they should aspire to run their own republics within the Soviet federal state. Even smaller groups, which had never known any form of independence, such as the Kalmyks or the Udmurts, also got their own territories. Russian ethnographers were hard at work identifying nationalities in order to give them their rights, promote their language, and provide education, all under the aegis of Communist advisers. A main enemy of the USSR, Lenin had stated, was Great-Russian chauvinism. He feared that after his death, "the infinitesimal percentage of Soviet and Sovietized workers will drown in that tide of chauvinistic Great-Russian riffraff like a fly in milk."[15] But in most cases the policy of *korenizatsiia* (nativization) continued into the early 1930s, in spite of Stalin's fears of independent authority in the republics.

But when Stalin in the 1930s turned to massive terror to uphold his dictatorship, the knell sounded for Asian national aspirations within the Soviet Union. Those who had argued for principles of national, religious, or cultural autonomy disappeared into the labor camps, as did many of their Russian advisers, as well as a sizeable number of foreign anticolonialists who had taken refuge in the USSR. Some prominent Soviet Muslim anti-imperialists, such as the Bashkir leader Mirsaid Sultan-Galiev, were executed in prison. Stalin wanted a unified Soviet state under his personal leadership, a state that could eventually challenge for hegemony in Europe. To the Georgian Communist Stalin, Europe was where the future of the world would be decided. The colonial world was at best a sideshow, and at worst a distraction. Inside the Soviet Union the former Russian colonials should be integrated into the Soviet state. Outside, anticolonialists were mainly of interest if they could further the security interests of the USSR. Even the massive postwar turn toward overthrowing European control in India, Indonesia, and China seemed of less consequence to Stalin. Although after 1945 he spoke about how anti-imperialism would weaken the United States and its allies, his gaze was firmly fixed on Europe.

Little wonder, then, that Stalin's successors felt that the *vozhd* had missed a trick with regard to the Third World. In what amounted to a direct, though implicit, criticism of the late dictator, Khrushchev and his colleagues set out to visit countries in Asia and the Middle East in the first few years after Stalin's death. Khrushchev himself went to India, Burma, and Afghanistan in 1955. While visiting newly independent states, Khrushchev's message was always the same: all those who broke away from colonialism could count on the support of the Soviet Union. Gone were the days when the Soviet Union mainly lectured its own truths to new countries. Now the emphasis was on practical cooperation, which would serve both sides alike, and which would, eventually, improve the conditions for a transition to socialism worldwide. "The peoples which achieved national independence have become a new and powerful force in the struggle for peace and social progress," Khrushchev told the Higher Party School in Moscow in January 1961. "The national liberation movement deals more and more blows against imperialism, helps consolidation of peace, contributes to speeding mankind's development along the path of social progress. Asia, Africa, and Latin America are now the most important centers of revolutionary struggle against imperialism."[16]

By 1960 the Soviet Union had expanded its reach into the Third World considerably. Even countries that opposed Cold War divisions and those that had pledged allegiance to the Bandung agenda were happy to turn to the Soviets for practical support. After the Suez crisis, Egypt had begun a long-term development program supported by the USSR. Indonesia, Cuba, and several west African states, including Ghana, Guinea, and Mali, began cooperating closely with the Soviets. In spite of its worsening relations with China, the USSR seemed to have no trouble finding friends in the Third World. India was one of the big prizes, and in spite of its nonaligned policy, Nehru's government had started drawing on the Soviet experience in building its own form of socialism. They expected the influence to go in both directions, however. The Indian ambassador to Moscow, K. P. S. Menon, reported that India's "friendship with the Soviet Union is paying dividends not only in the shape of . . . technical assistance but in a certain softening of the contours of Communism and the boring of a passage, through which goodwill—and good sense—can flow between the two Blocs."[17]

The crisis that would demonstrate both the reach and the limitations of Soviet power in the Third World happened in Congo. The poor and exploited Belgian colony got its independence suddenly in 1960, when there were no roads connecting the different parts of the vast country and little economic development, except in European-owned mines. Congo had a total of sixteen university graduates, no doctors, no high school teachers, no military officers, and no nation-wide political parties. Everything had been run by the Belgians. When the colonial administrators left, the new leadership, under Prime Minister Patrice Lumumba, did its best to avoid collapse. Lumumba was a radical Congolese nationalist, a former postal clerk who had campaigned for Congo's independence and who headed the only political party with at least some representation in most of the country's many provinces. The Belgians detested him, and preferred to work with separatist groups to keep their mining interests intact. The Americans opposed him, since they saw the Left-wing Lumumba as a possible conduit between Moscow and his country's mineral riches. Within weeks of independence, Congo was fragmenting. Lumumba appealed for, and got, the dispatching of UN troops, but not their assistance in keeping the country together. In desperation, he appealed publicly to the Soviets for assistance.

From the beginning of the Congo crisis, the Eisenhower Administration had viewed Lumumba as a threat to US interests in Africa. According to Secretary of State Dulles, it was "safe to go on the assumption that Lumumba had been bought by the Communists."[18] The United States tried to prevent him from coming to power and, when he was in power, tried to get him ousted through a military coup. Meanwhile, Lumumba condemned Western policies: "We know the objects of the West. Yesterday they divided us on the level of a tribe, clan and village. Today, with Africa liberating herself, they seek to divide us on the level of states. They want to create antagonistic blocs, satellites, and, having begun from that stage of the cold war, deepen the division in order to perpetuate their rule."[19] But the appeal for Soviet support—which started slowly arriving in Kinshasa—signed Lumumba's death warrant. The CIA planned an assassination attempt in September 1960, but, before it could be carried out, the prime minister was overthrown by the military. They handed him to his secessionist enemies in the province of Katanga, where he was tortured, and murdered three months later.

For Khrushchev and his advisers the Congo crisis was an eye-opener. A legitimate African government had appealed for Soviet support, and in July 1960 Khrushchev had promised to help: "If the states that are ingeniously carrying out an imperialist aggression against the Republic of Congo . . . continue their criminal actions, then the Soviet Union will not refrain from decisive measures to stop the aggression. The government of Congo can be sure that the Soviet government will offer to the Republic of Congo the necessary help that can be required for the triumph of your just cause."[20] Six months later Lumumba was dead, Congo was under the control of a US-supported military dictatorship, and the only thing the Soviets could do in response was to fulminate and name a new college for foreign students in Moscow after the martyred Congolese leader, Patrice Lumumba University. The Soviet Union did not yet have the logistic or military capacity to project its power to central Africa. It was a lesson those Central Committee staffers, Red Army officers, and KGB officials who had been involved would never forget.

For other Third World states, Congo's tragedy was also a sign of their own weakness. Ghana and Egypt had hoped to help Lumumba stay in power, but they were too weak and too slow to do so. The only way out, both Nkrumah and Nasser concluded, was to strengthen the economic development of their own countries. Other core Third World regimes, such as Ben Bella's Algeria, thought likewise. Only if national economic development could be jump-started through state intervention and planning could their countries grow powerful enough to satisfy the aspirations of their own peoples while also acting in solidarity with others. The Soviet economic experience had some of the keys to such growth, but these had to be invigorated and maximized through the abilities of the new states' own populations. A common Third World belief was that by removing colonial controls and creating a state that acted on behalf of the people, quick economic growth could be achieved. Instead many leaders found that their countries did not have the expertise needed to advance fast, especially in building new industries, and that the few resources they could export were still hostage to conditions set by multinational companies and international trade regimes. Almost from the beginning, many countries found that development efforts were hampered by increasing levels of official corruption. By the mid-1960s many Africans, especially, found that they were worse off in their daily lives than they had been under colonial rule. They were beginning to look for more stability, order, and incremental progress than the postcolonial regimes were able to offer.

Algeria is a good case in point. The man who emerged as the key leader of the FLN, Ahmed Ben Bella, had become radicalized when he served in the French army and later in France as a political prisoner. When the country finally got its independence, Ben Bella's government nationalized most industries and aimed for a gradual nationalization of Algeria's oil industry, the most important economic activity in the country. Land that had been abandoned by its European owners, most of whom fled to France after 1962, was given over to peasants' and laborers' self-managing collectives. Agricultural production dropped as a result of lack of expertise, equipment, and investments. The plans to build new industries were mainly unfulfilled, in part because those who were supposed to build them had enough to do fending for themselves and their families as prices rose and rapid urbanization drove rents up. The Algerian growth rate in the Ben Bella years was not low: a little bit less than 5 percent on average. But this was mainly due to oil exports. All other industries declined, and the state spent its oil income inefficiently and erratically. As doubts spread, Ben Bella himself became increasingly autocratic, given to long public speeches in which he sought support for the immediate implementation of policies ranging from the nationalization of newspapers to the introduction of compulsory membership in the

Muslim boy scouts. The crowds shouted "Long Live Ben Bella," but when the military deposed him in 1965 most Algerians seem to have drawn a sigh of relief.

In spite of its domestic failures, however, Ben Bella's Algeria became a centerpiece for Third World revolutionaries from Africa and the Middle East. Two of the main groups fighting against Portugal, which still held on to its African colonies, were headquartered there—the Popular Movement for the Liberation of Angola (MPLA) and the African Party for the Independence of Guinea and Cape Verde (PAIGC). Nelson Mandela, the leader of the South African National Congress (ANC), spent time in Algiers, where he received military training, as did revolutionaries from Congo, Rhodesia, and Palestine. Malcolm X and other African-American militants visited, and several of the leaders of the Black Panther movement later took refuge there. Many of Ben Bella's key advisers were western Europeans or Yugoslavs (but very few Soviets). Together with the Egyptians, the Indonesians, and the Indians, Algerian leaders underlined that only broad international solidarity and cooperation could complete the decolonization of Africa and break away from the stranglehold of the Cold War.

In 1961, the year before Algeria gained its independence, an extensive coalition of states had joined together to form what was to become the Non-Aligned Movement. All of them felt that the Cold War threatened their international interests and was in the way of their domestic development plans. Many of the same countries participated in the founding congress as had taken part in the Bandung Conference six years earlier. But nonalignment was not simply a follow-up to Bandung. Solidarity among peoples, and especially racial solidarity, was conspicuous by its absence. Instead the conference focused on the part of the Bandung agenda that underlined sovereign rights of states and the need for international peace as a precondition for the abolishment of all forms of colonialism and foreign intervention. With the first meeting held in the Yugoslav capital, Belgrade, the new initiative was intended to be much broader than just the independent countries of Asia and Africa. The purpose was to challenge the Cold

War system through new forms of international cooperation. China was not invited, but Cuba was a full member from the beginning, as was Cyprus and even conservative monarchies such as Ethiopia and Saudi Arabia. Sukarno summed it up in his address:

> Non-alignment is not directed against any one country, or against any one bloc, or against any particular type of social system. It is our common conviction that the policy of non-alignment is the best way for each of us to make a positive contribution toward the preservation of peace and the relaxation of international tension. And let us be quite frank: It is no mere accident that we countries gathered here happen to be the ones who have set ourselves on the path of non-alignment. . . . This is the era of emerging nations and a turbulence of anti-nationalism, the building of nations, and the breaking of empires.[21]

By the early 1960s decolonization had changed the world beyond what most people could have imagined in 1945. Not only were there many more independent countries around, but all of the new countries were led by non-Europeans. Europe, on the contrary, had lost much of its power, not least because the postcolonial states demanded their own say in world affairs. A majority of them disliked the international order that the Cold War had created. They felt constrained by it and believed it to be yet another form of European control. But at the same time the Cold War was inexorably engulfing them through conflicts at home and abroad. Already by the end of the 1960s rulers in what had constituted the Third World were searching for stability and new forms of economic growth, be it through Soviet or American models. Many of these second generation leaders were military men who preferred orderly change over revolution. The Third World was a moment; fifteen years after Bandung, more and more new states found it difficult to manage without strong links to one or the other Superpower.

11

Kennedy's Contingencies

The record of General Eisenhower's tenure as a US Cold War president was decidedly mixed. Backed up by his vast international experience, Eisenhower had avoided the sense of permanent crisis and frequent distress of his predecessor. He had extricated the United States from the Korean War and—equally importantly—avoided getting the country directly involved in new wars in Asia. But Eisenhower had also overseen a vast militarization of the Cold War, in which the US arsenal had expanded from 370 warheads in 1950 to more than 40,000 in 1960. He had alienated radical nationalists in the Middle East and Latin America through his covert interventions in Iran and Guatemala. And—mainly for domestic ideological reasons—he had failed to make use of the opportunities after Stalin's death for a real relaxation of the conflict with the Soviets.

Much of Eisenhower's more forward thinking seemed to come as an afterthought to the general. His attempts at reaching out to Third World leaders and arranging regular summits with the Soviets came right at the end of his presidency. Symbolically, his final meeting with Khrushchev had been cancelled because the USSR had shot down an American spy plane inside Soviet airspace. Having presided over the greatest buildup of military capacity in US history, Eisenhower in his farewell address went on to warn Americans that

We have been compelled to create a permanent armaments industry of vast proportions. Added to this, three and a half million men and women are directly engaged in the defense establishment. We annually spend on military security more than the net income of all United States corporations. This conjunction of an immense military establishment and a large arms industry is new in the American experience. . . . We must guard against the acquisition of unwarranted influence, whether sought or unsought, by the military-industrial complex. The potential for the disastrous rise of misplaced power exists and will persist.[1]

The legacy Eisenhower bequeathed to his successor was therefore a troubled one. The young president-elect, John F. Kennedy, struggled with contingencies left over from the last administration and those created by a rapidly changing world even before he took office in January 1961. He battled to understand, and then deal with, a crisis in Laos, where insurgents were threatening a US-supported government. He attempted to reach out to Congress to get its Democratic leaders to support a broader US involvement abroad, higher defense expenditures, and more aid to developing countries. And he tried to show a skeptical military and intelligence service that a young, Democratic, and Catholic president would not only be fully in charge but also better able to win the Cold War than his experienced predecessor. It was a frenetic first year in office, with promise and defeats in roughly equal measure.

John F. Kennedy was the first American president born in the twentieth century. He was also the youngest person ever elected president, a forty-three-year-old who took over from a man nearly thirty years his senior. As the first Catholic president, Kennedy's election was a sign that the US political elite was gradually extending into new demographic territory. From a wealthy Bostonian family of Irish immigrants, Kennedy would still get to know the slings and arrows aimed at him for being nouveau riche in a city where old money was revered. But he made up for it through a buoyant personality and a combative political demeanor. JFK—like some American presidents, he was known by his initials—had been brought up to win, in life as in politics, and he had the intelligence and charm that often allowed him to do so.

There was enormous enthusiasm across the country on Kennedy's election, even though it was a hard-fought contest against Eisenhower's vice president, Richard Nixon, and a very narrow win. Still, Kennedy's youth, his vigor, and his general attractiveness (not least alongside that of his wife, Jacqueline) enthused people, far beyond those who had supported him politically. His rhetoric was also scintillating. JFK spoke about the need for change and about America triumphant, always a winning combination in US politics (and a far cry from his predecessor's measured style). In his inaugural, the new president alerted the Soviets that he was

> unwilling to witness or permit the slow undoing of those human rights to which this nation has always been committed. . . . In the long history of the world, only a few generations have been granted the role of defending freedom in its hour of maximum danger. I do not shrink from this responsibility—I welcome it. I do not believe that any of us would exchange places with any other people or any other generation. The energy, the faith, the devotion which we bring to this endeavor will light our country and all who serve it—and the glow from that fire can truly light the world.[2]

As he had done in his campaign, after his election Kennedy spoke about the possibility of the United States losing out to the Soviets. Stability was not enough, he claimed, in an indirect attack on his predecessor. JFK wanted the United States to *win* the Cold War, though it was always unclear to him what such a victory would consist of. During the campaign he had claimed, quite inaccurately, that there was a "missile gap" that separated increased Soviet capabilities from those of the United States in terms of nuclear weapons. In fact the situation was the reverse, and Kennedy probably knew that. But he used the fictitious "gap" to illustrate his willingness to get one over on the Soviets in a competition for global power. To JFK, the 1960s was a decade of enormous danger and enormous opportunity. The world was plastic, and it was up to the United States to mold it into a new shape.

Over time, Kennedy's belligerent approach would be tempered by events. In a presidency tragically cut short, the defining moment was the Cuban missile crisis, when the Soviet Union and the United States got closer to nuclear war than at any other point during the Cold War. In the time that was left to him after that crisis in October 1962, Kennedy was more serious about seeking compromise and therefore a lasting peace. But he always remained strongly ideological. More of an intellectual than any other US Cold War president, Kennedy thrived on discussing ideas and trying to understand change. He believed in the Wilsonian creed, that it was only by making other countries more like the United States that his country could be secure and fulfill its historical mission. And the 1960s, more than any other decade, seemed to the young president to hold out the opportunities for doing so.

The first of the contingencies Kennedy had to deal with was the US relationship to countries in the Third World. As a senator, Kennedy had been an outspoken proponent of greater US engagement in the problems of newly independent states and in opposing colonialism, for instance with regard to Algeria. But his was not only an ideological and moral engagement. He also feared that the United States was missing a trick by not aligning more closely with the new states, and that the Soviets capitalized on US inaction. He had read *The Stages of Economic Growth*, by the MIT economic historian Walt Rostow, which argues that "traditional" societies are particularly susceptible to Communist infiltration at the very moment when they begin transitioning to modernity. He also read Khrushchev's January 1961 speech, in which the Soviet leader had pledged support even for non-Communist countries and movements in the Third World, and commented on it extensively. Reflecting his foreign policy inexperience, Kennedy saw the speech almost as a declaration of war against the United States. He instructed his advisers to "read, mark, learn and inwardly digest" Khrushchev's message. "You've got to understand it . . . ," the president kept repeating. "This is our clue to the Soviet Union."[3]

Kennedy believed that in order to win the Cold War, the United States had to prevent the postcolonial states from falling into the lap of the Soviet Union. Eisenhower had been too passive in that regard, the new president thought. His administration devised a policy that combined increased economic assistance with training US and local troops in anti-insurgency warfare. US development aid expenditure increased significantly, though only up to 0.6 percent of GDP.[4] A couple of months into his presidency, Kennedy launched the US Peace Corps as part of a larger effort to assist global development. The plan was to recruit American youth to work as volunteers in Africa, Asia, or Latin America, where they would provide skills training for the local population. As much of what Kennedy proposed, the Peace Corps was a call to action, an attempt at winning the Cold War by setting things right: "Every young American who participates in the Peace Corps will know that he or she is sharing in the great common task of bringing to man that decent way of life which is the foundation of freedom and a condition of peace."[5] By 1966 fifteen thousand Americans were serving in countries as diverse as Chile, Nigeria, Iran, and Thailand.

In security terms, Kennedy's initial focus was on southeast Asia, where rebellions against US-supported regimes had been brewing since the partition of Vietnam in 1954. The Laos crisis was to Kennedy a prime example of the kind of challenges the Cold War would lead to in the Third World. He viewed the Laotian Communists and their allies, the North Vietnamese, the Chinese, and the Soviets, as launching a direct provocation against him as a new president. It was a gauntlet thrown down that Kennedy was only too eager to pick up. He told his advisers he was "all for doing what we can in Laos," but he was very cautious about introducing US ground troops, hoping to force the Communists into a political settlement by threatening a US intervention.[6] As part of this strategy, the White House authorized a CIA covert operations program for Laos, which concentrated on the Chinese border areas. Kennedy also dispatched the US Seventh Fleet to the

South China Sea and placed combat troops in Okinawa on alert. Later he sent US troops to Thailand. Kennedy saw himself as threatening war in order to achieve peace, a policy of brinkmanship that he would also use in more serious conflicts during his presidency.

In Laos, JFK's carrot and stick approach worked, at least for a while. Khrushchev was in no mood for a battle over Laos, which he regarded—with some right—as the periphery's periphery. The Chinese were weakened after the disasters of the Great Leap Forward, and those temporarily in control in Beijing—Liu Shaoqi and Zhou Enlai—wanted to use the Laos crisis to indicate a continued willingness to work with the Soviets in international affairs. The North Vietnamese, although eager to help the Laotian radicals, were in no position to act on their own. The result was a conference at Geneva, at the end of which all powers involved—and the Laotians themselves—agreed to a neutralization of Laos, and the establishment of a coalition government. Very few people in Washington or Hanoi—and nobody in Laos—thought this would be the end of the story, and Kennedy deepened his commitment to South Vietnam as a result of the crisis. But, for now, one ball in the Superpower contest had been put out of play.

Kennedy's visions for Europe were much more limited than those for the Third World. He had no intention of attempting to change the balance of power there, and he suspected that Khrushchev was reasonably happy, at least for the time being, with current arrangements in Europe. The main outstanding issue was the control of the divided German capital Berlin, and Kennedy did not clearly understand how vexing this problem had become for his Soviet counterpart. Khrushchev viewed Berlin—the only part of Germany where people could still cross between East and West—as a wound to the heart of the German Democratic Republic, the eastern part of Germany, which was now a Communist state with 250,000 Red Army soldiers stationed within it. The problem was that East Germans, especially those with education or specialist training, continued to leave for the West in droves. In 1960 more than 190,000 had sought more freedom and better income in the western half of the city.

Both the East German leaders and members of his own leadership had been asking Khrushchev what he intended to do about the situation in Berlin. For the East German Communists, the situation was untenable: not only were a lot of talented people leaving, but their manner of leaving—in violation of controls and orders—derided the authority of Walter Ulbricht and the East Berlin government. But there was little they could do about it, as long as the subway, for instance, ran unimpeded throughout the whole city. As Ulbricht explained to Khrushchev in November 1960, "the situation in Berlin has become complicated, not in our favor. West Berlin has strengthened economically. This is seen in the fact that about 50,000 workers from East Berlin . . . go to work in West Berlin, since there are higher salaries there. Why don't we raise our salaries? . . . First of all, we don't have the means. Secondly, even if we raised their salary, we could not satisfy their purchasing power with the goods that we have, and they would buy things with that money in West Berlin."[7] Khrushchev met with Kennedy for the first time in a summit in Vienna in the summer of 1961. Kennedy had asked for the meeting. He told his advisers that he wanted to show the Soviet leader that "we can be just as tough as he is."[8] But their talks did not go well. Khrushchev was in an ebullient mood, with traces of distress. He was still upset over Lumumba's murder and the loss of Soviet positions in Congo. But the Soviet Union had just put the first man into space, and the United States had had its setbacks over Cuba and in relations with its European allies. Unwisely, Khrushchev tried to bully the much younger US president into making concessions. The Berlin problem was foremost on his mind.

First Khrushchev treated Kennedy to a lesson in ideology. In accusing the Soviet Union of promoting world revolution, he said, "the President drew the wrong conclusion. He believes that when people rise against tyrants, that is a result of Moscow's activities. This is not so. Failure by the US to understand this generates danger. The USSR does not foment revolution but the United States always looks for outside forces whenever certain upheavals occur."[9] Turning to Berlin, Khrushchev indicated that he was willing to negotiate, but at the end of the year "the USSR will sign a peace treaty unilaterally and all rights of access to Berlin will expire because the state of war will cease to exist." Kennedy responded with equal bluntness: "The United States cannot accept an ultimatum. Our leaving West Berlin would result in the US becoming isolated." "The USSR will sign a peace treaty," Khrushchev said, "and the sovereignty of the GDR will be observed. Any violation of that sovereignty will be regarded by the USSR as an act of open aggression against a peace-loving country, with all the consequences ensuing therefrom. . . . The USSR does not wish any change; it merely wants to formalize the situation which has resulted from World War II. The fact is that West Germany is in the Western group of nations and the USSR recognizes this. East Germany is an ally of the socialist countries and this should be recognized as a fait accompli." President Kennedy "concluded the conversation by observing that it would be a cold winter."[10]

"I never met a man like this," Kennedy exclaimed wearily after his meeting with Khrushchev.[11] The president found the Soviet leader overbearing, aggressive, but also eager to avoid war and sensitive to matters of prestige. On returning to the United States, Kennedy asked Congress for $3.5 billion in extra military expenditure in order to set up six new divisions for the army and two for the marines. He also planned to triple the draft and to call up the reserves. Khrushchev was fuming. "We helped elected Kennedy last year," he boasted to a group of scientists as he stated his intention to resume nuclear testing, which had been suspended by both countries since 1958. "Then we met with him in Vienna, a meeting that could have been a turning point. But what does he say? 'Don't ask me for too much. Don't put me in a bind. If I make too many concessions, I'll be turned out of office.' Quite a guy! He comes to a meeting but can't perform. What the hell do we need a guy like that for? Why waste time talking to him?"[12]

Khrushchev's underestimation of Kennedy made him act on Berlin in ways almost as self-defeating as Stalin's blockade in 1948. By the late summer of 1961 both leaders had been able to talk themselves into crisis mode over Germany. Neither side wanted military conflict, or even a standoff. But Khrushchev had to solve the East German emigration problem and Kennedy had to show his commitment to the

West German government and the NATO alliance. Khrushchev acted first. He picked up on a proposal that Ulbricht had made earlier about building a wall in order to physically separate East Berlin from West Berlin. Before signing off on the project, the Soviet leader went on an incognito visit to the German capital, driving into West Berlin, looking around. "I never got out of the car," he remembered later, "but I made a full tour and saw what the city was like."[13] On 13 August 1961, barbed wire started to go up along the dividing line separating the two parts of Berlin. The subway tunnels were quickly blocked off. The East German police shot at those who dared to cross. The city of Berlin had again become a victim of the Cold War. And this time its division seemed permanent.

But erecting the Berlin Wall signaled East Bloc weakness, not strength. The people of Berlin resisted as best they could. "There was this one street we used to go to," one of them remembers, "which was split down the middle by the wall. The street was in the west but the houses were in the east. The soldiers bricked up the front doors but people jumped out of the windows. There was a group of us on the western side who used to all try to knock off the top level of the wall before the cement had time to dry. We were a bit of a mob; we would all surge together and smash it."[14] The mayor of West Berlin, the Social-Democrat Willy Brandt, called the Wall "a shocking injustice." But in his radio address to all Berliners, Brandt also warned the East about the consequences:

> They have drawn through the heart of Berlin not just a border, but a fence, as in a concentration camp. With the support of the East Bloc states, the Ulbricht-regime has exacerbated the situation in Berlin and again broken with legal agreements and humanitarian obligations. The Senate of Berlin brings to the whole world its accusations against the illegal and inhuman actions of those who divide Germany, oppress East Berlin, and threaten West Berlin. . . . They will not succeed. We will in the future bring even more people from all over the world to Berlin to show them the cold, naked, and brutal reality of a system that has promised people heaven on earth.[15]

Khrushchev, however, thought he had found a way of solving his Berlin problem without a direct confrontation with the United States. He told his eastern European colleagues: "We should not force the conclusion of a peace treaty with Germany, but continue to move forward. . . . We should keep applying pressure. . . . We should carry on salami tactics with regard to the rights of the Western countries. . . . We have to pick our way through, divide them, exploit all the possibilities."[16] Kennedy refused to let US forces leave Berlin and insisted on access to East Berlin for American officers. For several months the Americans, the Soviets, and the East Germans played cat and mouse all over Berlin. Thirteen people were killed trying to leave the East right after the Wall went up. One of them was the twenty-five-year-old Werner Probst, who tried to swim across the Spree River. The East German border guards shot him just as he grabbed hold of a ladder on the western side. Willy Brandt ordered loudspeakers set up along the Wall, which kept repeating that "anyone who shoots dead a person who wants to go from Germany to Germany has committed murder. No one should think that he can claim to have acted on orders when he is called to account one day. Murder is murder, even if it has been ordered."[17] The East responded by firing tear gas into the western sector.

For Kennedy and Khrushchev the situation remained tense for several months. On 27 October there was a twenty-four-hour standoff between Soviet and American tanks right at Checkpoint Charlie in Friedrichstrasse, in the center of Berlin. It gradually became clear to the White House that the Soviets would not attempt to force the Americans out of Berlin, even as they tightened their grip on the city. Kennedy immediately saw the immense propaganda value of the Wall, but did not think there was much the United States could do about the situation, except assuring Brandt, the West German government, and its NATO allies that the United States would defend West Berlin in case of an East Bloc attack. Privately, the president mused that "it's not a very nice solution but a wall is a hell of a lot better than a war."[18] Brandt was disgusted with what he saw as cowardice on the president's part and feared for the future of his half-city. Other western European leaders, especially France's de Gaulle, also saw Kennedy as weak. The German people, de Gaulle said, "would be left with a sense of betrayal." He "would not be party to such an arrangement. The Germans would then in the future feel that at least they had one friend left in the West."[19]

In spite of the criticism, it is hard to see what more Kennedy could have done over Berlin except threatening war. The president did not want to be pushed around by Khrushchev. But Kennedy's view of what mattered in the Cold War was much more global than that of his predecessors, and his reading of the Vienna summit was that Khrushchev pushed on Berlin to solve East Germany's problems, not because he planned to upset overall stability in Europe. Prestige mattered to Kennedy, and it was at least as vital for him as for de Gaulle to keep West Germany in NATO and forestall any temptation on the side of the aging German chancellor Konrad Adenauer to negotiate directly with the Soviets in order to achieve reunification in return for German Cold War neutrality. But the walling off of East Berlin did not upset the balance in Europe, Kennedy concluded, however shocking it was in terms of human rights.

As could be expected from his thinking when he came into the presidency, Kennedy's level-headedness applied much more to Europe than to the Third World. His biggest challenge, by far, was to be the Cuban revolution, a regional problem Eisenhower had been eager to deal with but which had not been at the forefront of the general's mind. Gradually, Cuba was to become a significant participant in the Cold War in its own right, as a major Third World power and as an ally of the Soviet Union. But, as Kennedy came into office, the question in Washington was how to handle the Cuban revolution itself, an insurrection that had created a radical and militant regime in the most populous country in the Caribbean, ninety miles from the Florida coast.

The Cuban revolution was the result of years of misrule by Fulgencio Batista, a populist president whose methods had become increasingly dictatorial. It also reflected widespread poverty and social injustice in the countryside, though not more than was found in other

Latin American countries. From the beginning, nationalist opposition to US control played an important part in the revolution. Cuba had been occupied by the United States several times during its history, and some Cuban businesses, such the vital sugar industry, were dominated by US companies. During the latter part of his regime, Batista had drawn closer to the Americans, in part to offset his weaknesses at home. By the late 1950s Cuba seemed a country ripe for political change.

Those who came to fill this power gap were Fidel Castro and his group of exiled revolutionaries from Cuba and other Latin American countries. Castro was born in 1926, the son of a Spanish immigrant who had become a wealthy farmer in Cuba. As a very young man, Fidel Castro had become a radical student leader who opposed the government, campaigned for social justice and Latin American solidarity, and opposed US domination of Cuba. More of an insurrectionist than a Communist, the imperious youth commented to a friend that he would only become a Communist "if I could be Stalin."[20] Castro's activities forced him into exile in Mexico in 1955, from where he and a small band of revolutionaries attempted to return to Cuba clandestinely the following year. Arriving in December 1956 in a leaky yacht called *Granma*, bought from an American in Veracruz, only nineteen revolutionaries made it inland. The survivors settled in the Sierra Maestra, a mountain range in southeastern Cuba, where Castro, his brother Raúl, and the Argentinian Communist Ernesto "Che" Guevara proved themselves to be competent guerrilla leaders, skillfully setting up campaigns against Batista's regime and recruiting adherents among local peasants, workers on sugarcane plantations, and urban youth who traveled to join them. In 1958, when the Batista regime started to get into real trouble because of its economic incompetence, its internal divisions, and clashes with the Eisenhower Administration, Castro's forces began operating all over eastern Cuba. With his government collapsing around him, Batista left the country with as much of his vast fortune as he could grab. On 2 January 1959 the revolutionaries entered the capital, Havana, in triumph.

Their sudden victory came as much as a surprise to Castro as to everyone else. Spectacularly unprepared for government, the revolutionaries tried to draw on liberals and anti-Batista professionals to help run their regime. Having himself been drawn to Marxism, and influenced by his Communist brother Raúl, Castro also began working with members of the Cuban Communist Party. Che Guevara, who knew rather more about guerrilla tactics than economics, was made head of the Central Bank. But there was no doubt who was in charge, and who set the terms for the program of social change that was initiated by the new government. Fidel Castro wanted to cleanse Cuba of gambling, prostitution, and other ills that he saw as having been brought in by the Americans. He decreed radical land reform, rent reduction, and a minimum wage. He also set the new government to work on massive plans for expansion of education and health care. High-ranking members of the former regime were purged, and hundreds were executed by firing squad after brief "revolutionary" trials. Fidel's regime was authoritarian and at times brutal. A number of former allies broke with him and went into exile. The Castro brothers and their adherents claimed that the revolution needed to defend itself against its enemies.

The Eisenhower Administration was concerned about the radical and authoritarian aspects of the new regime, and what they considered the influence of Communists within it. But they also at first hoped that it would be possible to stunt these trends over time. Featured on America's most watched TV talk show right after the revolution, Castro, speaking in English, made much of his Catholic upbringing and his interest in baseball. In April 1959 he visited the United States and was feted as a pop star by the press and by large audiences wherever he went. Speaking to the *Wall Street Journal*, he encouraged US investment in Cuban industries and promised tax breaks for American companies. "He insists," says one of the reports, "he's a good friend of this country. He claims, in effect, he has only been pointing out past 'mistakes' in U.S. Policy toward Cuba."[21] But as Castro's exiled adversaries began flying military missions into his country

from Florida airports and US public criticism of his economic policies increased, the Cuban leader lost patience. In October 1959 he told
a mass rally in Havana:

> There are immigrants from everywhere in the United States. . . . And
> yet despite this Cuba is the only country which is being attacked by
> émigré planes. Why Cuba? If there is one country the United States
> should treat carefully, that country is Cuba. Cuba has just suffered a
> two-year war during which its cities and fields were bombed with
> American-made bombs, planes, and napalm. Thousands of citizens
> were killed by weapons which came from the United States. The least
> which we could expect after we destroyed the mercenary army, and
> after we freed our people from the tyranny, is that our people not
> continue to be bombed from bases on U.S. territory.[22]

By 1960 the Cuban-US relationship was in free fall. Eisenhower
wanted to get rid of Castro, and ordered the CIA's agents to attempt
to curtail his power on Cuba. When Cuba nationalized the land-
holdings of US-owned sugar cane companies, the United States responded by reducing the vital import quota of Cuban sugar. Castro
turned to the Soviet Union. His increasing fondness for orthodox
Marxism-Leninism would probably have led him there anyhow, but
strained relations with Washington helped him on his way. In February 1960 Soviet deputy premier Anastas Mikoyan visited Cuba,
where he promised loans and signed an agreement in which the
USSR would supply Cuba with cheap oil in return for Cuban exports
of sugar. Mikoyan sent elated reports back to Moscow. "This is a real
revolution," he told the KGB man who accompanied him. "Just like
ours. I feel as though I have returned to my youth!"[23] When the US-
owned refineries on Cuba refused to process Soviet oil, Castro nationalized them. Eisenhower responded with an embargo on trade
with Cuba in October 1960. Castro then nationalized all remaining
US property on the island. In January 1961, just before leaving office,
Eisenhower broke off diplomatic relations with Cuba.

When Kennedy came in, he discovered that Eisenhower had started an active covert operations program against Cuba in March 1960, right after Mikoyan's visit. The CIA provided military training for Cuban exiles and used its agents to sabotage arms shipments and industry on the island. They also began plotting to assassinate Fidel Castro, either by disaffected Cubans or by the help of US gangsters, who had had their activities on the island scuttled by the revolution. Eisenhower had not yet decided to go ahead with a full-scale attempt at overthrowing Castro, though he was obviously tempted by an operation similar to that which had overthrown Guatemalan president Jacobo Arbenz in 1953. Kennedy was presented with the plans to invade as if they were a fait accompli set up by the previous administration, making it harder for the new president to move in a different direction if he had so wanted.

In fact, there is almost no evidence that Kennedy wanted to act differently on Cuba than the plans his predecessor had drawn up. During the campaign, JFK had attacked Nixon (and implicitly Eisenhower) for failing Cuba, both by supporting Batista's regime and by not "getting results" against the Communists. "We never were on the side of freedom; we never used our influence when we could have used it most effectively—and today Cuba is lost for freedom," candidate Kennedy had said.[24] Both the military and the CIA recommended the invasion plan, and showed their willingness to amend it when President Kennedy indicated that he wanted there to be less visible evidence of a US involvement. Kennedy generally admired the intelligence community for its versatility and intellectual acumen, and had kept Eisenhower's director of central intelligence, Allen Dulles, in place in the new administration. "If I need some material fast or an idea fast, CIA is the place I have to go. The State Department is four or five days to answer a simple yes or no," Kennedy said.[25]

The plan that was implemented on 17 April 1961 was a failure from the beginning. Caught between his eagerness to remove Castro and his desire for deniability of direct US participation, Kennedy helped send 1,400 US-trained counterrevolutionary Cuban fighters across to the island from Guatemala. But, with the exception of bombing raids by US aircraft piloted by Cuban exiles, the president did not authorize US air support. There was no Cuban political organization to take charge of the operation. The CIA had expected that Kennedy would approve direct US involvement if the landings went badly. But JFK did no such thing. Instead, the invaders at Bahía de Cochinos (Bay of Pigs), 150 miles from Havana, were rounded up by Cuban troops, paraded on TV, and sent off to prison camps. Meeting with his new prisoners, Castro told them that "the people want the execution of all invaders. . . . It would be easy to execute you but it would only lessen our victory. The least guilty would pay for the most guilty."[26]

For the revolutionaries, the failed Bay of Pigs invasion opened up new opportunities. Meeting with US representatives that summer, Che Guevara said "that he wanted to thank us [the United States] very much for the invasion—that it had been a great political victory for them—enabled them to consolidate—and transformed them from an aggrieved little country to an equal."[27] Fidel Castro knew that the threat was not over. But he also knew that he could now be much more outspoken about his preferences and his international affiliations. "The danger of direct aggression could again gain momentum following this failure," he told the Cubans in a radio address. "We have said that imperialism will disappear. We do not wish it to commit suicide; we want it to die a natural death. . . . But their system demands production for war, not peace. How different from the Soviet Union . . ."[28]

While Castro used the Bay of Pigs to get closer to the Soviets, both in terms of industry and security, Kennedy had his own lessons. "Five minutes after it began to fall in, we all looked at each other and asked, 'How could we have been so stupid?'" the president told a friend. "When we saw the wide range of the failures we asked ourselves why it had not been apparent to somebody from the start. I guess you get walled off from reality when you want something to succeed too much."[29] Robert Kennedy, the president's brother, whom he had appointed attorney-general, pushed for further action to overthrow Castro. "Serious attention must be given to this problem immediately and not wait for the situation in Cuba to revert back to a time of relative peace and calm with the U.S. having been beaten off with her tail between her legs," Bobby Kennedy exhorted his brother. "The time has come for a showdown for in a year or two years the situation will be vastly worse. If we don't want Russia to set up missile bases in Cuba, we had better decide now what we are willing to do to stop it."[30]

Besides the gradual slide into the Vietnam War, the Bay of Pigs invasion was the biggest mistake of JFK's presidency. It solidified the Castro regime beyond anything Castro himself could have done, and was to lead to Kennedy's most dangerous confrontation with the Soviet Union. Part of Kennedy's problem was in terms of priorities. He felt that there were many challenges left over from the previous administration, and that he would have to deal with a great number of them at the start of his presidency.

One key issue, which preoccupied the young president much, was the extraordinary growth in the nuclear weapons arsenals of both Superpowers. Not only had the number of US nuclear warheads increased more than ten-fold over ten years, but by 1962 the Soviets had their own intercontinental ballistic missiles (ICBMs), though considerably fewer than Kennedy had claimed they had during his presidential campaign. Khrushchev commanded about one hundred missiles that could possibly reach the continental United States. Of these around thirty were based on Soviet submarines. Given the overwhelming preponderance of US ICBMs, plus shorter-range nuclear missiles placed around the Soviet Union from Greenland via Germany and Turkey to South Korea, and an estimated 144 nuclear submarines, Kennedy may not have had that much to worry about. But his concerns were increasingly with US strategic planning, which assumed that any war with the USSR would necessarily escalate into a full-scale nuclear conflict.

Kennedy wanted to move away from Eisenhower's reliance on the threat of massive nuclear retaliation to deter the Soviets. He wanted a more flexible response, a strategy outlined by his secretary of defense, Robert McNamara, as consisting of three parts, at least as far as Europe was concerned, in the event of war. First, an attempt to repulse Warsaw Pact forces by conventional (non-nuclear) means. If that failed, as McNamara assumed it would because of the Soviet conventional superiority in Europe, the United States would use smaller, tactical nuclear weapons. Only as a last resort would the Americans respond with an all-out nuclear attack on Soviet cities and military bases. The Kennedy Administration developed the Single Integrated Operational Plan, known as SIOP, which assumed that mutually assured destruction was not the only possible outcome in case of war.

Khrushchev was well aware of US strategic superiority in nuclear terms. His response was to combine bluffing and a war of nerves. The Soviets consistently claimed to have a greater nuclear capability than they actually possessed, and attempted to make up for what they lacked in precision and ballistic expertise by developing ever bigger nuclear weapons. The AN602 hydrogen bomb—the so-called *Tsar Bomba* or Emperor of Bombs—which the Soviets tested in October 1961, is the largest nuclear weapon ever produced, with an explosive power of about 1,500 times the combined yield of the weapons that destroyed Hiroshima and Nagasaki, or ten times the combined explosive power of all other weapons used during World War II. Khrushchev did not mind that *Tsar Bomba* was virtually undeployable for any practical military purpose. "I think the people with the strongest nerves will be the winners," he said. "That is the most important consideration in the power struggle of our time. The people with weak nerves will go to the wall."[31]

In April 1962 Khrushchev had an idea. Frustrated over events in Germany, angry with the Chinese who mocked him for his circumspection, and convinced that Kennedy was irresolute but also increasingly anti-Communist, Khrushchev wanted to act decisively to save the Cuban revolution. What if, he suggested to a somewhat incredulous Mikoyan, the Soviet Union were to deploy nuclear missiles on Cuba "very speedily"?[32] The United States had placed its nukes in Turkey, close to the Soviet border. Why could his country not guarantee Castro's survival by sending its own weapons to the island? There was, Khrushchev argued, no other way Havana could be protected—it was too close to the United States for the Soviets to be able to stave off an invasion by conventional means.

Having secured the Moscow leadership's approval, Castro was consulted, though in a form that made Khrushchev's plans almost into a done deal. Castro at first doubted the wisdom of provoking the Americans further, and worried about the reaction of other Latin American countries. But he was also pleased that the Soviets put such emphasis on Cuba and was ready to act "in solidarity" with his new comrades in Moscow. The plans went ahead. The first Soviet military personnel arrived, under great secrecy, in July 1962. Missiles began arriving in early September. At their peak more than forty thousand Soviets were building missile sites both for defensive and offensive purposes. The largest nuclear missiles that became functional on Cuba in October 1962 had a maximum radius of 1,200 miles, enough to reach cities in the southern and eastern United States from Houston to Baltimore.

Both the US military and the CIA had begun suspecting that the Soviets contemplated placing missiles on Cuba well before the summer of 1962. But when challenged on the issue, Soviet diplomats had been instructed to lie. In mid-October a US spy plane, a U-2, overflew the island and came back with clear evidence of missile sites under construction. The president, when alerted, wanted time to consider the US response. From the start of the crisis, Kennedy was certain that he had to get any Soviet missiles out of Cuba. The question was how to do that and avoid an all-out nuclear war between the United States and Soviet Union. When Kennedy saw Soviet foreign minister Anatolii Gromyko in the White House for a prearranged meeting on 18 October, Gromyko again lied about the Soviet deployment. The USSR "pursued solely the purpose of contributing to the defense capabilities of Cuba," Gromyko said.[33]

Gromyko's bold-faced lie convinced Kennedy that he had to go public. In a radio and television speech to the American people on 22 October, Kennedy addressed what he saw as an immediate danger emanating from Cuba. "Within the past week," the president said, "unmistakable evidence has established the fact that a series of offensive missile sites is now in preparation on that imprisoned island. The purpose of these bases can be none other than to provide a nuclear strike capability against the Western Hemisphere. . . . The 1930s taught us a clear lesson: aggressive conduct, if allowed to go unchecked and unchallenged, ultimately leads to war." His "unswerving objective," Kennedy said, was to "prevent the use of these missiles against this or any other country, and to secure their withdrawal or elimination from the Western Hemisphere." With the crisis now out in the open, Kennedy had put his credibility on the line: "I call upon Chairman Khrushchev to halt and eliminate this clandestine, reckless and provocative threat to world peace and to stable relations between our two nations. I call upon him further to abandon this course of world domination, and to join in an historic effort to end the perilous arms race and to transform the history of man. He has an opportunity now to move the world back from the abyss of destruction."[34]

Behind closed doors, attitudes hardened. In his speech, Kennedy had announced what he called a "quarantine" on shipments of weapons to Cuba. He also announced increased surveillance of the island, indicating that any attempts to prevent US violations of Cuban airspace would be regarded as an act of war. Neither Kennedy nor anyone in the so-called Executive Committee (ExComm) of top advisers that he had set up to deal with the crisis understood the Soviet dedication to defend the Cuban revolution or, for that matter, Cuba's need to defend its own sovereignty. The president and all of Washington viewed Soviet actions as preparations for an attack on the United States and a means through which (legitimate) US control of the Western Hemisphere could be thwarted. At the start of the crisis, they would rather risk war than accept compromise.

Kennedy's main strength throughout the Cuban missile crisis of 1962 was that, in spite of his hard line overall, he still gave diplomacy a chance. As the world held its breath on 23 October, waiting to see what would happen when Soviet ships bound for Cuba were intercepted by the US Navy, Kennedy secretly explored how the crisis could be resolved and nuclear war avoided. On the one hand, he needed to stave off hotheads on his own side who wanted to launch immediate airstrikes to disable the Soviet missiles on Cuba. Such an attack, Kennedy knew, would mean global nuclear war against the Soviet Union. On the other, he had to find a solution that removed the missiles and made the United States the winner. When Khrushchev, himself under pressure to avoid a confrontation, turned the Soviet ships back, the president thought he had made a breakthrough.

But Khrushchev had no intention of backing down. Like Kennedy, he needed breathing space, but he also sent a message to the president in which he rejected all of his demands and condemned the illegal US blockade of Cuba. Soviet and US military forces worldwide were put on full combat readiness. At the UN, US ambassador Adlai Stevenson confronted his Soviet counterpart, Valerii Zorin:

> **STEVENSON:** All right sir, let me ask you one simple question: Do you, Ambassador Zorin, deny that the USSR has placed and is placing medium- and intermediate-range missiles and sites in Cuba? Yes or no? Don't wait for the translation: Yes or no?
> **ZORIN:** I am not in an American courtroom, sir, and therefore I do not wish to answer a question that is put to me in the fashion in which a prosecutor does. In due course, sir, you will have your reply.[35]

Toward the end of the second week of the crisis, the buildup of US invasion forces against Cuba continued in Florida and along the Gulf coast. US overflights of Cuba intensified. Panic began to spread in US cities and elsewhere in the world, even in the Soviet Union, where the authorities tried to prevent news about the crisis getting to the population. Walter Cronkite, the CBS anchorman who reported on the crisis from minute to minute, began wondering what he would do in the TV studio when nuclear war broke out: "We have a utility room where the furnaces are, and we wondered whether we could make that into a bomb shelter of some form. We were learning for the first time the time that we would have after the explosion, before the fumes . . . [and the] heat would reach us."[36]

On 27 October an American U-2 overflying Cuba was shot down by a Soviet missile. Everyone involved thought war was getting very close. Castro wrote what sounded like a farewell letter to Khrushchev, where he urged him to launch a nuclear first strike against the United States after the Americans had begun invading Cuba. "I believe that the imperialists' aggressiveness makes them extremely dangerous, and that if they manage to carry out an invasion of Cuba . . . then that would be the moment to eliminate this danger forever, in an act of the most legitimate self-defense. However harsh and terrible the solution, there would be no other."[37]

But Kennedy was still playing for time. Contrary to orders issued earlier, he refused to permit the US Air Force to destroy the Soviet missile site that had shot down the U-2. Most of the ExComm members had not left the White House in a week. That evening Kennedy sent them home. McNamara remembered later: "It was a perfectly beautiful night, as fall nights are in Washington. I walked out of the president's Oval Office, and as I walked out, I thought I might never live to see another Saturday night."[38] Meanwhile, the same evening, Robert Kennedy met secretly with the Soviet ambassador to the United States, Anatolii Dobrynin. He offered a US pledge not to invade Cuba and an eventual removal of American missiles in Turkey in return for the Soviet withdrawal of all its missiles. Khrushchev, who knew the world was teetering on the brink of war, decided to accept. Conscious that time was running out, he had his acceptance read out on the open airwaves of Radio Moscow. He even had the broadcast repeated twice. On the morning of 28 October the immediate crisis was over.

The Cuban missile crisis was the most dangerous nuclear confrontation between the Soviet Union and the United States during the Cold War (though not the only one). Historians have been battling over who won and who lost. The real answer is, of course, that everyone won, since nuclear war was avoided. But it is also clear that, by being forced to take his missiles out of Cuba in such an open and visible fashion, Khrushchev lost the most. Why did he back down? He knew that the Soviet Union would suffer the most in case of a nuclear war, since its ability to inflict damage on the United States was far inferior to the reverse. He also feared for the survival of his regime in case of war. But the real reason was probably his Marxism. Khrushchev believed that Communism was on the up worldwide, and that his historic role was to steer the Soviet Union through a period in which, through the laws of history itself, the global balance of forces tipped in its direction. Nuclear war would destroy this historical achievement. Khrushchev wanted to celebrate the triumph of Communism, not eulogize at its funeral pyre.

Throughout the crisis, President Kennedy had proven himself to be a skillful leader and diplomat. He had taken great risks, and if Khrushchev had not backed down, it is likely that he would have taken his country into a nuclear war. But the risks he took were risks that most Americans seemed willing to take in order to preserve their increasingly global predominance. John Kennedy played the missile crisis well because he was broadly in line with the attitudes of those who had elected him, but also because he added to that the vital instruments of diplomacy, open and secret. It was through these instruments that a "solution"—fickle, incomplete, and tenuous—was in the end found.

According to his own testimony, Fidel Castro was furious. "We were irate. How did we learn about this? Through the radio, on the morning of the 28th. They broadcast that an agreement had been reached between the Soviet Union and the United States, that Kennedy was offering Khrushchev a guarantee. It really was a disgraceful agreement. It never crossed my mind they would do anything like this."[39] For the Cuban leader, it would have been better to die with honor than to live with disgrace. His relationship with the Soviets would never be the same, even though the countries remained close allies for the rest of the Cold War.[40]

John Kennedy was assassinated in November 1963. He was forty-six years old. If he had lived and been reelected in 1964, could he have been the president who brought the Cold War to an end? There is very little evidence for that, even though it was a more concerned and careful Kennedy who returned to his foreign policy agenda after

October 1962. Still, his aim was to win the Cold War, even if he had to do so while avoiding crises that could lead to an all-out conflict. Kennedy continued to believe that the Soviet Union constituted a global challenge to American interests, and that the United States had to push back when challenged. Reflecting on the missile crisis in a public speech a year later, the president said that he was "hoping for steady progress toward less critically dangerous relations with the Soviets, but never laboring under any illusions about Communist methods or Communist goals."[41]

One key change revealed by the crisis was just how much two sides knew about each other, both through espionage and through open sources. Spying had always played a key role in the Cold War, but in the 1960s and '70s it took on a new significance. In the immediate post-1945 era, the Soviets had had the main successes. Klaus Fuchs and other atomic spies had given Stalin what he needed to know about the US nuclear programs. Britain's Foreign Office had been utterly compromised when it had become clear, in 1951, that the head of its American Department, Donald Maclean, was a Soviet spy. Maclean escaped to Moscow, as did other members of the Cambridge Five spy ring that he belonged to, including Kim Philby, who had been the main British intelligence liaison with the United States. It is hard to imagine a greater disaster in intelligence terms.

In the 1960s the balance of spying power started to change. One possible reason was that the Soviet Union, post-Hungary, had lost some of its attraction to educated people in the West, making it harder to recruit ideologically minded spies. At the same time both western Europe and the United States seemed to be better able to deal with issues of social inequity than before: people like Fuchs and Maclean had been recruited to serve the Soviets in the 1930s in part because of their distaste for exploitative capitalism. In the 1960s, however, the most important spies were Soviets fed up with their own society. Anatolii Golitsyn, Oleg Penkovskii, Dmitrii Poliakov, and other Soviet intelligence officers who gave crucial information to the West all explained that they wanted the West to win the Cold War. Penkovskii explained that he saw himself as a "warrior for the cause of truth, for the ideals of a truly free world and of democracy. . . . I wish to make my contribution, perhaps a modest one but in my view an important one, to our mutual cause."[42] Poliakov, who ended up as a GRU major general, was, according to his American handler, "our crown jewel, . . . the best source at least to my knowledge that American intelligence has ever had and, I would submit, . . . the best source that any intelligence service has ever had."[43]

In spite of the advantages he had gained on his opponents, JFK's last year in office was taken by responding to domestic political crises, such as the growing African-American civil rights movement, by the widening war in Vietnam, and by attempts at finding some form of lasting stability in relations with the Soviet Union. He and Khrushchev agreed on a limited test ban treaty for nuclear weapons; a small step, granted, and one the Chinese felt was exclusively directed against them, since they were about to test their own first weapon. Even so, it was a sign that there were some matters on which the United States and the USSR could agree. Like Eisenhower, Kennedy regarded the Chinese Communists as being even more unreasonable than their Soviet brethren. In January 1963 he explained to the National Security Council that he thought the Chinese would be "our major antagonists of the late '60s and beyond."[44]

Were the Berlin and Cuban crises Cold War watersheds? Some say they were: the former in the sense that the European Cold War had now visibly stabilized, and the latter because both Americans and Soviets saw the necessity of some form of detente, or at least the need to avoid extreme nuclear crises in the future. But it did not necessarily look that way in the early 1960s: the Cold War continued and new crises could occur at any moment, though it was becoming increasingly likely that they would take place in the Third World and not in Europe. During Kennedy's time in office, the Cold War was becoming truly global, and the burdens it put on the material and mental resources of its main protagonists increased relentlessly.

12

Encountering Vietnam

The Vietnamese revolution started as a revolt against colonial oppression and ended as a set of wars deeply enmeshed with the global Cold War. Its origins were in the French colonization of Indochina in the nineteenth century, or perhaps even further back in Vietnam's long years of Chinese domination. At the core of the enterprise was a group of Vietnamese nationalist revolutionaries who in their youth became committed Marxists and admirers of the Soviet experience. For these young men and women, nationalism and Marxism were one. They believed that only by developing their movement, their nation, and their state according to Marxist laws of evolution could Vietnam truly succeed in the modern world. Their program was long-term, expansive, and utopian, but its implementation was dependent on first achieving independence and national unity. And it was for these latter aims that almost three million Vietnamese fought and died during the twentieth century.[1]

Although policy-makers worldwide did not see it at the time, Vietnam was in many ways different from the rest of Asia. It was the only place where Communism became a dominant outlet for nationalism almost from the beginning. Even in countries where the Communist movement grew very big, such as in China, Korea, or Indonesia, this was a much more gradual phenomenon and the rivals for power were stronger. But in Vietnam, the Communists' opponents were tainted by their collaboration with the French, and Ho Chi Minh could present his Viet Minh movement as authentically Vietnamese both culturally and politically. Irrespective of his long service as a Comintern agent, Ho reinvented himself after 1945 as the symbol of national independence and as an elder of his people who deserved respect, almost veneration, by all Vietnamese.

The US war in Vietnam was therefore folly from the beginning. Not because there were no anti-Communist Vietnamese who were willing to fight for their cause, but because they were a minority and were bound to lose out in any contest for nationalist authenticity. The Vietnamese Communists could also count on the assistance of the Communist Chinese next door and on Soviet help. But successive American Administrations believed that the United States had to act to avoid a Communist victory in Indochina. The domino theory, first invented for China, was moved to Vietnam. To them, the Cold War was a zero-sum game, in which a loss for one side was a gain for the other. And the Soviet Union, or, even worse, China, was seen as controlling Vietnamese Communism and standing to gain through its success.

INSIDE VIETNAM THINGS looked rather different. For Ho Chi Minh and those who had worked with him in the Communist movement of Vietnam since the 1920s, the 1954 Geneva Conference had been a disaster. Instead of getting the united, socialist Vietnam that they had fought for—and believed they had gained through their prowess on the battlefield—they received only half a country, and uncertain prospects of reunification anytime soon. And even worse: Moscow and Beijing, their two main foreign sponsors, had together forced them to accept this division. Although Hanoi was told that this was a temporary "consolidation" of revolutionary gains, no Vietnamese Communist was in any doubt that their country's unity had been sacrificed on the altar of Great Power politics. But the leaders also knew that they stood no chance of fighting on their own against the new regime in the south and its American backers. Ho Chi Minh was convinced that reunification would take time. First, Communist North Vietnam had to build a state, refine its army, and build strong links with its

Communist allies. Ho was under strong pressure from younger leaders, and especially those who themselves came from the south, for a more activist policy. He was a symbol rather than a state-builder; his power receded, and impatience grew, as North Vietnam developed in the late 1950s.

The North Vietnamese state, called the Democratic Republic of Vietnam, was Communist from the very beginning. In 1951 Ho Chi Minh had set up the Vietnam Workers' Party (VWP) to act as a Communist core within the Viet Minh front. From the Geneva Accords of 1954 on, the VWP was in charge of building the state, and the state it built north of the seventeenth parallel was a copy of the Soviet model as implemented in China after 1949. It controlled the army, the police, and had a large network of informers and political enforcers all over the country (including in large parts of the south). It imprisoned its opponents in labor camps of the Stalin type. Around fifteen thousand were executed, most of them during a hastily carried out land reform campaign patterned on China's. At least a million people fled to the south. Even the Soviets and the Chinese criticized the North Vietnamese for having gone too far too fast.

But the trouble the Vietnamese Communists put themselves in was overcome through cloaking it in a mantle of nationalism. All that was done, Ho declared, was done for the best of the nation, to make it rich, strong, and unified. Communist propaganda, both in the north and the south, hammered in the nationalist credentials of the Hanoi government and, equally importantly, the southern government's lack of them. Leaders in Hanoi remained convinced, probably correctly, that they would "win" an all-Vietnam election if one were to be held, which was the reason why the Eisenhower Administration opposed such elections, in spite of the Geneva Accords. By 1957 it was clear that national elections were an unlikely prospect, and that both the Soviets and the Americans easily accepted the status quo for Vietnam and the rest of Indochina. With his peace offensive underway, the last thing Khrushchev wanted was another Asian war.

The Americans, however, did have the problem of what to do with southern Vietnam. The French were gone, relieved to depart after their military humiliation. The former emperor, Bao Dai, was tainted by collaboration both with the French and the Japanese. Jointly, the emperor and his US advisers settled on Ngo Dinh Diem as prime minister. Diem was a Vietnamese nationalist who opposed the Viet Minh and who had been in exile, mostly in the United States, since 1950. His politics were nativist, Catholic, and conservative: Diem believed that in order to make Vietnam into the great power it deserved to be, it had to return to its traditional roots in a new and invigorated Catholic form. His new Vietnam was to be modern, along the patterns set by the West, but would also make use of the unique abilities the Vietnamese had to create a just and stable society. Soon Diem had pushed the emperor aside and set up a Republic of Vietnam in the south with himself as president. The United States began pouring significant aid into the new South Vietnamese state, but the reforms Diem had promised were slow in coming. His main aim was to solidify his own regime against all comers, including the Communists who remained in the south.

Irrespective of the advice from their international partners, the Vietnamese Communists slowly began to extend their campaigns against Diem's regime in the south. In 1956, encouraged by Khrushchev's de-Stalinization and insistence that each party had to find its own road to socialism, the southern Vietnamese Communist Le Duan composed a masterful manifesto of doublespeak. In it, he insisted on the correctness of the Soviet view that "all conflicts in the world at present can be resolved by peaceful means." But he also warned that, in the south, a "people's revolutionary movement definitely will rise up." In other words, the Communist party had to support the spontaneous mass movement in the south, shape it, and lead it.[2] By 1957, in response to Diem's attempts at wiping out Communism in the south, the party began a campaign of assassinations and bombings. Le Duan was made head of the party, gradually replacing Ho Chi Minh as the real center of power. In January 1959 the VWP approved of a "people's war" in the south and began infiltrating cadres into the south through Laos, along what became known as the "Ho Chi Minh trail." In July 1959 the southern Communists killed two US military advisers just outside the southern capital of Saigon. They were the first Americans to die in the new war in Vietnam.

The reason why Hanoi in 1960 could organize a general rebellion against Diem's government was the Sino-Soviet split. The Vietnamese skillfully began playing their two sponsors against each other in order to get the support they needed. There is little doubt that Le Duan and his leadership group were considerably closer to the Chinese than to the Soviets in terms of ideology, and that Mao's increasing radicalism inspired them to act forcefully. But Khrushchev was not just brought along by competition and circumstance. Because of Cuba, Algeria, and Congo, by 1960 the Soviets were much more alert to the potential for gains through "wars of national liberation" than they had been only a few years earlier. Hanoi's timing of a rebellion in the south was therefore close to perfect, even though neither Le Duan nor his foreign sponsors at this point expected anything but a long, drawn-out struggle with an uncertain outcome.

John Kennedy inherited his Vietnam quandary from President Eisenhower, and he never had time or occasion to concentrate on it to the extent of finding a firm strategy. Instead, Kennedy's Vietnam policy became a gradual slide toward greater US involvement, even though JFK resisted sending regular US troops to Indochina. He participated in negotiations for a neutralization of Laos, which gave some semblance of stability to the region. But Kennedy's greatest entanglement, in line with his overall approach to the Third World, was through attempts at reforming the South Vietnamese state and improving the fighting capacity of its army and air force. By 1963 the United States had sixteen thousand advisers in South Vietnam, up from six hundred when Kennedy took over. All main Vietnamese military units had US officers attached to them, and although the US advisers were not supposed to participate directly in fighting against Hanoi or the Communist-controlled National Liberation Front (NLF) in the south, they became increasingly indispensable to the South Vietnamese war effort. US aircraft and helicopters transported Vietnamese troops, including on raids into North Vietnam. The Americans also started using herbicides for crop destruction in order to starve the South Vietnamese rebels and their supporters, and began setting up "strategic villages" to which peasants "rescued" from NLF control could be relocated.

In spite of the increasing US support, by 1963 it was clear that the Diem regime was in serious trouble. Not only did the NLF expand its operations, especially in areas around the southern capital, Saigon. But the South Vietnamese president also clashed with the non-Communist political opposition, Buddhist groups, and student organizations. His relationship with his US sponsors also deteriorated; Diem insisted that South Vietnam was a sovereign country, and that he was ultimately in control of civilian and military planning. A number of Buddhist monks self-immolated on the streets of Saigon in protest against the regime, and their burning bodies were shown on US television news, making many Americans wonder about the success of the US involvement in Vietnam. In desperation, the Kennedy Administration quietly encouraged South Vietnamese generals to carry out a coup against Diem. On 1 November 1963 the South Vietnamese president was kidnapped and murdered by his own officers. Three weeks later Kennedy was shot in Dallas.

Kennedy's biggest mistake on Vietnam was always to view the south and the north as two different countries. From this followed that the northern military involvement in the south was an invasion, and that the Communist great powers—and China especially—were behind the aggression. This line of thinking, which the new president, Lyndon B. Johnson, took over from Kennedy, linked the Vietnam War directly to the Cold War. It also drew connections back to Korea, the Chinese civil war, and ultimately World War II. The lesson was supposed to be that if the United States did not stand up to Communist aggression, then its resolve would be doubted and its positions, including its ideological positions, eroded. But both Kennedy and Johnson believed that US Administrations, and especially Democratic Administrations, that were not seen to stand up to Communist aggression were punished by opinion-makers and voters. Both Kennedy and Johnson, in very different ways, had a great fear of weakness.

Quoting friends from his home state of Texas, Johnson liked to say that Americans "will forgive you for anything except being weak."[3]

In domestic terms, Lyndon Johnson was one of the best prepared presidents the United States has ever had. He had been in Congress since 1937 and was known as the master of the Senate, where he as majority leader had championed progressive causes in the FDR mold. As Kennedy's vice president he had served unhappily at the margins of power. With the president's assassination, he was thrown into the top seat of American politics, and he had a set of reforms that he wanted to carry out almost from the beginning. Some were plans that had been developed in the Kennedy Administration. But most were Johnson's own causes, and he had the experience, the toughness, and the wherewithal to push them through. Perhaps the most successful president in legislative terms in US history, Johnson saw through major initiatives on poverty reduction, civil rights, and health care, as well as immigration and education reform, dealing with thorny issues that had eluded his predecessor (or, for that matter, his successors). In the 1964 presidential elections, he crushed his Republican opponent and was reelected with the highest percentage of the popular vote ever.

But a solution to the escalating war in Vietnam seemed to elude Johnson, too. Although his political instincts told him to find a way out as fast as possible, he feared the consequences. His priorities were his domestic reforms, but he felt he would be unable to carry those out fully if he did not have a clean sheet on foreign policy. Discussing how to present the war to the American people, Johnson confided to an old buddy in the Senate:

> I think that I've got to say that I didn't get you in here, but we're in here by treaty [with South Vietnam] and our national honor's at stake. And if this treaty is no good, none of 'em are any good. Therefore we're there. And being there, we've got to conduct ourselves like men. That's number one. Number two, in our own revolution, we wanted freedom and we naturally look with sympathy with other people who want freedom and if you leave 'em alone and give 'em freedom, we'll get out tomorrow.[4]

During 1964 the Johnson Administration became increasingly convinced that the United States faced an all-out challenge from the Communist camp in Vietnam. The coup against Diem had led to little but increased instability. The rebellion in the Republic of Vietnam continued to spread. The evidence of the north supplying and directing that rebellion continued to mount. And behind Hanoi stood Beijing and Moscow, more or less in that order. Against plentiful evidence of a growing Sino-Soviet split, Johnson kept focusing on Vietnam as a Communist bloc problem. The difference between the Communist great powers, according to the Johnson Administration, was that the Soviets were practical and rational, while the Chinese were unreasonable and increasingly irrational. It is not difficult to see racial stereotypes behind this kind of thinking: the Soviets, after all, were at least led by Europeans, while the Chinese were Orientals who did not understand—or did not want to engage in—the normal give and take among powers. It was this irrationality more than anything, Johnson's secretary of defense Robert McNamara believed, that kept the war going.

By mid-1964, the president had become convinced that the only way to win the war in Vietnam was by showing an on the ground military willingness to do so. If the United States proved to Hanoi and to Moscow that they had nothing to gain by further aggression, they would come to the negotiating table, irrespective of howls of protest from the Chinese. McNamara and McGeorge Bundy, the president's national security adviser, both pushed for the bombing of North Vietnam, the deployment of US ground forces, and the widening of US participation in the war alongside South Vietnamese troops. In a draft presidential speech, Bundy argued that the United States was not "bound to give the aggressors any guarantee against joint and necessary reprisal for their repeated acts of war against free men in South Vietnam. What has been ordered from outside South Vietnam can be punished outside South Vietnam, by all the laws of nations, and by the elemental rule that men are answerable for what is done at their command. The aggressor in Hanoi knows his guilt, and the world knows it too."[5] Even Secretary of State Dean Rusk, a relative dove on foreign affairs, prodded the president. "The matter of war and peace lay in the Pacific," he told Johnson. "If we appeared to falter before the Soviet Union and Communist China this would be interpreted as a reward for the track they have been following, and this would increase the chance of war. If we were to make a move that would signal to Peiping [Beijing] that we are weakening, this would increase our danger."[6]

In August 1964 Johnson used inaccurate reports of North Vietnamese vessels firing on a US naval ship in international waters as an excuse to get Congressional authority for widening the war. The so-called Gulf of Tonkin resolution authorized the president "to take all necessary measures to repel any armed attack against the forces of the United States and to prevent further aggression."[7] In 1965 the US Air Force started bombing raids into North Vietnam, and the number of US troops increased to almost two hundred thousand. By the end of the year almost two thousand Americans had died in the fighting, and it was becoming clear to most people at home that this was a real war and not the kind of proxy conflict that the United States had engaged in globally over the past decade.

We know today that many of the US assumptions about the political and military calculus on the North Vietnamese, Soviet, and Chinese sides in the Vietnam War were mistaken. The North Vietnamese leaders viewed the war as a national struggle for liberation. They were aiming for a military victory, which they realized could only come about after a US disengagement. The Soviets realized that the war in Vietnam was to the US detriment in the global Cold War struggle, since it alienated Third World countries and movements, and made the Soviet Union seem a country that stood for peace and assistance to little Vietnam fighting the American Goliath. By almost every measure, the stakes in Vietnam were extremely low for the USSR and increasingly high for the United States. But Moscow was always wary of the war spreading elsewhere in southeast Asia, thereby forcing the Soviets to take a more active and visible role in defense of local revolutions. As things were, Khrushchev's successors were happy to condemn US aggression and provide limited aid to North Vietnam (in part to attempt to pry it away from its alliance with China), while privately telling Johnson that Moscow was trying to moderate Hanoi's behavior. The not-too-subtle Soviet message to the Americans was that Vietnam could be settled only if Washington was willing to work with Moscow on other Cold War issues.

It was the Chinese role in Vietnam that changed the most, in line with Beijing's topsy-turvy policies during the 1960s. In the first part of the decade, and especially after 1962, Mao Zedong increasingly used the war in Vietnam as a weapon against the Soviets. The Chinese Communists, Mao proclaimed, gave full support to Hanoi's attempts at fast-tracking its road to Communism and to liberating the south. The Chairman's message was that where Moscow prevaricated, Beijing acted. Chinese aid to North Vietnam increased significantly year on year, as Hanoi ideologically sided with China in its quarrels with the Soviets. But as the US engagement widened in 1964, Mao was keen to avoid a direct conflict with the Americans, as had happened in Korea. Beijing signaled to Washington that it would not get involved with its own forces unless the Americans invaded the north. In spite of his increasingly revolutionary stance domestically and internationally, Mao had a healthy respect for American power. Besides, with his confrontation with the Soviets worsening—mostly, it should be said, by his own actions—Mao Zedong had little appetite for an all-out war in Indochina. Therefore, China's policy came to consist of aiding the North Vietnamese and the NLF in the south, while egging them on to fight "relentlessly" against the Americans and eschew all negotiations. But Beijing had also learned from Korea not to take any chances. By 1967 China had 170,000 of its own troops stationed in Vietnam to help the North Vietnamese with their defense, while being prepared to fight in case the Americans crossed the dividing line between North and South Vietnam. "My fundamental idea," Chinese premier Zhou Enlai told the North Vietnamese, "is that we should be patient. Patience means victory. Patience can cause you more hardship, more sufferings. Yet, the sky will not collapse, the earth will not slide, and the people cannot be totally exterminated. So patience can be rewarded with victory thus causing historic changes, encouraging the Asian, African, and Latin American countries, and playing down the American imperialists."[8]

The Johnson Administration also saw the war in Vietnam in international terms. Through 1965 and '66, the president was convinced that weakness in Vietnam would translate into setbacks elsewhere in the Third World and possibly in Europe, too. Johnson principally saw this in alliance terms: if the word of the United States did not stand in southeast Asia, what would allies and potential enemies elsewhere think? But he also sensed—much encouraged by his advisers—that things might be about to turn to the benefit of the United States in some important regions of Asia, Africa, and Latin America. What was important, Johnson thought, was to hold the fort in Vietnam while other new countries—helped and encouraged by US assistance programs—turned away from radicalism and toward freedom and economic growth. Recognizing that foreign assistance was not popular among the general public or in Congress, the president issued a special message that was vintage LBJ both in form and content. "To those nations which do commit themselves to progress under freedom, help from us and from others can provide the margin of difference between failure and success," Johnson said. "This is the heart of the matter. . . . We will be laying up a harvest of woe for us and our children if we shrink from the task of grappling in the world community with poverty and ignorance. These are the grim recruiting sergeants of Communism. They flourish wherever we falter. If we default on our obligations, Communism will expand its ambitions. That is the stern equation which dominates our age, and from which there can be no escape in logic or in honor."[9]

The Administration was right in seeing the mid-1960s as a turning point in the Third World, even if they were wrong about the long-term effects of that turning for Vietnam and the rest of Indochina. In Algeria, long the tribune of Third World revolution, the army turned on President Ben Bella in June 1965 and ousted him in a coup. There was little resistance. The majority of Algerians felt that Ben Bella had been rich in rhetoric but poor in the execution of his plans. They wanted a more practical and pragmatic approach to economic development, which delivered tangible results for those had fought for so long for a state of their own. It was not so much the contents of the Algerian National Liberation Front's (FLN's) program that people objected to, as its poor execution and the increasing self-centeredness of the new revolutionary elite. Army head Houari Boumedienne, whose forces took over the Algerian capital under cover of acting as extras in the filming of the Gillo Pontecorvo film *The Battle of Algiers*, promised fewer speeches and more action, which is also what Algerians got over the years that followed. In its foreign policy and in much of its economic planning Algeria drew closer to the Soviet Union and away from Third World idealism.

In Ghana similar events took place. Kwame Nkrumah, for almost a decade the unchallenged leader of his country and a key Third World spokesman, was overthrown in a military coup in 1966. Nkrumah had lost much popular support because his economic policies were slow in bringing results and he was becoming increasingly dictatorial. In 1962 he sacked the chief justice. Two years later he banned all opposition parties and made Ghana a one-party state and himself president for life. The coup came when Nkrumah was on his way to China and North Vietnam, and the military officers who took over claimed that one of their purposes was to save Ghana from impending Communist control. In his book *Neo-Colonialism, the Last Stage of Imperialism*, published six months before his overthrow, Nkrumah accused his domestic opponents of being engulfed by "a flood of anti-liberation propaganda [that] emanates from the capital cities of the West, directed against China, Vietnam, Indonesia, Algeria, Ghana and all countries which hack out their own independent path to freedom. . . . Wherever there is armed struggle against the forces of reaction, the nationalists are referred to as rebels, terrorists, or frequently 'communist terrorists'!"[10]

The coups in Algeria and Ghana were windfalls for the Johnson Administration. Though there is no evidence that the CIA was directly involved in either event, the US government had encouraged and made clear its support for such action by the military. While the outcome in Ghana was a military dictatorship with close ties to the

United States, the Algerian result was more murky from a US perspective. Boumedienne was no pushover in international affairs, and his affinity for Soviet-style planning was well known to the Americans. Even so, Washington much preferred him over the Thirdworldist Ben Bella. In its review of the coup, the CIA commented that "in many areas of Algeria the army has probably already provided sounder leadership and administration than Ben Bella's government or the FLN party."[11] Thinking like the Soviets had become less of a challenge to the Johnson Administration outside of Europe than anti-imperialist revolutionaries and assorted friends of the Chinese or the Cubans. In spite of the Cold War continuing, Moscow had become a sort of "normal" enemy—European, straight-laced, and rather predictable—whereas the Third World was chaotic and given to excess. At the core of US fears lay the suspicion that future opposition to American global predominance might look more Chinese or Cuban than Soviet.

If any set of events should have given Washington pause in this kind of thinking, it was the defeats of the Left in Indonesia and Congo in 1965. Both still signaled that the future, at least in terms of a Communist challenge, might not lay with Beijing and Havana. They also, in different ways, indicated the beginning of the end of the Third World as a global political opposition. To Washington, counterrevolutions in Indonesia and Congo—and later in Bolivia—confirmed that US campaigns against Third World projects could work, if there were strong local allies, who fought against the radicals for their own reasons. It was the kind of lesson that conceptually could not be applied to Vietnam because such allies did not exist there and because an aggressive China was right next door. But the logical conclusion from this discrepancy, that the United States should withdraw its troops from Vietnam, was equally impossible to carry out because of the fear of being perceived as weak, irresolute, and defeatist in Cold War terms.

Ever since Lumumba's murder in 1960, Congo had seen sporadic fighting by Left-wing or separatist groups against a weak central government supported by the Americans, the Belgians, and European companies keen on exploiting the country's vast mineral wealth. By 1964 a full-scale rebellion had broken out in eastern Congo, headed by radicals who took over Kisangani (then called Leopoldville) and declared a People's Republic. As Congolese troops, aided by European and South African mercenaries and US advisers, approached Kisangani, the rebels took European hostages and threatened to execute them if the offensive continued. Prime Minister Moïse Tshombe, who had been responsible for the killing of Lumumba, appealed for Western intervention. In November 1964 President Johnson decided to have US planes airlift Belgian troops into eastern Congo to evacuate the hostages. "We couldn't just let the cannibals kill a lot of people," the president observed from his ranch in Texas.[12] While more than a thousand hostages were rescued, another two hundred were killed, alongside thousands of Congolese. Helped by a large CIA-led foreign operation, the Congolese government gradually took control of rebel territory and exacted its brutal revenge.

The US involvement in Congo led to angry reactions from the rest of Africa, not so much because of any love for the Congolese rebels, who were generally seen as a disorganized and mindless lot, but because of its association with the former Belgian colonial masters. The remaining Simbas (lions), as the survivors of the People's Republic called themselves, got help from the Egyptians and the Algerians, but also from the Cubans, who sent Che Guevara with a task force of more than one hundred to fight with them in April 1965. Che spent seven fruitless months in the eastern Congolese jungles, increasingly frustrated by the rebels' lack of coordination and their leaders' propensity for high living in Cairo rather than dire fighting in Congo. By the end of 1965 the rebellion had been defeated. The United States has been "licking [the] Congo rebellion," Johnson's deputy national security adviser, Robert Komer, told his bosses. "We and the Belgians have been practically calling the signals for Tshombe and providing him with everything he thought he needed—money, arms, advisors."[13]

A world away from Congo, Indonesia was even higher up the US list of international trouble spots. The Indonesian nationalists, led by the mercurial Sukarno, had achieved their independence from the

Netherlands in 1949 with the United States as a facilitator for liberation. Part of the reason why Washington had decided to push the
Dutch toward granting full independence to their former colony
was that Sukarno seemed a staunch anti-Communist. In 1948 his
forces had fought a brief civil war against the powerful Indonesian
Communist Party (PKI) and won a decisive victory. But as Sukarno
began to take more of an interest in anticolonial struggles globally
and radicalized his economic policies at home, Indonesia fell out of
American good graces. In Washington, the Bandung Conference, at
which Sukarno as host played the lead role, was seen as a challenge
to American foreign policy, and Sukarno became another bête noir
of the Eisenhower Administration. As the Indonesian president
turned toward a higher degree of centralization and cooperation
with the resurrected Communist Party in 1957, US patience was
running low. With the British and Dutch in tow, the Eisenhower
Administration carried out a covert program to help anti-Sukarno
Islamic rebels in Sumatra. "We must prevent Indonesia going over
to the Communists," Dulles told his British counterparts. "If Java
becomes Communist-dominated, the best thing to do was to undermine their system by building up the independence of the outer islands, beginning with Sumatra."[14]

The CIA's campaign against Sukarno failed, but, understandably,
left the Indonesian leader with an awareness that the Americans were
out to get him. In the 1960s his policies became even more intent on
building a strong central state for all Indonesians, which in his view
should include all of Borneo, New Guinea, and even peninsular Malaya. He sought to formalize the coalition that kept him in power, declaring his government to be based on *Nasakom*: nationalism, religion,
and Communism. When Malaysia became independent in 1963, Sukarno predictably denounced the new country as a neocolonialist
British puppet state and started a three-year-long low-grade war
against it, which Malay-speakers called *konfrontasi*, the confrontation. With Indonesian forces confronting British and Australian
forces in Borneo, and the Communist Party gaining ground politically in Indonesia, the United States was desperately searching for a

policy. The Johnson Administration vacillated. The president wanted to withdraw all aid to the country, but the Pentagon and the CIA recommended continuing contacts with the military, hoping that its officers would act against Sukarno.

But Washington was not the only power that hedged in its relations with the Third World firebrand. The Soviets resented being criticized by Sukarno for being old, white, and sluggish, and by the PKI, whose criticism was similar to the Chinese, for being revisionist. Still, the USSR was by far the largest supplier of weapons. Like the Americans, Moscow kept its lines open to officers in the Indonesian military but had little direct political influence. The Chinese, on the other hand, seemed close both to Sukarno and the Indonesian Communists. By the early 1960s, with the Sino-Soviet split visible, the Indonesian president imagined that he could pull Beijing over onto a Third World anti-imperialist and anti–Cold War platform. In speeches and writings he extolled China's significance. But Mao Zedong was not equally convinced about the relationship. As the Chairman moved further to the Left in the mid-1960s, Sukarno and his regime seemed less and less trustworthy, simply because it was a "bourgeois" and not a truly socialist government.

As tension mounted in Indonesia, Sukarno seemed to thrive on the anxious political situation. He dubbed 1965 "the year of living dangerously," and stepped up his commitment to political and economic change. His recklessness proved his undoing. In the summer of 1965, senior officers were unnerved by the president's proposal to create an armed people's militia to parallel the conventional military. The Communists, meanwhile, feared for Sukarno's health, based on information from his Chinese doctors. They assumed that with him gone, the generals would turn on them again. The PKI struck first, by sanctioning a coup attempt by Communist junior officers on 30 September 1965, in which six generals were murdered. But the remaining generals, led by Suharto, struck back and took control of Jakarta, "protecting" Sukarno and outlawing the Indonesian Communist Party.

The coup in Jakarta was followed by some of the worst killing of civilians during all of the Cold War. Right-wing nationalists in the military and some Muslim religious leaders fanned out and organized massacres of Communists who seem to have been mostly unprepared for the ferocity of the attacks. Minorities suspected, often without any reason, of having collaborated with the Communists were also set upon. The Chinese community was especially badly hit. In all, at least half a million people were killed, mostly by being beheaded or having their throats slit. "Like lightning," one eyewitness said, the execution-er's "machete cut through the neck of his victim, the one-eyed, power-less bicycle repairman. His head went into the sack. Then his hands were untied, so that it looked as though he died without first being bound. At first, his headless body disappeared beneath the surface of the water, then eventually it floated up. The next person killed was a woman; I don't know who she was."[15] In one part of the country, the rivers were so thick with bodies that it prevented the water from flow-ing. The US embassy contributed to the killings by providing the military with lists of Communists.[16]

Internationally, all sides seemed relieved that Sukarno was gone. The Americans had the most reason to be relieved. "We may at last have Sukarno on the run," Robert Komer wrote to President John-son. "It is hard to overestimate the potential significance of the ar-my's apparent victory over Sukarno. Indonesia . . . was well on the way to becoming another expansionist Communist state, which would have critically menaced the rear of the whole Western po-sition in mainland Southeast Asia. Now . . . this trend has been sharply reversed."[17] The Soviets licked their wounds but blamed Su-karno and the PKI for the disaster. The Chinese, from their paro-chial Maoist perspective, were also unperturbed. "I think it will be a good thing if Sukarno is overthrown," Foreign Minister Chen Yi said. "Sukarno could mediate between the right and the left. But the future of Indonesia depends on the armed struggle of the PKI. This is the most important thing."[18] Chen Yi's fantasies were soon dis-pelled. The most powerful Communist Party outside of the Soviet bloc was crushed forever, and Indonesia entered its thirty years of Right-wing dictatorial rule.

THE OVERTHROW OF so many Third World leaders in the mid-1960s meant a crisis for the movement as a whole. Tellingly, the Afro-Asian conference planned for Algiers in the autumn of 1965 never took place. The fiasco of the cancelled meeting was, said one of the delegates, "the tombstone of the Afro-Asian world."[19] More countries in the Afro-Asian group, such as Egypt, Algeria, Syria, Iraq, and India, began orienting themselves toward the Soviet Union, at least as far as assistance and models for development were concerned. The Cubans and the Yugoslavs, declared Communists although of very different ilks, also increased their influence. Other Third World countries began emphasizing their own economic interests more, usually connected to the export of resources such as oil. For the Americans this was an undoubted relief. But these victories had to be built on. "In expressing your pleasure to Sec[retary of] State and others over the Indonesia and Ghana coups," Robert Komer advised President Johnson, "you make clear that we ought to exploit such successes as quickly and as skillfully as possible."[20]

The turning away from Third World ideals in Asia and Africa hardened US approaches to Vietnam and Indochina. In hindsight it is easy to see that the Johnson Administration drew the wrong lessons from the mid-1960s turnaround. They thought that American resolve in Vietnam had contributed significantly to defections from radicalism elsewhere, though even the CIA found no evidence for that being the case. The lack of imagination in US policy on Vietnam from the mid-1960s on is striking. Faced with continued political instability in South Vietnam, Secretary of State Dean Rusk concluded in April 1966 that "vis-a-vis the threatened nations of Asia, we must ask ourselves whether failure in Viet-Nam because of clearly visible political difficulties not under our control would be any less serious than failure without this factor":

The question comes down, as it always has, to whether there is any tenable line of defense in Southeast Asia if Viet-Nam falls. Here we must recognize that the anti-Communist regime in Indonesia has been a tremendous "break" for us. . . . But for the next year or two any chance of holding the rest of Southeast Asia hinges on the same factors assessed a year ago, whether Thailand and Laos in the first instance and Malaysia, Singapore, and Burma close behind, would— in the face of a US failure for any reason in Viet-Nam—have any significant remaining will to resist the Chinese Communist pressures that would probably then be applied. . . . Thailand simply could not be held in these circumstances, and that the rest of Southeast Asia would probably follow in due course. In other words, the strategic stakes in Southeast Asia are fundamentally unchanged by the political nature of the causes for failure in Viet-Nam. The same is almost certainly true of the shockwaves that would arise against other free nations—Korea, Taiwan, Japan, and the Philippines—in the wider area of East Asia.[21]

The United States therefore fought on in Vietnam, even if victory seemed elusive. On the advice of the Pentagon, the Johnson Administration poured more manpower and resources into the country, building airports, deepwater ports, bases, and hospitals, plus civilian assistance to the South Vietnamese government, which seemed more and more given to in-fighting and less and less capable of defending itself. The US air campaign was widened, employing B-52 bombers against targets inside North Vietnam. The strategy—if it can be called such—was to deploy US troops to fight at the perimeter of the South Vietnamese defenses to inflict maximum damage on NLF and North Vietnamese units. The South Vietnamese army would then be able to handle the NLF fighters within the core parts of South Vietnam. As Communist casualties increased, the theory went, a point would be reached when Hanoi would have no choice but to come to the negotiating table on US terms.

None of the elements of this strategy worked. US troops under General William Westmoreland inflicted massive damage on the Communist forces. Eight hundred thousand North Vietnamese and NLF soldiers died during the war, against a total of fifty-eight thousand US troops. But the American battlefield victories could not be translated into the holding of territory. As soon as the Americans moved on, Communist units moved back in. There were whole areas that were held by the South Vietnamese and Americans by day, and by the NLF at night. The loyalty of the local population to the Saigon government was dubious all over the country. Although most peasants simply wanted to get away from the fighting, a substantial number of young men and women volunteered to fight for the Communists. To overcome their problems of control, the Americans and South Vietnamese started moving peasants into "strategic hamlets," where—ostensibly—they would benefit from better housing and education. In reality it was to keep the peasants from contact with the NLF. But the results of such wartime social engineering were often the opposite of what was desired, as South Vietnamese resented being moved from their ancestral farms and villages.

As in all Cold War conflicts, the civilian population suffered greatly. About fifty thousand North Vietnamese died in US bombing raids. The United States dropped more bombs on the north than it did on Japan during all of World War II. More than two hundred thousand died in Communist political campaigns, north and south. Hundreds of thousands became refugees in their own country, and tens of thousands were injured as a result of US napalm bombing or use of Agent Orange. The Vietnam War was one of the most tragic manifestations of the Cold War, fought, it now seems, with massive casualties and for no good purpose.

One key reason why US strategy did not work was support for North Vietnam from China and the Soviet Union. Le Duan negotiated his alliances skillfully. Although Moscow and Beijing were at odds during all of the American war in Vietnam, Hanoi continued to receive support from both, even after China and the Soviet Union nearly went to war against each other in 1969. Hanoi achieved this in part by making support for North Vietnam the litmus test of internationalist dedication to the cause and in part by playing the two Communist great powers against each other in terms of assistance. Up to 1965 Chinese military and civilian support for North Vietnam had been more significant than what arrived from the Soviet Union. Beijing and Hanoi had also been much closer politically, with Vietnamese Communist leaders supporting Chinese accusations against the Soviets for "revisionism" and "right-deviationism." But Mao's Cultural Revolution radicalism changed the relationship. The North Vietnamese resented being constantly reminded of how they should behave politically at home and how they should avoid "insulting" China by mentioning both Soviet and Chinese aid. Red Guards made up of Chinese advisers rallied in Hanoi and Haiphong to exhort the Vietnamese to condemn revisionism and learn from Chairman Mao. Meanwhile, the Maoists held back Soviet military supplies arriving through China. In Beijing, the Chairman still insisted that he be the ultimate judge of how the Vietnamese should fight their war. Meeting with North Vietnamese premier Pham Van Dong and General Vo Nguyen Giap in 1967, Mao told them that "fighting a war of attrition is like having meals: [it is best] not to have too big a bite. In fighting the US troops, you can have a bite the size of a platoon, a company, or a battalion. With regard to troops of the puppet regime, you can have a regiment-size bite. It means that fighting is similar to having meals, you should have one bite after another. After all, fighting is not too difficult an undertaking. The way of conducting it is just similar to the way you eat."[22]

Not surprisingly, the political leaders in Hanoi were left with the impression that China was willing to fight the war to the last Vietnamese. They therefore turned increasingly to the Soviet Union. And the Soviets were willing to reciprocate. They saw an opportunity to humiliate the Americans and chasten the Chinese. Soviet assistance to North Vietnam mounted dramatically in 1967, both on the military and the civilian side.[23] But at the same time Moscow advised Le Duan and his colleagues to negotiate if the opportunity arose. The Soviet aim was to ensure that the US war in Vietnam went badly, while holding out Moscow's role as a potential facilitator of talks. The North Vietnamese, understandably, made the decision to attempt to achieve substantial and sudden victories on the battlefield in order to empower them both in relation to their sponsors and vis-à-vis the South

Vietnamese and the Americans. Such gains, Le Duan thought, would be important if negotiations were to begin. But he also hoped for the collapse of the South Vietnamese regime and outright victory.

The North Vietnamese and NLF Tet offensive began in January 1968. Hanoi ordered a sweeping military assault and a general uprising in the south. Even though it never came close to meeting its maximum objectives, the offensive shook the South Vietnamese power structure and called into further doubt the efficiency of the US commitment to the regime in Saigon. Communist units attacked across the country, including in downtown areas of the capital. There they got inside the US embassy, took over the main radio station, and fought around the presidential palace. These operations, and similar "spectaculars" across South Vietnam, were de facto suicide missions, where the Communist fighters mainly were killed within a few hours. The reinforcements from larger units never arrived, and the general uprising failed to materialize. But the fighting in Saigon and other cities was shown on prime-time American television, where some news anchors were now starting to question the effectiveness of the war. CBS's Walter Cronkite, just returned from Vietnam, told his viewers that "we have been too often disappointed by the optimism of the American leaders, both in Vietnam and Washington, to have faith any longer in the silver linings they find in the darkest clouds. . . . For it seems now more certain than ever that the bloody experience of Vietnam is to end in a stalemate. . . . It is increasingly clear to this reporter that the only rational way out then will be to negotiate, not as victors, but as an honorable people who lived up to their pledge to defend democracy, and did the best they could."[24]

One thousand five hundred US soldiers died and seven thousand were wounded in the Tet offensive. Although the Communists may have lost twenty times as many, the impression that the war was unwinnable started to spread in the United States and among its allies. Since 1967 there had been large-scale demonstrations against the war all over the United States, organized by student organizations or by independent activist groups. Coming at the same time as the increased militancy of the African-American movement, many

Americans started feeling that the country had lost its direction and that chaos was threatening. To most protesters, the resistance against the war in Vietnam and racial oppression at home was one and the same. "Shoot them for what? They never called me nigger," the heavyweight boxing champion of the world, Muhammad Ali, told those who were trying to draft him.[25] Even Martin Luther King Jr., a moderate civil rights leader, declared in April 1967 that "a time comes when silence is betrayal":

> That time has come for us in relation to Vietnam. . . . We were taking the black young men who had been crippled by our society and sending them eight thousand miles away to guarantee liberties in Southeast Asia which they had not found in southwest Georgia and East Harlem. . . . I have tried to offer them my deepest compassion while maintaining my conviction that social change comes most meaningfully through nonviolent action. But they asked, and rightly so, "What about Vietnam?" They asked if our own nation wasn't using massive doses of violence to solve its problems, to bring about the changes it wanted. Their questions hit home, and I knew that I could never again raise my voice against the violence of the oppressed in the ghettos without having first spoken clearly to the greatest purveyor of violence in the world today: my own government.[26]

The war in Vietnam destroyed Lyndon Johnson's presidency and made him decide not to seek reelection in 1968. It was, in many ways, a tragedy: an Administration that had such high aspirations for a domestic transformation of the United States, and had accomplished so much, was destroyed by a foreign war that it fought out of ignorance and Cold War conventions. But there may be more consistency in Lyndon Johnson's approach to the world than he has usually been credited with. For him, as for Kennedy, domestic reform and fighting the Cold War went hand in hand. The United States could not fully succeed in one unless it succeeded in the other. The real tragedy of Vietnam in America was how it became the catalyst for failure on both scores. Johnson left his country more disoriented in terms of what could be achieved at home and feeling less secure in terms of how it could impact events abroad than it had ever been during the twentieth century.

The real tragedy of Vietnam is of course Vietnam's tragedy. As with Korea, Vietnam was torn apart by the Cold War, both through the Communist Party's brutality and failed development plans, and through American occupation and bombing. The difference with Korea was that the Vietnamese Communists had almost a monopoly on nationalist activism, and that the South Vietnamese leaders never were able to establish a credible government of their own. Could this have been different if South Vietnam had had more time to establish itself? There is no evidence for that. On the contrary, the United States spent more money and effort on Vietnam than on any other intervention during the Cold War. That it did not succeed was not because of a lack of endeavor. It was probably because Vietnam was the wrong place to intervene.

As the Vietnam War moved slowly toward real negotiations, it was clear that the American intervention there had meant a dramatic drop in support for the US role globally. It is an irony that just when much of Africa and Asia began to turn away from the Third World project and the Cubans failed to revolutionize Latin America, the United States got stuck in one of the few conflicts it could not win. Perceptually, it paid a high price for its folly. Many of America's European allies called for an unconditional end to the US bombing of North Vietnam. France's de Gaulle, with characteristic smugness after France's own disasters in Indochina, referred to the war as a Vietnamese "national resistance" against the United States, and US escalations as "illusions" that provoked China and the Soviet Union and were "condemned by a large number of the peoples of Europe, Africa, Latin America and is more and more threatening to world peace."[27]

In terms of the global Cold War, the US involvement in Indochina provided opportunities for the Soviet Union to reassert itself as the universal alternative to American domination and capitalist exploitation. From the Hungarian uprising to the Berlin Wall and the Congo crises, the Soviet Union seemed to fall behind. Challenged by US power, as well as by dissatisfaction in eastern Europe, the break with China, and the creation of the Third World, the Soviets and their system appeared to be out of tune with the way the world was turning. Vietnam gave them a chance to gain strength. That this reassertion happened less through their own gain than through the failures of others is of less relevance to the story at this point. If one thinks in bipolar terms, as many people did during the Cold War, it comes out as being more or less the same thing. America's loss was perceived as the Soviets' gain.

Even though the focus on Vietnam did not substantially divert US attention from Europe, where NATO remained strong in spite of challenges by de Gaulle and others, it arguably did prevent the Johnson Administration from fully engaging with other emerging crises. One such was the Palestinian refugee problem in the Middle East, where tension was again rising. Johnson had increased US support for Israel, which he saw as a Western-style island of stability in a chaotic region. The Israelis received more civilian assistance, as well as access to military hardware such as bombers and tanks. Johnson also deliberately turned a blind eye to the Israeli nuclear weapon program. In 1965 the president told one of his Jewish Cabinet members, Abraham Ribicoff, how much he appreciated working with the Israelis. "I had a long wire from [Israel prime minister Levi] Eshkol yesterday—a real good one—on my birthday. I have really saved him, and gone to bat with his equipment and stuff. I've done it quietly, and, I think, quite effectively."[28] The Palestinians simply did not figure in the equation.

Another omission was developments in southern Africa, where the Portuguese clung to their dilapidated empire and white supremacist regimes were developing in South Africa and Rhodesia. Southern Africa was the last great decolonization issue, and Johnson skirted it as best he could. While there is no doubt about his distaste for the South African apartheid regime—Johnson was, after all, the greatest civil rights president in US history—he felt that he needed both the South Africans and the Portuguese onboard in Cold War terms. Robert Komer put Johnson's dilemma to him succinctly: the Azores base, which the United States leased from Portugal, "makes it hard to be anti-Portuguese, while the UK's economic stake in Rhodesia and South Africa makes us reluctant to push them too hard. . . . To the extent that we can stay slightly ahead on these issues instead of being reluctantly dragged towards the inevitable, we can keep our African affairs in reasonably good repair."[29]

But events in southern Africa did not wait for the slow pace of change that the United States was trying to set out for matters of decolonization and racial equality. By 1968 liberation movements had taken up arms against the Portuguese in Angola, Mozambique, and Guinea Bissau. In South Africa the main anti-apartheid movement, the ANC, had committed itself to an armed struggle against the regime in Pretoria. Instead of showing solidarity with the oppressed, the Johnson Administration worried about Soviet and Chinese influence on the liberation movements. Like African-Americans, Africans should be grateful for what the president was trying to do for them, Johnson thought. As his presidency went down in flames over black and student unrest at home, coupled with an unwinnable war in Vietnam, Johnson lamented his fate. "I asked so little in return," he told his advisers. "Just a little thanks. Just a little appreciation. That's all. But look at what I got instead. Riots in 175 cities. Looting. Burning. Shooting. It ruined everything."[30] And as Johnson wondered why American cities burned, the Cold War looked set to take new turns abroad.

13

The Cold War and Latin America

After the Cuban revolution, no other event positioned Latin America more in terms of the Cold War than the 1973 coup in Chile. By overthrowing their elected government in the name of anti-Communism, Chilean officers brought the global conflict home to an extent that few of their compatriots had thought possible. They also brought terror and the mass violation of human rights to a country that had known few such crimes in the twentieth century. Supporters of the elected government were detained in sports arenas and assembly halls before being sent off to prison camps without any legal process. Many were tortured. "The torture took place daily," a female victim recounted. "We would be blindfolded, strapped to beds and then it would begin. There were electric shocks administered to all over our bodies, and then there would be a rape."[1] Even after a century of peace, Chileans could commit terrible atrocities against each other in the name of ideology.

BY 1973 SOUTH AMERICA was no newcomer to the Cold War. Growing out of an already established US hegemony on the continent, its roots go back to the late nineteenth century, when the United States gradually replaced Britain as the key power in the region. But the origins of the Cold War in Latin America are not all about the effects of US supremacy. They are also about class and ethnic conflict inside Latin American republics and about the growth of nationalism, populism, and the Left. On the whole, perhaps, the roots of the Latin American Cold War fed on high levels of inequality and social oppression. The region's greatest challenge has been to overcome extreme differences in levels of income and the political instability that such long-term inequities create.

What the Cold War added to this mix of dominance and resistance was the single-minded US preoccupation with Communism that became relentless from the late 1940s on. Successive US Administrations saw Latin American radicalism and Soviet-style Communism as natural allies of each other. This obsession became particularly important after the Cuban revolution, but it was visible well before then, for instance in the US intervention in Guatemala in 1954. It led the United States to ally itself with military regimes all over the continent. These regimes were the real tragedy of the Cold War in Latin America. They crippled the continent, even in those few cases when the time of their rule overlapped with economic advances. They disassociated their populations from participation in politics and from identifying with the state. They prevented the social progress that would have produced a more inclusive middle class. These regimes were not good for their countries nor for US relations with their countries. But the Cold War clouded the judgment of both Latin American elites and the US government, producing a symbiotic system of oppression that neither party benefitted from in the long run.

THE RISE OF US hegemony in Latin America was a much slower process than most people imagine. As late as 1939 the main European countries were more important than the United States for overall Latin American trade, even though US investment had increased strongly in the interwar period. In the early twentieth century, after the US invasion of Cuba in 1898, US influence spread gradually from the Caribbean, Mexico, and Central America to the countries in South America. But it was World War II that signaled the big breakthrough for US supremacy throughout the Americas. By then, not only was the US economy predominant over that of all of its Latin American partners (the Argentinian GDP per capita, which had been two-thirds that of the United States in 1900, had been reduced to half by 1950), but the war again cut the continent off from its trade with Europe, and Washington attempted to solidify its political grip in order to keep any influence by the German-led Axis Powers out of the American republics. The fully developed US hegemony in the Americas therefore coincided in time with the Cold War as an international system, and should be understood in light of it.

The special fear of postwar US administrations was of Communism seducing Latin Americans away from US-inspired models of development. According to views widely held in the United States, Latinos, like children, had to be guided onto the right path in terms of politics and economics, and North Americans had to do the guiding. If the US sense of purpose failed, then the Soviets and their allies could do what the Germans and Japanese had attempted to do during World War II: tempt the easily excitable Latin American republics in directions that would be disastrous for US economic and strategic interest and for the Latinos themselves. Just like in Europe, the ease with which US images of Nazi subversion melted into equally frightening depictions of Communist subversion is striking in US policymaking as well as in public assumptions. By 1948, both the State Department and the CIA were on the lookout for Communist influence in Latin America, but could so far, as they truthfully reported to President Harry Truman, see few signs of it.

For US Cold War presidents, Latin America was in a special zone in which US power had to reign supreme to protect basic US security and US global aims. Much as Russians in the USSR thought of the Slavic part of eastern Europe as a sphere with which they had special relations for ethnic and cultural reasons, many US leaders envisaged special relations between their own country and the countries to its south, not because of culture, but because of politics. The Latin American states were republics, just like their bigger brother to the north, and had liberated themselves from the European powers and initially shown much promise. But all of the promise of republicanism in Latin America had, in Washington's view, been squandered by the Latinos through their lethargy, caprice, and moral inadequacy. Good governance in Latin America needed a solid portion of US paternalism if it were not to be enticed away from its purpose.

But the US calling to guide Latin Americans toward their purpose was challenged by North American concepts of race and empire. From the nineteenth century on, white people in the United States had been wondering whether Latin Americans were capable of copying the US model of modernity. Could the "race" to which they belonged—a construct that Americans of north European origin placed far below themselves on the ethnic hierarchy—prevent Latin Americans from ever achieving order and prosperity, even if guided toward these standards? And furthermore: Was the US relationship with Latin America one in which normal boundaries for interstate behavior were valid? Could "republics" that in the US view had none of the founding virtues of good governance—personal autonomy, law, property rights—be regarded as equals of *the* American republic? Did the United States of America have natural borders, and—if so—where did these borders end? As late as 1864 US secretary of state William Seward had believed that "five years, ten years, twenty years hence, Mexico will be opening herself as cheerfully to American immigration as Montana and Idaho are now."[2] In the twentieth century, even if Latin Americans hoped that the United States was gradually being socialized into behaving more like a normal state in international affairs, many North Americans still questioned the validity of their neighbors' national aspirations.

As IF IN conscious response to US belittlement, the political agendas in Latin America have since the nineteenth century been dominated by nationalism. Similar to most other places, Latin American nationalisms have been intimately connected to the emergence of mass politics and have been manipulated by elites in order to strengthen their hold on power. The common themes of all of the different nationalisms south of the Rio Grande have been resistance to foreign pressure, especially that of the United States, and a belief in the national authority of military power. Especially in Spanish-speaking America, there has also been a strong sense of cultural unity, a pan–Latin

Americanism of great force, though colored by the specific national agendas and the geographical location of its activists. In the first half of the twentieth century, Latin American nationalisms became increasingly populist, often with very separate Right and Left components, as happened in Europe roughly at the same time. Just as US economic influence increased sharply, some of the internal political conflicts in Latin American countries were coming to a head.

If one believes that a substantial part of the Cold War in Latin America was domestic and ideological, then the 1920s and '30s were certainly the first Cold War era.[3] As workers organized and landless peasants protested against privilege and oppression, the Russian Revolution set an example for some. By 1929 small Communist parties had emerged in fifteen countries in the region. In some cases, such as in Brazil, Chile, Mexico, or Guatemala, they had an influence far greater than their numbers.[4]

Brazil became a focal point for class warfare in South America. There the young officers who took control of the main city São Paulo in 1924 were supported by Communist intellectuals. After being driven out of the city, the revolutionaries set out on a long march through the country, eventually ending up in Bolivia in 1927. Luís Carlos Prestes, who led the troops, later became the head of the Brazilian Communist Party and a central figure of the Comintern. But even where they gained some local support, the adherents of international Communism and the fronts they attempted to establish were usually no match for their political competitors, who often suppressed them cruelly. The main leaders of the new popular politics in Latin America emerging out of this period were not Communists but radical populists, who were as much inspired by the European radical Right as by the European Left. Vargas in Brazil, Perón in Argentina, Cárdenas in Mexico may, at times, have collaborated with Communists and other parts of the Left, but their aim was to strengthen the state and their own personal power.

But while Latin American populism increased in strength, so did US economic power in the region. During the 1920s and '30s—often seen as an isolationist era in US foreign affairs—American economic involvement in the southern republics increased steeply, much helped by new trade through the Panama Canal, which had opened in 1914. American investment increased, too, more than to any other part of the world. So did political ties, and not all of them were to the liking of the new Latin American radical nationalists. In countries as far away as Chile the North Americans tried to use their economic clout to fix prices on raw materials or intervene in elections. In Central America and the Caribbean the United States intervened militarily no fewer than thirteen times in the first three decades of the century. Under political pressure at home, at the Pan-American Conference in Havana in 1928 Mexico, Argentina, and other Latin American countries protested US interventionism. Before the conference, the Argentinian newspaper *La Prensa* wrote that US "imperialism has thrown down its mask and free people will reject it. . . . Orders by one government are [now] presented as valid for all." The United States was attempting to be the "global dispenser of justice" and the "supreme master through economic control . . . humiliating sovereignty with an arrogance unworthy of great nations."[5]

After 1933, the Franklin D. Roosevelt Administration attempted to reduce anger in the southern republics by its "good neighbor policy." In terms of relations with Latin American states quite a lot was achieved. Sensing that they had a more cooperative, or at least a more gracious, Administration in place in the White House, southern republics were more likely to go along with the isolation of enemy states in World War II. Nine Latin American states declared war on Japan and Germany right after the attack on Pearl Harbor. By the time the war ended eleven other states had joined the United States, though Argentina joined only in March 1945 and Chile the following month, after the fighting in Europe had ended.

The main US security preoccupation during the war was with Mexico. With a two-thousand-mile-long border with the United States, a large immigrant population, and with a history of opposing US foreign policy in the region, Mexico stood out as a country from where enemy agents could operate. Mexico had declared war on the Axis Powers in May 1942, but the US government remained suspicious of its southern neighbor's political orientation. And if Mexico seemed suspicious, then Argentina seemed positively alarming: having at first refused to join the Allies, Argentina was embargoed and Washington broke off diplomatic relations in 1944. The political instability in Buenos Aires also alarmed the Americans, especially after Juan Perón became vice president as the war was coming to an end. Colonel Perón represented the exact US image of a Latin American rabble-rouser. He had been involved in several military coups, was building organizations with a personal loyalty to him, and had been known to praise European Fascism and Nazism. When Perón was elected Argentinian president in 1946, he allowed escapees from Nazi Europe into Argentina, leading to another diplomatic crisis with Washington.

US policy toward Argentina under Perón set a pattern for its policies toward Latin American countries during the Cold War. As the US focus on subversion in the southern republics changed from Fascists to Communists in the late 1940s, much of the approach stayed the same. Latin Americans could not be trusted to come up with political preferences of their own, even through elections. Domestic and foreign subversives were waiting in the wings to take over the political stage, using radical populists as the warm-up act. The United States therefore had to be on its guard against any change that would allow Communists to get closer to power in any American republic. As the architect of the US containment policy, George F. Kennan, observed in 1950: "implicit in these communist activities is the possible wrecking of . . . the relationships . . . basic to Latin America's part in our global policies. . . . The danger lies less in the [Communist] conquest of mass support than in the clever infiltration of key positions, governmental and otherwise, from which to sabotage relations between these countries and the United States."[6]

The first test of the attention the United States paid to Latin America in a Cold War context came in Guatemala in 1954, when the Eisenhower Administration intervened against an elected radical reformist regime that had the support of the miniscule Guatemalan Communist Party. Led by Jacobo Árbenz, an officer from a wealthy family, the elected government attempted to introduce much needed social and land reform in what was probably the most unequal country in all of Latin America. In Guatemala 2.5 percent of the population owned more than 70 percent of the arable land, and the majority of the population was landless peasants. Since the late nineteenth century US companies, including the powerful United Fruit Company, had grown rich from production in Guatemala because of its good conditions for tropical fruit and its low wages. In 1952 President Árbenz expropriated uncultivated land—including some that belonged to US companies—against compensation that the owners found to be far too low. The Guatemalan government divided the expropriated land among one hundred thousand landless peasant families. Washington protested, but to no avail.

It was not the complaints of United Fruit executives, or the stories their PR department planted in North American newspapers, however, that made the US government decide to intervene. It was the fear of Communism. "In Guatemala," President Eisenhower told a Congressional delegation, "the Reds are in control and they are trying to spread their influence to San Salvador as a first step of the breaking out . . . to other South American countries."[7] By spring 1954 Eisenhower had given the green light to prepare the overthrow of Árbenz, and the CIA put together an operation that also involved military opponents of the Guatemalan president and parts of the civilian opposition. The United States organized the training of rebel troops, set up a propaganda radio station, and—after the Guatemalan government tried to boost its military capacity through buying arms from Czechoslovakia, a member of the Soviet bloc—declared a blockade against the country.

In June 1954 US-trained rebel troops crossed into Guatemala, with lists of Left-wingers marked for "elimination" by the CIA. US-piloted fighter planes strafed the capital. After a few weeks of fighting Árbenz resigned, mainly because he thought that was the only way to stave off a full-scale US invasion. He was replaced with a succession of military juntas that had the blessing of the United States. The military revoked most of Árbenz's social reforms. From the 1960s to the 1990s

Guatemala's inequities set off civil wars that devastated the country. The US-led overthrow of President Árbenz had created conflicts that neither the United States nor the Guatemalan Right could control. From his exile in Cuba, the former president concluded that it was US anti-Communism that had set off the intervention, not the need to protect American investments. "They would have overthrown us even if we had grown no bananas," Árbenz's close friend José Manuel Fortuny is quoted as saying.[8]

There is little doubt that Árbenz was right about what set off the US intervention. Secretary of State Dulles celebrated his overthrow as "the biggest success in the last five years against Communism."[9] But US diplomacy paid a significant price for its belligerence toward Guatemala. Even after the Czechoslovak weapons imports became known, Washington had a tough time getting even its allies in line. Uruguayan foreign minister Justino Jiménez de Aréchaga lauded "the intangible greatness of the principle of nonintervention" and chided those who indulged in "hysterical fear" or "use the phrase 'cold war' too generously."[10] Árbenz's foreign minister Guillermo Toriello "said many things some of the rest of us would like to say if we dared," one Latin American diplomat told the *New York Times*.[11] Even Winston Churchill's British government objected: "The Americans are making extraordinarily heavy weather over all this and acting in a manner which is likely to alienate world sympathy."[12] President Eisenhower, exasperated, told his staff that they were "being too damned nice to the British" and ordered the State Department to "show the British that they have no right to stick their nose into matters which concern this hemisphere entirely. . . . Let's give them a lesson."[13]

The Soviet Union had no role in the events in Guatemala; the distance was too great and its Communists regarded as too weak for Moscow to take much notice. It was the US intervention that set off a degree of Soviet interest. But even after Guatemala the general feeling in Moscow was that there was little that could be done to help Latin American revolutionaries, except through some increased support for the local Communist parties. Outside Europe, the Soviet focus was on Asia, where—following in the footsteps of the Chinese revolution—some of the great events of the future were expected to take place. Within this larger picture, Latin American Communists were left to fend for themselves. They helped organize, and sometimes had a significant impact within, the labor movements in their countries. But nowhere did they come close to holding political power or directing the general course of events.

The consolidation of the Cuban revolution changed all of that. By 1959 there was in Latin America a radical revolutionary government that operated in conjunction with local Communists. And even if the Cuban Communist Party as such had played a very limited role in the civil war—and was soon overshadowed by Fidel Castro's own revolutionary organization, with which it was to merge in 1961—Communists played a key role in the new regime from the beginning. The Soviets became Cuba's closest ally, in spite of policy differences that waxed and waned throughout the 1960s. Supported by most leading Latin American Communists, Moscow wanted a gradualist approach to revolution in other countries in the region and was skeptical of the insurrectionist guerrilla approach that the Cubans stood for. There was also the sense among South American radicals that Cuba was peripheral both geographically and historically to the main developments on the continent—it is quite clear that many Left-wingers in Argentina, Chile, or Brazil, at least to begin with, looked down their noses at the new leaders in Havana. But these conflicts and doubts were of minor importance compared to the big story: for the first time Latin America had seen a successful socialist revolution, which—with the active help of the Soviet Union—was able to defend itself against US attacks.

The Cuban revolution inspired radicals elsewhere, but not all of them were in Communist parties. In Venezuela, where free elections in 1959 had brought to power a reformist coalition headed by President Rómulo Betancourt, it was the youth wing of the president's own party that broke away and formed the Movimiento de Izquierda Revolucionaria (MIR). Accusing Betancourt of compromising with the United States, the military, and the Right, the young Marxist-Leninists in MIR—with Cuban support—launched an armed uprising against him. The Communist Party joined the revolt, but it was soon defeated by the Venezuelan military. The two parties turned to urban terrorism and guerrilla fighting in the countryside. Among their tactics were robbing banks, killing policemen, burning down government buildings, and kidnapping wealthy businessmen. Although both parties had some popular support at the outset, their tactics lost them the political game. Trade unions and peasant organizations campaigned for harsher measures against the rebels. Ninety-two percent of the voting population cast their ballots in the 1963 elections, which the insurrectionists tried to disrupt. By 1967 the extreme Left in Venezuela had been defeated and the insurrectionism often associated with the Cuban experience seemed a lost cause among most Latin Americans.

US worries about Cuba being replicated elsewhere knew no bounds, however. The Kennedy Administration was obsessed with the thought of Communist encroachment to its south. But it was also much more aware than its predecessors had been that it was poverty and social injustice that created the conditions under which radical political movements could operate successfully. In April 1961, just weeks before his Bay of Pigs attack on Cuba, the young US president launched what he called an Alliance for Progress between his country and Latin America. A ten-point program centering on development and economic assistance, while also promising to defend any country whose "independence is endangered," Kennedy's plan aimed to eradicate poverty in Latin America within ten years.

> If we are successful, if our effort is bold enough and determined enough, then the close of this decade will mark the beginning of a new era in the American experience. The living standards of every American family will be on the rise, basic education will be available to all, hunger will be a forgotten experience, the need for massive outside help will have passed, most nations will have entered a period of self-sustaining growth, and, although there will be still much to do, every American Republic will be the master of its own revolution and its own hope and progress.[14]

In spite of the president's lofty rhetoric, the aims of the Alliance for Progress were far too extensive to be realistic. Local elites feared what Kennedy's "revolution" would do to their own privileges. Radicals on the Left and the Right saw the Alliance as US imperialism by other means. The hierarchies of the Catholic church worried about moral decline and religious deviation in the wake of US Peace Corps volunteers and other North American experts. And the methods and technologies the United States sought to introduce were often unsuited for Latin American purposes. But in spite of all of this, some Alliance programs did have an impact, not least because they helped convince the emerging Latin American middle class that Cold War–inspired US policies could be to their advantage. The best of such programs—in education, health, transport, and housing—also showed a more open, less exclusive United States that was willing to work with its Latin American partners for mutual benefit.

The positive aspects of the Alliance for Progress were, however, entirely overshadowed by US willingness to support antidemocratic military regimes throughout the region. From the very beginning, military aid to resist Communism was an integral part of the Alliance plan. Under JFK's successor, Lyndon Johnson, the counterinsurgency aspect of the Alliance often came to dominate the civilian programs. Influenced by the widening war in Vietnam, LBJ was preoccupied with avoiding any Communist advances in Latin America on his watch. The president recognized the desperate social situation that drove young South Americans toward rebellion. But if the choice was between another "Castro revolution" and a right-wing dictator, then the United States should be with the latter any day, LBJ believed.

If any country in South America seemed prone to upheavals for purely social reasons it was Brazil. The country's inequality was the second-highest in the world, narrowly behind Sierra Leone.[15] A small white minority had income levels well beyond those in Europe or North America. Meanwhile the vast majority—white and black—lived in abject poverty, whether as landless laborers in the countryside or in the rapidly growing urban slums, the favelas of São Paulo or Rio de Janeiro. After years of dictatorship and military-influenced rule,

Brazil began to experiment with democracy in the 1950s. The president elected in 1956, Juscelino Kubitschek, started a number of state-led development projects, which led to strong economic growth but also to sharp rises in inflation. Kubitschek and his successor did little, however, to attack the social inequality that seemed to be at the root of so many of Brazil's problems. The Kennedy Administration, at the start of the Alliance for Progress, often commented on the need for social reform in Brazil.

When João Goulart became president in 1961, the Kennedys got more than they had bargained for. From the beginning of his presidency, President Goulart tried to get to grips with Brazil's social problems by mobilizing worker's organizations and supporting new and militant peasant groups that had grown up in rural areas during Brazil's brief democratic era. His aim was to counterbalance the many conservative forces in Brazilian politics, including some within his own party. He also wanted more political power for himself—Goulart was an impatient man, who had much to be impatient about. In foreign policy the Brazilian president wanted more independence from the United States, but was wary of both Cuba and the Soviet Union. Goulart was from a very wealthy landowning family in the south; he wanted reform but not revolution, and he kept the Communist Party under strict political control. His program, however—which included land reform and nationalization of utility companies—met increasing resistance from the Right. In a massive anti-Goulart demonstration in March 1964, organized by members of the Catholic clergy, a proclamation was read out: "This nation which God gave us . . . faces extreme danger. . . . Men of limitless ambition . . . have infiltrated our nation . . . with servants of totalitarianism, foreign to us and all consuming. . . . Mother of God preserve us from the fate and suffering of the martyred women of Cuba, Poland, Hungary and other enslaved Nations!"[16]

The Johnson Administration encouraged and supported a military coup against Goulart that month, as demonstrations and counter-demonstrations came to a head in cities all over Brazil. "I think we ought to take every step that we can, be prepared to do everything that we need to do" in order to support the coup-makers, President Johnson ordered. "We just can't take this one."[17] The fearmongering against Goulart that the United States had supported for several months helped ensure the rapid success of the coup. The downturn in the economy over the last eighteen months of his presidency also helped the military leaders depose him. The military dictatorship that inaugurated itself in 1964 was to last for twenty years, in which Brazil's most basic problems were shunted aside and the internal Cold War was stepped up.

If the United States played a central role in keeping the Brazilian dictatorship in power, it had an even more important position in Bolivia. One of the poorest countries in Latin America, Bolivia was ruled by General René Barrientos, who first came to power in a coup in 1964 and was elected president two years later. Barrientos was the Americans' kind of general, a young, energetic modernizer with real support in the population, who wanted to stress technology and land reform in an attempt to remake his country. US advisers flocked to Bolivia. But politically the Bolivian president kept his own counsel. Barrientos was a populist who presented himself as a staunch Christian while fathering dozens of children in extramarital relationships; a Quechua-speaking friend of the Indians who massacred peasants and miners when they objected to his rule; and a US-trained air force pilot and modernizer who easily engaged in anti-US rhetoric when politically expedient. By 1967 he was at the peak of his power—flying around the country in a helicopter he piloted himself, handing out footballs and radios, and shaking people's hands.

This was the political situation in Bolivia when the Cubans decided to make the country a test case for their doctrine of insurgency. The operation was spearheaded by Che Guevara, who had become increasingly restless in Cuba. Che thought of himself as an international revolutionary, linked both to pan–Latin Americanism and Communist internationalism. By 1966 Che and Cuban intelligence had begun to prepare support for an armed rebellion in Bolivia. Che rather abruptly—and against the advice of the Bolivian Communist Party—decided to lead the insurgency himself. He was smuggled into the Bolivian countryside in October 1966. From there a number of agents had been preparing the situation for months. Che's guerrillas scored some early victories against Bolivian military regulars and the insurgency gained the support of some militant miners, thanks to the Bolivian Communist Party's decision to throw its weight behind the Cuban operation. But otherwise everything went wrong for the guerrillas from the very beginning. Soon they were isolated in a couple of rural areas, not able to recruit from among Bolivian peasants, and cut off from contact with Havana.

For Barrientos the contest with the Cubans was a campaign he relished. Believing that he personified the Bolivian "revolution," as he called his program, he was doing battle against foreigners and invaders. He also liked the fact that as long as the Communist insurgency was under way, he had extra claims on US military and economic support. "The Fatherland is in danger," Barrientos proclaimed. "A vast Communist conspiracy, planned and funded by international extremism has exploited the good faith of some sectors of labor in trying to pit the people against the armed forces."[18] In October 1967—starving and almost out of ammunition—Che Guevara was captured by Barrientos's special forces and summarily executed. He told his interrogators, who included agents of the CIA, that his defeat was due to "the effective organization of Barrientos's political party . . . who took charge of warning the army about our movements."[19] Che Guevara lived on as a revolutionary icon, though his political defeat in Bolivia was another massive setback for those who believed in vanguard insurgencies as the path to Latin American socialist revolutions. It was also a signal that populist nationalism was a real match for Communism all over the continent. René Barrientos did not live long to savor his victory, though. His helicopter crashed in the mountains of central Bolivia in 1969, killing all onboard.

Che Guevara's death symbolized the final collapse of the *foco* approach to revolution—the belief that a small group of armed revolutionaries by themselves could provide a focus, *foco*, for discontent and lead an insurrection. But people drew different lessons from that collapse. In Chile, for instance, Socialists and Communists stressed that only a peaceful road to a socialist society would be possible. The United States government believed that Che's defeat meant that its policy of arming and supporting strong local leaders was working. It was nationalist anti-Communists who would defeat the Left, not US interventions. This conclusion fitted an intervention-weary Vietnam War generation of US leaders well. It also went with what some Americans thought were the general lessons of the mid-1960s, from Ghana to Indonesia, where local armies had overthrown their Leftist governments with US encouragement but little direct US support. Meanwhile, a successful direct US intervention in the small Dominican Republic in 1965 had been justified by anti-Communist rhetoric, but could as well be seen as one in a series of such invasions in the Caribbean going back to well before the Cold War. It was not an operation that could be replicated on the South American mainland, Washington believed.

Small groups on the radical Left drew different lessons from Guevara's defeat. They formed new clandestine organizations that aimed at destroying the existing order through armed combat, but now often in the cities, not in the countryside. In Guevara's homeland Argentina a number of youth movements challenged the government and some of them began using urban guerrilla methods. They came from a wide array of ideological backgrounds. Some were Trotskyist or Marxist-Leninist. Others were inspired by nationalism or by radical Catholicism. The largest movement, the Montoneros, were Peronists whose leaders had often emerged from the nationalist Right, but who by the late 1960s had begun taking up Left-wing revolutionary phrases in the quest for the return of their hero from his exile in Spain. Their leader, Mario Firmenich, liked the slogan *La patria socialista, sin Yanquis ni Marxistas* (A socialist nation without Yankees or Marxists).[20] Between them, these groups and the military's increasingly violent repression subjected Argentina to a time of terror.

At first the Montoneros gained some public support for their spectacular kidnapping and execution of Argentina's former military dictator Pedro Aramburu in 1970. He was widely hated as the man who had overthrown Perón in 1955. But as the urban guerrillas began a series of murders, kidnappings, bomb attacks, and bank robberies, their support evaporated. Still, they were able to recruit enough supporters to carry out a steady stream of terror, close to one attack per day in the early 1970s.[21] Nobody was safe. The Leftist guerrillas assassinated military officers, industrialists, trade unionists, priests, and foreign diplomats, almost seven hundred in total between 1969 and 1975. The terror did not abate after Perón *did* return as president in 1973. By 1975 Argentina seemed ungovernable, as did neighboring Uruguay, where the Tupamaros guerrilla group carried out similar attacks.

The first part of the Cold War conflict in Latin America was to come to a head, though, in Chile, on the other side of the Andes mountains. The country had a strong working class, parts of which had been organized in trade unions since the early interwar years. The political parties of the Left, Socialists and Communists, also commanded a substantial following. In the 1964 elections the candidate of their coalition, Salvador Allende, pulled more than 38 percent of the vote. He lost against the candidate of the Christian Democrats, Eduardo Frei, whose campaign was heavily backed by the CIA. But while the Johnson Administration was very afraid of the consequences if the Left won the election, the Christian Democrat Frei was no automatic supporter of American interests. As president he began many important domestic reforms that Allende could build on when he—in a sharply contested election—won the presidency in 1970, in spite of the CIA's attempts to stop him.

The new government was an alliance of Socialists and Communists dedicated to overcoming capitalism in Chile. While drawing inspiration from the Russian revolution, it intended to carry out a peaceful transition to a socialist state, through "the principle of legality, the development of institutions, political freedom, the prevention of violence, and the socialization of the means of production," as Allende noted in his first presidential address to Congress.[22] But Chile was a very conservative society, in which the old bourgeoisie and the new middle class had no intention of allowing a transition to socialism, peaceful or not. The reforms of Allende's government were met with growing protest, with the Chilean people split down the middle. Working-class and peasants' organizations supported Allende policies of nationalization and land reform, but all political groups outside the Left, including the Christian Democrats, opposed them. The government, the opposition claimed, "has sought to conquer absolute power with the obvious purpose of subjecting all citizens to the strictest political and economic control by the state and, in this manner, fulfilling the goal of establishing a totalitarian system."[23]

In Washington Allende's victory in the 1970 elections set off near panic. President Nixon thought Chile would develop into a second Cuba, with enormous consequences for Latin America and for the Cold War in the rest of the world. Détente with Moscow did not diminish this perspective. On the contrary, both Nixon and Kissinger believed that if Allende was able to succeed in Chile, then the Soviets would be less likely to cooperate with the United States elsewhere. With Allende's victory in a democratic election, the Soviets had a "Red sandwich" between Havana and Santiago, which could engulf all of Latin America, Nixon asserted later. Kissinger was, if anything, even more alarmist. The manner in which Allende had won his mandate made him even more dangerous than Castro, the US national security adviser claimed. Chile presented an "insidious" model that other Communists on the continent—or for that matter in western Europe—could follow later, Kissinger said.[24]

By 1973 it was clear that Chile's future would be decided by whether its armed forces would remain loyal to the constitution. The Chilean Right and the United States pushed for a military coup. Washington had set off considerable amounts of money through the CIA to create the conditions for a military takeover and had been doing its best to sabotage the Chilean economy, to "make the economy scream," as Nixon put it to CIA director Richard Helms.[25] Both the Soviets and the Cubans were dubious of the Allende government's chances of survival, and the Cubans advised it to arm the population against the threat of a coup. On its side, Brazil—the most powerful Right-wing military regime in South America—was supplying intelligence to a small group of dissident officers in Santiago, who were beginning to plan the removal of Allende by force. The CIA knew that coup-plotting was going on, but did not directly participate in it. The Agency only learned the date of the planned takeover a day before the plotters struck.

The Allende government was overthrown in a military coup on 11 September 1973 (a reason why the significance of 9/11 in Latin America and the United States differs). The main reason why the plotters succeeded was that they had won the support of General Augusto Pinochet, who had just been appointed Allende's commander in chief of the army. Pinochet betrayed his president with ease as soon as he became convinced that the coup stood a chance of succeeding. The general was convinced that Chile faced an existential battle against foreign Communists and internal subversives and made certain that maximum force was used against the government. President Allende killed himself when soldiers stormed the presidential palace. In Washington, the Nixon Administration drew a sigh of relief, and offered to assist the new regime.

Pinochet's dictatorship in Chile lasted seventeen years. In a country with a broad democratic tradition, its longevity and its brutality was a shock to most people, including some of those who had supported the coup. More than three thousand people were killed without any semblance of law or process. More than forty thousand were arrested, most in the three months following the coup, and many of them were tortured by the military.[26] "They stuck us in a room and forced us to remain standing, with our hands on our necks and without talking," one prisoner recounts. "Anyone who moved or talked was thrown on the floor and beaten with rifle butts and kicked. . . . [Among the prisoners] was a professor of literature at the University of Chile. There was also a Catholic priest, and another, a man named Juan, well known in the workers' districts of Valparaiso, who later died during a torture session. . . . There were unbelievable howls of pain, and they never stopped, day or night."[27]

By the late 1970s much of Latin America was ruled by military dictators. In Uruguay the military had also taken over in 1973. In Argentina they overthrew Juan Perón's widow, Isabel, in 1976, and established a military dictatorship under the drab but murderous general Jorge Videla. In all, fifteen out of twenty-one major states in Latin America were led by military dictators by the end of the decade. Most of them used their power to attack the Left. In Argentina almost ten thousand people were murdered by the junta in their "dirty war" between 1976 and 1983. The vast majority of them had nothing to do with the guerrillas who had terrorized the country; most were labor organizers, journalists, student leaders, or human rights activists. The same pattern was repeated by military dictators from Uruguay to Guatemala. Their violence was much more deadly than that of the Left-wing groups who had challenged the existing order. And it could be carried out because the military dictators knew that the United States would not break its ties with them in spite of their human rights abuses. Even a group of people as seriously lacking in talent as the Argentinian junta knew how to frame their terror in Cold War terms. General Orlando Agosti, who commanded the Argentinian air force, believed that he and his fellow officers had won a war "within the national territory but the aggressor is only a tentacle of a monster whose head and whose body are beyond the reach of our swords. . . . The armed combat is finished but the global confrontation continues."[28]

Brazil's military dictatorship, dating from 1964, followed a different trajectory. Its terror against the Left was widespread at first, with hundreds murdered and thousands imprisoned and sometimes tortured. Small Leftist groups responded by terror attacks, including the kidnapping of US, European, and Japanese diplomats. But during the early 1970s, with the war on the Left already won and détente reigning internationally, the Brazilian government began a more independent foreign policy and a more state-centered plan for economic development. Led by João Reis Velloso, the minister of planning, the country implemented import-substitution and national-development plans. Brazil was by far the biggest country in Latin America. The Brazilian generals were nationalists who wanted to strengthen the state and improve the country's international position. They were inspired by other Third World governments, of very different ideological persuasions, who saw state-planning, national control of resources, and a more fair economic world order as central to their countries' progress. To the great irritation of the United States, Brazil not only supported Third World demands at the UN, but under President Ernesto Geisel—a conservative anti-Communist of Prussian origin—it recognized the Marxist government in Angola, which the United States was trying to overthrow. Brazil wanted to be seen as a world power, even outside the Portuguese-speaking world. The United States responded by not renewing its military cooperation agreement with the country in 1977.

Outside of Cuba, the Soviet Union was more of an active bystander than a main participant in the Cold War in Latin America. It subvented the Communist parties and their fronts and alliances (including Allende's Unidad Popular in Chile) with money and with advice (sometimes welcome, sometimes not). It kept agents of the KGB and the GRU in the field in even the smallest of Latin American countries. Their task was more to report to Moscow than to influence local events, however. "The main thing," KGB chairman Iurii Andropov advised his Latin American operatives, "is to keep our finger on the pulse of events, and obtain multi-faceted and objective information about the situation there, and about the correlation of forces."[29] The Soviets were ready to attempt to steer the course of events and to grab opportunities whenever they arose. But in reality distance, priorities, and the relative balance of power made Moscow a restricted influence in Latin America during the Cold War.

But if the Soviet Union played a limited role in Latin America, so, in a different sense, did the United States. North American power was of course far superior to that of the Soviets, and in the Caribbean and Central America US military intervention was always a possibility. Elsewhere on the continent US economic influence was central, and Washington repeatedly attempted to use the extending or withholding of credit, investment, or trade as a political tool. It also on occasion tried to manipulate the prices of raw materials on which Latin American economies depended to gain political advantage. It trained Latin American officers and supplied their armies with weapons. The

CIA bribed politicians and officials and spent money to subvent the political campaigns of US favorites. But none of this enabled the United States to set the agenda in any major Latin American country on its own. Latin American nationalism—including that of the Right—precluded such a total predominance. Unlike the Soviet presence in Eastern Europe—with which it is often compared—the United States did not have subservient ideological allies in power in Latin America. A Betancourt, a Barrientos, or even otherwise despicable creatures such as a Videla or a Pinochet, were not straw men for the United States. They were nationalist Latin Americans, who opposed the Left for reasons that were altogether their own.

Mexico, with its long border with the United States, is perhaps the best case in point. Ruled since 1929 by the PRI, the Institutional Revolutionary Party, post–World War II Mexico was a jumble of capitalism and corporatism, centered on political compromises between the Right and the Left within the ruling party. But at the same time, Mexican elites became increasingly concerned with the threat of a challenge by the Left outside of the political system. In spite of its corruption and authoritarianism, the PRI took pride in having created a strong state, substantial economic progress, and defenses against US political and financial pressure. Its failure to create more social equality or more inclusive politics were its Achilles heel. When movements of students and workers began protesting in the late 1960s, the regime reacted with repression of dissent. The army was used against protesters, killing hundreds. In one of the main housing projects in Mexico City, Tlatelolco, scores were shot in a massacre on 2 October 1968. President Gustavo Díaz Ordaz's press secretary claimed that the "disturbances" were caused by "international Communist agitators . . . under the influence of foreign interests that the whole world should know."[30] With US assistance, the PRI organized anti-Communist militias, who acted against "Cuban infiltration" of Mexico. At one demonstration in 1968, they chanted "we want one, two, three dead Che's! Long live Christ the King! Long live Díaz Ordaz!"[31]

THE COLD WAR in Latin America was internal more than external. It centered on increasingly violent conflicts between the Right and the Left, parts of which became ever-more politically extreme. But Right and Left are complicated categories in Latin America. Within the Left were vicious provocateurs of the Montoneros kind and principled reformists such as Salvador Allende. The split between these two directions became increasingly deep in the latter stages of the Cold War. But the Right was deeply split as well. Some fought simply to keep their massive share of money and resources. Others were deeply ideologically committed to concepts of religion and nation. And some—especially in the small middle class in the Southern Cone—saw the United States as a direct inspiration in terms of politics and the organization of society.

As in so much else, the 1970s became a watershed for these political tendencies in Latin America. The advent of the military dictatorships did not mean "national unity," as they often proclaimed, but further fragmentation. Within the Left, there was an increasing split between those who believed in the democratic road and those who swore by revolutionary violence. Sometimes these differences were dictated by different histories or national backgrounds: it was a lot easier to believe in a peaceful return to democracy, say, in Uruguay, with its generations of parliamentary rule, than in Nicaragua, in spite of the ugliness of Montevideo's military rulers.

But often the splits on the Left were a matter of politics or ideology; those inspired by Cuba or by Che Guevara, or by liberation struggles in Africa or Asia, frequently opted for armed resistance. Those who organized in trade unions or within the church and those who belonged to the old Communist parties mostly preferred peaceful activities. Mario Firmenich, who had graduated top of his class at university in Buenos Aires, admired Che Guevara (and Juan Perón), and became the leader of the Montoneros guerrilla group. Luiz da Silva, known as Lula, who had no education, became head of the Steelworkers' Union in the Brazilian auto-manufacturing town of São Bernardo do Campo, and admired Gandhi and Dom Helder Camara, the radical archbishop of Recife. Lula became the first Left-wing president of Brazil. Firmenich became an economics lecturer in Spain.[32]

But if the Left was split, so was the Right. The brutal military dictatorships that dominated Latin America in the 1970s had little in common politically, except their disgust at the Left and general references to "order" and "Christian civilization." While all of them carried out bloody repressions, they had few ideas about how to actually govern their countries—some even sought advice from intellectuals who shared much of the general thinking that had inspired the Left. So it was, for instance, that the Brazilian military dictatorship came to emphasize centralized economic planning and a somewhat Thirdworldist foreign policy in the mid-1970s.

Chile under Pinochet took a very different direction. In a leap of faith it linked its economic future to radical Right-wing US economists that even many Americans regarded as extreme. Its policies led to the impoverishment of much of the working class and helped the regime defeat labor organizations. But at a time when much of the world slowly began to move in the same neoliberal direction, the experiments carried out by the "Chicago-boys" in Chile put the country's economy in an advantageous position. To the regime's surprise, however, the new middle class it helped create turned against it politically almost from the beginning. By the mid-1980s it was not just the working class and the Left that detested Pinochet; it was also many of those who had exploited the privatization of the Chilean economy, who now regarded the dictator and his violent methods as primitive embarrassments to their country.

The United States contributed significantly to the instability, uncertainty, and violence that characterized Latin America during the era of military dictatorships. It did so because of Cold War priorities. Washington saw the defeat of the Latin American Left as a defeat for Moscow, and it was willing to support the military dictatorships that achieved this victory in spite of the violence with which their campaigns were carried out. It was also willing to ignore its own immediate economic interest in the process; the Brazilian junta developed state-owned industries, practiced import-substitution, and manipulated its currency to gain advantage against the US dollar. All of it was accepted by Washington as long as the Brazilian military was regarded as a bulwark against Communist influence in Brazil. As so often in the Cold War, the logic of the conflict defeated both self-interest and common human decency.

14

The Age of Brezhnev

My students often balk when I call the late 1960s and '70s "the age of Brezhnev." Surely, they argue, there must be more significant figures to name an era after? What about Johnson, Nixon, or Kissinger? Or, maybe even more appropriately, and certainly with more approbation, Willy Brandt, Betty Friedan, or Julius Nyerere? They would be right in substance but wrong in illustration, as students sometimes are. Nixon or Brandt—in very different ways—may have contributed more. But it was Brezhnev who symbolized the spirit of the age within the Cold War. In a time when social and economic realities changed very rapidly, the Soviet leader stood out for his unwillingness to conform to the new conditions and his stubborn defense of his country's position within the Cold War system. Cautious, reactive, formulaic, and technocratic, Brezhnev is the very model of the middle Cold War, a time when leaders tried to impose order on uncertainty.

Leonid Illich Brezhnev was born to Russian working-class parents in 1906 in a hardscrabble town in eastern Ukraine. He was old enough to remember life before the revolution, but only vaguely; his whole life had been spent in the Soviet Union. As the first in his family he went to college, graduating as an engineer. He joined the Communist youth league at seventeen and the Communist Party at twenty-three, in 1929. Brezhnev passed through the Stalin purges unscathed—by sheer luck, he admitted later—though several of his friends were arrested. During the war he served as a political officer first in the

Caucasus and then on the Ukrainian front. By the time Germany capitulated, Brezhnev, not yet forty years old, had been promoted ma-
jor-general, after the Eighteenth Army, which he served with, had
fought all the way to western Czechoslovakia.

World War II was the decisive experience for Leonid Brezhnev, as
it was for all of his Soviet generation. It taught him about the need for
organization, discipline, and ruthlessness. It also taught him about the
horrors of war. There is no doubt that Brezhnev, even though he rarely
saw combat close up, carried the images of devastation with him for
the rest of his life, and they made him fear war. "I do not want to inflict that on my people again," he told US president Gerald Ford in
1974.[1] In war, Brezhnev said, "everyone loses."[2] But, while fearing the
ravages armed combat could bring, he also believed in the global mission of Communism and the need to defend Soviet achievements, including the control of eastern Europe. "When forces that are hostile to
socialism try to turn the development of some socialist country towards capitalism, it becomes not only a problem of the country concerned, but a common problem and concern of all socialist countries,"
he told the Poles in his usual clunky terms.[3]

Brezhnev became a member of the top Soviet leadership in 1956,
responsible for the defense industry. In 1960 Khrushchev, whose
protégé Brezhnev had been back in Ukraine, made him chairman of
the Presidium of the Supreme Soviet, meaning titular head of state. It
was a safe choice, Khrushchev thought, because of Brezhnev's low-key
style and proven loyalty. But as dissatisfaction with Khrushchev as
party chief mounted, more and more leaders saw Brezhnev as a possible successor. In October 1964 the majority of the Soviet leadership
rebelled against Khrushchev in what amounted to a palace coup. This
time the first secretary had no stomach for putting up a fight. "I thank
you for the opportunity you have given me to retire," he told his colleagues. "I ask you to write me a suitable statement, and I'll sign it."[4]
Brezhnev was made the new general secretary of the Communist
Party. Khrushchev retired to his dacha outside of Moscow.

It was the first peaceful change of power ever in the Soviet Union,
and one with enormous implications for the future, not just because

of how it happened, but also because of the meaning that the co-conspirators put into it. The main charges against Khrushchev had been that he was uncollegial and rash, that he disparaged other leaders and acted on his own. The mercurial, ever-present, high-handed Khrushchev was simply too much for them. They wanted a more collectivist leadership, with the party organization as the key institution. The accusations against Khrushchev had referred to domestic mistakes, but in the materials prepared there were also references to foreign affairs. In 1961 Khrushchev, it stated, had given "an ultimatum: either Berlin will be a free city by such and such a date, or even war will not stop us. We do not know what he was counting on, for we do not have such fools as think it necessary to fight for a 'free city of Berlin.'" Khrushchev, it continued, "wanted to frighten the Americans; however, they did not take fright, and we had to retreat, to suffer a palpable blow to the authority and prestige of the country, our policy, and our armed forces."[5]

Brezhnev and his colleagues' mandate was therefore quite clear. Those who had helped put them in power wanted more emphasis on planning, productivity growth, and welfare. They wanted a leadership that avoided unnecessary crises with the West, but also stood up for Soviet gains and those of Communism globally. Brezhnev was the ideal man for the purpose. As a leader, he liked to consult with others, even if only to bring them onboard with decisions already taken. After the menacing Stalin and the volatile Khrushchev, Brezhnev was likeable and "comradely"; he remembered colleagues' birthdays and the names of their wives and children. His favorite phrases were "normal development" and "according to plan." And the new leader was easily forgiven a certain vagueness in terms of overall reform plans as long as he emphasized stability and year-on-year growth in the Soviet economy.

Contrary to what is often believed, the Soviet economy was not a disaster zone during the long reign of Leonid Brezhnev and the leadership cohort who came into power with him. The evidence points to slow and limited but continuous growth, within the framework provided by the planned economy system. The best estimates that we have is that the Soviet economy as a whole grew on average 2.5 to 3 percent per year during the 1960s and '70s. This is lower than both the United States and western Europe during the same period, and considerably lower than the east Asian economies, but enough to keep the economy afloat and provide limited real growth in at least some sectors. In addition, the Soviet planned economy provided an even (though slowing) expansion, unlike the capitalist economies where unevenness year on year is part of the game.

But the Soviet system also had some intrinsic defects built into it. Inaccuracies in centralized resource allocation led to high levels of waste in production. And the economy was plagued by persistently low levels of productivity, which became more visible as the economy grew and capital became more abundant relative to labor. By the 1970s the diminishing returns of the planned economy had become obvious, even though Soviet leaders hoped that selective reform could reinvigorate it. In reality, though, the slowing growth rate was hard to reverse. The very high growth in the early years of the Soviet Union had probably stemmed from the exploitation of abundant resources and simple catching up with a lag created by years of war and dislocation. With the Soviet economy isolated from world markets of technology, education, capital, and investment, further growth was extremely hard to produce. This relative stagnation was an obvious challenge, especially for a country that claimed to represent the future of the world.

The direction of the output of the Soviet economy was almost entirely decided by political priorities. Like their predecessors, the Brezhnev leadership prioritized heavy industry and military hardware over consumer needs, even if they claimed to have other priorities. Therefore, though the economy as a whole expanded, consumer goods and certain types of food could at times be hard to find in the stores. "A woman walks into a food store," goes a favorite joke. "Do you have any meat?" "No, we don't." "What about milk?" "We only deal with meat. The store where they have no milk is across the street."

In the 1960s people hoped for better. The new Soviet premier, Aleksei Kosygin, in 1965 attempted reforms that could rationalize allocations, increase factory control over work methods and surplus, and reward those who worked hard. But even Kosygin's careful reforms never got full support from his colleagues. Soviet central planners were unwilling to change their habits. Some felt that such innovation could threaten their positions. Others were worried that rationalization and incentives would get in the way of ideological purity. The result was a planning system that did not stand the test of an increasingly complex economy. And when some bosses fell back on Stalinist methods of coercion, that, too, did not work. In Novocherkassk in 1962 workers had rebelled with the slogan "Milk, Meat, and Higher Wages." They had occupied party and police headquarters. At least thirty people had been shot as the KGB reestablished order. Soviet authorities did not want to see Novocherkassk repeated elsewhere in the country, and therefore were wary of demanding too much from the working class they professed to represent.

While the structural problems of the Soviet economy were clearly visible at the end of the 1960s, the overall living conditions for its citizens and its military strength both seemed to be improving. Compared to how they had lived a decade earlier, and not least compared with the war and with Stalin's terror, the common Soviet citizen lived a life of security and plenty under Brezhnev, in spite of the shortages. More expensive consumer goods—cars, fridges, television sets—while still in short supply, were sometimes available. Most people earned what they considered an acceptable salary and lived in decent apartments (again compared with the past). The state supplied free education, health care, housing, and even vacations. Most families had access to free day care and after-school programs. There was full employment, free and generous disability insurance, and early retirement age on full state pensions (55 for women and 60 for men). "It felt very stable and secure," said a friend of mine who grew up in Kiev in the 1960s. "We had most of what we needed. Nobody starved. And we always expected next year to be better than this year."

By the 1970s socialism had become the new normal in the Soviet Union and there were few outward signs of opposition. Like in Europe and North America, youth chafed under the conformity imposed on them by the government. But the astonishing lack of democracy or due process of law in a country that set itself up as the envy of the world did not seem to trouble too many Soviets. Although propaganda was everywhere, the Brezhnev regime was selective in its use of repression. Jews were sometimes singled out for persecution, in part because of engrained anti-Semitism and in part because of (mainly fictitious) links with Israel, which by now had become an enemy of the USSR. Political dissidents were imprisoned or otherwise punished, as were suspected nationalists or religious activists in the non-Russian republics. But overall the Soviet Union of the Brezhnev era seemed a country of remarkable, though somewhat deadening, calm, especially compared with the Russian past.

Eastern Europe under Soviet rule also seemed to have entered a new normality, even though it was not one that most of its people wanted. Soviet and Communist control were still seen as impositions by the majority. But people everywhere had learned to compromise with the regimes and make the best out of their situation. In this they were helped by modest but significant economic growth. Living standards were rising everywhere. Even if the eastern European economies suffered the same shortages of consumer goods as the Soviets did, they still, overall, had a higher standard of living than further east. This was especially true for the most advanced Soviet bloc countries, East Germany and Czechoslovakia, where average monthly salaries for technicians and skilled workers were substantially higher than in the USSR. Even in Poland engineers earned on average 15 percent more than their Soviet counterparts in 1964.[6] Still, people hoped for better, both in national and economic terms. Underground leaflets and proscribed books proliferated, in spite of the regimes' attempts to stop them and punish the distributors. Many eastern Europeans still resented their lot, but they did so within a world that had become more predictable and comfortable than before.

Even so, social and economic progress in eastern Europe paled in comparison with what was happening in the West. Since the 1940s western Europe and other countries in the capitalist zone (including Greece and Turkey) had gone through a profound transformation.

From being for the most part agricultural, localized, and oriented toward their own traditions and cultures, all of them by the 1960s were increasingly urban, industrial, mobile, and literate. This had happened on the back of strong economic growth, with the West German economy expanding 5.5 percent per year on average in the 1960s, the French 7 percent, and the Italian an astonishing 8 percent. For many countries the 1960s was the most intense growth period of all, part of what in France was called *Les Trente Glorieuses*, the glorious thirty postwar years of economic boom.

In the core countries of the western European economy, economic growth led to full employment and better conditions for workers, at least in terms of buying power. The regions at the periphery also benefitted, but on different terms: their benefit was as much in the export of labor as in local industrialization. Turkey, Greece, Yugoslavia, southern Italy, and all of Iberia sent workers to help build the western European miracle. Around 1970, money sent back by workers abroad constituted more than 50 percent of export earnings in Greece, Yugoslavia, and Portugal, and more than 90 percent in Turkey. It was Cold War alliances that made such migrations possible; Soviet-controlled eastern Europe saw nothing of the kind.

With full employment came a significant role for the trade unions, but in most cases (Britain being a partial exception) it was a less militant role than that of the interwar period. Negotiating from positions of strength, and with overall living standards for their members on the rise, most unions were happy to be integrated into mechanisms of collective bargaining within the capitalist system, rather than challenge that system from the outside. In this transformation they were much helped by the social welfare states that European political elites were building. Much of the impetus for the makeover in the role of the state came from the experience of wars and depression. But it also signaled that significant parts of the European Left and Right were willing to stand by their postwar dedication to new forms of social security networks as the economies began to grow. Indeed, it was the economic resurgence of western Europe that made the building of advanced welfare states possible. By 1970 all western European countries had developed systems of social security for the sick and elderly; they had free education up to college level, a guaranteed retirement age with benefits, and free or strongly subsidized health care.

The western European welfare state of the 1960s was only possible because of the combination of demographic growth, US consent, and fears over the ghosts of the past. Also, it demanded strong political leadership and an exchange of technology, products, and ideas across borders. Throughout western Europe, Social Democrats and Christian Democrats supplied the leadership necessary for creating a high degree of consensus around basic welfare provisions, while also preparing to fight the Cold War. And US leaders, as fearful of Europe's past as western European leaders themselves, put no obstacles in place for the expansion of the European state or for the expansion of European integration that seemed to go with it, even though such measures in the past had been foreign to American thinking. On the contrary, by the mid-1960s many of President Johnson's own US welfare programs seemed modeled on European prototypes.

In the 1960s, the only political challenge to the new form of capitalism that was being created in western Europe came from the French and Italian Communist parties. The other possible opposition, the Spanish and Portuguese Right-wing dictatorships, had long since capitulated to consumerism and welfare arrangements—it is very hard to be a Fascist if you have a complicated and negotiated social security system to look after. The French Communists were easily outmaneuvered by Charles de Gaulle, who assumed both the nationalist and the collectivist mantle. Only in Italy did the Communists present an electoral challenge. In 1972 they got 27 percent of the vote. And their key leader from the late 1960s, the young Sardinian aristocrat Enrico Berlinguer, was easily the most popular politician in the country.

But, while its working class popularity remained, the Italian Communist Party (PCI) was being refashioned from within. A new group of leaders, symbolized by Berlinguer, believed that Italy had to find its own way to socialism, and—increasingly—that the Soviet Union was a hindrance rather than a help in that process. The 1966 party program emphasized electoral politics, gradual reform, and the alliance of Communists, socialists, and "progressive" Catholics. While continuing to communicate closely with Moscow, and receiving much financial support from the Soviet Union, it was clear that the PCI wanted to set its own priorities, including in foreign policy, where Berlinguer began to downplay the party's opposition to Italy's NATO membership.

The Italian Communist position had much influence on political views among Communists elsewhere in Europe, west and east. The Spanish Communists in exile began thinking about a peaceful transition from the Franco dictatorship to pluralist democracy. The French party, still influential in the international Communist movement, defended the Italian position when it was attacked by Moscow, even though many French Communist leaders felt that Berlinguer was going too far in his criticism of Communist traditions. Still, it was clear by the late 1960s that at least some western European Communist parties thought they now had more in common with each other than any of them had with the Soviet Union, giving rise to the sobriquet "Eurocommunism" (a term the Italian, French, and Spanish Communists never gave a concrete definition, but which they were fond of brandishing when it suited their domestic purposes).

Some eastern European Communists were also starting to query what the future would hold for their parties. In Czechoslovakia, which had a strong domestic Communist tradition that went back much further than the 1948 coup, younger party leaders wanted to develop a Communist state that was more in line with popular priorities than had been the case before. To begin with, they had the support of the Brezhnev leadership in Moscow, which regarded the Czechoslovak Communist leader, Antonín Novotný, as somewhat old hat. The new party head whom the reformists put in place in January 1968 with Brezhnev's blessing, the Slovak Communist Alexander Dubček, at first tried to manage expectations, concentrating on economic reform along the lines of what had been proposed by Kosygin in the Soviet Union. But very soon he came under pressure to allow a more open political system and more freedom of expression. And, to everyone's surprise, including Dubček's own, the party majority seemed to agree with these demands.

In April 1968 Dubček launched what he called the party's "action program." Confirming the "leading role" of the Communist Party in state and society, the Czechoslovak Communists said that their country had to find its own way to advanced socialism:

> Democracy must provide more room for the activity of every individual, every collective, every link in the management, both at the lower and higher levels, and at the center too. People must have the opportunity to think for themselves and to express their opinions. We must radically change the practices that turned the people's initiative and critical comments and suggestions from below into words that met with the proverbial deaf ear. We must see to it that incompetent people . . . are really replaced by those who strive for socialism, who are concerned with its fate.[7]

Dubček and his colleagues aimed for a gradual reform of the economy and the political system, and hoped that their removal of press censorship, which took place in the spring, would help to give them the time they needed. They also believed that the majority of people supported socialism, even though they wanted to see it reformed. But the groundswell of criticism of the political system that quickly emerged in the press surprised them. The Soviets were horrified, especially when some Czech and Slovak commentators argued for their country's withdrawal from the Warsaw Pact. Reluctantly, Moscow began contingency preparations for military action against the new Prague leadership.

Dubček, who had started referring to his program of reform as "socialism with a human face," was certain that he could keep the situation under control. But the Soviets, who must have been wondering if they then represented "socialism with an inhuman face," were not so sure. Together with the leaders of the other Warsaw Pact countries, who were terrified that the "Prague Spring" would spread to their territories, they worked out plans for removing Dubček by force. At a hastily called meeting on the Soviet-Czechoslovak border in late July, Brezhnev demanded that "anti-Soviet statements" in Prague and Bratislava had to be stopped. Dubček and his delegation promised that they would stop. The Czechoslovaks tried to convince the Soviets that "events in our country are not moving in a direction that would result in the destruction of the gains of the revolution, much less does one observe even the slightest departure from the socialist camp or from the foundations of socialism." Kosygin acidly commented that the Czechoslovaks seemed more preoccupied with attracting Western tourists than defending the Warsaw Pact's common border.[8] After returning to Moscow, the Soviet leadership at first decided to take no further action. Even with all the preparations in place, Brezhnev still hoped that a full-scale invasion would be unnecessary. Such an action, he argued, might be required but would entail high political costs.

By the middle of August the Soviet leaders felt trapped. They wanted to stop a congress of the Czechoslovak Communist Party, scheduled for September, from going ahead, because they feared that it would enact further liberal reforms. Brezhnev called Dubček on the phone one last time. He insisted that the Czechoslovak leader immediately ban the most outspoken newspapers and throw dissidents out of the party. Dubček asked for more time. Brezhnev interrupted him.

> **BREZHNEV:** Sasha, I can't agree with this. Over the past two to three days, the newspapers I mentioned have been doggedly continuing to occupy themselves with the publication of defamatory ravings about the Soviet Union and the other fraternal countries. My comrades on the Politburo insist that we make an urgent approach to you on this matter. . . . This is just one more sign that you're deceiving us, and I can't regard it as anything other than that, let me say to you in all honesty. If you're not even able to resolve this matter now, then it seems to me that your Presidium in general has lost all its power.

DUBČEK: I don't see any deceit in this. We're trying to carry out the obligations we undertook. But we're carrying them out as best we can in a fundamentally changing situation.

BREZHNEV: But surely you understand that this arrangement, this way of fulfilling the obligations . . . will compel us to re-evaluate the whole situation and resort to new, independent measures . . . [9]

Brezhnev and Dubček agreed to speak again. Instead, in the morning of 21 August, troops from the Soviet Union, Poland, Hungary, and Bulgaria invaded Czechoslovakia and occupied the main cities. Dubček, President Ludvik Svoboda, and other members of the government were arrested and brought to Moscow, where they were forced to sign a protocol agreeing to the stationing of Soviet troops, the closing of newspapers, and the end of the most controversial reforms. There was sporadic resistance in the cities, in which seventy Czechoslovaks were killed. Seventy thousand fled across the border to western Europe. After he had been kept in place as a figurehead long enough for the Soviets to hope that he had been compromised among the Czechoslovaks who hated the invasion, Dubček was packed off to work for the Slovak forestry service. His successor, Gustáv Husák, handpicked by the Soviets, made Czechoslovakia the most repressive regime in the Soviet bloc.

The international reaction to the Soviet invasion of Czechoslovakia showed that the world was moving in new directions in the late 1960s. Different from the aftermath of Hungary in 1956, the United States' reaction was muted, almost nonchalant. When USSR ambassador Dobrynin visited President Johnson at the White House to inform him about the invasion, LBJ—consumed by the Vietnam War—barely took note and offered the astonished ambassador a mint julep. The main reaction was from ordinary western Europeans, who turned out in large numbers to protest the invasion. Even the majority of western European Communist parties condemned the Soviet action, with the PCI publicly calling it "unjustified" and noting its "strong dissent."[10] To Brezhnev's horror, Romania, a member of the

Warsaw Pact, also dissented, with its strongman, Nicolae Ceaușescu, calling the invasion a "grave error and a serious danger to peace in Europe and the destiny of world socialism."[11]

While the Soviets struggled to keep their bloc together, US influence in western Europe remained high, though American patience was at times sorely tested there. The United States was seen as a guarantor for European security against the Soviet Union, and support for the US military presence in Europe was strong. But western Europeans, and especially young people, also sought inspiration from the United States in terms of social trends, fashion, music, dance, and film. Obviously US propaganda agencies, like the United States Information Agency (USIA), tried to strengthen such biases further. But the reality was that they did not have to, and sometimes, when they tried, their ham-fisted ways did them more harm than good. Much more important than the USIA were US commercial television programs, which by the mid-1960s had become available to most Europeans. In the 1950s, Elvis Presley and Marlon Brando had became US cult figures in Europe, not least because of their rebelliousness. And when rock music conquered the world in the 1960s, most of its reference points were American, even for artists who were profoundly anti-establishment. A Bob Dylan or Jimi Hendrix was against most things that the US government was for, but for young Europeans of the 1960s, they opened a window to an America that outsiders wanted to be part of, culturally if not politically.

Lyndon Johnson's war in Vietnam dented this image but did not destroy it. Older western Europeans, at least at first, sympathized with the US effort in Indochina, because they likened it to what the Americans had done in Europe after World War II. But younger people increasingly disagreed, especially college students, who began staging protests, in part inspired by their US peers. What was fundamentally wrong with the US war in Vietnam, many people thought, was that a rich country was beating up a poor country. But some students felt that American behavior in Indochina was part of US imperialism, which Europe had also in their opinion been at the receiving end of. The protests against the Vietnam war in Europe were therefore, at least in part, a protest against what some people felt to be an over-whelming US influence in their own countries, a form of tutelage that could only be resented.

But the protests that were spreading among young people in the West in the 1960s were not only connected to what was seen as an un-just war in Vietnam. They also came out of a sense of powerlessness and lack of real democracy in their own societies. Because of the post-war baby boom there were far more young people around and a far higher percentage of them went to college, an influx that European and American universities were not prepared to handle. Very often protests that initially took aim at archaic forms of learning and gover-nance in universities were widened to become protests against soci-ety's and the state's oppression of young people. And gradually at least some of the youthful protesters began to see links between unfulfilled dreams of equality and representation for themselves and other mar-ginalized groups: ethnic minorities (especially African-Americans in the United States) and women, above all. The capitalist world may be delivering economic growth, their argument went, but not real de-mocracy or equality. The Port Huron Statement, put out by the US organization Students for a Democratic Society (SDS), in 1962 summed their accusations up well:

> Some would have us believe that Americans feel contentment amidst prosperity—but might it not better be called a glaze above deeply felt anxieties about their role in the new world? . . . The search for truly democratic alternatives to the present, and a commitment to social experimentation with them, is a worthy and fulfilling human enter-prise, one which moves us. . . . On such a basis do we offer . . . an ef-fort in understanding and changing the conditions of humanity in the late twentieth century, an effort rooted in the ancient, still unful-filled conception of man attaining determining influence over his circumstances of life.[12]

Although all western European countries saw youth protests during the 1960s, Paris in 1968 quickly became the symbol of what students and young people could (and could not) do. There students began protesting in the spring against conditions in the universities, and gradually also against consumerism, patriarchy, and a general lack of democracy. Police brutality against the protesters drew even more people to the streets. "To be free in 1968 means to participate!" was one of the slogans. "The boss needs you, you don't need him!" "Power to the imagination!" And, the inimitable "Be realistic, demand the impossible!" By late May, millions of workers had also gone on strike, against the advice of their unions, demanding more influence in the workplace and better pay. President de Gaulle panicked and left to join the French forces stationed in Germany, whom he hoped would be loyal to him. Power seemed to be in the streets; to some it seemed a classical French revolution.

But it was not. When new elections were held in June, de Gaulle won a decisive victory. The French Communists, who had tried to join the youth movement even though they had been politically attacked by it, lost half their seats. For most Frenchmen, who had been through profound social and economic change since 1945, the protests had provided an opportunity to speak out against conditions that they found oppressive, boring, or simply puzzling. But at the polling booth they confirmed their belief in the existing order, just like many young street fighters did indirectly when they donned their Levi's jeans or threw their Coca-Cola bottles at the police.

The real loser of May 1968 may have been the Communist Party. To young people it seemed old-fashioned, timid, and increasingly out of touch. Instead, some of the May protesters in Paris, alongside with their sympathizers elsewhere, championed a New Left, in which Marxism was seen as an instrument for personal as much as social liberation. The heroes of their imagination were Leon Trotsky and Che Guevara (both safely dead by 1968) or, remarkably enough, Mao Zedong, whose Cultural Revolution they equated with their own rebellion against authorities at home. Third World symbols and ideas received an afterlife among mostly bourgeois youth in western Europe, where they were seen as representing part of a global rebellion, in which some young Europeans also craved a role. While the shrinking working class mainly remained sympathetic with the old-style Communist parties in France and Italy, or the Social Democrats in West Germany or Scandinavia, youthful rebels formed small Maoist or Trotskyist parties of their own. As long as the Cold War lasted, none of these new radical parties—the Trotskyist Lutte Ouvrière in France, for instance, or the Maoist Communist Party of the Netherlands (Marxist-Leninist) and the Norwegian Workers' Communist Party (Marxist-Leninist)—ever got much support outside of university campuses.

The one social and political campaign of the 1960s that had a lasting impact, also on the Cold War, was the women's movement. While economic growth had exploded in the West in the postwar era, the position of women within this growth was still weak: in society, in the workplace, and in the family. One of the recurrent arguments of the Communists was that the Soviet bloc had abolished discrimination against women (an argument that barely held up but was useful for propaganda purposes). By the 1960s, autonomous women's groups in western Europe and North America had begun campaigning for a greater role for women in all walks of life. Though discrimination against women at work persisted, especially in terms of equal pay, these women's movements scored some stunning successes in terms of legal rights, family planning, and sexual liberation. The American feminist Betty Friedan was among the many women who gave direction to these groups. Could it be acceptable, Friedan asked in 1963, that women in industrial societies could not combine being a homemaker with a satisfying and well-paid job to which they were qualified through their education? "As she made the beds, shopped for groceries, matched slipcover material, ate peanut butter sandwiches with her children, chauffeured Cub Scouts and Brownies, lay beside her husband at night—she was afraid to ask even of herself the silent question: 'Is this all?'"[13]

By the 1970s thousands of women leaders all over the West had made sure that it was not all. The representation of women in skilled labor and in the professions exploded. In 1980 there were 32 percent women lawyers in West Germany (as against less than 7 percent in

1960). The changes in politics were equally dramatic. In Finland there were more than 30 percent female members of the national assembly in 1985 (compared with less than 15 percent in 1965). With better political representation—across the political spectrum—came more attention to issues that were especially important for women, such as child care, contraception and abortion, and the right to divorce. By the end of the Cold War, women were still discriminated against in terms of pay and career patterns (less than 15 percent of top executives in leading US companies are female even today). But the Communist argument that only socialism could end the unfair treatment of women had been proven false.

THE ACHIEVEMENTS OF social movements in the capitalist West did not prevent many political leaders from seeing the 1960s as a decade of increasing chaos and dislocation. The autonomy that many campaigning groups sought for themselves fueled elite concerns about society becoming ungovernable. Over time this pushed in the direction of finding new ways of stabilizing the Cold War, of making it less disruptive and dangerous, at least in Europe and in the relationship between the Superpowers. None of the events of the late 1960s seemed to push in the direction of an immediate Superpower confrontation, or a conflict across the division lines in Europe. No American thought that the Soviet Union was about to intervene in their all-consuming obsession, the war in Vietnam. And the Soviet invasion of Czechoslovakia in 1968 showed that even if western Europeans protested the crimes of the USSR, they were not up to doing anything about them. The nadir of disinterest was reached by western European student radicals, many of whom in 1968 were chanting not for Dubček but for Mao Zedong.

From a western European and Superpower perspective the idea of stabilizing the Cold War through a gradual lessening of tension between the blocs made sense in the late 1960s. Such a détente could enable leaders to better handle problems in their own societies, within their alliances, and in the Third World. It would reduce the chance of nuclear war and—crucially in a time when both the Americans and the Soviets were feeling the sting of military expenditure—reduce the cost of further military buildups. There were also those, at least in the West, who thought the two ideological systems would converge over time. Industrial society seemed to pose similar challenges to East and West, the thinking went. Some of the solutions, through technology and social engineering, were also likely to be similar, and therefore the states that carried them out would come to look more like each other, even if the political context was different.

The attempts at stabilizing the Cold War through a lasting détente began in Europe in the early 1960s. France's President de Gaulle—always upset at the thought of Superpower bipolarity and seeking a greater role for France in international affairs—attempted to reach out to the East on his own. Having successfully tested France's first nuclear weapon in 1960, de Gaulle felt that France should defend its foreign policy independence, even within the NATO alliance. The French president, a conservative with a deep-seated sense of the cultural unity of Europe, believed that the United States had become too predominant in the relationship with its partners. He wanted to see a more independent western Europe, under French leadership, that could balance the American role in NATO. De Gaulle's famous *non* to British attempts at joining the increasingly integrationist European Economic Community was based on his sense of London as a Trojan horse for Washington. France was the only country that could lead a more independent western Europe, de Gaulle thought, while keeping the US security guarantee and building bridges with the East.

In 1964, the French president began a more active program for technical and cultural cooperation with eastern Europe and with the Soviet Union. His aim, he declared at a dramatic press conference on the twentieth anniversary of the Yalta conference in 1965, was to overcome "Yalta" and bring an end to the division of Europe. "The reappearance of the nation with its hands free, which we again have become, clearly changes the global game, which, since Yalta, seemed henceforth limited to two partners."[14] The French president followed up with visits to Moscow, Warsaw, and Bucharest, where he received a hero's welcome from the regimes after he abruptly withdrew France from NATO's integrated military command in 1966. Europe's future, the general declared, was not in a bipolarity dominated by the Super-powers, but in "détente, entente, and cooperation." The practical re-sults of de Gaulle's policies, however, were few and far between. And by 1968 both Moscow and Washington took some pleasure in seeing de Gaulle's grandeur humbled by the May events. When he resigned the following year, after losing a referendum on administrative re-form, those who found solace in the European status quo drew a col-lective sigh of relief.

The reason why the Americans, though annoyed, could more or less disregard de Gaulle's shenanigans was that the future of the Euro-pean component of NATO seemed secure. President Johnson knew that the last thing the French president wanted, in spite of his com-plaints about "Yalta," was a US withdrawal from Europe. Johnson's hope, especially in light of rising US military expenditure in Indo-china, was to get western Europe (and Japan) to carry more of the economic burden for their defense themselves. But LBJ did not be-lieve that the United States ought to withdraw forces from Europe. When the Democratic leader of the Senate, Mike Mansfield, put for-ward a resolution calling for substantial troop reductions in Europe, Johnson scoffed to his staff: "I'm not one of those folks that are just sucked in by the Russians. I don't believe in the . . . whole goddamned theory that it's all over there. . . . I think those sons of bitches want to eat us any day they can."[15]

Johnson did believe, however, that Germany was less of an im-mediate Cold War issue because of West Germany's safe anchoring in NATO. While de Gaulle huffed and hawed and students—not least in West Germany—protested against US imperialism, both main parties in the Federal Republic, the Christian Democrats and the Social Democrats, saw their country's continued integration with the West as crucial for Germany's future. Indeed, de Gaulle's insistence on building his "new Europe" around a French-German axis seemed to confirm West Germany's place. Western European economic integration became an instrument both for further growth and for Cold War cohesion. Increasingly, the European integration project had West Germany's spectacular industrial and commercial success as its center. By 1970 the West German economy was almost 40 percent bigger than the French, and 65 percent bigger than the British economy.

Placing the German economic dynamo at the heart of European integration made good sense, both in terms of economics and politics. The 1957 Treaty of Rome had created a European Economic Community (EEC), which committed the members—Belgium, France, Italy, Luxembourg, the Netherlands, and West Germany—to set up a common market for goods, capital, and workers. In spite of Gaullist challenges and a slow, sometimes infuriating process of negotiation, ten years later the removal of internal tariffs was complete, with a full customs union inside what then was called the European Communities. The secret of the success was twofold. One was internal: allowing West Germany the free export of its industrial goods in return for it contributing heavily to subsidies for French and Italian farmers, the so-called Common Agricultural Policy. The other was external: the sense, in all western European capitals, that Europe could only regain a strong voice within the Cold War if it was more united.

It was therefore the combination of German economic strength and the Europeanization of Gaullist principles that under Cold War conditions created the new push toward European integration. After de Gaulle's resignation in 1969, Britain was allowed to reopen negotiations to join the EEC, and it joined, after a referendum, along with Denmark, in 1973. By then it was clear that the Communities would be the future of European integration, and that the European Free Trade Association, the other European trade bloc that Britain had cultivated as a less integrationist alternative, could not deliver the connection to European markets that Britain wanted. Britain's accession also convinced the Americans that they had little to fear, except perhaps in economic terms, from further western European integration. Britain in the EEC made the common market more of a European economic wing of NATO, increasing the attractiveness of the western European model for countries farther east.

West Germany's bigger role in Europe was also on the agenda of that country's domestic politics. In the 1965 elections the head of the Social Democrats (SPD), Willy Brandt, had argued for a policy of bridge-building with eastern Europe and the Soviet Union, both to further reduce military tension in Europe and to prepare the way for negotiations on German reunification. When Brandt became foreign minister in a grand coalition of Christian Democrats and Social Democrats in 1966, he was in a position to put some of this policy into practice. Having proven his anti-Communist credentials as mayor of West Berlin, Brandt felt that he could reach out to the East without creating a political backlash among West Germans who overall prioritized further economic growth and increase in welfare provisions over too much talk about German unity. It was going to be difficult, Brandt told SPD members in 1967. It would be about small steps, not big leaps. And a new West German eastern policy, *Ostpolitik*, was dependent on "a western policy oriented towards a European peace settlement."[16]

The 1969 elections in West Germany made Willy Brandt *Bundeskanzler*, the head of government. For the first time since 1930 a Social Democrat was in power in Germany, and Brandt was determined to use the opportunity both for domestic reform and for détente with the East. His Ostpolitik had been developed gradually in conversations with his closest advisers. Egon Bahr, whom Brandt had worked with in Berlin and who became his point man in contacts with the East, had spoken of *wandel durch annäherung* (change through rapprochement). This became a good summing-up of Brandt's policy: a careful building of trust among governments in the east and west of Europe, which would enable disarmament, increased trade, travel, and cultural contacts, and, eventually, German reunification and the full removal of Europe's Cold War divides. It was less than revolutionary, as Brandt's critics Left and Right were fond of pointing out. But it was also much more than Europe could have hoped for only a few years earlier.

Brandt knew that the road to East Berlin went through Moscow. In negotiations with Brezhnev in 1970, Brandt promised increased trade and economic cooperation and a treaty with the Soviet Union in which both sides agreed that the postwar borders in Europe, including the new Polish-German border and the border between East and West Germany, were inviolable. Brezhnev was delighted. A treaty with West Germany meant reducing the fear of German revanchism, and, even more important, the prospect that at some point a neutral Germany could tip the Cold War balance in Europe toward the Soviet Union. The Soviet leader bristled at those of his advisers who feared that the anti-Communist Brandt's aims were more insidious, namely the gradual loosening of the bonds that tied eastern Europe to the USSR. Even when Brandt before the signing of the treaty handed Brezhnev a note that said "this agreement is not contrary to the policy objective of the Federal Republic of Germany, which is to work toward a condition of peace in Europe under which the German people will regain its unity through free self-determination," the general secretary did not demur.[17] It was just words, Brezhnev argued. Germany needed the Soviet Union much more than the Soviets needed Germany.

If it had not been for the new Nixon Administration itself engaging in renewed efforts at détente with the Soviets, Brandt's policy could have been seen as positively treacherous in a NATO context. As things were, the Bundeskanzler could claim that he was building on initiatives launched by France and then by the United States itself. Even so, there was substantial weariness elsewhere in Europe and in Washington over Brandt's actions. The questions were not so much about what Brandt did now as with what his ultimate aim might be. Did the German Social Democrats want to make a grand bargain with the Soviets in return for reunification? If so, the future of the NATO alliance could be at stake. But Brandt was clever enough to use his credentials as a pro-American European, a man who had fought against his own country in World War II, in order to reduce the effects of these doubts, even if they never entirely went away.

Brandt followed up his Moscow treaty with a separate treaty with Poland, later in 1970. In it, the Federal Republic of Germany (FRG) restated its acceptance of Poland's western border and promised further peaceful cooperation between the two governments. But the most important aspect of the negotiations was Brandt's December 1970 visit to Warsaw. Insisting on going to the memorial for the 1943 uprising against German occupation in the Warsaw Jewish ghetto, Brandt placed a wreath honoring the resistance fighters. He then sank to his knees in the snow and slush, and remained there, silently, in front of the TV cameras. For Poles and others who watched in eastern Europe, it was a powerful symbol of a new German government intent on peace, headed by a man of a new generation who himself had no blame in Germany's wartime atrocities. It went further than any treaty in creating an image of a new West Germany for peoples in the east.

While all of this happened, the Communists in the German Democratic Republic (GDR) had been watching nervously from the wings. While they welcomed a less confrontational West German policy, they feared Brandt's immense popularity and his appeal among Germans in the East. They also feared that he was going above their heads when dealing with Moscow and Warsaw. To them, the achievements of Ostpolitik seemed a bit like the late Stalin-era discussions in Moscow about the purposes of the GDR. They refused to meet Brandt unless he gave full diplomatic recognition to the GDR first. By 1972, however, it was clear to Walter Ulbricht and the GDR leadership that they had to negotiate with Brandt, both to avoid Moscow's displeasure and to avoid undermining their position at home.

The result of these negotiations, mainly carried out by Egon Bahr on the West German side, was the Basic Agreement between the two German states in December 1972. To the East Germans the term "basic" meant that it contained the minimum of what they had to do. To Brandt it signaled the first step in a rapprochement between the FRG and the GDR. The treaty contained a promise by each government to respect the jurisdiction of the other on its territory and the mutual independence in international affairs. They also pledged to cooperate on a whole set of issues, ranging from science and sport to post and communications. The real significance of the treaty was that for the first time in twenty-five years the two German states were dealing directly with each other, even if full recognition was not forthcoming. And Brandt was right about it being a first step. Several other agreements between the two were reached during the 1970s, making it unlikely that one would return to the absolute confrontation of the earlier Cold War.

Brandt therefore seemed to have achieved quite a lot in his attempts at building bridges in Europe, even though it is unlikely that he could have achieved half as much if it were not for the overall spirit of détente in the early 1970s. The German chancellor also had his detractors among those who claimed that he was giving too much to the East and not standing up for human rights and freedom of expression. While Brandt and his successors negotiated with the East German authorities, forty-eight people were shot trying to cross into West Berlin and eleven thousand were imprisoned for speaking out against the Communist regime. What kind of change did the rapprochement bring, critics asked? Maybe the real change was in West Germany, where small extreme Left terrorist groups—secretly aided by the GDR—made the country more difficult to govern?

Brandt's answer was that one could not deal effectively with the eastern European governments if one at the same time was actively and openly encouraging their populations to overthrow them. The breaking down of Cold War divisions in Europe would take time, the Bundeskanzler argued. What mattered in the meantime was to avoid war and build people-to-people contacts. What Europe needed, Brandt argued at the UN on the occasion of the admission of both German states, finally, to that organization in 1973, was "a condition of day-to-day peace." The massive military budgets on both sides had to be reduced: "If we do succeed in reducing, through confidence building, the monstrous waste created by the lack of trust between antagonistic systems, then we will have set a historical example. . . . At the end of the Cold War . . . there will be neither victors nor vanquished. The truth is, that if one wants to achieve peace, one must not strive for victory for some and defeat for others, but rather for the victory of reason and moderation."[18]

Brandt's vision of a more peaceful Europe, so much based on his own experiences throughout the twentieth century, also contributed to what was undoubtedly the greatest achievement of European détente, the Conference on Security and Cooperation in Europe (CSCE). Back in the 1950s, the Soviets had launched a plan for an all-European security organization to replace the power blocs. It was a rather undisguised attempt at excluding the United States, as a "non-European" power, from discussions on Europe's future. The western Europeans saw it as such and rejected it out of hand. But in the late 1960s Soviet suggestions of talks found a better reception among Europeans west and east. With new attempts in Washington and Moscow at building a Superpower détente, European leaders were eager to avoid decisions being taken above their heads. Brandt's Ostpolitik had reduced the fear of Germany in eastern Europe. And, somewhat bizarrely, the invasion of Czechoslovakia had convinced many that there was no alternative to dealing with the Soviet Union if the partition of Europe was to be overcome.

The CSCE process was firmly anchored in the continued existence of NATO and the Warsaw Pact. But in spite of its skepticism both toward Ostpolitik and the CSCE process, the new US Administration of Richard Nixon was wise enough to let its European allies explore what was possible. One clear condition, which the Soviets grudgingly accepted, was the inclusion of the United States in the talks. Another was regular NATO consultations both on process and positions. The western European leaders had no problem accepting this framework. While eager to explore what could be achieved with the East, none of them wanted too many internal difficulties in the Western alliance.

The most surprising element on the road to the CSCE was the activism of the eastern European governments. That the Romanians, as dissidents within the bloc, came up with their own proposals was no surprise. But that Poland and Hungary, which had shown their Soviet loyalism when co-invading Prague in 1968, were eager to present their own plans for the gradual dismantling of Europe's Cold War divides was more astounding. Like the West, the East approached the talks through consultations in the Warsaw Pact and other Communist fora.

But by the early 1970s it was clear that if the Soviets ordered a unilateral halt to the process, there would be a considerable political price to pay in eastern Europe.

By 1973 the Soviets found themselves in a quandary. They had primarily wanted to use a negotiation process as a propaganda weapon against the United States. But as the deepening of their own engagement with the Americans proceeded and expectations for a continent-wide security conference spread in Europe, they had little choice but to go ahead with their participation. A number of smaller western European countries, followed by France, insisted on human rights and freedom of speech issues becoming part of the negotiations, alongside military confidence-building and economic cooperation. These then became "Basket III" of the negotiation process when, to everyone's surprise, the Soviets agreed to their inclusion. Brezhnev regarded talking about Basket III issues a small price to pay for making some headway on other concerns. Knowing how much the general secretary wanted an agreement, even the KGB concluded that "Basket III is dependent upon our interpretation. . . . These will be practical steps of the party and the organs of state security. Basket III gives no one the possibility of intervening in the internal affairs of another state. There are many references there to domestic legislation."[19]

The ratification of the Helsinki Final Act of the CSCE in mid-1975 was the high point of European détente. For Brezhnev it was the highlight of his political career. Thirty-five countries agreed to a Declaration on Principles Guiding Relations between Participating States. These principles included sovereign equality, inviolability of frontiers, and nonintervention in domestic affairs. All were propositions that the Soviets had put forward since the founding of their state. But the Final Act also included key paragraphs on the rights of the individual. The signatories, it declared,

> will respect human rights and fundamental freedoms, including the freedom of thought, conscience, religion or belief, for all without distinction as to race, sex, language or religion. They will promote

and encourage the effective exercise of civil, political, economic, social, cultural and other rights and freedoms all of which derive from the inherent dignity of the human person and are essential for his free and full development. . . . The participating States recognize the universal significance of human rights and fundamental freedoms, respect for which is an essential factor for the peace, justice and well-being necessary to ensure the development of friendly relations and co-operation among themselves as among all States. . . . They confirm the right of the individual to know and act upon his rights and duties in this field.[20]

Brezhnev told himself and others that it was just language, that it did not matter much. But in Cold War terms the Helsinki Final Act was to have consequences far beyond what anyone could have foreseen in 1975.

AS EUROPEANS STRUGGLED with managing their Cold War inheritance, the Third World project split further apart. With the enthusiasm for freedom and new opportunities now tempered by harsh postcolonial realities, the concepts of solidarity and transnational South-South cooperation developed during the anticolonial struggle receded into the past in most places. After the political turnarounds in the mid-1960s, most postcolonial governments prioritized their own state's interests and their own plans for economic development over the wider cooperation and cohesion imagined by Nehru, Nkrumah, or Sukarno. Countries in Africa, Asia, and Latin America could still cooperate against Cold War constrictions and against European predominance. But such cooperation would now be more narrowly conceived, and based primarily on each country's strategic or economic interests.

At the first meeting of the United Nations Conference on Trade and Development in 1964, a group of seventy-seven non-European countries promised to consult further among themselves on trade-related issues. At its first meeting as the Group of 77 in Algeria three years later, the new organization issued the Algiers Charter, which called for fairer prices for raw materials, acceptance of principles of political and legal sovereignty in global trade, and more open and equitable world markets. "The lot of more than a billion people of the developing world continues to deteriorate as a result of the trends in international economic relations," the charter noted.

> The rate of economic growth of the developing world has slowed down and the disparity between it and the affluent world is widening. . . . The international community has an obligation to rectify these unfavorable trends and to create conditions under which all nations can enjoy economic and social well-being, and have the means to develop their respective resources to enable their peoples to lead a life free from want and fear. In a world of increasing interdependence, peace, progress and freedom are common and indivisible. Consequently the development of developing countries will benefit the developed countries as well.[21]

Western European governments saw connections between their own wishes to reduce Cold War tensions in Europe and hopes in Africa, Asia, and Latin America for a more stable economic development. One point was to avoid revolutionary turbulence that could further complicate the global Cold War. Another, especially among European Social Democrats such as Willy Brandt and Sweden's Olof Palme, was that the Group of 77 was right in seeing global development as interconnected, irrespective of political and economic systems. In his 1973 UN speech, Brandt had underlined exactly this dimension by stressing that it would not much gain the West—and especially the Europeans—if East-West conflicts were replaced by North-South conflicts.

By the early 1970s the Group of 77 and other organizations working with it had developed a plan through which a fairer world economy could be initiated through the United Nations. The somewhat grandiosely termed New International Economic Order (NIEO), passed by a majority vote in the UN General Assembly in 1974, called for the right of states to control the extraction of their natural resources through state-managed resource cartels. It also wanted to see the regulation of transnational corporations, technology transfers from north to south, trade preferences, and debt forgiveness. In all, the NIEO charter aimed to create what Tanzanian president Julius Nyerere called a "trade union of the poor." Others called it, less charitably but probably more accurately, "socialism among states." The United States, predictably, rejected the demands, with its UN ambassador condemning the resolution as a "steamroller" representing the "tyranny of the majority."[22]

The demands for a New International Economic Order did have some positive effects. Pushed by Brandt and others, the EEC entered into a set of conventions with former European colonies in Africa and the Caribbean. These so-called Lomè Conventions, named after the Togolese capital, allowed duty-free imports into the EEC and set off $3.6 billion (almost $13.5 billion today) in aid and investment. But overall the immediate results were negative. By focusing on economic demands, the ailing Third World coalition blew itself apart. Countries that were dependent on cheap raw material imports for their burgeoning industries, say, Singapore, found that they had little in common with countries that relied on improving raw material prices, say, Zambia. Oil exporters found that their interests often clashed with those dependent on cheap oil. The 1970s therefore became a decade in which global economic as well as political roles changed dramatically, with considerable and sustained effects for how the Cold War was fought.

15

Nixon in Beijing

While the 1960s began changes that would transform Europe, the 1970s saw a metamorphosis that transformed Asia and with it, gradually, the world. Although China sidelined itself through its Cultural Revolution, other Asian countries had been preparing for an economic takeoff within the capitalist world system dominated by the United States. Japan had been in the forefront. During the 1960s its economy had grown 11 percent per year, one of the fastest growth rates ever known for what was, in essence, already a developed economy. But from the late 1960s other Asian countries joined Japan in rapid growth, borrowing some aspects of its export-driven economic principles. Within the span of a decade, South Korea, Taiwan, and Singapore went from being poor, resourceless countries to economic dynamos, mainly on the strength of their integrated industrial enterprises, government guidance, and hardworking, well-educated labor forces.

It is no surprise that all the "little tigers" of the rapidly growing east Asian economy were close political allies of the United States. Just like in the case of Japan, Cold War alliance with Washington meant access to US and other Western markets on preferential terms. It also meant that east Asian authoritarian governments, helped by US advisers and military support, could defend themselves against rebellions among their own populations. None of the American links would have been enough by themselves to create east Asian economic growth. That was caused mainly by domestic factors. Neither is it true, as sometimes claimed, that the US war in Vietnam bought time for successful capitalist industrialization elsewhere in Asia. In execution, as well as in consequence, these were unrelated phenomena, even though the demand for goods created by the Indochina wars did stimulate other economies in the region. But, in overall terms, the Cold War did help to make export-led growth a surer path to quick economic transformation, thereby creating global economic interaction on an ever-larger scale.

IN THE 1970S, many Americans grew increasingly fearful that the resurgence of western Europe and rapid growth in parts of Asia meant the loss of jobs and income in the United States. And in relative terms the US economy was becoming less predominant. In 1945 the United States had contributed a full third of the global economy. In 1970 the figure was less than a quarter and dropping. This ought not to have been surprising. Right after World War II all main competitors had been in ruins. A generation later they had rebuilt and could therefore compete more effectively. What really worried US policy-makers was their own country's combination of low domestic growth rates and high government expenditure, especially on defense. In 1970 the Japanese economy grew 10.7 percent, and the West German 2.6 percent. The US economy grew only 0.5 percent. The competitors were also catching up in terms of overall productivity.

In 1971 the US government acted to defend its own economic interest. By abruptly suspending the fixed rate of exchanging dollars for gold, it in effect devalued the US dollar against other currencies, helping American exporters and domestic business. It thereby deliberately destroyed the Bretton Woods system, in which most other currencies had been pegged to the dollar at a fixed exchange rate. For the first time since 1945 US leaders looked more to their own bottom line than to preserving and integrating the world economic system. Of course, it could be argued that successive US Administrations had upheld that system, because it first and foremost served the American economy. But by the early 1970s this seemed to no longer to be the case. The global economy entered a new and turbulent era.

The collapse of Bretton Woods had a significant effect on the Cold War. The global economy had been stable in terms of its structure since the late 1940s. Of course there had been fluctuations, both in volume and in profits. But it had been stable in the sense that the capitalist economies had gradually become more integrated through their common dependence on the US dollar. Although a slow process, it had facilitated the recovery of western Europe and Japan. It had also deflated the price of raw materials, giving industrialized countries an edge. So while the protection and expansion of the global capitalist system had been a core US objective in the Cold War, its pursuit of this aim had been hegemonic, not particularistic. The success of capitalism drove US policies much more than concerns about the profitability of American companies or even foreign expenditures of the American state.

All of this changed in the "long 1970s," from 1968 to 1982 or thereabouts. While the unsuccessful war in Indochina created a sense of US political and military weakness, unilateral action to prop up its own economic interests made the United States seem less predominant and more self-serving. These perceptions may have been less than true overall, but they were widely held at the time, both inside and outside the United States itself. More important than perceptions, though, were the new realities created by economic and technological change. The collapse of Bretton Woods and the floating of exchange rates were not a cause but a symptom of a global reshaping. In the capitalist West, the state-centered, tariff-oriented, capital-controls-dominated postwar world was giving way to international trade and international finance. World trade tripled from the mid-1960s to 1980, much helped by more effective forms of transport and by large amounts of currency, especially US dollars, held outside its country of origin. Overseas investments also increased dramatically, in part because improved communications provided investors with more information and therefore increased confidence. In the 1970s, capitalism went global, with consequences few could foresee. Over time, the United States would be a big beneficiary of this so-called "globalization." But at the beginning of the process this was hard to imagine, not least for Americans themselves, who felt that their country was slipping behind.

THE US ELECTIONS of 1968—like those in France the same year—delivered a conservative result on the back of deep societal upheaval. The civil rights leader Dr. Martin Luther King Jr. and the Democratic front-runner for their party's nomination as president, Robert F. Kennedy, the late president's brother, were both assassinated in the lead-up to the elections. Richard Nixon, the Republican candidate who had served as Eisenhower's vice president for eight years, was elected in a sharply fought three-way race. Nixon had the lowest percentage of popular votes since Woodrow Wilson in 1912. In his campaign, he had appealed to "the silent majority" who were afraid of change, tumult, and foreign wars. "We hear sirens in the night," he told his party's convention. "We see Americans dying on distant battlefields abroad. We see Americans hating each other; fighting each other; killing each other at home." Nixon promised stability in America and "an honorable peace" in Vietnam. His supporters, he said, would be "the great majority of Americans, the forgotten Americans—the non-shouters; the non-demonstrators. They are not racists or sick," Nixon assured them, "they are not guilty of the crime that plagues the land."[1]

To those who knew him, Nixon often stood out as small-minded and insecure, but by 1969 he had enormous political experience. His sense of desperation over his country's future made him an imaginative foreign policy-maker, who was willing to break barriers. Nixon wanted to fight and win the Cold War. But, alone among recent presidents, he thought of the United States as one country among many in the international system. It was the most powerful country, at least for now. But Nixon did not trust the American people, and especially its youth, to be willing to pay the price that Superpower status implied in the time ahead. He worried about a future in which lack of internal cohesion and the rise of powerful and more purposeful challengers could destroy US predominance. His policies of détente were intended to postpone that day and make an uncertain future more predictable and therefore less dangerous for the United States.

Nixon had made his name as a conservative Cold Warrior. His election campaign had been filled with pledges of restoring American greatness and with more than a whiff of prejudice against racial minorities at home and foreigners out to exploit the United States. But he knew that he would have to govern by leaving behind many of the tones he had struck in the campaign. Domestically, the new president kept most of the social reforms of the Johnson years, and even expanded some of them. Internationally, he, from the very beginning of his presidency, wanted to reshape the global framework so the United States could keep its preeminence at a lower cost than before. And Nixon knew that in order to do so, he would need to sit down with the Soviet leaders and negotiate some kind of temporary Cold War truce.

In his first instructions to his national security adviser, Harvard professor Henry Kissinger, Nixon underlined how all actions in foreign policy were connected. The new president's top priority was to disengage the United States from the wars in Indochina. But he felt that the road to get there did not go primarily through peace negotiations with Hanoi, but through Moscow and Beijing. Already before he became president, Nixon had begun thinking about exploring some form of relaxation of tension with China. In a 1967 article in the influential journal *Foreign Affairs*, he had argued that outside of Indochina, Asia was really a great success story from a US perspective. It had rapidly modernizing states with strong economic growth. Sooner or later China would join the others. "We simply cannot afford to leave China forever outside the family of nations. . . . There is no place on this small planet for a billion of its potentially most able people to live in angry isolation," Nixon argued.[2] If China wanted to talk, Nixon was ready to listen.

NIXON WAS RIGHT about the rest of Asia, or at least about some countries in its eastern half. It had taken longer there than in Europe to overcome the effects of war. But by the time Nixon was elected, domestically driven market economies were starting to transform the lives of people in South Korea, Taiwan, Hong Kong, and Singapore. It was hard to see the significance of this at the time. The Vietnam War overshadowed most other developments. And some bigger countries were barely affected by the changes, at least to begin with: China by choice, others by indigence. But the entry of Asia's "little tigers" into the capitalist world economy was to change the bigger picture, not least in terms of the global economic significance of eastern Asia. And none of this would have happened without the strictures and apertures of the Cold War.

Japan was the forerunner for much of this development. It provided a model, even though the other market economies were hardly just copies of the Japanese experience. When the United States ended its occupation of Japan in 1951, very few people in Asia or elsewhere would have predicted a glorious economic future for the island nation. Annual growth was slowing and political deadlock between Right and Left made the country hard to govern. But two things were happening that were going to change the future. The Japanese Right began to put aside its internal infighting, meaning that conservatives who had supported the war and those few who had seen it as a disaster joined in the same party. Their somewhat incongruously named Liberal Democratic Party (LDP) defeated the Left and established a political hegemony that lasted thirty-five years. The new government's industrial policy emphasized increasing productivity (in part by curbing the power of the trade unions) and a strong role for the state in guiding investment, production, and foreign exports.

At the same time as Japan got a stable government that emphasized long-term economic growth, some of the fundaments of expansion in the private sector started to come together. US needs during the Korean War had made some sectors of Japanese industry very profitable. Guided by the government, the big companies, the *zaibatsu*, used their profits to invest in rationalization and new technology. Meanwhile, the Eisenhower Administration—fearful of the influence of the Japanese Left—smoothed the way for Japanese exports not only to the United States, but to western Europe and southeast Asia as well. Few of the recipient countries were thrilled at the prospect of opening their markets to cheap imports from a former enemy. But the Americans insisted, telling them that strategic interests had to take priority over short-term balance-of-trade issues. US policy toward Japan, said a 1960 National Security Council (NSC) directive, encouraged "a strong, healthy, self-supporting and expanding economy which will permit improvement in Japan's living standards, provide more capital for the development of less-developed nations, and make a greater contribution to the strength of the Free World."[3]

1960 was the year of decision for the future of Japan. With the renewal of the US-Japanese Security Treaty pending, the Japanese Left mobilized its waning forces in an attempt to defeat it in parliament. The parliamentary clash over the future of the treaty set off protests by trade unionists, students, and government employees, who felt that the LDP had ridden rough-shod over their interests. The crisis led to violence on the streets and the cancellation of a planned visit by President Eisenhower. While it neither toppled the government nor blocked security treaty renewal, the 1960 crisis told the LDP grandees that they had to make Japan's reindustrialization more socially inclusive. The party got rid of Prime Minister Kishi Nobusuke, a wartime minister of munitions who had been all too eager to settle old scores with the Left. The new LDP government insisted that welfare for all was the aim of its economic policy, and promised that everyone's personal income would double within ten years.

With the Japanese economy now growing at double-digit figures, it took only seven years to realize the income doubling plan. During the 1960s and '70s Japan transformed itself from the sick man of the industrialized world to its foremost economic powerhouse. Helped by liberalizing trade regimes, government credit and export guidance, and strong and cohesive companies, Japan's access to international markets propelled it to become the world's second-largest economy and a global leader in technology and productivity by 1970. In 1960 Charles de Gaulle had disparagingly written off the visiting Japanese prime minister as a "transistor salesman." Twenty years later the

Japanese economy was twice the size of France's and its productivity a staggering 25 percent higher.[4]

TO MANY IN the West, Japan was still the exception that proved the rule of Asian underdevelopment. As late as the mid-1960s, when President Johnson made his fateful decision to send US ground troops to Vietnam, a commonly held view was that the rest of Asia would fall further and further behind North America, western Europe, and even the resource-rich states of the Middle East and Africa. The Asian countries were overpopulated, under-resourced, and very badly governed, argued US experts. This, in a sense, was why they were prime targets for Communist aggression and had to be defended by the United States. Asia was a region for Cold War expansion, not because of its importance but because of its weakness.

Those who held such views had not done their homework on South Korea, Taiwan, or the city-states of Hong Kong and Singapore. In 1954 South Korea had been the poorest country in eastern Asia, devastated by three years of war in which the front lines had moved through the whole country several times. Everyone had been affected by the cataclysm. Its GDP per capita was behind that of Ghana or Kenya and showed no sign of improving. But during the 1960s things changed, laying the groundwork for a massive economic expansion in the 1970s and '80s. The same can be said for Taiwan, a rump Chinese state ruled by refugees from mainland China. Some parts of their stories are similar to Japan's: state-led development, export-oriented growth, and high domestic savings rates. But others are distinct: the emphasis on building education, in some cases almost from scratch; the significance of social programs and welfare from the beginning of the economic expansion; and the rule of "development dictatorships," governed with an iron fist by their military leaders.

Both South Korea and Taiwan were front-line states in the Cold War. US assistance to both was significant. Between 1946 and 1978 South Korea received almost as much US aid as all of Africa put together.[5] But easy access to US and Japanese markets was at least as important. In 1970 three-quarters of South Korea's exports went to the

United States or Japan.[6] The middle part of the Cold War obviously gave the two economic opportunities that they otherwise would not have had. But it also posed challenges. The dictatorships were held in place in part by their access to US aid, including significant military assistance. The most important point, though, is that South Korea and Taiwan took the opportunities offered to them and made good use of their unanticipated advantage.

The same can be said, to an even higher degree, for Singapore and Hong Kong. Two unloved (and some would say unwashed) cities that had lost their strategic importance with the decline of the British empire saw it revived by the Cold War. Hong Kong became a listening post against China, ruled up to the end of the Cold War by Britain, in part in order to share its information cachet with the Americans. Singapore became, first, an unhappy member of the Malaysian federation, and then, from 1964, when they were thrown out of Malaysia, an independent city-state. From the birth of sovereign Singapore, its leader Lee Kuan Yew believed that, with the British leaving, only a US presence could save his new country. "Anyone who was not a Communist and wanted to see the US leave Southeast Asia was a fool," Lee told Indian prime minister Indira Gandhi.[7] Although of Chinese extraction himself, Lee feared Chinese dominance of his region.

But Singapore's real Cold War significance, at least in symbolic terms, was the degree to which the former labor organizer Lee Kuan Yew broke with ideals of Third World solidarity, which had much appealed to him in his youth, and moved toward market-led domestic development. At independence, Singapore had been dirt poor. It had no resources except its population. The US presence in his region provided both security and economic opportunity for Lee. By the early 1970s he no longer had any time for Third World demands for higher raw material prices or political nonalignment. Lee decided that only by embracing global markets could Singapore become rich and he himself more powerful.

WHILE OTHER EAST Asian countries experienced growth within a US-led world system, Mao's People's Republic of China had been exploring the depths of Marxist political rectitude. Although not the same kind of economic disaster as the Great Leap Forward campaign a decade earlier, the Cultural Revolution isolated China further from the world around it. It also quickly ran into trouble at home. While screaming students were carrying out Mao's orders to "bombard the headquarters" and senior Communists were dragged through the streets or punished as criminals, the country became increasingly ungovernable. With key functions such as railways or telephone services increasingly out of order, mainly because their staff was being hauled away for political reeducation, the Chairman started to worry about China's preparedness against a foreign attack. By 1969 many of the craziest aspects of the Cultural Revolution—public torture sessions, all-day political meetings, constant shouting of slogans—were brought to a halt, in part through the use of the army against Red Guard activists. Labor camps and reeducation sites remained, now sometimes populated by those who had been the Chairman's strongest supporters when the Cultural Revolution began. Even if Maoist terror was still in place, the political landscape in China was gradually changing.

Part of the reason for Mao's change of heart was a shift in his views of the Cold War. In 1965 Mao's main foreign preoccupation had been with the US intervention in Vietnam. But while he had predicted further American involvement there, he was surprised by the scale of it. Mao believed that the North Vietnamese stood no chance of winning without direct Chinese support, as in Korea. And, in the midst of Cultural Revolution chaos, he was loath to get into another war against the most powerful country on earth. But like Stalin in the Korean case, neither did the Chairman see any disadvantage in having the Americans bogged down in Indochina. When Hanoi in 1968, in the wake of the failed Tet offensive, agreed to tentative talks with the Johnson Administration, Chinese premier Zhou Enlai lambasted them for compromising the cause and imperiling their position. "Before their backbone has been broken, or before five or six of their fingers have been broken, [the Americans] will not accept defeat, and they will not leave," he told Xuan Thuy, the North Vietnamese chief negotiator. He even accused Hanoi's concessions of having caused both the murder of Martin Luther King Jr. and a stock market rise in the United States (a very bad thing in Chinese eyes).[8] No wonder that Le Duan, now convinced that Beijing wanted to fight the Vietnam War to the last Vietnamese, turned increasingly to their other sponsor, the Soviet Union, for assistance.

As in so many other matters, Mao Zedong's own actions brought about the results he feared the most. By late 1968 his attention had turned almost exclusively to the Soviet threat to China. The USSR, he believed, was the rising Superpower, while the United States was the declining one. Together they were completing the encirclement of China. China had to break out of the siege. Intent on showing Moscow that China did not fear its military might, Mao ordered Chinese soldiers to patrol disputed areas along the Sino-Soviet border. The Soviet countermeasures fueled Beijing's war scare of 1969.

That summer, fearful of a Soviet nuclear attack, Mao hauled four of his old military comrades back from the hovels to which they had been sent during the Cultural Revolution and ordered them to write a no-holds-barred secret report on China's international options. Entitled "A Preliminary Evaluation of the War Situation," their report began, prudently, by confirming Mao's worldview: the Superpowers hated China because of its successful Communism and the gains of its Cultural Revolution. The Soviet Union was, at the moment, more dangerous to China than the United States. War with the Soviets was coming, though it would not happen immediately. The Americans would prefer to see the two fight each other. "By 'sitting on top of the mountain to watch a fight between two tigers,' they will see the weakening of both China and the Soviet Union."

The four old marshals stressed the urgency of the situation. They compared it to China's position just prior to the Japanese attack in 1937. China, they said, had to improve its defensive stance. Although the Soviets and the Americans shared some interests, the conflict between them was "real and concrete." And Nixon, obsessed with the Vietnam War, "takes China as a 'potential threat,' rather than a real threat."[9] Chen Yi, Nie Rongzhen, and the other marshals sensibly left

Mao to draw his own conclusions. But their implication, that China may want to reduce its conflict with the United States in order to fight the Soviet Union, was clear.

IN WASHINGTON RICHARD NIXON had wasted no time in getting his new China initiatives going. Shocked by the Sino-Soviet border clashes in the spring of 1969 and fearful they could lead to nuclear war, he also saw huge opportunities for the United States. By the summer he had instructed US diplomats to signal that the United States was open to talks with Beijing. He also lessened trade and travel restrictions on the People's Republic. With a view to exit from the war in Indochina and improve relations with the Chinese, Nixon told South Vietnamese president Nguyen Van Thieu that the United States in the future would continue to support anti-Communist governments in Asia, but would not intervene to help them with its own troops. He then took off on a whirlwind tour around the world, meeting leaders in Pakistan and—as the first US president—in Communist Romania. In both places Nixon told his hosts in very direct language that he wanted to talk to Beijing, and asked for their help in relaying the message to Mao and Zhou Enlai.

With a new high in Sino-Soviet tension in the fall, and before the Chinese had responded to his feelers, Nixon began thinking about the longer-term implications of reaching out to China. With an eye always on domestic politics, the president realized that Soviet threats against China would make a moderation of US-China policy easier to accept by the American public. But he also told the NSC that the only country that could threaten the United States in the long run was the Soviet Union. Therefore, Nixon asked his team, "we must think through whether it is a safer world with China down, or should we look to keeping China strong?"[10] These were revolutionary thoughts by an American president, and indicated a plan that only Richard Nixon, with his conservative domestic record, could have any hope of achieving.

After the war scare of 1969 abated, the Chinese leaders held back from welcoming Nixon's overtures too openly. Mao's focus returned to domestic affairs and to the turmoil of the Cultural Revolution. Beijing was worried that Nixon was setting a trap for them, and that the real aim of his China policy was just to make it simpler for the United States to win the war in Vietnam. Nixon's attacks into Cambodia and Laos in 1970, undertaken primarily to cut off North Vietnam's supply lines to the south, seemed to confirm this view. Mao condemned Nixon's "Fascist aggression" and agreed to host Cambodia's exiled king, Sihanouk, in Beijing. Little concrete therefore happened in the Sino-American relationship at first, even though it was clear that new foundations had been laid for the future.

President Nixon was in some ways lucky that his China initiatives took some time to play themselves out. After all, his primary target for a global relaxation of tension was the Soviet Union, not China. And the Soviets had told him very directly about their wariness of any US messing about with their former Chinese clients. The veteran Soviet ambassador to the United States, Anatolii Dobrynin, had given the president a message from Moscow, which included stark warnings. "If someone in the United States is tempted to make profit from Soviet-Chinese relations at the Soviet Union's expense, and there are some signs of that, then we would like to frankly warn in advance that such line of conduct, if pursued, can lead to a very grave miscalculation and is in no way consistent with the goal of better relations between the US and the USSR."[11] Nixon hoped that the Soviets and the Chinese would attempt to overbid each other in a search for America's good graces. But at the same time he had to be careful not to play the China card in such a way that he upset the more important game, that with the Soviet Union.

Nixon wanted to find a stable balance in relations with the Soviets, at least for the immediate future. His aim was to reduce the risk of war and, over time, socialize Moscow into the international system that the United States had created. The Soviet Union, Nixon believed, was a postrevolutionary state, whose state interests counted for more than its ideology. As long as the Soviets did not challenge the global power of the United States, the president was happy to recognize it as the other Superpower and let it keep its hegemony in eastern Europe. The

Russian leadership of the Soviet Union was, after all, fellow Europeans, Nixon concluded. They were easier to talk to, and through, than assorted Third World radicals, including those in Vietnam.

But Nixon's détente policy toward the Soviet Union also took time to put in place. Although Brezhnev was eager for a stabilization of relations with the United States, there were many points of conflict that got in the way. The Soviet Union, Brezhnev insisted, would not accept a position of subservience to the United States in return for peace. It would continue to set its own positions in world politics on a global scale and defend socialism internationally, including in Cuba and the Middle East. Even in getting an agreement on limiting the number of strategic nuclear missiles, which Brezhnev himself had called for in the past, the Soviets would not be rushed. In Moscow, leaders believed circumstances favored them. "We got time," Brezhnev told his colleagues. "The Americans . . . try to push us. Now, we will not abandon the talks, but neither will we drive them forward."[12] By 1971, with his reelection campaign coming up, Nixon was getting impatient, especially on the nuclear talks. "Just make any kind of a damn deal," he told Henry Kissinger. "You know it doesn't make a goddamn bit of difference. We're going to agree to settle it anyway."[13]

It was Brezhnev's foot-dragging that pushed Nixon toward the greatest gamble of his political career. In April 1971 Mao had finally decided to respond to Nixon's overtures. Through the Pakistanis, he invited the president to visit Beijing for direct talks with the Chinese leadership. Nixon immediately decided to accept. He thought that reaching out to Beijing would put necessary pressure both on the Soviets and the North Vietnamese. "The difference between [the Chinese] and the Russians," Henry Kissinger explained, "is that if you drop some loose change, when you go to pick it up the Russians will step on your fingers and the Chinese won't. . . . The Russians squeeze us on every bloody move and it has just been stupid."[14]

In spite of Nixon's doubts about his national security adviser's negotiating skills, he decided to send Kissinger to Beijing as his advance man. The preparatory mission was to be secret, and Nixon knew that sending Kissinger was his best bet to keep it that way. On 8 July 1971, Kissinger flew to Pakistan for well publicized meetings with the leaders there. After the welcome reception on the first evening, Kissinger feigned illness, and his spokesman told reporters that he needed to rest outside Islamabad for a day or so. Instead, Kissinger that night flew secretly on a Pakistani aircraft straight to Beijing, where he was welcomed by Chinese premier Zhou Enlai. Awestruck at being the first American leader to visit Communist China, Kissinger began reading from a prepared text. Zhou cut him short. China, he said, was hoping for "coexistence, equality, and friendship." But for that to happen, the United States "must recognize the PRC as the sole legitimate government of China and not make any exceptions. Just as we recognize the United States as the sole legitimate government without considering Hawaii, the last state, an exception to your sovereignty, or still less, Long Island." In other words, the US relationship with Taiwan had to go.

On 15 July, with Kissinger back from his trip, Nixon astounded the world by going on live television to announce that he would visit the People's Republic of China soon. His aim, he said, was to further the cause of world peace. In Beijing the public announcement was shocking for those who had grown up with anti-Americanism as part of their basic beliefs. But it did strengthen Zhou Enlai's position in the frenzied infighting that the Chinese regime was going through due to the Cultural Revolution. As usual, Zhou had succeeded in carrying out Mao's wishes. Suspecting that he was falling out of favor, in part as a result of the US deal, Mao's designated successor Lin Biao made a dash for the Soviet border, only to die when the plane he was escaping on crashed in Mongolia. The chaos created by Lin's defection and death in September 1971 postponed Nixon's visit. It also reinforced Mao's hatred of the Soviet Union. Just like he had done in the case of Liu Shaoqi, Mao linked Lin's betrayal to Soviet social imperialism. Lin Biao had "wanted to compromise with the Soviet revisionists in defiance of our party's efforts to expose and criticize Soviet revisionism," Mao claimed.[15] When asked by Romania's Ceaușescu, who had helped with contacting the Americans, whether China, in due time, could also put things right with Moscow, the Chairman was adamant: "We will not put anything right, and will continue in our dogmatism; even [for] ten thousand years."[16]

On 21 February 1972 Nixon arrived in Beijing, the first US president ever to visit China. With arms limitation talks with the Soviets still ongoing, and no end to the war in Vietnam, the president needed a foreign policy success. He was determined to make this the one. Mao was ill, recovering from a severe lung infection, and only put in a brief appearance, during which he rambled about his weakness and incapacity. When the president gushed that "the Chairman's writings moved a nation and have changed the world," Mao responded that he had "not been able to change it. I've only been able to change a few places in the vicinity" of Beijing. Looking at Nixon, Mao pronounced that he liked him. "I like Rightists," the Chairman said. "I am comparatively happy when these people on the Right come into power. . . . We were not very happy with these presidents, Truman and Johnson."[17] Mao left the negotiations to Zhou, but kept a keen eye on what was happening.

Speaking to Zhou as if he were a congressman whom the president needed to win over to his side, Nixon stressed that the Chinese needed to deal with him, the president, directly. Other US politicians would oppose the understanding with China, Nixon said. Only he could deliver it. But in order to do so he needed to keep even some of his own cabinet members in the dark about what was going on. These included Secretary of State William Rogers, whose department Nixon suspected of leaking documents to the press in order to damage the president. Zhou listened to this unexpected and ingratiating performance, saying very little.

Then the president jumped straight into his view of why the United States and China had to cooperate. The Soviet Union was threatening world peace. "I believe," Nixon told Zhou, that "the interests of China as well as the interests of the U.S. urgently require that the U.S. maintains its military establishment at approximately its present levels and . . . [maintains] a military presence in Europe, in Japan, and of course our naval forces in the Pacific. I believe the interests of

China are just as great as those of the U.S. on that point," Nixon said. To him, the president explained, this was not about Taiwan, or east Asia, or even about the Vietnam War. It was about global stability.[18]

With Mao watching every move, it was hard even for a seasoned diplomat like Zhou Enlai to come up with much that the Americans wanted to hear, except attacks on the Soviets. On Indochina, Zhou told Nixon that the United States should withdraw, but that the Chinese would continue to support North Vietnam, the FNL, and the Cambodian and Laotian Communists. Japan, the premier said, should become "peaceful, independent, and neutral." Korea was an internal matter, for the Koreans to decide. And Taiwan would be "liberated" by the PRC after the United States broke its military links with Chiang Kai-shek's regime, something Zhou hoped would happen during Nixon's second term in office.

But Zhou did not have to offer much. Nixon needed a breakthrough with China for his own reasons. He hoped the positive press coverage of the visit in the United States would help him get reelected. But he also hoped the Soviets and the North Vietnamese would be concerned enough about the Sino-American contacts to seek their own settlements with Washington. The final statement of the visit, the Shanghai Communiqué, set out the views of the Chinese and US government separately at first. But it then concluded that the two countries would continue to work toward full normalization of their bilateral relations and cooperate on trade and technology. On the crucial issue of Taiwan, the communiqué made it clear that neither side wanted the island's future to be a barrier to current Sino-American interactions:

> The United States acknowledges that all Chinese on either side of the Taiwan Strait maintain there is but one China and that Taiwan is a part of China. The United States Government does not challenge that position. It reaffirms its interest in a peaceful settlement of the Taiwan question by the Chinese themselves. With this prospect in mind, it affirms the ultimate objective of the withdrawal of all U.S. forces and military installations from Taiwan. In the meantime, it

will progressively reduce its forces and military installations on Taiwan as the tension in the area diminishes.[19]

As with most diplomatic breakthroughs, neither side had fully got what they wanted. But Nixon was right about the value for the United States of starting an open-ended process in which China could be brought into play to serve American interests. Mao, on his side, had obtained increased security against the Soviet Union and at least some hope of recovering Taiwan soon. The Chairman remained puzzled, however, about the ultimate aims of the Americans. He could not understand why Nixon would support the "real" Communist revolution, his revolution, against the fake Communists in Moscow. "Kissinger," Mao had told the Vietnamese in 1970, "is a stinking scholar . . . a university professor who does not know anything about diplomacy."[20] Five years later, Mao accused Kissinger of "leaping to Moscow by way of our shoulders."[21] There was limited cooperation but almost no trust in the relationship, even after the Americans started to share highly sensitive intelligence with the Chinese.

For the rest of the world, and especially the rest of Asia, the breakthrough in Sino-American relations amounted to a strategic earthquake. For more than twenty years, Washington had been telling the Japanese, the South Koreans, and the southeast Asians that the Americans were in Asia to protect them against the expansionist plans of Chinese Communism. In Europe and elsewhere, the United States had protested any attempts by its allies or by neutrals to recognize the People's Republic of China. And now the US president appeared, smiling and saluting, in Beijing with Mao Zedong and Zhou Enlai. The Japanese prime minister, Sato Eisaku, who had been informed just a few minutes before Nixon's TV speech in 1971, had been in tears. "I have done everything they [the Americans] have asked," Sato said, but "they have let me down."[22]

For Japan, the "Niksonu Shokku," or Nixon Shocks, of 1971 led to some big discussions about the country's future, even within the ruling LDP. This was Japan's Cold War turning point. Nixon's departure from Bretton Woods was to a high extent directed against Japan's commercial interests. Seen from Washington, Japan had done too well under American tutelage. And Nixon's China adventure had left Japan high and dry diplomatically. Meanwhile Japan's domestic Cold War, between the LDP on the one side and the Communists, Socialists, and trade unions on the other, had abated (though much still divided them). The hapless Sato was in 1972 replaced by Tanaka Kakuei, who immediately set out for Beijing himself to make up for lost time. China and Japan agreed to establish full diplomatic relations, recognize Taiwan as a part of the PRC, and jointly oppose "hegemony" (shorthand for the Soviet Union) in the region.

Other Asians followed suit. Now encouraged by Beijing, the North Vietnamese decided that Nixon was serious about wanting out, and agreed to a peace deal with the Americans in Paris in January 1973. The Paris Accords were a curious mix of points inserted unilaterally by Washington and Hanoi, affirming both the unity of Vietnam and the sovereignty of South Vietnam. "The military demarcation line between the two zones at the 17th parallel is only provisional and not a political or territorial boundary," the text said. But it also said that "the South Vietnamese people's right to self-determination is sacred, inalienable, and shall be respected by all countries." Understandably, Nixon had to twist the South Vietnamese leaders' arms to get them to sign such a jerry-built agreement. In Beijing, Mao told the North Vietnamese that they should take a break for at least six months before they went on to conquer the whole country. But the Sino-Vietnamese relationship was already in free fall. As Vietnam neared forcible reunification under its Communists, Beijing suspected that their long-time allies had now teamed up with the Soviets to control all of Indochina.

Richard Nixon's opening to China had manifestly paid off in terms of what mattered most to the president. Suddenly fearful of losing out on the opportunity for détente with its main enemy, Leonid Brezhnev had pushed the arms limitation talks with the Americans toward agreement. When Nixon arrived in Moscow in May 1972, three months after his visit to Beijing, a Strategic Arms Limitation Treaty (SALT I) was ready for signing. For Brezhnev the summit was the highlight of his career as a statesman. Not only did the SALT agreement assume that the Soviet Union had reached parity with the United States in terms of strategic nuclear forces and was therefore militarily its equal, but the US president was willing to accept a general text, which included some of the key concepts that the Soviets had put forward in international relations over the past twenty years. "In the nuclear age," said the Basic Principles agreement signed in Moscow,

> there is no alternative to conducting [US-Soviet] mutual relations on the basis of peaceful coexistence. Differences in ideology and in the social systems of the USA and the USSR are not obstacles to the bilateral development of normal relations based on the principles of sovereignty, equality, non-interference in internal affairs and mutual advantage. . . . [The two countries] will always exercise restraint in their mutual relations, and will be prepared to negotiate and settle differences by peaceful means. Discussions and negotiations on outstanding issues will be conducted in a spirit of reciprocity, mutual accommodation and mutual benefit. Both sides recognize that efforts to obtain unilateral advantage at the expense of the other, directly or indirectly, are inconsistent with these objectives. The prerequisites for maintaining and strengthening peaceful relations between the USA and the USSR are the recognition of the security interests of the Parties based on the principle of equality and the renunciation of the use or threat of force.[23]

It was a remarkable declaration of a Cold War truce and of US recognition of the Soviet Union as an equal. For a country that throughout its twentieth-century history had built its foreign policy on concepts of uniqueness and, eventually, unrivaled power, this was a big step and, over time, a highly contested one domestically. But internationally it set off a moment during the Cold War where people in many different parts of the world for the first time thought that the conflict would be resolved by negotiation and mutual convergence. At this particular juncture it probably mattered less that neither Nixon nor Kissinger thought so. Their worlds remained ensconced within the Cold War. Elsewhere their actions helped some people start thinking beyond it.

One such departure in the 1970s stressed human and governmental interdependence across Cold War blocs. Humanity faced many challenges that were common to East and West alike, went the argument from some intellectuals and politicians. States were getting increasingly difficult to govern because they were getting more complex. Information flows were more difficult to harness, both for public and private activity, because there were more of them. Challenges of education, health, social care, urban planning, and transport were similar in all industrialized societies. Was it then not likely that East and West would become more similar over time, and that ideologies would matter less? The US economist John Kenneth Galbraith, who had served in the Kennedy Administration, had foreseen this already in his Reith Lectures for the BBC in 1966:

> The convergence between the two ostensibly different industrial systems, the one billed as socialism and that derived from capitalism, is a fact. And we must also assume that it is a good thing. In time, and perhaps in less time than may be imagined, it will dispose of the notion of inevitable conflict based on irreconcilable difference. . . . In the United States, were it not so celebrated in ideology, it would long since have been agreed that the line that now divides public from so-called private organization in military procurement, space exploration, and atomic energy is so indistinct as to be nearly imperceptible.[24]

Common perceptions of the centrality of science and technology would be key in bringing states of different persuasions closer together, Galbraith and others argued. But the arms race stood in the way of scientific cooperation. Distrust precluded common gains. Even though Nixon and Brezhnev moved toward arms control, many experts felt that such efforts were not moving fast enough. The Pugwash Conferences, in which scientists from East and West met without (at least visible) government interference, served to spread the idea that the scientific elite had a particular responsibility for world peace. In its 1969 report, the conference maintained that "effective deterrence can be obtained with a drastically reduced level of nuclear stockpiles. . . . The enormity of the destruction that would result from a full scale nuclear war with present stockpiles of nuclear weapons is simply not comprehended by the general public. Scientists have a great responsibility to help educate the public about this."[25]

The Pugwash scientists were undoubtedly right that US and Soviet nuclear stockpiles had reached unconscionable levels by the 1970s. The SALT negotiations, important as they were in building trust between the two sides, did nothing to reduce these levels. Their aspiration was simply to reduce future growth in the arsenals. During the 1960s the number of nuclear warheads had increased massively. Most of this increase was in the Soviet Union and the United States. The other nuclear powers—Britain, France, and China—had much smaller arsenals. The Soviets attempted to catch up with the US lead. In 1964 the United States had had ten times as many strategic nuclear warheads as the Soviet Union. Ten years later this advantage was reduced, though the Americans still had more than three times as many warheads, with much greater precision and deliverability. Between them, though, the increase was staggering, as the overall number of nuclear weapons had more than doubled during the 1960s. By 1975 there were nearly fifty thousand nuclear weapons. Some of these had six to ten independently targetable warheads. Their combined explosive power was more than enough to destroy all of the Earth's combined landmass.

But the perverted logic of the arms race did not stop with Earth. After the Soviet Union put the first satellite in orbit in 1957, the Cold War also threatened to spread into space. The rockets used to lift satellites into position was nearly identical to those propelling the Superpowers' intercontinental nuclear missiles. Both sides knew that making military use of such satellites would dramatically improve their position in the arms race. Very soon they were used not only for communications and missile guidance systems, but also for surveillance. Some experts on both sides argued for putting offensive weapons in space. Luckily, political leaders held back. One of the first signs of a coming era of détente was a UN-sponsored treaty in 1967 prohibiting the permanent stationing of weapons of mass destruction in space.

After the US moon landings in 1969 Nixon and Brezhnev realized that some cooperation on space exploration might be in the interest of both countries, and could provide a powerful symbol of a new era in Superpower relations. Pushed by scientists from both sides, the two leaders signed an agreement on cooperation in space research during Nixon's 1972 visit to Moscow. "That's got so much imagination to it," Kissinger crowed to his boss. "Kennedy," said Nixon, being Nixon, "Kennedy could never get even that, that space thing." Three years later space cooperation delivered one of the most striking images of détente, when a US Apollo spacecraft docked with a Soviet Soiuz and the astronauts shook hands through the opening hatch.

While some Cold War skeptics devoted themselves to promoting contact between societies, scientific exchange, or disarmament, others protested the Cold War as an extension of state control of the individual. The youth protest of the 1960s went through a transformation in the 1970s, at least for some of its protagonists. Out went the belief in Trotskyist or Maoist alternatives, at least for the Western world. In came a concern with state surveillance and state crimes. The French philosopher André Glucksmann, who had been chanting Maoist slogans in the streets in 1968, six years later wrote a book in which he compared Stalin's crimes to those of Hitler. Entitled *The Stove and the Cannibal: An Essay on the Connections Between the State, Marxism, and the Concentration Camps*, the book argued that Marxism in any form led to totalitarianism. In the United States, too, former socialists—like Georgetown professor Jean Kirkpatrick, and radicals like Daniel Patrick Moynihan, one of the architects of Johnson's War on Poverty—began stressing individual rights and choices over welfare provisions.

Some of the reinvigorated preoccupation with personal liberties in the West linked up with the critique of Stalinist society coming from

Soviets and east Europeans. The Soviet Nobel laureate Aleksandr Solzhenitsyn stood out as one of the bravest investigators of his government's crimes. His novel *One Day in the Life of Ivan Denisovich* revealed the inhuman conditions in Soviet labor camps, in which millions had served for no reason whatsoever. To Solzhenitsyn, the camp guards' cry became emblematic for the Soviet Union itself: "Attention, prisoners. Marching orders must be strictly obeyed. Keep to your ranks. No hurrying, keep a steady pace. No talking. Keep your eyes fixed ahead and your hands behind your backs. A step to right or left is considered an attempt to escape and the escort has orders to shoot without warning."[26]

Solzhenitsyn was expelled from the Soviet Union in 1974. Other writers followed suit. Andrei Amalrik was forced to go abroad two years later. His crime was that in an essay published in the West he had asked whether the Soviet Union could survive until George Orwell's infamous year 1984. A state so dependent on control and repression would sooner or later get into trouble, Amalrik argued. The longer authoritarianism and international isolation lasted, "the more rapid and decisive will be the collapse when confrontation with reality becomes inevitable." Against those both inside and outside the Soviet Union who said that "the situation is better now than it was ten years ago; therefore ten years from now it will be better still," Amalrik felt instead that the Russian Revolution had run its course, and that it had nothing more to offer the Soviet peoples.[27]

Other Cold War critics took their argument to the global level. They argued that neither socialism nor capitalism had been able to solve the big, common problems that humanity faced, and that the ideological competition rather distracted from their resolution. The damage to the environment caused by both forms of industrial development, the rapid increase in population, which many experts assumed contributed to hunger and turmoil, and the dire poverty in the postcolonial states convinced many in the West that the Cold War would soon be a thing of the past. The 1967–69 civil war in Nigeria, which was set off by resource competition and ethnic conflict rather than Superpower intervention, seemed more real than any potential clashes across the Cold War divide in Europe. The pictures of starving children in Biafra, broadcast worldwide by both East and West, seemed more of a threat to a common future than the arcane menace of a nuclear Armageddon.

But even for those who foresaw other threats as gaining in importance, détente between East and West stood out as a positive step. In the United States in 1973 almost 70 percent of the population believed that the United States and the USSR could work together for peace. There were even higher levels of support for SALT and for increased contacts in other fields, including trade and technological cooperation.[28] In western Europe opinion polls showed that many people thought the Cold War was over for good. Less than 10 percent of West Germans thought that the Soviet Union was a real threat to their country. Interestingly, when asked who they thought would be most powerful in fifty years' time, more than twice as many West Germans said the Soviet Union than said the United States.[29] But unlike in the 1950s, this prospect seemed no longer to fill them with horror.

At first, at least, even the increasingly visible foibles of détente's main protagonists in the West, President Nixon and West German chancellor Brandt, did not disturb public support for détente. Nixon's trouble with the law engulfed his presidency soon after his reelection in 1972. The president was found to have interfered with the investigation of a break-in at the headquarters of his Democratic opponents at the Watergate building in Washington. The burglary had been carried out on the orders of White House officials, and pressure on Nixon to testify increased. When it became clear that he faced impeachment and probable removal from office, Nixon resigned in August 1974. He was the first US president to resign and did so in disgrace.

Willy Brandt's chancellorship also ran aground on trouble of his own making. Like Nixon, he had been reelected in the autumn of 1972 with a solid public mandate. Brandt seemed uncertain, though, over where to move his *Ostpolitik* initiatives next. He did not want to challenge the US concept of a Superpower-led détente too directly, and he hoped to see more positive changes in the East, and especially in East Germany, before presenting new plans for East-West cooperation.

Meanwhile, Brandt's private life was increasingly messy. He drank too much and his extramarital affairs worried his colleagues, even before they found out that a key official in Brandt's office was an East German spy. Fearful of attempts at blackmail, Brandt resigned in May 1974. His replacement, Helmut Schmidt, supported Ostpolitik but was a marked skeptic over any eastern European and Soviet long-term willingness to reciprocate for Western concessions.

Nixon's successor in the White House, Gerald Ford, was also a strong supporter of further engagement with the Soviets and the Chinese. Henry Kissinger continued as foreign policy supremo, now as secretary of state, even though his position within the new Administration was gradually more curtailed. With Congress controlled by the Democrats and even many Republicans after Watergate critical of the strong executive Nixon had tried to put in place, the White House's room for maneuver in foreign policy became limited. In spite of this, the Ford Administration was able to complete the framework for a new SALT agreement, SALT II, which set equal and clear limits to the number of strategic nuclear weapons each side could possess, even in case of multiple warheads for each missile (MIRVs). The agreement also attempted to prevent the future deployment of new types of strategic weapons.

In November 1974 President Ford traveled to Vladivostok on the Soviet Pacific coast to sign the framework agreement for SALT II. In the negotiations there, both leaders attempted to move ahead as quickly as possible, sometimes against the advice of their own military experts. Brezhnev claimed that his aim was to settle the arms race so that the Soviet Union could turn more to domestic development. "We are spending billions on all these things, billions that would be much better spent for the benefit of the people," Brezhnev told Ford.[30] But the Soviet leader also wanted full equality in terms of all kinds of strategic weapons, including those where the Soviets in reality were lagging behind the United States. Full strategic parity therefore became a kind of trap for Brezhnev, if his aim was to salvage more funds for civilian purposes. The Soviet Union had to spend increasing amounts to reach the levels of weaponry they had falsely claimed, and the Americans generally believed, that the Red Army was already at.

By the mid-1970s proponents of détente had achieved much in ways that could not have been foreseen a decade earlier. It is too easy to say, as some do, that the time was ripe for such measures of confidence-building. Even though the détente process was haphazard and, on some critical issues, contradictory, it had taken real courage to bring it to where it was by 1975. The aging Brezhnev had made it into his life's work and believed it would preserve peace, even as he and his colleagues in Marxist terms began suspecting that global capitalism had entered a structural crisis that advantaged the Soviet Union in international affairs. The Chinese leaders also deserve some approbation for breaking with the past, even though they wanted to use the security they had gained for further nefarious purposes at home. It was, however, Richard Nixon who had made it all possible. Because he fundamentally distrusted his own people, Nixon had forced US foreign policy onto a track where, for the first time during the Cold War, it dealt with others on the assumption that US global hegemony would not last forever.

16

The Cold War and India

Different from what Henry Kissinger, President Nixon's national security adviser, often claimed, it was not China that was the global Cold War wild card. China under Mao was too ideological, too inward-looking, to serve that role. If there were a Cold War wild card it was India, a democracy of then more than four hundred million people, which had got its independence from Britain in 1947 and had largely adopted a British-style system of government. The new Indian leadership, under Prime Minister Jawaharlal Nehru and his Congress Party, defined itself as nonaligned, anticolonial, and socialist. While inspired to a significant degree by Soviet ideas of centralized planning, Nehru was fiercely opposed to the concept of power blocs. The Cold War, as an international system, repelled him. In Nehru's view, it was in its essence based on European preoccupations and drew attention away from the real problems the majority of the world's population faced: underdevelopment, hunger, and colonial oppression.

For the patrician Nehru, socialism was first and foremost about social assistance and equality in the broadest sense. Much inspired by British Left-wing traditions during his education at Harrow and Cambridge, the first Indian prime minister saw himself as "temperamentally and by training an individualist and intellectually a socialist. . . . I hope that socialism does not kill or suppress individuality. Indeed, I am attracted to it because it will release innumerable individuals from economic and cultural bondage."[1] In the Congress

Party resolution on economic policy, passed the year before the Second Five Year Plan started in 1956, "the national aim is a welfare state and a socialist economy. This can only be achieved by a considerable increase in income and much greater volume of goods and services and employment. Economic policy must, therefore, aim at plenty and at equitable distribution."[2]

To get the kind of development Nehru and the Congress leadership was looking for, Third World solidarity, national sovereignty, and freedom of action was essential. New India therefore in many ways defined itself in opposition to the Cold War, domestically and internationally. It was a key convener in assembling the Bandung Conference of 1955, and it became a founding member of the Non-Aligned Movement in 1961. In its foreign policy, it emphasized the role of inclusive international institutions, especially the UN. Well before European or Superpower détente set in, Nehru believed that the Cold War as an international system was detrimental to India's interests and those values he felt his country represented. Foreign leaders sometimes tired of Nehru's moralistic lectures and his insistence on India as an example. But his country was a power to be reckoned with, both in its Asian setting and through Nehru's insistence on India as a Cold War antidote.

WHILE SETTING UP India as an example for others seemed relatively easy, given the chaos that reigned in many parts of the postcolonial world, forging policies that would further Nehru's aims at home and abroad was more difficult. Under Nehru, Congress remained wedded to the British-style institutions that the country had adopted, including one person / one vote elections at least every fifth year. Some Indians argued that in a country with more than 80 percent illiteracy such a system was administratively ineffective and politically meaningless. The Indian Communist Party castigated Nehru for not doing enough to uproot entrenched social oppression in the countryside, especially through the caste system, or to curb exploitation of workers in the cities. The Communists built substantial support in many Indian states, such as Kerala and West Bengal, and was the largest opposition party in parliament. But they were always vulnerable to Nehru's attacks on them for supporting violence, disregarding Indian national interests, and oppressing individual freedoms. In the late 1950s, after the Communists won the elections in Kerala, Nehru intervened to have them unceremoniously booted out of office by the central government. His daughter, Indira Gandhi, who had been made president of the Congress Party with which the local Communists had been feuding, tolerated no resistance: "When Kerala is virtually on fire, it becomes the Center's duty to go to the aid of the people; the misrule of the Communist rulers of the state has created a situation which . . . does not brook legal quibbling."[3]

Brooking no resistance at home—from Communists, recalcitrant landowners and aristocrats, or from ethnic minority groups—Congress's main foreign challenge was fighting the consequences of the 1947 partition of India. Nehru claimed to have accepted the creation of Pakistan as an independent state, and indeed he did prefer it, as any sensible person would, over the continuation of the ethnic slaughter India had descended to during the year of independence. But the existence of a religious state, carved out of Indian territory both to the west and the east, vexed him as a radical secularist. He confessed privately that it would have been better if Pakistan had not existed. But, since it did exist, he insisted on treating it as an equal. What made such an approach difficult was the ongoing fighting in the state of Kashmir, located between India and Pakistan in the northwest. In 1947 Kashmir had acceded to India, but parts of its Muslim majority clamored for inclusion into Pakistan or independence. After a brief war, India controlled two-thirds of Kashmir, and Pakistan the remainder. For Pakistani leaders, fighting Indian control of Kashmir was a matter of national liberation. For Nehru, it was a matter of India's territorial integrity and its status as a noncommunal, multi-ethnic state. Nehru's own ancestors hailed from Kashmir. Though India offered a plebiscite to settle the matter, there was no way the prime minister, or his country, would give up Kashmir to Pakistani pressure.

On the world stage, Nehru stressed India's nonaligned foreign policy and the need for global solutions to world problems, preferably through the UN. His visit to the United States, during which he famously did not hit it off with his host, President Truman, was intended to socialize the Americans into the expanding community of nations. "Two tragic wars have demonstrated the futility of warfare," Nehru told the US Congress. "Victory without the will to peace achieves no lasting result. . . . May I venture to say that this is not an incorrect description of the world today? It is not flattering either to man's reason or to our common humanity. Must this unhappy state persist and the power of science and wealth continue to be harnessed to the service of destruction? . . . The greater a nation, the greater is its responsibility to find and to work for the right answer."[4]

India refused to come in on the US side in the Cold War, as Truman had hoped and almost expected. Bilateral US economic assistance continued. But "they expected something more than gratitude and goodwill," Nehru said on returning home, "and that more I could not supply them."[5]

The Americans did indeed hope for more. Truman and his secretary of state, Dean Acheson, found it very difficult to accept that non-alignment in the Indian case meant just that: an insistence on an independent foreign policy and a refusal to become subservient to either power bloc. On Korea, for instance, Nehru condemned the North Korean attack, but immediately began searching for a peaceful resolution of the conflict. Written off in Washington as hopelessly naive, the Indian initiatives did have an effect, especially on the cease-fire and prisoner of war negotiations at the end of the war. But Nehru's efforts to end the war did not leave much of an impression on Truman. "Nehru has sold us down the Hudson," the president reportedly complained in late 1950. "His attitude has been responsible for us losing the war in Korea."[6]

While Nehru kept his distance from the Americans, Pakistani leaders were happy to embrace them. Economically hobbled at home and feeling under pressure by India, the Muslim elite that had created the Pakistani state rushed to link up with US Cold War efforts. Pakistani envoys presented their country as a key link in the Cold War chain around the Soviet Union, especially since India had refused to contribute to the anti-Communist cause. Without US aid, they claimed, Pakistan could easily become a target for Soviet expansionism and the Soviet search for warm-water ports. In 1954 the Eisenhower Administration rewarded them with a Mutual Defense Assistance Agreement, under which Pakistan received substantial US military aid. Pakistan also joined the South East Asia Treaty Organization (SEATO) and the Baghdad Pact, which promised support from the United States and Britain in case of an attack on its territory. The other Asian members of these pacts were the Philippines, Thailand, Iran, Iraq, and Turkey. Nehru was livid. When receiving Eisenhower's secretary of state, John Foster Dulles, in New Delhi in 1956, the Indian prime minister castigated US policy. "He said he recognized that NATO might have been born of a real necessity," Dulles reported, but

> he doubted the genuine security value of any of the Asian arrangements. He bitterly deplored SEATO and Baghdad, which he felt Pakistan had entered not for security against the Soviet Communists but in order to get strength to use against India. He felt that the Pakistanis were a martial people and a fanatical people who could readily attack India. . . . He deplored the fact that United States armament of Pakistan was leading India to arm and to make large expenditures for defense when it wanted to concentrate its efforts on improving its economic and social condition. (In this discussion of Pakistan with which he dealt at length, he showed signs of strong emotion.)[7]

Much of Nehru's foreign policy was designed to break out of the south Asian strictures posed by partition. With some right, he blamed colonialism for south Asia's ills. It was the British, Nehru thought, who had set Muslims against Hindus, and who had set up independent states on the periphery of the subcontinent: Burma, Ceylon, Nepal, Bhutan, and Sikkim. They had accepted Goa as a Portuguese colony on the Indian west coast. They had given power to an assortment of territories ruled by princes and maharajas, whom the prime minister now had to tempt, cajole, and threaten into becoming full members of the Indian state. Anticolonial and Asian solidarity was therefore important to Nehru, first and foremost among the major Asian states. In his first years in power he reached out to Indonesia, which he saw as an equivalent to India in southeast Asia. He also wanted to work closely with China, in part in order to convince the Chinese Communists that they were Asians first and foremost. And he opposed the US Security Treaty with Japan, which he saw as a Cold War arrangement imposed on an Asian nation.

At Bandung in 1955, some participants came to view the conference as a bit too much of an Indian show, given Nehru's superstar status. His message to the conference was clear, though. The Cold War was against the interests of the Third World. Threatening the world with nuclear annihilation was not only immoral but it deflected from the real problems the postcolonial countries faced: poverty, illiteracy, epidemic illness, and social dislocation created by colonialism. The new postcolonial states had to work together to overcome both the ills left over from the colonial era and current Cold War threats. And the only way to get such cooperation going was for other countries to learn from India's nonalignment and its willingness to stand up for Third World principles even if the Cold War Superpowers told it not to. Somewhat sanctimoniously, Nehru told the leaders assembled at Bandung that on some issues they would have to give up their own national interests to support what was morally right and good for the common cause.

Nehru's key preoccupation in the follow-up from Bandung was to extend what he called practical solidarity to causes of decolonization, national unity, and opposition to foreign domination. At the UN, India lambasted the tardiness of European countries in setting African countries free. It spoke out against the increasing US role in Indochina, and welcomed the revolutions in Egypt and in Cuba. But unlike more radical Third World countries, Nehru continued to believe that cooperation with Europeans was possible, and that violent conflict should be avoided. Radicals such as Nasser were disappointed with India's position in favor of negotiations during the Suez Crisis or its lack of military support for African liberation movements. Nasser,

Ben Bella, and Nelson Mandela deplored India's emphasis on mediation and arbitration, and its continued willingness to remain within the British Commonwealth.

Within India itself, however, Nehru was moving further to the Left in his attempts to further his country's rapid development. Since the 1930s, the Congress leadership had been fascinated with Soviet planning models and the success these plans seemed to have in modernizing a backward country. After independence, Indian economists trained in Britain and influenced by Left-wing Labour ideas of state-centered development began putting together large-scale plans for how India could change into an industrial power while feeding its increasing population. But in spite of their British background, the Five Year Plans the Indian experts drew up were more GosPlan than LSE, more Lenin than Laski. The concrete and proven example of the Soviet experiment weighed heavier than vague and contested British schemes. In the Second Five Year Plan, from 1956, Nehru's chief planner, Prasanta Chandra Mahalanobis, outlined the aims of the enterprise:

> It must provide for a larger increase in production, in investment and in employment. Simultaneously, it must accelerate the institutional changes needed to make the economy more dynamic and more progressive in terms no less of social than of economic ends. Development is a continuous process; it touches all aspects of community life and has to be viewed comprehensively. Economic planning thus extends itself into extra-economic spheres, educational, social and cultural. Each plan for a limited period becomes the starting point for more sustained effort covering longer periods, and each step in advance opens out new vistas and brings into view new problems to be solved.[8]

The launch of the Second Five Year Plan coincided not only with India's championing of South-South solidarity, as at Bandung, but also with a substantial boosting of ties between India and the Soviet Bloc. Khrushchev visited India in 1955 and in spite of finding Nehru almost as difficult to deal with at the personal level as the Americans did, the Soviet leader was quick to declare a new era of Soviet-Indian friendship. Soviet aid began coming to India, although it for many years paled in comparison with development aid from North America and western Europe.[9] But Khrushchev went further than just money, technology, and experts. He also unequivocally supported the Indian position on international issues such as Kashmir. Somewhat cynically, the Indian embassy in Moscow told Nehru that "the Soviets are afraid that their eastern partner, China, with her enormous man-power and growing industrial strength might prove to be an uncomfortable friend. To cope with such a contingency when and if it arises, they want to establish counterbalancing conditions. . . . Who else could do it better than India? . . ."[10]

China had been a conundrum for Nehru ever since he became Indian prime minister. During the Chinese civil war, Nehru's sympathy had mainly been with the Communists because of their rural roots and their program for social justice. But first and foremost he deplored the violence of the war and the doctrinaire Marxist approach the CCP showed after its victory. In Nehru's mind the two were connected. War fostered extreme radicalism and aggression. He wanted to build closer relations with China as a fellow Asian country, but he was cautious because of the new Beijing regime's willingness to use terror to solve domestic problems and because of its ideological alliance with the Soviet Union. Even so, Nehru made it clear that China needed to be included in the Afro-Asian group of countries that he hoped to build. "I have no doubt at all," he told his colleagues, "that the Government and people of China desire peace."[11]

The status of Tibet, an autonomous borderland that China claimed as part of its sovereign territory, was a key problem in the Sino-Indian relationship. The Chinese Communist leaders feared that independent India was continuing British attempts at influencing Tibet for its purposes. Nehru, however, had no problems accepting China's sovereignty over the region, although he sympathized with the young Dalai Lama's attempts at keeping as much self-government as possible. The Indian prime minister was also keen that Tibet kept religious freedom for its largely Buddhist population. The Indian consulate in Lhasa, which served as a listening post for matters going on in Tibet, reported on the backwardness of the country and its need for development from "a curiously preserved antiquated feudal system more cruel than benign."[12] But it also stressed Tibet's role as a giant buffer zone between China and India.

When Chinese Communist troops entered Tibet in 1950, Nehru appealed for Chinese "forbearance and generosity" toward the Tibetans, but also advised the Tibetans to attempt to work with Beijing. To be on the safe side, he offered the Dalai Lama exile in India if needed. But he also authorized military support for the Tibetan government. "Supplies of arms and ammunition began to pour into Tibet by April 1950," according to the Indian consulate in Lhasa.[13] India's support did not help much, however, and by late 1950 much of Tibet was under control of the People's Liberation Army. Nehru refused US offers of joint support for the Tibetan resistance. Instead he advised the Dalai Lama, who was camped close to the Indian border, to return to Lhasa and agree to some of the Chinese demands in order to preserve as much as possible of Tibetan freedom.[14]

Mao Zedong was furious over Indian behavior on Tibet. In conversations with the Soviets, he referred to Nehru as a double-dealing imperialist agent and the "running dog" of British and American interests. The fact that Nehru had left the British diplomat and Tibetologist Hugh Richardson in place as Indian consul in Lhasa proved their case, the CCP leaders believed. While Beijing appreciated India's support in ending the war in Korea, it took a long time for any real trust to develop between the two sides.

In 1954, as part of China's contribution to the Soviet post-Stalin peace offensive, Beijing agreed to talks with Delhi on the Tibet issue. Nehru, who had been calling for such talks for a long time, was delighted with the newfound Chinese approach. He knew, of course, that China had now cemented its position in Tibet, and that Mao's sudden reasonableness was in part connected with this. But the Indian prime minister was genuinely surprised at how much the principles the Chinese put forward as general concepts for Sino-Indian cooperation did fit with his own ideas. Incorporated in the agreements were what Nehru began referring to, in Sanskrit, as *Panch Sheel*, the five virtues, and the Chinese, after consultation with the Soviets, as the Five Principles of Peaceful Coexistence. They included the principles of "mutual respect for each other's territorial integrity and sovereignty; mutual non-aggression; mutual non-interference in each other's internal affairs; equality and mutual benefit; and peaceful co-existence."[15]

At Bandung, Nehru highlighted the Panch Sheel principles as a basic foreign policy for the Afro-Asian countries and movements. In reality, of course, they were far less than a policy, but also more, in terms of common propositions, than East and West had been able to agree on during the Cold War. For the Indians, the Five Principles were principally a way of tying China into an outer circle of Third World cooperation. While truly independent and nonaligned countries like India, Indonesia, Egypt, and Ghana were to be the core of South-South networks, Nehru hoped that Asian states like China or Japan would be able to participate in spite of their Cold War alliances. The long-term aim, Nehru stated openly, was to break them away from their orientation toward the Cold War and bring them fully into an Afro-Asian partnership for global change.

India's foreign policy after Bandung aimed at building a closer cooperation among countries in Asia and Africa on issues of anti-colonialism, disarmament, and development. Congress leaders invited delegations from other new countries to visit India and to study its experience in science, technology, planning, and education. At the UN, Indian representatives pushed for international solutions to Cold War conflicts, and supported liberation movements in southern Africa, Algeria, and Indochina (where Delhi viewed the Vietnam conflict mainly as an issue of decolonization and opposed US involvement). Indian diplomats and activists also reported on US race issues. To most of them, the American unwillingness to face up to racial oppression in their own country was a sign of how little could be expected from Washington on questions of international decolonization. Nehru firmly believed that decolonization and human rights were linked in a global context. Even so, he remained a skeptic toward using UN human rights declarations as instruments of foreign policy because he believed that in most cases state sovereignty trumped international agreements on domestic matters. Nevertheless, Nehru found UN resolutions and conventions to be of great use since they could be turned against racial discrimination in South Africa or British colonial oppression in Kenya.

The other main aspect of Indian foreign policy was to build a broad bloc of nonaligned states in order to defeat the Cold War. This project was linked to the Third World initiatives coming out of Bandung, but it was still separate. Its intention was to get countries of very different political orientations to break with the Cold War dichotomy and declare themselves as nonaligned. This aim meant, for instance, that there was no room for China or Japan, but that Indonesia, Ghana, and Egypt played leading roles beside India. The big addition was Yugoslavia, whose flamboyant leader, Tito, became a key figure in the Non-Aligned Movement. His visit to India in 1954, during which he lauded all of his hosts' concepts of foreign policy, made him a hero in Delhi. Tito was, Indian diplomats observed, "the first great European statesman who came to Asia not as a representative of colonizers, but as a great friend of Asian nations."[16] In the summer of 1956, discussions among Nehru, Nasser, and Tito on the Yugoslav island of Brioni kicked off the idea of a more formal cooperation among countries committed to nonaligned principles, not only in Asia and Africa, but also in Europe and Latin America.

Since its expulsion from the Soviet bloc on Stalin's whim in 1948, Yugoslavia had lived a precarious existence on the margins of Europe: still Communist, but sustained by Western aid and defended by its own substantial army. Tito wanted his country to be more than a heroic outcast. He saw Yugoslavia as a beacon of independent socialist development and as a model for new countries in the Third World that did not want to subsume themselves in a Cold War dichotomy. It was possible to be socialist, independent, and respected by both power blocs, Tito claimed. After Khrushchev's 1955 admission that Stalin's accusations against Tito had been pure fantasy, Yugoslavia's stock in the Third World rose even higher.

For India and other new countries, Yugoslavia also played a major role as an arms exporter and supplier of military advisers. Up to Tito's death in 1980, his country was the militant wing of the Non-Aligned Movement, supplying equipment from its own plentiful military industry, not only to independent Third World countries, but also to liberation movements in Angola, Zimbabwe, and Guinea. In some cases Yugoslav military supplies rivaled those of the Soviet Union and provided a lifeline for countries that feared becoming too dependent on Moscow for their defense needs. Nehru and his successors regarded Tito as perhaps their closest ally. Nehru's daughter, Prime Minister Indira Gandhi, viewed the Yugoslav leader as a mentor in international affairs, almost like a substitute father.

But India also believed that it could have a more direct influence on the Soviet Union itself. Nehru never gave up hope on weaning the Soviets away from their Cold War behavior. Moscow reacted aggressively because it felt threatened, the Indian prime minister believed. "Whoever might have been responsible for this 'cold war,' the effect on the Soviet Union was to create apprehension and a continuing sense of danger," he told his chief ministers in 1955. Nehru found that it was "probable that if there is a marked improvement in world tensions and the cold war ceases, then internal developments and changes will take place in these East European states."[17] Indian diplomats saw Khrushchev's break with Stalin's policies at the Communist Party of the Soviet Union's Twentieth Congress in 1956 as a consequence of India's benign influence. Soviet leaders visiting India "must have been impressed at once by her progress and her abhorrence of violence. The theory that violence was not a prerequisite for the transformation of society was thus a recognition of a state of affairs which had come into existence. The conversations of the Soviet leaders with our Prime Minister and the intensive study of his books . . . must also have prompted Soviet leaders to discount the role of violence in the march towards socialism."[18]

The Soviet invasion of Hungary in 1956 dented the Indian image of the Soviet Union, but did not destroy it. India continued to receive Soviet aid for its development programs and to build its military capacity. But Nehru became even more preoccupied with the cause of nonalignment and the idea of building an anti–Cold War bloc. His doubts about the more radical approaches of Nasser, Nkrumah, or Sukarno did not lead to divergence. Rather, such doubts reinforced India's need to be close to the other nonaligned nations, in order to influence them. After all, Nehru concluded, what drove his fellow Third World leaders toward unnecessary radicalism was the unwillingness of the imperialist states to give up their positions and privileges. The 1960–61 Congo crisis was a case in point. Nehru was horrified at Lumumba's murder and placed the blame squarely on the Belgians and their US partners. India committed five thousand troops to UN peacekeeping operations in the country, on the condition that the secretary-general guaranteed Congo's national integrity.

The Congo crisis was the prod that led nonaligned countries to meet in Yugoslavia's capital, Belgrade, in 1961 to set up regular conferences and arrangements, later known as the Non-Aligned Movement. While strongly in favor of nonaligned cooperation, Nehru had been a skeptic toward setting up a more integrated organization, in part because he feared that it would reduce India's flexibility and independence in foreign affairs. Concerns over Congo had proven him wrong, even to himself. The non-bloc countries had to cooperate and take charge of the process of decolonization. If not, the Superpowers would exploit it for their own purposes. And the aborted Khrushchev-Eisenhower summit in Paris in 1960 proved that the Superpowers were not able to manage their own affairs, far less those of others. "War," said the final statement from the Belgrade meeting, "has never threatened mankind with graver consequences than today." But at the same time the participants stressed that "imperialism is weakening. Colonial empires and other forms of foreign oppression of peoples in Asia, Africa and Latin America are gradually disappearing from the stage of history."[19]

The fear of many of the founders of the Non-Aligned Movement in 1961 was that the death throes of colonialism could lead to new wars. While "a lasting peace can be achieved only if . . . the domination of colonialism-imperialism and neo-colonialism in all their manifestations is radically eliminated . . . the Conference resolutely rejects the view that war, including the 'cold war,' is inevitable, as this view reflects a sense both of helplessness and hopelessness. . . . They affirm their unwavering faith that the international community is able to organize its life without resorting to means which actually belong to a past epoch of human history."[20] For Nehru, the Belgrade declaration was both a design for a future without a Cold War and a warning about how fragile global peace actually was.

The nascent Non-Aligned Movement consisted of some strange bedfellows. While China had been excluded, Fidel Castro's Cubans made one of their international debuts at Belgrade. Only a year later, during the Cuban missile crisis, Castro would call on the Soviet Union to risk global nuclear war in defense of Cuban independence. But a number of conservative monarchies were also represented: Ethiopia, Morocco, and Saudi Arabia. Belgrade was not only different from Bandung because European and Latin American countries were represented; it was also different because the conference was more about the right to independence, sovereignty, and peace than about Third World solidarity. The state, in its various forms, played a more central place at Belgrade than it had done at Bandung. This was not surprising, perhaps, because of the sheer number of new states that had come into existence between 1955 and 1961. But, together with the Group of 77, it signaled a future in which states and their demands would rub up against a more radical reorganization of international affairs as envisaged in the early phase of decolonization.

For India, the need for security for its young state would become glaringly visible only a year after the founding of the Non-Aligned Movement. The 1962 war with China destroyed much of the optimism that Nehru's young assistants, though not always the prime minister himself, had shown about the future. Nehru was less concerned about the charges of naiveté leveled against him inside and outside of India than the effects the war would have on his country's international aspirations. As the Chinese armies advanced, Nehru despaired to the point of asking for a Soviet and then a US intervention. While the Soviets hedged their bets, not least because of the need for Chinese support in the concurrent Cuban crisis, the Kennedy Administration responded with airdrops of weapons for the Indian army. The president wanted to use India's urgent needs as a way of improving relations with Delhi. "By the Chinese action," Kennedy said, "the subcontinent has become a new area of major confrontation between the Free World and the Communists. . . . The Indians themselves are at long last fully aware of the Chinese Communist threat and appear to be determined to meet it."[21]

In spite of his government's considerable responsibility for its outbreak, it is true to say that the war broke Nehru's heart. He had hoped to be a peace-maker between East and West. And he had hoped that India, in its domestic as well as its foreign policy, would be an example of self-sufficiency and nonalignment for others to follow. Instead he was reduced to pleading for aid from the Superpowers to stem the military advance of another Asian country. "It is a tragedy," he noted, "that we who have stood for peace everywhere, should be attacked in this way and be compelled to resist attack by arms."[22] After the ceasefire, Nehru felt that his Asian policy was in tatters. Neither he nor his successors gave up on India's policy of nonalignment. But especially after Nehru's death in 1964 this policy was inoculated with a solid portion of Indian nationalism, particularly with regard to its own region.

Pakistan's response to the US military aid to India during the China crisis was to further build its own relations with Beijing. This was perhaps the Cold War's most unlikely romance. The Pakistani officers who engineered the alliance were conservative Muslims who had no interest in China's Communist excesses. And the Chinese accepted the Pakistani embrace simply on the principle that my enemy's enemy is my friend. When Washington, still Pakistan's main ally, demurred, the Pakistani military dictator, General Mohammed Ayub Khan, increased pressure on India in Kashmir. He wanted to show

Pakistan's military prowess to the Chinese and demonstrate to US president Johnson that his country was not dependent on American aid. Outwardly, the 1965 Pakistani incursion into Indian-controlled Kashmir was presented as a Kashmiri people's rebellion. But the Indian government knew better.

Nehru's successor, Lal Bahadur Shastri, an otherwise unassuming man, decided to strike back. He ordered large-scale attacks against Pakistani forces not just in Kashmir, but in western and eastern Pakistan simultaneously. With its forces defeated on the battlefield, Ayub Khan's regime was in trouble. The Americans refused to help, and the Chinese did not have the capacity. The Pakistanis' unlikely appeals to the Soviets for assistance just showed what dire straits they were in militarily. Ayub's desperation over his own folly did, however, give Moscow a rare Cold War opportunity to play the peace-maker. The terms for the cease-fire were negotiated under its auspices in the Soviet central Asian city of Tashkent. In territorial terms, the result was close to status quo. But Pakistan's weaknesses had been exposed, as had India's ability and intentions to be the predominant power within its region.

Indira Gandhi, Nehru's daughter, was chosen as prime minister after Shastri's sudden death, from a heart attack, during the Tashkent negotiations. India's new leader was a far tougher policy-maker than either of her predecessors. She was committed to a secular, socialist India that controlled its region and sought global influence through the UN and the Non-Aligned Movement in light of what she saw as its national interests. Even more than her father, she was profoundly skeptical about the US role in the world and viewed the Soviets as easier to work with, especially in light of the ongoing US alliance with Pakistan and Pakistan's flirtation with China. Gandhi's main security concern was Beijing, and the intensification of the Sino-Soviet conflict in the late 1960s alerted her to how much the Soviets and the Indians had in common strategically, even though she did not share Moscow's Communist ideology.

China's drift toward further radicalism and the Cultural Revolution frightened the Indian leaders, as it did many others. It convinced them that India would be even more of a target for Beijing than it had been in the past. Although they noted that China's self-inflicted damage "does not cause us any pain," they reacted sharply against harassment of Indians living in China, including the sacking of a Sikh temple in Shanghai and attacks on the Indian embassy in Beijing. Indira Gandhi made it clear that Indian policy toward China, including giving asylum to the Dalai Lama, would not change unless China stopped encouraging Pakistan to act aggressively and fomenting Communist rebellions within India itself. "India," noted the Ministry for External Affairs in Delhi, "is still the only sector in which the Chinese can indulge in military adventurism and hope to get away with it."[23]

The Non-Aligned Movement became Gandhi's favored foreign policy arena. As the movement expanded, she increasingly took a central place in it. The movement, she said, "means equality among nations, and the democratization of international relations, economic and political. It wants global cooperation for development on the basis of mutual benefit. It is a strategy for the recognition and preservation of the world's diversity."[24] But Gandhi was far too realistic to put all her eggs in one basket with regard to security and international affairs. Her Non-Aligned Movement strategy paralleled, but did not impede, increased cooperation with the Soviet Union on technology and defense. Gandhi made sure to keep her independence also vis-à-vis Moscow. She sharply criticized the Soviet occupation of Czechoslovakia in 1968. She also attacked any Soviet attempt to increase its influence in Pakistan, for instance through small-scale weapons sales to the regime in Islamabad. Even a "symbolic supply could be dangerous," the Indian foreign secretary admonished visiting Soviet leaders in 1969. "The prospect of Soviet tanks fighting Soviet tanks could not be welcome in the Soviet Union."[25] The United States remained a key supplier of civilian aid to India. This vital assistance came from the US government, from US contributions to multilateral organizations, and from private foundations. But US aid to India and its help during the war with China did little to improve the overall political relationship. India's criticism of US Asian policies grated many American leaders and made them regard the Indians as ungrateful. US attempts to get more sympathy from Delhi on its intervention in Indochina in the wake of the China war made no progress. When US vice president Hubert Humphrey was sent to India to solicit Indira Gandhi's support, "she confined herself to expressing concern at the likely escalation of the conflict in Vietnam and the need for a peaceful solution."[26] The US unwillingness to sacrifice its alliance with Pakistan also got in the way of a closer US-India relationship. And Indians commented sharply on what they saw as a lack of racial justice in the United States and the lack of a US commitment to racial equality worldwide. The United States, said a 1969 overview of US internal changes by Indian diplomats, "has reached a stage, where a dangerous relationship exists between . . . black rage and white fear. The confrontationist tactics of the one evoke a reactionary response in the other." It was this response, Gandhi believed, that had produced Richard Nixon's election victory in 1968.[27]

But Indira Gandhi's main challenge as she fastened her grip on Congress and Indian politics was not the relationship with the United States. It was domestic development in India. First and foremost she felt the need to make more progress in battling her country's chronic problems with poverty and hunger. India had avoided China's development disasters, but also it had made much less progress in promoting health and education. A country priding itself on its democratic development was still dependent on food aid from abroad. Gandhi was convinced that the Indian development model would pay off if the political conditions were right. But in India, as in Pakistan and much of the Middle East, extreme forms of social oppression were left untouched in spite of the leaders' socialist rhetoric. Congress politicians were promising opportunities for all, especially at election time, but then allied themselves with local elites to the detriment of the low-caste poor. Instead of being an instrument for social change, the Congress Party had become a tool for families who had ruled and exploited their neighbors for generations under colonial rule.

Indira Gandhi was determined to root out these shortcomings, but she felt she needed more power in order to do so. In 1969 she nationalized key banks and concentrated executive power within her own secretariat. When her more radical policies led to a split in the Congress Party, Gandhi's faction won the 1971 national elections hands-down on the slogan "Get Rid of Poverty." She moved the country closer to a strict centralized planning regime, in which the government was responsible for most economic activities. When accused of betraying her father's more liberal policy, Indira bristled. "My father was a statesman," she responded. "I'm a political woman. My father was a saint. I'm not."[28]

The 1971 Bangladesh war, the biggest crisis in south Asia since independence, gave Indira Gandhi the chance to prove that she was indeed no saint. The crisis had its origins in the Cold War, and especially in the relationships among Pakistan, India, China, the United States, and the Soviet Union. Although the trigger that set the war off was the Pakistani generals' abysmal treatment of the people in the eastern half of their country, the scene had been set by the sudden rapprochement between the United States and China through Kissinger's Beijing visit in July 1971. This harmonization was what Indian leaders had feared most. From the mid-1960s on, Indian security advisers had warned that "the great temptation before the Western world would be to prop up China as a counterweight to the USSR."

> We felt, however, that this might be a dangerous move, because there was an essential difference between these two countries, which needed to be recognized. The USSR also had its world-wide ambitions, but they were pursuing these in a more peaceful manner than the Chinese. Perhaps this was due to the fact that they had had 40 years in which to develop, during which they also had built up some prosperity for themselves; perhaps it was due to the realization of the dangers of nuclear war. But ultimately the USSR presented less of a danger to the world community than China, particularly with regard to the issue of war and peace. China, far more than [the] USSR, would pursue her course with ruthless determination, quite undeterred by the prospect of a large scale war.[29]

The specific danger, for India, lay in Pakistan's close relations with both the United States and China. The symbolism of Kissinger leaving for Beijing from Islamabad was not lost on India's leaders. But, in spite of its centrality in international affairs, as a state Pakistan had been going downhill ever since its inception in 1947. When the generals had tried to democratize in 1970, the result was an election victory for the Awami League, an eastern Pakistani movement that wanted to make the country into a democratic confederation, in which the Bengali population of the east had a genuine say. Predictably, the western Pakistani general who was president, Yahya Khan, nullified the result and arrested Sheikh Mujibur Rahman, the leader of the Awami League. When unrest broke out in eastern Pakistan, the generals introduced martial law. Soldiers began attacking neighborhoods in the east that had a high percentage of Bengali nationalists or Pakistani Hindus. Large numbers of refugees started crossing over to India. Both in public and in private Indira Gandhi began describing Pakistan's policy toward the Bengalis as "genocide," and started preparing a military intervention. Her motives were both humanitarian and strategic.

The Nixon Administration was blind to the disasters the Pakistani generals inflicted on their own countrymen, but saw the Cold War strategic setback the splitting up of Pakistan could lead to for the United States. Visiting Delhi on his way to Pakistan and, secretly, from there to Beijing, Kissinger tried to strike a pose of uncertainty on how far the United States would go to assist Pakistan in case of a war. The Indians would have nothing of it. When Kissinger claimed that he had been unaware of continued US weapons' shipments to Pakistan during the crisis, the Indian foreign minister shot back: "It is surprising that such a high placed official as you are not given full facts. . . . The embarrassment over all this is . . . for you. Yet it is a serious blow to our relations." Pakistan, Foreign Minister Swaran Singh said, "has been sustained wholly by you." With seven million refugees and increased fighting along the eastern border, "there is a limit to what we can take. . . . We would like to know whether we are coming in the way of your interests. If we are, we would like to take a second look at our own policies."[30]

A week later Washington and Beijing jointly announced Nixon's forthcoming visit to China. Kissinger told the Indian ambassador that the United States would not help his country if China intervened in an Indian war with Pakistan. The Indian response was swift. Picking up on proposals made earlier by the Soviets, Gandhi agreed to a treaty of friendship between India and the Soviet Union. "In the event of either being subjected to an attack or a threat thereof," said the treaty, the two sides "shall immediately enter into mutual consultations in order to remove such threat."[31] India also started a large-scale program for training Bengali guerrillas to fight in eastern Pakistan. And on the prime minister's orders, the Indian military began preparations for a full-scale invasion of Pakistan if diplomatic efforts to solve the crisis did not succeed fast. "The Indo-Soviet Treaty appears to have taken both Beijing and Washington by surprise," reported the Indian embassy in the US capital. "The treaty represents a certain reassurance for India and a certain advance for the Soviet Union in Asia and a corresponding setback to Sino-US maneuvers."[32]

On 4 December 1971 India launched a combined ground, sea, and air operation against eastern Pakistan. Within a few days, the Pakistani military in the east was crushed and a Bengali administration began ruling the territory as independent Bangladesh. Seeing the jubilant crowds in the capital, Dacca, it was difficult for anyone not to see the Indian intervention as a liberation. But Nixon and Kissinger viewed it as Indian aggression. They moved parts of the US Seventh Fleet into the Indian Ocean and told their new Chinese friends that "we are afraid that if nothing is done to stop it, eastern Pakistan will become a Bhutan and western Pakistan will become a Nepal. And India with Soviet help would be free to turn its energies elsewhere."[33] But the Chinese knew that an intervention this late in the game would be risky, and with all her military objectives reached, Indira Gandhi quickly accepted a cease-fire. South Asia settled into a new status quo, with India even more predominant, still nonaligned but also closer to the USSR than ever before.

Nixon and Kissinger, in conversations that oozed racism and misogyny, fumed that "the bitch" had tricked them. "We'll be paying for it for a long time. . . . It will be interesting," Kissinger told the NSC, "to see how all those people who were so horrified at what the Paks were doing in East Pakistan react when the Indians take over there."[34] "What we are seeing here," Kissinger told the president, "is a Soviet-Indian power play to humiliate the Chinese and also somewhat us. . . . And the effect of that will be on all other countries watching it is that the friends of China and the United States have been clobbered by India and the Soviet Union."[35] The Nixon Administration set out to punish India as best it could.

The sense of enmity in Washington was reciprocated in Delhi. "Military aid to Pakistan from the US has been one of the potent causes of the military getting the upper hand in the internal affairs of Pakistan and in sustaining its unnatural hostile posture towards India and ambitions over Kashmir," said one Indian Ministry of External Affairs report to the prime minister.[36] "China and USA both do not mind sacrificing Indian interests if it holds them tighter close."[37] Indians, claimed another Delhi policy review, have "been bewildered and shocked by the persistent stand of the US administration against India, against the freedom struggle of Bangladesh and in support of the Yahya regime [in Pakistan]."[38] Indira Gandhi was not going to seek American friendship anytime soon.

Instead the Indian prime minister turned increasingly authoritarian in domestic affairs and friendly toward the Soviet Union internationally. The high point of Soviet-Indian cooperation was in the mid-1970s, as the USSR expanded its military and economic cooperation with India, including the building of steel plants and the exploitation of oil and coal reserves. The Soviets were also instrumental in providing assistance for India's "peaceful nuclear test" in 1974. "The Soviet Union," said a 1974 Indian government report, "continued to support India's policy of non-alignment and her contribution to the strengthening of world peace and to the struggle for the removal of all vestiges of colonialism, neo-colonialism and racism."[39]

When Indira Gandhi in 1975 responded to a Supreme Court decision invalidating the last elections by refusing a new vote, restricting civil liberties, and ruling by decree under a state of emergency, the

Soviets began hoping that India would follow in the footsteps of the People's Democracies and some postcolonial states by introducing socialism through a one-party system. "Should small groups with the backing of big finance, press and foreign friends, but without support of the masses, be allowed to force their ideas upon the majority?" Indira Gandhi asked her party. "Will there be democracy, when India is weakened?"[40] But Indian democracy was far too robust even for a leader of Indira Gandhi's stature to put aside. Under pressure from increasing political unrest at home, she called an election in 1977, which she felt certain she would win, but ended up losing to an opposition alliance headed by former Congress minister Morarji Desai. The first non-Congress government since independence had little to offer in terms of new policies. But it managed to rebuild Indian democracy after the Emergency, while keeping its international policies in place. The aging Desai and his advisers were afraid that the Soviets would break their links with India with Indira Gandhi out. "Indo-Soviet relations are characterized by deep understanding and close identity or broad similarity of views," said a policy overview from the new foreign minister. "Friendship and understanding with the Soviet Union has hitherto been one of the main directions of India's foreign policy. This has both emotional content and hard-headed logic. . . . Today there is a vast spectrum of inter-weaving relations from which both political and economic advantages have accrued to India."[41]

The new Desai government was not going to throw these advantages overboard. The Indian foreign secretary met Soviet diplomats and told them that "while a number of important events have taken place in India . . . it was important to remember that India remained where it was and its foreign policy remained unchanged." The Desai government would "preserve the character of India's foreign policy not merely because they have inherited it but because they realized its rationale in terms of India's interests." The Soviets and the Indians, the foreign secretary said, "could have continued confidence in each other and look forward to the further development [of] the many different links of cooperation between the two countries in the interest of mutual benefit."[42]

At a carefully managed meeting with the similarly senescent Brezhnev in Moscow in 1979, the Indian prime minister tried to make sense of a rapidly changing world. The Soviet-Indian partnership was confirmed. Both were frightened by the rise of political Islam in nearby Iran. Asked by Desai what was really going on in Iran, the Soviet leader confessed, "The devil only knows. . . . There was that uprising of the people. Thousands demonstrated. . . . We always had good relations with Iran, with the Shah also. He came to us and I went to him. . . . [Now] the Shah is not there. The Americans supported him! Now there is the new regime and the Americans would like to adapt themselves to the new regime also. The Rightists [Islamists] have made their appearance there and they want to have close relations with the USA."[43]

To nobody's surprise, Indira Gandhi was back in charge after the 1980 elections in India. The prime minister was not exactly chastened, but certainly more aware of her role as "a political woman" than ever. She also feared for India's unity and cohesion in a world where issues of identity, religion, and nation had started to replace the Cold War ideological divide. The rise of Islamism frightened her as much as it had Brezhnev and Desai. Already before the elections in India, the Indian Foreign Ministry had warned the Soviets about the resistance that the new Communist government in Afghanistan was giving rise to. "While we could not openly say so . . . , our own principles of secularism did not necessarily rejoice at the emergence of the religious fervor in many countries which both India and the Soviet Union considered as important," Indian foreign secretary Jagat Singh Mehta told the Soviet ambassador.[44] But some of the damage was self-inflicted. "In many Arab countries," Mehta continued, "there was a strong feeling that Islam was being threatened by the [Communist Afghan] Khalqi government. This was of course not India's view but we were bringing it to their notice as a friend."

For India, and especially for the new Indira Gandhi government after 1980, the world was turning faster than they would like to see. Most Indian leaders, including many of those who had opposed Congress, were wedded to India's planned economy development model.

They liked to see centralized states abroad, with whom they could negotiate on trade and security issues. Although they complained endlessly about Sino-American rapprochement, Soviet-American détente was in many ways in India's interest. Indira Gandhi hoped that over time her country could develop good working relations with the Americans also, possibly by way of Moscow. Ethnic and religious mobilization in south Asia and the Middle East could get in the way of such hopes, the prime minister feared.

But in returning as prime minister, she also still felt the influence of the Cold War on India. Gandhi deplored "the unceasing effort of other countries to mold our policies to fit in with their global strategies." She saw more "uncritical acceptance of foreign postulates" within India than before. "We should not imitate other countries or other systems, nor is it our aim to become improved editions of them," Gandhi warned.[45] But, just as for her predecessors, Indira Gandhi's room for maneuver remained circumscribed by the Cold War. In spite of its many efforts, even a country as significant as India was never able to fully break away from the global conflict molding its policies.

17

Middle East Maelstroms

As everywhere else in Asia and Africa, the Cold War in the Middle East must be understood as part of a long-term struggle between colonialism and its opponents. What set it apart was the intensity of its conflicts, both domestic and international, and the significance these conflicts achieved at the global level. At times, such as around the 1967 and 1973 wars, it seemed as if the Cold War in the Middle East had hijacked the bipolar world for its purposes. And although not all clashes in the region were linked to the global ideological divide, many political leaders did their utmost to make it sound that way, both for purposes of domestic mobilization and in order to build alliances against their regional enemies. For Soviets and Americans, the Middle East was a maelstrom that threatened to pull them in toward its vortex, driven by forces they firmly believed they had an interest in, but still always found hard to gauge.

At the end of World War II, most of the Middle East had been controlled by foreign powers. British forces backed up French influence in Syria and Lebanon, as well as further west in the Maghreb. The British themselves occupied Palestine and dominated the governments in Egypt, Iraq, Jordan, and the Gulf states. Most of the Arabian peninsula was controlled by the conservative, religious Saudi monarchy in alliance with US oil companies. Iran was occupied by the Soviets in the north and the British in the south, ostensibly to keep its oil riches from falling into German hands. It was a colonial world through and through, where Arabs and Persians were always reminded of their status as dominated and controlled.

A decade or so later this political landscape was transformed. British and French domination was increasingly a thing of the past, and the 1956 Suez Crisis confirmed European frailties. So did France's failing colonial war in Algeria. Arab nationalist revolutions were driving politics in Egypt, Syria, and Iraq. Palestine was divided between the new religiously defined state of Israel and territories occupied by Egypt and Jordan. In this rapidly changing Middle East successive US Administrations, and their European and Japanese allies, believed that it was critical to secure oil supplies and retain a Western strategic presence. The Soviets, meanwhile, hoped that radical nationalists would break away from capitalist control and form alliances with Moscow. Some CPSU theoreticians thought that shutting off cheap Middle Eastern oil could help produce the ultimate crisis of capitalism, while Red Army planners knew that in case of war NATO armies depended on imported oil. On both sides, it was a heady mix of dreams and apprehensions that linked the Middle East's nightmarish politics with the Cold War conflict.

In addition to its oil supplies, there were two other main connectors between the Middle East and Cold War. One was the conflict within the region between secular and religious politics. In every country in the Middle East, secularists—mainly, but not always, socialists—confronted those who believed that government should be organized according to religious prescripts. In the Arab world, the nationalists who had the upper hand were socialist secularists who admitted some role for religion, but generally persecuted the Islamists, the minority who believed in religious rule. An exception was Saudi Arabia, but even there the conservative aristocrats in power were far too preoccupied securing their own income from the country's oil wealth and exploiting their US alliance for domestic security purposes to risk any independent Islamist activity. In Iran, set apart from the Arab Middle East by language, culture, and confession, a young monarch intent on modernizing his country under US auspices ruthlessly persecuted those members of the Shia clergy who believed in religious rule. The Shah felt, with good reason in the 1950s and '60s, that the majority of conservative mullahs would support him against his arch enemies, the Left and the Iranian Communist Party.

The other connector was the creation of a new Jewish state in the Middle East. Both the United States and the Soviet Union had supported the state of Israel at its inception. But they had done so for very different reasons. For the Americans, Israel was a refuge for Jews from the European Holocaust and, at least for some, the fulfillment of the biblical prophesy of the Jews' return to their ancestral homeland. It was also the introduction of Western modernity into the Middle East and a potential ally for US foreign policy in the region. For the Soviets, Israel—at least at first—meant more trouble for the British and a victory for a kind of Left-wing Zionism with which even the deeply anti-Semitic Stalin thought he could work with over time. Israel might also be a solution to his own Jewish problem. Stalin had nothing against the thought of sending elderly, infirm, or politically undesirable Soviet Jews to Israel, just like he had moved whole peoples around inside the Soviet Union.

Both Americans and Soviets turned out to have been very mistaken in terms of the significance of the Jewish state for themselves and for the region. Israel's defeat of the Arab countries in 1948 and the strength and cohesion of Israeli society made it into a force to be reckoned with on its own terms. Israel was beholden to US assistance but not dependent on it, at least not until the 1967 war. It confronted anti-Semitism in the Soviet bloc, simply because it existed there more than anywhere else. But the biggest mistake of the Superpowers in the Middle East was to misjudge the vigor and advance of Arab nationalism, fueled in part by the creation of a Jewish state on Arab territory. For many Arabs, the existence and success of Israel, paired with the number of Palestinian Arab refugees, served as constant reminders of the need to create a unified and powerful Arab nationalist movement that could redeem the Arab nation and speed it toward a modernity of its own.

Arab nationalism, like other forms of European and Asian nationalisms, came out of the nineteenth century. It found its contemporary form in the years after World War I, after the collapse of the Ottoman Empire. When European countries refused to give Arab countries their independence, but instead proceeded with a full-scale recolonization of the Middle East, nationalist groups staged open revolts. In 1919 massive demonstrations in Egypt demanded full autonomy and the end of British control. In Iraq the population rebelled the following year. The British crushed the uprising with up to ten thousand Iraqis dead. The 1925 Syrian and Lebanese revolt against French rule cost at least six thousand lives. By the end of World War II, if not before, nationalism was in command of local politics all over the Arab world, and the colonial regimes were receding.

But Arab nationalism did not stop with demands for national independence. For many Arab nationalists, the monarchical regimes that gradually replaced direct colonial rule were almost as bad as the British and French. Nationalist leaders viewed these kings and sheikhs as outgrowths of the colonial presence, who were keen on striking compromises with the former colonial powers for their own personal gain. One by one Arab kings were overthrown by movements that criticized their "society of the half percent" and demanded rapid modernization alongside social equality. The young officers who removed Egypt's King Farouk in 1952 stressed anti-imperialism, anti-feudalism, and abolition of monopolies as their policy. They also saw the Arab monarchies' failure to win against Israel in 1948 as a sign of moral decay. "The Arab peoples entered Palestine with the same degree of enthusiasm," wrote Gamal Abdel Nasser, the leader of the 1952 Egyptian revolution. "They did so on the basis of . . . a common estimate shared by all as to the outer borders of their security. These peoples left Palestine with a common bitterness and disappointment; then, each in its own internal affairs encountered the same factors, the same ruling forces that had brought about their defeat, and forced them to bow their heads in humiliation and shame."[1]

Nasser's speeches on Palestine made clear how far he and other nationalists had come in regarding all Arabs as *one* people. Even though the Arab world had been politically disunited since the thir-teenth century, it was quite natural that revolutionaries who wanted rapid change hoped that Arab cultural unity could be translated into a common purpose, not least because it would give added significance to themselves and to their movements. "When the struggle was over in Palestine," wrote Nasser, "the Arab circle in my eyes had become a single entity. . . . I have followed developments in the Arab countries, and I find they match, point for point. What happened in Cairo had its counterpart in Damascus the next day, and in Beirut, Amman, Baghdad and elsewhere. . . . It is a single region. The same circum-stances, the same factors, even the same forces, united against all of it . . . the foremost of these forces was imperialism."[2]

Born in 1918, Nasser was an army officer with strong Egyptian na-tionalist and Pan-Arab views. He saw the struggle for Egyptian inde-pendence as part of a wider Arab liberation struggle, which in turn linked to global anti-imperialist and Third World concerns. From the beginning of his political career, Nasser believed in a vague form of socialism, but it had to be a form of governance developed by Arabs themselves in accordance with the principles of Islam. Although Nasser admired the Soviet economic system, he was fearful of Com-munist political influence in Egypt, and on several occasions impris-oned Left-wing leaders when he thought they went too far in their criticism of the government. But his main domestic enemy was what he considered the religious Right. Nasser openly mocked the Muslim Brotherhood and banned all Islamist organizations after an infuriated member of the Brotherhood tried to assassinate him in 1954. For the Egyptian leader, Islam was first and foremost an inspiration for Arab liberation and regional unity. He abolished Sharia courts and made the religious authorities in Egypt—seen by many worldwide as the main Islamic theologians—issue a fatwa, which said that all Muslims, whether Sunni, Shia, or sectarian, belonged to the same Muslim community.

Nasser's views on the Cold War were straightforward. He be-lieved that the United States, Britain, and France would attempt to control the Arab world even after the end of colonialism. He saw the conservative Muslim monarchies in Saudi Arabia, Iran, Jordan, and the Gulf states as instruments in this political and economic oppression. Like the Indians and Indonesia under Sukarno, Nasser turned to the Soviet Union because he believed that Moscow could be an alternative supplier of economic and military aid and know-how. The Soviets, for Nasser, were a likely ally in the struggle for his political aims in the Arab world. His form of nonalignment was one in which he guarded his independence, united with other Third World countries, and worked ever-more closely with the Soviets in the pursuit of Nasser's own aims. Domestically, his proof of his Cold War policies' success was the Soviet financing of the Aswan Dam, the world's largest dam project, which Nasser sought and received after he felt that the Americans would attach political strings to their aid. When the Eisenhower Administration furiously withdrew its offer of assistance, the Soviets designed and helped build the dam, which was completed in 1970.

Internationally, Nasser also benefitted from his increasing closeness with the Soviet Union. In the 1960s Egypt fought an outdrawn conflict with the Saudis in support of the revolution in Yemen. Nasser's aim was to show the other regional powers that Egypt was in control of the fate of the Arab revolution all over the Middle East. The Soviets and other Communist countries gave substantial support to the more than seventy thousand Egyptian troops who served in Yemen. The Yemeni royalists were supported by Britain and the United States, as well as Jordan and Iran, in addition to the Saudis. Nasser's intervention got entangled in Yemeni tribal relations and clan differences, and was at a logistical disadvantage due to Saudi proximity across Yemen's northern border and British access from its colony in Aden. The Egyptian president fumed that even the shoes of the dead Egyptian soldiers "are more honorable than the crowns of King Saud and King Hussein."[3] But by the late 1960s Nasser's effort in Yemen had fizzled out, with big losses and few achievements, even though the Egyptian presence left behind reservoirs of radicalism in the south of Arabia.

But other movements than Nasser's also had their eyes on the cause of Pan-Arabism. The Arab Ba'ath [Renaissance] Party was founded in Damascus in 1940 by Michel Aflaq, a former Communist from a Christian Syrian family who believed in a regimented mass movement that would renew the Arab quest for political and cultural unity. Aflaq and his followers welcomed the revolution in Egypt but criticized Nasser for being self-serving and too centered on Egyptian interests. Instead, the Ba'ath leadership wanted to build Arab unity from below, with branches of the party in each country, all intent on taking power and unifying the Arab world around an authoritarian, nationalist, and socialist program. The Ba'ath leaders were the vanguard who would break with generations of backwardness, fragmentation, and European domination. They, Aflaq said, have "the will that the nation lacked, as a daring model and example of movement from passiveness and slumber to awakening and action."[4]

As is often the case with parties that put unity above all other virtues, the Ba'ath experienced its fair share of infighting from the very beginning of the party's existence. Some of its members supported the merger of Syria and Egypt into a United Arab Republic in 1958, in spite of the party's criticism of Nasser. That union ended in acrimony three years later. In Iraq some members supported the 1958 revolution, which overthrew the monarchy, only to see the party crushed there a year later. But in spite of its disunity, the influence of the various branches of the Ba'ath Party increased in many Arab countries in the late 1950s and early 1960s. For many Arabs who wanted revolutionary change without embracing Communism, Ba'athist thinking served their purposes well.

The revolution in Iraq in 1958 was a watershed in the Cold War in the Middle East. The military regime that took power allied itself with the miniscule Iraqi Communist Party, in part because the new president, Abd al-Karim Qasim, distrusted the Ba'ath. Qasim also wanted an alliance with the Soviets to protect his regime against Western intervention, like the one in Iran five years earlier. The revolution was bloody. The king and fourteen members of his family were gunned down at the palace. The British embassy was sacked. US leaders, understandably, were horrified. Within weeks, Iraq had gone from being a US ally central to its security architecture to joining with its opponents, Nasser and the Soviets. "We either act now or get out of the Middle East," President Eisenhower told his advisers. "To lose this area by inaction would be far worse than the loss in China, because of the strategic position and resources of the Middle East."[5] Always watchful for falling dominoes, Eisenhower wanted to confront what he saw as a direct Soviet challenge to US power in the Middle East. "Our military advisers," Secretary of State Dulles told Congress, "believe we now hold a considerable superiority which the USSR would not want to challenge. . . . So, it is a probability that if we act decisively and promptly, they may figure that Nasser has gone too fast. They may withdraw before their prestige is engaged and general war risked."[6]

The immediate US response showed clearly the limitations of American foreign policy in the Middle East. Acting on a request from Lebanon's president Chamoun, Eisenhower sent eight thousand US marines to land in Beirut. The president referred to Communist subversion of Lebanon and the need to "preserve its territorial integrity and political independence."[7] But in reality the landing was an almost desperate attempt to demonstrate US power and purpose in the Middle East. The aim was to frighten the Soviets from too deep an involvement with Middle Eastern revolutions and to warn the new Iraqi leaders away from taking possession of Kuwait, an oil-rich sheikdom that most Iraqis regarded as part of their national territory. More than half of Britain's oil imports came from Kuwait, and its loss would mean that western Europe and Japan would be in dire straits in terms of energy supplies.

In Moscow, Khrushchev observed the revolutions in the Middle East with satisfaction and not a little glee. "Can we imagine a Baghdad Pact without Baghdad? This consideration alone is enough to give Dulles a nervous breakdown," the Soviet leader grinned to his comrades in Moscow.[8] But Khrushchev was not about to give the new Iraqi leaders, or their Egyptian backers, any hard guarantees against

US interventions. He told Nasser, who flew to Moscow for an urgent meeting in the wake of the US troop landings in Lebanon, that he would not provide sophisticated weapons systems for Arab use. "If the need arises," the Soviet leader argued, "then it would be better to launch [these weapons] from our territory. . . . [And] you can be assured that if aggressors start a war against your country, then we will help you by means of these rockets."[9] Khrushchev found the Middle East to be a hopeful but confusing region, where Soviet power could do little but prod the new regimes in the direction of social reform, socialist planning, and ever-closer military, political, and economic relations with the Soviet Union.

Soviet room for action in the Middle East was caught between its experts' Marxist analysis of class-struggle and the political and strategic aims of its leaders. Both the Arab and the Persian Middle East were seen as too backward for genuine socialist revolutions. Their immediate future would be nationalist revolutions against Western imperialist domination carried out by the local bourgeoisie and its allies. The Soviet Union should be a backer of such revolutions, although it had to realize their character, which was defined by the narrow local self-interest of their protagonists. But while Middle Eastern bourgeois nationalists could not have the same global class perspective as Soviet or eastern European Communists, they could still be part of an international front against the West. Soviet purposes in the Middle East did not need true socialist revolutions. They only needed movements and regimes that rebelled against Western control of their resources, and that sought Soviet support in doing so.

Soviet and American views of Israel also attempted to fit complex local realities into shallow Cold War frameworks. At least up to the Suez Crisis, the Soviets retained some hope that the Zionist state could be amenable to Moscow's positions in international affairs, thereby making it possible for them to broker a settlement between it and its Arab neighbors. This view was not as far-fetched as it sounds today. Bolshevism and Zionism had grown up politically side by side in Russia and eastern Europe, as socialist rivals and sometimes as enemies. "The struggle between the Zionist and Bolshevik Jews," Churchill had proclaimed back in 1920, "is little less than a struggle for the soul of the Jewish people."[10] But up to 1948 British imperial policies, not the Arabs or the Soviets, had been Zionism's deadliest enemy. The willingness of an Israeli Labor government under Ben-Gurion to align itself totally with the British and French at Suez therefore came as a bit of a shock to Moscow.

Knowing what was going on in Israel, the country's alliances should not have come as a surprise. For Israel's Labor government, confronting the country's Arab neighbors was a question of survival. And to uphold this confrontation, Western support was necessary. "When we are isolated," explained Ben-Gurion, "the Arabs think that we can be destroyed and the Soviets exploit this card. If a great power stood behind us, and the Arabs knew that we are a fact that cannot be altered, Russia will cease her hostility towards us, because this hostility would no longer buy the heart of the Arabs."[11] The Israeli leaders' suspicions were confirmed through Soviet agreements with Egypt in the wake of the 1956 war. The Zionists felt that they had to move closer to the Americans. Soviet anti-Semitism, which Khrushchev never confronted openly, also helped convince Ben-Gurion and other Jewish leaders that the Communist state could never become a friend of Israel.

For Gamal Abdel Nasser, the Soviet alliance brought its frustrations. He had hoped to use Soviet military and economic aid to position Egypt as the primary power within the region.[12] Instead, the economy took a downward turn in the 1960s, mainly caused by low productivity, corruption, high military expenditure, and excessive free distribution of goods and services. Meanwhile, the long war in Yemen impressed nobody; the United Arab Republic was dissolved by the Syrians in 1961; and Qasim was overthrown and murdered in Iraq in 1963. In both Syria and Iraq the Ba'ath Party was in ascendance, in spite of both Egyptian and Soviet disapproval. By the mid-1960s, Ba'ath governments were in place in both Damascus and Baghdad, even though they saw eye to eye on few things, except persecuting Communists, Islamic leaders, and ethnic minorities.

The Cold War in the 1960s gave Nasser a chance to reset his international stature. While continuing to work closely with the Soviets, the Egyptian leader intensified his engagement with and on behalf of revolutionary movements in the Third World. Such positions, Nasser felt, enabled him to break out of a local framework that he often found irksome. Especially after the fall of Ben Bella in Algeria in 1965, Cairo became the meeting point of African revolutionaries from Angola to Morocco. The Afro-Asian Peoples' Solidarity Organization (AAPSO) was headquartered in Cairo, and even though Soviet influence in the association increased in the late 1960s, Nasser always made sure that he could put his personal imprimatur on its usually nebulous proceedings.[13]

Nasser's Third World engagements and his need to be seen as the principal champion of all Arabs, especially after the Yemeni debacle, led him to focus more than he had in the past on the plight of the Palestinians. Since 1948, more than a million stateless Palestinians had lived as refugees all over the Arab world. Their existence was precarious. Most Arab regimes refused them the right of citizenship and they were often exploited in terms of work and living conditions. But by the mid-1960s Palestinian organizations had become more visible, and one of them, Fatah, led by a former student at Cairo University, Yasir Arafat, had begun small-scale armed attacks against Israel. "We will not put down our arms as long as Palestine is not liberated and until Palestine occupies the status it deserves in the heart of the Arab nation," Arafat declared.[14]

The origins of the 1967 Middle East war are to be found in the intersection between the Arab rediscovery of the Palestinian cause and the intensifying Cold War in the region. Playing Arab leaders against each other in their search for support, in 1966 Fatah had relocated from Egypt to Syria, where a radical faction of the Ba'ath Party was now in command. In spite of the difficult relationship between them and the Ba'ath Party in the past, the Soviets also threw their weight behind the new regime in Damascus, hoping it would mean a Ba'athist realignment with Moscow. If that were to be the case, the balance in the Middle Eastern Cold War would tip decisively toward the Soviets,

Brezhnev believed. Soviet arms deliveries to both Syria and Egypt intensified, as did Arab rhetoric against Jewish occupation of Palestine.

In April 1967 Israel responded to Fatah incursions from Syria and Jordan by strafing the forces of the two countries with aircraft and tanks. Israeli jet fighters overflew Damascus. The Soviets believed the Israelis were preparing a full-scale attack on Syria, and warned their local allies. Fearful of being seen as less anti-Israel than the Ba'athists and alarmed by the information from Moscow, Nasser moved his troops toward the Israeli border and blockaded its sea access from the Gulf of Aqaba. The Soviets and the Syrians hoped that Egyptian pressure on Israel would temper Israeli bellicosity elsewhere.

Instead, fear of a concerted Arab action made Israel decide to strike first. On 5 June 1967, in a surprise attack, its air force destroyed the Egyptian air force on the ground. Its armies then conquered the Sinai peninsula, threatening Cairo, and responded to shelling from the Jordanian side by conquering East Jerusalem and the West Bank of the river Jordan. In the north Israeli troops routed the Syrians, taking possession of the Golan Heights. In less than a week of fighting, Israel's Arab neighbors had suffered a total military defeat. In the Sinai Desert, row after row of burned-out T-34 tanks, supplied by the Soviets to the Egyptian army, bore witness to the scale of the Arab humiliation and its Cold War significance.

The United States had stayed out of the war as best it could. But even if the only US casualties were the crew on a Navy spy ship accidentally (it was claimed) sunk by the Israelis, US public opinion was firmly on the side of Israel. Though the Jewish state was undoubtedly the aggressor, the scale of its victory against much larger forces made it a David fighting Goliath. Americans also liked that the Israelis did what the United States itself seemed incapable of doing in Indochina: giving a licking to the Soviet Union and its allies. The humiliation of aggressively anti-American Arab regimes also suited Washington. "We're going to start sorting these people out a bit," President Johnson's national security adviser McGeorge Bundy told his White House colleagues.[15]

For the new Soviet leadership the Arab defeat was a massive set-back. The lead-up to the war had shown Moscow's diplomacy to be fumbling and uncertain. While advising Egypt and Syria to tone down their rhetoric so as to avoid war, the Soviets' warning about an impending Israeli attack had helped make that attack a reality. But first and foremost it was the scale of the Arab losses that shocked Moscow. "The data at our disposal," an exasperated Leonid Brezhnev explained to his Warsaw Pact colleagues on 20 June, "shows clearly that due to this generous aid rendered by the USSR and other countries, Arab countries were indisputably superior to Israel in weapons and military personnel prior to the outbreak of hostilities." The Arab leaders had failed because of lack of coordination among themselves and with the Soviet Union. Only a Soviet ultimatum, sent to the Americans, brought the Israeli offensive to an end. But the Soviets, Brezhnev said, would continue to support the "progressive" Arab states, since Moscow was convinced that the United States had encouraged and facilitated the Israeli attack.[16]

Nasser offered to resign but stayed on after massive demonstrations in Cairo and other cities demanded that he remain. The defeat may have dented the president's popularity but had not destroyed it. Together with the Syrians, and with Soviet support, the Egyptians kept their confrontational stance toward Israel. The "War of Attrition," as Nasser called it, consisted of small-scale attacks on Israeli forces, while avoiding an all-out war. In each case the Israelis struck back with what the new Labor prime minister, Golda Meir, straightforwardly called an asymmetrical response: to do more damage to the Arabs than what they could do to Israel. Meir refused to withdraw her troops from the occupied territories. "There is no substitute for our consolidation along the cease-fire lines in view of the fact that the Arabs still refuse to make peace," she claimed.[17]

The 1967 war added to the Palestinian tragedy. New refugees, this time from the West Bank and Gaza, settled in the surrounding Arab states. In Jordan and Lebanon they became a key part of the population, and their Palestinian Liberation Organization (PLO) a key part of the political landscape. The PLO was a loose confederation of Fatah and other groups, with Yasir Arafat as the leader. They continued to carry out small-scale attacks against Israel. But the PLO became increasingly fractious. One group, the Patriotic Front for the Liberation of Palestine (PFLP), a self-declared Marxist-Leninist party that claimed Che Guevara among its heroes, hijacked a US plane in 1969 and forced it to land in Damascus, where the group was headquartered. A year later the PFLP pulled off a much larger operation: it hijacked four Western planes and flew three of them to Jordan, where they blew them up.

Even though all the hostages were released, the terror operation provided Jordan's King Hussein with the excuse he had been waiting for to tame the Palestinian presence in his country. Accusing the PLO and other Palestinian groups of behaving as a state within the state, the king sent his forces to drive them out of Jordan. To the surprise of most observers, the Jordanians succeeded, in spite of Syrian threats to intervene. "Black September," as the Palestinians called it, was a landmark in the Middle Eastern Cold War. Arab unity had been broken. The PLO leadership, even though it had been opposed to terror against foreign targets, was tainted by its conflict with other Arabs and its links with international terrorist organizations. The Soviet Union, which had cautiously begun to build links with the PLO, was again humiliated in the Middle East, this time by a "plucky little king" whom they considered a relic of the past in the region.

The Soviets responded to Black September by intensifying their buildup of the Egyptian and Syrian forces. Internally, Brezhnev explained his policies by stressing that the Soviet Union wanted a political compromise in the Middle East, and that a diplomatic solution could only be possible when Israel and its US backers realized that there was a true balance of power in the region. The increasing Soviet involvement was not contrary to détente, he explained. "Our party has always . . . proven that the policy of peaceful co-existence is not in opposition to, but rather strengthens the process of global revolution," Brezhnev told his colleagues.[18] By 1970 the Soviets had resupplied the Egyptian army and air force, and provided much more advanced missiles than the Egyptians had had before. Red Army personnel manned Egyptian positions along the Suez Canal. "At Nikolayev," one of them recounted later, "they dressed us in civvies, issued us smart foreign-tailored suits (from Socialist-bloc countries). The enlisted men got berets and the officers, hats. We turned in all our personal effects and military documents and boarded the cruise liner Admiral Nakhimov as tourists. My surveillance station was masked as an ambulance."[19]

With Soviet S-125 anti-aircraft missiles in place and Soviet pilots flying missions over Egypt the balance in the Middle East did begin to shift. There is no doubt that the cease-fire that Israel agreed to in August 1970, which allowed the S-125 missiles to remain on the canal banks, was a product of the new Soviet intervention. About twenty thousand Soviet advisers served in Egypt between 1967 and 1971, most of them in military positions. Negotiations began on a defense treaty that would make Egypt the closest thing to a Soviet ally outside of the Warsaw Pact. The Nixon Administration stepped up its military support for Israel, while trying to get Soviet support for a peace deal. A "settlement which is painful to both sides and Soviets sell to UAR [Egypt] would be in our interest," Henry Kissinger explained to the NSC. "From point of view of our overall relationship, we want a settlement that is unpalatable to UAR and Soviets have paid the price of selling it."[20]

The sudden death of Gamal Abdel Nasser in October 1970 dramatically changed politics in Egypt. His successor, Anwar Sadat, was caught in an ironic situation. On the one hand, he wanted to put pressure on the Soviets to further increase their military support for his regime. On the other, he believed the Egyptians at some point would have to talk with Washington to get an overall peace agreement for the Middle East. After signing the new defense treaty with the Soviets in 1971, a year later he protested against Soviet reluctance to supply advanced longer-range missiles to Egypt by capriciously expelling some (but not all) Soviet military advisers. He also opened secret channels of communication with the Americans. President Nixon, impatient with Israeli reluctance to negotiate with the Arabs, suspended US military aid to put pressure on Golda Meir. For Nixon it was much more important to get the Soviets out of Egypt, and eventually out of the Middle East, than to make Israel invulnerable to an attack.

The ultimate irony of Sadat's first years in power is that he wanted peace with Israel based on the pre-1967 borders, but saw no other way to achieve his objective than through forcing a military solution. Convinced that the Arab armies now were up to the task of if not defeating, then causing serious damage to the Israelis, he began preparing an attack. With the Soviet position much reduced and the Americans still on the sidelines, there was little that could hold Sadat back. On 6 October 1973, on the eve of Yom Kippur, the holiest day in Judaism, the Egyptian and Syrian armies attacked across the cease-fire lines. The Israeli army was pushed back both in the Sinai and on the Golan Heights, with substantial losses. It was clear that Israel had problems assembling enough men and materiel to fight effectively on both fronts. By 9 October Meir ordered the Israeli nuclear forces, which the country had developed secretly in the late 1960s, to be readied. Her move was both an attempt to force the Americans to provide military assistance and an ultimate guarantee against a full-scale Arab invasion. At Kissinger's insistence, US military resupplies started that day. The Soviets had already begun resupplying their Arab allies.

The surprising Israeli setbacks in the first phase of the October War meant that the conflict quickly took on a Cold War dimension. "The Arabs may even be smelling a victory, not a stalemate," Kissinger said. "That means the Soviet Union has won. For us to have gone in to have saved the Arabs' ass would have been perfect."[21] But, as things were, the Americans even refused to join the Soviets in a UN Security Council call for an immediate cease-fire. Washington wanted status quo restored because even a small loss of occupied territory for Israeli would have meant a victory for the Soviet Union.

With US resupplies underway, Israel could go on the offensive. On 11 October its forces crossed the former cease-fire line on the Golan Heights and headed toward Damascus. On 15 October the Israelis crossed the Suez Canal and began pushing toward Ismailia and Cairo.

The Soviets bristled at what they saw as US-Israeli collusion to secure even further territorial gains for the Jewish state or, possibly, over-throw the regimes in Syria and Egypt. When the Americans finally agreed to a UN cease-fire resolution, which was accepted by all par-ties, the Israelis continued their advance in some sectors. This brought their troops to within forty kilometers of Damascus and one hundred kilometers of Cairo. The Egyptian Third Army, thirty-five thousand men, was surrounded. Brezhnev sent Nixon a message. In it he threat-ened a direct Red Army intervention if the Israeli offensives did not end. US intelligence reported that they believed Soviet troops were being readied to be sent to the Middle East.

On the evening of 25 October, Nixon responded by putting US forces worldwide on alert. Strategic Air Command, Continental Air Defense Command, European Command, and the Sixth Fleet all went to DEFCON 3, the highest level of combat readiness since the Cuban missile crisis. With Nixon already beleaguered by the Watergate scan-dal, Kissinger believed that "the overall strategy of the Soviets now appears to be one of throwing détente on the table since we have no functional President, in their eyes, and, consequently, we must pre-vent them from getting away with this."[22] While Nixon signaled to the Soviets that Red Army troops in the Middle East would mean war with the United States, Kissinger put maximum pressure on the Israe-lis to cease their violations of the truce.

In Moscow, the Politburo was shocked when they picked up the US nuclear alert. The discussion that followed made it clear that the Soviet leaders had not reached any decision on sending troops to the Middle East; theirs had been merely threats and contingency planning. "It is not reasonable to become engaged in a war with the United States because of Egypt and Syria," Kosygin said.[23] Brezhnev summed up by saying that the Soviet warnings had, after all, had the intended effect: the Americans were reining in the Israelis. But the Soviet Union was quick to accept a US-sponsored resolution that gave the UN the responsibility of separating the fighting armies. In a rambling press conference in Washington, Nixon credited his détente policy with resolving the crisis. It was, he said, because he and Brezhnev "have had this personal contact, that notes exchanged in that way result in a settlement rather than a confrontation."[24] But neither side was in doubt that the 1973 war had exposed some of the limitations of détente.

The despair within Arab states over the outcome of the October War was palatable. Libya had announced an embargo on oil exports to the United States and others who were backing Israel. To Kissinger's horror all other Arab oil producers followed suit, including stalwart US allies such as Saudi Arabia. The embargo led to a massive increase in the price of oil, which in itself contributed to the West's economic woes during the mid-1970s. In spite of US pressure, the Organization of Petroleum Exporting Countries (OPEC) was keen to regulate production to keep prices high even after the embargo ended. Oil, which in spite of increases in demand had been cheap and abundant ever since the 1940s, now doubled in price. OPEC's price policies encouraged those in the Third World who sought a new international economic order based on higher prices for raw materials. It also made the installation of a real US hegemony in the Middle East a more pressing concern for Washington.

Kissinger had realized that the United States needed to be seen as contributing to some form of peace deal in the Middle East if the Soviet Union were to be pushed back. And putting pressure on the Israelis to withdraw from at least some of the occupied territories was essential for any negotiations to work, the secretary of state thought. The 1973 war could help convince Golda Meir that her country needed a deal. The Israelis, Kissinger said, "have lost their invincibility and the Arabs have lost their sense of inferiority."[25] But Meir's government refused to play ball, except on military disengagement agreements, which Kissinger skillfully negotiated. Even with Sadat's Egypt increasingly turning away from the Soviet Union, in spite of the support it had given during the war, the Americans got little help from the Israelis to completely turn the tables on Moscow.

"The Middle East," Kissinger explained to President Gerald Ford right after he had taken office in August 1974, "is the worst problem we face. The oil situation is the worst we face. . . . But we can't afford another embargo. If we are faced with that, we may have to take some oil fields."[26] When Meir's Labor successor, Yitzhak Rabin, refused to agree to an interim accord with the Egyptians in March 1975, as proposed by Washington, President Ford lost patience. He wrote to Rabin "to convey my deep disappointment over the position taken by Israel during the course of the negotiations. . . . The failure to achieve an agreement is bound to have far-reaching effects in the area and on our relations. I have directed an immediate reassessment of U.S. . . . relations with Israel, with a view to assuring that the overall interests of America in the Middle East and globally will be protected. You will be informed of our decisions."[27]

But the US president was increasingly under pressure at home from those who believed that the global détente policy had given too much to the Soviets. With Kissinger protesting furiously that his Middle East policy rather aimed at taking something *away* from the Soviet Union, seventy-six senators from both parties wrote to President Ford attempting to undermine his new stance. "We believe," they said, "that a strong Israel constitutes a most reliable barrier to domination of the area by outside parties. Given the recent heavy flow of Soviet weaponry to Arab states, it is imperative that we not permit the military balance to shift against Israel. We believe that preserving the peace requires that Israel obtain a level of military and economic support adequate to deter a renewal of war by Israel's neighbors."[28]

For an unelected president hoping to win the presidency in 1976, this pressure was too much to bear. The American Israel Public Affairs Committee and some Jewish organizations in the United States were able to link their fear of the United States not being supportive enough of Israel with the rising criticism of détente. Groups on the Right, often called neoconservatives because of their eclectic background in libertarian thinking, human rights promotion, and foreign policy militancy, took up these allegations. In their eyes, Nixon, Ford, and Kissinger were bartering away support for the only true friend the United States had in the Middle East, just like they had bartered away support for oppressed people in eastern Europe and the Soviet Union. Standing tall against the Soviet Union meant standing with

Israel. President Ford's own rhetoric became remarkably more pro-Israel as the presidential campaign got underway.

The development in American politics was in a way a parallel to what was happening in Israel itself. The Cold War came to overwhelm the democratic promise of Israel. From a republic fighting for the right to self-determination, Israel after 1967 became an occupying power whose politics moved significantly to the Right. Rabin's Labor Party lost the 1977 elections to a conservative coalition, the Likud. It was the first time since the founding of Israel that Labor was out of government. The new prime minister, Menachem Begin, had been the leader of Irgun, one of the terrorist organizations fighting for Israel's independence before 1948, and had been marginalized in Israeli politics ever since because of his extreme views. The Likud's election manifesto had made clear that "the right of the Jewish people to the Land of Israel is eternal, and is an integral part of its right to security and peace. Judea and Samaria [the West Bank] shall therefore not be relinquished to foreign rule; between the sea and the Jordan, there will be Jewish sovereignty alone."[29] As he took office, Begin had made up his mind that he wanted peace with Israel's neighbors, but not at the expense of the new conquests in the east.

The Palestinian organizations, meanwhile, made any form of negotiations harder to achieve. This was in part because of Arafat's despair over lack of support from Arab states. But it was also because he feared that any settlement that would be made with the Israelis would happen at great cost to the Palestinians. His people's only hope, Arafat thought, was that the Cold War would prevent Arab countries from seeking separate deals with their enemies. Palestinian terrorism was most of all intent on making it more difficult to ignore their cause. In 1972 a terrorist group attacked Israeli athletes at the Munich Olympics, killing twelve people, and there were a series of hijackings of international flights. Not all of these were carried out by the PLO, but Arafat refused to condemn any form of Palestinian violence. In the short term, this strategy without a doubt gave prominence to the Palestinian cause and dominated the news media, but in the longer term it proved catastrophic, as its recklessness and nihilism alienated many states and individuals who might otherwise have sympathized with the Palestinians' plight.

With Sadat's Egypt attempting to get US support for a peace with Israel, other Arab countries moved closer to the Soviet Union.[30] Two different factions of the Ba'ath Party were in power in Syria and Iraq. Syria's leader Hafez al-Assad despised his Iraqi colleagues, and they hated him back in equal measure. Saddam Hussein, who became the key leader in Iraq in the mid-1970s, believed that the Syrians were out to kill him and force a unification of the two countries under Assad's leadership. Both countries, however, turned to the Soviets and eastern Europeans to help them out, both in terms of security and economic development. For the Soviets, close links with these two regimes served to mitigate—perhaps essentially in their own minds—the disaster of Sadat's defection to the US side. Soviet experts were of course aware of the self-serving fickleness of both Ba'ath regimes. They knew how the Syrians and the Iraqis persecuted Communists, about high-level corruption, and about the nepotism of the leaders. But the International Department of the Soviet Communist Party, in particular, argued that the Ba'athists were bourgeois nationalists who had broken with imperialism, and therefore worthy of Soviet support.

By the late 1970s extensive Soviet-led support programs were in place for both countries. To a higher degree than before, the Soviets delegated some of the assistance for Syria and Iraq to the eastern European states, especially to East Germany and Bulgaria. Of the three thousand Soviet bloc advisers in Syria in 1979, seven hundred were from the GDR.[31] Although the Soviets' inability to get the Iraqis and the Syrians to cooperate sometimes drove them to distraction— Assad, especially, had a tendency to get on Brezhnev's nerves—they patiently continued to supply aid to both countries. Younger leaders gave some hope for the future. Saddam Hussein was, according to the Hungarian Communists, a "progressive, nationalist patriot" from whom much could be expected.[32] By 1980 Syria and Iraq were among the biggest recipients of Soviet backing globally, although the amounts paled in comparison with US assistance to Israel and Egypt.

If Syria and Iraq were troubled alliances for the Soviets, a revolution in the south of Arabia for a while, at least, seemed to set hearts fluttering in Moscow. In 1967 Britain beat another hasty retreat, this time from its colony in Aden, on the southern tip of the Arabian peninsula. The National Liberation Front, which took over power, declared their country to be a people's republic, and sought close relations with the Soviets and their allies. The People's Democratic Republic of Yemen (PDRY), as the country became know, was different from the other "progressive" Arab regimes in Communist eyes. The heads of the PDRY "are guided in their activity mainly by Marxist-Leninist theory, rather than by nationalist and religious views," declared the Hungarian leaders, who engaged in a big assistance program for South Yemen.[33] For the Soviets, access to the important port of Aden for naval purposes was also a substantial advantage, just like its naval base in Tartus on the Syrian coast.

Both the United States and the Soviet Union were looking for their own kind of regimes in the Middle East and finding very few of them. The Americans were finding democracy in Israel and the Soviets Marxism-Leninism in South Yemen, but that helped them little as long as both were small states actively engaged in antagonizing their neighbors. From an overall strategic point of view, neither Superpower could hope to achieve much, except in a negative sense. By the 1970s, both the Soviets and the Americans needed, for their own reasons, to forestall another Middle East war. Each hoped, gradually, to force the other power out of the region, which would give them advantages in the global Cold War (though not very many in the Middle East, as long as no fundamental political and economic changes took place there). For both Superpowers, the Middle East was a zone of confusion and fluidity, where lasting advantages seemed very hard to achieve.

The lack of much economic progress, except in Israel and, through extreme oil revenues, in some of the Gulf states, was more significant for the future of the region than the shifting Cold War allegiances of Middle Eastern states. Much as in other Third World countries, the secular nationalist regimes in the Middle East failed to deliver the

kind of improvements in their daily lives that most people were looking for. Instead they got increasingly high-handed and undemocratic
governments, in alliances with foreign powers to whom the lives of
their peoples seemed to count for little. Not surprisingly, some
younger people began looking for other forms of authority and purpose to dedicate themselves to. Especially after the 1973 war, a sense of
hopelessness and humiliation drove thousands to attend Islamic
schools and mosques where preachers blamed the failures of Arab regimes on their detachment from God.

Contemporary political interpretations of Islam were of course
nothing new among Muslims in the Middle East or elsewhere. But up
to the mid-1970s such groups—the so-called Islamists—were small
and persecuted minorities. Even in Saudi Arabia, where the king
claimed to base his whole political system on Islam, only government-
approved Islamists were allowed. Egypt, Syria, and Iraq had all banned
the Muslim Brotherhood, and those who believed in a political role
for Muslim leaders disappeared into the regimes' prisons, or worse.
Gradually Islamists turned toward underground organization and
terrorism. In Syria the Ba'athists allegedly used chemical weapons
among other armaments to put down an Islamist rebellion in the west
in 1982. At least ten thousand people were killed.

But the pressure various Islamist organizations were put under by
Middle Eastern governments only seemed to strengthen them. Their
faith, and the belief that God was the ultimate authority of all things
political, made persecution easier to bear. Some groups, such as the
Brotherhood in Egypt, also began to extend their popularity through
assistance programs in poor neighborhoods. When those using such
services were arrested by the regime, they admitted that they would
rather support Muslims who did something for the poor than a regime that talked loudly but did very little. The regimes were also vulnerable to criticism of corruption, subservience to foreign powers,
and their now famous inability to destroy Israel.

Some key Islamist leaders made the Cold War the foremost sign of
the depravation of Middle Eastern regimes. Sayyid Qutb, an Egyptian
who had traveled in the United States (where the way of life repelled

him) and who wrote extensively, mostly from prison, claimed that only Islam had the answer to the world's ills.

> Mankind today is on the brink of a precipice, not [only] because of the danger of complete annihilation which is hanging over its head . . . but because humanity is devoid of vital values. . . . Democracy in the West has become infertile to such an extent that it is borrowing from the systems of the Eastern bloc, especially in the economic system, under the name of socialism. It is the same with the Eastern bloc. . . . Marxism in the beginning attracted not only a large number of people from the East but also from the West, as it was a way of life based on a creed. . . . This theory conflicts with man's nature and its needs. This ideology prospers only in a degenerate society or in a society which has become cowed as a result of some form of prolonged dictatorship. But now, even under these circumstances, its materialistic economic system is failing.[34]

Qutb was hanged in an Egyptian prison in 1966. But his ideas spread further in the 1970s, as the secular states in the Middle East came under pressure from within because of their poor economic performance. The United States did not view the Islamists as a main threat. On the contrary, the Islamists might be useful because they opposed Left-wing nationalist regimes that the Americans themselves despised and wanted to see removed. Their social conservatism and anti-Communism also fitted American purposes. The arch-enemies of the Islamists were the Communist parties, especially in Iraq and Iran. For the Soviets, the Islamists were reactionary relics of the past. They would have no role in progressive societies moving—under Soviet guidance—toward socialism.

By the late 1970s the Cold War in the Middle East had fashioned a region with hard, almost intractable problems. The area was divided into US and Soviet allies, much as were Europe and eastern Asia. Both powers supported regimes that did not serve their own populations well. Neither power had a real interest in solving the Arab-Israeli conflict, except to the degree that negotiations helped their own position versus the other Superpower. The United States refused to speak with the Palestinian leaders, whom they considered terrorists. The Soviets claimed to support the Palestinian cause, but only to the extent that they could control the Palestinian organizations. The American obsession with securing Middle Eastern oil supplies made dictatorships such as Iran and Saudi Arabia natural US allies. It was an explosive mix, which made sure that the region would stay highly volatile up toward the end of the Cold War and beyond.

18

Defeating Détente

By the mid-1970s it seemed as if the Cold War had become an entrenched international system, although at significantly lower levels of tension than before. Some people believed that détente would, over time, help end the conflict, through social and economic convergence or through the dismantling of iron curtains through trust building and human contact. But even those who thought that the Cold War was there to stay claimed that the conflict had been transformed. Instead of ever-higher global tension, the world seemed headed for some form of duopoly, in which the United States and the Soviet Union shared responsibility for limiting regional conflicts, making sure that nuclear weapons did not proliferate, and avoiding restlessness within their own ranks. Rivalry would continue, even precarious rivalry as that in the Middle East. But the Cold War was manageable and stable. Very few people believed that Leonid Brezhnev or Gerald Ford ultimately would set the world on fire because of their beliefs. Brezhnev, the *New York Times*' Moscow correspondent reported in 1973, "has gained a reputation in the West for his taste for food, drink, hunting and fast cars, and problems with weight and smoking. A rising flow of Western visitors has found him gregarious and talkative and has come away . . . struck by his warm smile."[1] A man, it seemed, who enjoyed life so much that ideology was of less consequence.

There were of course dissidents to this ameliorated view of the Cold War. In the Soviet Union and eastern Europe some people opposed the authoritarian rule of Communist bosses. The Chinese, set on their own course, cursed the prospect of a Soviet-US global condominium. The Islamists condemned the rule of infidel powers that tried to prevent the return of Muslims to God. In the United States neoconservatives raged against the compromises with evil that the Nixon Administration had carried out. America, they claimed, was selling its birthright for a short period of peace with the enemy. The Soviet Union, claimed Ronald Reagan in his race against Gerald Ford for the Republican nomination in 1976, had its sights set on global hegemony. It was for the United States to resist it. "We did not seek world leadership," Reagan said, "it was thrust upon us. It has been our destiny almost from the first moment this land was settled. If we fail to keep our rendezvous with destiny or, as John Winthrop said in 1630, 'Deal falsely with our God,' we shall be made 'a story and byword throughout the world.' Americans are hungry to feel once again a sense of mission and greatness."[2]

Although the détente policies of Nixon and Brezhnev had their enemies in various places, it is difficult to imagine the collapse of détente without the changes in US politics that took place between 1973 and 1976. The Watergate affair convinced many Americans that there was something fundamentally wrong with the way the country was governed. Nixon, Kissinger, and the secrecy with which the agreements with the Soviet Union had been carried out were part of the problem. Senator Henry Jackson, a Democrat from Washington State, attacked the Administration for not realizing that the Soviet Union consistently violated human rights and therefore could not be trusted in international affairs. Détente was one of the many ways in which Nixon and his successor had hoodwinked the American people, Jackson believed. In 1974 Jackson and a majority in the Senate forced through an amendment stipulating that the United States could not grant Most Favored Nation status in trade to countries that had a bad human rights record. This included the Soviet Union, which, however, was given an eighteen-month waiver to improve its practices, including the right to emigrate. The Soviets were furious, but Kissinger told them that the Administration would overcome these problems.

In the election campaign of 1976 Ford came under increasing pressure from fellow Republicans who wanted to repudiate détente. The problem with Nixon's approach, they claimed, was that it made the United States into just another country in the world. Ronald Reagan, the former governor of California who ran against Ford for the nomination in 1976, claimed on the campaign trail that

> under Messrs. Kissinger and Ford this nation has become number two in military power in a world where it is dangerous—if not fatal—to be second best. . . . Our nation is in danger. Peace does not come from weakness or from retreat. It comes from restoration of American military superiority. . . . Ask the people of Latvia, Estonia, Lithuania, Czechoslovakia, Poland, Hungary all the others: East Germany, Bulgaria, Romania ask them what it's like to live in a world where the Soviet Union is Number One. I don't want to live in that kind of world; and I don't think you do either. . . . I believe God had a divine purpose in placing this land between the two great oceans to be found by those who had a special love of freedom and the courage to leave the countries of their birth. From our forefathers to our modern-day immigrants, we've come from every corner of the earth, from every race and every ethnic background, and we've become a new breed in the world. We're Americans and we have a rendezvous with destiny.[3]

Reagan's rhetoric did not earn him his party's presidential nomination in 1976. Ford was nominated, but then proceeded to lose the election to the Democratic neophyte Jimmy Carter, in part because of the damage the Republican Right had done to their own candidate. By the 1976 election, the neoconservative coalition had become a force to be reckoned with in American politics. They opposed domestic reforms to advantage women and ethnic minorities and felt that the upheavals of the 1960s had made the United States almost ungovernable. The country could therefore easily be taken advantage of by the

Soviets or by Third World states that attacked America but were happy to receive US aid when needed.

This sense of being beleaguered from without and abandoned by their own leaders was shared by many Americans, even those who did not support Reagan in 1976. Economic growth was sluggish and inflation higher than it had been for three decades, reaching 13 percent toward the end of the decade. The Ford Administration's critics started using the term "stagflation," symbolizing all that was wrong with the US economy. Although almost all major economies experienced the same combination of low growth and high inflation during the 1970s, critics of the US Administration presented it as if it were a particular US phenomenon, and a telltale sign of Washington's weakness vis-à-vis other countries. In reality, stagflation was a product of free-floating currencies, globalization of capital and investment, increasing raw material prices, and, over time, increasing international competition. Gradually, these developments would actually help the US economy recover faster than many others. But seen from the mid-1970s, it all seemed to be doom and gloom. The price and wage freezes that the Nixon Administration introduced did not help, either with the economy or the public mood.[4]

THE AMERICAN SENSE of their country being poorly led and taken advantage of was also advanced by real developments in international affairs that made the United States look wayward and weak. In Indochina, after a brief lull in the fighting after the completion of the US withdrawal in 1973, the revolutionary armies went on the offensive. Although both of North Vietnam's allies, the Soviet Union and China, had urged caution, the North Vietnamese armies started an all-out attack on South Vietnam in December 1974. The guarantee of increases in Soviet supplies were of critical importance in Hanoi's decision-making. For the Soviets, expanding support for North Vietnam was not a break with the détente policy; indeed, as Brezhnev pointed out repeatedly, Moscow had never promised to reduce its aid to Vietnam. On the contrary, Soviet advisers in Hanoi increasingly agreed with their Vietnamese hosts that the South was ripe for picking. The Chinese also continued their assistance, in part to rival the Soviets. No wonder Le Duan and the other Vietnamese Communist leaders saw 1975 as a unique opportunity to reunify their country, one that might not come back soon, especially given the increasing political dissonance between them and leaders in Beijing.

The North Vietnamese offensive was in complete violation of the agreements that country had signed only a year earlier. Although the South Vietnamese armies on paper seemed well placed to defend their territory, the lack of coordination among their military units, the massive refugee problem that the offensive created, and the psychological blow of the US withdrawal combined to defeat South Vietnam fast. Although the North Vietnamese were aware of their strategic superiority, they were still surprised at how quickly resistance folded. By March 1975 the South Vietnamese forces had been driven out of the central highlands. Their enemies then proceeded to swallow up the coastal cities and bases one by one. In April the North Vietnamese leadership ordered all their forces to head straight for Saigon.

South Vietnamese president Nguyen Van Thieu resigned 21 April, accusing his former American backers of being "unfair . . . inhumane . . . irresponsible." "You ran away and left us to do the job that you could not do," Thieu said.[5] Congress had already cut assistance for South Vietnam in half in 1974, and further US aid in 1975 probably would not have made much of a difference on the battlefield. South Vietnam's calls for the United States to live up to Nixon's unofficial promises of military support in case of a northern attack went unheeded in Washington. Just after Thieu's bitter resignation, President Ford told university students that "America can regain the sense of pride that existed before Vietnam. But it cannot be achieved by refighting a war that is finished as far as America is concerned. . . . The fate of responsible men and women everywhere, in the final decision, rests in their own hands, not in ours."[6]

North Vietnamese forces, supported by the South Vietnamese National Liberation Front, took Saigon 30 April 1975. Images of American helicopters airlifting out US personnel and as many terrified

South Vietnamese officials as they could carry did no good for America's standing in the world. Whatever way it was construed, the end of the Vietnam wars was a defeat for American power in Asia. At home, critics attacked the Administration for apathy and cowardice. And although their claims that US Cold War policies had fallen from omnipotence to impotence were certainly exaggerated, the flight from Saigon was undoubtedly the nadir of US foreign policy in the postwar era. Communists and Third World revolutionaries celebrated, as did many young people in the United States and Europe who had opposed the war. But for the two and a half million Americans who served in Vietnam, not to mention for the families of the fifty thousand who died and the seventy-five thousand who were left severely disabled, the fall of Saigon left a bitterness toward their own political leaders that never quite disappeared.

For the majority of Vietnamese who sympathized in one form or another with national liberation as outlined by the Communists, Hanoi's victory proved a mixed blessing. Their country was reunified and at peace. But the northern leaders took complete control and left little to the southern Liberation Front. They wanted a quick reunification in social and political terms as well as militarily. The country was declared to be a Socialist Republic under the leadership of the Communist Party. Their form of socialism was distinctly Soviet. The economy was directed through centralized planning. Private ownership was abolished and agriculture collectivized. Trade and markets were all put under government control.[7] At least a million people in the south—former military men, business people, and teachers—were sent to reeducation camps. As a result, the southern economy collapsed. Two million Vietnamese fled abroad, some out of fear but most out of economic necessity.

If many Vietnamese had an unhappy time after 1975, conditions were ten times worse across the border in Cambodia. There a fanatical group of Communists, inspired by the more extreme forms of Maoism and China's Cultural Revolution, took power after the US-supported regime collapsed. Their leader, who called himself Pol Pot, believed that the combination of imperialist influence and rapacious neighbors threatened the Cambodian people with extinction. His was a form of Maoism that put exceptional emphasis on autarky, racial purity, and eugenics. On taking power, Pol Pot's Communist Party of Kampuchea (known by its French sobriquet, Khmer Rouge) emptied the cities and drove everyone into the countryside to engage in basic agricultural work. In spite of the assistance they had received from Hanoi during the war, they turned viciously on all national minorities in Cambodia, including the Vietnamese and the Chinese who lived there. It is estimated that almost two and half million people, a third of the population, died as a result of Khmer Rouge policies.[8]

It took time before Western public opinion began to realize the enormity of what was happening in Cambodia. So intense had the condemnation of the US war in Indochina been, that many did not want to believe the full extent of the Khmer Rouge's genocides. But when the gruesome facts began to be known, they contributed significantly to the overall critique of Communism, not least in Europe. Still, Cambodia did not dominate the news pages the way it should have, in part because the events there were overshadowed by the crises in the Middle East and the seeming implosion of the US system of government after Watergate. And in the middle of all this, a revolution took place in Portugal, the consequences of which had more of an impact on the Cold War than even the end of the conflict in Indochina.

Portugal had been a fascist-style dictatorship since 1933. Running the poorest country in Europe, the regime clung on to its colonies, which it believed gave it status and a hope for economic expansion in the future. Even after the other European states were forced to decolonize, Portugal insisted on keeping its African possessions (Angola, Mozambique, Guinea-Bissau, Cape Verde, and São Tomé and Príncipe) as well as East Timor in the Indonesian archipelago. The regime told its people, and the United States and its NATO allies, that the liberation movements fighting in these countries were Communists, directed by Moscow. But patience with what seemed expensive, unwinnable colonial wars was wearing thin among the population and in the military. The event that broke the regime's back was the 1973 oil crisis. Portugal could simply not afford to keep its population with subsidized gas as well as provide for its forces fighting in Africa.

On 25 April 1974 a group of younger officers, all of whom had served overseas, acted against the regime. In a bloodless coup, later called the Carnation Revolution, they removed the government and set up a National Salvation Junta of leading generals to rule the country. The colonies were promised independence. But General António de Spínola and the moderates who headed the new administration were soon confronted by some of the junior officers who had put them in place. The younger men wanted more rapid change in Portuguese society. Some of them allied themselves with the Portuguese Communist Party, a pro-Moscow party that preached revolution without much of a plan for taking power. Portugal went through a period of continuous political instability, during which confrontations between the Left and the Right made the country almost ungovernable.

Meanwhile the Portuguese colonies in Africa seceded one by one. In Guinea-Bissau and Cape Verde the transition was smooth. The united liberation front took power and transformed itself into a Marxist regime, closely linked to Cuba and the Soviet Union. The Front for the Liberation of Mozambique (FRELIMO) took power there and declared a People's Republic. Though aligned with the Soviet bloc, its leaders guarded their independence. In Angola, however, a civil war had been underway between competing liberation movements even before the Portuguese revolution. In 1974, as the Portuguese were preparing to withdraw, this war became a conflagration that threatened to engulf neighboring African countries as well as the Superpowers.

Angola was by far the richest of Portugal's former African colonies in terms of resources. The population, however, was poor, and the colonizers had done their best to stimulate rivalry among its main ethnic groups. The only liberation movement that had support among all groups, including the white and mixed-race elite in the capital, Luanda, was the Popular Movement for the Liberation of Angola (MPLA). The MPLA was a front led by Marxist intellectuals with close connections to the Portuguese Communist Party. It had received Soviet, Cuban, and Yugoslav support since the early 1960s but had seen its fair share of infighting and splits. Just after the Soviets had begun increasing their support for the movement, in 1970, the MPLA went through one of its ruptures. When the Carnation Revolution took place, the movement was therefore at a disadvantage compared with its opponents, the National Front for the Liberation of Angola (FNLA), a nativist group that was supported by Zaire's president, Mobutu Sese Seko, and the National Union for the Total Independence of Angola (UNITA), which drew most of its support from the Ovimbundu tribe.

When the Angolan civil war broke out among these groups in 1974, the MPLA soon improved its position. It controlled the capital and the areas around it, and it was able to work smoothly with the Portuguese officers representing the new government in Lisbon. By the summer of 1975 it dominated eleven out of fifteen Angolan provinces. But the governments in Zaire and South Africa intervened, with covert US support, sending troops into Angola to fight against the MPLA. Neither wanted a Communist-led country on their borders. The Soviets and the Cubans scrambled to get support in to their allies. When the MPLA's leader Aghostino Neto declared his People's Republic of Angola on 11 November 1975, the Cubans began airlifting troops and weapons to Luanda.

The South Africans almost reached the Angolan capital before the Cubans counterattacked. But helped by the Soviets who supplied aircraft and artillery, the Cuban and MPLA response was decisive. The South Africans withdrew southward, feeling betrayed by the United States. There, Congress had prohibited further military support for the Angolan opposition, in spite of White House protests. By spring 1976 the MPLA was in control of the country, supported by almost thirty thousand Cubans and an increasing number of Soviet and eastern European advisers. The Ford Administration was incensed. They saw Angola as a new form of Soviet intervention, carried out across thousands of miles, with the Cubans as proxies. "It is an awful situation," Kissinger told the South African ambassador, "and ultimately the Russians will be able to ride the momentum of the victory in Angola to defeat the powerful leaders in Africa, resulting in total victory in Africa. . . . The American people in certain situations become divided, like with Vietnam, and then there will be no action taken by them. We therefore cannot count on them."[9]

The Americans were right in seeing Angola as a new form of Soviet intervention, although in Moscow it had happened almost as an afterthought. The Cubans had been the driving force, not the Soviets.[10] The Angolan intervention, Karen Brutents, the deputy head of the CPSU's International Department, explained later, "became a fact without any master plan."[11] The main point from Moscow's perspective was the need to back up the Cubans, and not let them down "a second time," as Brutents said.[12] The Cuban missile crisis still rankled in Moscow, as did the 1973 October War. Even though Brezhnev was skeptical to begin with about putting too much emphasis on Angola, the Cuban and MPLA success on the ground made him and many in Moscow feel that this was "payback time." The United States had intervened globally for a generation or more. Now the Soviets had shown that they could do so, too, in support of their strategic and ideological interests.

Along with the fall of Indochina, the intervention in Angola helped the powerful backlash against détente already underway in Washington. President Ford, running for the presidency, banned the use of the term "détente" in his campaign. His opponent, the Democratic governor Jimmy Carter, who had no foreign policy experience, castigated the Administration's policies. "We've become fearful to compete with the Soviet Union on an equal basis," Carter claimed in the televised debates with Ford. "We talk about détente. The Soviet Union knows what they want in détente, and they've been getting it. We have not known what we've wanted and we've been out-traded in almost every instance."[13] Carter wanted to do away with the secrecy of the Kissinger years. He wanted the United States to emphasize its own values in foreign affairs: human rights, freedom of religion and emigration, self-determination. American principles, not "balance of power politics," would restore the respect the United States had lost in the world, Carter believed.

Jimmy Carter won a close election in 1976. From the beginning of his presidency, he sought to set relations with the Soviet Union on what he considered a safer ground. In his first letters to Brezhnev, Carter expressed a wish to move beyond the Cold War. There was, the US president said, much that the two countries could cooperate on: "development, better nutrition, and a more meaningful life for the less fortunate portions of mankind."[14] As to the SALT negotiations, Carter felt they did not go far enough. He preferred, he told Brezhnev, deep cuts in nuclear arsenals on both sides. Carter's new proposals horrified the Soviets. They believed basic agreement had already been reached on a new SALT treaty. And they were fearful that the new proposals were a ruse. They knew full well that Soviet nuclear missiles were much less accurate in targeting than US missiles. Having a lot of missiles therefore made the Soviets feel safer. Brezhnev was angry with Carter's moving away from the status quo, as he saw it. Carter's secretary of state, the experienced diplomat Cyrus Vance, recalled that when he tried to bring up the issue in Moscow, he "got a wet rag in the face and was told to go home."[15]

But things were going to get much worse between Carter and the Soviets. In order to emphasize his human rights policy, the new president chose to send a message to the Soviet dissident Andrei Sakharov, in which he underlined his "firm commitment to promote respect for human rights not only in our own country but also abroad. We shall use our good offices," Carter said, "to seek the release of prisoners of conscience."[16] The Kremlin was livid. It was an "an attempt to harass us, to embarrass us," their US ambassador Anatolii Dobrynin said later.[17] All preparations for an early meeting between the two presidents were put on hold by Moscow.

Some of the early problems in Carter's Soviet policy came out of inexperience. Nobody in Carter's inner team of advisers had any background on foreign affairs or, worse, on thinking about foreign affairs in terms of domestic politics. The growing power and influence of the US Jewish lobby seems, for instance, to have taken the new

Administration by surprise. "It is something that was not a part of our Georgia and Southern political experience and consequently not well understood," Carter's chief of staff admitted to the Georgia-born president.[18] Both in his Soviet and his Middle East policy, Carter quickly learned that he needed allies from special interest groups, but he was not always good at winning them over.

Carter's difficulties grew because from day one of his Administration he was getting conflicting advice from his key foreign policy aides. Cyrus Vance believed that a lot had been achieved through détente and that Carter had to be very careful not to throw it away for little gain. An old-school diplomat, the secretary of state presumed that antagonizing the Soviets unless absolutely necessary would not be in America's interest. Zbigniew Brzezinski, the Harvard professor who became Carter's national security adviser, had a different view and temperament. Of Polish origin, Brzezinski was closer to the president's conviction that the Soviet Union, like any other country, had to be confronted when it behaved in ways that were contrary to the international norms that the United States was promoting. Brzezinski encouraged what he deemed a tough, realistic foreign policy because, as he explained to Carter, the Soviet Union needed détente even more than the United States did.

From the very beginning, the Carter Administration was under pressure from a growing public opinion at home that thought the Soviet Union was taking advantage of America's weakness. Although a majority was still in favor of arms limitation talks with the Soviets, almost 70 percent of Americans in 1978 thought that the Soviet Union could not be trusted to live up to its agreements.[19] In many ways the fear and distrust of the Soviet Union was a reflection of the worries many Americans had about conflict, decline, and powerlessness in their own society. But it took activist groups to give voice to these frustrations. One such group, the Committee on the Present Danger (CPD), included both Republicans and Democrats who believed that the Soviet Union was on the offensive worldwide. Led by Paul Nitze, Jeane Kirkpatrick, and President Johnson's former undersecretary of state Eugene Rostow, the CPD became a powerful lobbying group critical of the SALT negotiations and Soviet human rights violations, and supportive of increased military expenditure and links with Israel.

Carter had hoped to spend time dealing with the broader issues on his foreign policy agenda, first and foremost US energy security, peace in the Middle East, and human rights on a global scale. Instead, with his ratings slipping in the polls, he was forced back to national security issues dealing with the Soviet Union. With SALT negotiations near a standstill, the Soviets, on their side, were losing hope that much could be achieved under this president. This realization, in turn, provided incentive for those in Moscow who wanted a more assertive Soviet policy, especially with regard to Africa and Asia. The world, some of them claimed, was turning toward socialism, and the USSR had to be there to help the process.

Seen from a Soviet perspective, the global situation in the mid-1970s could indeed seem hopeful. There had been setbacks in the Middle East, but these, it was explained to Brezhnev, were because of imperialist perfidy, not because of the class-struggle in Arab countries. Syria and Iraq were working more closely with the Soviets. South Yemen was a People's Republic. All the freshly independent African countries were governed by Marxist-Leninists. Vietnam was reunified under Communist rule. India had become a Soviet ally. In Somalia, across from Yemen on the Horn of Africa, the Revolutionary Socialist Party held power and invited the Soviet navy to station ships at the port of Berbera. Internationally things looked good for the Soviet Union. For some younger Communists there, these global advances made up for an increasing disillusionment with the practice of socialism in the Soviet Union itself.

The Ethiopian revolution had its origin in the changes that were sweeping all of Africa in the 1970s. Younger leaders, especially in the military, were impatient with the lack of social and economic progress and frustrated by their own lack of status. For some of these, Soviet-style Marxism-Leninism was more attractive than vaguer forms of African socialism. Cuba was a great inspiration, both as a multiracial society and as a planned economy. The idea of forcing through necessary social change rapidly and efficiently was inspiring for these leaders. Ethiopia, which had been an orthodox Christian monarchy for centuries, with little social and economic change, seemed to them to be ripe for such a reshaping.

Ethiopia's 1974 revolution overthrew the emperor Haile Selassie and replaced him with a group of younger officers who called themselves the Dergue, or Committee. The aging emperor was murdered in prison a year later and buried beneath the latrines in his former palace. Mengistu Haile Mariam, a thirty-seven-year-old major, made himself the leader of the new government. He sought close relations with the Soviet Union, eastern Europe, and Cuba. Moscow was unenthusiastic to begin with. The Soviet leaders doubted the Ethiopians' dedication to Marxism-Leninism and feared that too-close links with Ethiopia would create problems for their existing alliance with neighboring Somalia, with whom the Dergue was increasingly at odds. By 1977, however, the Soviets had begun to supply weapons and military training to the Ethiopians, and the Cubans were sending advisers.

Concerned by the increasing closeness between Addis Ababa and Moscow, the Somalians decided to act. They wanted to unite Ogaden, a mainly Somali region in southern Ethiopia, with their own country, and thought the chaos created by the Ethiopian revolution would give them the chance to do so. The Soviets and the Cubans warned Somalian president Siad Barre against such an attack and hoped to mediate a solution. But by July 1977 it was clear that Ethiopia was facing an all-out Somalian invasion.

The Soviets decided to help save the Ethiopian revolution. They broke off relations with Siad Barre and began freighting advanced weapons to Addis Ababa by an air-bridge, the biggest such operation since the 1973 assistance to Egypt. At least fifteen thousand Cuban soldiers arrived, and Soviet officers were commanding Ethiopian and Cuban troops. The Somalians resisted fiercely, but by early 1978 they were being driven back across the border. Meanwhile, the Soviet relationship with Ethiopia widened into support for all parts of the Ethiopian government. Some Soviet leaders, especially in the International Department of the Communist Party, believed that Ethiopia could become a showcase for Soviet-inspired modernization in the Third World. Although they had misgivings about Mengistu's brutality and his constant warfare against minority groups, the head of the International Department, Boris Ponomarev, agreed to send "a group of experienced comrades of the CPSU" to help build the Dergue into a Communist Party in the future.[20]

As could be expected, the Soviet involvement in the Horn of Africa set off alarm bells in Washington. Brzezinski told the president that he saw a pattern of behavior on the Soviet side that pushed in the direction of more aggression worldwide. Carter agreed. Even though he was eager to move forward in bilateral relations with the Soviet Union, he worried about Soviet behavior in the Third World. The president believed that détente included principles of nonintervention in regional conflicts. "The Soviets' violating of these principles," he told the press, "would be a cause of concern to me, would lessen the confidence of the American people in the word and peaceful intentions of the Soviet Union, would make it more difficult to ratify a SALT agreement or comprehensive test ban agreement if concluded, and therefore, the two are linked because of actions by the Soviets. We don't initiate the linkage."[21]

The Horn of Africa crisis highlighted the conflicts within Carter's own Administration. Secretary of State Cyrus Vance simply could not understand why Brzezinski and the president threatened to let the Horn overshadow other developments that were much more important to the United States. Linking Soviet interventions and SALT would be disastrous, Vance told them. "We will end up losing SALT and that will be the worst thing that could happen. If we do not get a SALT treaty in the President's first four years, that will be a blemish on his record forever."[22] But Vance's voice counted for less and less in the Administration.

One way in which the United States could pay the Soviets back for their perceived Third World activism was through improving relations with China. Carter at first wanted to go slow with the issue of full recognition of the People's Republic. He was concerned about the Chinese Communists' human rights record and understood that working more closely with the Chinese would be a red rag to Brezhnev. The new Chinese leaders who came to power after Mao Zedong's death in 1976 were keen to extend their contacts with the Americans. While Mao had thought of links with the United States first and foremost in terms of security for China, his successor, Deng Xiaoping, wanted US technology and trade. Deng needed US help to make China rich and strong. A more extensive relationship with the United States would assist in China's modernization, Deng concluded.

After Ethiopia, US preparations for a full recognition of the People's Republic of China moved into high gear. Even though recognition did not change much in practical terms between the two countries, it was a powerful symbolic act and it opened new possibilities. Deng told his closest advisers that he wanted to dramatically expand cooperation with the Americans, if they were willing to reciprocate. The Chinese leader feared the massive strengthening of Soviet power that he saw on a global scale. He was particularly preoccupied with the increasing closeness of the Soviet-Vietnamese relationship, and suspected it was part of a Soviet master plan for surrounding China.

Relations between Vietnam and China had been in free fall since 1975. To the astonishment of US leaders who had fought their war in Vietnam to a large extent to contain Chinese Communist expansionism, this falling out got increasingly militarized. By 1978 the two sides were trading insults and sending troops to their border. Then, in what must have been the most harebrained strategic plan of the century, the Khmer Rouge regime in Cambodia followed up the expulsion of people of Vietnamese ancestry with military incursions into Vietnam. The Vietnamese military, ten times stronger, fought back. As their forces penetrated into Cambodia, they were horrified by the levels of Khmer Rouge violence against its own people. By the end of 1978 the leadership in Hanoi had decided to remove Pol Pot's regime, both because it was a security threat to Vietnam and because of its genocidal policies. In just two weeks the war was over. The remnants of the Khmer Rouge fled to the borders with Thailand, and a new pro-Vietnam regime was put in place in Cambodia.

Though it had acted for its own reasons, Vietnam had saved Cambodia from one of the most murderous regimes in the twentieth century. Deng Xiaoping, however, was furious. The Khmer Rouge had been China's allies, of a sort, and Deng was convinced the Soviets were behind the Vietnamese invasion. He decided, in his own words, to teach Vietnam "an appropriate limited lesson."[23] On the US side, Zbigniew Brzezinski also worried that if Vietnam got away with its occupation of Cambodia, then it could also attack other countries. It was, in a sense, a revival of domino theories, only this time China and the United States were on the same side, and Vietnam was to be punished for having removed a murderous Maoist dictatorship.

When Deng Xiaoping came to Washington to inaugurate the new relationship with the United States in January 1979, the Chinese leader straightforwardly informed his hosts that China would attack Vietnam to teach it a lesson. It would be a limited attack with limited objectives, and China would withdraw before the Soviet Union could act in the north. Commenting on the overall situation with regard to the Soviets, Deng said that he saw "no possibility of détente. We can say that the situation is becoming more tense year by year. . . . We believe the Soviet Union will launch a war. But if we act well and properly, it is possible to postpone it. China hopes to postpone a war for twenty-two years."[24]

President Carter could not condone an outright Chinese attack on Vietnam. But he also told Deng that he understood that China "cannot allow Vietnam to pursue aggression with impunity."[25] The United States ended up publicly deploring China's attack the following month, but in private Carter shared intelligence with the Chinese and assured them that the United States would back them up if the Soviets threatened them from the north. The Chinese invasion turned out to be a disaster for Beijing, however. Over the course of a month of fighting, China lost almost half as many soldiers as the United States did in all of its war in Vietnam. There is little doubt that if Deng had not decided that the "lesson" for Vietnam was complete, the Chinese losses would have increased even further. China's war in Vietnam not only showed how woefully unprepared for actual fighting the People's Liberation Army was. It also set Sino-Vietnamese relations on a course of intense hostility that has lasted ever since.

With tension mounting both in Washington and Moscow, negotiators were still able to finish a SALT II agreement that both sides would sign. In June 1979 Carter and Brezhnev traveled to Vienna for the signing ceremony and the first summit in almost five years. Their meetings did not work well. Brezhnev, aging, tired, emotional, was deeply suspicious of Carter's commitment to détente. "It had not been a simple thing to start restructuring Soviet-American relations which had been burdened by the inertia of the Cold War," Brezhnev said at their first meeting.[26] He accused the Americans of neglecting the principles of détente, as he saw them: "complete equality, equal security, respect for each other's legitimate interests, and non-interference in each other's affairs." Carter responded that it was equally important that "we exercise restraint in regional political competition, that we restrict our military intervention in trouble spots in the world, either directly or by proxy. It was important that we take care not to deprive either of our countries or, for that matter, any other country, of access to crucial natural resources."[27] SALT II was signed, but—perhaps not surprisingly, given the public mood in the United States—the US Senate held up ratification.

Carter's reference to natural resources signaled his increasing preoccupation with political turbulence in the Middle East. Egypt's president, Anwar Sadat, had broken with the other Arab countries in November 1977 and traveled to Israel to begin direct negotiations with Prime Minister Begin. This brave act made Egypt an outcast in the Arab world, but it also secured US assistance in negotiating a separate peace accord with Israel. Egypt got the Sinai peninsula back. It also got massive increases in US assistance after the accords were signed at Camp David in March 1979. But by then another Middle East country, Iran, was ablaze with revolt. The Shah, in power since the US-sponsored coup that overthrew Mossadegh in 1953, had been facing massive demonstrations against his autocratic regime. In September 1978 he had declared martial law. But with even the support of the Iranian army in doubt, the Shah had fled the country in January 1979.

The Iranian revolution led to another massive increase in oil prices. The Americans worried that the powerful Iranian Communist Party, the Tudeh, would take power in the chaos that followed the Shah's departure. But instead Shia Islamist organizations were in the driver's seat. Their focal point was Ayatollah Ruhollah Khomeini, a seventy-seven-year-old Shia cleric who believed that Iran should be made into an Islamic republic under his charismatic leadership. Khomeini saw himself as the guardian of Islam in Iran. In his sermons, spread illegally in Iran through audio and videotape, he condemned both the United States and the Soviet Union as devils who were out to destroy all Muslims. Khomeini's slogan was "neither Left, nor Right, but Islam!" His triumphant return to Tehran from exile in February 1979 immediately made him the country's de facto leader.

The Islamic revolution in Iran was a deliberate attempt at breaking with the Cold War order. Khomeini appealed to all Muslims to help defend the new regime: "We have turned our backs on East and West, on the Soviet Union and America, in order to run our country ourselves," Khomeini declared. "The position we have attained is a historical exception, given the current conditions in the world, but our goal will certainly not be lost if we are to die, martyred and defeated."[28] To begin with, neither Washington nor Moscow thought that Khomeini's regime would last. Many, in both capitals, thought that he would do like Muslim conservatives in the past and eventually turn to the United States for support. But they were wrong. Khomeini saw himself as the real revolutionary against a world of falseness. In November 1979 some of his supporters occupied the US embassy in Tehran and took its diplomats hostage. Khomeini supported the occupation, in part to make sure that any reconciliation with Carter would be as difficult as possible.

The hostage crisis undid Carter's presidency. He was seen as weak and indecisive because he did not respond by attacking Iranian territory or forcing some kind of showdown with Ayatollah Khomeini, as if that would have helped the hostages. Instead, Carter struggled to understand what was going on in Iran. He did not want to drive the Iranians into the arms of the Soviets. The Cold War was still uppermost in his mind. In the end he settled on a military rescue operation, which failed spectacularly when two US aircraft collided in the Iranian desert. The botched effort in April 1980 led to Vance's resignation as secretary of state and probably doomed Carter's chances for reelection. A month later Ronald Reagan, vowing to break with détente and make America great again, won the Republican nomination for president.

But if the Americans had trouble with Islamism in Iran, the Soviets faced such trouble of their own farther north. In Afghanistan a Marxist party had come to power through a military coup in April 1978. The new regime started to work closely with the Soviets, who advised them to go slow on implementing substantial reform in the countryside. The Soviet advisers believed that the Afghan people were not ready for large-scale secular initiatives such as land reform, education for women, and outlawing child marriages. But the Afghan Communists persisted. By early 1979 they faced a growing Islamist rebellion, organized from neighboring Pakistan and Iran. The Afghan Islamists believed in an Islamic revolution, like what had happened in Iran (even though they regarded the Shia as sectarians). They were mostly educated in the Middle East, in Egypt or Saudi Arabia, and they wanted to shake up Afghan society as much as the Communists did—though in the direction of *more* Islam, not less.

As Islamist attacks against government installations in Afghanistan intensified, more Soviet advisers arrived to help the Afghan Communists out. Even though the political haste of Mohammad Taraki, the Afghan president, exasperated the Soviets, they were committed to supporting the regime. They saw opportunity as well as danger. "Angola, in combination with Ethiopia, was the way to Afghanistan," Karen Brutents, the deputy head of the CPSU's International Department, observed later.[29] But when Taraki himself was killed in factional infighting with his deputy, Hafizullah Amin, in September 1979, Soviet advisers on the spot sounded the alarm. Amin claimed to pursue an even more extreme Marxist-Leninist policy than Taraki, but the KGB suspected him of contacts with the Americans and of planning to "do a Sadat" on the Soviet Union. With Islamist guerrillas advancing, the Soviets began preparing to remove Amin by force and put in place a new Afghan Communist leadership more loyal to the Soviet Union and more effective in fighting the Islamist rebellion.

The Soviet intervention began on Christmas Eve 1979. The Carter Administration had been able to follow the troop buildup on the Soviet side of the border through its new spy satellites, so the invasion came as no surprise. The president was still horrified at the Soviet action. Brzezinski had been describing to him what he called an "arc of crisis," in which the Soviets were hoping to insert their power, stretching from the Horn of Africa, across the Red Sea, to the shores of the Indian Ocean. The Afghanistan invasion seemed to prove such Soviet intentions. Some US analysts believed that the real objectives of the Red Army operation were ports on the Indian Ocean and control of the Gulf's oil. However far-fetched such suggestions were, they had an effect in the frenzied White House atmosphere during the hostage crisis.

Carter addressed the American people in a television address on the evening of 4 January 1980. He called the Soviet invasion "an extremely serious threat to peace." The reason for this, he said, was not just the events in Afghanistan themselves. It was

> because of the threat of further Soviet expansion into neighboring countries in Southwest Asia and also because such an aggressive military policy is unsettling to other peoples throughout the world. This is a callous violation of international law and the United Nations Charter. It is a deliberate effort of a powerful atheistic government to subjugate an independent Islamic people. We must recognize the strategic importance of Afghanistan to stability and peace. A Soviet-occupied Afghanistan threatens both Iran and Pakistan and is a steppingstone to possible control over much of the world's oil supplies.[30]

Two weeks later, in his state of the union address, Carter underlined that "the implications of the Soviet invasion of Afghanistan could pose the most serious threat to the peace since the Second World War."[31] The president asked his advisers for actions that could be taken to punish the Soviets, and when proposals came in, he signed off on every one of them, so that even Brzezinski was taken aback at the president's fury. He stopped trade and cultural exchanges, barred exports of grain, technology, and transport equipment, halted space cooperation, banned Soviet fishing boats in US waters, and threatened to boycott the Moscow Olympics. He also withdrew the SALT II treaty from consideration in the Senate. "History," Carter said, "teaches . . . very few clear lessons. But surely one such lesson learned by the world at great cost is that aggression, unopposed, becomes a contagious disease."[32]

If it were not for previous events, starting with the Soviet Angola operation in 1975, Carter's reaction could have been seen as exaggerated and hyperbolic. The Soviet Union had had broad influence in Afghanistan for two generations, and the Afghan Islamists, whom the United States had started supporting even before the Soviet invasion, were not necessarily a better alternative for Afghanistan than Communist rule. But none of that mattered within the overall Cold War framework that Carter applied. Ever since he became president, he had suspected that the Soviets were mounting an outright challenge to the US position in the world. By the time of the Ethiopian crisis, détente, from the US perspective, had already been in deep trouble. US military expenditure, in decline since the beginning of détente, had started to rise again. In Carter's fourth budget it rose by almost 12 percent adjusted for inflation, an increase unprecedented in peacetime.[33] Zbigniew Brzezinski's summing up in his memoirs, that "détente lies buried in the sands of the Ogaden," might seem outrageous, especially to those who have visited that bleak part of the world. But in describing President Carter's view at the time it may hold more than a grain of truth.

And still Carter's emphasis on the Cold War did him so little good in US political terms. In the presidential election he got clobbered by

Ronald Reagan, who claimed that inflation, the rise of Soviet power, and the oil shocks all were due to the president's incompetence. But worse, Reagan insisted, Carter did not really believe in America.

> They say that the United States has had its day in the sun, that our nation has passed its zenith. They expect you to tell your children that the American people no longer have the will to cope with their problems, that the future will be one of sacrifice and few opportunities. . . . The time is now, my fellow Americans, to recapture our destiny, to take it into our own hands. . . . Can we doubt that only a Divine Providence placed this land, this island of freedom, here as a refuge for all those people in the world who yearn to breathe free? Jews and Christians enduring persecution behind the Iron Curtain; the boat people of Southeast Asia, of Cuba, and of Haiti; the victims of drought and famine in Africa; the freedom fighters in Afghanistan; and our own countrymen held in savage captivity.[34]

Reagan's rhetoric was a throwback to an earlier time, but for many Americans it captured the moment perfectly. They wanted to be brought back to a world of more certainty and away from foreign and domestic challenges that were transforming the country they lived in. Never mind that Reagan had very few concrete solutions to offer for America's ills. Like Margaret Thatcher in Britain, he stood for a kind of conservative rebellion against those, he claimed, who had been holding the country back. In that sense Reagan's first cabinet was the most radical American Administration since the New Deal. It promised to dramatically lower taxes, eliminate the public deficit, abolish all price controls, and do away with most government regulations of the economy. Both his supporters and his opponents spoke of the Reagan Revolution, although in reality much less happened than had been promised.

Reagan from the very beginning of his presidency believed that the United States had to strengthen its defense and its international prestige in order to negotiate with the Soviet Union from an advantageous position. Supremely self-confident, he thought that he would succeed where, in his view, Nixon, Ford, and Carter had failed. He did not take into consideration the effect his rhetoric had on the other side. Reagan's tough talk really frightened the aging leadership in Moscow, who, for the first time, started believing that the world might be heading toward a total war between the Superpowers. When Reagan said, at the start of his presidency, that Americans should "begin planning for a world where our adversaries are remembered only for their role in a sad and rather bizarre chapter in human history," Soviet leaders took him very seriously.[35]

Part of the reason for the Soviet fear of Reagan's policies was their own failure in Afghanistan. Instead of a short intervention that would set things right in that country, as he had been promised by his advisers, Brezhnev got a long and deepening war. The brutality of Soviet warfare created a massive refugee problem, which the Islamists could make use of to get adherents for their cause. The Soviet problems widened in 1982 and '83, when Reagan stepped up the support for the Afghan Islamists, the mujahedin, and their backers in Pakistan. Although the Reagan Administration was aware that some of these Islamists were at least as anti-American as they were anti-Soviet, they had concluded that assisting them was essential in pushing back Soviet power. "Here is the beauty of the Afghan operation," said William Casey, Reagan's head of the CIA, to his colleagues. "Usually it looks like the big bad Americans are beating up on the natives. Afghanistan is just the reverse. The Russians are beating up on the little guys. We don't make it our war. The mujahedin have all the motivation they need. All we have to do is to give them help, only more of it."[36]

Afghanistan was not the only place where Reagan wanted to push back against Left-wing revolutions. In Nicaragua, one of Latin America's poorest countries, a group of Marxist-inspired rebels had taken power in 1979 after ousting a deeply unpopular dictator who had been supported by the United States. The Sandinista Front, as Nicaragua's new leaders called themselves, had a radical program of nationalizations and land reform. They wanted close relations with Cuba and the Soviet bloc, even though Fidel Castro warned them against moving so fast that the United States would intervene.[37] The Sandinistas tried to avoid a direct confrontation with Washington, but the Reagan Administration had them in their gun sights from the moment they took office. Reagan's point of attack was the Nicaraguan support for a rebel movement in neighboring El Salvador. The president claimed that he had evidence of the involvement of "the Soviet Union, of Cuba, of the PLO, of, even Qadhafi in Libya, and others in the Communist bloc nations to bring about this terrorism down there."[38] But his main culprits were the Sandinistas.

By late 1981 the United States had helped organize a counterrevolutionary force in Nicaragua, the so-called Contras, and was beginning to supply them with weapons and training. The immediate aim was to put pressure on the Sandinista government to stop its involvement in El Salvador, but soon the goal shifted to the overthrow of the Nicaraguan government itself. The Sandinistas were helped by revolutionary volunteers from the rest of Latin America, by the Cubans, and, to a very limited extent, by the Soviets. Though not all Sandinista reforms were equally popular with the Nicaraguans, most of the population seems to have believed, at least to begin with, that their new leadership was standing up to US bullying. The underlying reason for the support of the Left in Central America was of course the immense poverty that most people lived under. More than half of all Nicaraguan children were malnourished in the 1970s. The contrast with life a few hundred miles farther north was striking. In a world where the average person in Central America consumed less meat than what the average American fed to his pet, protesting social injustice easily became a protest against US hegemony.

Détente was defeated by a number of circumstances, some of which were outside of Superpower control. Revolutions in the Third World unsettled the process of rapprochement, and rapid economic change helped undermine it. It is also clear that from the very beginning, leaders in the United States and the USSR had read somewhat different things into détente. The Soviets believed that they had got acceptance for true equality between the two powers. Most leaders in the United States thought that the Soviets had signed up to cooperate with a world-system that was led by the Americans. But the Soviets were also consciously willing to take great risks in their relations with Washington for the sake of assisting revolutions elsewhere and expanding their own power.

Ultimately, though, détente was defeated by politics in the United States. Nixon and Kissinger had gone further in attempting to manage the Cold War together with the Soviet Union than most Americans were willing to accept. After Watergate the American distrust of its government, *all* government, reached fever pitch. Détente was a victim of this process, although it seems likely that rapprochement would have come to a standstill at some point even without Nixon's disgrace. Most Americans were simply not willing to tolerate that the United States could have an equal in international affairs, in the 1970s or ever. And they elected Ronald Reagan president to make sure that such a devaluation of the American purpose would not happen again.

19

European Portents

By 1982 many people were saying that the Cold War had returned to where it had been before the détente process began. Some were even arguing that Reagan had started a "new Cold War," as if the conflict had ever gone away completely. But even for those who had observed the fighting of the Cold War in the Middle East, Africa, Latin America, and south and southeast Asia in the 1970s, the conflict in the 1980s seemed to take on a new and more dangerous dimension. There was the relentless military buildup, which had taken a new and hazardous turn. The threat of nuclear war was ever more immediate, especially as both sides were developing new, lighter, and more easily targetable weapons. And there was the rhetoric, which by 1982–83 had reached fever pitch. Reagan spoke of the USSR as "the focus of evil in the modern world." The Soviets spoke of Reagan as the new Hitler. "Reagan's vulgar speeches show the true face of the military-industrial complex. They have long sought such a figure. Now, they have finally found it in the form of Reagan," said Iurii Andropov, who after Brezhnev's death in 1982 replaced him as Soviet leader.[1]

The Cold War in the early 1980s was very perilous, probably more so than at any other time since the Cuban missile crisis of 1962. But there were other trends as well. China began to move away from the hypercentralization of economic power that had been its ideal under Mao. Some countries that had identified themselves as belonging to the Third World began experimenting with reforms that opened them to market practices both domestically and internationally. But first and foremost there was the beginning transformation of Europe, where western European integration and economic expansion increasingly created an irresistible attraction for countries east of the Iron Curtain. So strong was the pull that even the reinvigorated Superpower Cold War could not entirely deter it, especially since one Superpower—the USSR—was no longer altogether certain what its aims in Europe truly were.

LIKE THE INTENSIFICATION of the Superpower conflict, the transformation of the Cold War in Europe can be traced back to the Portuguese revolution of 1974. For Europeans, much less preoccupied with events in Africa than the Superpowers were, the issue was not so much the character of the regimes in Luanda or Maputo. It was what would come out of the change of government in Lisbon. While most western Europeans celebrated Portugal's turn away from a Fascist-style dictatorship, they also worried about the effect a Communist takeover outside the Soviet zone could have on the continent's future. The issue was not so much about the Portuguese Left overall. It was mainly about the resurgent Portuguese Communist Party, which went out of its way to proclaim its support for the USSR and its ideals at a time when patience with these ideals ran thin outside of the Soviet bloc.

The Portuguese revolution happened at a time when significant parts of the western European radical Left had begun to feel that the legacy of the Russian October Revolution was becoming less and less relevant for their own political practice. The so-called New Left of the 1960s had of course proclaimed this already, but their reach was limited. When the Italian Communist Party (PCI), followed by the Spanish and the French, in the late 1960s began saying that they believed in a transition to socialism only through elections and parliaments, the effect was much greater. But the new PCI leader, the charismatic and vigorous Enrico Berlinguer, did not stop there. Berlinguer wanted to re-create western European Communism as a democratic alternative in the West. He also wanted to put pressure on the eastern European parties to reform and respect human and democratic rights. Especially after the Chilean coup in 1973, in which the Left had been destroyed, Berlinguer argued for a "historic compromise" between Catholic and Communist parties in Europe to safeguard democracy. His Eurocommunism proved popular in Italy and beyond.

On a European level, the Portuguese revolution pitted Berlinguer's Eurocommunists against Soviet support for the doctrinaire Portuguese Communist Party. Privately, to other like-minded Communists and Social Democrats, including West Germany's Brandt and Sweden's Olof Palme, Berlinguer admitted that it would be a disaster for the Left in Europe if the Portuguese Communists came to power. In a sure sign of how western European politics was shifting, the opposition to Communist rule in Portugal brought together some strange bedfellows: Eurocommunists, Social Democrats, Catholic groups, and the CIA all in different ways attempted to strengthen the non-Communist alternatives. When the Portuguese Socialists under Mario Soares came to power in 1976, with a radical Social Democratic agenda, there were sighs of relief all around in the western European capitals, as well as in Washington.

In spite of their community of purpose over Portugal, successive US Administrations nonetheless distrusted and feared the Eurocommunists. The Americans believed that Berlinguer's real aim was to become part of the government and then to seize power from within. The Soviets had even more reason to dislike the constant hectoring from the Italians about their own policies. Brezhnev was shocked when Berlinguer said openly, in Moscow, that democracy was a "historically universal value upon which to base an original socialist society" and furious when the Italian called NATO a "shield useful for constructing socialism in freedom."[2] Even so, Moscow had little alternative but to continue to support the western European Communist parties both politically and financially, for fear of losing all influence among them.

In the United States the main worry concerning Europe was to hold the NATO alliance together as the Cold War grew colder in the late 1970s. Ever since the 1940s some US policy-makers had worried about western European, and especially West German, instincts for compromising with the Soviets rather than confronting them. Most often such suspicions had been misplaced. The western Europeans had, after all, built NATO, together with the Americans, in order to defend themselves against what they saw as a threat from the East. Very often the differences on key defense issues between the United States and its main allies had been in terms of tone, not content. And even if the Americans bore by far the greatest military and financial burden in the defense of western Europe, Washington had been keen to let the Europeans be part of making decisions. The deliberative decision-making within NATO helped convince all allies that they were there on equal terms, and not just as staffage in a global Cold War.

But as Superpower détente began to collapse, many western European leaders were worried about what would follow. Détente, they thought, had served Europe well. It had opened up new avenues for contact across the Iron Curtain. Trust-building measures between the military alliances had made Europeans feel more secure, and these western European leaders were themselves vested in the détente processes. It was *their* project, not just the Superpowers'. Not surprisingly, they were looking for ways to keep European détente alive even when relations between Moscow and Washington seemed to be in free fall.

The Helsinki process, as it was often called after the conference held there in 1975, was one way of keeping lines to the East open. The right to send observers to military exercises, participation in academic conferences, exchanges in science and technology, and the right for western Europeans to travel freely to eastern Europe (but not, in practice, the other way around) should be upheld in spite of conflicts in other areas, most western European leaders thought. Chiefly, they were preoccupied with trade and economic interaction. And since trade between the blocs in Europe tended to be a one-way street, with the export of western European goods to the east, both sides were keen to find products that could flow in the opposite direction. The one that stood out was Soviet oil and gas, and plans for gas pipelines from Siberia to western Europe had been underway since the mid-1970s. Reagan, predictably, put his foot down. When the western Europeans refused to cancel the project, in 1981 Reagan slapped US sanctions on all companies, including European companies, that contributed to building the pipelines. Although the Americans later relented, considerable damage was done to the perception of transatlantic unity.

In terms of discussion of military strategy the Americans had much less to fear from their allies, although they did not always realize that this was so. When the Carter Administration in 1977 wanted to introduce high-radiation nuclear weapons for battlefield use (so-called neutron bombs) in Europe, most western Europeans leaders went along. They feared the Soviet advantage in conventional forces, especially if there were to be deep cuts in the strategic nuclear arsenals, and believed the neutron bomb could help offset that advantage. Public opinion in almost all western European countries was of a different view. The neutron bomb was decried as an inhumane weapon that killed people and spared property. Exactly the kind of weapon, the western European Left argued, that US capitalists would like to see. When Carter unilaterally cancelled the deployment a year later, those western European leaders who had supported the proposal were furious. They felt that they had gone out on a political limb for nothing.

The German chancellor, Helmut Schmidt, was especially angry. He had weathered public opinion on the neutron bomb and felt betrayed. Schmidt, who regarded himself as an expert on strategic matters (and on most other matters, too), had already formed a very low opinion of Carter as a leader. But the West German chancellor, who was by far the most powerful politician in Europe, was also concerned about Soviet intentions. He was especially worried that a combination of Carter's naiveté and Soviet military strength in Europe could tempt the Americans to compromise with the Soviets, to western Europe's disadvantage. Schmidt believed that the US position in the world was slipping and that Europeans had to prepare to fend more for themselves. But he was also keen to keep the Americans in Europe to the highest degree possible for strategic reasons, as long as Schmidt himself could influence key decisions in NATO.

What particularly worried western European strategic planners was that the Soviet and Warsaw Pact advantage in conventional forces was being augmented by Brezhnev's introduction of new highly mobile medium-range ballistic missiles, the SS-20s. The Soviets deployed the new weapons because they knew the missiles they replaced were of very poor quality, and because there were no treaties that prohibited them from doing so. But it was a political mistake because western European leaders felt it to be an attempt at intimidation in troubled times. It was Helmut Schmidt, more than anyone, who cobbled together the NATO response, the so-called double-track decision of December 1979. In it, the NATO partners said they would prepare the deployment of US medium-range Pershing II and cruise missiles in western Europe in response to the Soviet deployment. At the same time, NATO invited negotiations on limiting the number of all medium-range nuclear missiles in Europe on an equal basis, as part of what would be the SALT III talks. This was an important decision. It kept NATO united, sent a clear message to the Soviets, and—maybe most importantly—made it plain that western European leaders more than ever took responsibility for their own defense.

There was to be no SALT III, however. Two weeks after NATO's double-track decision, the Soviets invaded Afghanistan. Most western European leaders, except Britain's new prime minister, Margaret Thatcher, thought Carter overreacted to the Soviet action. "We will not permit ten years of détente and defense policy to be destroyed," Helmut Schmidt told his colleagues.[3] Schmidt, who was in essence Germany's most pro-American chancellor since Konrad Adenauer, felt that Washington was failing in consulting its allies. He also really started to fear that the world was heading toward Superpower war. He told Carter that West Germany would agree to joint NATO measures against the invasion, but that he himself would keep communication lines with Moscow open. Against US wishes, Schmidt traveled to Moscow in June 1980 to meet with Brezhnev. With his usual bluntness, Schmidt told the aging Soviet leader that he thought the invasion of Afghanistan had been a grave mistake. But he also asked for, and got, Soviet concessions on discussing nuclear arms in Europe.

The USSR was willing to talk, Brezhnev said, as long as *all* nuclear weapons in Europe were part of the discussion.

Brezhnev's willingness to talk indicated his worry about how fast tensions were rising on a global scale. But the form the initiative took was also meant to pry open differences in NATO. France and Britain had their own nuclear weapons, which they did not want to negotiate over. West Germany did not. The Soviets were still hoping that West Germany's dependence on the United States and Germany's position as a Cold War front line state could help Moscow appeal to German nationalist instincts. But the 1980 initiatives on medium-range missiles were soon overtaken by further increases in tension between the two power blocs. By 1983 Cold War anxiety in Europe was at its highest level since the early 1960s because of the rhetorical confrontation between Reagan and the Soviet leaders. More than half of all western Europeans polled believed they would see a war between the Superpowers in their lifetime.

Leonid Brezhnev died in November 1982 after eighteen years as Soviet leader. He was not mourned by many. Even his closest colleagues had begun to sense that the Soviet Union had come to a standstill during the final phase of his leadership. Brezhnev had without doubt improved the international position of the Soviet Union and made it a military Superpower at a level his predecessors could only have dreamt about. But the foreign expansion of the USSR had taken place at great economic cost and, many Communists felt, at the expense of solving problems at home. Brezhnev's successor, Iurii Andropov, was selected because his colleagues thought he could handle foreign affairs and provide impetus for necessary adjustments at home. As chairman of the secret police, the KGB, for fifteen years, Andropov had the skill and the ruthlessness needed to shake things up, his aging Politburo colleagues believed.

But Andropov, though aware of the need for domestic reform, was a sick man already when he was made general secretary, and therefore incapable of doing much. He died in February 1984. His replacement, Konstantin Chernenko, was an apparatchik and Brezhnev crony who wanted to keep a steady ship without much thought of reform. Chernenko was also unwell when he was elected. He died after little more than a year in office. Not surprisingly the party cadre and the population in general thought that leadership of the party was drifting. A friend of mine, who lived in Moscow at the time, claimed that his six-year-old son got so used to hearing Chopin's funeral march on television that he thought it was the Soviet national anthem.

And while an elderly Politburo struggled to stay alive physically and politically, Cold War tensions kept on rising. The Soviets began worrying in earnest about the risk of a US surprise nuclear attack, and took steps to increase surveillance of key Western institutions. The KGB was ordered to keep watch for political, financial, and religious leaders traveling toward nuclear shelters or safe zones, for any increases in the capacity of blood banks, and for hospitals being readied. This intelligence operation, called RIaN (short, in Russian, for "nuclear missile attack"), probably helped convince Soviet leaders that no immediate attack was underway. But tensions remained high. In September 1983 the Soviet air force shot down a civilian Korean airliner that had strayed into Soviet airspace. The Soviets had mistaken it for a US spy plane. All 269 people aboard were killed, 61 of them Americans, including a US congressman.

The Soviets made this terrible case of mass murder even worse in Cold War terms through initially lying about their involvement, claiming that they had not shot down the plane. US Cold War hawks had a field day. Reagan's UN ambassador, the neoconservative Jeane Kirkpatrick, played US intelligence recordings of transmissions between the Soviet pilots and their air defense command at the UN Security Council. Reagan himself went on national television, calling it "the Korean airline massacre, the attack by the Soviet Union against 269 innocent men, women, and children aboard an unarmed Korean passenger plane. This crime against humanity must never be forgotten, here or throughout the world."[4]

In November 1983 things got really ugly. For years NATO had held military exercises, usually in the fall, in order to test alliance readiness to withstand a sudden Warsaw Pact attack. The 1983 version, codenamed Able Archer '83, simulated conflict escalation up to the point when nuclear strikes were launched. The Soviets had been notified about the exercise beforehand, and knew quite a bit about it from their own intelligence sources. Still, when Able Archer got underway, tensions grew. The CIA reported later that Moscow had placed "Soviet air units in East Germany and Poland on heightened readiness."[5] There is no reason to believe that the Soviet leaders thought an attack was imminent, but Moscow's reaction showed just how volatile and dangerous the overall situation was. The world, and Europe especially, was closer to a situation where nuclear war could break out accidentally than it had been for a long time.

The fear that was engulfing the Soviet leaders was not just a product of the pressure they were under from the West. It also came about because the economic and social system they represented seemed to be in trouble. Economic growth was slowing. A decline in oil prices sharply reduced the Soviet state's foreign income. Andropov and others castigated sloth, corruption, and drunkenness. While no Soviet leader thought that the system they had inherited needed fundamental change, most were aware that it needed reform. The Soviet state, many Communist leaders agreed, was overextended. The high degree of centralization in planning hobbled the economy. Military expenditure was growing too quickly, and the Soviet Union supported too many Third World states and movements that were becoming accustomed to living off Moscow's largesse. But while questions abounded, few had any answers. And even the questions could not be posed too loudly. The Soviet Union was a dictatorship, and the currency for promotion was loyalty.

If things were not looking too good in the Soviet Union, they were beginning to look even worse in eastern Europe. Granted, many eastern Europeans, in Hungary and Czechoslovakia, for instance, had a standard of living that Soviet citizens could only dream of. But even so, the sense spread of the leaders' inability to deal with the most pressing problems, including secure and stable supplies of consumer goods. It was not that eastern Europeans on a whole were living worse lives than before. It was that many of them knew how much better people in western Europe were living and how quickly progress was made there. The increased contacts across the Iron Curtain after Helsinki had convinced many eastern Europeans, especially professionals, teachers, and managers, that their lives were much poorer than those lived across the borders in the West. More than before they compared themselves not with their own past, or with the Soviet Union, but with other Europeans whose lives they thought they knew, through glimpses on television, film, or chance encounters.

Something else had changed, too. The fear of German revanchism and expansionism, so much touted by the Soviets, had ceased having much of an impact on younger eastern Europeans. This was important, especially in Poland. Over a third of Polish territory had been German before the war. But Brandt's *Ostpolitik* and the high level of interaction with both Germanies had done away with much of the unease that had existed in the past. It left Poles free to be concerned about their own affairs, and they had much to complain about, especially workers and their families. Poland had fallen behind most other eastern European countries in terms of growth. In 1970, when the government tried to raise prices on ordinary goods, workers protested. "What is communism?" went the joke in Warsaw. "It is when everything will be available in stores. In other words, like it was before the revolution."

The large-scale workers' protests in 1970 frightened the Polish government. With Soviet consent, it tried to borrow its way out of the crisis. Just like countries in Latin America, the Poles and other East Bloc governments found western banks and institutions eager to lend money in the 1970s. Poland was seen as a solid borrower: it had a stable system of government and at least some products that could be exported (coal, ships, and agricultural produce). Nobody really considered the inefficiency of production and the shoddiness of the products, which led to nobody outside the East Bloc wanting to buy their goods. The Polish Communists borrowed about $20 billion up to 1977, when the patience of their Western creditors started to run out. The regime had to increase prices, again, in order to pay back its loans.

Like in 1970, Polish workers would not accept worse conditions without a fight. They felt things were bad enough already. And by 1978 they had a new inspiration for their struggle. The deeply Catholic Polish working class that year celebrated the election of a Polish Pope. The first non-Italian elected since the sixteenth century, Karol Cardinal Wojtyła took the name John Paul II. He had been the archbishop of Kraków, a vigorous and athletic man of fifty-eight, a theological conservative who had always been close to workers in his home country. The Communist leaders simply did not dare refuse him permission to visit Poland after his election. More than a quarter of the Polish population saw him in person to celebrate mass during his tour of the country in 1979. "If we accept all that I have dared to affirm in this moment, how many great duties and obligations arise?" the pontiff asked his countrymen. "Are we capable of them? . . . It is impossible without Christ to understand this nation with its past so full of splendor and also of terrible difficulties. . . . Let your Spirit descend," prayed John Paul, "and renew the face of the earth, the face of this land." His audience chanted: "We want God, we want God."[6]

In August 1980 the workers at the Lenin Shipyard in Gdansk went on strike. Led by the young electrician Lech Wałęsa, the workers occupied the shipyard and demanded improved pay and working conditions. When other factories joined in the strike, the demands were expanded to include free trade unions, freedom of expression, and the release of political prisoners. With strikes spreading and other groups joining the workers, the Polish Communist Party gave in to some of the demands. Desperate to get its working class to cooperate in increasing production, the government felt that it had little choice but to give in. At the end of the month, Communist negotiators had agreed to a new independent trade union, Solidarity, as well as the release of prisoners and most of the workers' economic demands. The talks inside the shipyard, with Wałęsa and other workers' leaders challenging the profusely sweating Communist cadre in their suits and ties, were shown live on television. It was a sight most Poles never thought they would live to see.

By 1981 Solidarity had almost ten million members and its own publications and publishing houses. The Communist government tried to keep censorship in place, but with less and less success. The party itself was badly split on how to handle the Solidarity challenge. Some leading members, including the new first secretary, Stanisław Kania, wanted to build a lasting compromise with Solidarity and other non-Communist groups. They wanted all parts of Polish society to be responsible for the dire economic situation the country was in. They still wanted the Communist Party in charge in order to stave off a Soviet intervention. But all other matters were negotiable, at least over time. As could be expected, Moscow and the other Warsaw Pact capitals brought enormous pressure to bear on the Poles. They wanted Kania replaced, Solidarity banned, and censorship expanded. Their support went to the defense minister, General Wojciech Jaruzelski, who replaced Kania as first secretary in October 1981.

On 13 December 1981 Jaruzelski introduced martial law and cracked down on Solidarity. Five thousand of its leaders were arrested. The new regime brought back heavy censorship, and military units patrolled the streets. To disgruntled Communist Party members, Jaruzelski claimed that he had introduced martial law because of the clear and immediate risk of a Soviet Red Army invasion. This was almost certainly untrue. When Jaruzelski developed the plan for martial law together with the Soviets, they pushed him to implement it, while making it clear that if the operation failed the Red Army would not intervene to bail him out. After Afghanistan, with economic problems mounting and Superpower tension increasing, the Soviet Union simply could not risk moving their forces into Poland. Andropov had put it in very clear terms to the Moscow Politburo on 10 December:

We cannot risk such a step. We do not intend to introduce troops into Poland. That is the proper position, and we must adhere to it until the end. I do not know how things will turn out in Poland, but even if Poland falls under the control of "Solidarity," that is the way it will be. And if the capitalist countries pounce on the Soviet Union, and you know they have already reached agreement on a variety of economic and political sanctions, that will be very burdensome for us. We must be concerned above all with our own country and about the strengthening of the Soviet Union.[7]

Perspectives were starting to shift in other eastern European countries, too, though more slowly than in Poland. Hungary under János Kádár had long had the most liberal political regime in the Warsaw Pact. In the 1980s its economy was slowing, and like Poland, it had made up for the shortfall through Western loans. But Hungary also had more economic interaction with the West than any other Soviet bloc country. Since 1976 the Buda Heights, so destroyed in the fighting in 1945, had had its own Budapest Hilton Hotel. Visitors from other eastern European countries used to scramble up the hillside just to gawk at its turrets. Hungarians themselves were relatively free to travel. In 1985 more than five million Hungarians traveled abroad, about a third of them to western Europe. One of them reported later on her experiences: "I was so overwhelmed when I went to the West for the first time that I couldn't even process all the information I was bombarded with during those three weeks. . . . In Eastern Europe we had to fight to have the very rights Westerners took almost for granted. . . . There was fresh food in the markets, even at weekends, and I didn't have to stand in a long queue to buy a loaf of bread."[8]

The people of Hungary or Czechoslovakia regarded themselves less and less as "eastern Europeans" left by others for Soviet domination. Instead they began recasting themselves as central Europeans, under occupation by a strange, oriental Soviet culture. If, say, Norway or Portugal were part of the European mainstream, why were not they? In Hungary the opposition was mainly intellectual or commercial. In Czechoslovakia, after 1968 a much harsher dictatorship, the opposition demanded political rights and the undoing of the regime imposed after the Soviet invasion. Charta '77 was a manifesto of political dissidents, ranging from underground rock bands to leading opposition figures, such as the playwright Václav Havel. It condemned political oppression in Czechoslovakia: "Freedom of public expression is inhibited by the centralized control of all the communication media and of publishing and cultural institutions. No philosophical, political or scientific view or artistic activity that departs ever so slightly from the narrow bounds of official ideology or aesthetics is allowed to be published; no open criticism can be made of abnormal social phenomena; no public defense is possible against false and insulting charges made in official propaganda."[9]

The Prague rock group Plastic People of the Universe put it more succinctly: "Whoever is now twenty, he wants to vomit with disgust."[10] The band members were arrested. Havel was arrested, too. He was sentenced to four years' imprisonment in 1979.

The Soviet and eastern European attacks on dissidents helped delegitimize Marxism-Leninism in the eyes of most people elsewhere. In the USSR the few outspoken political dissidents who existed were imprisoned or exiled. In some cases they were committed to psychiatric hospitals, where they were pumped with drugs intended to make them docile and cooperative. Vladimir Bukovsky, a Soviet dissident who in 1976 was "exchanged" for the imprisoned Chilean Communist leader Luis Corvalán, had spent years in psychiatric institutions. So had General Piotr Grigorenko, a Red Army officer who protested political oppression in the Soviet Union. The physicist Andrei Sakharov, one of the founders of the Moscow Helsinki Group, a dissident body set up to monitor Soviet (non-) compliance with the 1975 Helsinki Accords, was spared such humiliating treatment. But that was only because he was one of the fathers of the Soviet nuclear program and the winner of the 1975 Nobel Peace Prize. Instead Sakharov was sent in internal exile to the city of Gorky (now Nizhny Novgorod), where he was kept under strict surveillance and away from the international press. In his Nobel Prize acceptance speech, read by his wife Elena Bonner, Sakharov stressed "the link between defense of peace and defense of human rights, . . . [only] the defense of human rights guarantees a solid ground for genuine long-term international cooperation."[11]

The East German authorities prided themselves both on economic progress and on sophisticated methods of controlling any potential opposition. But from the late 1970s on it was clear that at least the former of these aims was in trouble. Compared to other countries in the Soviet bloc the GDR was still doing well. Its people had the highest standard of living and the highest productivity. But the all-pervasive secret police, the Stasi (short for State Security Service), which kept individual files on more than a third of all East Germans, reported that all was not well. The curious shortages that people were subjected to (coffee disappeared from the shelves for a while in 1976, bananas and oranges in 1979) made some East Germans unhappy, especially as many of them could watch on television the abundance of goods in West Germany. The Stasi was still able to contain any kind of open opposition and East Germans did, on the whole, obey the government. But the East German leaders knew that they had to improve the economy. As they grumbled among themselves, what the GDR competed against was not Poland or Bulgaria, but the most advanced industrial economy in the Western world, which also happened to be German.

Like most other eastern European countries, the GDR tried to stimulate its economy by getting loans from the West, and especially from West Germany. The East German problem in the 1980s was not, by itself, the level of indebtedness, but the decline in hard currency exports that would make it possible to service this debt. In the 1950s and '60s East Germany had lots of products, from optics to cars, that could be sold outside the Soviet bloc. These exports slowed in the 1970s. By the 1980s East Germany was entirely outcompeted by southern European and Asian countries that could make better products for a lower price. The East German attempt at using its technological know-how to produce computers for export failed entirely. Nobody wanted big and clunky East Germans machines that were not compatible with anything produced outside the Soviet bloc.

For the East German leaders, keeping détente alive increasingly became a not-too-sophisticated form of blackmail against West Germany. West Germans were allowed to visit the East, but only if they exchanged a certain sum of hard currency into East German marks, worthless outside of the GDR. East Berlin threatened to cut off contacts if West Germany did not provide further loans or agree to economic deals, always with the East German mark rated at parity with the West German deutschmark. The new conservative West German government under Helmut Kohl, who replaced Helmut Schmidt in 1982, continued these concessions to East Berlin. Like Schmidt, Kohl believed that some form of contact was better than no contact. Most shocking of all, the West German government had to pay in hard currency for each East German who was allowed to leave for the West. Not surprising that by the mid-1980s some Germans in the east had started feeling that they, as a people, were quite literally held hostage by a failed government. But almost all of them restricted their complaints to family and close friends alone.

East Germany's fundamental problem was that it was simply too close to the biggest success story in Europe, the Federal Republic of Germany. And through the FRG, it was too close to the processes of European integration that by the mid-1970s had been swinging into high gear. On its own, compared to countries on the European periphery or outside of Europe, the GDR might still look OK. But compared to the industrial and financial powerhouse in the west, it seemed almost like a failed state. And West Germany was now building on its success to advance further integration among all the capitalist states in Europe, exactly the kind of system that East Germany could not be part of.

After the expansion of the European Community (EC) to include Britain, Ireland, and Denmark in 1973, the European Commission pushed ahead with plans for further integration. Helped by the West German and French governments, plans for direct elections to the European Parliament were passed. So were plans for a single western European market in which people, goods, services, and capital could move freely across borders. Such steps were needed, many European leaders thought, if their countries were not to fall behind the United States and Japan in economic development. While these plans took time to be fully implemented, just moving toward them undoubtedly stimulated European economies, including the West German, which otherwise would have been seen as stagnating (at least compared with the growth of the three previous decades). They also encouraged

competition, heightened efficiency, and facilitated the spread of technology. But first and foremost the work to create a union of European
states signaled the strength of a common set of ideas, which had not
always been visible in European cooperation before. In their Stuttgart
Declaration from 1983, western European leaders committed themselves "to create a united Europe, which is more than ever necessary
in order to meet the dangers of the world situation, capable of assum-
ing the responsibilities incumbent on it by virtue of its political role,
its economic potential and its manifold links with other peoples."[12]

The sense that the intensification of the Cold War created a pressure to speed up both the form and the extent of European integration was visible in all western European capitals. Greece was
fast-forwarded to become a full member of the EC in 1981. Spain
and Portugal joined in 1986. These were to a high extent Cold War
decisions (which US leaders, by the way, very strongly supported).
In being offered EC membership, the countries of southern Europe
signed up to a form of socially responsible capitalism, in which they
would receive aid if, but only if, they forwent the revolutionary alternative. And aid they did get, both before and after they became
full members of the EC. By the late 1980s these poorest countries in
Europe were seeing a massive lift in enterprise, welfare, and average
income. I remember a Portuguese farmer from impoverished
Alentejo explaining to me in 1988 why he no longer supported the
Communist Party: European aid, he said, made hope of a better life
possible.

The expansion of the EC to encompass southern Europe was of
enormous significance for the Cold War. For eastern Europeans it held
out the promise that they, too, could join a European community. For
people in Prague or Budapest it was difficult to understand why farmers in Alentejo or fishermen in Crete could benefit from European integration while they could not. This perception was a time bomb under
Soviet rule in eastern Europe. It signaled that the alternative to a division of Europe into power blocs might not be war or dislocation, but a
world in which countries joined up to decide their own future without
Superpower control. The worst enemy of Communist control was not

NATO military maneuvers, but the promise of affluence when walls through Europe were removed.

Another consequence of the speeding up of the European integration process was the expansion of regional identities. Instead of focusing solely on the state they lived within, more and more Europeans began thinking of themselves as members of regions that either transcended state borders or stood out within these borders. German-speaking Italians in South Tyrol could link up more closely to people on the other side of the Austrian border. French-speaking Walloons in Belgium connected to their counterparts in France. In Spain Catalans and Basques demanded recognition as separate nationalities. Some of this led to conflict, but in most cases the concept of there being a common European integration process within which smaller nationalities could find their place even without full national independence helped ameliorate the tension between regions and states.

The question, however, was what would happen where Cold War division lines separated distinct European regions. By the mid-1980s the many links that had historically connected Bratislava, Budapest, and Vienna, three old capitals at the heart of Europe, became easier to see. Writers in all three countries began referring to their location in central Europe, even if the Cold War borders that separated them were still in place. In the Balkans identity issues were becoming increasingly complex. Hungarians in Romania were protesting the harsh treatment they received from the Ceaușescu government. Albanians in Yugoslavia had begun demanding independent rights. And elsewhere inside Yugoslavia agitation for the rights of the individual nations, Croats and Slovenes especially, had been stepped up. Some believed that such problems could only be solved within a wider framework for European integration. But so far the Cold War stood in the way, and the capacities of the European institutions were in no way up to the task of breaking down such barriers on their own.

Not all governments in Europe saw their interests served by a deepening integration in all areas, as the Stuttgart Declaration had called for. Margaret Thatcher, the free market ideologue who had become British prime minister in 1979, was a strong supporter of a western European common market. She also believed that the EC could help "realizing our common European strength to ensure the further spread of democracy and freedom and justice," as she put it to the European Parliament in 1986.[13] But she was profoundly skeptical of further political integration and feared both for British sovereignty and its "special relationship" with the United States. The latter was mirrored in the close personal relationship Thatcher had with Ronald Reagan, who other western European leaders, at least at first, regarded as a dogmatic dimwit.

Thatcher's status was augmented by her successful war against Argentina for control of the Falkland Islands in the South Atlantic. It was a conflict that in the eyes of the rest of the world, at least, came out of nowhere. After the Argentinian military regime took over the British-controlled islands of roughly 1,800 people in 1982, Thatcher sent a full British naval expedition eight thousand miles to reconquer them. The Reagan Administration, focused on the Cold War and worried about the stability of the Argentinian military regime against its Leftist challengers, wanted time for mediation. "I think an effort to show we're all still willing to seek a settlement," Reagan told the British prime minister on the telephone, " . . . would undercut the effort of . . . the Leftists in South America who are actively seeking to exploit the crisis." Thatcher would have nothing of it. "This is [about] democracy and our island, and the very worst thing for democracy would be if we failed now," she told the president.[14] The British took back the islands, with almost a thousand lives lost, most of them Argentinians. The war did little damage to the British-American relationship, but it did remind Reagan that there were other conflicts that needed handling besides the Cold War.

French leaders' biggest concern with the European integration process was how to prevent West Germany from becoming too predominant politically as well as economically. France had been a driver for European integration, and this approach continued under François Mitterrand, the Socialist who was elected president in 1981. Mitterrand at first seemed to set out on a more Left-wing course for France, and to the consternation of the Americans included several Communists in his government. But after his first year and a half in power, with the French economy in real trouble, the new president switched tack. Instead of talking about tax increases and nationalizations, Mitterrand moved toward fiscal and monetary prudence in an attempt to make French industry more competitive within Europe. The Communists were quietly dropped from his government, and the concept of a French Left alternative to "Anglo-Saxon" capitalism went out the window. All over western Europe, Mitterrand's Right turn was of great significance. It meant that a free market social and economic model would be in the driver's seat in an expanded EC, even if there were still marked differences between Mitterrand's France and Thatcher's Britain.

It is tempting to see the increase in small-scale terrorist activities in western Europe in the late 1970s as a reaction against the end of the sharp Left/Right divides in official politics. The small minorities of the extreme Left or Right who believed that the postwar western European states were illegitimate and exploitative had moved toward terrorism in the 1960s. But it was only a decade later that groups such as the West German Rote Armee Fraktion, also known as the Baader-Meinhof Group, and the Italian Brigate Rosse were firmly established. The spectacular acts of terrorism that they, and their rivals on the Right, carried out up to the end of the 1980s were probably a sign of how such groups were losing out within ordinary political competition. But even so, the murders of the head of the German Employers' Union Hanns Martin Schleyer by Baader-Meinhof in 1977 and of the former Italian prime minister Aldo Moro by the Brigate Rosse the following year shook up politics all over Europe.

But much worse for East-West relations were the suspicions in Bonn and elsewhere of collaboration between the Communist regimes in the East and terrorists in the West. Several Baader-Meinhof terrorists received military training in the East, and the East German Stasi supplied them with information about West German attempts at capturing them. East Germany and Bulgaria also facilitated links between western European terrorists and extremist movements in the

Middle East and Japan, such as the Palestinian PFLP-GC (the Abu Nidal group) and the Japanese Red Army, a tiny terrorist organization operating in the Middle East. This was a dangerous game. Some eastern European and Soviet officials may have believed that it would help them destabilize societies in the West. In reality it reminded western leaders of the illegitimate character of the eastern regimes themselves and helped make the Cold War more risky.

Western European terrorism also helped governments undermine other challenges to their policies. But attempting to taint young people's protest movements of the 1970s and '80s with smears of terrorist links backfired in the longer run. Especially after Ronald Reagan became US president, groups that advocated nuclear disarmament moved into the mainstream, as did environmental movements. In October 1983, more than three million western Europeans participated in rallies against NATO missile deployments. In London and in Bonn at least 250,000 people marched, under slogans such as "Ban the Bomb" and "Stop Nuclear Suicide." The West German Green Party, which was founded in 1980, linked disarmament with ending environmental destruction on both sides of the Iron Curtain. They got significant support for their positions: two-thirds of all West Germans polled in 1983 opposed new NATO missiles in Europe under any circumstance.[15]

What was new with the western European protest movement in the 1980s was that it was increasingly directed against militarism and oppression both in the West and the East. The campaign group European Nuclear Disarmament (END), launched in 1980, demanded the withdrawal of Soviet SS-20 missiles as well as saying no to new NATO weapons. What was worse from a Soviet perspective, many of the END leaders had close contacts with dissidents in eastern Europe. E. P. Thompson, a veteran British peace campaigner and former Communist, declared that "there is an immediate link between real disarmament and the development of democratic movements in the Socialist states. Furthermore, the creation of democratic movements in them is a precondition for forcing the Socialist states to disarm."[16] In the 1980s, the European Left seemed to have rediscovered the link between rights and liberties and Left-wing politics. The Helsinki process gave nuclear protesters an opportunity to meet with dissidents such as Havel in Czechoslovakia or with disenchanted members of the Communist Party in Hungary. They discovered that they had much in common on a broad set of concerns.

One such issue was the environmental degradation that the Cold War in Europe had contributed to. Not only were military industries big polluters, but nuclear energy, toxic waste, and deforestation were in many people's minds connected to the Cold War competition for production. Political parties such as the Greens and movements such as END made these links in their campaigns, sometimes criticizing the East as much as the West. But environmental criticism of the Cold War also found its way into the political mainstream. The youth wings of all the main West German parties believed that East-West agreements on "common security" were a precondition for solving acute environmental problems. Even the West German Christian Democrats, now in power under Helmut Kohl, in its 1984 program saw the reduction in polluting industries and the universal use of catalytic converters in cars as part of Germany's core international policies.[17]

But it was not only Europeans who were concerned about the wider effects of the Cold War. To a degree that would have astonished his European detractors, US president Ronald Reagan had begun worrying that nuclear war could break out by accident, or that the Soviet Union could feel pushed into launching a first strike on the West. Reagan believed that the United States was winning the Cold War. A sunny optimist by nature, the president felt that America's greatness had been restored by his election and by his actions during his first two years in office, including the military buildup. He also believed that the rest of the world was gradually turning in America's direction, toward free markets and democracy. Any nuclear conflict would destroy these natural processes, Reagan thought. Especially after the Able Archer affair, the president began thinking more seriously about how conflict could be avoided. "I feel the Soviet are so defense minded, so paranoid about being attacked," Reagan wrote in his diary, "that without being in any way soft on them we ought to tell them no one here has any intention of doing anything like that. What the hell have they got that anyone would want?"[18]

Ever since he became president, Reagan had been preoccupied with finding ways in which the United States could be protected against a nuclear attack. He found the principles of mutually assured destruction to be morally contentious and personally repugnant. The thought of himself ever having to use the nuclear launch codes horrified Reagan, who as president avoided most briefings or simulations in which he would have to do so. Instead, the president in 1983 commissioned a Strategic Defense Initiative (SDI), which would focus on preventing nuclear missiles from ever reaching the US mainland. Dubbed "Star Wars" by its detractors, these plans imagined the use of space-based lasers to destroy incoming missiles. Even some of the president's own science advisers suggested that it would not work, or at least not within a generation or so. But Reagan persisted, pouring billions into his new pet program.

SDI horrified the Soviets. Not only did it break with the principles they had got so used to during the SALT negotiations, and therefore, in their view, made the world a more dangerous place; but they also knew that their side did not have the technology to compete and could not afford massive new investments in science and technology in order to catch up with the United States. Like their US counterparts, most Soviet experts doubted that SDI was implementable, at least anytime soon. But Soviet leaders could not take the risk of the Americans getting such weapons without any response. Such retaliation, most experts believed, could only come through new offensive technologies or through massive increases in the throw weight of Soviet missiles, well beyond what the SALT agreements would allow for.

Moscow's reaction to Reagan's dreams of a space-based interceptor program against nuclear missiles exemplified the widening gap in technology between West and East. By the mid-1980s the West was ahead in most fields, from satellites to fiber-optic cables to computers. These advances were made possible by alliances between government funding—often military—and commercial companies that delivered the goods. Soviet scientists and engineers had no problem understanding the progress that was made in the West. They could probably have delivered the same results for the Soviet Union, if there had been a system in place flexible enough to put such technology into production. It was at the production end that the Soviet Union was lagging behind, by design as much as by inertia.

Satellites provide a good example. Up to the 1970s the Soviet Union was ahead in satellite technology. Its Ekran satellites delivered television to millions of Soviet citizens in Siberia and the Pacific provinces well before any such system existed in the West. But the Soviets, intentionally, did not see satellite TV as a means for commercial purposes, and its international propaganda broadcasts were more likely to make viewers turn their TVs off than on. In the early 1980s American satellite stations began sending US news, sports, series, and movies across the globe, in many cases accessible for anyone who could afford a satellite dish. The message of consumerism was an integral part of the new TV stations' appeal. And it was eagerly received by most of those who could receive it.

The successes of commercial television indicated that in many parts of the world people's priorities were beginning to change. This turn toward consumerism went along with fundamental changes in the global economy that got underway in the 1970s. As we have seen, the breakdown of the Bretton Woods system of fixed rates, regulated trade, and capital controls led to a sense of crisis in the West, and especially in the United States. But it also reflected a relative improvement in the economic position of others, above all in Asia. All over the globe, except in the Communist countries, people were reinventing themselves as consumers of products that earlier on had either not existed or been out of reach for anyone but the top layers of society. From clothes to electronics, from cosmetics to air conditioners, prices fell as competition and the number of potential consumers both increased. Not surprisingly, container-shipping capacity almost tripled during the 1980s.

Much of what happened in the global economy after the early 1970s privileged the United States. Although its economic position as a country relative to others continued to slip, its position at the center of the world's financial system continued. The dollar remained the world currency, and freed from previous constraints, the US government made sure its value remained low in order to encourage both US exports and foreign investments in the United States. But the United States could also draw advantages from the globalization of trade and finance in the 1980s. US banks and, especially from the mid-1980s, US investment companies could easily invest in foreign markets, knowing that they had access to the one currency most other people wanted. New financial instruments and technologies from the United States predominated worldwide.

The global financial revolution of the 1980s transformed the world economy and thereby changed the landscape of one of the main battlefields of the Cold War. The massive increase in investments, often in forms that nobody would have thought of before the 1970s, was made possible by a combination of government deregulation and advances in information technologies. Well before electronic information became a consumer staple, financial services put it to work in providing investors with real-time information on markets and economic trends. The combination of telecommunication and computing power—what we today know as the Internet—was first developed in the United States for military purposes. But it was as revolutionary for financial services as for defense networks, and it tied the world of capital together around American inventions and American principles.

The turn toward consumerism outside of the United States also helped US businesses. Makers of more traditional goods often complained that they were outcompeted by cheap imports, and even top-notch electronics and cars were often produced better and cheaper outside the United States. But the ideas, designs, and technologies on which they were built were often American. Personal computers, for instance, were mainly based on American (or at least US-owned) technology, giving rise to companies such as Apple and Microsoft. What seemed a revitalization of the world's hunger for American products, including its music and film, helped sustain Reagan's rhetoric about freedom and choice being quintessential American values.

By the mid-1980s neoconservative politics upheld neoliberal economics, and vice versa.

The United States did not create globalization, or consumerism for that matter, as economic weapons in the Cold War. But the Reagan Administration did use its influence over major financial institutions to limit the economic room for maneuver of anyone outside of Europe suspected of choosing a socialist development model allied with the Soviet Union. The access to credit for countries such as Cuba, Nicaragua, Angola, or Vietnam was next to nonexistent, forcing them to rely on support from the Soviets and eastern Europeans, which was less and less forthcoming. Even more important, however, for the opponents of capitalism worldwide was the sense that global trends and norms were moving in opposition to them and their ideals. Margaret Thatcher's mantra that "there is no alternative" to capitalism in its neoliberal form seemed to be a self-fulfilling prophesy, including for those who resented its implications.

Even though these sentiments had come on rather suddenly and would turn out to be a passing phase, at least in their most doctrinaire form, they were remarkably powerful by the mid-1980s. To begin with, both Reagan and Thatcher seemed to struggle to get control of the economy, and their monetarist remedies were widely ridiculed. The 1982–83 recession was the deepest the United States had experienced since the late 1950s. What created the recovery, it could be argued, was less monetarist principles than massive US deficit spending, mainly for military purposes, combined with the creation of global markets, not least in financial terms. But this did not matter to those who believed that monetarism and other forms of neoliberal economics would save the world from the threat of Communism and from the insidious introduction of socialism in the West. Neither did it matter much to them that Reagan borrowed more money than all his predecessors combined, or that the cost of public services grew significantly during Thatcher's time in power. Their message far overshadowed their practices. And that message—that individual freedom mattered more than society's needs—resonated far beyond those who had ever heard about monetarist policies.

20

Gorbachev

By the early 1980s the Soviet Union was roughly where the United States had been a decade before. Its economy seemed set on a downward turn. Its politics seemed dysfunctional, to the point that real leadership and direction were hard to attain. And the public mood was dismal. People who had been proud of Soviet achievements and at least tolerant of the system's imperfections now started to doubt the future of Communism and their own role within it. Like in the United States a decade earlier, few Soviet people could envisage any alternative form of state and society. But there was a distinct doubt about whether the regime could continue as it was for much longer.

The Soviet Union in the 1980s also had two additional challenges that the United States had not had to face in the previous decade. Never having been tested at the voting booth, the Communist Party of the Soviet Union (CPSU) had much less legitimacy than the US government, even under weak presidents such as Gerald Ford or Jimmy Carter. The Communists had of course created the Soviet state and the advances that went with it, in science, education, welfare, and military power, but ever since Stalin's time Soviet leaders had seemed afraid of their own people and in no way convinced of the support the CPSU would get from them in a time of crisis.

Internationally the Soviet Union also had challenges that the United States had not had, even in the 1970s. Granted, Brezhnev's détente policies, and the massive Soviet military buildup that had accompanied them, had genuinely made the Soviet Union the other Superpower. It had by far the most powerful forces in Europe or Asia and had shown that it was capable of intervening globally when it so wished. But the USSR was isolated from the global economic system to a degree that even its eastern European allies were not. In 1985 only 4 percent of the Soviet gross national product was connected to foreign trade outside the East Bloc. Foreign investments were negligible. Even the much-vaunted gas exports to western Europe were slow to make an impact. By 1985 the Soviets supplied less than 3 percent of western Europe's natural gas.

This isolation happened partly by the Soviets' own design and partly through enforcement by others. Soviet leaders were concerned that economic interaction with the capitalist world, and especially a foreign presence inside the Soviet Union, would lead to the spread of capitalist thinking and practices. Such a development could usher in political unrest and eventually foment a counterrevolution against the Communists. Foreign trade was of course acceptable and the Soviets would have liked to expand it, but only on their conditions of state-led initiatives and strict reciprocity. Any Communist official charged with handling foreign commercial links had to be doubly careful. Not only did political rectitude have to be shown at all times, but any whiff of corruption by foreign interests had to be avoided, or the KGB would swoop. No wonder some Soviet officials preferred safety over ambition, even if that meant dealing with collective enterprises in Omsk rather than more enticing foreign ventures.

But the Western allies, and especially the United States, also tried to prevent the Soviet Union from benefitting too much from economic interaction with the West. Since the late 1940s, the Coordinating Committee for Multilateral Export Controls (CoCom) had placed restrictions on products countries allied with the United States would be allowed to export to the Soviet Union. These lists were quite extensive, ranging from advanced agricultural equipment to aircraft components to computers and software. Some of it the Soviets were able to get through industrial espionage, but by no means all. At the same time, direct trade with the United States nose-dived with the collapse of détente. Already in 1974 the US Congress introduced an act (the Jackson-Vanik amendment to the Trade Act) that restricted normal trade relations with countries that did not allow free emigration (read, the USSR). In 1980 President Carter embargoed US grain sales to the Soviet Union as a reaction to the invasion of Afghanistan. Although Ronald Reagan lifted the embargo the following year, having found that it did more damage to US farmers than to the Soviets, it did much to undermine Soviet trade relations with the West.

Up to the late 1970s the Soviets could ignore economic relations with the rest of the world, although they had done so at their peril. They could claim that their own form of modern development, a socialist, centralized planned economy, could deliver economic progress at least to the same extent as the capitalist West. But as capitalist globalization grew and more and more regions were linked up through it, Soviet isolation began to stand out. The USSR, after all, had been designed to *overtake* capitalism, not to fall further and further behind. Especially as the US economy began a very strong expansion from 1984 on, it seemed as if the Americans were benefitting from trends the Soviets could not be part of. Almost as bad, from a Soviet perspective, was the growth in the eastern Asian economies, where even small countries that the Soviets had never been much concerned about had growth rates three or four times the USSR's average.

Domestically, leaders of the Andropov kind had believed that they could will the Soviet economy to work better. Their campaigns against corruption, drunkenness, and slovenliness showed little result in terms of output, however. Before the 1917 revolution Russia had been a grain exporter. By 1985 it was entirely dependent on foreign imports, bringing in more than forty-five million tons that year alone. It also imported nine hundred thousand tons of meat just to feed its population.[1] And real reform was not forthcoming. The aging Politburo simply refused to experiment with the economy in any meaningful sense. Even limited reforms such as those in eastern Europe, not to mention China, were off the table.

Ironically, one real danger for the Soviet economy was its increasing dependence on oil and gas exports for access to hard currency. As we have seen, Soviet foreign trade was small in size. But it needed hard currency income in order to service its import credits. The profits from energy exports, in good times, had also been used to expand beyond the plan in domestic production of high-end consumer goods, which the plan itself did not allow much room for. When oil prices nose-dived in 1981, these parts of the Soviet economy had taken a real hit, even though the planning bureaucracy tried to explain it as a temporary setback. But people, especially in the cities, noticed that stores emptied out even quicker and that lines for consumer products were longer than they had been even during the 1950s.

And then there was the war in Afghanistan. Brezhnev had been promised a short intervention, the sending of a "limited contingent" of Red Army troops to help the "real Communists" in the Afghan party set things right. They would be out within months, according to the materials the Politburo discussed in December 1979, when the final decision to intervene was taken. But by 1985 Soviet soldiers in Afghanistan had been fighting there for five years, and the chances of any withdrawal seemed remote. Both Brezhnev, in the waning years of his life, and his successor, Iurii Andropov, had been keen to arrange a negotiated withdrawal. But the overall direction of the Cold War counted against it. The Afghan Communist regime feared it would collapse without Soviet troops in the country. And the Soviets would only withdraw if the Americans and the Pakistanis agreed to stop supplying the Afghan Islamist resistance. Chances for a withdrawal anytime soon seemed remote.

By 1985 the Red Army had more than one hundred thousand troops in Afghanistan. Most of the country seemed to be under control by them and by the government army of the Afghan Communist Party, led by the vain and ineffectual Babrak Karmal. But that was only during the day and when Communist troops were nearby. At night, or when these troops had to be concentrated or redeployed, the resistance had begun to move into villages all over Afghanistan. Some of this resistance was local, tribal, or clan-based. People were defending their own areas against infidel foreigners and what they saw as a rapacious atheist regime in Kabul. But increasingly these local fighters joined up with one of the several Islamist parties based across the border in Peshawar, Pakistan, in order to get access to weapons and supplies. In turn, these links changed the tenor of the resistance ideology. In the 1970s nobody would have thought that Islamism in its Middle Eastern form would have stood much of a chance in idiosyncratic and recondite Afghanistan. But in the decade that followed, groups such as the Hizb-i-Islami (the Islamic Party)—with slogans borrowed from the Islamic Brotherhood, from extremist preachers in Saudi Arabia, and even from the otherwise much maligned Iranian Shia revolution—began to dominate the resistance discourse in Afghanistan.

A key reason why the Afghan Islamists won out over other groups in the resistance was the support they received from the Pakistanis and the Americans. For the Reagan Administration the calculus was simple: The Islamist groups seemed the best organized and the most effective part of the resistance. They were less corrupt and less likely to engage in the thousand local compromises that warfare in Afghanistan normally demanded. Mostly they killed more Soviets. "We had a very . . . cold-blooded view of things," commented Charles Cogan, the CIA's south Asia chief in the early 1980s. "Our interest was in reversing the tables on the Russians, after Vietnam."[2]

The Pakistani military dictator Muhammad Zia-ul-Haq encouraged CIA director William Casey and Reagan in seeing the Afghan liberation struggle as a battle of religion against Communist atheism. Zia used conservative religious authorities as tools for ruling Pakistan, especially after he had his democratically elected predecessor, Zulfikar Ali Bhutto, hanged in prison in 1979. The following year he introduced Sharia courts, a novelty (to put it mildly) in Pakistani jurisprudence. A US-trained officer with a particular fixation on the Indian threat to Pakistan, Zia believed that it was only through increased support from Washington that his country could maintain its independence. The Soviet invasion of Afghanistan was Zia's lucky break. With considerable success, he presented his case to Reagan: the real Soviet aim, Zia claimed, was to destroy Pakistan in cooperation with India. In that way the Soviets could dominate the Indian Ocean and control oil transports from the Gulf.

Even though they did not accept all of Zia's pretentious claims of his country's importance, the Americans knew that without the Pakistani dictator's cooperation, there was no way US supplies could get to the Afghan resistance. By 1985 these supplies had become a major operation. Reagan believed that by hitting Afghanistan and other Soviet-supported regimes in Asia and Africa, he could increase the price the Soviets paid for their foreign involvements. Although there is no evidence that the president thought the United States could force the Soviets to withdraw entirely, Reagan did expect that US arming of anti-Leftist guerrilla forces could discourage Moscow from such interventions in the future.

The Reagan Administration's aid for the Afghan mujahedin soon got entangled with a dramatic stepping up of US assistance to other movements worldwide. By 1985 this had turned into a major US offensive against the Left in what used to be the Third World. In Angola the United States supported, armed, and trained the guerrilla fighters of Jonas Savimbi's National Union for the Total Independence of Angola (UNITA), who were fighting against the Cuban-supported government. In Cambodia the Americans helped the forces fighting against the Vietnamese-supported government, including (at least indirectly) the remnants of the notorious Khmer Rouge. In both of these countries, the opposition stood no chance of winning outright militarily. But their access to US weapons and military training ensured that the Left-wing governments were unable to consolidate their hold on all of their territory. It also prevented all forms of economic growth and increased the cost to the Soviets, Cubans, and Vietnamese of keeping their allies in power. For the moment, at least, this was good enough for Washington. The United States was now using the same methods to put pressure on the Soviets that the USSR had used against America in the 1970s, Reagan believed.

Central America was a different case, and US aims were much wider. Since Nicaragua and El Salvador were nearly on America's doorstep, Reagan's appetite grew, from ensuring the Sandinistas end their support for Left-wing rebels in El Salvador to the overthrow of the Nicaraguan regime itself. In 1984 the CIA secretly mined

Nicaraguan harbors to cut it off from the outside world. But Reagan's problem was that Congress, increasingly wary of another Vietnam-style quagmire, balked at funding the US allies in Nicaragua, the Contras. In spite of his overall popularity, Reagan could not get Congress to budge. The 1984 Boland amendment prohibited any US government measure that "would have the effect of supporting, directly or indirectly, military or paramilitary operations in Nicaragua by any nation, group, organization, movement, or individual."[3] The CIA reported that the Contras, "even with American support, cannot overthrow the Sandinistas." The only solution, the Agency's chief analyst Robert Gates believed, was to "acknowledge openly . . . that the existence of a Marxist-Leninist regime in Nicaragua . . . is unacceptable to the United States and that the United States will do everything in its power short of invasion to put that regime out."[4]

With the president's tacit encouragement, the Reagan White House and the CIA put in place a network for increased support for the Contras that was badly thought out and almost certainly illegal. The centerpiece of the system was donations, and sometimes weapons, that the administration had solicited from friendly countries, such as Saudi Arabia and Brunei. These supplies could be used covertly to aid not only the Contras but also UNITA and the Afghan mujahedin. By late 1985 the White House had expanded this system into a totally harebrained scheme to sell weapons to Islamist Iran, now fighting for its life against an Iraqi attack, and give the proceeds secretly to the Contras. The aim would be to reach out to Iranian "moderates" to engage them in the Cold War against the Soviets and get them to assist with the release of US hostages held by Islamist terrorist groups in the Middle East. The plans failed, and the ensuing political fallout came to threaten the political survival of the Reagan presidency. But they showed clearly how far Reagan and his assistants were willing to go to in battling Soviet associates worldwide.

The aging leadership group in Moscow therefore feared not only Reagan's rhetoric and America's technological advances; they were also looking closely at what the US president was doing in Asia, Africa, and Latin America. They understood it as a counterrevolutionary offensive and associated it with a decisive US break with détente. On this matters had been turned upside down as well. In the 1970s Ford and Carter had been complaining of the Soviets risking détente for Angola or Ethiopia. Now Andropov's successor, Konstantin Chernenko, claimed that Reagan's aggression risked war. But the Soviet leader neither was nor seemed to be in a position to stand up to the United States. Chernenko, born in 1911—the same year as Ronald Reagan—was fading. He could hardly read his prepared texts in public. The day he was appointed leader of the CPSU, Chernenko had shuffled along to Andropov's graveside, where he nearly fell in and had to be steadied by other old-timers in the Politburo. These were not men to face down such a massive US challenge.

On 10 March 1985 Chernenko died. When the Politburo members met to consider his successor, it was already clear that a younger man would have to be found. The seventy-six-year-old Andrei Gromyko, who had been foreign minister since 1957, nominated Mikhail Gorbachev, who at fifty-four was the youngest member of the Politburo. When each individual member, as usual, spoke to confirm his support for a decision that had already been taken by the top leaders, Vladimir Dolgikh, one of the lesser lights of Soviet politics, in a somewhat tragi-comic manner provided the best summing up. "We are all united," he said, "in the opinion that he [Gorbachev] not only has great experience in his past, but he also has a future. Today our country needs an energetic leader who would be capable of going deeply into the substance of problems, a leader who is sincere, courageous and demanding."[5] And that was exactly what the CPSU got in Gorbachev, to a degree that nobody in March 1985 could have imagined possible.

Mikhail Sergeevich Gorbachev was born in Stavropol in southern Russia in a mixed Russian-Ukrainian family. Both of his grandfathers were purged during the Stalin era, and one of them was sent in exile to Siberia. Gorbachev studied law at the prestigious Moscow State University, making him the first Soviet leader with a university degree. While there, he married the Ukrainian Raisa Titarenko, a philosophy graduate who would have a great influence on her husband's career. And he joined the Communist Party, which by 1970 had made Gorbachev the party leader in his hometown and a member of the CPSU Central Committee at the ridiculously young age of forty.

Ten years later Gorbachev was a member of the ruling Politburo. His portfolio was agriculture, and one might guess that this notoriously unrewarding assignment was given him at least in part to balance the fact that his rise as a party leader was unprecedentedly quick. But in between the stages in his meteoric political rise, Gorbachev also found time to do what young people in 1960s and '70s USSR longed to do above all else: go abroad. In the summers of 1977 and '78 he and his wife traveled through France and Italy as tourists, seeing the sights but also meeting with ordinary people in a way that few other Soviet leaders-in-training had done. The Gorbachevs could of course make these trips only because they were especially trusted by the state; ordinary Soviets could only dream of such an opportunity. But even so they wondered about what they saw and about the reasons why it had so little impact in the Soviet Union. "It seemed," wrote Gorbachev later, "that our aged leaders were not especially worried about our undeniably lower living standards, our unsatisfactory way of life, and our falling behind in the field of advanced technologies."[6]

These concerns were precisely what the Gorbachevs set out to deal with after Mikhail's election as general secretary. Gorbachev believed that Soviet society needed to be invigorated through the strict oversight of the Communist Party. People's morale needed to be rebuilt and their faith in the future strengthened. He had few concrete proposals at first, and those he had were taken straight out of Andropov's playbook: an anticorruption campaign, a campaign against alcoholism. The latter, by the way, did not exactly improve the new general secretary's popularity, earning him the nickname "General Secretary Mineral Water." "There was this long line for vodka, and one guy just could not stand it any longer," went a favorite Moscow joke. "'I am going to the Kremlin, to kill Gorbachev,' he said. An hour later, the guy came back. The line was still there, and everyone asked him, 'Did you kill the General Secretary?' 'Kill him?' he responded. 'The line for that is much longer than this one!'"

To begin with, Gorbachev's style was more important than his substance. He was young, vigorous, and liked to be seen outside talking to people. But he was also authoritarian and impatient. When a representative from the Ministry of Finance pointed out that a significant part of government taxes came from alcohol consumption, Gorbachev interrupted him: "There is nothing new in what you have just said. Each of us knows that there is nothing to be purchased for the cash held by people. But you are not proposing anything other than forcing people to drink. So just report your ideas briefly, you are not in the Finance Ministry, but at the Politburo session."[7]

But the Finance Ministry was not the only part of Soviet bureaucracy that Gorbachev was impatient with. Party secretaries and ministers were bombarded with letters and instructions about improving their performance, and threatened with severe sanctions if they did not. Before the 1986 Party Congress he purged many of the older leaders in the Politburo and replaced them with his own people, selected from the younger generation. Gromyko, who supposedly had remarked that Gorbachev had a nice smile, but teeth of steel, was promoted to the largely ceremonial role of Soviet president. His replacement as foreign minister was the reform-oriented party head of the Soviet republic of Georgia, Eduard Shevardnadze. Shevardnadze made up for his lack of foreign experience through his dedication to the Communist Party organization. For the new foreign minister, as for many Soviets who had waited almost a generation for a dynamic and decisive leader, the general secretary's authoritarian manner was easy to accept. And Shevardnadze was a quick learner, someone Gorbachev could turn to with his ideas for a dramatic change in the flagging international fortunes of the Soviet Union.

Gorbachev understood from the very beginning of his tenure that the USSR needed to reduce its expenses in the arms race and in support for revolutionary movements abroad. But he wanted to do so in ways that did not reduce the international status of the Soviet Union or its position as a global Superpower. The key, Gorbachev believed, was to get the Soviet economy going again. And to make that happen, some form of cooperation with the West was unavoidable. The general secretary doubted that much could be achieved with the Americans. He described them to his colleagues as "not serious." But he was hopeful that western European governments, both in their own interest and in the interest of peace, would reach out to the Soviet Union. "The European direction of our diplomatic, political and other actions is extremely important for us. Here we have to be much more consistent and flexible" than in the past, Gorbachev said.[8]

In Washington, Reagan hoped for an early summit with the new general secretary. In a personal letter to Gorbachev, the president invited him to an early summit and referred, somewhat whimsically, to a common "goal of eliminating nuclear weapons."[9] Ever since the Able Archer incident, Reagan had been looking for concrete ways of getting negotiations going with the Soviets on nuclear weapons. The threat of nuclear war worried him deeply. After watching the ABC drama *The Day After*, which depicts Lawrence, Kansas, after a nuclear attack, Reagan noted that it "left me greatly depressed."[10] In January 1984, in his State of the Union address, Reagan turned directly to the Soviets with his appeal: "People of the Soviet Union, there is only one sane policy, for your country and mine, to preserve our civilization in this modern age: A nuclear war cannot be won and must never be fought. The only value in our two nations possessing nuclear weapons is to make sure they will never be used. But then would it not be better to do away with them entirely?"[11]

Gorbachev, for some very good reasons, doubted the sincerity in Reagan's appeal. But he worried about the increases in defense spending that the Strategic Defense Initiative (SDI) program would inflict on the Soviet Union. He also needed time to develop his European initiatives, which he hoped would split the western Europeans from the United States in what he saw as Reagan's warlike attitude to the Soviet Union. Although little progress had been made at the off-and-on negotiations between the two sides on nuclear weapons' issues in Geneva, Gorbachev agreed to a summit meeting with the American president there, to take place in November 1985. It would be the first meeting between the top US and Soviet leaders for six years. Neither side expected much in terms of concrete results.

The Geneva summit allowed the two leaders to take the measure of each other, even though, as expected, it delivered very little in practical terms. Reagan, warm, breezy, and at times mundane, did little to impress Gorbachev, who came away with a sense of a president who was the hostage of his advisers. The only time Reagan really got through to him was when they parted. Past summits had not achieved very much, Reagan said. The president "suggested that he and Gorbachev say 'To hell with the past,' we'll do it our way and get something done."[12] It was an expression of Reagan's frustrations with what he found to be a plodding, detail-oriented Soviet negotiating style. But it was also an indication of the president's belief that he could deal with Gorbachev at the personal level and bring about results.

In his first year in power Gorbachev got increasingly impatient with the lack of progress that he witnessed in the Soviet Union. Gorbachev had believed that the new and inspirational leadership he provided would mean that people would be willing to work harder to achieve economic results within the plan. Instead Soviet economic growth continued to stall and shortages were as visible as before. Impatiently, Gorbachev rounded on his advisers. If they could not provide him with results, they were not only failing him, they were failing the greatness of Soviet society, he told them. At the twenty-seventh CPSU Party Congress in the spring of 1986, Gorbachev called for "a qualitatively new state of the Soviet socialist society." But he also warned the delegates about "the shortcomings in our political and practical activities [and] the unfavorable tendencies in the economy and the social and moral sphere."[13] It was a very new form of report from the CPSU's general secretary, who also used the Congress to underline his own leading position. After a year in power, Gorbachev had unequivocally nailed his colors to the mast of reform.

Already at his first meetings after taking over as head of the party, Gorbachev had referred to the war in Afghanistan as "a bleeding wound." But that did not mean that he had given up on winning the war by securing the Communist regime and bringing the Red Army home in triumph. In meetings with his generals during the summer of 1985, Gorbachev told them they had a year to come up with a military strategy that actually worked in defeating the Islamist insurgency. He allowed them to attack the mujahedin closer to, and sometimes across, the Pakistani border, and agreed to more air support and more weapons for the Afghan Communist army. But he also made it entirely clear that if the new and more aggressive strategy did not work, then he would aim for a negotiated withdrawal of Soviet troops, even if the political aims for securing the regime had not been met.

A year later, Afghanistan was as much of a mess as it had been when Gorbachev took over. The Soviet offensive had simply led to more suffering for Afghan civilians, more refugees for the mujahedin to recruit from, and higher numbers of Red Army casualties. It had also led to more US, Chinese, and Pakistani support for the insurgents. In a move that shocked even its British allies, the Reagan Administration had supplied the Afghan Islamists with sophisticated portable ground-to-air missiles, Stingers, that had a range of twenty-six thousand feet. Soviet air operations had become much more risky. And a government victory on the ground was not in sight. In June 1986, Gorbachev told the Politburo that "we have to get out of there."[14]

> GORBACHEV: We got ourselves into this mess—we did not calculate it right, and exposed ourselves in all aspects. We weren't even able to use our military forces appropriately. But now it's time to get out. . . . We've got to get out of this mess!
>
> [MARSHAL SERGEI] AKHROMEIEV [chief of the general staff of the Red Army]: After seven years in Afghanistan, there is not one square kilometer left untouched by a boot of a Soviet soldier. But as soon as they leave a place, the enemy returns and restores it

all back the way it used to be. We have lost this battle. The majority of the Afghan people support the counter-revolution now. We lost the peasantry, who has not benefited from the revolution at all. 80 percent of the country is in the hands of the counter-revolution, and the peasant's situation is better there than in the government-controlled areas.[15]

In October 1986 Gorbachev met Reagan for a summit in Reykjavik. The meeting had originally been suggested by the Soviets as a preparatory meeting for a visit by Gorbachev to Washington. But it turned into something much more substantial. Gorbachev had decided to go all-out to break the dynamics of the arms race and prevent the militarization of space. He offered an agreement to remove *all* Superpower intermediate-range nuclear weapons from Europe, without including British and French weapons. He also proposed a 50 percent cut in intercontinental missiles. The condition was that the Americans did not deploy SDI in any form for the next ten years. Taken aback, Reagan, on his own initiative, proposed a deal to eliminate all ballistic missiles within ten years. Gorbachev, almost immediately, suggested eliminating all nuclear weapons within a decade.

But Reagan would not budge on SDI.

[REAGAN:] If we have eliminated all nuclear weapons, why should you be worried by the desire by one of the sides to make itself safe—just in case—from weapons which neither of us have anymore? Someone else could create missiles. . . . I can imagine both of us in 10 years getting together again in Iceland to destroy the last Soviet and American missiles. . . . By then I'll be so old that you won't even recognize me. And you will ask in surprise, "Hey, Ron, is that really you? What are you doing here?" And we will have a big celebration over it. . . .

GORBACHEV: We cannot go along with what you propose. If you will agree to banning tests in space, we will sign the document in two minutes. . . . I have a clear conscience before my people and before you. I have done everything I could.

REAGAN: It's too bad we have to part this way. We were so close to an agreement. I think you didn't want to achieve an agreement anyway. . . . I don't know when we'll ever have another chance like this and whether we will meet soon.

GORBACHEV: I don't either.[16]

But Reykjavik was not entirely a failure. The fact that Soviet and US leaders could now negotiate outside the framework set by a generation of arms control talks pointed to a future where even the most basic of Cold War concepts could change very rapidly. The discussion, driven by the two leaders' political and personal preoccupation with abolishing the risk of nuclear war, also alerted their assistants that the Soviet-American conflict was moving into a new phase with real opportunities for settling acute points of conflict. Although most advisers on both sides were mightily relieved that such a radical nuclear denouement was not achieved, at least not there and then, they all understood that from now on they were in new and entirely unchartered territory as to what could happen between the two sides.

Part of the reason for Gorbachev's radicalism at Reykjavik was that he wanted a big foreign affairs victory to underpin his new, more radical initiatives at home. Throughout late 1986 Gorbachev and his advisers had been working on new initiatives in what they called *perestroika* (restructuring) and *glasnost* (openness). At a Central Committee Plenum in January 1987 the general secretary announced that a fundamental restructuring of the Soviet economy was necessary to overcome years of deterioration. Perestroika, Gorbachev said, was "a resolute overcoming of the processes of stagnation, destruction of the retarding mechanism, and the creation of dependable and efficient machinery for expediting the social and economic progress of Soviet society. The main aim of our strategy is to combine the achievements of the scientific and technological revolution with a plan-based economy and set the entire potential of socialism in motion."[17]

But what was the concrete content of the restructuring to be? And how much openness would be allowed? At the January plenum Gorbachev had spoken about "free labor and free thought in a free country." But he had also defended the Soviet past and the achievements of socialism. Besides, there was intransigence and outright opposition to fundamental reform within the Communist Party, the government, and not least the economic planning system. During 1987 and 1988 Gorbachev and his closest advisers, Aleksandr Iakovlev—a reformist former ambassador to Canada—Vadim Medvedev, and Georgii Shakhnazarov, began formulating a new strategy for the Soviet economy. In 1987 enterprises got more autonomy to set their own production goals and to sell any surplus production directly to consumers, but they also became responsible for balancing their own budgets. The following year the Communist Party allowed private ownership of businesses in some sectors, encouraged joint enterprises with foreign companies, and supported the transfer of control over some state-owned enterprises to workers' collectives. Critics accused them of abandoning Communism. Gorbachev retorted that what he did, and *only* what he did, would save Communism. Continuing as before was simply not an option.

Gorbachev undoubtedly had a point. After oil prices fell by two-thirds from 1985 to 1986, the pressure on the Soviet economy increased. Gorbachev's gamble was that new forms of enterprise and foreign investments would make the economy grow, so that dramatic cuts in state expenditure would not be necessary. But past thinking was hard to avoid. High taxes discouraged enterprise. Gorbachev's refusal to increase state-mandated prices on food and key consumer goods kept shelves empty. The Central Bank kept printing money to make up for the shortfall in state finances. As a result, inflation rose and the black market became increasingly predominant in the cities. Reforming the Soviet system, Gorbachev soon learned, was a gargantuan task.

Some of the reform plans probably weakened the Soviet economy rather than strengthening it. GosPlan, the previously all-powerful State Planning Committee, was reduced to only "setting priorities," rather than detailed planning of output at the factory level. By the late 1980s this was almost certainly a necessary reform. But the haste and lack of preparation with which it was implemented led to confusion and increased the lack of interaction among production units that was necessary for increasing output. By late 1988 the Soviet economy was changing fast. But not all of it was for the better. And none of it, thus far, contributed much to ordinary citizens feeling better off than they had been before.

Gorbachev's energy and appetite for change seemed to know no boundaries. His policy of glasnost was originally intended to open up criticism of previous practices in order to stimulate support for perestroika. But soon the reduction in censorship opened the floodgates for criticism of Communist principles and for investigations of the crimes of the Soviet past. Gorbachev kept insisting that there were limits to criticism and that only "constructive" ideas should be put forward. But in reality he did very little to limit the outpouring of re-crimination that Soviet citizens had pent up for so many years. Khrushchev, he believed, had been removed because he had not had enough people to support him against party conservatives. Exposing the misdeeds of the past would only strengthen his own position. And, crucially for Gorbachev, he thought it was the right thing to do. The more he learned about the true content of Soviet repression, the more horrified he was by it.

In the Soviet press, cautiously at first, journalists began digging into the secrets of the past. New accounts of the horrors of Stalin-era prisoner camps were printed (prompting Gorbachev to release the last remaining political prisoners and allow others to return from exile). The 1930s purges were discussed openly, as was the woeful unpreparedness of the USSR to withstand the German attack in 1941. But some of most sensitive topics still took time to appear. The secret protocols of the Molotov-Ribbentrop Pact, in which the Nazis and the Soviets divided up eastern Europe between them, were not admitted to before 1989. And it took up to 1990 for Soviet responsibility for the massacre of Polish officers at Katyn to be accepted. The Soviet government, Gorbachev then said, "expresses deep regret over the tragedy, and assesses it as one of the worst Stalinist outrages."[18] But for some Soviets it was too much, too fast. In a letter to a newspaper in March 1988, the chemistry professor Nina Andreeva deplored the new tendencies. "Recently," she wrote, "one of my girl students puzzled me by frankly saying that the class struggle was an antiquated conception, like the leading role of the proletariat."[19] Andreeva wanted the basic Marxist principles to be kept in place, and many Soviet citizens, especially in Russia, agreed with her.

For Gorbachev it was important, though, that he and the party served *all* Soviet republics and not just Russia. Believing that some of his reforms would be more popular in the periphery than in the center, he and his closest advisers traveled much around the country, including to the Caucasus and to central Asia. Gorbachev also believed that the Soviet Union had to develop into a real federal union of equal republics, and that these republics should be as self-governing as possible. He kept telling his Moscow colleagues that reform, and especially political reform, could only be guaranteed from below, and that with the right kind of leadership much could be achieved in and through the republics. By the end of 1988 some of the republics had begun to assert themselves more than in the past, both in support of reform and in support of their own interests.

Two entirely unforeseen events also contributed to the speeding up of reform in the Soviet Union. In April 1986 reactor number four at the Chernobyl nuclear power plant on the Ukraine-Belorussian border exploded, sending massive amounts of highly radioactive fallout into the atmosphere. Through the heroic efforts of firefighters and military personnel the ensuing fire was brought under control. But everything else backfired. Authorities were slow in carrying out a general evacuation of the population in the worst affected area. For two days Soviet leaders said nothing about the accident. They only did so after high levels of radiation were picked up in faraway Sweden. Gorbachev, who had been unusually reticent himself as the crisis broke, later used the Chernobyl example as a telltale of why glasnost was needed throughout Soviet bureaucracy. For Soviet citizens, and for Europeans in general, it was a stark reminder of the terrible environmental record of the USSR.

A year after the Chernobyl disaster a German teenager, Mathias Rust, managed to fly a small airplane undetected from Helsinki to

Moscow, and landed unopposed in the middle of Red Square. Rust said he did it for the sake of peace. For the Soviet military it was a public relations disaster. Gorbachev made use of the opportunity to pension off half the general staff and promote people he believed in, such as Marshal Sergei Akhromeev, a thinking man's general if there ever was one. But the idea that the Red Army had created an impenetrable fortress lost some of its luster, in Russia especially. Rather, the generals became the aim of a new barrage of jokes. Groups of Russians, it was said, were now loitering around Red Square waiting for the next flight to Hamburg. Or that Red Square should be renamed Sheremetevo 3, since the new Terminal 2 at Moscow's Sheremetevo Airport was already crumbling.

In eastern Europe people were watching in disbelief as the Gorbachev phenomenon was unfolding. To begin with, most people inside and outside the Communist parties believed that the reforms would lead to the strengthening of Soviet power and therefore of its hold on other countries. Even after Gorbachev himself began speaking openly about the need for eastern European leaders to reform their own countries, indicating that they would be allowed a great deal of leeway in choosing their own path, he was widely disbelieved. Eastern Europeans had seen periods of Soviet liberalization before and knew where they had all ended. But by 1987 it began to dawn, first inside the Communist parties, that Gorbachev was something completely new. For the party members who wanted reform, Gorbachev seemed the answer to their dreams. But for the party leaders, who feared change, perestroika and glasnost were the stuff of nightmares. When Gorbachev's impish press secretary Gennadi Gerasimov, in Czechoslovakia, was asked what was the difference between Gorbachev's reforms and Dubček's in 1968, his response was "nineteen years." Antireform Communists in eastern Europe had much to fear.

For Gorbachev, what mattered most with eastern Europe was to fit the states there into a more successful European socialist community, which could rival the achievements the general secretary saw in the capitalist western European Community. He wanted to learn from the practices of the more advanced states, first and foremost the GDR, in terms of technology and its implementation. But he was also aware that economically all eastern European states got a good economic deal from cooperating with the Soviet Union, especially in terms of energy and raw material prices set far below world standards. Fairness meant that prices within the Communist economic community, the ComEcon, should be similar to prices in international markets, Gorbachev thought, and paid in hard currency. Politically, the eastern Europeans should solve their own problems within the Warsaw Pact and the ComEcon, while adhering to the international policies of the USSR. In 1986, Gorbachev told East German leader Erich Honecker that he should "do what he regards as right for themselves, just like we do what we regard as right for us. It is best if we have confidence in each other."[20] But the Soviet leader's advice was that eastern European Communists needed to broaden the base for their own rule, just like he was trying to do at home.

Although all East Bloc leaders paid lip-service to the Soviet initiatives, in reality most of them tried to stave off any meaningful change for as long as possible. They knew that they could not liberalize their regimes without the risk of losing control. Their hope was that perestroika and glasnost would stall or be reined in inside the USSR. The relationship between Gorbachev and Honecker soon soured. Gorbachev tired of the East German leader's constant reminders of the need for the USSR to support the GDR. Honecker also complained about less-than-flattering treatment of the GDR in Soviet papers. When Reagan dared the Soviet leader to end the division of Germany in a 1987 speech at the Brandenburg Gate—"Mr. Gorbachev, tear down this wall"—Gorbachev bristled. He told his advisers that he would not let the Americans set his European policy. But even so, Gorbachev's closest foreign affairs aide, Anatolii Cherniaev, wrote in his diary, "He feels it in his heart that the problem cannot be removed and that someday the Germans will reunite."[21]

What really galled Gorbachev was that East German intransigence prevented him from doing what he considered really important for the Soviet Union, not least economically: to draw closer to West Germany and, through the Germans, to western Europe. Gorbachev had not given up on the age-old Soviet Cold War dream of somehow politically detaching the Europeans from the Americans. But as his economic needs grew, especially for trade and credits, his priorities began to shift. Gorbachev was aware that the West German economy was the dynamo at the heart of the European Community, and also the source of much of the credit that had flowed into eastern Europe. Not believing that the United States would be a source of economic assistance, Gorbachev's thinking concentrated more and more on West Germany and, perhaps in a longer perspective, Japan.

Still, it took up to late 1988 to arrange a proper meeting between Gorbachev and West German chancellor Helmut Kohl. East Germany was one big obstacle. Another was that Kohl feared the influence Gorbachev could have in western Europe through his enormous popularity there. "Gorbymania" in the West was at its peak in 1986–87. In West Germany, opinion polls showed that he was by far the most popular figure in world politics, well ahead of Reagan, Kohl, and Thatcher. In an offhand remark that really angered Gorbachev, Kohl in 1986 had said that the Soviet leader was only "a modern Communist leader who understands public relations. Goebbels," added the chancellor tactlessly, ". . . was an expert in public relations, too."[22]

Gorbachev's closest contacts in the West were with the two countries he had visited as a tourist twenty years before, France and Italy. The leaders there had experienced the moderation and political integration of their own Communist parties into the national mainstream, and therefore believed they could help socialize the Soviet Union into status quo world affairs as well. The Italian leader Giulio Andreotti and the French president François Mitterrand were probably among the most cynical entrepreneurs of power in postwar Europe, but their experience and insights fitted Gorbachev's purpose of learning more about how the West actually operated. Margaret Thatcher, too, was a favored interlocutor, even if the general secretary expected to get less, both in terms of useful advice and support, from the prime minister the Soviet press had dubbed "the Iron Lady."

Still, Gorbachev was realistic enough to understand that he needed to concentrate on relations with the United States if he were to achieve the two key breakthroughs he was looking for: nuclear disarmament and reduction of military tension, both in Europe and elsewhere. In late 1987 the Soviet leader went to Washington for his first summit on US soil. The official purpose was to sign a treaty on eliminating most intermediate nuclear forces, such as the SS-20s and Pershings, in itself a huge step forward for arms control. But the summit ranged much wider. Gorbachev told Reagan about his plans for democratic government in the USSR and spoke openly about his difficulties. The president was impressed both with his dedication and with his frankness. He startled Reagan by saying that the Soviet Union expected to withdraw fully from Afghanistan within twelve months (although Gorbachev's appeals for the Americans to stop arming the mujahedin fell on deaf ears). Above all he got Reagan's attention when he declared that he would "like to work together with the President to resolve regional conflicts." In follow-ups from the summit the Soviets and the Americans for the first time sat down to discuss how they together could work to draw down the conflicts in Indochina, in southern Africa, and in Central America.

After the Washington summit, the two sides began to view each other, at least to a limited extent, as partners seeking solutions to world problems. There was little doubt that the Americans were in the driver's seat. The Soviets often took over US positions or ameliorated them, at most. This reflected both genuine changes in Soviet views of regional conflicts and a sense of weakness on their side. Though under pressure toward the end of his presidency, Reagan had nothing like the problems Gorbachev had at home. But also just getting to know each other better actually did deliver results. Military to military contacts flourished, during which the generals discovered that some of their worst fears did not appear in the strategy of the other side, or that some procedures were merely mirror images of each other. Enemy stereotypes started to give way, although it was still unclear what they would be replaced by. For some allies of both countries, and especially for Soviet allies in Africa and Asia, the process seemed to happen with bewildering, unnerving speed.

Only six months after the Washington summit Ronald Reagan traveled to Moscow for the first visit to the Soviet capital by a US president in sixteen years. Although the two sides made progress on arms control and general bilateral relations, the real breakthrough was in political atmospherics. At a speech at Moscow State University, broadcast directly by Soviet television, Reagan lauded the new relationship between the two sides. They were now partners and friends, he said. "People do not make wars," Reagan argued, "governments do. And no mother would ever willingly sacrifice her sons for territorial gain, for economic advantage, for ideology. A people free to choose will always choose peace."[23] When asked by a reporter, as he walked across Red Square, whether he still believed the Soviet Union was an evil empire, Reagan said, "No. You are talking about another time, another era."[24] He put his arm around Gorbachev and announced that "there is good chemistry between us."[25]

Reagan's willingness to embrace the Soviet side did not extend to regional conflicts, however. When Gorbachev tried to explain to him that politics in Muslim countries was already moving from Cold War confrontations to a risk of new fundamentalist regimes, Reagan refused to listen. Gorbachev highlighted the dangers that existed in Afghanistan. But, the general secretary continued with some relief, "Afghanistan is now a thing of the past. We have reached our agreement. Let's untie the Afghanistan knot and use it as a basis of untying other regional knots." "The Soviet Union," Gorbachev said, "was willing to act with the United States, but the US seemed uninterested or unwilling to work cooperatively."[26]

Gorbachev was right that Afghanistan did not set a good precedent for cooperation with the United States on regional conflicts. In April 1988 the Pakistanis and the Afghans had signed the Geneva Accords, guaranteed by the USSR and the United States. All sides promised to respect principles of sovereignty and noninterference, and the Soviets stated that they would withdraw their troops no later than May 1989. Any internal settlement was left up to the Afghans themselves. Washington refused to stop arming the mujahedin, noting simply that "should the Soviet Union exercise restraint in providing military assistance to parties in Afghanistan, the United States similarly will exercise restraint."[27] It was a sham of an agreement, which allowed the Afghan civil war to continue as before, minus the presence of Soviet troops. But for Gorbachev it was still a victory of sorts: it allowed him to bring the soldiers home and to draw a line under the Afghanistan fiasco. The withdrawal was completed by 15 February 1989, three months ahead of the deadline.

Gorbachev's supporters had hoped that the Afghan settlement, if it could be called that, and Reagan's public embrace of the Soviet leader in Moscow would give the general secretary some slack in dealing with domestic affairs. That was not to be the case. In late 1988 and early 1989 problems seemed to be peaking on the home front, with food shortages in the cities and growing political unrest in some of the republics. Much of the dissatisfaction was concentrated on Gorbachev himself. He had promised so much and delivered so little, many people thought. Some had already forgot that only a few years earlier such sentiments openly expressed could have landed them in prison or worse. Now, the reforms themselves seemed to be under threat because the Soviet state was breaking apart at the seams.

The only leader who seemed undaunted by these difficulties was Gorbachev himself. He spent much time in the winter of 1988–89 thinking about political reform and the decentralization of power to the republics. In March 1989 the Soviet Union held its first ever contested elections for a new parliament, the Congress of People's Deputies. The CPSU won in most precincts, often by dubious methods, but about 20 percent of the seats were won by independents. One of them was Andrei Sakharov, the dissident physicist and Nobel Peace Prize winner, who had been released from internal exile only two years before. Another was the rebellious Boris Yeltsin, a former Moscow party chief and member of the Politburo who back in 1987 had threatened to resign in protest against the slow pace of reform and as a consequence had been fired by Gorbachev. The party's monopoly on power had been broken. And the breaking had been designed by the man who was the Communist Party's general secretary and the country's supreme leader.

In his first years in power, Mikhail Gorbachev had attempted to redraw the political map inside and outside of the Soviet Union. To him, the Cold War no longer made sense, at least not in its classical form of global confrontation and lack of interaction. His starting point was Marxist-Leninist, or rather, Marxist *and* Leninist. He believed in materialist analyses but also in the ability of a small and determined minority to act on behalf of society as a whole. And he found that the USSR needed to adopt some of the practices of the West in order to retain and develop Soviet socialism. Learning and adapting was not a sign of weakness, Gorbachev believed, but a source of strength. His leadership qualities and the authority of the Communist Party would make perestroika a success.

Three things happened domestically to undermine Gorbachev's project. The Soviet economy took a turn for the worse, in part because of the dislocation produced by uncertain reforms. Across the Soviet Union people began turning against the party's hierarchical structures. And a sizeable number of Soviet leaders, including some of Gorbachev's close advisers, had begun losing faith in even the basic tenets of socialism. The general secretary was caught between party conservatives, who wanted stability and political control, and those who were willing to abandon the party in order to pursue their own plans for the future of their countries and for their own future. Gorbachev himself wanted political, economic, and legal reform, but without throwing overboard the achievements of Soviet socialism. His aim, increasingly openly expressed, was a state ruled by law, in which the power of the party was not removed but curtailed. In October 1988 Gorbachev told the Politburo that "the reorganization of the apparatus is connected with the formation of a rule-of-law state. . . . The entire structure of our society and state must work on a legitimate basis, i.e., within the limits of the law. No-one has the right to go beyond the boundaries of the law, to break the law. And the most important violator . . . is sitting here, at this table—the Politburo, and also the Secretariat, of the Central Committee."[28]

In his international policies Gorbachev aimed to overcome the Cold War and move the Soviet Union closer to western Europe and especially to European social democracy. In conversations with the former West German chancellor Willy Brandt, now head of the Socialist International, and with Spain's socialist prime minister Felipe González, he admitted that "talking with you is both easy and hard for us. Easy because the level of mutual understanding allows us to communicate like friends, openly, discussing any subject. But it is difficult because we cannot gloss over problems with general phrases. . . . Perhaps," the general secretary told Willy Brandt in 1989, "it is time to consider what needs to be done to overcome the schism of 1914."[29] Gorbachev saw his policies as part of Russia's age-old linking up with Europe, but also as a coming together of socialists who had been split apart by their responses to World War I, at the dawn of the Cold War ideological conflict.

But Gorbachev's plans for an international reordering reached beyond Europe. To him, getting rid of the Cold War meant more than a return to concepts of state interest, of the sort that had existed in the late nineteenth century, before the Cold War took hold. His vision was for a better-organized world, in which the UN and comprehensive international agreements regulated international affairs and prevented the kind of indiscriminate killing that both sides had engaged in far too often in regional conflicts during the Cold War. Given the US conviction that the world at large was turning toward American concepts of freedom and free market practices, Gorbachev's vision might seem naïve. But it was another striking example of how, within the span of only a few years, a vigorous leader had been able to redefine the very purpose of what the Soviet state stood for and how Soviet power should be understood.

21

Global Transformations

The world had changed tremendously in the 1970s and early 1980s, and in the late 1980s it changed even more. New technologies began to transform the way many people got information, did business, or thought about the future. New forms of economic practices, centered on capital and investment, spread worldwide. New centers of industrial production, especially in Asia, began to take over some of the functions that Europe and North America had developed for more than a century. And, as we have already seen in the Soviet Union, political ideologies also began to change, slowly at first, but then more and more rapidly. By the time the Cold War ended, the world had already changed in ways that made the global ideological conflict less relevant for a large number of people, while other conflicts—ethnic, religious, national, or economic—had become more important.

These late-twentieth-century global transformations implied many things at once. In North America and Europe they meant the spread of market practices less encumbered by social welfare provisions. As a result, when these practices spread further, to countries in which they had so far played less of a role for the individual—the Middle East, India, China, southeast Asia—they were presented as inflexible and unceasing: the harder edge of capitalism. The amazing spread of information through film and television, including global news broadcasts and satellite connections, confronted people with lives of alternatives and affluence in forms few had seen before. To most people, obviously, the lifestyles of *Dynasty* or *Baywatch* were quite literally undreamed of. But the global spread of daytime television also helped to put in sharp relief the lives that people actually lived across the globe. And by 1989 many people wanted a better life for themselves and their families, over and beyond what the great socialist and collectivist projects could offer.

The information explosion contributed significantly to the end of the Cold War, especially in the sense that people's priorities shifted. But a better informed public is not always a more knowledgeable one. Sometimes a sudden flourish of information that immediately and demonstrably contradicts values you have long held dear can lead to cynicism and callousness. Likewise, the breakdown of social structures held in place by authoritarian leaders can create dramatic redefinitions of purpose both within and among preexisting communities. The world experienced all of this—from the Soviet Union to Yugoslavia to China to Latin America—as the Cold War came to an end. Although the conclusion of the global Cold War facilitated the resolution of old confrontations, it also gave rise to new forms of tension worldwide.

The global changes of the 1980s contributed to a general crisis for socialist states. This was not just an eastern European crisis, it was global, in the sense that new socialist states such as Nicaragua, Ethiopia, Mozambique, or Vietnam also came under tremendous pressure to modify or abandon their political choices. As we have already seen, some of this came out of the global antirevolutionary offensive of the Reagan Administration. But the crisis went deeper than that. And in many ways the initial changes in socialist countries of the Global South *preceded* the changes that took place in eastern Europe. China is of course the big example. But even countries that were aligned with the Soviet Union in the early 1980s began to introduce incentives and markets into their economies. Mozambique is a case in point. By 1982–83 small-scale private enterprise was allowed. In 1986 the country signed a deal with the International Monetary Fund, which, in return for loans and investment, privatized major industries, reduced state spending, and deregulated trade as well as the general economy.

In Vietnam, the government had already begun liberalizing trade and agricultural production in 1981. By 1986, before there were any major changes in the USSR and eastern Europe, Vietnam introduced the Đổi Mới (Renovation) program, which brought market principles to much of the economy.

These changes away from the plan and toward the market happened at the same time as the beginning of a major shift in the center of the world's economic activity from the North Atlantic states to eastern Asia. This transition is a long process, which is still ongoing. But its origins, at least in a full-scale form, can be traced back to the decade before the Cold War ended. The shift had many causes. The global spread of capital and technology was one. Developments in transport and patterns of consumption were others. The easy exploitation of reasonably well-skilled pools of labor under authoritarian, market-friendly regimes in Asia also stimulated capitalist growth. But perhaps most important was the unprecedented access to markets in Western countries that made export-led models of growth possible. And the latter was a direct consequence of the way the Cold War was fought in its final stage, when the United States built crucial alliances with Asian countries to keep the Soviet Union and its allies at bay.

The massive expansion of global markets coincided with the expansion of US power globally. Contrary to what many had thought in the 1970s (and would think again in the 2010s), the reorientation of the world's key nodes of industrial production away from the United States did little to harm America's centrality in world affairs. Since many of the ideas, practices, technologies, and products that spread worldwide were in their origins *American*, the United States appeared to be more important than ever. And the massive deficit spending the Reagan Administration undertook, mainly for military purposes, stimulated both domestic consumption and foreign investments in the United States. It also, of course, expanded the American position as by far the most powerful country in terms of its armed forces.

The US economic benefits from globalization would, in hindsight, stand out as a moment more than a general trend. But it was enormously significant because of the timing: the full extent of US global hegemony was at its peak when the Cold War came to an end. This is, of course, different from arguing that US power, pure and simple, ended the Cold War. But the two are obviously related. The same global developments that undermined the socialist countries and that made eastern Asia a hub for the further expansion of capitalism also made the Reagan expansion possible. And it was this expansion that convinced many, including former enemies, that US economic practices on most things from marketing, to corporate management, to financial (de)regulation were worth emulating. The global transformations at the end of the Cold War therefore seemed to privilege the United States in ways that former US leaders could hardly believe was achievable.

THE CLEAREST EVIDENCE for the centrality of the United States could, ironically enough, be found in China. After the Maoist regime had made anti-Americanism the staple of its foreign policy and had broken with the Soviets to a large extent because Khrushchev attempted to stabilize relations with the Americans, Mao himself toward the end of his life began cooperating with the United States to improve China's security. Deng Xiaoping, Mao's successor as Chinese leader, took the cooperation with the Americans much further than Mao in his wildest imagination would have thought possible. Deng's aims were mostly economic. He believed that China's technological backwardness weakened it and made it a more likely victim for Soviet aggression. But he also wanted to improve the standard of living for the Chinese people. As his plane took off for his first visit to the United States in 1979, Deng instructed his advisers in what he saw as a key lesson of the twentieth century: "Whoever work with the Americans will gain, while those who try to oppose them will fail."[1]

Deng Xiaoping was born in 1904 in a small village in northeastern Sichuan Province. He had worked in France in his youth, where he joined the Communist Party, and later served the Comintern in Moscow. Back in China he worked loyally with Mao Zedong, even though he admitted that he found some of the Chairman's more recondite plans difficult to understand. Purged twice as a "Rightist" during the Cultural Revolution, Deng came back with a vengeance after Mao's death in 1976. A fiery man with an iron work ethic, Deng had been dubbed "little red pepper" by his workmates in France. This was not only because he stood barely five feet tall and liked his home province's spicy cuisine; it was also because he was, always, a man in a hurry, for himself and for his country. By 1978 the leaders of the Maoist Left, including the Chairman's wife, Jiang Qing, had been arrested, and China put on a new course toward economic reform.

To begin with, Deng and his advisers had few clear ideas about how to change China. What they did know was that the past had been a disaster. The common realization of how bad things were was in a way their most important weapon. Instead of catching up with the advanced economies, China in the 1960s and '70s had fallen further and further behind. It was as if all their efforts, all the intensity of the political campaigns, all the willingness to sacrifice for the common good, especially among young people, had led to nothing. On his visit to the United States, Deng saw an affluence and abundance that was almost beyond comprehension. He could not sleep at night, he reported to his colleagues. The thought of how much China had to do to catch up kept him awake.

Deng's greatest strength in moving China forward was his willingness to experiment. And unlike Gorbachev in Moscow ten years later, the Chinese leader had something to build on that was outside of the Plan. As Communist authority fragmented during the Cultural Revolution, a few communes and work collectives in the southern provinces had clandestinely begun to introduce market mechanisms in their business practices. They had done so not so much to earn lots of money but rather out of sheer self-preservation. If the Maoist campaigns were to return, they thought, they had to have something to live on. In the 1960s their children had died of hunger. They were determined that should not happen again. By 1974 some of these units had set up barter agreements and indirect credit arrangements, as well as different forms of fee-charging services. In border areas some units engaged in smuggling and currency fraud. Some agricultural commutes allowed families to sell produce they had cultivated themselves, and keep the profit.

This was the market as conscious rebellion against a system that simply did not deliver. It was small-scale and easily snuffed out. In cases when inspectors or zealots caught those responsible, they could go to prison for years. But when the central government, slowly and tentatively, began experimenting with market concepts after 1978, these people were ready. With others who had similar ideas, the *getihu* (private traders, or, perhaps better, guerrilla entrepreneurs) began diversifying and investing. After 1981 many of their activities were legalized, even though for years some of what they did was in a legal gray zone. Most of them did not mind, as long as they could earn money without being threatened with prison or execution.

In Beijing, China's reformist leaders did not make policy with these people in mind, though the getihu represented the kind of dynamism that some of them would like to see more of. Deng's reform plans had three main aims: to get access to modern technology, to increase production, and to keep the Communist Party in power unopposed. Under these main aims, there were distinct subsections. Deng wanted to increase exports (to earn hard currency) and strengthen the military (to guard against a Soviet attack and keep the party in power). He also wanted to decentralize economic decision-making. One of the key targets for Deng's ridicule was the Beijing bureaucrat who now, safe from Cultural Revolution upheavals, simply added another half percent to planned output for each year.

But the road to reform was in no way straightforward. The party was faction-ridden and politically divided. Many of Deng's colleagues, not surprisingly, thought that models for socialist China should be sought in socialist Yugoslavia or Hungary, not in the capitalist West. Allowing private enterprise was especially difficult. The Chinese name for the Communist Party, Gongchandang, literally means "the Party of Common Property." Under Mao, party leaders had spent years denouncing market experiments in other socialist countries. To now turn around and endorse such practices in China was hard. But Deng drove them on. "We permit some people and some regions to become prosperous first, for the purpose of achieving common prosperity faster," he told CBS's Mike Wallace in 1986.[2]

Deng's first steps, beyond allowing small-scale private enterprise in trade and services, was to decollectivize agriculture. He dissolved the People's Communes and introduced a household responsibility system. This meant that families were allocated a plot of land from which they had to deliver a set output to the state, but were free to trade any surplus privately. Agricultural production shot up. Farmers started to save money. Sometimes they pooled their money to start small enterprises in their villages or the nearest town. State-owned enterprises were allowed to sell surplus products and set their own prices for them. Foreign investment was encouraged in special economic zones, where foreign companies could invest freely and retrieve their profits, as long as they were willing to share their technological know-how with Chinese companies.

While Deng was a daring experimenter in economic policy, he was much less certain in international affairs. He knew that he needed a good relationship with the United States and linked Chinese foreign policy closely to that of Washington. Having imbibed Mao's perception of the Soviet Union as a deadly threat to China, Deng believed that working with the Americans provided protection as well as economic opportunities. And the United States was happy to oblige. For both Carter and Reagan, China was the key Cold War ally, equal if not greater in importance than western Europe or Japan. Having at first been shocked at Chinese poverty and underdevelopment, the Americans assisted growth through loans, technology transfers, and access to foreign markets. If China was to work with the United States to put pressure on the Soviet Union, then its domestic situation had to improve.

The beginning of the Chinese economic expansion, which later was to produce such earthshaking consequences for the global economy as a whole, was therefore intimately connected to how the Cold War was fought. As the market took hold in China, and as the overall economy began expanding, the Chinese attraction to Western, and especially American, methods of production, management, and marketing also increased. By the late 1980s, Chinese society was already a very different place from the wearisome, terrorized setting it had been a decade earlier. Some people suffered as social security provisions faded. But more people wanted to make use of the new opportunities that Deng's reforms offered. Even though most of the economy was still state-controlled, and the Communist Party refused to give up its monopoly on power, China had started a transformation that marked a definitive break with socialist planning models. Its choices were strongly to influence other socialist countries that wanted higher growth through participation in the global economy.

Still, China was not the main focus of those who looked for economic models for the future in the 1980s. Next door, in Japan, an already developed economy was experiencing continuous high growth rates of around 5 percent. At the beginning of the decade, the Harvard social scientist Ezra Vogel had argued that Japan, in many respects, was already the number one country globally. Japan, he argued, "has dealt more successfully with more of the basic problems of post-industrial society than any other country."[3] Comparing the influence of global powers eight years later, the Yale historian Paul Kennedy saw Japan as "enormously productive and prosperous, and getting much more so."[4] It was hard not to conclude that the future, at least in some ways, belonged to Japan.

The argument that Japan had achieved its extraordinary position in spite of (some would say because of) not prioritizing military affairs was tremendously powerful in the debates of the 1980s. It implied that what made countries successful in the late twentieth century was not military power but economic achievement. It also implied that an export-led process of economic growth could lift countries not just out of poverty, but could help them to overtake the major powers of the world. In 1990 Japan's GDP per capita was higher than that of the United States, and almost seven times higher than that of the USSR. Not surprisingly, other countries wanted to learn from the Japanese model.

A main reason why Japan could concentrate on its own economic growth was of course that the United States not only protected the country militarily but also had facilitated its access to international markets, first and foremost its own. And even though the Reagan Administration publicly voiced its displeasure with Japan's trading practices, it was very careful to not let economic issues endanger the close alliance between the two countries. This was particularly true after Nakasone Yasuhiro became Japanese prime minister in 1982. Nakasone wanted to keep the US alliance in place but was more of a nationalist both in political and economic terms than his Liberal Democratic Party predecessors. He wanted to improve Japan's relations with China and the rest of mainland Asia, not least to improve the prospects for Japan's exports if the United States should prove less amenable as a market in the future. By 1987 Japan was China's largest trading partner and the second-biggest foreign investor, after the United States. Japan also had extraordinary importance for China as a supplier of loans and technology. No wonder Deng Xiaoping underlined the importance of the relationship while meeting with Nakasone. "The historical friendly relations between Japan and China must continue onto the 21st century, and then to the 22nd, 23rd, 33rd, and 43rd century," Deng said. "Currently, Japan and China do not have urgent problems. The development of Japan-China relations into the 21st century is more important than all other issues."[5]

But by the 1980s Japan and China were not the only Asian economies that grew. Most impressive in terms of growth were the east and southeast Asian "little tigers." In 1987 Hong Kong's per capita GDP grew 12.1 percent, South Korea's 11.2 percent, Taiwan's 11 percent, and Singapore's 9.1 percent. All of them had market-oriented economies and export-led industrial growth, with a strong element of state guidance of the overall economy. In other words, they looked a bit like Japan (even though all of them were different in their own ways) but were very unlike the centralized planned economies of the socialist world. None of the little tigers had been expected by economists to do well in international competition; they had few resources and they were far away from most of their markets. But the 1970s had positioned them to take advantage of the changes in the global economy in the decade that followed. They all had well-educated populations, low production costs, and well-managed, ambitious companies. Their businessmen already had commercial contacts in the United States and western Europe, with which their countries had been allied in the Cold War. The little tigers were well placed to roam.

The little big tigers, South Korea and Taiwan, also benefitted enormously from the social and political stability created by successful transitions to democracy. Up to the late Cold War era both had been military dictatorships supported, at least indirectly, by the United States. Thousands of people had died in the struggle for democratic rights. But as the Cold War waned and international tension in the region declined, both South Korea and Taiwan moved to forms of democratic government, the former in 1987 and the latter four years later. The transitions were initiated by the regimes themselves, in part because they believed that their countries would be stronger if they were more democratic. Their gamble that democracy would create better laws and institutions paid off. Both countries are today among the wealthiest in the world.

With the exception of the city-state of Singapore, southeast Asia had not benefitted much from the global changes of the 1970s. Part of the reason was the ongoing wars in Indochina, where Vietnam went almost straight from a war against the United States to a war against the Khmer Rouge in Cambodia. No other part of the world suffered more, and for longer, as a result of Cold War conflicts. And the suffering there continued into the 1980s, mainly as a result of Reagan's Third World strategy. In one of the most perverse twists of the Cold War, the remnants of the genocidal Khmer Rouge regime, who were fighting the Vietnam-supported government in Cambodia, survived up to 1991 thanks to US and Chinese backing. Hitting back at Vietnam for its alliance with the Soviet Union was the main purpose of this nefarious partnership, but it was also a way for Reagan to tell the Chinese that he was serious about containing the Soviets on the ground. The result was more misery for the Cambodians, and also an undeclared border war between Vietnam and Thailand, from where most of the Cambodian opposition operated.

The perceived threat from a heavily militarized Vietnam made the anti-Communist countries in southeast Asia pull more closely together. The Association of Southeast Asian Nations (ASEAN), which had been set up in 1967, aimed at ensuring "their stability and security from external interference in any form or manifestation in order to preserve their national identities in accordance with the ideals and aspirations of their peoples."[6] But in reality this had meant working closely with the United States against what the leaders of these countries saw as Soviet and Chinese threats. In the 1980s, however, Deng Xiaoping managed to turn generations of distrust between China and conservative southeast Asian leaders around. As the economic interaction between China and southeast Asia grew, the diplomatic relationship also became closer. By 1985 it was clear that Vietnam was facing coordinated pressure from the north and the south to withdraw from Cambodia.

The Vietnamese leadership's response to this challenge was to deepen reform at home and to prepare to end its military presence in the neighboring countries. Even before Gorbachev was elected in the USSR, the new generation of leaders in Hanoi realized that the Soviet Union would only be of limited value to them in standing up to foreign pressure. The Đổi Mới reforms, which liberalized the Vietnamese economy in the late 1980s and gave significant room for private enterprise, was built on Deng's experiments in China but even more so on the experience of the main ASEAN countries. In a move unprecedented for any Communist state, Vietnam increasingly based its negotiations for a withdrawal from Cambodia on the need to draw closer to ASEAN. The first meetings were held in Jakarta, and by 1989 the Vietnamese had made it clear that they would withdraw unilaterally irrespective of the squabbling among the various Cambodian factions. By September 1989 all Vietnamese forces had left. By 1992 Vietnam had a Treaty of Amity and Cooperation with ASEAN and had also normalized its relations with China.

In the early 1980s India also began to step further away from the Cold War. Granted, India had always been an uncomfortable customer at the Cold War table, intent on setting its own rules for its foreign engagements. But since the 1960s it had increasingly come to see its links with the Soviet Union as important to its national security. When Indira Gandhi returned to power in 1980, she began a gradual loosening of the ties to Moscow. Part of this was in response to the renewed intensity of the Cold War. Gandhi did not want India to be seen as too tied to the USSR as matters heated up. In spite of her abhorrence of Islamism and sympathy with the secular reform aims of the Communist Afghan government, she was uneasy at the effects of the Soviet invasion. In particular, the Indian prime minister was concerned with the unprecedented US support for Pakistan that the invasion produced. In her meetings with President Reagan in 1982, Gandhi went out of her way to stress that India wanted good relations with the United States, and that she wanted the Soviets to withdraw from Afghanistan.

But India's new rebalancing of its foreign relations came up against Reagan's insistence on providing ever more advanced military aid to Pakistan. After Indira Gandhi was assassinated in 1984, the new prime minister, her son Rajiv Gandhi, began seeing Gorbachev as the answer to India's foreign policy dilemmas. Here was a new Soviet leader who deemphasized strict ideological concerns and placed economic development at the core of his foreign policy agenda. Rajiv Gandhi saw, earlier than most, some of the transformation of the global economy that was going on, and wanted India to go through its own perestroika, giving more room to markets, private initiative, and economic globalization. He believed Gorbachev to be a kindred spirit. The Delhi Declaration the two signed in 1986 shows more Indian influence than Soviet:

1. In the nuclear age, mankind must develop a new political thinking and a new concept of the world that provides sound guarantees for the survival of mankind.
2. The world we have inherited belongs to present and future generations alike—hence we must give priority to universal human values.

3. Human life must be acknowledged [as] the supreme value.
4. Non-violence must become the basis of human co-existence.[7]

Though Gorbachev and Gandhi may have been right that the abolition of the Cold War would lead to a more peaceful world, other events in Asia did not exactly point in that direction. The war between Iraq and Iran that broke out in 1980 has been called the first post–Cold War war, and this is correct as far as the lack of ideological motives are concerned. The Iraqi attack on Iran was largely motivated by the prospect of territorial gain and the fear of Iranian collusion with Iraq's minority Shia Muslims. The Soviets, who had been big supporters of Saddam Hussein's Iraq, told the Iraqis they did not see much sense or meaning in the war. Moscow was afraid that the Iraqi attack would push Iran back into the arms of the United States. The Reagan Administration, on the other hand, did not warm to either of the two belligerents, though it was more concerned about the prospects of Iranian expansion than anything Saddam was doing. One Administration official is said to have quipped that it was a pity that both sides could not lose. Meanwhile the war developed into a form of confessional conflict, with Sunni Arabs battling Shia Persians. Almost a million people died in a needless, aimless struggle, in which the two sides took turns in having the upper hand and the only people to prosper were European and Asian arms manufacturers.

The slow end to the Cold War brought little but misery to the Middle East. In Africa the situation was very similar to begin with, but ended with some rays of hope. Since the 1960s Superpower interventionism, projects of European racial supremacy, and misguided high modern development concepts had wreaked havoc with the continent. For most of the 1980s this situation continued. In southern Africa the white supremacist regime in South Africa continued to wage war against its neighbors and oppress the black majority. The United States assisted the survival of the regime through trade and investment, and by opposing international sanctions. In Zaire (Congo) Mobutu continued his rampant exploitation of his own people, supported through a Cold War partnership with Washington.

And in Ethiopia the officers of the Dergue clung to their project of socialist transformation, assisted by the USSR, while their country slowly fell to pieces around them. Elsewhere, military dictatorships abounded. Lieutenant Jerry Rawlings took power in Ghana in 1979, aged thirty-two. Master Sergeant Samuel Doe did the same in Liberia the following year, aged twenty-nine. It was not a pretty picture.

In southern Africa the situation was especially acute. After their debacle in Angola in 1975–76, where they were defeated by a combination of local and Cuban forces, the apartheid regime in South Africa withdrew into the areas it controlled militarily. The new prime minister, P. W. Botha, was a racial ideologue, who believed that white South Africa was better off the less contact it had with the rest of the continent. For him, the *vesting Suid-Afrika* (fortress South Africa) was what was important, not what his supporters disparagingly termed "civilizing blacks elsewhere." In 1979 Botha helped the British and Americans push the white settler regime in Rhodesia to accept the Lancaster House Agreement, by which the country became majority-governed Zimbabwe in 1980. Their assumption, later proved correct, was that the election winner, Robert Mugabe, was more intent on establishing his own power than risking it through any form of cooperation with the Soviet Union.

On other matters, internal and external, the Cold War became increasingly important in southern Africa in the 1980s. Botha viewed his own regime as essentially anti-Communist. His argument for clinging to the fiction of "independent" homelands for blacks within South Africa was that majority rule would mean a victory for Nelson Mandela's African National Congress (ANC), which was in alliance with the South African Communist Party. South Africa also continued to occupy the neighboring country of Namibia (also known as South West Africa), in spite of countless UN resolutions demanding its withdrawal. Meanwhile, Botha stepped up the policy of trying to destabilize the next-door countries of Angola and Mozambique, on the pretext that they were allied with the Soviet Union and gave refuge to ANC exiles. The South African military carried out hundreds of incursions into the territory of neighboring states, with the explicit aim of killing leaders of the ANC resistance or soldiers of the South West Africa People's Organization (SWAPO). Southern Africa seemed to be a powder keg ready to explode.

Besides South Africa itself, Angola was the center point of the Cold War in Africa. The MPLA government that had taken power with Cuban help in 1975 was closely allied with Havana and Moscow. Although the South African regime seemed ready to live with that as a fact, the Reagan Administration's support for the Angolan opposition led to a flaring up of the civil war there. The leader of the opposition UNITA movement, Jonas Savimbi, was one of the poster boys of Reagan's antirevolutionary offensive in the postcolonial world. By 1984 Savimbi's guerrillas were receiving money, weapons, and training from the CIA. As Reagan put it to his advisers the following year: "We want Savimbi to know that the cavalry is coming."[8] In 1986 the Americans even supplied UNITA with fifty anti-aircraft Stinger missiles. The fact that UNITA was allied with the South Africans and was responsible for massive human rights violations in the areas it controlled did not matter to Reagan. The important thing was to use the conflict to put further pressure on the Soviets and on the Cubans to withdraw from Africa.

P. W. Botha was a reluctant participant in Angola's renewed civil war. He cherished the idea of destabilizing the regime in Luanda, but was worried about trusting the Americans or engaging too many of his own troops. What tipped the balance was the increased warfare in South African–controlled Namibia. To alleviate the pressure on themselves, the Angolan government had allowed SWAPO guerrillas to increase strikes from Angolan territory into their homeland. In 1987 Botha decided to teach the MPLA a lesson, while helping UNITA, which was on the defensive in spite of recent US aid. The South African invasion quickly turned into a stalemate. In the Battle of Cuito Cuanavale—the largest military engagement in Africa since World War II—Cuban and Angolan troops held their own against the advancing South African forces. Inside South Africa public opinion quickly turned against the war, especially after Botha had to call up the reserves in early 1988. Even to white South Africans, Botha's regime increasingly seemed to deliver little but war, instability at home, and continued international isolation.

To many observers, both in Africa and elsewhere, it seemed strange that the Reagan Administration continued to fan the flames of war in southern Africa while talking peace with the Soviets in Moscow. To some extent this difference in policy was the result of real divisions within the Administration, with key State Department officials pushing for negotiations to end regional conflicts while many NSC staffers continued to emphasize covert operations in support of anti-Communists. But it is doubtful whether the president himself perceived it as a split in policy. For Reagan, forcing the Soviets and Cubans out of Africa had always been a key aim. In his view, Gorbachev could only become a US partner if he agreed to a full withdrawal from Africa, Asia, and Latin America. Reagan's approach was maximalist: he wanted to benefit as much as possible from Soviet weakness when the opportunity was there.

After Cuito Cuanavale, all sides in the Angolan conflict began slowly to edge toward a negotiated solution. The improved relationship between the United States and the Soviet Union played a decisive role. Both sides pushed their allies toward an agreement. On the US side, Reagan was under increasing pressure from Congress, which had already imposed comprehensive sanctions on South Africa against the president's wishes. The two diplomats in charge of coordinating Soviet-US cooperation on Africa, Chester Crocker and Anatolii Adamishin, also hit it off personally. Crocker played "a brilliant role," according to Adamishin.[9] In December 1988 the parties reached a linked agreement on Cuban withdrawal from Angola and Namibian independence.

The southern African agreement was a high point in dismantling Cold War conflict in the Third World. It would of course not have been possible without years of careful work through the UN and in international public opinion by those who opposed the apartheid regime. It would also have been unlikely without the Cubans matching South African military power at Cuito Cuanavale. But in essence it symbolized Gorbachev's commitment to a withdrawal from the Third

World. "I personally don't think they are going to build socialism in this part of the world," admitted Adamishin at the signing of the accords. Fidel Castro went along with the process, in part because he believed Cuba had achieved what it had sought in southern Africa all along: security for Angola and independence for Namibia. But he resented the manner in which the Soviets had acted above his head, and expressed his concern in letters to Gorbachev. The Soviet leader's key foreign policy adviser Anatolii Cherniaev was scathing:

> "The Beard" [Castro] wasted the revolution and now he is ruining the country, which is spiraling toward a total mess. It's true that he will not stop in his demagoguery about orthodox Marxism-Leninism and going "to the end"; since this is the last thing he can use to preserve his "revolutionary halo." But this halo is already a myth. . . . Nobody reckons with Cuba in South America, it is no longer setting any kind of example. The Cuban factor has waned. A break in relations? . . . he is only going to harm himself. We will only win, and save 5 billion doing it. Are people going to grumble about this? Yes, some will: the dogmatists and dissenters from the "revolutionary camp" and the Communist Parties that are becoming extinct, whose time has passed.[10]

Against Cherniaev's advice, Gorbachev decided to go to Cuba to see Castro in April 1989. With the southern Africa deal done, neither side found it useful to rehash their differences over that event. Instead Castro, who knew how dependent his regime was on Soviet support, took the initiative in discussing a solution to the crisis in Central America. He knew that Gorbachev would like to see such a solution, which was one of the key concerns of the new US Administration of George H. W. Bush. But Castro also hoped that Cuba would be able to extricate itself before it was left alone in support of the Nicaraguan Sandinistas and their revolutionary allies in Central America as Soviet assistance waned. Castro had always been a skeptic about the chances of survival for Left-wing regimes in Central America without some kind of settlement with the United States. As the Cold War receded, the Cuban leader hoped that such an arrangement could be found.

The Sandinista government in Nicaragua had been fighting for its life against a US-led onslaught since the early years of the revolution. Not only did the United States arm, train, and equip Nicaraguan counterrevolutionaries (the Contras), but it also attempted to strangle the country economically through preventing Nicaraguan exports. The ostensible reason for US hostility, the way Reagan portrayed it, was Nicaraguan support of Left-wing guerrillas in neighboring El Salvador, who were fighting the military and paramilitary Right-wing groups. El Salvador—one of the most socially unequal and politically unstable countries in Latin America—would probably have seen massive unrest even if there had been no Nicaraguan support for the Left. But Reagan used the El Salvador crisis to put further pressure on the Sandinistas.

Reagan's problem was that the US intervention in Central America was far from popular among Americans, who were weary of a Vietnam-like scenario closer to home. A 1984 poll showed that only 30 percent supported Reagan's policy there.[11] The massive human rights violations of the Salvadorian military also harmed the Administration's attempts at supporting them against Left-wing guerrillas. The murder of the antiregime Salvadoran archbishop Oscar Romero, as he celebrated mass in the San Salvador cathedral in 1980, was an atrocity too far for many Americans, as was the killing, by sniper fire, of thirty-five mourners at his funeral. Throughout the 1980s, Reagan had to fight Congressional attempts to cut all US aid to the Contras and to the Salvadoran government. By the time the Iran-Contra scandal broke, in the fall of 1986, it was clear that the president would not be able to fund his Central American campaign much longer without serious conflict with US lawmakers. Reagan still persisted, but his efforts were less and less effective, both with regard to US public opinion and toward the fighting parties in Central America.

Indicative of how the Cold War ended, it was initiatives by regional groups of countries that finally began resolving the civil wars in Central America. Mexico, as the biggest country in the region, played a key role, but it was Costa Rica's president Óscar Arias who in 1988 presented the peace plan that would underpin negotiated solutions. When Castro and Gorbachev met in Havana in February 1989 this was, in effect, the plan they chose to support. The Sandinistas had little choice but to go along, as had the Contras, whom Congress threatened with losing all support if they did not agree to lay down their weapons in exchange for free and fair elections to be held in 1990.

While the end of the decade brought some hope for the peoples of Central America, the situation in Latin America as a whole during the 1980s was contradictory and confusing. The region as a whole saw a series of dramatic ends to years of military dictatorships and a gradual return to civilian rule. In Peru in 1980, Bolivia in 1982, Uruguay in 1984, and Brazil in 1985, new governments were elected. In Argentina the military junta, which had been guilty of countless human rights violations in the name of anti-Communism and the Cold War, collapsed in the wake of their attempt to seize the Falklands in 1982. Even Chile, where a ruthless military government under Augusto Pinochet had been in place since the 1973 coup, was transformed in 1988 when the dictator lost what was intended to be a mere pro forma referendum on his continued rule. Pinochet's Cold War rhetoric against the Left no longer impressed the Chilean middle classes. Like middle classes elsewhere, they sought stability, legality, and international recognition. Pinochet's regime could not deliver any of these standards.

Pinochet's fall was surprising to his supporters in Washington. They believed that in spite of the regime's brutality, Pinochet would be forgiven by the majority because of the market-oriented economic reforms his advisers had carried out. But like almost all Latin American countries, whatever their economic orientation, Chile had turned out to be profoundly susceptible to the international debt crisis of the early 1980s. During the previous decade, governments in Latin America had borrowed heavily to finance economic expansion and public investments, especially in infrastructure and education. Many countries of different ideological persuasions, such as the Right-wing military dictatorship in Brazil, the radical nationalist dictatorship in Peru, and the semidemocratic government in Mexico, had aimed at centrally planned, state-led industrialization processes. State-owned companies were at the forefront of this expansion. By the early 1980s there were more than six hundred state enterprises in Brazil, making up almost half of all bigger companies. In Mexico there were more than a thousand, a fivefold increase since the early 1970s. Even though many of these companies did reasonably well in commercial terms (especially, of course, those that were monopolies or near monopolies), they were dependent on massive amounts of capital for their expansion, according to plans set by the governments.

Until the early 1980s, the international lending market continuously expanded. The influx of hard currency deposits from oil-rich Middle Eastern countries to Western and Japanese banks, the so-called petro-dollars, made for easy money. And, for most of the decade, the return through interest or investments in Europe or the United States was low, thereby privileging more risky but also more potentially rewarding lending to developing countries, especially in Latin America. But in 1979 interest rates in the United States increased dramatically, in some cases going up to 20 percent, a fourfold hike in less than two years. At the same time instability in raw material prices, on which most Latin America economies still depended, grew further. These fluctuations, within a long-term downward trend, made it more difficult either to pay back loans or get new ones. By 1982 many big banks refused to lend more. In August that year Mexico defaulted on its debts. This set off a chain reaction, in which the US government scrambled to prop up the banks, while pushing for debt negotiations among the debtor countries, the banks, and the international financial institutions, especially the IMF.

For the Reagan Administration, the Latin American defaults were not only the result of Latin profligacy and waste; they were also welcome opportunities to spread the gospel of free markets and neoliberal economies. The price the IMF exacted for helping Latin American restructure their debt was called "structural adjustment," meaning the recipient countries accepted neoliberal elements in their domestic economies, such as privatization, import liberalization, and abolishing subsidies and social spending. The short-term results were catastrophic for the Latin American economies. Economic growth stagnated. Incomes dropped, especially in urban areas, and unemployment rose to very high levels. Inflation hit the middle class and working class alike. The only good outcome of what Latin Americans call La Década Perdida (the Lost Decade) was the collapse of the military dictatorships, which, by common consent, had helped cause the economic meltdown and did not have the power to stand up against US demands.

The moves away from dictatorship and toward more accountable forms of government in many parts of the world at the end of the Cold War were much helped by invigorated international debates on rights and norms. Many of these debates questioned the strong and in some places almost overwhelming role of the state in Cold War politics. The Cold War had helped states to expand their power over people and communities almost everywhere. Even in the United States, where so many ideological positions privileged individual freedoms and rights, the practice had been toward an enlargement of the capacity of the federal government. The argument, everywhere, had been won by the combined needs of military preparedness and social improvement. The former was to fend off enemy expansion. The latter was to organize society better and to present it as the model for the future. But by the 1980s these forms of thinking were coming under pressure both in the East and the West. In the Soviet Union, Gorbachev began to reconsider the established belief that more state power was the solution to all problems. In the United States and Britain neoliberals challenged the very foundation that postwar state interventionism was built on: that capitalism functioned better if it was regulated by governments. While before the state seemed to be the answer (or at least a part of it), now, for some, it was the mother of all ills.

But the shift in thinking was not only connected to economic or social issues. It also dealt with human rights and legal protections for the individual. And most surprisingly, perhaps, nongovernmental organizations and pressure groups often took the lead in pushing states, of both ideological persuasions, to respect such rights and norms.

Amnesty International, which had existed since 1961, expanded its membership dramatically from the late 1970s on. Other groups, such as Human Rights Watch and Helsinki Watch, appeared in the wake of the 1975 Conference on Security and Cooperation in Europe. Campaigns against the human rights violations of Latin American dictatorships, such as Chile or Argentina, grew in the region itself as well as in western Europe and North America. In some cases, the campaigners were the same young people who had protested against Soviet attempts at silencing its domestic opposition. They celebrated the physicist Andrei Sakharov and his wife Elena Bonner, who had helped set up a group to monitor their country's compliance with the Helsinki Accords in Moscow in 1976. These were important signs that the Cold War divide was, at least to some people, becoming less important than universal rights and duties. Dissidents in Czechoslovakia or Poland could count on increasing support across the political spectrum in the West. Meanwhile, other identities manifested themselves in protests for basic rights. In Catholic Poland as well as in Protestant East Germany, Christian churches affirmed the rights of their countrymen as citizens. In Muslim countries clerics began to speak out against unlawful imprisonments. "Rights talk" seemed, at least for a while, to overtake the insistence on Cold War ideological rectitude.

Nothing exemplifies the shifts in the political terrain better than the success of the international campaigns to end apartheid in South Africa. For years the main Western countries, and especially the United States and Britain, had turned a mostly deaf ear to protests against the blatant forms of racism through which the white minority there ruled. South Africa was too strategically important and too mineral rich to be put beyond the pale. More often than not, Western leaders had felt a certain empathy with white South Africans, even though they objected to the methods they used to rule the black majority. But by the mid-1980s, as global protests spread against the injustice with which South Africa was ruled, the policy of "constructive engagement" with white South Africa came under increasing pressure. While the UN demanded economic sanctions and an embargo against South Africa, the international anti-apartheid movement got increasing attention for its cause. The 1988 pop concert at Wembley Stadium in London to celebrate the seventieth birthday of imprisoned ANC leader Nelson Mandela became a global sensation, watched live by more than six hundred million people around the world. Featuring a stunning array of artists, from the Bee Gees to Whitney Houston and Eric Clapton, the event made it more difficult to condemn Mandela as a "Communist," as both Ronald Reagan and Margaret Thatcher had done in the past. By the end of the 1980s, even those who had shown sympathy with the South African government in the past were turning against it, accepting that the abolition of apartheid was a common task across Cold War boundaries.

1980s "rights talk" was connected to the other emerging global discourse, which could be called "identity talk." With the Cold War ideological divide receding, more and more groups reacted against states that had ignored individual and group identities, be it along religious, linguistic, or ethnic lines. While human rights activists spoke about universal principles, nationalists or religious activists spoke about rights and duties embedded in them on behalf of their communities. The state they lived in had suppressed these communities, went the argument, and now they needed to reassert themselves. In some cases, such as among Basques or Catalans in Spain, or in the Baltic republics in the USSR, the Cold War was seen as having been an argument for their suppression. In other cases, the Cold War was seen as a kind of emergency, a frozen world that kept states together well beyond their "sell by" date. The most striking example was the federal republic of Yugoslavia, where centrifugal forces were soon to cause disastrous results. Even the Serbs, the largest population group in Yugoslavia, worried about their future. In a 1986 memorandum, the Serbian Academy of Arts and Sciences said,

> Unlike national minorities, portions of the Serbian people, who live in other republics in large numbers, do not have the right to use their own language and alphabet, to organize politically and culturally, and to develop the unique culture of their nation. Considering the existing forms of national discrimination, present-day Yugoslavia

cannot be considered a democratic state. . . . The guiding principle behind this policy has been "a weak Serbia, a strong Yugoslavia" and this has evolved into an influential mind-set: if rapid economic growth were permitted the Serbs, who are the largest nation, it would pose a danger to the other nations of Yugoslavia. And so all possibilities are grasped to place increasing obstacles in the way of their economic development and political consolidation.[12]

But the main region for a massive shift from a Left-Right divide to a new form of politics was in the Middle East. There the Islamist revolution in Iran had provided inspiration for new groups based on religious identity and on a new, political and fundamentalist interpretation of the Quran. Up to the early 1980s political interpretations of Islam, both Sunni and Shia, had mainly identified with the Cold War political Right. The Sunni Muslim Brotherhood, for instance, was a profoundly conservative organization that battled the Middle Eastern Left, whether Communist, socialist, or Ba'athist. But during the 1980s Islamists increasingly turned against both socialism and capitalism, and against both the Soviet Union and the United States. Egyptian and Saudi extremists played an important role in this turn. For them, the United States was at least as guilty in helping infidel Arab regimes suppress real Muslims as was the Soviet Union. They wished to wage war against Israel and its American supporters. But they also wanted to fight the Soviet occupation of Afghanistan. One of them, Abdullah Azzam, a Palestinian Islamist who headed a key Pakistan-based support network for the Afghan mujahedin, argued that "whoever can, from among the Arabs, fight jihad in Palestine, then he must start there. And, if he is not capable, then he must set out for Afghanistan. For the rest of the Muslims, I believe they should start their jihad in Afghanistan. . . . The sin upon this present generation, for not advancing towards Afghanistan, Palestine, the Philippines, Kashmir, Lebanon, Chad, Eritrea, etc., is greater than the sin inherited from the loss of the lands which have previously fallen into the possession of the Kuffar [the infidels]."[13]

By the time the Soviet withdrawal from Afghanistan got underway, networks of internationalist Islamists were being formed in Afghanistan and in neighboring Pakistan. Osama bin-Laden, a Saudi who was a sometime collaborator and sometime rival of Azzam, organized his own group, which he called al-Qaeda (the Base). Bin-Laden had been allied with the Afghan Islamist radicals Abdul Rasul Sayyaf and Gulbuddin Hekmatyar, who—while receiving plentiful weapons and supplies from the United States—had turned increasingly anti-American. Like Azzam, bin-Laden and his sponsors saw Afghanistan as just one battle in the war to liberate Muslims from foreign control. But taking Kabul, the capital, was first on their list of priorities, and with the Soviet pullout in 1989 they believed that their time had come.

Even without the Red Army, the Islamist conquest of Afghanistan turned out to be more complicated than the somewhat naïve jihadists first believed. Facing its moment of truth, the Afghan Communist government fought better than its opponents. Even if Washington and the Pakistanis continued their support for the mujahedin, while the Soviet Union gradually ended most of its involvement, the opposition was not able to take Kabul. Some local Afghan leaders found, not surprisingly, that they feared the more radical Islamists and their foreign jihadi friends more than they feared Najibullah's government. As their offensives failed, the mujahedin started to fragment. By 1991, when the Communists finally started running out of supplies, there was already a full-blown civil war among some of the opposition groups. The mujahedin's final rush toward Kabul in April 1992 saw Afghanistan descend into total chaos. Hekmatyar, who wanted to take the city on his own, clashed with a coalition of other factions, including some of his former Islamist friends, and lost. His response was to shell the capital using heavy artillery he had taken from the former government forces. It was an unedifying spectacle, leading to a US disengagement and the despair of foreign Islamists. For Osama bin-Laden the Afghan debacle was an important lesson. Only through ideological training, committed internationalism, and strict organization could the cause of jihad be furthered in the future, he believed. Bin-Laden set out for Sudan but was to return to Afghanistan, and to history, five years later.

The processes that ended the Cold War were manifold and complex, just like its origins had been. The end of the global conflict created enormous opportunities for good, as witnessed in southern Africa or southeast Asia. But not all issues were resolved, and some regional legacies lingered, such as in Korea, in the Middle East, or in the Balkans. Sometimes the outcome was contradictory. The economic hardships imposed on many Latin Americans often outweighed the celebrations over the return to more democratic and responsive forms of government. And some of the ideologies that overtook the Cold War dichotomy, religious fanaticism or nationalist self-obsession first among them, were as dangerous for the people caught up in them as the ideological struggles between capitalism and socialism had been. Still, the end of the Cold War opened up new possibilities for people everywhere. In some cases they made use of them to make a better world. This is not least true for Europe, the continent where the Cold War arguably began and where it was to end.

22

European Realities

The Cold War in Europe ended because years of closer association between East and West had reduced the fear that the two sides had for each other, and because of western Europe's proven record of success-fully integrating peripheral countries into a European Community. It ended in 1989 because the peoples in eastern Europe rebelled and Gorbachev did nothing to save the Communist regimes. On the con-trary, the Soviet leader insisted that popular sovereignty was unavoid-able both in eastern Europe and in the Soviet Union itself. The eastern European regimes had shown that they could not reform. Therefore, the head of the CPSU found, it was not unnatural for them to fall. It was a remarkable turn of events, but one that had its portents in the beginning transformations of the détente era. The end of Commu-nism could happen so quickly in Europe because the ground had al-ready been laid and because the support of the regimes in the East was already wafer-thin. Unless the Soviets would act to rescue them, they could not defend themselves successfully.

By 1989, Gorbachev insisted that to him the Cold War was over. His attention was increasingly being drawn to how to deepen reform within the Soviet Union itself. His main preoccupation was with po-litical changes. Gorbachev wanted to make the USSR a democratic, federal state and to pull the Communist Party, which he still headed, along in the process. But his lofty aims were quickly overtaken by eco-nomic hardships, nationalisms, and competing bureaucracies. With

Gorbachev refusing to budge, and without substantial aid coming in from elsewhere, the Soviet state was soon in serious trouble. By 1991 its very existence seemed threatened. This was a remarkable turnaround for the Soviet people and for the world, and it all happened within less than a decade.

Overall, the people's revolutions in eastern Europe were astonishingly peaceful and nonviolent. The one big exception was Yugoslavia, where nationalist demagogues in their hurry to kill off the federal state set off waves of violence that were to last a decade, inflicting terrible suffering on most Yugoslavs. Yugoslavia was the prime example of a country that the Cold War had helped hold together. Confronted with Soviet power in eastern Europe, as they had been since 1948, most Yugoslavs had preferred sticking together in their own, homegrown, federal state, even if they did not always like their neighbors. But as the Cold War receded, some members of each Yugoslav nationality began to worry about the consequences if one or more of the other groups within that federal state got the upper hand on themselves. Yugoslavia had been held together not by trust but by fear, and with the object of that fear shifting, the country descended into destruction and fratricide.

OTHERS HAD MUCH to be grateful for. In America, the year 1989 began on a cheerful note. Ronald Reagan was stepping down as president after eight years in office, and was widely celebrated for his achievements. The election of his vice president, George H. W. Bush, as his successor confirmed that most Americans had forgiven Reagan for his involvement in the Iran-Contra scandal as well as the increasingly hands-off leadership style in his last years in office. What they remembered, they thought, was a president who had fixed the economy and removed the threat of nuclear destruction. No other president since Woodrow Wilson had changed his foreign policy views more during his time in office. In his farewell address, Reagan spoke about the Soviets as partners. "My view," the departing president told the American people, is that President Gorbachev is different from previous Soviet leaders. I think he knows some of the things wrong with his society and is trying to fix them. We wish him well. And we'll continue to work to make sure that the Soviet Union that eventually emerges from this process is a less threatening one. What it all boils down to is this: I want the new closeness to continue. And it will, as long as we make it clear that we will continue to act in a certain way as long as they continue to act in a helpful manner.[1]

President Bush was less certain. At the beginning of his presidency, he wanted time to consider how US policy toward the Soviets should develop under the new circumstances. A much more traditional Cold Warrior than Reagan, Bush was not sure that the "new closeness" would continue. On the contrary, as he noted at the beginning of his presidency, the Soviet Union "presents a new and complicated political challenge to us in Europe and elsewhere. My own sense is that the Soviet challenge may be even greater than before because it is more varied."[2] "The Cold War is not over," warned Bush's national security adviser Brent Scowcroft. There may be "light at the end of the tunnel. But I think it depends partly on how we behave, whether the light is the sun or an incoming locomotive."[3] Bush and Scowcroft feared that perestroika and glasnost might be *too* successful, so that the Western alliances lowered their guard too much.

Gorbachev was disappointed at Bush's "strategic pause." Why, he asked himself, were the Americans hesitating now when he needed them most? In western Europe Gorbachev was still regarded as a hero, and got a hero's welcome everywhere. Even British prime minister Margaret Thatcher went out of her way to heap praise on Gorbachev during their meetings in London in April 1989. When Gorbachev complained about Bush, Thatcher responded that "your success is in our interest. It is in our interest that the Soviet Union become more peaceful, more affluent, more open to change so that this would go together with personal freedoms, with more openness, and exchanges. Continue your course, and we will support your line. The prize will be enormous."[4] Gorbachev's chief foreign policy aide, Anatolii Cherniaev, confided to his diary that "Russia has no other option left. It has to become like everybody else. If this happens, then the October and Stalin syndromes will disappear from world politics. The world will truly be completely different."[5]

But Gorbachev needed foreign support to turn around his flagging fortunes at home. The CPSU still held a predominant position in the Congress of People's Deputies. Gorbachev wanted to move ahead with creating a more democratic Soviet Union as soon as possible, including in the republics. He also wanted to reform the economy, making some room for private enterprise. But while loans and investments from abroad were very slow in arriving, the domestic economy eroded further. High inflation and an increasing dependence on the black market hindered the development of consumerism at home. Government deficits increased, especially at the federal level, since taxes were withheld or embezzled. And meanwhile resistance against Gorbachev's leadership grew, both from leaders in the republics, who wanted more power for themselves, and from within the Communist Party at the central level, where traditionalists accused him of throwing away the achievements of Soviet rule.

Nationalist unrest in a few of the Soviet republics also began to undermine Gorbachev's position. In the Baltic states, forced to join the USSR after World War II, most of the protest was peaceful, but determined. Already in 1988 the Communist-controlled Supreme Soviet of Estonia had declared that the laws of their republic took precedence over Soviet laws. During the elections to the new federal assembly, more than 80 percent of the seats in neighboring Lithuania went to non-Communist candidates. In a further sign that even inside the Soviet Union nationalism trumped ideology, the two Communist-led republics of Armenia and Azerbaijan began confronting each other over control of the Armenian-populated enclave of Nagorno-Karabakh inside Azerbaijan. Tens of thousands of people fled from their homes and hundreds were killed, including some by the Red Army, whom Gorbachev sent in to enforce the peace. The crackdown bought some time for Moscow, but at the cost of both sides accusing Gorbachev of siding with their enemies.[6]

While Gorbachev attempted to march on with his reforms in the Soviet Union, his Communist colleagues in eastern Europe had less and less room for maneuver. Their economies were in trouble, with high debt payments and stagnant production. By 1987 there was nearly no growth at all, across the East Bloc, from Poland to Bulgaria. Although living standards varied greatly, with East Germans, Czechoslovaks, and Hungarians still doing better than, say, the poorer countries in the European Community, the overall trend was downward. Further loans from the West were hard to obtain, and the Soviets had made it clear that they would look after their own urgent needs first. In the late 1980s the economic situation started to spill over into politics. Some Communist leaders, often of the younger generation, started to feel that they needed to mobilize the whole people if an economic collapse were to be avoided. And the only way such a mobilization could happen was through political inclusiveness.

As always, it was Poland that went first. The leaders of the Polish Communist Party found themselves in a desperate economic situation, in which they were unable to repay their foreign loans while paying ever more in wages and social services to prevent workers from rebelling against them. In November 1987, encouraged by Moscow, they set up a referendum in which they asked the population to vote yes to two questions: Are you in favor of radical economic reform? Are you for a deep democratization of political life? But Poles distrusted their government so much that they would not even answer such questions in the affirmative. In desperation, Poland's president, General Jaruzelski, appointed a new government that would introduce market-based reforms in the economy. But Polish workers welcomed the government with a wave of strikes in 1988. It was clear that even the policy of buying off the working class was failing.

Jaruzelski's final gamble was to arrange negotiations with the opposition so that at least some groups could be persuaded to help take responsibility for the economic crisis. He believed that although the workers were still rebellious, the old leadership of Solidarity—most of whom had been in prison since 1981—would no longer be the key leaders. The government even allowed a televised debate in November 1988 between the head of their official trade union and Lech Wałęsa, the former head of Solidarity. The result was another disaster. Wałęsa trounced his opponent.

> **OFFICIAL:** Is trade union pluralism the only solution to all Polish problems? It is also necessary to see opportunities in the party, where significant transformations are happening and will be happening. . . .
> **WAŁĘSA:** When I speak of pluralism, I have in mind three spheres: the economy, trade unions, and politics. We have to understand that, because those ideals will triumph sooner or later. One organization will never have a copyright on all knowledge. That is why we fight for pluralism—whether you like it or not. . . .
> **OFFICIAL:** But you understand that, given the very impulsive nature of Poles, diversity must be found in unity. Otherwise, we will tear each other apart.
> **WAŁĘSA:** We will not make people happy by force. Give them freedom, and we will stop stumbling in place. . . .
> **OFFICIAL:** Do you not see here essential structural changes moving in the direction of democracy?
> **WAŁĘSA:** What I see is that we are going by foot, while others go by car.[7]

Forced by public opinion, encouraged by the Soviets, and entreated by their own senior leaders, the Polish Communist Party's Central Committee agreed to formal negotiations with the opposition to begin in February 1989. With Solidarity still banned, the movement appointed prominent Polish intellectuals and Catholic clergy to represent them. Walesa co-chaired the roundtable meetings with General Czesław Kiszczak, the Communist minister of interior who had put him in prison in 1981. The negotiations moved slowly at first. The Communists attempted to keep constitutional reform from being discussed. Solidarity was split between the Wałęsa mainstream and more radical factions that denounced any compromise with the authorities. But slowly a compromise was reached, in which Solidarity would be legalized and free elections held, to begin with, for 35 percent of the seats in the lower house of parliament (the Sejm) and for all of the seats in the new Senate. It was a risky enterprise, both for the Communists and for Solidarity. Jaruzelski hoped to legitimize the Communists' hold on power. Wałęsa wanted to show Solidarity's strength in elections, set for 4 June 1989.

While Communists and their opponents battled for power in Poland, the Hungarian Communist Party was slowly feeling its way toward a compromise with its own population. Hungary had long been the most liberal of the East Bloc countries. But even there the limit had been set at questioning the Communist Party's monopoly on power. However, by 1988 younger leaders in the Hungarian party, inspired by Gorbachev, wanted to go further in terms of liberalization. They thought that by transforming the party, they stood a good chance of hanging on to power, even if the opposition was allowed to organize. In May 1988 the aging leader János Kádár, who had been in charge since the Soviet invasion more than thirty years earlier, was replaced by the reformer Károly Grósz. The new head of the party praised Gorbachev's reforms. By February 1989 Hungary had introduced freedom of speech and legalized some non-Communist groups. In May travel restrictions to Austria were lifted, meaning that Hungarians were the first people in the Warsaw Pact who could move freely across the borders to a non-Communist country.

In June 1989 the Hungarian Communist authorities took a step that dramatically indicated their break with the past. In Budapest, under great official fanfare, the leader of the 1956 revolution, Imre Nagy, was reburied. Nagy, who had been executed after the Soviet invasion, stood for many as the symbol of Hungarian nationalism and resistance against Moscow's domination. Gorbachev had only gradually come around to reevaluating the events of 1956, but he let the Hungarians know that the Soviets had no objections. Already in February 1989 he had made it clear that the USSR was seeking "a restructuring of its relations with the socialist countries" that emphasized "unconditional independence, full equality, strict non-interference in internal affairs, and rectification of deformities and mistakes linked with earlier periods in the history of socialism."[8] Young Hungarians were out to test these intentions. Viktor Orbán, a twenty-five-year-old who spoke on behalf of the youth at Nagy's funeral, accused the Communists of having robbed young people of their future through their "blind obedience to the Russian empire and [to] the dictatorship of a single party."[9]

As late as the summer of 1989 Gorbachev remained convinced that his aim of a qualitatively new alliance among socialist states could be made a reality. He wanted a reconstituted socialist community, in which not only eastern Europe (including Yugoslavia) but also China could find a place. Although Sino-Soviet relations had improved during Gorbachev's time in power, he was, as usual, impatient, and wanted more of a breakthrough than his assistants had been able to give him with the skeptical Chinese. In 1989 he decided to go to China himself in order to normalize relations and get off to a new start through meeting with Deng Xiaoping. "One has to understand the Chinese," Gorbachev told the Politburo. "They have a right to become a great power." The Chinese were "getting stronger," the Soviet leader said. "Everyone can see it."[10]

Gorbachev was undoubtedly right that China was getting stronger as a result of Deng's economic reforms. But many of the most basic problems in Chinese society remained similar to those the Soviets were trying to deal with at home. After all, the People's Republic of China had been set up as almost a direct copy of the USSR. By the late 1980s many young Chinese were impatient for political and social reforms of the kind Gorbachev was attempting to carry out in the Soviet Union. They demanded freedom of speech and association, and deplored the corruption and inequality that had come with the new direction in the economy. Deng would have nothing of it. To him, reform meant strengthening, not weakening, the Communist Party's grip on power. In 1986 he had unceremoniously fired the party's general secretary, the popular Hu Yaobang, for having moved too far in allowing an open debate of China's problems. Students who protested were thrown in prison and workers who attempted to organize independently of the party were harassed.

When Hu Yaobang died suddenly in April 1989, student activists made his passing an occasion for lamenting the lack of democracy in China. But the small memorial gatherings they organized quickly turned into a broader protest against one-party dictatorship. By May large rallies staged by students, workers, and young professionals were taking place in the major cities, and protesters occupied the central square in Beijing, at Tian'anmen. Their slogans would not have been out of place in eastern Europe: Long live democracy! Patriotism is not criminal! Oppose corruption! We are the people! The Communist Party leadership hesitated on what to do. Deng wanted an immediate crackdown, but the new secretary general, Deng's protégé Zhao Ziyang, hoped to find a way of compromising with the protesters. Meanwhile, Mikhail Gorbachev arrived in Beijing on the first visit of a Soviet leader for more than thirty years.

Instead of being a stunning international triumph, the May 1989 visit turned into a quandary for the guests. With Tian'anmen off limits, the Soviet delegation had to be smuggled into the Great Hall of the People through a back entrance. From there, Gorbachev could hear the protesting students chanting his name. He sympathized with the protesters, but could not run the risk of criticizing his hosts. Instead he took refuge in platitudes, talking about the friendship between the Soviet and Chinese peoples. In private he wondered how long the Chinese Communists would remain in power. "Some of those present here," he told his colleagues in a meeting at the Soviet embassy on 15 May, "have promoted the idea of taking the Chinese road. We saw today where this road leads. I do not want Red Square to look like Tian'anmen Square."[11] Luckily for Gorbachev, his host was intent on compromise. The questions of the past, Deng said, somewhat lamely, were not "ideological disagreements. We were also wrong. . . . The Soviet Union incorrectly perceived China's place in the world. . . . The essence of all problems was that we were unequal, that we were subjected to coercion and pressure."[12]

With Gorbachev hurrying back to Moscow, Deng Xiaoping had cleared the deck for his assault. For his hesitation, the party leader Zhao Ziyang was dispatched in the same way as his predecessor: he was to spend the next fifteen years under house arrest. Drawing on his military connections, Deng made all the decisions. On 4 June tanks moved in to clear Tian'anmen Square. Hundreds of prodemocracy protesters were killed as troops occupied central Beijing. Thousands were imprisoned or went into exile. The new party leadership was handpicked by Deng and his associates. China's international status dropped considerably, but the country was too important to isolate entirely, especially for the Bush Administration, which still believed that it needed China to balance the USSR. Most importantly for the Americans, Deng may have crushed the democratic aspirations of his countrymen, but he was not about to give up on economic market reform. A couple of years later, at the age of eighty-eight, he went on a tour of the southern provinces and extolled their reformist zeal. "Are such things as securities and stocks good, do they cause danger, are they things unique to capitalism, can socialism make use of them?" he mused. "It is permissible to judge, but we must be resolute in having a try."[13]

In eastern Europe, however, economic reform was no longer enough to preserve Communist rule. Poland's first multiparty elections since the start of the Cold War were held on the same day as the crackdown in Beijing. The result was a disaster for the Communists, far beyond anything they or Moscow had imagined. Of all the 161 contested seats in the Sejm, Solidarity took 160. In the Senate, where all the seats were contested, they won 99 out of 100. The final seat went to an independent candidate. The Polish Communist Party, in power since 1945, was not just defeated but humiliated. It tried to put together a new government from its nominal majority in the Sejm, but allies and even party members began to desert the sinking ship. On 24 August 1989 the Communists capitulated, and the Sejm voted in a non-Communist government, headed by the Solidarity activist Tadeusz Mazowiecki. Everyone held their breath to see what the Soviet reaction would be to the Communists' loss of power.

But Gorbachev's position was already clear. In a speech to the Council of Europe after the Polish elections the Soviet leader reminded his astonished listeners that "the social and political orders of certain countries [in Europe] changed in the past, and may change again in the future. However, this is exclusively a matter for the peoples themselves to decide; it is their choice. Any interference in internal affairs, or any attempts to limit the sovereignty of states—including friends and allies, or anyone else—is impermissible."[14] His press spokesman, Gennadi Gerasimov, was even clearer: "We will maintain ties with any Polish government that emerges after the recent elections. This is purely a Polish internal affair. Any solution adopted by our Polish friends will be acceptable to us."[15] Gorbachev's chief foreign policy adviser, Anatolii Cherniaev, noted in his diary that he thought "a complete dismantling of socialism as a factor of world development is in process. Maybe this is inevitable and good. For this is a matter of humanity uniting on the basis of common sense. And this process was started by a regular guy from Stavropol."[16]

Both in western Europe and in the United States the reaction to events in Poland was one of disbelief. Nobody had expected that the Polish Communists would capitulate so fully or that Gorbachev would be the midwife for a non-Communist Poland. The Bush Administration's approach was, as usual, cautious. The president worried more about possible unrest that could lead to a backlash from the Red Army in Poland or against Gorbachev in the USSR than he did about assistance to the new Polish government, which western Europeans were pressing hard for. During his visit to Poland and Hungary in July 1989 Bush kept stressing the need for moderate and realistic aims, and underlined that what the United States could do to help was limited, not least financially. To some Europeans, east and west, it was all too much caution. "Bush, as a President, has a very big drawback," Mitterrand confided to Gorbachev, "he lacks original thinking altogether."[17]

But on some issues the western Europeans were cautious themselves. This was especially true for any issue that touched on the status of Germany. The settlement of borders in Europe as a result of World War II, including the borders that divided Germany, had kept the peace, some leaders believed. It had also been helpful to the sense of western Europe as a community of equals that West Germany had a not dissimilar population size to France, Britain, and Italy, even if it had a larger economy. As unrest began increasing in East Germany in early September 1989, both western and eastern European leaders, including Thatcher and Mitterrand, underlined to Gorbachev that German unification was not on the cards. Gorbachev agreed, but his main problem was the stability of East Germany. Its leader, Erich Honecker, had stubbornly refused to go along with any of the Soviet leader's tempered suggestions that reforms were needed. By the late summer of 1989 Gorbachev was losing patience with Honecker and his constant sniping at Gorbachev's own policies. The GDR had even started banning Soviet publications from entering the country. Gorbachev wanted Honecker replaced, but he could not express this wish openly for fear of destabilizing the entire East German state.

As it turned out, the citizens of East Germany were even more impatient with their leader. Throughout the summer of 1989 groups of East Germans had traveled to other eastern European countries in order to get to West Germany from there. On 19 August the Hungarian authorities, acting in part from humanitarian motives and in part in order to get West German loans, allowed 900 of these refugees to cross the border to Austria. Honecker was furious and accused the Hungarians of being traitors to socialism. But there was little he could do about it. Inside East Germany open defiance of the regime had begun to spread. In Leipzig, where the churches had organized groups around human rights and disarmament, demonstrations began in early September. First the slogan was "We Want to Leave." But then, almost unperceptively, it shifted to "Down with Stasi," "We Are Going Nowhere," and, unyieldingly and climactically, "We Are the People." Thousands were arrested and some were beaten up. But the protests continued.

The East German regime had nowhere to turn. Gorbachev despised most of the leaders there. The West, including West Germany, would not come to their rescue, even though Chancellor Helmut Kohl feared that Honecker could use massive force to stay in power. For a while a "Chinese solution" was indeed contemplated in East Berlin, but it was stranded on Gorbachev's known position and on increasing worries among younger Communist leaders that they could personally be held responsible for any bloodshed. Honecker still believed he could ride out the storm. But the upcoming fortieth anniversary of the GDR, which he had planned to celebrate with all pomp possible, put him in a difficult spot. It gave the opposition an aim for their mobilization. And, worse, it would bring Gorbachev to Berlin as the guest of honor, in the middle of Honecker's attempts at crushing the dissent.

As usual, Gorbachev avoided criticizing his hosts openly. The furthest he would go was in telling a TV reporter on 6 October that the "only danger is not to react to life itself." But it was clear to all who attended the closed-session meetings that Honecker did not have the Soviet leader's trust. After Gorbachev's visit the GDR police and military gave up trying to stop the demonstrators. At least 70,000 marched in Leipzig 9 October. A week later the number was 120,000. And a week after that more than 300,000. By then Honecker was gone, voted out by the Central Committee of his own party. The new party chief, Egon Krenz, promised negotiations with the opposition. He also made it clear that the East German authorities were preparing new and more liberal travel arrangements for its citizens to visit West Germany, including West Berlin. At a 9 November press conference, Günter Schabowski, the GDR government's chief spokesman, said it had already been decided that people with proper permission would be allowed to cross the border. Asked repeatedly when the new regulations would come into force, Schabowski finally said that he thought it would be "immediately, forthwith."

That evening thousands of jubilant East Berliners moved toward the checkpoints in the Wall, disregarding the need to apply for permission. At first, GDR border guards, having no instructions on how to handle the situation, tried to fend them off, threatening to shoot if the crowds surged forward. They then began letting the loudest protestors pass through individually and very slowly, in the hopes that doing so would reduce tension. But the crowds just grew and were pushing up against the Forbidden Zone around the checkpoints. Around 11:00 p.m., fearing for their own safety, the East German officers gave up and lifted the barriers.[18] Large groups of people began crossing from east to west without any documents whatsoever. That evening they embraced their surprised western countrymen along the main avenues in West Berlin. "What I will never forget is this," one East Berliner remembers. "The taste of my first strawberry yoghurt! It tasted so good that I lived on it for a week!"[19] Already the next morning some enterprising Berliners began hacking away at the Wall itself. East German guards tried to chase them away for another few days. But by the end of the following week the guards themselves were seen dismantling parts of the Wall. One of the most shameful symbols of the Cold War was nearing its end.

The accidental opening of the Berlin Wall was, literally, the main breakthrough in the miraculous year 1989. With the Wall down, relations between East and West Germany were certain to be transformed. How far and how fast nobody could tell, but there was no way things could stay the way they had been before. People and policy-makers on both sides of the Iron Curtain began to imagine very different kinds of futures. Almost everyone celebrated the opportunities, but there were also concerns. For all its drawbacks and human costs, the Cold War international system had kept the peace in Europe for almost fifty years. People born in 1900 had seen two cataclysmic wars, in which more than sixty million Europeans died. People born fifty years later had seen none.

The end of the Cold War in Europe first and foremost meant an opportunity to end the German problem. The Cold War had kept Germany divided, against the wishes of most of its population. The opening of the Berlin Wall foretold some ending of that abnormal situation. But European leaders were wary of Germany's size and its economic power, especially if unified. For the leaders in the European Community, except Thatcher, who was profoundly skeptical of Germany reuniting at all, the solution had to be further European integration. Within a deeper form of community, which would make nation-states parts of a European political, economic, and monetary union, Germany's strengths would be Europe's strength. Helmut Kohl agreed. In a speech to the Bundestag in November 1989, where he launched a ten-point plan for German unity, Kohl stressed Germany's essential European-ness: "The future architecture of Germany must fit into the future architecture of Europe. . . . Linking the German question to the development of Europe as a whole . . . makes possible an organic development that takes into account the interests of everyone involved"[20]

The Single European Act, which had come into force in the European Community in 1987, was the most ambitious expansion of the integration process for thirty years. The agreement committed the members to move toward a full European Union, with all tariffs and border controls removed, and with free movement of goods, people, services, and capital. The Union would also aim for a common monetary policy and help coordinate common foreign and defense policies. It was a big step, which helped reduce concern with an overmighty Germany sitting astride Europe and pointed toward the Maastricht agreement of 1992. "Economic and monetary union will be a linchpin in favor of political integration," insisted France's president, François Mitterrand. "It will mean that a decisive step will have been taken toward achieving a real union—that is, a European political union."[21]

The French president was probably among the first European leaders who realized that some form of German unification would be impossible to avoid. But he wanted to get the maximum in return, for himself and for France, in order to agree to such a rearrangement. He therefore played on Thatcher's doubt about German reunification in order, later, to act as mediator on behalf of the Germans. This scheme, Mitterrand thought, would connect a unified Germany even more closely to France and help deliver French aims, such as monetary union and stronger political integration. "The sudden prospect of reunification had delivered a sort of mental shock to the Germans. Its effect had been to turn them once again into the 'bad' Germans they used to be," the French president told Thatcher in January 1990. "He had said to [Kohl] that no doubt Germany could if it wished achieve reunification, bring Austria into the European Community and even regain other territories which it had lost as a result of the war. They might make even more ground than had Hitler. But they would have to bear in mind the implications."[22]

The devious Mitterrand had of course said no such thing. In public, as in private to the West German leaders, he had from the very beginning stressed Germany's right to self-determination.[23] What really limited the significance of the French president's scheming, however, was George Bush's surprisingly clear and immediate support of Kohl's policies. Already in November 1989 Bush had told the German leader that he was "very supportive of your general approach. . . . We are on the same wavelength. I appreciated your ten points and your exposition on the future of Germany."[24] More importantly, Bush told both the US public and members of his own Administration not to fear German unification. And already by February 1990 he instructed his secretary of state, James Baker, that the US aim was "a unified Germany in the Western alliance."[25] The US president's position left Thatcher fuming on the sidelines and Kohl free to develop his policy for unification. The big question was how Mikhail Gorbachev would react to the German plans.

While East Germany was collapsing, the onslaught against the other eastern European Communist regimes continued. The Hungarian regime, which had been one of the forerunners for reform, avoided further protest by simply dissolving the Communist Party and the People's Republic already in October 1989. The party was reborn as the Socialist Party, within a reconstituted Republic of Hungary. The new government set May 1990 as the month for Hungary's first free elections for over forty years. The reaction in the Kremlin, so different from 1956, was simply to congratulate the Hungarian party with its courage and foresight. Soviet foreign minister Shevardnadze declared that "each country has the right to absolute freedom of choice."[26]

In Czechoslovakia, where the regime had resisted reform for as long as it could, the end was different but synchronous. Being burdened with the responsibility for the crackdown after the Soviet invasion in 1968, the Communist Party was even more unpopular in Czechoslovakia than elsewhere in eastern Europe. The man who had been in charge of the persecution, Gustáv Husák, had been forced to resign as party leader in 1987, in part because he was personally anathema to Gorbachev. But the leaders who replaced him were entirely hapless, especially Miloš Jakeš, the new general secretary, whose bumbling speeches were the cause of much mirth across the country. A week after the Berlin Wall had come down, demonstrations against the government broke out in Prague. They soon spread to others parts of the country. Prominent intellectuals, among them the playwright Václav Havel, who had several times been imprisoned for dissent, formed a Civic Forum, which demanded talks with the regime. Journalists took over some of the newspapers and began spreading the message of the opposition, including calling for a general strike. Jakeš and some members of the party leadership wanted to use the police and military against the demonstrators, but found that they could not be trusted. On 24 November Jakeš and the entire party presidium resigned, and the new leaders began negotiating with the opposition.

The next day it became clear that the balance of power in Czechoslovakia had changed forever. In Prague alone, eight hundred thousand people marched against the Communist Party, chanting slogans such as "We Want Democracy," "Back to Europe," and "Havel for President." Alexander Dubček, the party leader who had been forced out by the Soviets after 1968, joined with the demonstrators. In speeches both in his native Slovakia and in Prague, Dubček called for change and nonviolence. "If there once was light, why should there be darkness again?" Dubček told the crowds. "Let us act . . . to bring back the light."[27] On 29 November the Czechoslovak Federal Assembly, still dominated by Communists, voted to introduce multiparty democracy. A month later the same assembly voted in the former dissident Václav Havel as new president of the country. A whole generation of Communist officials slunk away into the shadows. In his first speech as president, Havel gave his harsh verdict on what Czechoslovakia's "velvet revolution" had inherited: "Our country is not flourishing. The enormous creative and spiritual potential of our nations is not being used sensibly. Entire branches of industry are producing goods that are of no interest to anyone, while we are lacking the things we need.

A state which calls itself a workers' state humiliates and exploits workers. Our obsolete economy is wasting the little energy we have available. . . . We have polluted the soil, rivers and forests bequeathed to us by our ancestors, and we have today the most contaminated environment in Europe." The only solution, Havel said, was to create "a republic of well-rounded people, because without such people it is impossible to solve any of our problems—human, economic, ecological, social, or political."[28]

In Bulgaria the end of Communism came in a different way, and more slowly. The poorest of the East Bloc countries, Bulgaria had benefitted more than any of the others from exchanges among them. Even in the 1980s, many Bulgarians saw Communism as a relatively successful development program, even though they resented the authoritarianism and oppression of the government. Most Bulgarians also felt a distinct kinship with the Russians for cultural and historical reasons. With Gorbachev in power in Moscow, this sense of closeness could lead to unexpected results, though. On 10 November, one day after the fall of the Berlin Wall, younger Communist leaders ousted party head Todor Zhivkov for his failure to instigate Gorbachev-style reforms. Zhivkov had lead the party for more than thirty-five years. He was a father figure for many Bulgarians and not widely hated like a Husak or a Jaruzelski. The new leaders wanted to build on the successes of Bulgarian socialism, while moving closer to the European Community, and position themselves to remain in power after a multiparty system had been introduced.

The Bulgarian Communists succeeded to a remarkable degree with their plans, though they did so by nefarious means. By initiating roundtable negotiations along the Polish model, they bought time so that the party could reconstitute itself as a Socialist Party in time for the first free elections in June 1990. Uniquely in the former Soviet bloc, the former Bulgarian Communists not only won the first free election but helped oversee the transition to a new market-based economic system. But a main reason for their success was an unprecedented Communist campaign to force Muslim Bulgarians to give up their identity and take Christian names. Starting in 1984, Zhivkov's regime had prohibited the use of Turkish in public and closed many mosques. In 1989, as it came under pressure, the Communist Party began forcibly deporting Muslim activists to Turkey. Several people were killed in clashes with the police. In the panic that followed at least three hundred thousand Bulgarian Muslims were expelled or fled across the border. It linked the Communist Party with Bulgarian nationalism and foreshadowed the terrible crimes that would happen further west in the Balkans a few years later.

Even worse violence took place in Romania, as the Communist Party there tried to cling on to power. The Romanian leader Nicolae Ceaușescu prided himself on his country's independence from Moscow. Although nominally a member of the Warsaw Pact, Romania had condemned the invasion of Czechoslovakia in 1968 and later criticized Soviet involvement in the Horn of Africa and in the Middle East. Romanian insubordination was of course welcomed in the West, and Ceaușescu was rewarded with access to Western technology and invitations to foreign capitals. In 1978 the increasingly erratic dictator was even granted a visit with Queen Elizabeth at Buckingham Palace—having been tipped off in advance, the palace staff reportedly removed all valuables from the guest rooms so that Ceaușescu and his wife Elena would not bring them back to their poverty-stricken country. For while Ceaușescu was being feted abroad, Romania was falling deeper and deeper into destitution, not least because their leader insisted on spending enormous amounts on gigantic vanity projects, such as the construction of the world's largest parliament building in the capital, Bucharest.

Ceaușescu believed he was safe from the sort of upheavals that happened elsewhere in eastern Europe in the fall of 1989, since his regime was not dependent on Soviet support. But Romanians were running out of patience. Living standards had declined for more than a decade and shortages were acute. Besides Albania, Romania's GDP was the lowest in Europe, roughly on a par with Jordan or Jamaica. And Ceaușescu's insistence on being treated like a godlike figure even by other Communist Party leaders made some of them long to get rid of him. The end therefore came quickly when it came. After a week's unrest in the city of Timişoara, Ceauşescu addressed the people of Bucharest in front of his new Parliament building. At first things looked normal. Hundreds of people were holding up posters with Ceauşescu's portrait, as they always had done at such events. The party leader saluted the revolutionary courage of the capital's population. Then:

> **CEAUŞESCU:** I also want to thank the initiators and organizers of this great event from Bucharest, considering it as a . . . , as a. . . .
>
> **CROWD:** Ti-mi-şoa-ra! Ti-mi-şoa-ra!
>
> **BODYGUARD:** Move back into the office, sir.
>
> **CEAUŞESCU:** What? No, wait.
>
> **BODYGUARD:** Why are they screaming?
>
> **CROWD:** We want bread!
>
> **ELENA** Ceauşescu, to crowd: Silence!
>
> **CEAUŞESCU:** Hallo!
>
> **CROWD:** Down with Ceauşescu!
>
> **ELENA:** Silence!
>
> **CEAUŞESCU,** to Elena: Hush! Shut up!
>
> **CEAUŞESCU:** Comrades! Sit down quietly![29]

All of this was in front of live microphones and therefore broadcast to the whole country.

Fighting broke out around the square and engulfed the city overnight. Nobody could quite say who was fighting whom because some military units joined the protesters. Hundreds of people were killed. There were rumors of snipers from Ceauşescu's dreaded secret police, the Securitate, firing on people from rooftops. The next morning the crowds stormed the Central Committee building, where the Ceauşescus had been hiding out. But they had already fled by helicopter. On landing in a small town 75 kilometers northwest of Bucharest, the president and his wife were taken prisoner by the local military. On Christmas Day 1989 they were both shot after a summary trial. The film of their trial is a sad sight: an elderly, bewildered couple who do not quite understand what is happening to them. As the verdict is read, they ask to be executed together. Communist Romania ended, as it had begun, in blood.

While eastern Europe liberated itself, the Soviet and the US leaders finally met for a proper summit, on ships anchored at Malta in the Mediterranean in December 1989. At their first meeting, onboard the Soviet ship *Maksim Gorkii*, Bush and Gorbachev agreed that the Cold War was over. But they drew different conclusions as to what that meant. For Bush, it seemed as if removing the USSR as a consistent adversary simply freed the United States to get more of what it wanted elsewhere. To Gorbachev's amazement, in view of the historic changes in Europe, one of Bush's main points was to end Soviet support for Nicaragua (and hopefully also for Cuba). It seemed as if to the US president the Cold War had simply returned to where it had been before World War II—a global ideological struggle, rather than a conflict between two Superpowers. For the Soviet president, the stakes were much higher. This was principally because he faced a battle for reform inside the USSR. But it was also because he believed that the world was turning away from what had produced the Cold War. "We see today that reliance on force, on military superiority, was wrong," Gorbachev told Bush.

> It did not justify itself. . . . The emphasis on confrontation based on our different ideologies is wrong. We had reached a dangerous point, and it is good that we stopped to reach an understanding. Reliance on nonequal exchange between the developed countries and the developing world cannot go on. It has collapsed. Look at how many problems there are in the developing world that affect all of us. Overall, my conclusion is that strategically and philosophically, the methods of the Cold War were defeated . . . [though] we face problems of survival, including the environment and problems of resources.[30]

At Malta, the two sides agreed to intensify arms control negotiations, consult on German questions, and open up for increased trade and technological exchanges. The summit went off well. But it was also clear that the two men had less to talk about than at earlier Soviet-American summits. The Cold War international system was fading fast. Gorbachev was facing the battle of his life in reforming and uniting the Soviet Union, while transitioning it to a democratic form of government. There is no doubt that Bush genuinely wished him well in that enterprise. Bush believed that the United States had won the inter-state Cold War, and his inherent caution made him disinclined to believe that high levels of conflict inside the USSR at this stage would necessarily be to the US advantage. Some of his advisers thought that only the breakup of the Soviet Union would mean a final end to the Cold War. But the president was not on their side. Bush, as always, preferred stability over any kind of risk-taking.

When Gorbachev returned to Moscow, problems were piling up. In the Caucasus, the Soviet republic of Azerbaijan was blockading the Soviet republic of Armenia, creating massive economic dislocation. In the Baltic states, the demand for independence was getting increasingly vocal. In August 1989 people across Estonia, Latvia, and Lithuania joined hands, quite literally, and formed the longest human chain ever. They sang songs of freedom and independence, and of telling the truth about history. "Three sisters woke up from their sleep, now come to stand for themselves," went one of them.[31] In Moscow, the CPSU Central Committee condemned what they called mindless nationalism. But even the Communists in the Baltic states understood which way the wind was blowing. In December 1989, just after Gorbachev returned from the Malta summit, the Lithuanian Communist Party broke with the CPSU and asserted its full independence. Like in eastern Europe, the Baltic Communists had begun to believe that the only way they could remain relevant was by joining the national revolution.

Given the high level of nationalist agitation that took place in some of the European and Caucasian republics, many CPSU leaders advised Gorbachev to postpone the free elections that he had promised they would hold in 1990. But Gorbachev held firm. He feared that taking a step back now would lead to him losing control over the CPSU at the central union level. To his advisers, Gorbachev explained that only if he could play the democrats against the party apparatus did he stand a chance of success. It was clear that he did not fully trust his own party any longer. In the Baltic republics the elections went as could be expected. In all of them non-Communist parties won. These parties then proceeded to do what they had promised their electorate: to assert national independence. Lithuania went first and furthest. In March 1990 its elected Supreme Soviet reconstituted itself as the Supreme Council, which promptly declared that "the sovereign powers of the State of Lithuania, abolished by foreign forces in 1940, is reestablished, and henceforth Lithuania is again an independent state."[32] Nobody in the council voted against the declaration of independence. Two weeks later the Estonian assembly proclaimed the Soviet occupation of their country illegal, and the Latvians followed suit in May 1990. Gorbachev had a very big challenge on his hands.

Gorbachev's aim in 1990 was to force the CPSU, the party of which he was still the general secretary, to give up its monopoly on power. The Soviet leader was in many ways inspired by the events in eastern Europe. He wanted democracy, but he also wanted a strong Communist Party capable of winning elections and defending the achievements of the socialist era. He wanted to devolve power to the republics, but keep the USSR united as a state. On the economy, he wanted foreign loans to help the country back on its feet, and the introduction of gradual market reforms. Remarkably, Gorbachev seemed politically deaf to just how much damage the economic deterioration did to his ability to the lead the Soviet Union. He believed that political reform and the new sense of freedom all over the USSR would make up for the absence of consumer goods, at least in the short term.

On this the Soviet leader was almost certainly wrong. The more Soviet citizens learned about how far behind other countries they were in terms of what they could buy in their shops and markets, the more they blamed Gorbachev and the CPSU leadership for it. Opinions polls, freely conducted in the USSR for the first time, showed that a massive majority of citizens believed that things were getting more difficult and that the weakest were suffering the consequences. Outside of the cities, very few people joined in the political ferment.

"We didn't pay much attention," said one villager from Volgoda. "Our kolkhoz director would tell us that perestroika and glasnost were important, but why would we believe him? We watched the rallies and speeches on television, but it was nothing to do with our lives."[33]

Meanwhile, in Moscow Gorbachev was facing increasing challenges, even after the Congress of People's Deputies elected him president of the USSR in March 1990. In the new assembly, opinions were strongly divided between liberals, who believed that Gorbachev was moving too slowly, and conservatives, who thought he was moving too fast. Inside the Communist Party apparatus, many were horrified at how easily Gorbachev had let eastern Europe go and feared that he would also give up on keeping the Soviet Union together. In the Russian Republic, one of the fifteen constituent republics of the USSR, liberal reformers had the upper hand in the republic's assembly after the elections in the spring of 1990, but, instead of supporting Gorbachev, they elected Boris Yeltsin chairman. Yeltsin engineered a Russian declaration of sovereignty, in which the biggest of the republics, covering three quarters of Soviet territory, declared that the laws of the Russian Republic took precedence over Soviet laws. Yeltsin then in a dramatic speech resigned from the Communist Party of the USSR. At the time, many thought that all of this was mainly showmanship on the part of the flamboyant Yeltsin. But over the months that followed, with other republics following Russia's example, the issue of Soviet legitimacy became more and more complicated.

At first Gorbachev stood firm. He refused to accept independence for Lithuania or claims of full sovereignty for republics elsewhere. In 1989 the Red Army had used force to break up nationalist demonstrations in Georgia. Twenty people were killed. In January 1990, after months of unrest and ethnic clashes between Azeris and Armenians, Soviet special forces took control of the Azerbaijan capital of Baku against strong Azeri nationalist opposition. The Soviet minister of defense, Dmitrii Iazov, personally directed the operations. At least 130 civilians were killed, along with 30 Red Army soldiers. The bloody crackdown did little to stem Azerbaijan's drift toward asserting its national sovereignty. But it did, at least temporarily, strengthen Gorbachev's hand against party hard-liners in the Kremlin.

The image of Gorbachev as a hapless victim of events after the Communist collapse in eastern Europe does not hold up to scrutiny. Gorbachev had *wanted* the democratization of the eastern European countries and the removal of the Iron Curtain. He also wanted the democratization of the Soviet Union along lines similar to what was happening further west. In the summer of 1990 he made his views clear in a speech to the Twenty-eighth Congress of the Communist Party:

> In place of the Stalinist model of socialism we are coming to a citizens' society of free people. The political system is being transformed radically, genuine democracy with free elections, the existence of many parties and human rights is becoming established and real people's power is being revived. . . . The transformation of the super-centralised state into a true union state founded on self-determination and the voluntary unity of the peoples has begun. In place of an atmosphere of ideological dictatorship we have come to freedom of thought and glasnost and openness about information in society.[34]

But Gorbachev did not just trust his ideals. As events in Georgia and Azerbaijan showed, he still had the loyalty of the Red Army both when he wanted to use force and when he did not want to use it. Subservience to the country's political leadership was so deeply engrained in the Soviet military that they did not question orders, nor did they assume political responsibilities on their own. The same was true for the KGB. But that organization was increasingly split. Some old-timers, such as KGB chairman Vladimir Kriuchkov, put the preservation of the USSR above all other duties. A younger generation of secret police officers realized both that change was inevitable and that they had skills and information that would serve them well as individuals whatever the outcome of the political struggles at the top. By late 1990 a number of them were in touch with managers of enterprises planning to privatize or with foreigners hoping to invest in a new economy.

Gorbachev's main problem was therefore not disloyalty in the "ministries of power" but the political contest going on within the Soviet leadership. As CPSU general secretary he was increasingly caught between two groups. His liberal advisers—Aleksandr Iakovlev, Georgii Shakhnazarov, Anatolii Cherniaev, and others—wanted him to ditch the Communist Party, call a snap union-wide presidential election, and contest it as a democratic socialist. The top members of his government, the Defense Ministry, and the KGB wanted him to reinstall discipline in the Communist Party and crush the national independence movements. Gorbachev was caught in the middle. He would not give up on the CPSU because he believed it was still key to holding the union together. If not the CPSU, what is there, he challenged his more impatient acolytes. At the same time, he refused to give permission for an all-out assault against the nationalists in the republics. He was willing to authorize crackdowns, but only when ethnic violence or a chance for real secession demanded it. Massive bloodshed was not on the agenda.

In international affairs Gorbachev's main strategy from 1990 on was to link the Soviet Union more closely to Europe. Like his liberal advisers, he had always seen the Soviet future in Europe, and the liberation of eastern Europe had made a closer connection with the main European countries possible. Gorbachev spoke often, and well, about "a common European home, from the Atlantic to the Urals," a Gaullist phrase that was intended to appeal to European self-interest in assisting the Soviet transformation. But the Soviet leader knew that the realization of such a concept was inconceivable without a solution to the German problem. Not only was West Germany the major economic power in Europe, but East Germany still stood as a constant reminder of a failed Soviet European policy, in which it had busied itself building walls across the continent instead of tearing them down.

By February 1990 Mikhail Gorbachev had concluded that some form of German unification was inevitable, and that the USSR would be best served by playing a positive role in the process. What made the undertaking speed up beyond what most observers, including most German observers, had imagined possible was the combined effect of the breakdown in the East German economy and the elections there in March 1990. With access to West German products they deemed superior, few people in the east wanted to buy eastern goods anymore. Production stalled. Still, the more expensive consumer items from the west were unobtainable for East Germans because their money was near worthless when exchanged for the deutschmark. In the election more than 40 percent of East Germans voted for Kohl's CDU—a party that had nearly no base in the east—simply because they thought doing so would speed up unification. The result astonished Europe. With the same party now ruling both East and West Germany, it was clear that unification was not an issue for the future. It was an issue for the here and now.

With Britain's Margaret Thatcher indignant on the sidelines, all western European leaders fell in step behind President Bush and West German *Bundeskanzler* Helmut Kohl in starting an international process to agree to the conditions for Germany's full reunification. The so-called "Two-Plus-Four" negotiations (the two Germanies plus the victorious Great Powers from World War II) began in May 1990, with the real sticking points being whether a united Germany could be a member of NATO and the pace and format of the actual unification procedures. To the surprise of the Western powers (and to the dismay of the British and to some extent the French), Gorbachev agreed not only to a united Germany in NATO but also to the process being completed within the year. West German promises of further economic assistance to the USSR helped pave the way. But even more significant was Gorbachev's conviction that NATO or Germany were no longer enemies of the Soviets. They were friends and partners. In their meeting in July 1990 near Stavropol, where Gorbachev was born, Kohl put it well: "One may not forget history.

For without a knowledge of history the present could not be understood nor the future be shaped. Most of those present at this table roughly belonged to his generation—they had still experienced the war as children, too young to become guilty, but old enough to understand. It was the task of this generation to settle some things at the end of this century before passing the baton on to the next generation."[35]

Emotional as he was about unification and a new German-Russian relationship, Kohl did not neglect creating facts on the ground to make the unification process irreversible. In the summer of 1990 the deutschmark was made the official currency of East Germany and a full "monetary, economic, and social union" between the two states came into being. West German laws were gradually introduced in East Germany, and in August the East German parliament made a formal request to the West German government to be incorporated into the Federal Republic of Germany. Kohl knew such brisk moves would raise criticism even among his Western allies. But he felt it was a risk worth taking. There were still hundreds of thousands of Soviet soldiers stationed in East Germany. If something happened to Gorbachev, Kohl needed to be able to deal with whatever government replaced him in Moscow.

Right up to the final negotiations in Moscow in September 1990 it was unclear whether all of Germany would be NATO territory and whether Germany would regain its full sovereignty immediately upon reunification. The British, truculent to the finish, insisted on the right of allied NATO troops to enter what would soon be the former East Germany, knowing that the Soviets would turn this down. The veteran West German foreign minister Hans-Dietrich Genscher would have nothing of these tactics. Himself born in eastern Germany, Genscher wanted no delay in reunification. He insisted on an immediate agreement and on full German sovereignty. Working with the Soviets and the French, Genscher pushed back on the British demands. In the end, the parties agreed to a last-minute fudge: non-German troops would not be permanently stationed or deployed in the east, but the definition of the term "deployed" would be decided by the German government, "in a reasonable and responsible way, taking into consideration the security interests" of each of the powers.[36] On 12 September 1990 the Two-Plus-Four Treaty was signed, opening for German unification three weeks later. Even the seasoned diplomat Genscher was moved at the signing: "This is a historic moment for the whole of Europe and a happy one for the Germans. Together we have come a long way in a short time. . . . On 3 October we Germans will again be living in one democratic state, for the first time in 57 years. . . . [Now] we want nothing more than to live in freedom, democracy and peace with all other nations."[37]

But if German unification seemed almost a miracle in its simplicity and smoothness, trouble was brewing elsewhere in Europe. A bit like in the Soviet Union, the republics of the Yugoslav federation had been drifting apart for several years. But even inside the bigger republics there were ethnic tensions. In Albanian-majority Kosovo, then a part of the Yugoslav Serbian republic, Albanian miners went on strike in 1989 to demand more rights for their community. The Kosovo miners were supported by non-Communist nationalist groups in the Yugoslav republics of Slovenia and Croatia farther north. In Serbia, the leader of the Communist Party there, Slobodan Milošević, saw the Kosovo demands as yet another attempt at undermining Serbia's position within Yugoslavia. In a 1989 speech he condemned those who wanted to split Yugoslavia and claimed that the Serbs had sacrificed more than others to keep the country free and united. The concessions "the Serbian leaders made at the expense of their people could not be accepted historically and ethically by any nation in the world, especially because the Serbs have never in the whole of their history conquered and exploited others."[38]

But Milošević could not stem the centrifugal forces in Yugoslavia. On the contrary, his own nationalist rhetoric contributed to them. In January 1990 the Slovenian and Croatian Communist parties broke away from the Communist Party of Yugoslavia. In April free elections in both republics led to non-Communist majorities. In Serbia, on the other hand, Milošević and the now rump Communist Party solidified their hold on power. The scene was set for a showdown. In December

1990 a referendum in Slovenia delivered a 95 percent vote for independence. In Croatia nationalists also won an independence referendum, but substantial non-Croat minorities, among them the fifth of the population who were of Serbian origin, boycotted the vote. When Slovenia and Croatia, with encouragement from a newly reunited Germany, declared full independence the following year, the scene was set for the Yugoslav wars, which devastated the former federal republic over the next ten years. At least 140,000 people died and several million were displaced in the worst warfare in Europe since World War II, wars that the new European institutions altogether failed to stop.

In Moscow Gorbachev was battling on to avoid a similar fate for the Soviet Union. After the deal on Germany, he hoped that West German credits and international political support would help him stabilize the situation internally in the Soviet Union. But until the economy stabilized, Gorbachev's plan was to hold the Communist Party together through compromises with party traditionalists and with moderate nationalists in the republics. The new CPSU Politburo, elected at the Twenty-eighth Party Congress in the summer of 1990, was a mix of the two groups, with very few of the general secretary's reformist allies onboard. In December 1990, after Gorbachev picked the conservative nonentity Gennadii Ianaev as his vice president, Foreign Minister Shevardnadze resigned, publicly accusing Gorbachev of leading the country back toward a dictatorship. In a rambling speech, Shevardnadze claimed that "nobody knows what this dictatorship will be like, what kind of dictator will come to power and what kind of order will be established."[39] Shevardnadze's resignation was a hard blow for Gorbachev. The two had worked together to implement perestroika since Gorbachev's election in 1985. And, worse, the foreign minister was followed out the door in early 1991 by many other reformers, who either resigned or were thrown out by the new party leadership.

In the Russian Republic the increasingly populist Boris Yeltsin made promises of improved services and a better economy if, and only if, Russia took more power for itself within the union. Entirely free from the pressures of compromise and incumbency that dogged Gorbachev, Yeltsin could promise all things to all men, but he was also a shrewd politician who knew that he needed to solidify his position within Russia in preparation for whatever upheavals were to come within the Soviet state. In neighboring Ukraine, the second-largest of the Slavic republics in the USSR, the leader of its parliament Leonid Kravchuk had similar thoughts. Still a member of the Communist Party, Kravchuk was far less willing to attack the Soviet Union than Yeltsin was. But even he had accepted Ukraine's declaration of full sovereignty in the summer of 1990, a month after Russia. In November the two had signed a separate pact of mutual support and friendship. And when Gorbachev again attempted to use force in the Baltics in January 1991, the leaders of Russia and Ukraine protested jointly. Yeltsin went to Tallinn, the capital of Estonia, where in usual dramatic fashion he recognized the independence of the Baltic republics and exhorted Russian Red Army soldiers to disobey orders from the Kremlin. In Moscow more than one hundred thousand people marched in support of independence for the Balts.

Besides using the Red Army, Gorbachev had one final method by which he hoped to keep the union together. That was to appeal directly to the people in a referendum. In March 1991, against much resistance among his advisers, both liberal and conservative, he went to the country with the following question: "Do you consider necessary the preservation of the Union of Soviet Socialist Republics as a renewed federation of equal sovereign republics in which the rights and freedom of an individual of any nationality will be fully guaranteed?" It was, to put it mildly, a leading question, and not surprisingly the Balts, the Georgians, and the Armenians refused to participate. But the results in the other republics were still a massive popular vote for the union, with "yes" collecting more than three-quarters of the votes. In Russia 73 percent voted in favor of the union, which perhaps was not surprising given that Russia had constituted the USSR in the first place. But votes in Ukraine (71 percent yes) and in Central Asia (between 95 and 98 percent yes) were surprises, and gave Gorbachev hope as he worked over the summer on revising the union treaty in line with the referendum question.

The Cold War's central logic had been that one of the Superpowers had to lose for the other to win. For many US leaders this had in reality meant that there could be no lasting peace in the Cold War until the Soviet Union had ceased to exist. But in 1991, as the scenario of a Soviet collapse stopped being entirely implausible, the cautious George H. W. Bush quickly moved away from believing that the end of the USSR would in fact be in the US interest. Gorbachev's Soviet Union was of course already a very different state from that of Stalin. But the real issue was with new challenges arising, also for the United States, as the Cold War receded. In January 1991 the Americans had gone to war against Iraq in response to Saddam Hussein's invasion of Kuwait. Even though he worked hard to avoid war through an Iraqi withdrawal—Iraq was after all an old Soviet ally—Gorbachev sided almost completely with the United States as soon as US operations in the Gulf began. "Our doubts, yours and mine, about Saddam Hussein have proven right," he told President Bush. "He is the kind of person against whom force is necessary. I have a full understanding of this burden to the nations of the world."[40]

After the US victory in the Gulf War, Bush's attention was even more taken by the need for some degree of Soviet stability to help the United States tackle international crises and prevent the spread of weapons of mass destruction. Bush began to consider seriously what might happen to Soviet nuclear arsenals if conflict spread inside the USSR. He therefore cold-shouldered Yeltsin and some of the more extreme of Gorbachev's opponents, even after Yeltsin had been elected president by the people of the Russian Republic in June 1991. During a visit to the Ukrainian capital, Kiev, at the beginning of August, Bush spoke to the Ukrainian parliament, which the previous year had declared Ukraine a sovereign republic. "We will maintain the strongest possible relationship with the Soviet Government of President Gorbachev," Bush told the Ukrainians. "Freedom is not the same as independence. Americans will not support those who seek independence in order to replace a far-off tyranny with a local despotism." Bush hoped that the Soviet "Republics will combine greater autonomy with greater voluntary interaction—political, social, cultural, economic— rather than pursuing the hopeless course of isolation."[41] Nationalist Ukrainians were flabbergasted and angry, and in Washington conservatives referred to Bush's address as the "Chicken Kiev speech." But for the US president Soviet dissolution now seemed more dangerous than Soviet power, with the potential for civil and interstate wars breaking out on a vast scale across Eurasia. That these fears were not realized is something we now take for granted, but it was not necessarily the case that the Soviet bloc would on the whole avoid the eventual fate of Yugoslavia.

As Gorbachev prepared to put his signature to the new union treaty, he had reason to be cautiously optimistic about the future of his balancing act. Gorbachev thought that it would all come down to the economy: with the union secured within a new framework, gradual economic reform would proceed, helped by European, American, and Asian investments. Gorbachev foresaw a future split in the Communist Party, both at the union and the republic levels, with himself leading an all-union socialist party that he hoped would compete successfully within a democratic system. On 4 August 1991 the general secretary went on vacation to the Crimea, as he had done every year since he came to office. He expected to finish his work on the new union treaty while there.

Two weeks later Moscow awoke to news that a nationwide state of emergency had been declared. Gorbachev, said the news bulletins, had gone on sick leave. In his place, a government committee, headed by Vice President Ianaev, was in charge. Muscovites, and the whole country, had little doubt that there had been a coup d'état. In Moscow, citizens took to the streets, meeting in front of the Russian parliament building, where Yeltsin and his advisers had barricaded themselves. Censorship was reintroduced and leaders of the opposition arrested by the KGB. Paratroopers took up positions at key intersections.

In reality Gorbachev was kept prisoner in his Crimean dacha. The day before the coup was announced, a delegation, including his own chief of staff, had been sent by the plotters to demand his acquiescence to their plans. Gorbachev had refused. He had known that the KGB and the military had been preparing plans to crack down on unrest in the republics, but had never thought they would act against him. With Gorbachev's refusal, the plotters' plans started to go awry even before they had been announced. In the late afternoon on the day of the coup, the commander of a tank battalion sent to disperse the crowds in front of the Russian parliament declared his loyalty to the Russian Republic. Yeltsin climbed on top of one of the tanks and denounced the takeover. "We are dealing with a rightist, reactionary, anti-constitutional coup," Yeltsin shouted. "Such methods of force are unacceptable. They . . . return us to the Cold War era along with the Soviet Union's isolation in the world community. . . . I call on all Russians to give a dignified answer to the putschists and demand that the country be returned to normal constitutional order."[42] It was his finest hour. Some of his aides commented, not incorrectly, that it was the role Yeltsin was born to play.

From then on everything went wrong for the coup-makers. The Moscow curfew they tried to impose was not observed. More and more barricades went up in the capital. Military units were reluctant to follow orders. The KGB hesitated. Leaders in the republics did not return their calls. From inside the Russian parliament—the Belyi Dom, or White House, as it was called in Russian—Boris Yeltsin organized the resistance. He announced the setting up of Russian, as distinct from Soviet, armed forces and appointed himself commander in chief. On the third day the members of the government committee simply gave up. Some flew to the Crimea to meet with Gorbachev, who greeted them with ice-cold contempt. Others simply slunk away and were later arrested by the police. Boris Pugo, the interior minister, and his wife committed suicide, as did Gorbachev's chief military aide, Marshal Sergei Akhromeev, who had offered his services to the committee.

Gorbachev flew back to Moscow on a plane sent by the Russian leaders. His mood was grim. His wife, Raisa, his closest friend and ally, had collapsed during their incarceration, suffering from hypertension. He thought about all those whom he had appointed to high office who had betrayed him. On arrival he went home to make sure Raisa was properly looked after. It was a very human thing to do, but it was a dreadful political mistake. It disappointed his supporters who had put their lives on the line for him, and allowed Yeltsin to take political control of Moscow. The Russian president worked through the night. When Gorbachev reported for duty the next day, Russia was already taking over the USSR.

Yeltsin's first order was to suspend all activities of the CPSU on Russian territory. Party offices were closed and the Central Committee building in Moscow sealed. Its archives and documents were taken over by Yeltsin loyalists. The head of the KGB, Vladimir Kriuchkov, who had been among the coup-plotters, was arrested and the KGB was later dissolved. Hundreds of KGB officers inside the headquarters at Lubianka first thought the angry crowds would storm the building. Instead Muscovites were diverted by the sight of cranes, ordered there by Yeltsin, dismembering the statue of Feliks Dzherzhinskii, the founder of the secret police, in the square outside. In the Kremlin Yeltsin forced Gorbachev to rescind his appointments of new heads of the Soviet military and the security service, and appoint officers close to Yeltsin instead. When Gorbachev appeared before the Russian parliament to thank them for their fortitude, he was heckled by the representatives and openly mocked by Yeltsin, who signed further orders to outlaw CPSU activities in the general secretary's presence. When Gorbachev claimed, from the rostrum, that he could not determine the full extent of the CPSU's culpability in the coup because he had not yet read the relevant documents, Yeltsin walked across the podium with transcripts from party meetings. "Read this!" said the Russian president, and forced Gorbachev to read out to the assembly evidence of how his Communist colleagues had betrayed him.[43] Power was palpably shifting in the USSR.

The final drama of the Cold War became a purely Soviet tragedy. As Yeltsin worked with other leaders in the republics to set up a new commonwealth of sovereign states, bypassing the USSR entirely, Gorbachev's power waned. After the coup, he resigned as general secretary and did not challenge Yeltsin's wholesale expropriation of the

CPSU's funds and properties in Russia. In September 1991 the Congress of People's Deputies, the elected union assembly Gorbachev had invested so much faith in as a new democratic parliament of the USSR, dissolved itself. Politics in the republics was taking precedence, also for the politicians. The Baltic states had already reestablished themselves as fully independent countries during the August coup. In the Central Asian republics, so unwilling to see the Soviet Union go in March, national elites coming out of the Communist Party declared full sovereignty during the autumn of 1991. Their situation was similar to the effects of British or French decolonization thirty years earlier: the imperial center gave up ruling, and therefore local elites set up new states based, in main part, on lessons learned during the late imperial era. The last nail in the Soviet coffin was the 1 December referendum in Ukraine, in which the population voted overwhelmingly for full independence.

Throughout all of this Gorbachev could have tried to use force to keep the union together. He was still the president of the USSR. He himself believed that the Red Army would have obeyed him, as would, at least up to a point, the security services. But he steadfastly refused to do so. To him, an involuntary union was no alternative to a Soviet Union. He repeatedly told his diminishing group of advisers—now again mainly his old liberal friends—that using force would endanger everything they had stood for. He would not preside over a dictatorship; he would rather see the union disappear and be replaced by some form of confederation, as Gorbachev believed was Yeltsin's aim. Maybe it could prevent the USSR turning into another Yugoslavia, where civil wars were now already raging. Also, Gorbachev was exhausted. After the betrayal by people to whom he had been close, and with his beloved wife ill, even he did not have the strength to fight on.

On 8 December 1991 the leaders of Russia, Ukraine, and Belarus met secretly at a government guest house in the Belavezha Forest near the Polish-Belorussian border. They met there because all of them still feared that the security services, on Gorbachev's orders, would show up to arrest them. In the document they hastily signed, the Soviet Union was dissolved in a subclause, in which the three simply ascertained "that the USSR as a subject of international law and a geo-political reality no longer exists." Instead they set up a Common-wealth of Independent States, which other Soviet republics could join at will. They pledged to cooperate politically and economically, to ex-tend the same rights to everyone residing in their respective repub-lics, irrespective of their national origin, and to fully respect the territorial integrity of each other and of all countries.[44] Russia ratified the treaty on 12 December, the same day as it withdrew from the So-viet Union. Within weeks Armenia, Azerbaijan, Kazakhstan, Kyrgyz-stan, Moldova, Tajikistan, Turkmenistan, and Uzbekistan had all joined the new commonwealth.

After some last-minute hesitation, Gorbachev decided to resign as Soviet president. In a televised resignation speech to the Soviet people in the evening on 25 December, the president said that he had fought for "the preservation of the union state and the integrity of this coun-try." But

> developments took a different course. The policy prevailed of dis-membering this country and disuniting the state, which is some-thing I cannot subscribe to. . . . Destiny so ruled that when I found myself at the helm of this state it already was clear that something was wrong. . . . [It] was going nowhere and we could not possibly live the way we did. We had to change everything radically. . . . An effort of historical importance has been carried out. The totalitarian sys-tem has been eliminated, which prevented this country from becom-ing a prosperous and well-to-do country a long time ago. . . . I am positive that sooner or later, some day, our common efforts will bear fruit and our nations will live in a prosperous, democratic society. I wish everyone all the best.[45]

Before broadcasting his speech, Gorbachev had called President Bush and explained what would happen. Soviet nuclear weapons were safe, he told him. Authority would be transferred to Yeltsin immedi-ately. His usual noncommittal self, Bush responded to Gorbachev's emotional Christmas Day call by speaking in generalities, as if to a public meeting: "And so, at this time of year and at this historic time, we salute you and thank you for what you have done for world peace. Thank you very much."[46]

As Gorbachev finished his televised address, his military aides carrying the suitcases with the nuclear codes stole quietly away, looking for their new boss in another part of the Kremlin. Gorbachev went alone to the Walnut Room, where members of the Soviet Politburo had often met, for a drink with five of his closest aides. Then, before midnight, he went home, as ex-president of a former country.[47]

THE DISSOLUTION OF the Soviet Union removed the last vestige of the Cold War as an international system. For two generations it had dominated international affairs, and the ideological struggle that preceded it and on which it fed had lasted even longer. As in most great changes in world politics, the end was sudden but the antecedents were long. As a dominant aspect in human affairs, the Cold War had ailed for some time, at least since profound global economic and political changes began in the mid-1970s. But the Soviet collapse brought it to a definite conclusion. There was no country left to challenge the United States globally in the name of a radically different ideology. Conflicts and tensions that had grown from the Cold War would remain, as would its nightmarish weapons and curbed strategies, but time had moved on, and new forms of global interaction had taken the place of the old.

The World the Cold War Made

As an international system of states, the Cold War ended on that cold and gray December day in Moscow when Mikhail Gorbachev signed the Soviet Union out of existence. But the ideological Cold War, which predated this state system by almost two generations, disappeared only in part. Granted, Communism in its Marxist-Leninist form had ceased to exist as a practical ideal for how to organize society. But on the US side, not so much changed on that day in December 1991. American foreign policy rolled on, unperturbed by any significant adjustments in strategic vision or political aims. The Cold War was over, and the United States had won it. But most Americans still believed that they could only be safe if the world looked significantly more like their own country and if the world's governments abided by the will of the United States. By almost every measure, the ideas and assumptions built up over generations stayed wholly unreformed, despite the disappearance of a major external threat. Instead of a more limited and therefore achievable US foreign policy, the majority of policymakers from either party believed this was a unipolar moment, where the United States could, at minimal cost, act on its urges.

US post–Cold War triumphalism came in two versions. One could be called the Clinton version, which emphasized US-style capitalist prosperity and market values on a global scale. Its lack of specific purpose in international affairs was striking, as was its lack of discipline in achieving even its economic aims. Instead of building broad and stable frameworks for the conduct of US foreign policy, through the UN, the international monetary institutions, and long-term agreements with other Great Powers (in general China and Russia), the Clinton Administration concentrated on its prosperity agenda. Its political instincts in doing so, at home at least, were probably right: Americans were tired of the international campaigns of the past and wanted to enjoy what some called "the peace dividend." But internationally the 1990s was a lost opportunity for institutionalizing cooperation, as it was for using the peace dividend globally to combat disease, poverty, and inequality. The most glaring examples of these omissions were former Cold War battlefields like Afghanistan, Congo, or Nicaragua, where the United States—or most others for that matter—could not have cared less about what happened immediately after the Cold War was over.

The second form of US post–Cold War triumphalism could be called the Bush version. Where Clinton emphasized prosperity, Bush emphasized predominance. In between, of course, stands 9/11. It is possible that the Bush version would never have come into being if it were not for the terrorist attacks on New York and Washington carried out by Islamist fanatics—in fact by a renegade faction of one of the US Cold War alliances. What is clear is that the Cold War experience conditioned the response of the United States to these atrocities. Instead of a combination of targeted military strikes and global police cooperation, which would have been the most sensible reaction, the Bush Administration chose to use the unipolar moment to lash out at its enemies and occupy Afghanistan and Iraq. These actions had no meaning in a strategic sense, in effect creating two twenty-first-century colonies under the rule of a Great Power with no appetite for or interest in colonial rule. Most independent observers with any experience of the two countries told Washington that the occupations would lead to more Islamist activity, not less. But the United States did not act out of strategic purpose. It acted because its people, understandably, were angry and fearful. And it acted because it could. The direction of the actions were decided by Bush's foreign policy advisers, people like Dick Cheney, Donald Rumsfeld, and Paul

Wolfowitz, who all thought of the world mainly in Cold War terms. They stressed power projection, territorial control, and regime change, in cases where the combination of regional alliance-building, strict economic embargos, international policing, and punitive air strikes would have done the job more effectively.

Put together, the 1990s and 2000s were as if the United States had lost a global purpose—the Cold War—and not yet found a new one. In the meantime, old habits and ways of thinking remained in place, more or less unchanged. There are those, of course, who would insist that the United States cannot behave internationally in any other manner. Because of its distinctly ideological character as a nation, founded on values and political principles rather than on a long heritage of common culture and language, it is in itself a kind of permanent Cold War against all opponents. The United States cannot get a Gorbachev moment of introspection and doubt, it is claimed, because such questioning of the purpose of the nation would go against the very being of America. The post–Cold War era was therefore not an aberration but a confirmation of an absolute historical purpose for the United States, in which the Cold War was just one episode and where global hegemony or defeat are the only two possible outcomes.

Those who claim such consistency in the international role of the United States are almost certainly wrong. Its foreign policies have, after all, shifted over time, dependent on domestic concepts of political purpose, military capabilities, and actual foreign threats. It could be argued, and I would agree, that the democratic promise of the United States—unfulfilled as it has often been—negates such a determinism. But the lack of self-reflection and specific debate, which Cold War triumphalism gave rise to, meant that necessary changes in policy after the Cold War were more difficult to carry out. Such a view is not arguing against the long-term significance of ideology in US foreign policy, which I have written about at great length in this book and elsewhere. But it is to see US post–Cold War rudderlessness as a consequence of a lack of imaginative leadership, not as something essential or predetermined.

Some people would say that asking for a post–Cold War reorientation of US foreign policy was asking too much, and that critiques of triumphalism are too easy. The United States, after all, won the Cold War, and therefore would have little demand for altering its course. The USSR needed Gorbachev's reforms, and collapsed when they failed. But the United States had no use for such wholesale changes. If it ain't broke, don't fix it.

But such a position takes far too narrow a view of the US Cold War experience. Like its enemy, the United States had its portion of Cold War successes and failures. It is just that the balance sheet came out differently, and better, than that of the other side. Post–Cold War mythologies, often employed, for instance, with regard to Iraq and Afghanistan, and, I am sure, other conflicts in the future, stress Reagan's military buildup and willingness to confront the USSR as the root cause of the US Cold War victory. This book has stressed, even (or maybe especially) for the Reagan era, long-term alliances, technological advances, economic growth, and the willingness to negotiate as more important weapons in the US arsenal. Whatever direction the thinking goes in, it is clear that the United States failed to use the better lessons of how it conducted the Cold War in order to get a grip on its role in the post–Cold War era.

This book has shown that the main reason the Cold War ended was that the world as a whole was changing. From the 1970s on, global economic transformations were taking place, which first privileged the United States but then provided increasing advantages for China and other Asian countries. Gradually, over the course of the generation that has passed since the Cold War, the United States can less and less afford global predominance. Increasingly, it has to position itself to work with others within a multipolar constellation of states. The self-indulgence of the 1990s and the failed attempts at rearranging the Islamic world by force of the 2000s meant that the United States squandered many chances to prepare for a new century in which its relative power will be reduced. Lessons from the Cold War indicate that its main aim should have been to tie others into the kinds of principles for international behavior that the United States would like to see long term, especially as its own power diminishes.

Instead the United States did what declining Superpowers often do: engage in futile, needless wars far from its borders, in which short-term security (or even convenience) is mistaken for long-term strategic goals. The US preoccupation with absolute security (which cannot be had) and cheap oil, which was, at best, a limited fix, led it to disregard the broader picture, especially as far as Asia was concerned. The consequence is a United States that is less prepared than it could have been to deal with the big challenges of the future: the rise of China and India, the transfer of economic power from West to East, or systemic tests such as climate change and epidemics.

If the United States won the Cold War, as I think it did, then the Soviet Union, or rather Russia, lost it, and lost it big. The main reason this happened was that its political leaders, in the Communist Party, did not give its own population a political, economic, or social system that was fit for purpose. The Soviet peoples had sacrificed immensely during the twentieth century in an attempt at building a state and society of which they could be proud. The vast majority of citizens had believed that their hard work and defense of their achievements had created both a Superpower with a global reach and a better future for themselves. The ability to believe in improvement under Soviet rule, which would also be the pinnacle of Russian achievement, kept doubts away for the majority, even for those who ought to have known better. The crimes of the Soviet state were ignored by rulers and ruled alike, in a mutual conspiracy of silence.

Then, in the 1980s, it all came crashing down. Conditions at home got worse, not better. The state, which many had thought to be near omnipotent, failed at carrying out even the simplest tasks. Afghanistan and the cost of international isolation deprived the young of the future they wanted. And when necessary reform set in under Gorbachev, it too failed to deliver the progress that citizens craved. Although many Soviets embraced the freedom to speak openly, to vote, to form organizations, to practice their religion, or to watch films and read literature that had been banned, there was a gaping hole at the core of Gorbachev's perestroika. Without bread, what freedom?, some of them asked, increasingly often.[1]

And then the Communist Party self-destructed and the Soviet government suddenly was no more. With the exception of the Baltic states, independence came to the Soviet republics not as a preexisting demand from below, but more as an effect of the ongoing Soviet collapse. After December 1991 fifteen republics, all former parts of the USSR, suddenly had to find their own way in the world. Nationalism came to most of them as a justification for national independence, not the other way around. In that way the collapse of the Soviet Union was indeed a case of decolonization, reminiscent of what had happened to the British or French empires. No wonder that almost all of the post-Soviet states struggle with high levels of ethnic and political tension even after a generation of sovereignty.

It was worst for Russia itself. The collapse left Russians feeling *déclassée*, robbed of their position, whether they lived in Russia itself or were among the many who inhabited other new post-Soviet states. One day they had been the elite in a Superpower. The next they had neither purpose nor position. Materially things were bad, too. Old people did not get their pensions. Some starved to death. Malnutrition and alcoholism reduced the average life span for a Russian man from sixty-six in 1985 to less than fifty-eight ten years later. To Russians used to a remarkable degree of (sometimes depressing) stability, theft, violence, and pornographic movies seemed to be the greatest achievements of post-Soviet freedom.

Among the thefts was one that will safely qualify as the raid of the century. This was the privatization of Russian industry and of its natural resources. Privatization had to come, some of its defenders say. After the USSR collapsed, its planned economy was moribund. But even if one accepts this argument, the way privatization happened was indefensible. As the socialist state was being dismantled, ownership of Russia's riches was taken over by a new oligarchy emerging from party institutions, planning bureaus, and centers of science and technology. Instead of being used to cure some of the country's many ills, resources were given away to the well-connected, especially among the friends and supporters of President Boris Yeltsin. Value created by generations was transferred to individuals who had no connection with the local community (but plenty of connections with those in power). Very often the new owners stripped their possessions of what they could sell and closed down whatever production was left. Unemployment rose from zero to 30 percent within three years. And all this happened while the West applauded Yeltsin's economic reform.

In hindsight, at least, it is clear that the economic transition to capitalism was a catastrophe for most Russians. It is also clear that the West should have dealt with post–Cold War Russia better than it did. It is hard, however, to specify what alternative paths would have looked like. The key, I think, would have been the realization, so often lacking in the 1990s, that Russia would under all circumstances remain a crucial state in any international system because of its sheer size. It would therefore have been in the interest of the West, and especially the Europeans, to begin integrating the country into European security and trade arrangements as soon as possible after 1991. Such an approach would have demanded a lot of money and even more patience, given the chaos that reigned in Russia. Some argue that it would have been politically impossible, both within the West and within Russia itself. An effort the size of the Marshall Plan was certainly not in the offing. But both the West and Russia would have been considerably more secure today if the chance for Russia to join the European Union and possibly also NATO in some form had at least been kept open in the 1990s.

Instead Russia was kept out of the processes of military and economic integration that eventually extended all the way to its borders. It has given Russians the sense of being outcasts and has left the country sulking at Europe's door. In turn, this has given credence to Russian jingoists and bigots, such as its current president Vladimir Putin, who see all the disasters that have befallen the country over the past generation as part of some preconceived US plan to reduce and isolate it. Putin's authoritarianism and bellicosity have been sustained by genuine popular support. Most Russians would like to believe that all that has happened to them is someone else's fault, instead of dealing with the immense problems in Russian society and in the Russian state themselves. The shocks of the 1990s have given way to a peculiar Russian form of uninhibited cynicism, which not only encompasses a deep distrust of their fellow citizens, but sees long-term, effective conspiracies against themselves everywhere in the world, often contrary to fact and reason. Over half of all Russians now believe Leonid Brezhnev was their best leader in the twentieth century, followed by Lenin and Stalin. Gorbachev is at the bottom of the list.[2]

For others around the world, the end of the Cold War undoubtedly came as a relief. With the threat of global nuclear annihilation gone, one of the big challenges to human existence had been removed, or at least suspended. There was also reason to hope, especially during the 1990s, that Great Power interventionism would be reduced, and that principles of sovereignty and self-determination would be respected. Europe and Japan had gained much from the Cold War itself, as had China in its latter phase. The division of Europe, and of Germany, had been a tragedy, as had the imposition of dictatorial regimes in the East. But the international system had given Europe almost fifty years of peace, unknown there during the first part of the century. And protected by that peace, resilient societies had grown up that were able to handle post–Cold War transformations remarkably well, including the unsparing transition to capitalism in the East and the unification of Germany, the biggest single project of the post–Cold War era. Japan, shorn of the distinct international economic advantages that the Cold War era had bestowed upon it, entered a period of low growth. But it did so from a very high level of development, which in 1995 saw the country's GDP per capita still stand at more than 30 percent above that of the United States. "If this is a recession," commented an African friend of mine, living in Tokyo, "we want one, too!"

China is often seen as one of the main beneficiaries of the Cold War. This is not entirely true, of course. The country saw imposed on it a European-style Marxist-Leninist dictatorship that was mostly out of tune with its needs. The result, during the Maoist era, were some of the most terrible crimes of the Cold War, in which millions died. But during the 1970s and 1980s, Deng Xiaoping's China benefitted massively from its de facto alliance with the United States both in terms of security and development programs. The end of the Cold War came as a complete shock to the Chinese leaders, who suddenly realized that they—in part due to their own efforts combatting the Soviets—would be left to face the Americans in a unipolar world. From the Chinese perspective the wrong Superpower collapsed: they had believed that, at least long-term, the USSR was in ascendance, while the United States was declining. From the 1990s on, the Chinese Communist Party was terrified that US influence would subvert its rule at home and hem it in abroad, including among its Asian neighbors.

In the multipolar world that is now establishing itself, it seems likely that the United States and China will be the strongest powers. Unless they stumble at home, and both may easily do so, their competition for influence in Asia will define the outlook for the world. But the US relationship with China, or with Russia for that matter, is unlikely to develop into any form of Cold War. Both have political systems very different from the United States (or from each other). But both China and Russia are well integrated into the capitalist world system, and many of their leaders' interests are linked to further integration. Unlike the USSR, these people are not likely to seek isolation or global confrontation. They will attempt to nibble away at US interests and dominate within their regions. But neither are, by themselves, willing or capable to institute global ideological conflict or militarized alliance systems. Rivalries, most certainly, which may lead to conflicts or even localized wars, but not of the Cold War kind.

Throughout the Cold War, it was the battleground regions that suffered most. Korea, Indochina, Afghanistan, much of Africa and Central America were left devastated. Some recovered, but for others devastation left cynicism in its wake. US Cold War clients may have been best at sheer plunder. Just dictators whose names start with the letter M—Mobutu (Congo), Marcos (Philippines), and Mubarak (Egypt)—among them amassed fortunes of an estimated $17 billion, according to recent estimates. But Soviet clients were not far behind. Angola, one of the countries most ravaged by the Cold War, could have been among the wealthiest parts of the world due to its mineral and energy resources. But today most of its population remain desperately poor. Meanwhile, the daughter of the president is reported to be the richest woman in Africa. Her net fortune is estimated at around $3 billion.

The ease with which many former Marxists adapted themselves to a post–Cold War market system begs the question whether this had been an avoidable conflict in the first place. What is clear is that the outcome was not worth the sacrifice, not in Angola, but probably not in Vietnam, Nicaragua, or for that matter Russia either. "If I had to do it over again," confessed Bulgaria's long-time Communist boss Todor Zhivkov, "I would not even be a Communist, and if Lenin were alive today he would say the same thing. . . . I must now admit that we started from the wrong basis, from the wrong premise. The foundation of socialism was wrong. I believe that at its very conception the idea of socialism was stillborn."[3] Even among those who were on the winning side the costs and risks have sometimes seemed too high: in lives, in expenditure, and in the threat of nuclear war.

But was it avoidable back in the 1940s, when the Cold War went from an ideological conflict to a permanent military confrontation? While post–World War II clashes and rivalries were certainly unavoidable—Stalin's policies alone were enough to produce those—it is hard to argue that a global Cold War that was to last for almost fifty years and threaten the obliteration of the world could not in any form have been avoided. There were points along the way when leaders could have held back, especially on military rivalry and the arms race. But the ideological conflict that was at the bottom of the post–World War II tension made such sensible thinking very difficult to achieve. In that sense, it was its ideological origins that made the Cold War special and hyperdangerous. People of goodwill on both sides believed that they were representing an idea whose very existence was threatened. It led them to take otherwise avoidable risks with their own lives and the lives of others.

Another big question is whether the Cold War actually was, as one key book title has it, "the division of the world."[4] Some argue that state leaders (and historians) were too blinded by the Cold War as an organizing principle for a period of history to see the diversity and hybridity that went on beside it. This book has argued that although the Cold War between capitalism and socialism influenced most things in the twentieth century, it did not decide everything. The two world wars, the Great Depression, decolonization, and the transfer of wealth and power from West to East may well have happened even without the Cold War (but obviously not in the form that they eventually got). Likewise, some polities refused to take part, at least fully. India, for instance, was in many ways established as an anti–Cold War state. Others had systems that allowed for significant levels of state control while remaining capitalist in essence, such as in Scandinavia. Capitalist Norway has more state ownership of companies than socialist China. And, percentage-wise, Sweden's government spends two times more than China's out of the country's total GDP.

And yet the Cold War did influence most things because of the centrality of its ideologies and the intensity of its adherents. A number of countries and movements went to war against US-led capitalism in the twentieth century. By 1945 they had been defeated, Germany and Japan first among them. Sitting in his bunker in Berlin in 1945, just before killing himself, even Hitler admitted that in the future "there will remain in the world only two Great Powers capable of confronting each other—the United States and Soviet Russia."[5] The reason why this was so clear to everyone was not just the strategic capabilities of the two states. It was also because each symbolized a distinct way of organizing society and the state. The United States was in 1945 and throughout the Cold War the more powerful of the two. But the USSR was on most counts a credible challenge right up to the end.

The most important reason why the Cold War affected everyone in the world was the threat of nuclear destruction that it implied. In this sense, nobody was safe from the Cold War. The greatest victory of Gorbachev's generation was that nuclear war was avoided. Historically, most Great Power rivalries end in a cataclysm. The Cold War did not (which is the reason why I can write about these events now from the relative safety of my Harvard study). Even so, there is no doubt that the nuclear arms race was profoundly dangerous. On a couple of occasions, we were much closer to nuclear devastation than anyone but a few people realized. Nuclear war could have broken out by accident, or as a result of intelligence failures. When awarded the Nobel Peace Prize in 1985, the organization International Physicians for the Prevention of Nuclear War outlined the medical consequences: "A horror-stricken and dust-covered Earth, burned bodies of the dead and wounded, and people slowly dying of radiation disease."[6] Or, in pop culture, Depeche Mode sang about the two-minute warning before destruction and of the world afterward: "The dawning of another year . . . one in four still here."[7]

Why were leaders willing to take such unconscionable risks with the fate of the earth? Why did so many people believe in ideologies which the same people at other times would have realized could not hold all the solutions they were looking for? The answer, I think, is that the Cold War world, like the world today, obviously had a lot of ills. As injustice and oppression became more visible in the twentieth century, people—and especially young people—felt the need to remedy these ills. Cold War ideologies offered immediate solutions to complex problems. For most, it was a bit like buying a car (which I happen to be doing at the moment). In my heart, I would like a bit of Volvo, and a bit of Ford, and a bit of Toyota. But I cannot have that, since manufacturers refuse to sell their new cars in parts. And, even if they did, I am not an expert mechanic. Though I trust (or at least hope) that the automakers' mechanics are top-notch. The Cold War was a bit like that. Most people had to take what was available, even if it conflicted with specific needs or even with common sense.

What did not change with the end of the Cold War were the conflicts between the haves and the have-nots in international affairs. Now in some parts of the world such conflicts are made more intense by the upsurge of religious and ethnic movements, which threaten to destroy whole communities. Unrestrained by Cold War universalisms, which at least pretended that all people could enter their promised paradise, these groups are palpably exclusionist or racist. Some, in the Middle East, Europe, south Asia, or in the United States, remind us a bit about what the world was like before the Cold War became an international system. Stakes are higher now, not least because of weapons of mass destruction. And solutions are even more difficult to find, though most realize that at some point negotiations and compromise will have to come into play. But compromise is hard, because supporters of these groups or states believe that great injustices have been done to them in the past, which somehow justify their present outrages.

Before, during, and after the Cold War, everyone wants their place in the sun. A chance to be counted. Respect for what they consider as theirs, whether in religion, lifestyle, or territory. Often people, and especially young people, need to be part of something bigger than themselves or even their families, some immense idea to devote one's life to. The Cold War shows what happens when such notions get perverted for the sake of power, influence, and control. But that does not mean that these very human urges are in themselves worthless. On the contrary, if the plan had been to heal the sick, abolish poverty, or give everyone a chance in life *without* threatening the world with nuclear annihilation, then we would probably have summed up much of the efforts that went into the Cold War as good. History is complex. We do not always know where ideas will lead us. Better, then, to consider carefully the risks we are willing to take to achieve good results, in order not to replicate the terrible toll that the twentieth century took in its search for perfection.

Approaches and
Acknowledgments

Writing world history is never easy, even when the focus is on a set of events that are limited in time and effect. Although the author is of course responsible for the conclusions, the work is necessarily dependent on the research of those who know infinitely more about parts of the story than any one person can aspire to investigate in a lifetime. World history is therefore always a collective enterprise, implicitly or explicitly. Anyone who believes that they alone can be the judge of all the detail in big history are fools. But likewise, those experts who think that big history cannot or should not be done are poorer for it. They limit their own understanding, just like they limit the uses of history for potential readers.

For me, that usefulness is key to what I do. It can of course be achieved through many kinds of history writing, big and small, broad and narrow, with different focus points in terms of individuals, communities, states, or social classes. But world history, like its cousins international and transnational history, has a particular significance because it allows the historian and the reader to put things into context beyond individual countries or even regions. This is what I strive to do in this book: to tell the history of the global Cold War on all continents and within a broad chronology, in ways that make plain the differences in how groups of people experienced the conflict. It has been a difficult task and it is now up to the readers to judge how well it is done.

I HAVE TALLIED up a great amount of intellectual debts during the time it has taken me to write this book. My first debt, as always, is to my teachers and mentors: Michael Hunt in Chapel Hill, Geir Lundestad and Helge Pharo in Oslo, and Mick Cox in London. My colleagues at the London School of Economics and Political Science (LSE) and at Harvard have helped develop different aspects of the book (sometimes in ways that are not easy to recognize). I am particularly grateful to the extraordinary group of people who, together with Mick and myself, created LSE IDEAS: Svetozar Rajak, Emilia Knight, Tiha Franulovic, Gordon Barrass, and many, many others. Working in IDEAS was one of the highlights of my academic career, not least because the study of the Cold War as an international system is an IDEAS mainstay. In the Department of International History at LSE most of my colleagues had some input to this book, especially Piers Ludlow, Tanya Harmer, Antony Best, Vladislav Zubok, Kirsten Schulze, Nigel Ashton, MacGregor Knox, David Stevenson, Steven Casey, Kristina Spohr, Gagan Sood, and Roham Alvandi.

Much of my understanding of the Cold War has come through two extraordinary projects that I have been lucky enough to be part of. One was the setting up of the journal *Cold War History*, in publication since 2000. I have learned much from all the members of the editorial board and from generations of managing editors who have done an outstanding job in establishing the journal. I have also, of course, learned much from the contributors (including some of those who in the end did not get published!). The late Saki Dockrill drove the journal forward. I cherish her memory.

I was also very lucky to co-edit the massive *Cambridge History of the Cold War* with Melvyn Leffler. Working with the seventy-plus authors was an intense learning experience, both (I must confess) with regard to knowledge and patience. Working with Mel as co-editor was a joy throughout. He is one of my favorite colleagues: erudite, meticulous, and always supportive.

I am also indebted to the many students at LSE and now at Harvard who have joined in my classes on the Cold War. Learning is always a two-way street. A lot of the insights that have helped create this book have come to me by way of undergraduate or graduate students during lively discussions in class, or through the supervision of PhD students. I am among those who find it difficult to write without teaching: being in the classroom is a way of testing out ideas, frameworks, and structure, which benefits most things that I do, this book not least.

During my time at LSE IDEAS I was lucky enough (thanks to the generosity of Emmanuel Roman) to link up with a remarkable array of visiting professors who all had an impact on how this book was written: Paul Kennedy (more than anyone), Chen Jian, Gilles Kepel, Niall Ferguson, Ramachandra Guha, Anne Applebaum, and Matthew Connelly.

My new colleagues at Harvard have been very helpful in the final stages of the process. Tony Saich and the Ash Center at the Harvard Kennedy School have provided a congenial and creative atmosphere in which to work. Even before I myself moved to Harvard in 2015, I drew on the remarkable knowledge and insights of Mark Kramer and his Cold War project here.

I have benefitted enormously from the help of colleagues around the world who have facilitated my research, often putting their own work aside to help me during my visits. I am especially grateful to Niu Jun, Zhang Baijia, and Niu Ke in Beijing, Alexander Chubarian and Vladimir Pechatnov in Moscow, Silvio Pons in Rome, Jordan Baev in Sofia, Nguyen Vu Tung in Hanoi, Ljubodrag Dimić and Miladin Milošević in Belgrade, Srinath Raghavan in Delhi, Khaled Fahmy in Cairo, and Matias Spektor in Rio de Janeiro.

A number of colleagues and friends have been kind enough to read and comment on parts of the manuscript as it was being created. They have helped me make it a better book and avoid (I hope) too many mistakes in the text. I am very much indebted to Vladislav Zubok, Serhii Plokhy, Csaba Békés, Stephen Walt, Christopher Goscha, Chen Jian, Piers Ludlow, Fred Logevall, Mary Sarotte, Daniel Sargent, Vanni Pettinà, Anton Harder, David Engerman, Niu Jun, Mark Kramer, Sulmaan Khan, Tanya Harmer, and Tarek Masoud.

I have been helped by fantastic research assistants for parts of this project. I am grateful to Sandeep Bhardwaj (in Delhi), Khadiga Omar (in Cairo), and Maria Terzieva (in Sofia). The latter two also helped with translations, as did Laszlo Horvath (Hungarian) and Jan Cornelius (Afrikaans). Trung Chi Tran helped at Harvard during the final stages. The research for the Korean part of the book received a generous grant from the Academy of Korean Studies (AKS-2010-DZZ-3104).

When most needed, friends provided wonderful locations in which to write: Sue and Mike Potts in St. Marcel, Cathie and Enrique Pani in Mexico, and Hina and Nilesh Patel in Norfolk. I am very grateful to them.

One of the fun things about working on the global history of the Cold War over the past twenty years has been that so much work is collaborative. This is not least due to two remarkable institutions in Washington, DC: the Cold War International History Project at the Woodrow Wilson Center and the National Security Archive. I, and countless other historians, have benefitted enormously from the help and diligence of these two institutions, which have done so much to make US and foreign documents on the Cold War available to the public. I am particularly grateful to Christian Ostermann and (before him) James Hershberg at the Wilson Center, and to Thomas Blanton, Malcolm Byrne, and Svetlana Savranskaya at the archive.

My literary agent, Sarah Chalfant of the Wylie Agency, has made this book happen in more ways than I think she herself realizes. In the latter stages of production, I have been extraordinarily lucky to work with two terrific publishers, Lara Heimert at Basic Books in New York and Simon Winder at Penguin in London. Bill Warhop has done an expert job with the copyediting.

Finally, I have been truly blessed to have worked with outstanding administrative assistants throughout the research for this book. Tiha Franulovic at LSE was the bedrock of my professional existence for more than a decade. At Harvard, first Lia Tjahjana and now Samantha Gammons have assisted with ability and dedication. They are the facilitators on whom scholars depend to get things done.

LET ME END with a few remarks on conventions and approaches throughout the book. In the endnotes, I have aimed at simplicity and precision. I had to avoid making an overlong book even longer through massive amounts of archival citations, but also to make it possible for other scholars to retrieve documents where I have found them. Materials I have had access to in archives are cited by their original archival location. Documents I have had access to through other depositories, such as library collections, CWIHP, the National Security Archive, or other online sites, have been cited with their current (November 2016) physical or online location.

Translations from original sources are my own, except when noted. I have, however, on occasion consulted other translations or sought the help of native speakers to improve accuracy and readability.

I have not always been able to give enough credit where credit is due to those many who have assembled, edited, or translated collections of documents. These are the workers upon whom everyone else in this business depend. I myself have been among their number, so I know. Again, my weak excuse is that I could not make this book even lengthier. So, that said, let me express my allegiance and gratitude to those many, whether in Washington, or Beijing, or Moscow, who are working hard and unselfishly to make formerly secret government information publicly available.

O. A. Westad
Cambridge, Massachusetts
January 2017

Notes

WORLD MAKING

1. See for instance John Lewis Gaddis, *The Long Peace: Inquiries into the History of the Cold War* (New York: Oxford University Press, 1987). Although I agree with many of Gaddis's points about what kept superpower war from breaking out, I strongly disagree with the "long peace" designation.

2. Odd Arne Westad, *The Global Cold War: Third World Interventions and the Making of Our Times* (Cambridge: Cambridge University Press, 2005).

3. *Marx/Engels Selected Works* (Moscow: Progress, 1969), 1:26.

4. Karl Marx, interview with the *Chicago Tribune*, December 1878, *Karl Marx, Friedrich Engels: Collected Works* (New York: International Publishers, 1989), 24:578.

5. *Protokoll des Parteitages der Sozialdemokratischen Partei Deutschlands: Abgehalten zu Erfurt vom 14. bis 20. Oktober 1891* [Minutes of the Party Congress of the Social Democratic Party of Germany: Held in Erfurt from October 14–October 20, 1891]. (Berlin: Verlag der Expedition des "Vorwärts," 1891), 3–6.

6. Friedrich Engels, "A Critique of the Draft Social-Democratic Program of 1891," in *Karl Marx, Friedrich Engels: Collected Works* (New York: International Publishers, 1990), 27:227.

7. For an overview from a US perspective, see Andrew Preston, *Sword of the Spirit, Shield of Faith: Religion in American War and Diplomacy* (New York: Alfred A. Knopf, 2012).

8. Henry James, "The American," *Atlantic Monthly* 37 (June 1876): 667.

CHAPTER 1: STARTING POINTS

1. Quoted in Robert W. Tucker, *Woodrow Wilson and the Great War: Reconsidering America's Neutrality, 1914–1917* (Charlottesville: University of Virginia Press, 2007), 213.

2. Vladimir Ilich Lenin, *What Is to Be Done?: Burning Questions of Our Movement* (New York: International Publishers, 1929; Russian original 1902), 1.

3. Quoted in John Ellis, *Eye-Deep in Hell: Trench Warfare in World War I* (Baltimore, MD: JHU Press, 1976), 102.

4. Karl Liebknecht, "Begründung der Ablehnung der Kriegskredite" [Reasons for the Rejection of the War Credits], *Vorwärts*, 3 December 1914.

5. Wilson quoted in Robert L. Willett, *Russian Sideshow: America's Undeclared War, 1918–1920* (Washington, DC: Brassey's, 2003), xxxi.

6. Fordism, commented the imprisoned Italian Communist Antonio Gramsci in 1934, is ultimately an American challenge to Europe. "Europe wants to have its cake and eat it, to have all the benefits which Fordism brings to its competitive power while retaining its army of [social] parasites who, by consuming vast sums of surplus value, aggravate initial costs and reduce competitive power on the international market." David Forgacs, ed., *The Gramsci Reader: Selected Writings 1916–1935* (New York: New York University Press, 2000), 277. For a further discussion, see Charles S. Maier, "Between Taylorism and Technocracy: European Ideologies and the Vision of Industrial Productivity in the 1920s," *Journal of Contemporary History* 5, no. 2 (1970): 27–61.

7. Ole Hanson, *Americanism versus Bolshevism* (Garden City, NY: Doubleday, 1920), p. viii.

8. Churchill, "Bolshevism and Imperial Sedition," *Winston S. Churchill: His Complete Speeches, 1897–1963*, ed. Robert Rhodes James (New York: Chelsea House, 1974), 3:3026.

9. Bertrand Russell, *Bolshevism: Practice and Theory* (New York: Harcourt, Brace and Howe, 1920), 4.

10. Ho Chi Minh, "The Path Which Led Me to Leninism," Edward Miller, ed., *The Vietnam War: A Documentary Reader* (Malden, MA: John Wiley & Sons, 2016), 8.

11. Rudolf Nilsen, "Voice of the Revolution," transl. Anthony Thompson, in *Modern Scandinavian Poetry* (Oslo: Dreyer, 1982), 185. Used with permission of copyright holder Jens Allwood. Volume edited and published by his late father, Martin Allwood.

12. "Manifesto of the Communist Party of South Africa, adopted at the inaugural conference of the Party, Cape Town, 30 July 1921," at http://www.sahistory .org.za/article/manifesto-communist-party-south-africa.

13. W. Bruce Lincoln, *Red Victory: A History of the Russian Civil War* (New York: Da Capo Press, 1989), 384.

14. Dimitry Manuilsky, *The Communist Parties and the Crisis of Capitalism: Speech Delivered on the First Item of the Agenda of the XI Plenum of the E.C.C.I. held in March–April 1931* (London: Modern Books, 1931), 37. Manuilsky was the head of the Comintern from 1929 to 1934.

15. *Report of Court Proceedings in the Case of the Anti-Soviet "Bloc of Rights and Trotskyites" Heard before the Military Collegium of the Supreme Court of the U.S.S.R. Moscow, March 2–13, 1938* (Moscow: People's Commissariat of Justice, 1938), 775.

16. Steven Casey, *Cautious Crusade: Franklin D. Roosevelt, American Public Opinion, and the War Against Nazi Germany* (Oxford: Oxford University Press, 2001), 23.

17. Editorial, *New York Times*, 24 August 1939.

18. Entry for 7 September 1939, Georgi Dimitrov, *The Diary of Georgi Dimitrov, 1933–1949*, ed. Ivo Banac (New Haven, CT: Yale University Press, 2008), 115.

19. Will Kaufman, *Woody Guthrie, American Radical* (Champaign: University of Illinois Press, 2011), 1.

20. 21 July 1940 Declaration of Workers' Organizations, in Torgrim Titlestad, *Stalin midt imot: Peder Furubotn 1938–41* [Against Stalin: Peder Furubotn, 1938–1941] (Oslo: Gyldendal, 1977), 42.

21. Fridrikh Firsov, ed., *Secret Cables of the Comintern, 1933–1943.* (New Haven, CT: Yale University Press, 2014), 152.

22. The German Communist Margarete Buber-Neumann, for instance, was first arrested in Stalin's purges in 1938 and then spent two years in the Soviet labor camp Karaganda before she was extradited to Nazi Germany, where she spent five years in the Ravensbrück concentration camp.

23. Dmitrii Volkogonov, Triumf i tragediia: politicheskii portret I.V. Stalina [Triumph and Tragedy: A Political Portrait of I.V. Stalin] (Moscow: Novosti, 1989), 2:169.

24. Rodric Braithwaite, *Moscow 1941: A City and Its People at War* (New York: Vintage, 2007), 82.

CHAPTER 2: TESTS OF WAR

1. Churchill's radio address to the British people, 22 June 1941, in Winston Churchill, *Never Give In!: The Best of Winston Churchill's Speeches* (New York: Hyperion, 2003), 289.

2. Winston Churchill, *The Second World War. Volume III: The Grand Alliance* (Boston, MA: Houghton Mifflin, 1950), 370.

3. Ibid., 330.

4. Ibid., 394.

5. Woody Guthrie, "All You Fascists" (1944), Woody Guthrie Publications, http://woodyguthrie.org/Lyrics/All_You_Fascists.htm.

6. Vladimir Pechatnov, "How Stalin and Molotov Wrote Messages to Churchill," *Russia in International Affairs* 7, no. 3 (2009): 162–73.

7. Minutes of meeting at Kremlin, 11:15 p.m., 13 August 1942, CAB127/23, Cabinet Papers, National Archives of the United Kingdom.

8. Compared with Churchill, Roosevelt was more realistic in his understanding of Stalin's aims. The British prime minister seems, at least for some time, to have believed that he had struck a deal with Stalin on the percentage-wise influence of the Great Powers in eastern Europe during a drunken session in Moscow in October 1944.

9. Bohlen minutes, Stalin-FDR, 1 December 1943, Tehran, *Foreign Relations of the United States* (hereafter *FRUS*): *The Conferences at Cairo and Tehran*, 594.

10. Communiqué Issued at the End of the Yalta Conference, 11 February 1945, *FRUS: The Conference of Berlin (the Potsdam Conference), 1945*, 2:1578.

11. William D. Leahy, *I Was There* (New York: Whittlesey House, 1950), 315–16.

12. Quoted in Rick Atkinson, *The Guns at Last Light: The War in Western Europe, 1944–1945* (New York: Picador, 2013), 521.

13. Milovan Djilas, *Conversations with Stalin* (New York: Harcourt, Brace & World, 1962), 114.

14. Mandelstam was one of the greatest Russian poets of his generation. He died in a Siberian prison camp in 1938. Prior to his arrest, he had told his wife that "only in Russia is poetry respected. It gets people killed. Is there anywhere else where poetry is so common a motive for murder?" Nadezhda Mandelstam, *Hope Against Hope: A Memoir* (New York: Atheneum, 1970), 159.

15. Quoted in Steven Merritt Miner, *Stalin's Holy War: Religion, Nationalism and Alliance Politics, 1941–1945* (Chapel Hill: University of North Carolina Press, 2003), 51. The head of the Russian Orthodox Church from 1945 to 1970, Patriarch Aleksii I, worked closely with the Soviet authorities.

16. Original "Quit India" resolution drafted by Gandhi, April 1942, *New York Times*, 5 August 1942.

17. Joint Declaration by President Roosevelt and Prime Minister Churchill, as broadcast 14 August 1941, https://fdrlibrary.org/atlantic-charter.

18. Diary, 17 July 1945, box 333, President's Secretary's Files, Truman Papers, Harry S. Truman Library, Independence, MO (hereafter Truman Library).

19. Record of conversation, Truman–Molotov, 23 April 1945, *FRUS 1945*, 5:258.

20. Quoted in Arnold Offner, *Another Such Victory: President Truman and the Cold War, 1945–1953* (Stanford, CA: Stanford University Press, 2002), 34.

21. Prime Minister to President Truman, 12 May 1945, CHAR 20/218/109, Churchill Papers, Churchill College Archives, Cambridge, UK.

22. Memorandum by the President's Adviser and Assistant (Hopkins) of a Conversation During Dinner at the Kremlin in *FRUS: The Conference of Berlin (The Potsdam Conference), 1945*, 1:57–59.

23. Pechatnov, "How Stalin and Molotov Wrote Messages to Churchill," 172.

24. Entry for 28 January 1945, in Georgi Dimitrov, *The Diary of Georgi Dimitrov, 1933–1949*, ed. Ivo Banac (New Haven, CT: Yale University Press, 2008), 358.

25. Hugh Dalton, *High Tide and After: Memoirs, 1945–1960* (London: F. Muller, 1962), 157.

26. Richard N. Gardner, *Sterling-Dollar Diplomacy; the Origins and the Prospects of Our International Economic Order*, new and expanded (New York: McGraw-Hill, 1969), xvii.

27. Ritchie Ovendale, *The English-Speaking Alliance: Britain, the United States, the Dominions and the Cold War 1945–1951* (London: Routledge, 1985), 43.

CHAPTER 3: EUROPE'S ASYMMETRIES

1. John Vachon, *Poland, 1946: The Photographs and Letters of John Vachon* (Washington, DC: Smithsonian Institution Press, 1995), 5.

2. Quoted in Keith Lowe, *Savage Continent: Europe in the Aftermath of World War II* (London: St. Martin's Press, 2012), 31.

3. Henri Van der Zee, *The Hunger Winter: Occupied Holland 1944–5* (London: J. Norman & Hobhouse, 1982), 304–5.

4. Speech at Vélodrome d'hiver, 2 October 1945, in Maurice Thorez, *Oeuvres*, book 5, volume 21 (Paris: Editions sociales, 1959), 203.

5. Lowe, *Savage Continent*, 283.

6. Quoted in William I. Hitchcock, *The Bitter Road to Freedom: The Human Cost of Allied Victory in World War II Europe* (New York: Free Press, 2009), 163.

7. Record of conversation, Stalin–Hebrang, 9 January 1945, G. P. Murashko et al. (eds.), *Vostochnaia Evropa v dokumentakh rossiiskikh arkhivov, 1944–1953* [Eastern Europe in Documents from the Russian Archives, 1944–1953] (Novosibirsk: Sibirskii khronograf, 1997), 1:118–33.

8. Mark Kramer, "Stalin, Soviet Policy, and the Consolidation of a Communist Bloc in Eastern Europe, 1944–53," in *Stalinism Revisited: The Establishment of Communist Regimes in East-Central Europe*, ed. Vladimir Tismaneanu (Budapest: Central European University Press, 2009), 69.

9. Quoted in Adam Ulam, *Understanding the Cold War: A Historian's Personal Reflections* (New York: Transaction Publishers, 2002), 277.

10. Michael Dobbs, *Six Months in 1945: FDR, Stalin, Churchill, and Truman, from World War to Cold War* (New York: Random House, 2012), 121.

11. The German Ambassador in the Soviet Union (Schulenburg) to the German Foreign Office, 10 September 1939, frames 69811–69813, serial 127, Microfilm Publication T120, Records of the German Foreign Office Received by the Department of State, US National Archives.

12. William D. Leahy, *I Was There* (New York: Whittlesey House, 1950), 315–16.

13. Patryk Babiracki, *Soviet Soft Power in Poland: Culture and the Making of Stalin's New Empire, 1943–1957* (Chapel Hill: University of North Carolina Press, 2015), 56.

14. Conversation between Władysław Gomułka and Stalin on 14 November 1945, *Cold War International History Project Bulletin*, 11 (1998), 135.

15. Quoted in Tony Judt, *Postwar: A History of Europe Since 1945* (London: Penguin, 2006), 200.

16. Babiracki, *Soviet Soft Power in Poland*, 61.

17. Quoted in László Borhi, *Hungary in the Cold War, 1945–1956: Between the United States and the Soviet Union* (Budapest: Central European University Press, 2004), 35.

18. Quoted in István Vida, "K. J. Vorosilov marsall jelentései a Tildy kormány megalakulsásáról" [Marshal K. J. Voroshilov Reports on the Formation of the Tildy Government], *Társadalmi Szemle*, 1996, 2:86.

19. Council of Foreign Ministers, Second Session, Thirteenth Informal Meeting, Palais du Luxembourg, Paris, 26 June 1946, *FRUS 1946*, 2:646.

20. Harry S. Truman, *Memoirs* (Garden City, NY: Doubleday, 1955), 1:493.

21. Winston Churchill, *Never Give In!: The Best of Winston Churchill's Speeches* (New York: Hyperion, 2003), 413.

22. The full text of Kennan's original telegram is in Kenneth M. Jensen, ed., *Origins of the Cold War: The Novikov, Kennan, and Roberts "Long Telegrams" of 1946*, revised edition (Washington, DC: United States Institute of Peace, 1993), 17–32.

23. Ibid.

24. Special Message to the Congress on Greece and Turkey, 12 March 1947, in *Public Papers of the Presidents* (hereafter *PPP*) *Truman 1947*, 179.

25. Summary of meeting between President and Congressional Delegation, 28 February 1947, box 1, Joseph M. Jones Papers, Truman Library.

26. Memorandum by the Under Secretary of State for Economic Affairs (Clayton), 27 May 1947, *FRUS 1947*, 3:230–32.

27. Quoted in Edward Taborský, *Communism in Czechoslovakia, 1948–1960* (Princeton, NJ: Princeton University Press, 1961), 20.

28. Quoted in Olaf Solumsmoen and Olav Larssen, eds., *Med Einar Gerhardsen gjennom 20 år* [With Einar Gerhardsen through Twenty Years] (Oslo: Tiden, 1967), 61–62.

29. Zhdanov on the Founding of the Cominform, September 1947, in Jussi M. Hanhimäki and Odd Arne Westad, eds., *The Cold War: A History in Documents and Eyewitness Accounts* (Oxford: Oxford University Press, 2003), 51–52.

30. Quoted in Philip J. Jaffe, "The Rise and Fall of Earl Browder," *Survey* 18, no. 12 (1972): 56.

CHAPTER 4: RECONSTRUCTIONS

1. Summary Record of the Ninety-First Meeting of the Third Committee, 2 October 1948, in William Schabas, ed., *The Universal Declaration of Human Rights: The Travaux Préparatoires* (Cambridge: Cambridge University Press, 2013), 3:2058.

2. Quoted in John C. Culver and John Hyde, *American Dreamer: The Life and Times of Henry A. Wallace* (New York: Norton, 2001), 457.

3. On Nitze, see David Milne, *Worldmaking: The Art and Science of American Diplomacy* (New York: Farrar, Straus and Giroux, 2015), 268–325.

4. NSC 68: "United States Objectives and Programs for National Security: A Report to the President" (April 7, 1950). *FRUS 1950*, 1:235–311.

5. Ibid.

6. The best overview is David Kynaston, *Austerity Britain, 1945–51* (London: Bloomsbury, 2007).

7. Quoted in Michael Dobbs, *Six Months in 1945: FDR, Stalin, Churchill, and Truman—from World War to Cold War* (New York: Knopf, 2012), 205.

8. *Hansard*, series 5, vol. 452, House of Commons Debates, 30 June 1948, 2226.

9. Barry Eichengreen, *The European Economy Since 1945: Coordinated Capitalism and Beyond* (Princeton, NJ: Princeton University Press, 2007), especially 52–84.

10. Alessandro Brogi, *Confronting America: The Cold War Between the United States and the Communists in France and Italy* (Chapel Hill, NC: University of North Carolina Press, 2011), 116.

11. Raymond Aron, *The Opium of the Intellectuals* (New York: Transaction, 2011 [1955]), 55.

12. Entry for 8 August 1947, in Georgi Dimitrov, *The Diary of Georgi Dimitrov, 1933–1949*, ed. Ivo Banac (New Haven, CT: Yale University Press, 2008), 422.

13. "The Situation of the Writer in 1947," in Jean Paul Sartre, *What Is Literature?* (Charleston, SC: Nabu Press, 2011 [1947]), 225.

14. Thomas Assheuer and Hans Sarkowicz, *Rechtsradikale in Deutschland: die alte und die neue Rechte* [Right-wing Radicals in Germany: The Old and the New Right] (Munich: Beck, 1990), 112.

15. Willy Brandt, *My Road to Berlin* (Garden City, NY: Doubleday, 1960), 184–98.

16. Quoted in Lawrence S. Kaplan, *NATO 1948: The Birth of the Transatlantic Alliance* (Lanham, MD: Rowman & Littlefield, 2007), 208.

17. Togliatti speech, 12 March 1949, Royal Institute of International Affairs, ed., *Documents on International Affairs 1949–50*, 254–56.

18. *The Papers of General Lucius D. Clay: Germany, 1945–1949*, ed. Jean Edward Smith (Bloomington, IN: Indiana University Press, 1974), 568–69.

19. Senator Joseph McCarthy speech, 9 February 1950, in William T. Walker, ed., *McCarthyism and the Red Scare: A Reference Guide* (Santa Barbara, CA: ABC-CLIO, 2011), 137–42.

20. Amir Weiner, "Saving Private Ivan: From What, Why, and How?," *Kritika: Explorations in Russian and Eurasian History* 1, no. 2 (2000): 305–36; Amir Weiner, "The Empires Pay a Visit: Gulag Returnees, East European Rebellions, and Soviet Frontier Politics," *Journal of Modern History* 78, no. 2 (2006): 333–76; and Elena Zubkova, *Russia After the War: Hopes, Illusions and Disappointments, 1945–1957* (Armonk, NY: M.E. Sharpe, 1998), 106.

21. Dimitrov, *Diary of Georgi Dimitrov, 1933–1949*, 414.

22. Ibid., 437.

23. Mark Harrison, "The Soviet Union after 1945: Economic Recovery and Political Repression," *Past & Present* 210, no. 6 (2011): 103–20; Vladimir Popov, "Life Cycle of the Centrally Planned Economy: Why Soviet Growth Rates Peaked in the 1950s," CEFIR/NES Working Paper Series (Moscow: Centre for Economic and Financial Research at the New Economic School, 2010).

CHAPTER 5: NEW ASIA

1. Quoted in Mark Gayn, *Japan Diary* (New York: W. Sloane Associates, 1948), 227.

2. "Basic Initial Post-Surrender Directive," August 1945, *Political Reorientation of Japan. Report of the Government Section, Supreme Commander for the Allied Powers*, vol. 2 (Washington, DC: U.S. Government Printing Office, 1949), appendix A, 423–26.

3. Quoted in Gayn, *Japan Diary*, 231.

4. George Kennan, "Recommendations with Respect to U.S. Policy Toward Japan," 25 March 1948, *FRUS 1948*, 6:692.

5. *Security Treaty Between the United States of America and Japan*. Treaties and Other International Acts Series, 2491 N (Washington, DC: US Government Printing Office, 1952).

6. Quoted in Odd Arne Westad, *Decisive Encounters: The Chinese Civil War, 1946–1950* (Stanford, CA: Stanford University Press, 2003), 160.

7. Record of conversation, Mikoyan—Mao Zedong, 5 February 1949 (Xibaipo), Arkhiv Prezidenta Rossiiskoi Federatsii [Archives of the President of the Russian Federation] (hereafter APRF), fond 39, opis 1, delo 39, p. 71.

8. Frank Dikötter, *The Tragedy of Liberation: A History of the Chinese Revolution, 1945–57* (London: Bloomsbury, 2014), 100.

9. Among them was the seventy-four-year-old businessman and philanthropist Tan Kah Kee (Chen Jiageng), whose rubber plantations and steel mills had made him the richest man in southeast Asia. See Lim Jin Li, "New China and Its *Qiaowu*: The Political Economy of Overseas Chinese Policy in the People's Republic of China, 1949–1959," PhD thesis, London School of Economics, 2016.

10. Quoted in V. N. Khanna, *Foreign Policy of India*, 6th ed. (New Delhi: Vikas, 2007), 112.

11. *Le Figaro*, 5 January 1950.

12. E. E. Spalding, *The First Cold Warrior: Harry Truman, Containment, and the Remaking of Liberal Internationalism* (Lexington, KY: University Press of Kentucky, 2007), 181.

13. NSC 68: "United States Objectives and Programs for National Security: A Report to the President," 7 April 1950, *FRUS 1950*, 1:260.

14. Jonathan Bell, *The Liberal State on Trial: The Cold War and American Politics in the Truman Years* (New York: Columbia University Press, 2013), 92.

15. *The Wall Street Journal*, 8 August 1949.

16. The best overview is Fredrik Logevall, *Embers of War: The Fall of an Empire and the Making of America's Vietnam* (New York: Random House, 2012).

17. Eisenhower to Hazlett, 27 April 1954, in *The Papers of Dwight D. Eisenhower* (Baltimore, MA: Johns Hopkins University Press, 1996), 15:1044.

18. Eisenhower news conference, 7 April 1954, in *FRUS 1952–1954*, vol. 8, part 1, 1281.

19. Quoted in Robert Beisner, *Dean Acheson: A Life in the Cold War* (Oxford: Oxford University Press, 2009), 217.

20. Berry to Matthews, 8 February 1952, *FRUS 1952–1954*, vol. 11, part 2, 1634.

21. Diary entry for 21 July 1947, Harry S. Truman diary, Truman Library, at http://www. trumanlibrary. org/diary/page21.htm.

22. Quoted in J. Philipp Rosenberg, "The Cheshire Ultimatum: Truman's Message to Stalin in the 1946 Azerbaijan Crisis," *Journal of Politics* 41, no. 3 (1979): 933–40.

23. Stalin to Pishevari (Democratic Party of Azerbaijian), 8 May 1946, Arkhiv vneshnei politiki Rossiiskoi Federatsii [Foreign Policy Archive of the Russian Federation] (hereafter AVPRF), f. 06, op. 7, pa. 34, d. 544, pp. 8–9.

24. Gabriel Gorodetsky, "The Soviet Union's Role in the Creation of the State of Israel," *Journal of Israeli History* 22, no. 1 (2003): 4–20.

25. Jawaharlal Nehru, *The Discovery of India* (Calcutta: Signet Press, 1948), 12–13.

26. Ibid.

27. Eisenhower notes, 29 April 1950, *The Papers of Dwight D. Eisenhower* (Baltimore, MA: Johns Hopkins University Press, 1981), 11:1092.

CHAPTER 6: KOREAN TRAGEDY

1. Quoted in Young Ick Lew, *The Making of the First Korean President: Syngman Rhee's Quest for Independence, 1875–1948* (Honolulu: University of Hawai'i Press, 2014), 194.

2. Rhee to US State Department, 5 June 1945, quoted in Young Ick Lew, *The Making of the First Korean President*, 232.

3. Quoted in Vladimir Tikhonov, *Modern Korea and Its Others: Perceptions of the Neighbouring Countries and Korean Modernity* (London: Routledge, 2015), 21.

4. Instructions for ambassador in Korea (Shtykov), 24 September 1949, AVPRF, f. 059a, op. 5a, pa. 11, d. 3, p. 76.

5. The best overview is still Chen Jian, *China's Road to the Korean War: The Making of the Sino-American Confrontation* (New York: Columbia University Press, 1994).

6. Shen Zhihua, *Mao Zedong, Sidalin yu Han zhan: ZhongSu zuigao jimi dangan* [Mao Zedong, Stalin, and the Korean War: Top Secret Chinese and Soviet Archives] (Hong Kong: Tiandi, 1998), 130.

7. Stalin to Mao Zedong, 1 October 1950, APRF, f. 45, op. 1, d. 334, pp. 99–103.

8. Mao Zedong to Stalin, 2 October 1950, APRF, f. 45, op. 1, d. 334, pp. 105–6.

9. Stalin to Mao Zedong, 5 October 1950, quoted in Stalin to Kim Il-sung, 7 October 1950, APRF, f. 45, op. 1, d. 347, pp. 65–67.

10. Quoted in "Historical Notes: Giving Them More Hell," *Time*, 3 December 1973.

11. Stalin to Mao Zedong, 5 June 1951, APRF, f. 45, op. 1, d. 339, pp. 17–18.

12. Quoted in Hajimu Masuda, *Cold War Crucible: The Korean Conflict and the Postwar World* (Cambridge, MA: Harvard University Press, 2015), 85.

13. Radio and Television Report to the American People on the National Emergency, 15 December 1950, *Public Papers of the Presidents of the United States. Harry S. Truman. Containing the Public Messages, Speeches, and Statements of the President, January 1 to December 31, 1950* (Washington, DC: United States Government Printing Office, 1965) (hereafter only *PPP [president, year]*), 741.

14. De Gaulle in *Le Monde*, 13 July 1950.

15. Quoted from Richard Peters and Xiaobing Li, eds., *Voices from the Korean War: Personal Stories of American, Korean, and Chinese Soldiers* (Lexington: University Press of Kentucky, 2014), 184.

16. Marguerite Higgins, "Reds in Seoul Forcing G.I.s to Blast City Apart," *New York Herald Tribune*, 25 September 1950.

17. Quoted from Peters and Li, *Voices from the Korean War*, 245.

18. Steven Casey, *Selling the Korean War: Propaganda, Politics, and Public Opinion in the United States, 1950–1953* (Oxford: Oxford University Press, 2010), 205–6.

19. Jim G. Lucas, "One Misstep Spells Death in Korea, *New York World-Telegram*, 7 January 1953.

20. See Byoung-Lo Philo Kim, *Two Koreas in Development: A Comparative Study of Principles and Strategies of Capitalist and Communist Third World Development* (New York: Transaction, 1995), 168.

CHAPTER 7: EASTERN SPHERES

1. For reasons of space, I have not been able to explore the fate of Albanian Communism in this book. I refer readers who are interested to Elidor Mëhilli's excellent book *From Stalin to Mao: Albania and the Socialist World* (Ithaca, NY: Cornell University Press, 2017).

2. Martin Mevius, *Agents of Moscow: The Hungarian Communist Party and the Origins of Socialist Patriotism 1941–1953* (Oxford: Oxford University Press, 2005), 81.

3. The British philosopher Isaiah Berlin commented: "And then to destruction, blood—eggs are broken, but the omelette is not in sight, there is only an infinite number of eggs, human lives, ready for the breaking. And in the end the passionate idealists forget the omelette, and just go on breaking eggs." "A Message to the 21st Century," *The New York Review of Books*, 23 October 2014.

4. The big exception was Poland, where the figure was never greater than 63 percent.

5. Otto Grotewohl, *Im Kampf um die einige Deutsche Demokratische Republik. Reden und Aufsätze* [In Battle for the United German Democratic Republic: Speeches and Publications], vol. 1 (Berlin: Dietz, 1954), 510.

6. Stefan Doernberg and Deutsches Institut für Zeitgeschichte, *Kurze Geschichte der DDR* [Short History of the GDR] (Berlin: Dietz, 1968), 239, 241.

7. "Die Lösung" [The Solution], Bertolt Brecht, in *Gedichte* [Poems], vol. 7 (Frankfurt am Main: Suhrkamp, 1964), 9.

8. Michael Parrish, *The Lesser Terror: Soviet State Security, 1939–1953* (Westport, CT: Greenwood Publishing Group, 1996), 270.

9. Quoted in Miriam Dobson, *Khrushchev's Cold Summer: Gulag Returnees, Crime, and the Fate of Reform After Stalin* (Ithaca, NY: Cornell University Press, 2009), 30.

10. Quoted in William Taubman, *Khrushchev: The Man and His Era* (New York: Norton, 2003), 242.

11. Quoted in Alexander V. Pantsov and Steven I. Levine, *Mao: The Real Story* (New York: Simon & Schuster, 2012), 409.

12. See Csaba Békés, "East Central Europe, 1953–1956," in *The Cambridge History of the Cold War*, ed. Melvyn P. Leffler and Odd Arne Westad, vol. 1 (Cambridge: Cambridge University Press, 2010), 334–52.

13. See Laurien Crump, *The Warsaw Pact Reconsidered: International Relations in Eastern Europe, 1955–1969* (New York: Routledge, 2015).

14. The best overviews of Soviet foreign policy are Vladislav Zubok, *A Failed Empire: The Soviet Union in the Cold War from Stalin to Gorbachev* (Chapel Hill: University of North Carolina Press, 2007), and Jonathan Haslam, *Russia's Cold War: From the October Revolution to the Fall of the Wall* (New Haven, CT: Yale University Press, 2011).

15. *For a Lasting Peace, for a People's Democracy!*, no. 41 (1951): 1–4.

16. Radio Free Europe background report, 6 June 1958, quoting the Yugoslav paper *Slovenski poročevalec*, 72-4-242, RFE Collection, Open Society Archives, Budapest.

17. See Svetozar Rajak, *Yugoslavia and the Soviet Union in the Early Cold War: Reconciliation, Comradeship, Confrontation, 1953–57* (London: Routledge, 2011).

18. Transcript of CPSU Central Committee Plenum, 12 July 1955, f.2, op.1, d.176, pp. 282–95, Russian State Archive of Contemporary History (hereafter RGANI).

19. Khrushchev's full speech is entered into [US] *Congressional Record: Proceedings and Debates of the 84th Congress, 2nd Session (May 22, 1956–June 11, 1956)*, C11, Part 7 (June 4, 1956), 9389–403.

20. Record of Conversation, Mao Zedong–Pavel Iudin, 31 March 1956, AVPRF, f. 0100, op. 49, pa. 410, d. 9, pp. 87–98.

21. "Gomułka's Notes from the 19–20 October [1956] Polish-Soviet Talks," 19 October 1956, Cold War International History Project Digital Archives, Woodrow Wilson International Center for Scholars, (hereafter CWIHP-DA), http://digitalarchive.wilsoncenter.org/document/116002.

22. Sándor Petőfi, "The Nemzeti Dal" [National Song], 1848, trans. Laszlo Korossy, http://laszlokorossy.net/magyar/nemzetidal.html.

23. "Account of a Meeting at the CPSU CC, on the Situation in Poland and Hungary," 24 October 1956, CWIHP-DA, http://digitalarchive.wilsoncenter.org /document/112196.

24. Quoted in Békés, "East Central Europe, 1953–1956," 350.

25. John Sadovy, quoted in Carl Mydans and Shelley Mydans, *The Violent Peace* (New York: Atheneum, 1968), 194.

26. Ibid.

27. Csaba Békés, "The 1956 Hungarian Revolution and the Declaration of Neutrality," *Cold War History* 6, no. 4 (2006): 477–500.

28. Quoted in Paul Lendvai, *One Day That Shook the Communist World: The 1956 Hungarian Uprising and Its Legacy* (Princeton, NJ: Princeton University Press, 2010), 152.

29. Leonid Brezhnev, *Tselina* [Virgin Lands] (Moscow: Politizdat, 1978), 12.

30. Roald Sagdeev, *The Making of a Soviet Scientist: My Adventures in Nuclear Fusion and Space from Stalin to Star Wars* (New York: Wiley, 1994), 286.

CHAPTER 8: THE MAKING OF THE WEST

1. Tom Lehrer, "MLF Lullaby," on *That Was the Year That Was*, 1965 recording, at http://www.metrolyrics.com/mlf-lullaby-lyrics-tom-lehrer.html.

2. *The Schuman Declaration* (Brussels: European Commission, 2015), 17.

3. 20 September 1949: Regierungserklärung des Bundeskanzlers vor dem Deutschen Bundestag [Government Policy Statement to the German Parliament], http://www.konrad-adenauer.de/dokumente/erklarungen/regierungserk larung.

4. De Gaulle radio broadcast 19 April 1963, in Charles de Gaulle, *Discours et messages* (Paris: Plon, 1970), 4:95.

5. Quoted in Giovanni Arrighi, "The World Economy and the Cold War, 1970–1990," in *The Cambridge History of the Cold War*, ed. Melvyn P. Leffler and Odd Arne Westad (Cambridge: Cambridge University Press, 2010), 3:23–44.

6. John Foster Dulles speech at the Council on Foreign Relations, in *State Department Bulletin*, vol. 30, no. 761, 25 January 1954, 107–10.

7. James C. Hagerty, diary entry for 25 February 1954, James C. Hagerty Papers, box 1, January 1–April 6, 1954, Dwight D. Eisenhower Library, Abilene, Kansas (hereafter Eisenhower Library).

8. Quoted in Thomas Borstelmann, *The Cold War and the Color Line: American Race Relations in the Global Arena* (Cambridge, MA: Harvard University Press, 2009), 90.

9. Remarks of Senator John F. Kennedy in the Senate, 14 August 1958, John F. Kennedy Library, Boston, MA (hereafter Kennedy Library), https://www.jfklibrary.org/Research/Research-Aids/JFK-Speeches/United-States-Senate-Military-Power_19580814.aspx.

10. Churchill to Eisenhower, 13 April 1953, *FRUS 1952–54*, vol. 6, part 1, 973.

11. Memorandum for the record of the President's dinner, President's villa, Geneva, 18 July 1955, *FRUS 1955–1957*, 5:376.

12. Memorandum of Conference with President Eisenhower, 3 January 1961, *FRUS 1961–1963*, 24:5.

13. Quoted in Fred I. Greenstein and Richard H. Immerman, "What Did Eisenhower Tell Kennedy about Indochina? The Politics of Misperception," *Journal of American History* 79, no. 2 (1992): 576.

14. Memorandum of Cabinet Meeting, 19 January 1961, *FRUS 1961–1963*, 24:21.

CHAPTER 9: CHINA'S SCOURGE

1. See R. J. Rummel, *Death by Government*, at http://www.hawaii.edu/powerkills/NOTE1.HTM.

2. The best overview is Niu Jun, *LengZhan yu xin Zhongguo waijiao de yuanqi (1949–1955)* [The Cold War and the Origins of New China's Foreign Policy, 1949–1955] (Beijing: Shehui kexue wenxian, 2012).

3. See Frederick C. Teiwes and Warren Sun, *The Politics of Agricultural Cooperativization in China: Mao, Deng Zihui, and the "High Tide" of 1955* (Armonk, NY: M.E. Sharpe, 1993).

4. Quoted in Zhu Dandan, "The Double Crisis: China and the Hungarian Revolution of 1956" (PhD thesis, LSE, 2009), 181. See also her *1956: Mao's China and the Hungarian Crisis*, Cornell East Asia Series, vol. 170 (Ithaca, NY: East Asia Program, Cornell University, 2013).

5. Zhihua Shen and Yafeng Xia, "The Great Leap Forward, the People's Commune and the Sino-Soviet Split," *Journal of Contemporary China* 20, no. 72 (2011): 865.

6. See the harrowing accounts in Yang Jisheng, *Tombstone: The Great Chinese Famine, 1958–1962* (New York: Farrar, Straus and Giroux, 2012).

7. Quoted in Zhihua Shen and Yafeng Xia, *Mao and the Sino–Soviet Partnership, 1945–1959: A New History* (Lanham, MD: Lexington Books, 2015), 289.

8. Shen and Xia, "The Great Leap Forward, the People's Commune and the Sino-Soviet Split," 868, 874.

9. Record of conversation, Mao Zedong–Pavel Iudin, 22 July 1958, in Odd Arne Westad, ed., *Brothers in Arms: The Rise and Fall of the Sino-Soviet Alliance, 1945–1963* (Stanford, CA: Stanford University Press, 2000), 348.

10. Mao quoted in Westad, *Brothers in Arms*, 23.

11. Record of conversation, Mao Zedong–N.S. Khrushchev, 2 July 1959, APRF, f. 52, op. 1, d. 499, pp. 1–33.

12. Mao notes, quoted in Westad, *Brothers in Arms*, 24.

13. Mao Zedong, "A lu shih" [Winter Clouds], 26 December 1962, at Marxist Internet Archive, https://www.marxists.org/reference/archive/mao/selected-works/poems/poems33.htm.

14. Quoted in Jeremy Friedman, *Shadow Cold War: The Sino-Soviet Competition for the Third World* (Chapel Hill: The University of North Carolina Press, 2015), 170.

15. Record of conversation, Mao-Khrushchev, 2 October 1959, CWIHP-DA, http://digitalarchive.wilsoncenter.org/document/112088.

16. Niu Jun, *1962: The Eve of the Left Turn in China's Foreign Policy*, Cold War International History Project Working Paper 48 (Washington, DC: Woodrow Wilson Center, 2005), 33.

17. Quoted in Dong Wang, "From Enmity to Rapprochement: Grand Strategy, Power Politics, and U.S.-China Relations, 1961–1974" (PhD dissertation, University of California, Los Angeles, 2007), 201.

18. "Mao zhuxi de tanhua 21/12/1965 yu Hangzhou" [Chairman Mao's Speech at Hangzhou 21 December 1965], mimeograph copy in author's possession.

19. Quoted in Roderick MacFarquhar and Michael Schoenhals, *Mao's Last Revolution* (Cambridge, MA: Belknap Press of Harvard University Press, 2006), 47.

20. Quoted in Michael Schoenhals, ed., *China's Cultural Revolution, 1966–1969: Not a Dinner Party* (Armonk, NY: M.E. Sharpe, 1996), 106.

21. See Donald S. Sutton, "Consuming Counterrevolution: The Ritual and Culture of Cannibalism in Wuxuan, Guangxi, China, May to July 1968," *Comparative Studies in Society and History* 37, no. 1 (1995): 136–72.

22. "The DPRK Attitude Toward the So-Called 'Cultural Revolution' in China," 7 March 1967, CWIHP-DA, http://digitalarchive.wilsoncenter.org/document/114570.

23. Quoted in Yang Kuisong, "The Sino-Soviet Border Clash of 1969: From Zhenbao Island to Sino-American Rapprochement," *Cold War History* 1, no. 1 (2000): 23.

24. Quoted in MacFarquhar and Schoenhals, *Mao's Last Revolution*, 335.

25. *Klassekampen* [newspaper], 19 September 1973.

CHAPTER 10: BREAKING EMPIRES

1. Quoted in William Roger Louis and Judith Brown, *The Oxford History of the British Empire, Volume IV: The Twentieth Century* (Oxford: Oxford University Press, 1999), 331.

2. Quoted in Louis and Brown, *Oxford History of the British Empire*, 4:350.

3. Quoted in Ebrahim Norouzi, The Mossadegh Project, 11 October 2011, http://www.mohammadmossadegh.com/biography/tudeh/.

4. *Africa-Asia Speaks from Bandung* (Jakarta: Indonesian Ministry of Foreign Affairs, 1955), 19–29.

5. Discours de Gamal Abdel Nasser, 26 juillet 1956, in La Documentation française, eds., "Notes et études documentaires: Écrits et Discours du colonel Nasser," 20.08.1956, no. 2.206 (Paris: La Documentation française, 1956), 16–21.

6. Quoted in Donald Neff, *Warriors at Suez: Eisenhower Takes America into the Middle East* (New York: Simon and Schuster, 1981), 376.

7. The Egyptian embassy in Washington had been kept well informed about US thinking; see Egyptian Embassy Washington to Ministry of Foreign Affairs, 17 August 1956, 0078-032203-0034, National Archives of Egypt, Cairo.

8. Eisenhower televised address, 20 February 1957, *Public Papers of the Presidents: Dwight D. Eisenhower, 1957*, pp. 151–52.

9. Prime Minister's Lok Sabha speech, 19 November 1956, *Selected Works of Jawaharlal Nehru* (New Delhi: Oxford University Press, 2006), 2nd series, 35:362.

10. Prime Minister's Lok Sabha speech, 20 November 1956, *Selected Works of Jawaharlal Nehru*, 2nd series, 35:372.

11. Quoted in Jean-Pierre Vernant, *Passé et présent: contributions à une psychologie historique* (Rome: Edizioni di Storia e Letteratura, 1995), 1:112.

12. Aimé Césaire's letter to Maurice Thorez, 24 October 1956, *Social Text* 103, vol. 28, no. 2 (2010): 148.

13. NSC 5910/1, "Statement of U.S. policy on France," 4 November 1959, *FRUS 1958–1960*, volume 7, part 2.

14. Quoted in J. Ayodele Langley, *Ideologies of Liberation in Black Africa, 1856–1970: Documents on Modern African Political Thought from Colonial Times to the Present* (London: R. Collings, 1979), 25–26.

15. Lenin note, 30 December 1922, *Lenin: Collected Works* (Moscow: Progress, 1970), 36:593–611.

16. "Khrushchev Report on Moscow Conference, 6 January 1961," USSR: Khrushchev reports, 1961, Countries, President's Office Files, Presidential Papers, Papers of John F. Kennedy, Kennedy Library.

17. KPS Menon to Ministry of External Affairs, 24 February 1956, MEA 26(22) Eur/56(Secret), p. 8, National Archives of India, New Delhi.

18. Memorandum of Discussion at the 452d Meeting of the National Security Council, 21 July 1960, *FRUS 1958–1960*, vol. 14:339.

19. Speech at the opening of the All-African Conference in Leopoldville, 25 August 1960, *Patrice Lumumba: Fighter for Africa's Freedom* (Moscow: Progress Publishers, 1961), 19–25.

20. Khrushchev to Lumumba, 15 July 1960, in Vladimir Brykin, ed., *SSSR i strany Afriki, 1946–1962 gg. : dokumenty i materialy* [The USSR and African Countries, 1946–1962: Documents and Materials] (Moscow: Gosudarstvennoe izdatel'stvo politicheskoi i nauchnoi literatury, 1963), 1:562.

21. "Sukarno, 1 September 1961," Non-Aligned Nations summit meeting, Belgrade, 1961, Subjects, President's Office Files, Presidential Papers, Papers of John F. Kennedy, Kennedy Library.

CHAPTER 11: KENNEDY'S CONTINGENCIES

1. Eisenhower televised address, 17 January 1961, *Public Papers of the Presidents: Dwight D. Eisenhower 1960–1961*, 421.

2. John F. Kennedy inaugural address, 20 January 1961, *Public Papers of the Presidents: John F. Kennedy 1961*, 1–2.

3. Robert F. Kennedy Oral History Interview, JFK #1, John F. Kennedy Library.

4. James A. Yunker, *Common Progress: The Case for a World Economic Equalization Program* (Westport, CT: Greenwood Publishing Group, 2000), 37.

5. Statement by the President, 1 March 1961, *Public Papers of the Presidents: John F. Kennedy 1961*, 135.

6. Memorandum of Conference with President Kennedy, 25 January 1961, *FRUS 1961–1963*, 24:43.

7. Record of Meeting of Comrade N. S. Khrushchev with Comrade W. Ulbricht, 30 November 1960, CWIHP-DA, http://digitalarchive.wilsoncenter.org /document/112352.

8. Quoted in William Taubman, *Khrushchev: The Man and His Era* (New York: Norton, 2003), 488.

9. Kennedy-Khrushchev meeting, Vienna, 3 June 1961, *FRUS 1961–1963*, 5:184.

10. Kennedy-Khrushchev meeting, Vienna, 4 June 1961, *FRUS 1961–1963*, 5:230.

11. Quoted in Taubman, *Khrushchev*, 500.

12. Ibid., 503.

13. Ibid., 505.

14. Quoted in Helen Pidd, "Berlin Wall 50 Years on: Families Divided, Loved Ones Lost," *The Guardian*, 12 August 2011.

15. Brandt speech, 13 August 1961, Chronik der Mauer, http://www.chronik-der-mauer.de.

16. "Rough Notes from a Conversation (Gromyko, Khrushchev and Gomulka) on the International Situation, [October 1961]," CWIHP-DA, http://digitalarchive.wilsoncenter.org/document/112004.

17. 16 October 1961 (mobile loudspeaker stations), Chronik der Mauer, http://www.chronik-der-mauer.de.

18. Quoted in Michael Beschloss, *The Crisis Years: Kennedy and Khrushchev, 1960–1963* (New York: Edward Burlingame Books, 1991), 278.

19. Quoted in Marc Trachtenberg, *A Constructed Peace: The Making of the European Settlement, 1945–1963* (Princeton, NJ: Princeton University Press, 1999), 334.

20. Quoted in Leycester Coltman, *The Real Fidel Castro* (New Haven, CT: Yale University Press, 2003), 39.

21. Ed Cony, "A Chat on a Train: Dr. Castro Describes His Plans for Cuba," *Wall Street Journal,* 22 April 1959.

22. Speech by Premier Fidel Castro at mass rally in Havana, 27 October 1959, Castro Speech Database, http://lanic.utexas.edu/project/castro/db/1959/19591027.html.

23. Quoted in Christopher M. Andrew and Vasili Mitrokhin, *The World Was Going Our Way: The KGB and the Battle for the Third World* (New York: Basic Books, 2005), 36.

24. 7 October 1960 Debate Transcript, Commission on Presidential Debates, http://www.debates.org/index.php?page=october-7–1960-debate-transcript.

25. Quoted in Christopher M. Andrew, *For the President's Eyes Only: Secret Intelligence and the American Presidency from Washington to Bush* (New York: HarperCollins, 1995), 259.

26. Castro Interrogates Invasion Prisoners, 27 April 1961, Castro Speeches Database, http://lanic.utexas.edu/project/castro/db/1961/19610427.html.

27. Conversation with Commandante Ernesto Guevara, 22 August 1961, National Security Archive Digital Archive (hereafter NSA-DA), https://nsarchive.wordpress.com/2012/02/03/document-friday-che-guevara-thanks-the-united-states-for-the-bay-of-pigs-invasion/.

28. Castro Denounces US Aggression, 23 April 1961, Castro Speeches Database, http://lanic.utexas.edu/project/castro/db/1961/19610423.html.

29. Hugh Sidey, "The Lesson John Kennedy Learned from the Bay of Pigs," *Time*, 16 April 2001.

30. Memorandum from the Attorney General (Kennedy) to President Kennedy, 19 April 1961, *FRUS 1961–1963*, 10:304.

31. Quoted in Muhammad Haykal, *The Sphinx and the Commissar: The Rise and Fall of Soviet Influence in the Middle East* (New York: Harper & Row, 1978), 98.

32. Quoted in Taubman, *Khrushchev*, 541.

33. Record of conversation, Kennedy–Gromyko, 18 October 1962, *FRUS 1961–1963*, 11:112.

34. Kennedy televised address, 22 October 1962, *Public Papers of the Presidents: John F. Kennedy 1962*, 808.

35. Adlai Stevenson Addresses the United Nations Security Council, 22 October 1962, https://www.youtube.com/watch?v=xgR8NjNw__I.

36. Interview with Walter Cronkite, CNN *Cold War* series, episode 10 ("Cuba 1959–1962"), http://nsarchive.gwu.edu/coldwar/interviews/episode-10/cronkite1.html.

37. Castro to Khrushchev, quoted at John F. Kennedy Library website, http://microsites.jfklibrary.org/cmc/oct26/doc2.html.

38. McNamara, CNN *Cold War* series, episode 10 ("Cuba 1959–1962").

39. Castro, CNN *Cold War* series, episode 10 ("Cuba 1959–1962").

40. Elsewhere, even Third World radicals hoped for more stable relations between the USSR and the United States in the wake of the missile crisis. See, for instance, Ministry of Foreign Affairs report 18 December 1962, 078–048418 –0010, National Archives of Egypt, Cairo.

41. Kennedy address at the University of Maine, 19 October 1963, *Public Papers of the Presidents: John F. Kennedy 1963*, 797.

42. Declassified Penkovskii materials, CIA Library, http://www.foia.cia.gov /sites/default/files/document_conversions/89801/DOC_0000012267.pdf.

43. Grimes, CNN *Cold War* series, episode 21 ("Spies 1944–1994").

44. Record of the 508th Meeting of the National Security Council, 22 January 1963, *FRUS 1961_1963*, 8:462.

CHAPTER 12: ENCOUNTERING VIETNAM

1. The best overview is Christopher Goscha, *Vietnam: A New History* (New York: Basic Books, 2016).

2. Le Duan, "Duong loi cach mang mien Nam" [The Path of Revolution in the South], circa 1956, http://vi.uh.edu/pages/buzzmat/southrevo.htm.

3. Quoted in Robert D. Dean, "An Assertion of Manhood," in *Light at the End of the Tunnel: A Vietnam War Anthology*, ed. Andrew J. Rotter, 3rd ed. (Rowman & Littlefield, 2010), 367.

4. Quoted in Michael Beschloss, ed., *Taking Charge: The Johnson White House Tapes, 1963–1964* (New York: Simon & Schuster, 1998), 401–3.

5. Quoted in Andrew Preston, *The War Council: McGeorge Bundy, the NSC, and Vietnam* (Cambridge, MA: Harvard University Press, 2006), 163.

6. Quoted in David E. Kaiser, *American Tragedy: Kennedy, Johnson, and the Origins of the Vietnam War* (Cambridge, MA: Belknap Press of Harvard University Press, 2000), 361.

7. Joint Resolution of Congress H.J. RES 1145 7 August 1964, http://avalon.law.yale.edu/20th_century/tonkin-g.asp.

8. Record of conversation, Zhou Enlai and Pham Van Dong et al., 23 August 1966, Odd Arne Westad et al., eds., *77 Conversations Between Chinese and Foreign Leaders on the Wars in Indochina, 1964–1977* (Working Paper 22, Washington, DC: Cold War International History Project, Woodrow Wilson International Center for Scholars, 1998), 97.

9. Special message to Congress on foreign aid, 19 March 1964, *Public Papers of the Presidents: Lyndon B. Johnson 1963–1964*, 393.

10. Kwame Nkrumah, *Neo-Colonialism: The Last Stage of Imperialism* (New York: International Publishers, 1965), 247.

11. Intelligence Memorandum Prepared in the Central Intelligence Agency, 19 June 1965, *FRUS 1964–1968*, 24:42.

12. Record of telephone conversation, Johnson and Walter Reuther (UAW president), 24 November 1964, tape number 6474, Lyndon B. Johnson Presidential Library, Austin, Texas (hereafter Johnson Library).

13. Robert Komer, "Talking Points (Preparation for McGeorge Bundy talk with Senator Dodds)," 31 August 1965, box 85, Congo, Africa, Country File, NSC, Presidential Papers, Johnson Library.

14. Quoted in Matthew Jones, "'Maximum Disavowable Aid': Britain, the United States and the Indonesian Rebellion, 1957–58," *The English Historical Review* 114, no. 459 (1999): 1192.

15. Quoted in Robert Cribb, "The Indonesian Massacres," in *Century of Genocide: Critical Essays and Eyewitness Accounts*, ed. Samuel Totten, William S. Parsons, and Israel W. Charny, 2nd ed. (New York: Routledge, 2004), 252.

16. See Michael Wines, "CIA Tie Asserted in Indonesia Purge," *New York Times*, 12 July 1990, and John Prados, *Lost Crusader: The Secret Wars of CIA Director William Colby* (Oxford: Oxford University Press, 2003), 156.

17. Memorandum from the President's Deputy Special Assistant for National Security Affairs (Komer) to President Johnson, 12 March 1966, *FRUS 1964–1968*, 26:418.

18. Quoted in Taomo Zhou, "China and the Thirtieth of September Movement," *Indonesia* 98, no. 1 (2014): 29–58, quote on p. 53–54.

19. Eric Gettig, "'Trouble Ahead in Afro-Asia': The United States, the Second Bandung Conference, and the Struggle for the Third World, 1964–1965," *Diplomatic History* 39, no. 1 (2015): 126–56, quote on pp. 150.

20. Memorandum From the President's Acting Special Assistant for National Security Affairs (Komer) to President Johnson 12 March 1966, *FRUS 1964–1968*, 26:457–58.

21. Memorandum from Secretary of State Rusk to President Johnson, April 1966, *FRUS 1964–1968*, vol. 4:365.

22. Record of Conversation, Mao Zedong and Pham Van Dong, Vo Nguyen Giap, 11 April 1967, Westad et al., *77 Conversations Between Chinese and Foreign Leaders on the Wars in Indochina, 1964–1977*, 102.

23. Nicholas Khoo, *Collateral Damage: Sino-Soviet Rivalry and the Termination of the Sino-Vietnamese Alliance* (New York: Columbia University Press, 2011), 87.

24. Cronkite's editorial on the Vietnam War, February 1968, *CBS News*, http://www.cbsnews.com/news/highlights-of-some-cronkite-broadcasts/.

25. Quoted in Krishnadev Calamur, "Muhammad Ali and Vietnam," *The Atlantic*, 4 June 2016.

26. Martin Luther King Jr., "Beyond Vietnam," 4 April 1967, in *A Call to Conscience: The Landmark Speeches of Dr. Martin Luther King, Jr.*, ed. Clayborne Carson and Kris Shepard (New York: Warner Books, 2001), 133–40.

27. Charles de Gaulle, Speech in Phnom Penh, 1 September 1966, Fondation Charles de Gaulle, http://www.charles-de-gaulle.org/pages/l-homme/accueil/discours/le-president-de-la-cinquieme-republique-1958–1969/discours-de-phnom-penh-1er-septembre-1966.php.

28. Quoted in Robert David Johnson, *Lyndon Johnson and Israel: The Secret Presidential Recordings*, Research Paper, no. 3 (Tel Aviv: S. Daniel Abraham Center for International and Regional Studies, Tel Aviv University, 2008), 33.

29. Quoted in Thomas Borstelmann, *The Cold War and the Color Line: American Race Relations in the Global Arena* (Cambridge, MA: Harvard University Press, 2009), 182.

30. Quoted in Borstelmann, *The Cold War and the Color Line*, 173.

CHAPTER 13: THE COLD WAR AND LATIN AMERICA

1. Christina Godoy-Navarrete, quoted in Kim Sengupta, "Victims of Pinochet's Police Prepare to Reveal Details of Rape and Torture," *The Independent* (London), 9 November 1998.

2. Quoted in Walter LaFeber, *The American Search for Opportunity, 1815–1913* (Cambridge: Cambridge University Press, 1993), 9.

3. See Gilbert M. Joseph and Daniela Spenser, eds., *In From the Cold: Latin America's New Encounter with the Cold War* (Durham, NC: Duke University Press, 2007), 20.

4. See Eric Zolov, "Expanding Our Conceptual Horizons: The Shift from an Old to a New Left in Latin America," *A Contra Corriente* 5, no. 2 (n.d.): 47–73.

5. *La Prensa*, 13 January 1927.

6. Memorandum by the Counselor of the Department (Kennan) to the Secretary of State, 29 March 1950, *FRUS 1950*, 2:598–624. As John Lewis Gaddis points out in *George F. Kennan: An American Life* (New York: Penguin, 2011), 386, there is little evidence that Kennan's recommendations on Latin America influenced US policy. But his summing up of the situation undoubtedly reflected much of the concerns in Washington at the time.

7. Excerpt from the diary of James C. Hagerty, Press Secretary to the President, 26 April 1954, *FRUS 1952–1954*, 4:1102.

8. Quoted in Piero Gleijeses, *Shattered Hope: The Guatemalan Revolution and the United States, 1944–1954* (Princeton University Press, 1992), 4.

9. Quoted in Max Paul Friedman, "Fracas in Caracas: Latin American Diplomatic Resistance to United States Intervention in Guatemala in 1954," *Diplomacy & Statecraft* 21, no. 4 (2010): 681.

10. Quoted in Friedman, "Fracas in Caracas," 679.

11. "Interamerican Tension Mounting at Caracas," *New York Times*, 7 March 1954.

12. Quoted in Friedman, "Fracas in Caracas," 672.

13. James C. Hagerty Diary, 24 June 1954, Box 1, Hagerty Papers, Dwight D. Eisenhower Library, Abilene, Kansas.

14. Address at a reception for the diplomatic corps of the Latin American republics, 13 March 1961, *Public Papers of the Presidents: John F. Kennedy 1961*, 172.

15. See Francisco H. G. Ferreira and Julie A. Litchfield, "The Rise and Fall of Brazilian Inequality, 1981–2004" (Policy Research Working Paper Series, The World Bank, 2006).

16. Quoted in Robert M. Levine, *The History of Brazil* (London: Palgrave Macmillan, 2003), 126.

17. Recording of telephone conversation between Lyndon B. Johnson, George Ball, and Thomas Mann, 31 March 1964, tape number 2718, Johnson Library.

18. Quoted in James Dunkerley, *Warriors and Scribes: Essays on the History and Politics of Latin America* (London: Verso, 2000), 4.

19. Quoted in Jon Lee Anderson, *Che Guevara: A Revolutionary Life* (New York: Grove Press, 1997), 768.

20. Quoted in David Rock, *Authoritarian Argentina: The Nationalist Movement, Its History and Its Impact* (Berkeley: University of California Press, 1993), 218.

21. Quoted in Paul H. Lewis, *Guerrillas and Generals: The "Dirty War" in Argentina* (Westport, CT: Praeger, 2001), 51.

22. Allende, "First Annual Message to the National Congress, 21 May 1971," James D. Cockcroft and Jane Canning, eds., *Salvador Allende Reader* (New York: Ocean Press, 2000), 96.

23. 22 August 1973 resolution in Chilean Chamber of Deputies, *La Nacion* (Santiago), 25 August 1973.

24. Quoted in Tanya Harmer, *Allende's Chile and the Inter-American Cold War* (Chapel Hill: The University of North Carolina Press, 2011), 63.

25. Notes on Meeting with the President on Chile, 15 September 1970, NSA-DA, http://nsarchive.gwu.edu/NSAEBB/NSAEBB8/nsaebb8i.htm.

26. Comisión Nacional Sobre Prisón Politica y Tortura, http://www.indh.cl /informacion-comision-valech.

27. Róbinson Rojas Sandford, *The Murder of Allende and the End of the Chilean Way to Socialism* (New York: Harper & Row, 1976), 208.

28. Federico Finchelstein, *The Ideological Origins of the Dirty War: Fascism, Populism, and Dictatorship in Twentieth Century Argentina* (Oxford: Oxford University Press, 2014), 152.

29. Christopher M. Andrew and Vasili Mitrokhin, *The World Was Going Our Way: The KGB and the Battle for the Third World* (New York: Basic Books, 2005), 78.

30. Quoted in Renata Keller, *Mexico's Cold War: Cuba, the United States, and the Legacy of the Mexican Revolution*, Cambridge Studies in US Foreign Relations (Cambridge: Cambridge University Press, 2015), 211.

31. Quoted in Keller, *Mexico's Cold War*, 223.

32. Some did move from one position to the other. José Mujica, a former urban guerrilla who became president of Uruguay, concluded that "it's one thing to overturn a government or block the streets. But it's a different matter altogether to create and build a better society, one that needs organization, discipline, and long-term work. Let's not confuse the two." Krishna Andavolu, "Uruguay and Its Ex-Terrorist Head of State May Hold the Key to Ending the Global Drug War," *Vice*, 9 May 2014, http://www.vice.com/read/president-chill-jose-pepe-mujica -uruguay-0000323-v21n5.

CHAPTER 14: THE AGE OF BREZHNEV

1. Quoted in Melvyn P. Leffler, *For the Soul of Mankind: The United States, the Soviet Union, and the Cold War* (New York: Hill & Wang, 2008), 247.

2. Record of conversation, Brezhnev and Kissinger, 24 October 1974, William Burr, ed., *Kissinger Transcripts: The Top Secret Talks with Beijing and Moscow* (New York: New Press, 1998), 327–42.

3. *Pravda*, 25 September 1968.

4. Quoted in William Taubman, *Khrushchev: The Man and His Era* (New York: Norton, 2003), 16.

5. Quoted in David Holloway, "Nuclear Weapons and the Escalation of the Cold War, 1945–1962," in *The Cambridge History of the Cold War*, ed. Melvyn P. Leffler and Odd Arne Westad (Cambridge: Cambridge University Press, 2010), 376–97.

6. See Henry Phelps Brown, *The Inequality of Pay* (Oxford: Oxford University Press, 1977), 38–51.

7. Quoted in *Marxism Today*, July 1968, 205–17.

8. Negotiations at Čierna nad Tisou, 29 July 1968, Jaromír Navrátil, ed., *The Prague Spring 1968: A National Security Archive Documents Reader* (Budapest: Central European University Press, 1998).

9. Transcript of Leonid Brezhnev's Telephone Conversation with Alexander Dubček, August 13, 1968, ibid., 345–56.

10. Vladimir Tismaneanu, ed., *Promises of 1968: Crisis, Illusion, and Utopia* (Budapest: Central European University Press, 2011), 394.

11. Nicolae Ceaușescu, *Romania on the Way of Completing Socialist Construction: Reports, Speeches, Articles* (Bucharest: Meridiane, 1969), 3:415–18.

12. SDS, "The Port Huron Statement," in Timothy Patrick McCarthy and John Campbell McMillian, eds., *The Radical Reader: A Documentary History of the American Radical Tradition* (New York: The New Press, 2003), 468–76.

13. Betty Friedan, *The Feminine Mystique* (New York: Norton, 1963), 1.

14. Maurice Vaïsse, *La grandeur: politique étrangère du général de Gaulle, 1958–1969* [Greatness: The Foreign Policy of General de Gaulle, 1958–1969] (Paris: Fayard, 1998), 360–61.

15. Quoted in Thomas Alan Schwartz, *Lyndon Johnson and Europe: In the Shadow of Vietnam* (Cambridge, MA: Harvard University Press, 2003), 123.

16. Brandt speech to the SPD Bundestag members, 11 April 1967, in Willy Brandt, *Berliner Ausgabe*, ed. Helga Grebing et al. (Bonn: Dietz, 2000), 6:129.

17. Quoted in Willy Brandt, *People and Politics: The Years 1960–75* (London: HarperCollins, 1978), 238.

18. Brandt's speech to the UN General Assembly, 26 September 1973, in Brandt, *Berliner Ausgabe*, vol. 6, pp. 6:498–511.

19. Record of conversation, Mielke-Kriuchkov, 19 September 1983, CWIHP-DA, http://digitalarchive.wilsoncenter.org/document/115718.

20. "Conference on Security and Co-Operation in Europe: Final Act," *American Journal of International Law* 70, no. 2 (1976): 417–21.

21. Charter of Algiers, 25 October 1967, in Mourad Ahmia, ed., *The Collected Documents of the Group of 77* (Oxford: Oxford University Press, 2015), 6:22–39.

22. Quoted in Nils Gilman, "The New International Economic Order: A Reintroduction," *Humanity* 6, no. 1 (2015): 1–16.

CHAPTER 15: NIXON IN BEIJING

1. Richard Nixon's address accepting the presidential nomination at the Republican National Convention in Miami Beach, 8 August 1968, The American Presidency Project, http://www.presidency.ucsb.edu/ws/?pid=25968.

2. Richard Nixon, "Asia After Viet Nam," *Foreign Affairs* 46, no. 1 (1967): 113–25.

3. National Security Council Report, United States Policy toward Japan, June 1960, *FRUS 1958–1960*, 18:347.

4. See Gilbert Cette et al., "A Comparison of Productivity in France, Japan, the United Kingdom, and the United States over the Past Century," paper presented at the 14e Colloque de l'Association de comptabilité nationale (6–8 June 2012), Paris, France, www.insee.fr/en/insee-statistique-publique/connaitre/colloques /acn/pdf14/acn14-session1-3-diaporama.pdf.

5. Mark Tran, "South Korea: A Model of Development?," *The Guardian*, 28 November 2011.

6. Young-Iob Chung, *South Korea in the Fast Lane : Economic Development and Capital Formation* (Oxford: Oxford University Press, 2007), 30.

7. Ang Cheng Guan, "Singapore and the Vietnam War," *Journal of Southeast Asian Studies* 40, no. 2 (June 2009): 365.

8. Odd Arne Westad et al., eds., *77 Conversations Between Chinese and Foreign Leaders on the Wars in Indochina, 1964–1977* (Working Paper 22, Washington, DC: Cold War International History Project, Woodrow Wilson Center, 1998), 132–33.

9. Xiong Xianghui, "Dakai ZhongMei guanxi de qianzou [Prelude to the Opening of US-China Relations]," *Zhonggong dangshi ziliao*, no. 42 (1992): 72–75.

10. Minutes of meeting of the National Security Council, San Clemente, 14 August 1969, *FRUS 1969–1976*, 12:226.

11. Record of conversation, Nixon-Dobrynin, 20 October 1969, *FRUS 1969–1976*, 12:285.

12. Record of conversation, Leonid Brezhnev and other Communist leaders, Crimea, 2 August 1971, SAPMO-BArch, DY 30 J IV 2/20, p. 9.

13. Nixon-Kissinger telephone conversation, 12 March 1971, in Luke Nichter and Douglas Brinkley, eds., *The Nixon Tapes, 1971–1972* (Boston: Houghton Mifflin Harcourt, 2014), 41.

14. Nixon-Kissinger telephone conversation, 27 April 1971, ibid., 108.

15. CCP Central Committee Document 24, July 1971, in James T. Myers, Jürgen Domes, and Erik von Groeling, *Chinese Politics: Ninth Party Congress (1969) to the Death of Mao (1976)* (Columbia: University of South Carolina Press, 1986), 171.

16. Record of conversation, Mao–Ceauşescu, 3 June 1971, CWIHP-DA, http://digitalarchive.wilsoncenter.org/document/117763.

17. Record of conversation, Mao-Nixon, 21 February 1972, *FRUS 1969–1976*, 17:680–81.

18. Record of conversation, Nixon–Zhou Enlai, 22 February 1972, *FRUS 1969–1976*, 17:362.

19. Ibid., 812–13.

20. Record of conversation, Mao Zedong–Pham Van Dong, 23 September 1970, Westad et al., eds., *77 Conversations Between Chinese and Foreign Leaders on the Wars in Indochina, 1964–1977*, 175.

21. Record of conversation, Mao Zedong–Kissinger, 21 October 1975, *FRUS 1969–1976*, 18:789.

22. Michael Schaller, "The Nixon 'Shocks' and U.S.-Japan Strategic Relations, 1969–74," National Security Archive Working Paper No. 2 (1996), http://nsarchive.gwu.edu/japan/schaller.htm.

23. *PPP Nixon 1972*, 633.

24. John Kenneth Galbraith, "Reith Lectures 1966: The New Industrial State. Lecture 6: The Cultural Impact," transmitted 18 December 1966, downloads.bbc.co.uk/rmhttp/radio4/transcripts/1966_reith6.pdf.

25. "19th Pugwash Conference on Science and World Affairs," in *Science and Public Affairs*, April 1970, 21–24.

26. Aleksandr Solzhenitsyn, *One Day in the Life of Ivan Denisovitch*, trans. by Ralph Parker (New York: Dutton, 1963), 42.

27. Andrei Amalrik, *Will the Soviet Union Survive Until 1984?* (New York: Harper & Row, 1970), 41, 5–6.

28. Tom W. Smith, "The Polls: American Attitudes Toward the Soviet Union and Communism," *Public Opinion Quarterly* 47, no. 2 (1983): 277–92.

29. See Werner D. Lippert, "Richard Nixon's Détente and Willy Brandt's Ostpolitik: The Politics and Economic Diplomacy of Engaging the East" (PhD thesis, Vanderbilt University, 2005), appendix.

30. Record of conversation, Brezhnev-Ford, 23 November 1974, *FRUS 1969–1976*, 16:325.

CHAPTER 16: THE COLD WAR AND INDIA

1. Quoted in Jag Mohan, "Jawaharlal Nehru and His Socialism," *India International Centre Quarterly* 2, no. 3 (1975): 183–92.

2. Quoted in ibid.

3. Quoted in Karl Ernest Meyer and Shareen Blair Brysac, *Pax Ethnica: Where and How Diversity Succeeds* (New York: PublicAffairs, 2012), 52.

4. Nehru speech to US Congress, 13 October 1949, *Selected Works of Jawaharlal Nehru*, 2nd series (New Delhi: Jawaharlal Nehru Memorial Fund, 1992), 13:304.

5. Quoted in Robert J. McMahon, *The Cold War on the Periphery: The United States, India, and Pakistan* (New York: Columbia University Press, 1994), 57.

6. Quoted in Andrew J. Rotter, *Comrades at Odds: The United States and India, 1947–1964* (Ithaca, NY: Cornell University Press, 2000), 214.

7. Record of conversation, Nehru-Dulles, 9 March 1956, *FRUS 1955–1957*, 8:307.

8. Indian Planning Commission, *Second Five Year Plan: A Draft Outline* (New Delhi: The Commission, 1956), 1.

9. See David C. Engerman, "Learning from the East: Soviet Experts and India in the Era of Competitive Coexistence," *Comparative Studies of South Asia, Africa and the Middle East* 33, no. 2 (2013): 227–38.

10. Ratnam to Dutt, 22 December 1955, Ministry of External Affairs (hereafter MEA), P(98)-Eur/55, pp. 4–5, National Archives of India, New Delhi (hereafter NAI).

11. Jawaharlal Nehru, *Letters to Chief Ministers, 1947–1964*, ed. G. Parthasarathi (New Delhi: Oxford University Press, 1985), 4:86. For an overview, see Anton Harder, "Defining Independence in Cold War South Asia: Sino-Indian Relations, 1949–1962" (PhD thesis, LSE, 2016).

12. Indian Mission, Lhasa, Annual Report for 1950, MEA 3(18)-R&I/51, NAI.

13. Ibid.

14. The best overview of the early phase in the Sino-Indian rivalry over the region is Sulmaan Wasif Khan, *Muslim, Trader, Nomad, Spy: China's Cold War and the People of the Tibetan Borderlands* (Chapel Hill: The University of North Carolina Press, 2015).

15. "Treaty 4307: Agreement on Trade and Intercourse between Tibet Region of China and India, 29 April 1954," *UN Treaty Series*, 229 (1958): 70.

16. Quoted in Jovan Čavoški, "Between Great Powers and Third World Neutralists: Yugoslavia and the Belgrade Conference of the Non-Aligned Movement, 1961," in *The Non-Aligned Movement and the Cold War: Delhi-Bandung-Belgrade*, ed. Natasa Miskovic et al. (London: Routledge, 2014), 187.

17. Nehru, *Letters to Chief Ministers, 1947–1964*, 4:197, 240.

18. Indian embassy Moscow to Ministry of External Affairs, 24 February 1956, MEA, 26(22)Eur/56(Secret), NAI.

19. "Non-Aligned Countries Declaration, 1961," Edmund Jan Osmańczyk, ed., *Encyclopedia of the United Nations and International Agreements*, 3rd ed. (London: Taylor & Francis, 2003), 3:1572.

20. Ibid.

21. Rusk to Harriman, 25 November 1962, *FRUS 1961–1963*, 19:406.

22. Nehru, *Letters to Chief Ministers, 1947–1964*, 5:537.

23. East Asia Division to Foreign Secretary, 6 February 1967, MEA WII/104/3/67, NAI.

24. Quoted in Renu Srivastava, *India and the Nonaligned Summits: Belgrade to Jakarta* (Delhi: Northern Book Centre, 1995), 85.

25. Record of conversation, T.N. Kaul-A.A. Fomin, 8 March 1969, MEA WI/101(39)69 vol. 2, p. 84, NAI.

26. Foreign Secretary to (Indian) Embassy Washington, Summary Record of Prime Minister's talks with Vice President Humphrey, 17 February 1966, MEA WII/121(21)/66, p. 60, NAI.

27. Indian Embassy, Washington, to Foreign Secretary, n.d. (October 1969), "Internal Developments in the United States," MEA WII/104(14)/69 vol. 2, NAI.

28. Quoted in Oriana Fallaci, "Indira's Coup," *New York Review of Books*, 18 September 1975.

29. Record of conversation, Foreign Secretary–General Adams, 12 November 1963, MEA 101(34)-WII/63, p. 34, NAI.

30. Record of conversation, Singh-Kissinger, 7 July 1971, MEA, WII/121(54)71, p. 55, NAI.

31. Treaty of Peace, Friendship and Cooperation Between the Government of India and the Government of the Union of Soviet Socialist Republics, 9 August 1971, http://mea.gov.in/bilateral-documents.htm?dtl/5139/Treaty+of+.

32. Minister for Political Affairs report, 18 August 1971, MEA, WII/104/34/71, NAI.

33. Record of conversation, Kissinger–Huang, 10 December 1971, *FRUS 1969–1976*, 11:756.

34. Minutes of Washington Special Actions Group meeting, 4 December 1971, *FRUS 1969–1976*, 11:620–26.

35. Record of telephone conversation, Nixon-Kissinger, 5 December 1971, *FRUS 1969–1976*, 11:638.

36. "Indo-Pakistan Relations," n.d. (March 1972?), WII/103/17/72, p. 8, NAI.

37. "Sino-US Relations and Implications," 6 March 1972, ibid., 14.

38. "Impact of Sino-American, Indo-Soviet, and Indo-Pakistan Relations on Indo-US Relations," n.d. (March 1972?), ibid., 31.

39. East Europe Division, Ministry of External Affairs, Annual Report (3 February 1975), MEA WI/103/5/75-EE vol. 1, NAI.

40. Quoted in Vojtech Mastny, "The Soviet Union's Partnership with India," *Journal of Cold War Studies* 12, no. 3 (2010): 73–74.

41. "Indo-Soviet Relations—A Critical Analysis," 12 April 1977, MEA, WI/103/10/77/EE, p. 53, NAI.

42. Record of conversation, Mehta-Sudarikov (head of South Asia Division, Soviet Foreign Ministry), 21 April 1977, MEA WI/103/10/77/EE, p. 45, NAI.

43. Record of conversation, Brezhnev–Desai, 12 June 1979, MEA WI/103/4/79(EE) vol. 1, pp. 234–49, NAI.

44. Record of conversation, Mehta-Vorontsov, 20 March 1979, MEA WI/103/4/79(EE) vol. 1, pp. 98–102, NAI.

45. Indira Gandhi speech in Delhi, 1 April 1980, at Indian National Congress, http://inc.in/resources/speeches/298-What-Makes-an-Indian.

CHAPTER 17: MIDDLE EAST MAELSTROMS

1. Nasser, "Falsafat al-Thawra [The Philosophy of the Revolution]," quoted in Reem Abou-El-Fadl, "Early Pan-Arabism in Egypt's July Revolution: The Free Officers' Political Formation and Policy-Making, 1946–54," *Nations and Nationalism* 21, no. 2 (2015): 296.

2. Quoted in ibid., 295.

3. Nasser speech 23 December 1962, at https://www.youtube.com/watch?v=voUNkFuhg1E.

4. Aflaq speech, 1 February 1950, Michel Aflaq, *Choice of Texts from the Ba'th Party Founder's Thought* (Baghdad: Arab Ba'th Socialist Party, 1977), 86.

5. Quoted in Douglas Little, "His Finest Hour? Eisenhower, Lebanon, and the 1958 Middle East Crisis," in *Empire and Revolution: The United States and the Third World Since 1945*, ed. Peter L. Hahn and Mary Ann Heiss (Columbus: Ohio State University Press, 2001), 32.

6. Quoted in Aleksandr Fursenko and Timothy Naftali, *Khrushchev's Cold War: The Inside Story of an American Adversary* (New York: Norton, 2006), 164.

7. Statement by the President, 15 July 1958, *Public Papers of the Presidents: Dwight D. Eisenhower 1958*, 553.

8. Quoted in Fursenko and Naftali, *Khrushchev's Cold War*, 159.

9. Quoted in ibid., 169.

10. Quoted in Sharman Kadish, *Bolsheviks and British Jews: The Anglo-Jewish Community, Britain, and the Russian Revolution* (London: Psychology Press, 1992), 135.

11. Quoted in Avi Shlaim, "Israel, the Great Powers, and the Middle East Crisis of 1958," *Journal of Imperial and Commonwealth History* 27, no. 2 (1999): 177–92.

12. For Egyptian priorities in terms of Soviet assistance, see M. Khalil (Egyptian Deputy Prime Minister) to S. Skatchkov (Chairman, Soviet State Committee on Foreign Economic Relations), May 1966, 3022–000557, National Archives of Egypt, Cairo.

13. For Egyptian relations with African countries in 1963–65, see the Ministry of Foreign Affairs reports in 0078-048408, National Archives of Egypt, Cairo, and on military support, see report from 18 September 1965, 0078-048418-408, ibid.

14. Quoted in Ghassan Khatib, *Palestinian Politics and the Middle East Peace Process: Consensus and Competition in the Palestinian Negotiating Team* (London: Routledge, 2010), 27.

15. Notes of a meeting of the Special Committee of the National Security Council, 9 June 1967, *FRUS 1964–1968*, 19:399.

16. "On Soviet Policy Following the Israeli Aggression in the Middle East," 20 June 1967, CWIHP-DA, http://digitalarchive.wilsoncenter.org/document/112654.

17. Statement to the Knesset by Prime Minister Golda Meir, 5 May 1969, Israel Foreign Ministry, http://www.mfa.gov.il/mfa/foreignpolicy/mfadocuments /yearbook1/pages/8%20statement%20to%20the%20knesset%20by%20prime%20 minister%20golda.aspx.

18. "On Soviet Policy Following the Israeli Aggression in the Middle East," 20 June 1967, CWIHP-DA, http://digitalarchive.wilsoncenter.org/document/113381.

19. Quoted in Isabella Ginor, "'Under the Yellow Arab Helmet Gleamed Blue Russian Eyes': Operation Kavkaz and the War of Attrition, 1969–70," *Cold War History* 3, no. 1 (2002): 138.

20. Minutes of a National Security Council Meeting, 25 April 1969, *FRUS 1969–1976*, 23:92.

21. Record of conversation, Kissinger, Schlesinger, Colby, 13 October 1973, *FRUS 1969–1976*, 25:483.

22. Memorandum for the record, 24/25 October 1973, *FRUS 1969–1976*, 25:741.

23. Quoted in Victor Israelyan, *Inside the Kremlin During the Yom Kippur War* (Philadelphia, PA: Penn State Press, 2010), 180.

24. The President's news conference of 26 October 1973, *Public Papers of the Presidents: Richard Nixon 1973*, 902–3.

25. Memorandum of conversation, 9 October 1973, *FRUS 1969–1976*, 25:413.

26. Memorandum of conversation, 12 August 1974, *FRUS 1969–1976*, 26:406.

27. Letter From President Ford to Israeli Prime Minister Rabin, 21 March 1975, ibid., 553.

28. Letter to President Ford by 76 Members of the US Senate, 22 May 1975, Israeli Foreign Ministry, http://mfa.gov.il/MFA/ForeignPolicy/MFADocuments /Yearbook2/Pages/84%20Letter%20to%20President%20Ford%20by%2076%20 Members%20of%20the%20U.aspx.

29. Quoted in Efraim Karsh, *Israel: The First Hundred Years* (London: Frank Cass, 2002), 3:103.

30. As did many of the Palestinian organizations; for an insider's view, see record of conversations, George Habash (PFLP)–Chudomir Aleksandrov (BCP Politburo), 17 November 1981, Sofia, f. 1b, op. 60, an. 287, pp. 1–60, Central State Archives, Sofia, Bulgaria (hereafter CDA, Sofia).

31. Massimiliano Trentin, "La République démocratique allemande et la Syrie du parti Baas," *Les cahiers Irice*, no. 10 (2013): 19.

32. "Saddam Hussein's political portrait—compiled for Foreign Minister Frigyes Puja prior to the Iraqi leader's visit to Hungary in May 1975," 26 March 1975, CWIHP-DA, http://digitalarchive.wilsoncenter.org/document/122524.

33. "Policy Statement on the Bulgarian Relations with Angola, Ethiopia, Mozambique, and PDR of Yemen," 1 October 1978, CWIHP-DA, http://digital archive.wilsoncenter.org/document/113582.

34. Quoted by Joanne Jay Meyerowitz, *History and September 11th* (Philadelphia, PA: Temple University Press, 2003), 231.

CHAPTER 18: DEFEATING DÉTENTE

1. Hedrick Smith, *New York Times*, 13 June 1973.

2. Reagan speech to second annual CPAC Convention, 1 March 1975, http://reagan2020.us/speeches/Let_Them_Go_Their_Way.asp.

3. Reagan's campaign address, 31 March 1976, Ronald Reagan Library, https://reaganlibrary.gov/curriculum-smenu?catid=0&id=7.

4. See Daniel J. Sargent, *A Superpower Transformed: The Remaking of American Foreign Relations in the 1970s* (Oxford: Oxford University Press, 2015).

5. Quoted in George J. Church, "Saigon," *Time*, 24 June 2001.

6. Address at a Tulane University Convocation, 23 April 1975, *PPP: Ford 1975*, 568.

7. For this, see record of conversation, Todor Zhivkov–Le Duan, 8–9 October 1975, Sofia, pp. 1–45, a.n. 186, op. 60, f. 1, CDA, Sofia.

8. See R. J. Rummel, "Statistics of Cambodian Democide: Estimates, Calculations, and Sources," at https://www.hawaii.edu/powerkills/SOD.CHAP4.HTM.

9. South African UN mission to the Secretary of Foreign Affairs, Cape Town, 15 May 1976, Record of conversation with Kissinger and Scowcroft, 1/33/3, vol. 33, South African Department of Foreign Affairs Archives, Pretoria.

10. For the Cuban summing up of these relationships, see record of conversations, Fidel Castro–Todor Zhivkov, 11 March 1976, Sofia, f. 1b. op. 60, an. 194, pp. 1–38, CDA, Sofia.

11. "US-Soviet Relations and Soviet Foreign Policy towards the Middle East and Africa in the 1970s. Transcript of the Proceedings of the First Lysebu Conference of the Carter-Brezhnev Project. Oslo, Norway, 1–3 October 1994," 45 (hereafter Lysebu I).

12. Ibid., 47.

13. Commission on Presidential Debates: The Second Carter-Ford Presidential Debate, 6 October 1976, http://www.debates.org/index.php?page=october-6-1976-debate-transcript.

14. Carter to Brezhnev, 26 January 1977, *FRUS 1977–1980*, 6:2.

15. Quoted in "SALT II and the Growth of Mistrust. Transcript of the Proceedings of the Musgrove Conference of the Carter-Brezhnev Project. Musgrove Plantation, St. Simon's Island, Georgia, 7–9 May 1994," p. 62.

16. Carter to Sakharov, 5 February 1977, *FRUS 1977–1980*, 6:17.

17. Quoted in "The Collapse of Detente. Transcript of the Proceedings of the Pocantico Conference of the Carter-Brezhnev Project. The Rockefeller Estate, Pocantico Hills, NY, 22–24 October 1992," p. 13.

18. Hamilton Jordan to Carter, June 1977, Container 34a, Foreign Policy/Domestic Politics Memo, Hamilton Jordan's Confidential Files, Office of the Chief of Staff Files, Jimmy Carter Library, Atlanta, Georgia.

19. Tom W. Smith, "The Polls—American Attitudes Toward the Soviet Union and Communism," *Public Opinion Quarterly* 47, no. 2: 277–92.

20. Record of conversation, Markovski-Ponomarev, 10 February 1978, CWIHP-DA, http://digitalarchive.wilsoncenter.org/document/110967.

21. The President's News Conference, 2 March 1978, *PPP Carter 1978*, 1:442.

22. Meeting of the Special Coordination Committee of the National Security Council, 2 March 1978, quoted in Jussi M. Hanhimäki and Odd Arne Westad, eds., *The Cold War: A History in Documents and Eyewitness Accounts* (Oxford: Oxford University Press, 2003), 542–44.

23. Record of conversation, Carter–Deng Xiaoping, 29 January 1979, *FRUS 1977–1980*, 8:768.

24. Ibid., 8:747.

25. Ibid., 8:770.

26. Record of conversation, Carter-Brezhnev, 15 June 1979, *FRUS 1977–1980*, 6:551.

27. Record of conversation, Carter-Brezhnev, 16 June 1979, *FRUS 1977–1980*, 6:581, 578.

28. Hamid Algar, ed., *Islam and Revolution: Writings and Declarations of Imam Khomeini* (Berkeley, CA: Mizan Press, 1981), 300–6.

29. Lysebu I, 34.

30. Jimmy Carter televised address, 4 January 1980, *PPP Carter 1980–81*, 1:22.

31. Jimmy Carter, "State of the Union Address," 23 January 1980, *PPP Carter 1980*, 1:196.

32. Jimmy Carter televised address, 4 January 1980, *PPP Carter 1980–81*, 1:24.

33. See SIPRI Military Expenditure Database, http://www.sipri.org/research/armaments/milex/milex_database.

34. Ronald Reagan, "Address Accepting the Presidential Nomination at the Republican National Convention in Detroit," 17 July 1980, The American Presidency Project, http://www.presidency.ucsb.edu/ws/?pid=25970.

35. "Toasts of the President and Prime Minister Margaret Thatcher of the United Kingdom at the Dinner Honoring the President," 27 February 1981, The

American Presidency Project, http://www.presidency.ucsb.edu/ws/index
.php?pid=43471. For the initial Soviet reactions to Reagan's election, see record
of conversation, Todor Zhivkov–Andrei Gromyko, 23 December 1980, f. 1b, op.
60, an. 277, pp. 1–22, CDA, Sofia.

36. Quoted in Steve Coll, *Ghost Wars: The Secret History of the CIA, Afghanistan, and Bin Laden, from the Soviet Invasion to September 10, 2001* (New York:
Penguin, 2004), 99.

37. For an overview of what the Sandinistas wanted from the Soviets and eastern Europeans, see record of conversations, Henry Ruiz (Nicaraguan Minister of
Foreign Assistance)–Aleksandr Lilov (Deputy Head of the Bulgarian Communist Party), 18–19 October 1979, f. 1b, op. 60, an. 257, pp. 1–83, CDA, Sofia. For
Castro's views, see summary of conversations, Fidel Castro–Todor Zhivkov, Havana, 7–11 April 1979, f. 1b, op. 66, an. 1674, pp. 23–35, CDA, Sofia.

38. Excerpts from an interview with Walter Cronkite of *CBS News*, 3 March
1981, *PPP Reagan 1981*, 191.

CHAPTER 19: EUROPEAN PORTENTS

1. "Stasi Note on Meeting Between Minister Mielke and KGB Chairman
Andropov," 11 July 1981, CWIHP-DA, http://digitalarchive.wilsoncenter.org
/document/115717.

2. Quoted in Silvio Pons, "The Rise and Fall of Eurocommunism," in *The
Cambridge History of the Cold War*, ed. Melvyn P. Leffler and Odd Arne Westad
(Cambridge: Cambridge University Press, 2010), 2:55.

3. Quoted in Kristina Spohr, *The Global Chancellor: Helmut Schmidt and the
Reshaping of the International Order* (Oxford: Oxford University Press, 2016), 111.

4. Ronald Reagan, televised address 5 September 1983, *PPP Reagan 1983*, 1227.

5. Quoted in Nate Jones, "First Page of Paramount Able Archer 83 Report Declassified by British Archive," 27 October 2014, https://nsarchive.wordpress
.com/2014/10/27/first-page-of-paramount-able-archer-83-report-declassified
-by-british-archive-remainder-of-the-detection-of-soviet-preparations-for-war
-against-nato-withheld/. See also Nate Jones, ed., *Able Archer 83: The Secret History of the NATO Exercise That Almost Triggered Nuclear War* (New York: New
Press, 2016).

6. Homily of His Holiness John Paul II, Warsaw, 2 June 1979, https://w2
.vatican.va/content/john-paul-ii/en.html.

7. "Session of the CPSU CC Politburo," 10 December 1981, CWIHP-DA, http://
digitalarchive.wilsoncenter.org/document/110482.

8. Interviews, http://www.academia.edu/7966890/Interviews_about
_travelling_to_West_under_communism_Hungary_in_Europe_Divided_Then
_and_Now.

9. Declaration of Charter 77, 1 January 1977, https://chnm.gmu.edu/1989 /archive/files/declaration-of-charter-77_4346bae392.pdf.

10. Plastic People of the Universe, "Komu je dnes dvacet" [Whoever is Now Twenty], http://www.karaoketexty.cz/texty-pisni/plastic-people-of-the-universe -the/komu-je-dnes-dvacet-188129.

11. Acceptance speech, 10 December 1975, Oslo, http://www.nobelprize.org /nobel_prizes/peace/laureates/1975/sakharov-acceptance.html.

12. "Solemn Declaration on European Union (Stuttgart, 19 June 1983)," *Bulletin of the European Communities*, no. 6 (June 1983): 24–29. An overview of developments in the late 1970s is N. Piers Ludlow, *Roy Jenkins and the European Commission Presidency, 1976–1980: At the Heart of Europe* (London: Palgrave Macmillan, 2016).

13. Thatcher speech to the European Parliament, 9 December 1986, http:// www.margaretthatcher.org/document/106534.

14. Quoted in Ian Glover-James, "Falklands: Reagan Phone Call to Thatcher," *Sunday Times*, 8 March 1992.

15. James M. Markham, "Germans Enlist Poll-Takers in Missile Debate," *New York Times*, 23 September 1983.

16. Quoted in Christopher Flockton, Eva Kolinsky, and Rosalind M. O. Pritchard, *The New Germany in the East: Policy Agendas and Social Developments Since Unification* (London: Taylor & Francis, 2000), 178.

17. "Tagesprotokoll, 32. Bundesparteitag, Mai 1984, Stuttgart, CDU," at www .kas.de/Protokolle_Bundesparteitage.

18. Entry for 18 November 1983, Ronald Reagan, *The Reagan Diaries* (New York: HarperCollins, 2007), 199.

CHAPTER 20: GORBACHEV

1. See Yegor Gaidar, *Collapse of an Empire: Lessons for Modern Russia* (Washington, DC: Brookings Institution Press, 2010).

2. Interview with Dr. Charles Cogan, August 1997, National Security Archive, http://nsarchive.gwu.edu/coldwar/interviews/episode-20/cogan1.html.

3. Boland amendment, Public Law 98-473, 12 October 1984, uscode.house .gov/statutes/pl/98/473.pdf.

4. Quoted in Malcolm Byrne, *Iran-Contra: Reagan's Scandal and the Unchecked Abuse of Presidential Power* (Lawrence: University Press of Kansas, 2014), 45.

5. Session of the Politburo of the CC CPSU, 11 March 1985, http://digital archive.wilsoncenter.org/document/120771.

6. Mikhail Gorbachev, *Memoirs* (New York: Doubleday, 1996), 102–3.

7. Session of the Politburo of the CC CPSU, 4 April 1985, NSA-DA, nsarchive .gwu.edu/NSAEBB/NSAEBB172/Doc8.pdf.

8. "Conference of Secretaries of the CC CPSU," 15 March 1985, CWIHP-DA, http://digitalarchive.wilsoncenter.org/document/121966.

9. Reagan to Gorbachev, 11 March 195, NSA-DA, http://nsarchive.gwu.edu/dc .html?doc=2755702-Document-02.

10. Entry for 10 October 1983, Ronald Reagan, *The Reagan Diaries* (New York: HarperCollins, 2007), 186.

11. Reagan State of the Union address, 25 January 1984, *PPP Reagan 1984*, 1:93.

12. Record of conversation, Reagan–Gorbachev, 20 November 1985, Geneva, in Svetlana Savranskaya and Thomas Blanton, eds., *The Last Superpower Summits. Gorbachev, Reagan, and Bush. Conversations That Ended the Cold* War (Budapest: Central European Press, 2016), 112.

13. Mikhail Gorbachev, *Political Report of the CPSU Central Committee to the 27th Party Congress* (Moscow: Novosti, 1986), 5, 6.

14. [CPSU CC] Politburo Session, 26 June 1986, Notes of Anatoly S. Chernyaev, NSA-DA, http://nsarchive.gwu.edu/NSAEBB/NSAEBB272/Doc%204%20 1986–06–26%20Politburo%20Session%20on%20Afganistan.pdf. Four months later, Gorbachev told the other leaders that the USSR had to "pull our forces out in one or, at most, two years."

15. Politburo Session, 13 November 1986, Notes of Anatoly S. Chernyaev, NSA-DA, http://nsarchive.gwu.edu/NSAEBB/NSAEBB272/Doc%205%201986 -11-13%20Politburo%20on%20Afghanistan.pdf.

16. Russian transcript of Reagan–Gorbachev Summit in Reykjavik, 12 October 1986 (afternoon), published in FBIS-USR-93-121, 20 September 1993.

17. "Excerpts from a speech given by Mikhail Gorbachev to the Central Committee of the Communist Party of the Soviet Union," http://chnm.gmu.edu /tah-loudoun/blog/psas/end-of-the-cold-war/.

18. "Soviets Admit Blame in Massacre of Polish Officers in World War II," *New York Times*, 13 April 1990.

19. N. Andreeva, "Ne mogu postupatsia printsipami" [I Cannot Give Up My Principles], *Sovetskaia Rossiia*, 13 March 1988.

20. Record of conversation, Gorbachev-Honecker, 3 October 1986 (in German), *Chronik der Mauer*, http://www.chronik-der-mauer.de/material/178876 /niederschrift-ueber-ein-gespraech-zwischen-erich-honecker-und-michail -gorbatschow-3-oktober-1986.

21. "The Diary of Anatoly S. Chernyaev, 1987–1988," translated and edited by Svetlana Savranskaya [hereafter Cherniaev Diaries], NSA-DA, http://nsarchive .gwu.edu/NSAEBB/NSAEBB250/index.htm.

22. Quoted in David H. Shumaker, *Gorbachev and the German Question: Soviet-West German Relations, 1985–1990* (Westport, CT: Greenwood Publishing Group, 1995), 36.

23. Reagan, "Remarks and a Question-and-Answer Session with the Students and Faculty at Moscow State University," 31 May 1988, *PPP Reagan 1988*, 1:687.

24. Quoted in Stanley Meisner, "Reagan Recants 'Evil Empire' Description," *Los Angeles Times*, 1 June 1988.

25. Quoted in Igor Korchilov, *Translating History: 30 Years on the Front Lines of Diplomacy with a Top Russian Interpreter* (New York: Simon and Schuster, 1999), 167.

26. Record of conversation, Gorbachev-Reagan, 1 June 1988, NSA-DA, http://nsarchive.gwu.edu/NSAEBB/NSAEBB251/.

27. Quoted from Amin Saikal and William Maley, eds., *The Soviet Withdrawal from Afghanistan* (Cambridge: Cambridge University Press, 1989), 19.

28. Quoted in Archie Brown, "Did Gorbachev as General Secretary Become a Social Democrat?," *Europe-Asia Studies* 65, no. 2 (2013): 209.

29. Record of conversation, Gorbachev-Brandt, 17 October 1989, NSA-DA, nsarchive.gwu.edu/NSAEBB/NSAEBB293/doc06.pdf.

CHAPTER 21: GLOBAL TRANSFORMATIONS

1. Ambassador Wu Jianmin in conversation with the author, London, October 2013.

2. *Selected Works of Deng Xiaoping, 1982–1992* (Beijing: Foreign Languages Press, 1994), 174.

3. Ezra F. Vogel, *Japan as Number One: Lessons for America* (Cambridge, MA: Harvard University Press, 1979), vii.

4. Paul Kennedy, *The Rise and Fall of the Great Powers: Economic Change and Military Conflict from 1500 to 2000* (New York: Random House, 1987), 467–68.

5. "Cable from Ambassador Katori to the Foreign Minister, 'Prime Minister Visit to China (Conversation with Chairman Deng Xiaoping),'" 25 March 1984, CWIHP-DA, http://digitalarchive.wilsoncenter.org/document/118849.

6. ASEAN Bangkok Declaration, 8 August 1967, in Michael Leifer, ed., *Dictionary of the Modern Politics of Southeast Asia*, 3rd ed. (London: Routledge, 2001), 69.

7. Quoted in K. Natwar Singh, "Revisiting Russia," *Business Standard*, 5 March 2011.

8. John Prados, *Safe for Democracy: The Secret Wars of the CIA* (Chicago, IL: Ivan R. Dee, 2006), 503.

9. Quoted in *The Philadelphia Inquirer*, 19 December 1988.

10. Cherniaev Diaries, 1989, http://nsarchive.gwu.edu/NSAEBB/NSAEBB275/.

11. See Kevin J. Middlebrook and Carlos Rico, *The United States and Latin America in the 1980s* (Pittsburgh, PA: University of Pittsburgh Press, 1986), 50.

12. "Serbian Academy of Arts and Sciences (SANU) Memorandum 1986," Making the History of 1989, https://chnm.gmu.edu/1989/items/show/674.

13. Abdullah Azzam, "Defense of the Muslim Lands," https://archive.org/stream/Defense_of_the_Muslim_Lands/Defense_of_the_Muslim_Lands_djvu.txt.

CHAPTER 22: EUROPEAN REALITIES

1. Reagan, "Farewell Address to the Nation," 11 January 1989, *PPP Reagan 1988–89*, 2:1720.

2. National Security Review 3, 15 February 1989, GHW Bush Library, https://bush41library.tamu.edu/archives/nsr.

3. Quoted in Sarah B. Snyder, "Beyond Containment? The First Bush Administration's Sceptical Approach to the CSCE," *Cold War History* 13, no. 4 (2013): 466.

4. Record of conversation, Gorbachev-Thatcher, 5 April 1989, NSA-DA, http://nsarchive.gwu.edu/NSAEBB/NSAEBB422/.

5. Cherniaev Diaries, 1989, http://nsarchive.gwu.edu/NSAEBB/NSAEBB275/.

6. The best overview is Serhii Plokhy, *Last Empire: The Final Days of the Soviet Union* (New York: Basic Books, 2014).

7. "Excerpts from debate between Lech Walesa and Alfred Miodowicz, 30 November 1988," Making the History of 1989, https://chnm.gmu.edu/1989/items/show/540.

8. Quoted in Mark Kramer, "The Demise of the Soviet Bloc," *Journal of Modern History* 83, no. 4 (2011): 804.

9. Viktor Orbán, "The Reburial of Imre Nagy," in *The Democracy Reader*, ed. Diane Ravitch and Abigail Thernstrom (New York: HarperCollins, 1992), 249.

10. Quoted in Sergey Radchenko, *Unwanted Visionaries: The Soviet Failure in Asia at the End of the Cold War* (Oxford: Oxford University Press, 2014), 161.

11. Quoted in ibid., 163.

12. Quoted in ibid., 167.

13. Quoted in Odd Arne Westad, "Deng Xiaoping and the China He Made," in *Makers of Modern Asia*, ed. Ramachandra Guha (Cambridge, MA: Harvard University Press, 2014), 199–214.

14. Quoted in Kramer, "The Demise of the Soviet Bloc," 827.

15. Ibid., 828.

16. Cherniaev Diaries, 1989, http://nsarchive.gwu.edu/NSAEBB/NSAEBB275/.

17. "From the Conversation of M. S. Gorbachev and François Mitterrand," 5 July 1989, Making the History of 1989, https://chnm.gmu.edu/1989/items/show/380.

18. See Mary Elise Sarotte, *The Collapse: The Accidental Opening of the Berlin Wall* (New York: Basic Books, 2014), 146–49.

19. Petra Ruder, quoted in Kai Diekmann and Ralf Georg Reuth, eds., *Die längste Nacht, der grösste Tag: Deutschland am 9 November 1989* [The Longest Night, the Greatest Day: Germany on 9 November 1989] (Munich: Piper, 2009), 167.

20. Helmut Kohl's Ten-Point Plan for German Unity (28 November 1989), German History in Documents and Images, http://germanhistorydocs.ghi-dc.org/docpage.cfm?docpage_id=118.

21. Quoted in R.C. Longworth, "France Stepping Up Pressure for a United States of Europe," *Chicago Tribune*, 30 October 1989.

22. Charles Powell to Stephen Wall, 20 January 1990, Margaret Thatcher Foundation, http://www.margaretthatcher.org/document/113883.

23. See Frédéric Bozo, *Mitterrand, the End of the Cold War and German Unification* (New York: Berghahn Books, 2009).

24. Record of telephone conversation, Bush-Kohl, 29 November 1989, Memcons and Telcons, https://bush41library.tamu.edu/archives/memcons-telcons (hereafter Bush Memcons), Bush Library.

25. Quoted in Mary Sarotte, *1989: The Struggle to Create Post-Cold War Europe* (Princeton, NJ: Princeton University Press, 2009), 111.

26. Quoted in "Hungary Declares Independence," *Chicago Tribune*, 25 October 1989.

27. Quoted in Steven Greenhouse, "350,000 at Rally Cheer Dubcek," *New York Times*, 25 November 1989.

28. "New Year's Address to the Nation, 1990," Havel's Selected Speeches and Writings, http://old.hrad.cz/president/Havel/speeches/index_uk.html.

29. Transcribed from video recording, 21 December 1989, https://www.youtube.com/watch?v=wWIbCtz_Xwk.

30. Record of conversation, 2 December 1989, first meeting, Bush Memcons, Bush Library.

31. Transcribed video recording, https://www.youtube.com/watch?v=UKtd BAJGK9I.

32. Supreme Council of the Republic of Lithuania, "Act on the Re-establishment of the Independent State of Lithuania," 11 March 1990, http://www.lrkt.lt/en/legal-information/lithuanias-independence-acts/act-of-11-march/366.

33. Quoted in Bridget Kendall, "Foreword," Irina Prokhorova, ed., *1990: Russians Remember a Turning Point* (London: MacLehose, 2013), 12.

34. Quoted in Archie Brown, "Did Gorbachev as General Secretary Become a Social Democrat?," *Europe-Asia Studies* 65, no. 2 (2013): 198–220.

35. Quoted in Hanns Jürgen Küsters, "The Kohl-Gorbachev Meetings in Moscow and in the Caucasus, 1990," *Cold War History* 2, no. 2 (2002): 195–235.

36. "Treaty on the Final Settlement with Regard to Germany," *United Nations Treaty Series*, vol. 1696, I-29226.

37. "Address given by Hans-Dietrich Genscher at the signing of the Two Plus Four Treaty," 12 September 1990, CVCE website, http://www.cvce.eu/obj/address _given_by_hans_dietrich_genscher_at_the_signing_of_the_two_plus_four _treaty_moscow_12_september_1990-en-e14baf8d-c613–4c0d-9816–8830a7f233 e6.html.

38. Milosevic's Speech, Kosovo Field, 28 June 1989, http://www.slobodan -milosevic.org/spch-kosovo1989.htm.

39. Quoted in David Thomas Twining, *Beyond Glasnost: Soviet Reform and Security Issues* (Westport, CT: Greenwood, 1992), 26.

40. Record of telephone conversation, 18 January 1991, Bush Memcons, Bush Library.

41. Bush, "Remarks to the Supreme Soviet of the Republic of Ukraine," 1 August 1991, *PPP Bush 1991*, 2:1007.

42. "Yeltsin's address to the Russian people," 19 August 1991, https://web.viu .ca/davies/H102/Yelstin.speech.1991.htm.

43. Quoted from *The New York Times*, 24 August 1991.

44. Soglashenie o Sozdanii Sodruzhestva Nezavisimykh Gosudarstv [Agreement on the Establishment of the Commonwealth of Independent States], 8 December 1991, http://www.worldcourts.com/eccis/rus/conventions/1991.12.08 _Agreement_CIS.htm.

45. "End of the Soviet Union: Text of Gorbachev's Farewell Speech," *New York Times*, 26 December 1991.

46. Record of telephone conversation, Gorbachev-Bush, 25 December 1991, Bush Memcons, Bush Library.

47. Andrei S. Grachev, *Final Days: The Inside Story of the Collapse of the Soviet Union* (Boulder, CO: Westview, 1995), 192.

THE WORLD THE COLD WAR MADE

1. Constantine Pleshakov, *There Is No Freedom Without Bread!: 1989 and the Civil War That Brought Down Communism* (New York: Farrar, Straus and Giroux, 2009).

2. "Russians Name Brezhnev Best 20th-Century Leader, Gorbachev Worst," 22 May 2013, *Russia Today*, https://www.rt.com/politics/brezhnev-stalin-gorbachev -soviet-638/.

3. Quoted in Chuck Sudetic, "Evolution in Europe: Bulgarian Communist Stalwart Says He'd Do It All Differently," *New York Times*, 28 November 1990.

4. Wilfried Loth, *Die Teilung der Welt: Geschichte des Kalten Krieges 1941–1955* [The Division of the World: The History of the Cold War 1941–1955] (Munich: Deutscher Taschenbuch-Verlag, 1980).

5. François Genoud, ed., *The Testament of Adolf Hitler; the Hitler-Bormann Documents, February–April 1945* (London: Cassell, 1961), 103.

6. Yevgeny Chazov, Nobel Lecture, 11 December 1985, https://www.nobelprize .org/nobel_prizes/peace/laureates/1985/physicians-lecture.html.

7. Depeche Mode (Alan Wilder), "Two Minute Warning," from *Construction Time Again*, Mute Records, 1983.

Index

ODD ARNE WESTAD is the ST Lee Professor of US-Asia Relations at Harvard University. He is the author or editor of eleven books, including *Restless Empire* and *The Global Cold War*, which won the Bancroft Prize, the Harrington Award, and the Akira Iriye International History Award. Westad lives in Cambridge, Massachusetts.